Boggy Slough

MYRNA AND DAVID K. LANGFORD BOOKS ON WORKING LANDS

Publication of this book is supported by
T. L. L. Temple Foundation
Texas Natural Resource Conservation Publication Endowment, Texas State University

Boggy Slough

*A Forest, a Family, and a
Foundation for Land Conservation*

Jonathan K. Gerland

TEXAS A&M UNIVERSITY PRESS
College Station

This paper meets the requirements of ANSI/NISO
Z39.48–1992 (Permanence of Paper).
Binding materials have been chosen for durability.

Manufactured in China

Library of Congress Cataloging-in-Publication Data
LCCN 2021040677
ISBN 978-1-62349-995-2 (cloth)
ISBN 978-1-62349-996-9 (ebook)

Contents

Acknowledgments

IT IS RARE TO HAVE access to such a wealth of historical records as I have had in researching and writing this book. Acknowledgements go first to several generations of the Temple family who donated some 200 cubic feet of lumber company records to Stephen F. Austin State University during the 1960s and some 1,300 cubic feet of additional business and family records to The History Center at Diboll beginning in the 1980s. The story of Boggy Slough as a land of change could not have been discovered or told without both of these important resources. Likewise, the T. L. L. Temple Foundation, through its ongoing support of East Texas initiatives such as environmental conservation and The History Center, preserved not only the land, but also the history of its people.

Many individuals also contributed to the making of this book. Foremost was Ellen Temple, who early on inspired me to write an environmental history of Boggy Slough and provided the necessary and steadfast encouragement to see it through. Her love of the land and passion for East Texas history and archives are unsurpassed. In many ways great and small, this book simply would not exist if not for her.

Next, I owe much gratitude to Charlie Harber, a true native of the land I wrote about, who first introduced me to Boggy Slough. Through many summertime excursions, rambling through briar patches, dodging cottonmouths, and eating sack lunches under ancient post oaks, my knowledge of the place began with him. Charlie also helped me find Joe Silvers of Henderson, who generously donated a treasure trove of family photographs of the Rayville Ranch to The History Center, where I work. Our understanding of Boggy Slough owes much to both of these men.

I humbly thank Richard Donovan, among my dearest friends, whose encouragement I experienced like a son. He aided me in innumerable ways—from introducing me to the Neches River of his youth to inspiring me to an even greater appreciation of the place we call home. I also thank our mutual friend Larry Shelton of the Texas Conservation Alliance, for accompanying me during site visits, providing important ecology lessons, and participating in several years' worth of lengthy email exchanges. Richard's and Larry's knowledge and experiences would fill a multitude of books, and this book is better for the wisdom and encouragement that they shared.

Also contributing to my ecological understanding and assisting in plant identifications was Eric Keith of Raven Environmental Services, who never let one of my many inquiries go unanswered. Jason Singhurst, chief botanist of Texas Parks & Wildlife, also contributed in important ways, as did Ike McWhorter of the US Forest Service. I also thank dendrochronologists Dr. Rebecca Kidd of Stephen F. Austin State University and Dr. Charles Lafon of Texas A&M University, who helped me understand the hickory and walnut composition of the East Texas forests as recorded by Spanish and French observers during the seventeenth and eighteenth centuries.

I also thank William Cronon, environmental historian at the University of Wisconsin at Madison. Although I have never met him, his excellent books, articles, and online resources—including classroom lecture notes—made me a student of the land, teaching me how to read a landscape and reminding me that the work of environmental history is performed as much on the ground and in the fields, streams, and forests as it is in the archives.

Always eager to help dig up an obscure Trinity County record was Susanne Waller, librarian and archivist of the Trinity County Historical

Commission, who shared not only her archives and time but her passion for local history. I am also grateful to Liz Holcomb of the Trinity County Abstract Company, who so kindly allowed me to spend several days researching and photographing her exhaustive land record files. I thank Joe Scott Evans of Groveton for helping me answer a few legal questions, and I am also grateful to Clay Kenley of Mustang Prairie Ranch, who assisted my understanding of East Texas cattle raising during the early and middle twentieth century.

Patrick Walsh and Brian Stauffer provided much-appreciated assistance with the records of the Texas General Land Office in Austin. For additional land records guidance and assistance with the Spanish language, I was kindly aided by Jesús F. "Frank" de la Teja of Texas State University, Francis X. Galán of Texas A&M University at San Antonio, and Jorge L. Garciá Ruiz of the National Autonomous University of Mexico at San Antonio. George Werner of Katy, Texas, and Murry Hammond of Los Angeles freely shared with me their vast knowledge of Texas railroad history and their many decades of meticulous research.

I am also indebted to Kayce Halstead of Stephen F. Austin State University's Steen Library for providing access to several important early state forest service documents. For similar assistance with other rare government records and publications, I owe thanks to Carter Smith and Cliff Shackelford of the Texas Parks & Wildlife Department and Nancy Koerth of the US Forest Service. Gratitude also goes to Julie Shackelford of the Conservation Fund, Nacogdoches, who helped me understand some important land conservation matters.

I am grateful to my staff at The History Center—Patsy Colbert, Louis Landers, Emily Hyatt, and Allison Grimes—who each assisted in meaningful ways. I am especially indebted to Emily, who not only read and corrected numerous manuscript drafts and listened patiently to many long stories of discovery in the archives and forests, but also provided invaluable insight, which made the book far better than I could have made it alone. I also thank the present and past staffs of the East Texas Research Center at Stephen F. Austin State University for providing me access to the vast Forest History Collections since the 1980s.

Many former Temple company foresters and wildlife managers also assisted in numerous ways. I owe much appreciation to Darryl Stanley, Stan Cook, Bill Goodrum, Don Dietz, Richard Capps, Joe Hamrick, and Norman Davis. I am equally grateful to Robert Sanders of the T. L. L. Temple Foundation and Jason Sebesta of International Paper, who kindly accommodated my many site visits during recent years. And, early in my writing, Justin Penick and Holly Wahl of Acorn Forestry provided helpful maps and aerial photographs.

I also thank Jay Dew and his staff at Texas A&M University Press for all their work to bring this book to fruition. I especially thank the reviewers, Dan K. Utley and Thad Sitton. Their encouragement and discerning criticism meant the world to me, and they too made the finished product much better.

This book also would not have been possible without the encouragement, support, and understanding of my wife, Jill, son Joseph, and daughter Jolie. They graciously allowed my absences and missed holidays, weekends, and vacations. Jill, especially, boosted my spirits at just the right times and kept the hearth and home wonderfully intact. Joseph created the fine maps for the book and shared his own environmental knowledge and a few of his college textbooks.

Lastly, I want to thank all the people and organizations I fear I have somehow forgotten at such a time as this. I especially thank the many descendants of Sullivan's Bluff families whom I met and corresponded with over the past couple of decades, particularly the descendants of the Christie sisters, whose simple words written more than a century ago taught me again to appreciate the beauty and wonder of "flowers on hillsides" and "pretty little birds singing."

To all the peoples who ever called Boggy Slough home, this book is fondly dedicated.

Boggy Slough

CHAPTER 1

A Story of the Land

The idea of nature contains, though often unnoticed,
an extraordinary amount of human history.

—RAYMOND WILLIAMS (1980)

Boggy Slough, a 19,055-acre conservation area in Houston and Trinity Counties, was once a nameless land that stretched between nameless streams. Nameless river-bottom lakes and marshes reflected nameless forests of nameless trees, and the wind blew across nameless hills and prairies of nameless grasses and flowers. Then men and women came, and in their own voices, tongues, and traditions, they gave names to the land and waters, and to the plants, trees, and animals. Their names conveyed meaning, identity, and a sense of place. Through the ages, people lived and died among these places they named. New generations, and at times people from far away, inherited the land. They kept and reshaped certain names, discarded and forgot others, and assigned new ones as they preferred. As the people and cultures changed, so did the land and its names.[1]

In time people speaking and writing the Spanish language arrived and bestowed new names, as they were instructed by their political and religious leaders, often changing even their own names to suit changing inclinations. They did not understand many of the names provided by earlier inhabitants, including those of the Caddo people, who for a thousand years called the entire region home. The Spanish named a large federation of these people Tejas, which was their spelling of a word they heard spoken as a greeting, interpreted as "ally" or "friend." French speakers also came, but the Spanish so jealously guarded the land they called Provincia de los Tejas that when the French left, most of their names left with them.[2]

Eventually Boggy Slough became inhabited by a people who called themselves Americans. They followed the ways of the English more than any others, especially in their speech and in the way they bound the land within irregular patterns of measured ownership surveys to which they assigned their personal names. They did not know many of the land's earlier names or its inhabitants. Several centuries of converging European empires on a land once dominated by peoples and cultures that gradually disappeared left a dearth of understanding.[3]

The Americans did retain a few earlier names. To the river that had fundamentally shaped the land, they kept the name Neches, the Spanish understanding of the tribal name of Tejas people who farmed and hunted along the middle and upper stretches of the stream valley for centuries. The name had replaced the Neches tribe's own word for the river, Nachawi, as well as the earlier Spanish names of Rio San Miguel Arcangel—named for the leader of heaven's forces in their triumph over the powers of hell—and Rio de los Tejas, the River of the Texas people.[4] Concerning Cochino

Bayou, which divides the conservation area into northern and southern sections defined as much by custom as by geography, the Americans also kept part of the Spanish name, Arroyo de los Cochinos, meaning stream of pigs, and merged it with the French derivation of the Choctaw word *bayuk*, meaning slow-moving waters.[5]

Early land surveyors chose the names of important trees they found, such as cedar and elm, to identify other streams. To one particular slough they gave a geological and topographical term brought from old England—boggy. To other streams and backwater lakes, homesteading families gave their surnames, such as Britton and Franklin, while to a cemetery, as well as a school district, they gave the biblical name Mount Pisgah—named for a mountain peak above the Jordan River valley from which Moses could see the Promised Land he was forbidden to enter.[6]

Other physical and cultural features also received names. For many decades a river bluff, a ferry crossing, and a post office located four miles north of Cochino Bayou carried the name Sullivan, given by a large family who settled there in 1853. In 1894, a new generation of Sullivans received a new post office and named it Tesla, for the Serbian American scientist Nikola Tesla, whose exhibits of alternating electrical current at the World's Columbian Exposition in Chicago the previous year had enthralled all humankind. When a railroad bypassed Tesla seven years later, however, it took away not only the community's post office and name but also its sons and daughters before any of them experienced the arrival of rural electricity.[7]

Two large saline prairies, located in the plains of Cedar Creek near another bluff of the Neches River, received the names Bluff Prairie and Cedar Brake Prairie.[8] In 1904, Bluff Prairie became the site, as well as the name, of a short-lived oil field and an oil company that drilled two wells into the poorly drained soils.[9] Several decades after a gas blowout occurred in one of the wells, drainage patterns altered by the relocation of a state highway formed what many people called Prairie Lake. In 1951, following the construction of an earthen causeway across the wet prairie, the United States Geological Survey published a new topographical map of the area and named the dammed waters Black Cat Lake, perhaps for the occasional mysterious sightings of black cats there.[10]

Twentieth-century railroad and lumber companies—which came from afar to tap the natural wealth stored in the land's newly commoditized pine trees—also conferred names, mainly for stations and logging camps. Redgate was named simply for a nearby red gate, while places like Neff, Rayville, and Walkerton were named for company officers and managers.[11] In 1910, at the logging camp of Walkerton, Southern Pine Lumber Company employees dug a pond to serve as a water station for steam railroad locomotives, and, through an amusing transformation of toponyms, a mapmaker some six decades later identified Walkerton Pond as Walden Pond, perhaps thinking of the much larger and deeper natural water body in Concord, Massachusetts, popularized by naturalist Henry David Thoreau's 1854 classic, *Walden; or, Life in the Woods*. Similarities between the two places were few, but each did have railroads, to which even Thoreau was transcendentally drawn, fancying himself "a track-repairer somewhere in the orbit of the earth." But whereas Thoreau "heard the rattle of the railroad cars . . . conveying travelers from Boston to the country," residents of Walkerton and the children at the nearby Mount Pisgah schoolhouse heard the rattle of cars carrying logs from the forest to Diboll. At both Walden and Walkerton, the whistles and bells of locomotives sounded the death knell of an old world and the birth of something new. The land and its people were never the same again.[12]

Following the industrial removal of Boggy Slough's largest trees, herds of cattle and brush-eating goats by the thousands displaced not only the land's human inhabitants but also much of its rural virtues.[13] For several decades, while land managers waited for the smaller pines to reach merchantable size, some 32,000 acres of the cutover and barbed-wire-fenced land became known simply as "the ranch," where ecological

Pine Lumber Company's high-profile guests than as a timber factory for its sawmills, the land demonstrated remarkable resiliency in regenerating not only trees, but also a whole forest ecosystem, especially after livestock was removed during the early 1960s and an ecological fire regime was restored during the early 1980s. Ultimately, the cutover land once grazed by large herds of Brahman cattle became home instead to some of the state's largest pine trees and oldest second-growth industrial hardwood bottomland forests, with a surprising collection of rare and endangered plants and animals.

Following the early-twenty-first century breakup of Temple-Inland, one of the nation's largest and most successful forest products corporations, the T. L. L. Temple Foundation, led by a new and more environmentally conscious generation, acquired 19,055 acres of Boggy Slough in 2013 and established the Boggy Slough Conservation Area to adjoin some 693 acres of additional Boggy Slough land owned by the descendants of Arthur Temple Jr., a grandson of T. L. L. Temple.[14] In many ways Boggy Slough was the crown jewel of what was once Temple-Inland's dynasty of some 1.25 million acres of forestland in Texas, and it had been a special place in the forest for the Temple family

fire was excluded and an experiment in converting former forests into shortgrass grazing pastures ultimately failed. At the same time, the fences that kept cattle in and people out also protected the highly adaptable white-tailed deer from overhunting. Soon, the members of an elite hunting club, named for Boggy Slough, where the club's first hunting lodge was built in 1922, applied the stream's name to about 20,000 acres of prime hunting ground along more than 18 miles of the Neches River between Texas State Highways 94 and 7. Managed more as a hunting club for Southern

Boggy Slough's history, the land shaped and defined people as much as people shaped and defined the land. A diverse forest of hardwoods and pines that grew on mixed soils and varied topography afforded all resident generations with everything needed to establish homes as well as prosperous societies. The fertile and dappled land made the agricultural Caddo the most culturally advanced peoples in Texas in the eyes of European visitors, and it provided later American settlers with ample means to produce what they needed for their society. Each generation of inhabitants, as well as later industrial managers, adapted to the land and also modified it to meet their needs, all the while cultivating and shaping it into a landscape that reflected their culture, which itself was a product of the land.

This history of *Boggy Slough* considers climate, soils, and topography, as well as animals and the seeds and roots of trees and plants. At its heart, however, it is a tale of caretaking, of the continuing relationships between people and nature, of natural processes and systems and of how men and women sought to manipulate them. It is a story of the life-giving energy of the sun and how people and corporations sought to direct nature with fire and other tools to increase the amount of sunlight that shone on the grasses, plants, and trees they desired the most, which influenced the kinds of wildlife and domesticated livestock they preferred to have nearby. It is also a story of time and the daily and seasonal cycles of life and of vegetation growth and dormancy. It is the story of a rooted forest, where death merely composted the process of renewal and new birth, where living trees shed their leaves annually, "repaying the earth with interest

since T. L. L. Temple began purchasing it for his Southern Pine Lumber Company in 1902. It was "the best land," Temple's great-grandson Buddy Temple declared upon the foundation's acquisition of it, and he outlined a vision for making it even better by restoring native floral and faunal biodiversity while at the same time maintaining a conservation-focused "working forest." The family and the foundation would use the conservation area to demonstrate "conservation forestry" management practices that would balance ecological and social benefits and share the results of scientific research independent of industry and public stock market demands. At its core, the conservation area would serve as an anchor for the Neches River Corridor project, an effort by the T. L. L. Temple Foundation and The Conservation Fund to protect critical hardwood bottomland habitats along one of the most unspoiled rivers in Texas, linking conservation lands to the north, such as the Neches River National Wildlife Refuge, with protected lands to the south, including the Big Thicket National Preserve.

Boggy Slough: A Forest, a Family, and a Foundation for Land Conservation is a story about the connections between people and the land that made their lives possible and meaningful. Throughout

A view of the stream Boggy Slough from a kayak, October 2016. *Photo by the author.*

what they have taken from it," as Thoreau famously wrote.[15]

Railroads also played a part in the story of the land. Fundamentally linked to nature, they were built on products of the earth, including 3,200 wooden crossties in every mile of track, which harnessed the work of "iron horses." Even their construction followed the earth's topography, whereby humans decided the route but the lay of the land determined the way. Railroads at Boggy Slough, as well as elsewhere, were more than a technology. They were social engines that connected the land's timbered wealth to sawmills and manufactured products to markets, where people decided the monetary value of nature and the rates of exchange. Everywhere their tracks extended, railroads transformed lives as well as landscapes.[16]

A black-crowned night-heron perches on the bank of Boggy Slough, October 2016. *Photo by the author.*

The history of Boggy Slough is also a story of how nature changed humans as much as humans changed nature. People may have commodified Boggy Slough's trees during the late nineteenth century, but it was the forest's mixed-species composition that influenced who would market those trees and how. Ironically, it was Boggy Slough's ecological diversity—which earlier generations had prized—that caused most industrialists to overlook its hardwood bottomlands, lowland glades, and mixed-forest uplands. Instead, they preferred lands with the highest possible concentration of large pine trees, which held the highest profit margins. Consequently, Boggy Slough was acquired later than other industrial forests, by T. L. L. Temple of Texarkana, whose earlier lumber ventures in northeast Texas had all failed because of exhausted timber resources and overextended contractual obligations. Those past experiences, combined with the Panic of 1907—one of the worst economic depressions in American history—which coincided with the beginning of logging operations at Boggy Slough, influenced Temple's conservative approach to harvesting, whereby his loggers saved some smaller trees for a later cutting.

But while the land itself determined when and how it was industrially harvested, and despite its particular advantages being not yet fully realized, Temple's managers sought to reshape it according to their own vision of what it should be. Thus, while waiting for a young "second crop" of pine trees to grow to merchantable size, they exerted great influence on the forces and cycles of nature, understanding only later that they were incapable of controlling even the consequences of their actions. Attempting to support large herds of cattle on the cutover lands, managers fenced the land and waged a costly war against emergent hardwood brush that shaded the grass. They excluded fire and introduced thousands of Spanish goats to consume the unwanted vegetation and then went to Laredo and hired more than one hundred migrant workers from Mexico to chop out what the goats could not control. It was all part of their "land clearing scheme," managers said. In an effort to have sufficient year-round feed for the cattle, managers introduced nonnative "improved" forage plants, including kudzu, and Temple bought five cotton seed oil mills in Oklahoma and Arkansas, as well as 27,000 acres of additional grassland in South Texas—all merely to feed Boggy Slough's cattle, a losing effort that required natural and human resources from two other states and one foreign country. Managers learned the hard way that they could change Boggy Slough only so much, before the land changed their minds instead.

This story also tells of the natural and cultural conflicts that resulted from differing visions of Boggy Slough and its natural resources. Proponents of preserving open range herding and woodland commons hunting traditions resisted Boggy Slough's unnatural fences with a vengeance because the stretched barbed wires abruptly redefined their customary exercise of usufruct rights as criminal acts of trespassing and poaching.[17] Conflicts developed even within Southern Pine Lumber Company between local management and absentee ownership classes, specifically whether or not the land actually required cattle and their human keepers in order to successfully guard deer and protect trees. Another contention was the question of who should be allowed to legally kill a deer—employees, to keep them contented, loyal, and prevent them from joining labor unions, or influential politicians and business leaders, to gain and maintain their "bonds of friendship." Definite answers were not forthcoming, or accepted, for decades, and fences and their implications remain a concern today.

As with any patch of earth where men and women—and even corporations—have chosen to live, to work, and to make their homes, Boggy Slough is ultimately a story of both mistakes and successes. While each generation decided the definition of home by taking the land as they found it, shaping it to their desires, and seeking to sustain it, they also sought to pass on, in the words of environmental historian William Cronon, "what was best in it (and in themselves) to their children."[18] At Boggy Slough, it was the enduring forest, despite all that had once threatened it, that proved most resilient and worthy of passing on to future generations. The growth of trees "covered up a lot of ignorance on our part over the years, fantastic mistakes that Mother Nature has recouped for us," Arthur Temple Jr. once confessed.[19] Nature's regenerative canopy of trees not only hid human blunders but in time also delivered redemption and produced gratitude.[20]

Finally, Boggy Slough remains a land of varied cultural overlays. There are as many different stories of Boggy Slough as there are people who have known the place. These diverse, rich stories continue to confront the managers of the conservation area on a daily basis. While tales of mighty deer hunts and rousing clubhouse parties persist, the land itself continues to speak to all who will listen.

At the Mount Pisgah Cemetery, on a hill among pines and scattered hickories, the stems of assorted wildflowers and the dried stalks and seed heads of past seasons sway gently as odes and elegies among modest gravestones that mark the lives of the people who once lived on the surrounding hillsides between elm-shaded creeks and branches. All around, the inseparability of natural and cultural history is evident—in words etched in stone, in the aroma of yellow jessamine in early spring and the scent of warm pine straw in late summer, in the sounds of birds and insects, and in breaths of wind sighing through pine boughs. Inside the cemetery's fences, in the middle of an altered but recovering landscape that is as much cultural as it is natural, there is a beautiful pine savannah relic, a tiny patch of understory that once carpeted much of the surrounding forest. This story of Boggy Slough is not just of what has been lost, but of what can still be found.[21]

CHAPTER 2

A Land of Provision

It is not what you look at [that matters],
but what you see.

—HENRY DAVID THOREAU (1851)

Many centuries before the first Europeans arrived to record their observations in journals and letters, the place now called the Boggy Slough Conservation Area was home to the southwestern tribes of the great Hasinai Confederacy of Caddo peoples. These Hasinai Caddos used the land as they found it while also manipulating it to support thriving agricultural societies.[1] The Neches River valley's mixed pine and hardwood forests, along with their interconnected ecosystems, furnished a cornucopia of easily exploited resources. Foremost was the great diversity of plants and trees, which in varying stages of succession and symbiotic relationships provided reliable food and domestic supplies as well as ideal habitat for large populations of wildlife, including game animals. Never far away, the river and bottomland lakes and sloughs offered ample populations of fish, turtles, and mussels. Furthermore, hardwood trees, by annually shedding their leaves over the course of centuries, had created and were sustained by moist forest soils easily adapted to cultivation practices that employed only wood, bone, and stone tilling implements. Upon first seeing the flourishing Hasinai villages and agricultural fields, Spaniards believed the Neches valley soil was "capable of growing anything that may be planted."[2]

Spanish and French visitors found the forests of the middle Neches valley in a centuries-long process of becoming variably open and diverse. They described vast portions of the landscape as "an open forest" comprising a great assortment of shade-intolerant trees and plants that produced easily gathered nuts, berries, seeds, and fruits.[3] They observed the Hasinai people actively and passively using fire just as any other natural tool, essentially to expand the abundance and predictability of food and other life resources. By subjecting the forests to frequent fire intervals of between two and twenty years, the Hasinai eliminated pine leaf litter and fallen branches from the forest floor, which created and maintained an open and grassy woodland structure that was ideal for travel, game management, and hunting. Far from being model ecologists, the Hasinai nevertheless managed fire well enough to avoid burning their homes while clearing areas for cultivation and favoring certain vegetation over others.[4] To the Spanish, who identified the Hasinai peoples as "Tejas," this much-altered and impressively managed land was renowned as "The Kingdom of the Tejas," from which an even larger region eventually took its name.[5]

———————

Although Boggy Slough has not yet been the subject of proper archaeological studies, ceramic pottery sherds and various stone hunting points, knives, scrapers, and other tools found widely

A sampling of Indian artifacts found by a Temple-Inland forester during road work along a terrace at the south end of Franklin Slough during the 1990s. *Courtesy of The History Center, Diboll.*

across the property suggest human habitation back to at least the Late Archaic Period (between 3000 BCE and 500 BCE).[6] Most of the artifacts, especially those found on a gently sloping terrace along the western bank of Franklin Slough near Cochino Bayou, just north of the Eastern Texas Railroad, date to what archaeologists call the Woodland Period (between 500 BCE and 800 CE).[7] Some of the pottery sherds found along this terrace and nearby bluff, as well as at a terrace bluff at the northern end of the three-mile-long Franklin Slough, indicate a Caddo presence of a more recent era (between 800 CE and 1700 CE). Red mulberry, swamp chestnut oak, and many other valuable trees of the Hasinai landscape still occupy these sites today, as do channels of former springs that drained down the terraces toward the slough and river.[8]

The formal archaeological studies of Caddo sites near Boggy Slough indicate that Caddo groups in varying sizes were distributed across a wide region. One Caddo village and burial site less than five miles due east of Boggy Slough Island, in Angelina County, contained burial mounds, skeletons, and nearly two hundred Caddo manufactured and decorated ceramic sherds, when it was discovered during the 1920s and studied during the 1930s.[9] Official archeological investigations will undoubtedly help researchers better understand Boggy Slough's earlier history, but until then the written records of European visitors beginning in the 1680s provide important insight into the land's earlier peoples and the environments in which they lived.

Much of the land described by French and Spanish soldiers and missionaries during the late seventeenth and early eighteenth centuries was in the middle Neches River valley, in present-day Houston and Cherokee Counties, where several tribes of the Hasinai Confederacy of Caddos settled several hundred years earlier, about the year 800 CE. These were the people the Spanish identified collectively as Tejas, and they lived in villages spread out over a dozen miles or more in all directions, each within scattered forest clearings along distinctive landforms near the river, creeks, and sloughs. As one Spanish missionary to the Hasinai described the locations "where the Indians live[d]," they were "open spaces and stretches of sand and marshes." Some villages were described as inhabiting "delightful" sites with running water within "fine woods with plum trees (*Prunus angustifolia*)."[10] While some of the larger villages identified during the sixteenth and seventeenth centuries are believed to have been situated about sixteen miles north and northwest of the Boggy Slough lands, other villages, such as those of the Nacono and Nechaui tribes, were closer and probably embraced at least the northern section of today's Boggy Slough Conservation Area.[11] Regardless of the named villages' exact locations, which certainly moved from time to time across the centuries, the geographies described by their earliest European observers are indistinguishable from what is already known about the Boggy Slough land. The conservation area's topography, soils, and forest composition, nurtured by more than 18 miles of the Neches River, contain important and unmistakable elements of Hasinai Country.[12]

Europeans saw the land of the middle Neches valley as forested in pines and many varieties of upland and bottomland hardwoods, with open understories made and preserved by the Indians. There were many "clearings" in the forest, including upland prairies as well as lowland meadows. In certain flat areas along the river and creek bottoms, where drainage patterns and soil conditions tended to favor herbaceous plants rather than woody vegetation, there were notable saline glades. The moist forest soils between the higher and lower elevations, when cleared of trees by the Indian practice of girdling, produced easily cultivated crops of fast-growing corn, beans, squash, sunflowers, and tobacco. The Indians maintained

the prairies, agricultural fields, and surrounding forests in various levels of succession by selectively setting fires at various intervals. By regulating the frequency and seasonal scheduling of the fires, they controlled the intensity and results of the burns, which molded the landscape, especially on the edges and margins of woods and savannas, to produce diverse ecosystems that supported permanent human habitation.[13]

The open wooded environment that closely surrounded the many Hasinai villages was immensely diverse and seemed remarkable to most Europeans. Writing from the west bank of the Neches River in 1691, Fray Francisco Casañas de Jesús María said the forests were filled with "walnuts (*Juglans* and *Carya* spp.) and nearly all the different species of nut-bearing trees," also "many species of acorns (*Quercus*), all of them good [to eat]." There were in addition "many mulberries (*Morus*) and other kinds of fruit trees, such as chestnuts [chinquapins (*Castanea pumila*)]," as well as other plants, some producing berries, "such as the blackberry bush." There were also "innumerable other vines," Casañas continued, "some entangled among the trees, and others in the form of stubby vines growing in the open spaces." There were so many, he said, "they look[ed] as if they had been planted by hand."[14]

Other Spanish observers described the land in similar fashion. Fray Francisco Hidalgo wrote in 1716, saying the wooded areas surrounding Hasinai villages were "filled with different kinds of trees: oaks, chestnuts [chinquapins], pines, cottonwoods, medlars [persimmon], cherries, and many other kinds of trees that I do not know the names of."[15] Also in 1716, Fray Isidro Felis Espinosa wrote of "a forest of scattered pines, walnut trees, grapevines, common oaks and evergreen oaks (*Quercus nigra*)."[16] Seeing the same ground at the same time as Espinosa, Captain Domingo Ramón described the region as "land famous for its abundance of watering holes, valleys, [and] good woods of walnuts and grapevines." Captain Ramón was especially impressed by the frequency, abundance, and size of the grapes, mentioning them often in his reports and recording some were "as large as pigeon eggs."[17] In 1718 Fray Francisco Céliz recorded seeing "valleys, ravines, and clearings with open woods of oaks and many pecans." During mid-October, he said the pecans and chinquapin nuts "were so plentiful that they covered the ground" and were "very delicious."[18] Writing in 1722, Espinosa provided more detail than he had six years earlier, describing the Neches landscape as "filled with various kinds of trees, such as oaks, pines, cottonwoods, live oaks, large nut [tree]s—which yield the thick shelled nuts—and another kind of tree which yields the small, thin shelled nuts."[19] Espinosa added that besides the nut-bearing trees, such as walnuts and hickories ("thick shelled") and pecans ("thin shelled"), there were many fruit trees, "like the medlar [persimmon], the plum, and the large wild cherry" as well as other woody plants, bushes, and vines that grew grapes, including "a white grape that looks like a muscatel, red and white mulberries, and large blackberries."[20]

The bounty of edible nuts, fruits, and berries that Europeans found enveloping the Indian villages and the forests connecting them might seem unimaginable today. Yet today's landscape has been so greatly altered to suit the active and passive desires of a recent economy, just as the land 325 years ago was shaped to fit the requirements of an earlier way of life. Significantly, nearly all of the important plant and tree species observed were shade intolerant, and many were full-sun dependent. Undoubtedly the growth of mast- and fruit-producing trees, as well as berry- and grape-producing vines and shrubs, was encouraged by the Hasinai Caddo as the preferred vegetation near their villages. The berry-producing vines and shrubs growing in forest openings that Fray Casañas wrote about in 1691 may have appeared to him as "planted by hand" because they likely were planted by hand.[21]

Spanish officials in Mexico had heard reports of the Hasinai "gardens" well before their missionaries saw them because other tribes, such as the highly mobile Jumano, informed them.[22] Writing later and more confidently than Casañas, Fray Gaspar José De Solís confirmed the reports, recording Neches valley tribes indeed maintained "orchards of various kinds," which grew "peaches, plums, persimmons, figs, chestnuts [chinquapin], ash, pomegranates, and other fruit."[23] After such orchards and coppices were eventually abandoned by their gardeners, as tribes customarily relocated their villages from time to time, later Euro-Americans instinctively knew the locations of former village sites—and what they believed to be fertile ground—by looking for conspicuous stands of mulberries, mayhaws, persimmons, plums, elderberry, and beautyberry, as well as black walnut and certain hickories.[24]

Beyond gardens and agricultural fields, the Hasinai also created and managed the forests and "open spaces" through the selective use of fire to create a diversity of overlapping habitats. The Indian forested landscape was far different from most of what is seen today throughout East Texas, where fire exclusion and loblolly pine plantation management has predominated for three-quarters of the last century, resulting in a profusion of early successional upland sweetgum and other understory woody plant thickets that have adversely affected the habitats of such creatures as quail, turkey, and the red cockaded woodpecker, to name only a few. By the time of European contact, the people of the Neches valley had learned to increase the rate of natural disturbances such as lightning-caused fire to encourage the growth of certain plants and trees near their villages, which not only provided food for themselves but also for game, such as deer, turkey, squirrel, and quail, which in turn could be hunted for food. After centuries of experience, Indians knew well that fire-disturbed sites provided more food than old growth vegetation; that seed, berry, acorn, and nut growth was stimulated; and game yields were higher in areas kept in a state of constant vegetative succession. Furthermore, pine, oak, and hickory—which were the majority of tree species utilized as boundary witnesses and recorded by Boggy Slough's presettlement nineteenth-century land grant surveyors—were

A white-tailed deer enjoys fresh herbage following a late winter prescribed burn near Rayville, March 2018. *Photo by the author.*

highly driven by disturbance, required abundant sunlight to grow, and were unable to regenerate under shade (including their own). In fact, ecologists have long argued that the dominance of pine, oak, and hickory forest types such as Boggy Slough's, in virtually every region on earth, is due primarily to fire.[25] As the forest ecologist Stephen Spurr affirmed in 1964, "Fire is the dominant fact of forest history."[26]

European descriptions of the Neches valley's "clear pine forests," "good pasturage," and "clearings with open woods" of pines, hickories, oaks, and chinquapins, along with areas of pines that were "scattered" and found in "groves" suggest a patchwork-patterned application of a fire regime of periodic low-intensity surface burns of short duration, wherein mature trees suffered rarely more than charred bark. Many of the trees mentioned by the Europeans had a thick, insulating bark, which protected those trees' cambium layers from the relatively low heat of surface fires. Also, the broad, cupped leaves of many oaks—once fallen—were far less flammable than fallen pine straw and provided a damp carpet of protection all around mature oak trunks. If trees did die from very hot

fires, chinquapin and most of the oaks and hickories resprouted vigorously from roots, while the top-killed saplings of shortleaf pines resprouted repeatedly from the root collar, a unique ability among the southern pine species. Furthermore, shortleaf pines contained low amounts of resin, grew rapidly when young, and produced abundant seeds that were easily dispersed—all advantages contributing to the tree's special tolerance of fire.[27]

Shortleaf pines (*Pinus echinata*) once covered a vast portion of the continent—from East Texas to Florida and up the Eastern Seaboard to New Jersey—and were the dominant species in Boggy Slough's preindustrial uplands. In 1687, French army officer Henri Joutel surely noticed shortleaf pines when he wrote of seeing "tall pine groves" that were "quite lovely" growing in the uplands west of the Neches River as he approached Hasinai villages from the southwest. Through a keen eye, he observed the trees were "very straight, but their cones very small."[28] More than two centuries later, T. L. L. Temple's managers commented similarly on Boggy Slough's shortleaf pines—although seen as commodities, something priced, bought, and sold—describing them as "long, clean bodies" of "fine shortleaf timber."[29]

A few stands of the not only fire-tolerant but also fire-dependent longleaf pines also grew in Boggy Slough's preindustrial forests, being at the far northwestern reaches of their native domain in Texas. When a journalist photographed a stand of these long-needled pines just north of Cochino Bayou in November 1907 just before they were cut, at least one of them measured four feet in diameter—nearly a foot wider than a longleaf pine located just south of Cochino Bayou today, which is a Texas Forest Service state co-champion tree.[30]

Repeated fires tended to prevent the establishment of thin-barked, shallow-rooted, shade-tolerant species, which often lacked the ability to resprout from fire. Soil became warmer and drier when burned regularly, so that trees and woody vegetation that preferred a certain level of moisture did not grow. Loblolly pine (*Pinus taeda*), with a name origin meaning "mud puddle," did not grow in the regularly burned uplands in the Indian landscape and was instead confined to the less frequently burned and moister sites nearest the bottoms. Sweetgum (*Liquidambar styraciflua*), too, was affected by the Indian burning, and was found almost exclusively in the bottoms, long before its ubiquitous presence throughout twenty-first-century landscapes following industrial logging and many subsequent years of fire exclusion.[31] Under Indian fire management, Boggy Slough's drier and sandier upland sites became dominated by shortleaf pine and the drier oak and hickory species. As evidence, 40 percent of the trees cited in the earliest General Land Office boundary surveys for parcels in the Boggy Slough Conservation Area's nearly 20,000 acres were the upland post oak, hickory, and red oak species, each cited about 13 percent of the time by surveyors marking corners and bearings. Surveyors utilized pine in the same areas about 19 percent of the time. By comparison, surveyors of the bottomland tracts frequently utilized the wetter overcup, water, and willow oaks; sweetgum, ash, and elms; and rarely pine.[32]

In addition to shaping the composition of tree stands, the Indian selective use of fire also served to naturally prune certain desired plants while at the same time increasing the rate at which nutrients were absorbed into the soil, so that shrubs and grasses thrived in the wake of fire. From centuries of experience, Hasinai Caddos knew the varying frequencies required to provide the vegetation they desired most. For instance they knew that fields of berries and certain other gatherable foods produced abundant yields if burned in cycles two to three years apart, instead of annually, since many were biennially fruiting plants. For establishing and maintaining grasslands, they knew that annual fires were best. Grasses like most of the bluestems (*Andropogon* and *Schizachyrium* spp.) were rare in mature closed-canopy forests, but in a forest burned regularly by Indians they were abundant, since their characteristic late-summer accumulation of dry, coarse, dead growth created the perfect fuel through which fire readily ran, burning away not only the grasses' own dead growth, which encouraged regeneration, but also diminishing woody plants that might compete for sunlight.[33] Henri Joutel was glad to find that the Hasinai practice of regularly burning their forests produced "lovely" grass that was "very fine" for his horse while he sojourned among the Neches valley tribes during the spring of 1687. He recorded the Hasinai burned the areas immediately around their settlements annually "during the fall," which resulted in grass early the following spring that was "very beautiful and green."[34]

The practice of burning, especially of grasslands annually, was for many centuries widespread across much of North America and was later practiced in varying degrees by American settlers throughout much of the nineteenth century.[35] Witnessing similar spring landscapes as Joutel some 170 years later, the noted American landscape architect Frederick Law Olmsted traveled on horseback across Texas during the mid-1850s, crossing the middle Neches valley in present-day Cherokee and Houston Counties. Olmsted wrote that the beauty of burnt prairies in spring "has never been and never will be expressed. It is inexpressible." The sight so overwhelmed him, however, he attempted to describe it anyway, writing, "Although once dreary . . . the . . . repulsive black changed at once to a vivid green" and created an almost unimaginable "cheering effect." Olmsted also keenly observed that the bursting forth of spring grasses in "the unburnt districts, covered with the thick mat of last year's growth," was "a month behind."[36]

Most importantly, the Hasinai's selective use of fire also created what ecologists call the "edge effect," where two ecosystems overlap to produce an even greater diversity of life.[37] Indian burning increased the boundary areas between forests and grasslands, making ideal site conditions for many species of plants, which in turn created ideal habitats for numerous species of wildlife. In such ways the Hasinai increased the productivity of the land simply by imitating natural processes such as lightning-caused fire, windfall, and tree mortality and disease events, all of which created forest openings. Selective Indian burning thus promoted a further patchwork pattern to the forest and a mosaic quality of ecosystems, producing forests in various levels of ecological succession, which contributed to sustaining the Hasinai's settled life.[38]

The open understory landscape of the Hasinai people remains one of their defining, yet often overlooked, cultural characteristics.[39] Fire was a significant, even sacred, tool of the Hasinai in clearing lands and shaping vegetation, cooking, firing pottery, drying and preserving food, making weapons and tools, maintaining mosquito-repelling smoke around their villages, and a host of other uses and customs. Fire was so central to the lifeways of the Hasinai, the Spanish believed that they actually worshipped it, describing in great detail and with fascination how the inhabitants of each house maintained "a perpetual fire" inside their homes, regardless of the season. Within a great fire temple, "like that of a parish church," as Espinosa described, Hasinai leaders preserved an inextinguishable fire from which flaming embers were carried with wooden tongs in all directions to the surrounding villages and to each new house at the time of its construction. Members of each household took immense care to preserve their fire, fearing great calamity would befall all inhabitants if it burned out. The Spanish priests recorded that the Hasinai sacrificed to these fires the first harvests of crops and other plant foods as well as the first of all the game they killed. They are "deluded," Espinosa wrote in 1716, for "they claim that fire created all of these things."[40] Ironically, in an ecological sense, Espinosa probably did not realize that fire had indeed "created all of these things."

The spatial extent of the Hasinai-managed lands was vast. The widespread Indian villages and communities, which contained a dozen or more large houses each, along with the surrounding lands variously shaped by fire, occupied many acres. The Hasinai located their villages and fields near the river, creeks, and sloughs on gentle moist slopes and terraces between frequently flooded bottomlands and well-drained uplands, which made ideal sites for their staple crops of corn, beans, squash, melons,

and sunflowers.[41] The Caddo sites discovered along Franklin Slough in North Boggy are prime examples of that habitat. The cultivated fields, cleared of all living trees by girdling, were nearest the scattered dwellings and were burned annually along with surrounding grasslands near marshes and shallow lakes, which the Spanish called *lagunas* and nineteenth-century Boggy Slough land surveyors called "river swamps" and "lakes in swamp."[42] The annual Indian burning also controlled fleas, ticks, and other pests nearest their villages. Next were areas burned every two to three years, because some plants, such as the biennially fruiting blackberries, would have been eliminated through annual burning, but produced abundantly when pruned by fire every second or third year. This second level of managed land also provided relatively open areas for defensive purposes. Lands utilized for small game hunting and upland mast foraging followed, and then lands beyond for larger game.

The Hasinai burned each outer management area less frequently and at different seasons, depending on the desired result and the amount of fuel accumulation, up to intervals of five, ten, and twenty years. The cycles of repeated surface burns in varying intervals was surely broken occasionally when fire escaped in the outer perimeters, especially during times of drought, which historically was about every ten to fifteen years, potentially causing conflagrations not extinguished until rains quenched them or they reached major streams. Because the villages were located near frequently flooded bottomlands where fire rarely traveled except for intentional firings of cane brakes to stimulate and increase supplies of giant cane (*Arundinaria gigantea*), a good provision of gatherable deciduous firewood was preserved and readily at hand for reasonably long periods of time, even though the perpetual fires within each dwelling and ceremonial house certainly consumed large quantities of firewood through the generations.[43]

The altered landscape mosaic shifted occasionally, such as when the Hasinai relocated their villages during times of disease, when crops failed, or when fuel wood eventually diminished. The result

A lone cardinal flower blooms in the light of a setting sun along the banks of the Neches River near Britton Slough in October 2017. *Photo by the author.*

The resulting landscape fabric was quite large. In 1686 Anastase Douay, one of LaSalle's priests, recorded that the distance between the Hasinai tribes west of the Neches River and the tribes east of the Angelina River was 52 miles. Douay said the Hasinai countryside of connected "hamlets" was "one of the largest and most populous [he had] seen in America."[45] When the Spanish embraced the same landscape a few years later, they estimated it to be some 720 square miles, or half a million acres, covering an area north and south of the most traveled east–west paths between the most visited villages.[46]

Paths connecting the widely spread villages were also noticeably open, as were the larger landscapes through which they passed. In 1687, when LaSalle's brother, Jean Cavelier, traveled between the villages along the Neches and those along the Angelina, he reported Hasinai escorts led him over "as well beaten a road as that from Orleans to Paris." For a distance of more than 50 miles, woodlands were almost unnoticeable, he said, for "we rode the whole way through beautiful and vast prairies."[47] In 1727 the Spanish cartographic engineer Francisco Barreiro surveyed the territory and provided further description when he produced a beautiful map of "Provincia De Los Tejas" and wrote in his accompanying report, "Al-

of moving was an expansion over many miles of a landscape in various stages of forest succession, altered by fire and other human, as well as natural, disturbances such as wind, drought, ice, tree disease, and insect infestations. Abandoned crop fields, no longer burned annually, became forested landscapes again, while river and creek bottoms, no longer constantly gathered for fuel and exploited for cane resources, also returned to later successional stages. Over the course of decades and centuries, later generations returned to former village sites, repeating and spreading again the successional process.[44]

though the greater part of its land is a continuous woods, this is so sparse that it is no trouble at all to cross it, even when there is no road or path." He also added that there was no "elevation, mountain, or hill which cannot be ascended while riding a horse at full speed."[48] Barreiro's studied observations suggest that although a few early Spaniards may have become lost in the East Texas forests, the experience may have resulted from losing a particular "road or path" within an open understory rather than within a dense understory where worn pathways would have been more pronounced.[49]

The open Hasinai landscape endured at least into the early nineteenth century, in spite of a decreasing Hasinai population, which may have lessened the frequency of their understory-clearing forest firings.[50] When Stephen F. Austin rode horseback through East Texas for the first time in 1821, he saw "handsome, smooth prairies" and "good pasturage" within the timbered uplands west of Nacogdoches and "very little undergrowth" in the forests along the many branches between the Angelina and Neches Rivers, noting open stands of oak, hickory, elm, and black walnut, as well as "rich bottoms" that were both "large" and "wide." During several days of riding, he saw the grass as "more abundant and of a ranker and more luxuriant growth than I have ever seen before in any country."[51] In 1834 a traveler from the northeastern United States recorded riding westward from Nacogdoches and still finding open forests of pine, oak, and hickory interspersed by small prairies. Wherever he found groves of pines, he noted the trees were "straight and tall, but standing so far apart that a carriage might go almost anywhere among them. The grass grew beneath them, and we could see a great distance as we passed along. And thus it continued for about twenty miles."[52] Upon reaching the east bank of the swollen Neches River, this traveler said he could see across the waters, "a house half a mile distant, through the woods."[53]

Not all East Texas river bottoms held such a vista through open woods. Although travelers during the late seventeenth to the early nineteenth centuries routinely wrote of easy passage across Hasinai country, especially between Nacogdoches and the Neches River, they noted sections of "very dense woods" along the middle and lower Trinity and Brazos Rivers and southwest of the Neches River in present-day Tyler County.[54] These woods, especially sections along the middle and lower Trinity, were home to the Bidai tribes, who did not share the Hasinai affinity of intensive landscape shaping. It is no coincidence that the word *bidai* is Caddoan, meaning "brushwood" or "brush people." That the Hasinai would assign such a name to their nearest neighbors indicates the clear distinction they saw between differing landscapes and between themselves and others.[55] The Bidai lived only a partially settled life and moved seasonally along the lower stretches of the Trinity and San Jacinto Rivers, keeping in contact with the even less settled Orcoquisac peoples along the coast. French traders, too, moved in relative secrecy among these Bidai and Orcoquisac tribes, often coming by canoes from the coast, as land approaches were difficult because of the dense vegetation, which later Anglo-Americans would call "the Big Thicket." It is also no coincidence that since nomadic forest-dwelling peoples tended to clear land less, they relied more on water transportation than did more settled peoples such as the Hasinai Caddo. There is little evidence to suggest the Hasinai depended on rivers for any long-distance travel, and there is no evidence of others reaching them by canoe. In fact, the historical record suggests that all peoples—Spanish, French, Jumano, Bidai, as well as the Hasinai themselves—traveled mostly *across* rivers rather than on them when moving through Hasinai territory. It was partly for this reason—a long-established open forest understory and a network of trails—that the Spanish marked their various royal roads, or "King's" highways, across Hasinai country and not through the less-managed lands of others.[56]

Dense, highly shaded forests held little value in the Hasinai economy, which benefited most from younger to middle-aged trees in varying stages of succession, which were more productive and manageable. A younger successional forest provided more mast, fruits, and other resources than an older closed-canopy forest, which eventually became sterile.[57] Some hickories for instance, although capable of living five hundred years, are most productive between the ages of 40 and 125 years and cease producing nuts by about 225 years of age. Joutel thought the oaks, hickories, and walnuts east of the Trinity River, especially those nearest the Neches, were not as large as those west of the Trinity. He wondered about soil conditions as the reason, but the Hasinai's land exploitation practices may have also been factors.[58] The Hasinai's stone axes and other cutting tools worked best on smaller trees, which provided conveniently sized limbs, roots, and bark resources, which were easily procured and put to numerous purposes, including house and furniture construction, as well as making medicines, tools, fishing lines, ropes, and lashings. The Hasinai made strong cordage in various sizes and strengths from long strips of the fibrous cambium layer between the sapwood and outer bark of many different tree species, such as elm, basswood (also known as linden or linn), walnut, ash, and cedar, and the Spanish believed it was as strong as any rope manufactured in Europe. Joutel said the Hasinai made "very strong rope" from "little walnut trees," noting that the tribes avoided the use of leather in fashioning various lashings and straps to prevent their dogs, which were domesticated wolves and coyotes, from gnawing the leather and destroying tools, furniture, and homes.[59]

Although the Hasinai worked and managed their environment more intently than any other indigenous people of Texas, their forested home, no matter how open, remained nevertheless unsuitable to the majority of Spanish standards of civilization and city building. Eager in his missionary zeal, Fray Mazanet initially believed missions could be established in East Texas more economically than anywhere else, because, as he wrote in 1690, "the Tejas are people inclined to work."[60] Mazanet soon learned, however, that the Hasinai had no desire to congregate and move to compact pueblo-style housing such as the Spanish

had experienced along the Rio Grande. Mazanet saw the fertile soils of the forest and the "work" of the Hasinai perhaps without realizing subtle but important ecological connections between plants, trees, and soils or the differences in value systems between two cultures. In fact, the trees themselves, which did as much to produce the soils as the soils did to create the trees, were seen as a liability through European eyes. Writing to the Viceroy of Mexico in August 1691, Casañas described the land of the middle Neches valley as an almost ideal colony location. The soil was rich and fertile, even "better" than the soil of Spain, he dared to say. "It has but one fault," he cautioned, "that of being very thickly covered with a great variety of trees."[61] Casañas correctly stated that the Hasinai would never consent to city dwelling if it meant changing their culture, but while he saw the reason merely as a determined refusal to clear more trees, it could be that the Hasinai simply rejected Spanish appeals to forsake a way of life proven by centuries of experience. Meanwhile, other priests, such as Hidalgo, also tempered their initial prospects, seeing the Neches valley's trees as prohibitive to extensive sheep and cattle ranching, although they did feel the region was most favorable to raising large herds of swine.[62]

Some military captains, too, held the Hasinai forested homeland in disfavor, judging the many openings too small to accommodate large camps of traveling armies with their numerous packs of trade goods and hundreds, sometimes thousands, of accompanying livestock, including spare horses, in tow. In 1691 Governor Terán de los Ríos felt uneasy camping spread out within the Hasinai forests, fearing Indian thievery under the cover of darkness. When Governor Aguayo passed through the middle Neches River valley in 1721, an incredible entourage of five hundred mounted soldiers, four thousand spare horses, fourteen hundred mules (six hundred carrying packs), nine hundred sheep, and six hundred cattle followed behind him. Strung out for miles, his army spent sixteen days crossing the swollen Trinity River. When they came to the Neches, they spent six days building a timber bridge across it. This large entrada of so many men and beasts was not so much concerned about moving through any forest but with simply avoiding the obliteration of Hasinai cornfields.[63]

Written observations of the land during Aguayo's epic journey through East Texas illustrate again differences in perspective. Whereas Casañas had seen great numbers of trees that negatively affected European civilization building, one of Aguayo's priests, Fray Juan Antonio Peña, described the same landscape as "a country thinly covered with trees" and "woods thinly settled with trees."[64] With such conflicting views—thickly versus thinly—it is clear that even the most basic understanding, and appreciation, of a forest was in the eyes of the beholder, saying as much about the observers as it did about the landscapes observed.[65]

Dissimilar ideas and even preferences against a forest environment persisted into the Mexican era. Although Jose María Sánchez, the French naturalist Jean-Louis Berlandier's draftsman, could pronounce the East Texas forests as "vast and majestic" and even "beautiful" during his travels in 1828, he utterly detested "the terrible floods caused by the rivers which form horrible marshes and lakes, where immense numbers of mosquitoes, ticks, red bugs, gadflies and etc. breed."[66] Even Mexican General Manuel Mier y Terán, who found aesthetic beauty as well as spiritual and contemplative bliss in "the eternal forests of Tejas," complained also of humidity and insects.[67] The various Indian practices of repelling mosquitoes by smearing on their bodies concoctions involving alligator grease, mud, and the oils from various crushed plant leaves—such as from American beautyberry or southern wax myrtle—did not appeal to Spanish proprieties, nor did the smoke that constantly filled Hasinai houses and surrounded their villages along the floodplains.[68]

Aside from descriptions of the general climate and landscape, most of the observations made by Neches valley writers during the seventeenth and eighteenth centuries focused on specific forest grasses, plants, trees, and wildlife, because their authors saw firsthand the importance of such things to the Hasinai way of life.[69] In addition to the various berries, grapes, plums, and other fruits, the nuts from walnut, chinquapin, pecan, and several types of hickory trees were high in protein, calories, carbohydrates, and especially fat. The vegetable fat and protein in nuts made them an important part of the Hasinai diet, because they supplemented the low-fat protein of the white-tailed deer and the high carbohydrates of wild roots, fruits, and garden vegetables. Nuts were readily collected during high mast years (variably by species, every two to seven years), usually by women, in significant enough quantities to be stored to last during seasons of low mast. Some were eaten raw, but they were also crushed and made into meal and oils. When mixed with other ingredients, such as with cornmeal, as well as with the seeds from various grasses and sunflowers and with berries and grapes, the concoction made a fine trail food, something that was easily carried while hunting and traveling. When boiled, the nut meal and oils made a variety of "butters," "milks," and warm drinks. To grind the nuts, the Indians made large mortars, or bowls, from the trunks of hardwood trees, such as from walnut (*Juglans nigra*), hickory (*Carya* spp.), and black gum (*Nyssa sylvatica*), hollowed out with fire. Hasinai women used pestles, or poles, five or more feet in length, made also from walnut, hickory, and black gum to grind and mash the various nuts, as well as corn and sunflower and grass seeds. Black gum was a favorite corn-grinding resource because of the sweet taste the wood imparted to cornmeal when utilized in that manner. Hasinai women usually performed the meal-grinding work outside, but in inclement weather they took their work inside the large huts. Acorns, too, were abundant and held sufficient caloric as well as protein values to be depended on as a type of starvation food, in case the cultivated crops of corn, beans, and squash failed. As food, acorns from swamp chestnut oak and other white oaks were probably preferred over those from red oaks because of the higher volume of acidic tannin in red oaks, although the tannin was not too difficult to remove through grinding and boiling.[70]

Hasinai men and women utilized the tannin from red oak bark (an important commodity in the Hasinai economy), along with deer and buffalo brains, to treat animal hides and make leather that was extremely soft, supple, resistant to wear and tear, and impervious to water and putrefaction.[71] They used acorn shells as well as walnut husks, bark, and roots to dye deer skins, often a rich black color that impressed the Europeans. In addition to making articles of soft clothing, some of which were adorned with ornaments of shells and later beads, the Indians made practical as well as decorative bags, curtains, mats, and bedding covers from the various animal skins.[72] Indian men used the tines of deer antlers to knap and shape chert into sharp arrow points, knives, and scrapers, and they utilized larger antlers to rive wood. They also used whole deer heads and body skins to disguise themselves in stalking and hunting deer, which was a great fascination to Spanish observers.[73]

The Hasinai were great hunters, not just of deer, but also of bear and buffalo and many birds, including turkeys. They were cunning and took great care to go unnoticed by game while hunting. Just as they concealed themselves in deer skins and heads to hunt deer, they dressed in a camouflage of feathers when hunting turkeys. Before crossing prairies and other forest openings, they remained at the edges of the trees for some time, carefully observing the land for anything out of the ordinary. Upon seeing free passage, they cut a large tree branch, which they carried across the opening, crouching and hiding beneath it. They also climbed tall trees from which they could "see everything," one Spaniard wrote, without themselves being observed.[74] Through centuries of experience they were excellent marksmen with bows and arrows and later with rifles. They hunted bear fearlessly, which also impressed the Spanish, who were themselves proud when one of their own people killed one, or more. Admitting he might be boasting, Fray Espinosa wrote once that "while accompanied by a number of Indians who, with their dogs, had treed two bears, I killed them both with my own hands at one shot; and, from behind the protection of an oak, I succeeded in hitting another bear in the head when he was coming down a pathway alone."[75] In addition to using dogs, which the Indians domesticated from wolves and coyotes, to hunt bear, Hasinai warriors employed them also to carry home hides and meat, especially buffalo meat from areas west of the Trinity River. Even after obtaining horses, the Hasinai continued to employ dogs in transporting meat and hides, and some still preferred to hunt buffalo by foot because of their stealthy and proven stalking abilities.[76]

Just as deer provided food, clothing, and other resources, bear and buffalo also supplied many needs. Bear fat, especially, was highly prized. Hasinai used it in food seasoning and cooking year round. Women stored it in earthen pots inside their houses and rolled it in small blankets of moss for travel. They used bear fat to fry fresh fish that they caught in the river and bottomland lakes and sloughs, and their venison and buffalo meat cooked in bear fat was considered a delicacy. Bear fat became so valuable on the American frontier that by the middle eighteenth century the French were obtaining two thousand barrels of it every year from the Hasinai in trade, no doubt adding to the significant depopulation of bear. Although bear fat made all foods tastier, it was buffalo meat that held "first rank for its flavor," the Europeans said. When not fried, it was roasted or boiled. In addition to being a tasty source of high protein food, buffalo held other valuable uses. The Hasinai made spoons, cups, and flasks from horns, glue for arrow tips from hooves, bow strings from ligaments, and shields, boots, shoes, and, later, saddles from buffalo hides. The Hasinai also made great rugs from both bear and buffalo skins and effective agricultural hoes from their shoulder bones.[77]

Seventeenth- and eighteenth-century Europeans found turkeys in great abundance in the middle Neches and Angelina valleys, where the large fowl and the forest-shaping Hasinai experienced a synergistic relationship. Spaniards mentioned finding the birds "in flocks" throughout the forests and plains, where they were often the primary food source to travelers over successive days.[78] A modern

Hasinai in the 1980s wrote that the turkey remained more closely associated with her people "than any other animal" because the two "lived in close proximity for centuries." Enjoying the same diverse and open forest habitat, turkeys came to locate their roosts and the Hasinai located their villages and cornfields never too far apart. Turkey roosts offered nearby Hasinai villages a natural protective warning from intruders in the night, while Hasinai cornfields surely attracted turkeys. Certain bands of Hasinai tribes may have even domesticated some flocks.[79]

Hasinai villages, while being near turkey roosts, were also adjacent to sloughs, creeks, and bottomland lakes, which make up a large portion of today's Boggy Slough Conservation Area. The Spanish said these bodies of water were "full of fish of every kind," similar to the ones that swam in the river, sometimes calling the slack waters, "lagoons, where different kinds of fish abound." The Hasinai made weirs from cane, river birch, or willow sticks to trap fish in stagnant and slow-moving backwaters, and they used crushed walnut shells and red buckeye seeds and roots as a toxin to stun the fish for easy catching. During summer months, whole families of Hasinai camped along the Neches River, where they enjoyed several days of fish catching and feasting. Fish they didn't eat immediately, they smoked and dried in scaffolds on the river bank for carrying back to the main villages.[80] Centuries later, Boggy Slough's American settlers enjoyed a similar Neches River ritual, as families journeyed overland down to the Neches' banks for tent camping and fishing, carrying their grease and frying pans.[81] The Hasinai also ate of the river's abundant mussels and turtles, which were so numerous that the earliest European visitors believed they held real commercial possibilities.[82]

In addition to the incrementally burned village landscape, other defining Hasinai characteristics were their conical-shaped thatched grass houses and their nearby agricultural fields. Pine trees, which provided abundant leaf needles on the forest floor to carry Indian fires and maintain a desired

ecosystem, also provided the building material of tall straight pole frames for Hasinai houses, as well as public buildings for social and civic gatherings, receptions, and religious purposes. Hasinai men assembled pine poles having a base diameter of about a man's lower thigh, and set them in holes dug in the ground in a circular pattern. The tops were pulled and bent toward the center of the circle and lashed together with strong tree cambium bark cordage. A tree trunk with limbs was placed temporarily in the center, on which workers mounted to assemble and tie the tops of the poles together. This center tree was removed when the assembly work was completed. Crosswise slender poles or laths were used to further bind and brace the vertical poles together, to which long grasses (canes and reeds) were attached on the outside of the house as siding. Women generally performed the grass thatching, beginning at the bottom and climbing up the horizontal laths.[83] Up to six families may have resided in each conical-shaped house, which were about 40 to 60 feet in diameter and 50 feet high. Europeans described their appearance as being like large beehives or extremely high haycocks. The houses contained no windows and only one door, and featured an opening in the center of the roof to let out smoke from the continually burning fires. Inside, the floors were kept clean and well swept. There were mats of cane, reeds, and animal hides for sitting, and rooms were occasionally partitioned by hanging mats made of reeds, often highly decorative. Hidalgo felt the colorful reed mats, which were dyed black, red, and yellow, and often checkered, were beautiful enough to adorn "ladies drawing rooms" in Europe. Around the walls were platform beds made from wood frames, covered with mats of reeds and cane under buffalo hides. Benches, tables, and chests were also made of wood, cane, and reeds, while the wood from black walnut trees provided plates and platters and various decorative carvings, often in the forms of "little ducks" as well as alligators.[84]

Hasinai house building was a communal activity. Fray Espinosa recorded the process in 1722,

A grove of young pines glow in the golden morning sunlight as the moon sets behind them, at Rayville in the Boggy Slough Conservation Area, September 2017. *Photo by the author.*

saying that when a family decided it was time to construct a house, they first informed the chiefs of their intentions. These community leaders then set the date for the project and instructed messengers to alert the tribe so they would help in the construction. The messengers went from house to house throughout the village and left small sticks, signifying the quantity and size of the poles and laths to secure, trim, and clean and when to bring them to the construction site. Further instructions were provided so that everyone knew who was responsible for the various types of construction work to be done and what preparations were necessary. The messengers then slept at the building site the night before the appointed day of construction. At dawn, the messengers rose and called all the people together. "Upon the first call," said Espinosa, each man came running with his pole on his shoulder and placed it in the hole which he

had previously dug. In this fashion, the pole setting took little more than an hour, followed by securing all the lath and horizontal bracing poles, working from the bottom up. Women then joined in the work by attaching the long grass siding, to a thickness of eight to twelve inches. By midday the house was finished, and all participants were treated to a feast prepared by the new home dwellers.[85]

The Hasinai took great care in their personal appearance, especially in their clothes. Hasinai women carefully treated and dyed animal skins, which when finished were soft and resembled "fine cloth." They often cut fringes along the edges of the soft clothing, decorating them with shells and dyed reeds, making dresses that were "very pretty," said one priest. Women were nearly always modestly dressed and usually wore soft deerskin skirts as well as deerskin blouses. In the warmest months men went naked indoors, while they usually wore at least some form of breechcloth outdoors. Women kept their hair long and well combed into a braid tied together with a string of rabbit's hair. Men usually kept their hair short, and they shaved using sharp mussel shells. They especially liked to wear colorful feathers as a head covering, and they stored the finest of the feathers in hollow reeds for special occasions. Women usually tattooed their upper bodies and faces by forcing fine charcoal under pricked skin. Men were occasionally tattooed but they seemed to have preferred temporary face and body painting instead, using red ochre.[86]

The Spanish were quick to identify the desirability of Hasinai lands for religious mission work and potential settlement, while they also, at least initially, accepted the Hasinai belief that the Neches valley land was "the best in the world."[87] In their agricultural fields, which they kept productive through rotational planting, Hasinai men and women planted fast-growing, quick-maturing food crops, including two varieties of corn that matured at different seasons—an early "little corn" harvested between May and July and a later "flour corn" harvested between July and September—and six varieties of beans, as well as squash, oily seed plants such as sunflowers, and starchy seed plants such as panic grass. In addition to such field crops and the berry and fruit orchards, the Hasinai also grew a little tobacco for religious and diplomatic uses and also bottle gourds that served in making many different utility vessels.[88] For bean poles to support climbing bean plants, the Hasinai cut stalks of switch and river cane, about seven feet in length, leaving the sturdy forked branches of the cane attached. Once the canes were dried, the Hasinai placed the stalks in the ground next to their bean vines. Since the forks of the cane stalks provided additional area for the vines to climb and spread, the Europeans believed the practice yielded higher production than using any other resource to train climbing vines. At harvest time, the Indians simply cut the vines at the ground, leaving them attached to the cane stalks, then gathered the stalks in bunches and carried them inside their houses. There, the beans were picked and placed inside cane and reed baskets with sturdy lids to keep out rats, after first being covered with siftings of ashes to ward off weevils. Corn was dried on large cribs made from small wood or dried cane that reached up to ten feet above smoky fires. After drying, the shelled corn, like the beans, was placed separately inside cane and reed baskets and covered with ashes for preservation. The Hasinai strung the best ears of corn together, leaving the shucks on, and hung them in the middle of their houses to be near the smoke, preserving enough seed for two years' worth of plantings, in case of crop failures.[89]

The Hasinai uses of the Neches valley's natural resources are too numerous to include every one, but a few more examples pertinent to Boggy Slough deserve at least passing mention. Saline glades and prairies, such as those between Boggy and Britton Sloughs, home to the rare and endangered Texas prairie dawn-flower (*Hymenoxys texana*), and the larger Bluff Prairie Saline north and east of Cedar Creek, home to the rare Neches River rose mallow (*Hibiscus dasycalyx*), provided important salt resources. The earliest land surveyors noted these open flat places in their field notes, setting posts "in the prairie[s]," since trees were absent for use as corner witnesses. These areas were exceptionally wet and mushy during winter and spring and were extremely dry and hard during the summer and fall. They were places where drainage patterns and slow evaporation rates created unique soil compositions of surface salts and low pimple mounds among the coarse sands and compacted clays, which discouraged the growth of woody plants and trees. During his East Texas visit during the early nineteenth century, General Terán noted that indigenous peoples as well as Mexican and Anglo-American settlers extracted salt "in abundance" from such places, which he called "fields that abound in a lime clay."[90]

Giant cane, or river cane (*Arundinaria gigantea*), was an extremely important resource to the Hasinai, and it was abundant all along the Neches River and the bottoms of its feeder streams. In 1886 a land surveyor noted that Boggy Slough Island was "covered with large cane."[91] To the indigenous peoples, cane fields offered a supermarket of goods. Besides the Hasinai use of cane in the construction of houses, furniture, mats, crates, woven baskets, service platters, and fish traps, the plants' shoots and seeds provided food and medicines, while the stalks served in making smoking pipes, musical flutes, candles, toys, and clothing and hair decorations, as well as arrow shafts, blowguns, and darts for small game hunting. The judicious harvest of cane by the Indians advantageously pruned the stands and also promoted vigorous new growth. Periodic Indian burning of canebrakes about every five to ten years also rejuvenated and sustained healthy stands.[92]

Besides using cane to make musical flutes, the Hasinai created other instruments from a variety of additional resources. They utilized the hollow bones of various wetland wading birds—herons, egrets, and cranes—to make additional flutes. From bottle gourds and little rocks they fashioned rattles and other percussive instruments, and by stretching wet animal hides across hollowed tree kettles they formed large drums. A favored species for such large drums was bottomland black gum (*Nyssa sylvatica*) because of the wood's distinctive resonance qualities.[93]

Other notable wood uses included river birch (*Betula nigra*) that grew in abundance along the sandy banks of the river and streams. Indians used the bark, sap, and leaves medicinally, and the papery peeling bark provided excellent fire tinder, wet or dry. River birch bark was probably also used as a medium to communicate written or drawn spatial relations, such as when LaSalle asked a Nabadache chief near the Neches River to "draw on bark a map of their country, of that of their neighbors, and of the river Colbert, or Mississippi, with which they were acquainted," as recorded by Father Anastase Douay in 1686.[94] Osage orange (*Maclura pomifera*), or bois d'arc as known by the French, meaning "wood of the bow," was highly prized by the Hasinai and many other North American tribes for making high-quality bows and war clubs. Hasinai and other tribes traded the valuable wood as far away as present-day New York. Although it is believed the original native range of Osage orange was primarily in Oklahoma, northern Texas, southwestern Arkansas, and northwestern Louisiana, the tree is easily transplanted and cultivated, and was probably planted by some Hasinai tribes along the Neches. John R. Swanton, the noted early-twentieth-century anthropologist, believed the Caddoan word for Osage orange was Nachawi (Natca' wi), which was also their native name for the Neches River.[95]

Clay deposits suitable for making pottery occurred widely throughout the Neches valley and were easily obtained from bluff and bank exposures along the river and streams and by digging shallow pits. Hasinai knew well where to find the best quality clays and how to prepare them. Anthropologists consider the pottery made by Hasinai women to be some of the finest aboriginal pottery manufactured in North America, because of its high-quality material construction, design, and pure artistry. Using local clays tempered with varying consistencies of burned and pulverized

bone and mussel shell fragments, Hasinai women and girls mixed precise amounts of water to form all kinds of basic cookware and storage vessels, as well as finely crafted and highly decorative serving plates, bowls, cups, and bottles that were engraved and incised. They used smooth pebbles and small stones from the creeks to burnish the pottery before final drying, tediously polishing the outside surfaces to a desired level of luster. To obtain the hottest fires to cure their ceramics, they burned wood from hickory and Osage orange trees.

Archaeologists and anthropologists estimate the population of the East Texas Caddos between eighteen thousand and sixty thousand prior to their exposure to European diseases early in the sixteenth century, and then their number plummeted to about ten thousand by the end of the seventeenth century.[96] Unfortunately for the Caddos and the other indigenous peoples of America, their isolation from the Old World had prevented their exposure to deadly diseases to which Europeans over the centuries had developed immunities. Diseases such as smallpox, measles, and cholera found new victims in the Caddo, who lacked biological resources to fight them. Epidemics resulted, causing significant death rates and declining fertility. As Caddo historian F. Todd Smith said, "more than any other factor, disease caused the Indians to weaken and decline, opening the door for invasion and displacement by the Europeans."[97]

As the land's longtime distinctive managers steadily declined in number and influence, the land also changed. The diseases and vices of the Europeans took a heavy toll on the Hasinai, and they soon abandoned their old ways of using the land. They along with other Caddos that survived soon embraced an exchange-based economy with the Spanish and French that began an unsustainable drain on the land's natural resources. Vast populations of wildlife that were once common also declined, and in their places came herds of European grazing animals that required something different from the plants and soils. Food became scarce for the Hasinai, resulting in malnutrition and further decline.

A new economy based on the value of deer skins—from which the English word "buck" originated as an expression of money—emerged whereby the Hasinai traded both directly and as middlemen in supplying animal hides to the French and Spanish in exchange for manufactured goods and horses. Hasinai women desired things such as metal axes, knives, kettles, and needles to lighten the toil of their daily work, and Hasinai men desired horses, guns, powder, and bullets to assist them in their hunting and defense against other tribes who were also pressured under European influences.[98]

Deer and other wild game in Boggy Slough and surrounding areas became hunted almost solely for their hides. When the Mexican General Manuel de Mier Y Terán visited East Texas in 1828 he reported eighty thousand deer skins were traded in one year alone between Nacogdoches and Natchitoches. Terán acknowledged to Mexican President Guadalupe Victoria the number seemed unimaginably high, but his personal inspection of the Nacogdoches merchants' books confirmed the count.[99] Terán expressed concern about the sustainability of such hunting activities, and he predicted deer in East Texas would eventually be extinct, as they were already becoming scarce in the United States. Along with the deer skins, Terán also recorded some fifteen hundred bearskins and twelve hundred otter and six hundred beaver pelts were traded annually. He thought the otter and beaver numbers would have been even higher, but those animals were already "almost eradicated" along the Neches, Angelina, and Trinity Rivers, he said, "because of the relentless pursuit of American trappers."[100]

Meanwhile, feral hogs were overrunning the land. They were already well established in East Texas by the late seventeenth century, probably having descended from swine that escaped from the DeSoto-Moscoso entrada from Florida into East Texas in 1542. By the 1680s, when the Talon brothers of France lived among the Hasinai peoples along the Neches, they said they saw "runaway pigs all over the country." In 1691 Fray Casañas included "wild hogs" among the Neches River's "various kinds of animals that [were] good to eat," and he described them as "quite large and savage like those in New Spain."[101] Similar descriptions of East Texas wild swine were given for at least the next 160 years, perhaps none more famous than Frederick Law Olmsted's account of tangling with "savage" hogs at a Neches River camp one night in December 1853. Olmsted wrote that the wild hogs were "a disgusting annoyance beyond all description," being "frantic and delirious with hunger." They were so vicious that some "ran directly through the fire" and carried away a chicken while it was still roasting. Others managed to take half the corn that was being fed to the horses, even though two men stood guard. "The fiercest" hog, Olmsted said, resisted "even a clubbing" and continued to eat and squeal "through the blows."[102]

By the 1820s some herdsmen along the Neches River were raising hogs for commercial gain, and it may have been during this time, certainly no later than early in the 1830s, that Boggy Slough's most important stream besides the Neches River— Arroyo de los Cochinos, or Cochino Bayou, meaning "stream of pigs"—received its name.[103] In 1828 General Terán observed that some immigrant Alabama tribes along the Neches River, downriver from Boggy Slough, were already cultivating large fields of corn and sweet potatoes, which were fenced to keep out their sizable herds of cattle and hogs, being raised to support the Nacogdoches markets.[104] It was now clear that Hasinai land that was once a land of provision was becoming instead a land of production.

As the newly formed United States government continued to extinguish Indian titles to lands within its expanding borders during the late eighteenth century, many displaced and weakened tribes, such as the Shawnee, Cherokee, Biloxi, Delaware, Kickapoo, Alabama, and Coushatta, moved west into Spanish and later Mexican Texas, further pressuring the lands of the native Hasinai. Of these tribes, only the Alabama and Coushatta were allowed an eventual home in Texas, as the others, like the Hasinai, were pushed into northern Texas and then expelled to Oklahoma by the

1850s. Regrettably, the disappearance of the Hasinai from East Texas, which had been their homeland for more than a millennium, was so rapid that the onrushing American frontier hardly noticed their passing, naming several prairies and creeks in the middle Neches valley, as well as a county, after the immigrant tribes who lived there only briefly. Even the US Department of Agriculture's name of a bottomland soil type, Pophers, which makes up 26 percent of Boggy Slough's land today, was named for an immigrant Shawnee chief.[105]

For thousands of years the Hasinai and their Woodland ancestors had experimented with the soils, plants, trees, and waters of Boggy Slough to learn what resources worked best for their people's survival and success. Their experience taught them the precious value of sunlight and how the powerful use of broadcast fire would provide the plant and animal resources they favored. They knew that the selective use of fire in varying intervals and intensities caused a patchwork of "edges" within the forest, where different environments overlapped to create an even greater diversity of plant and animal life. By encouraging certain natural processes to the disfavor of others, the Hasinai did much to shape the forests that later American settlers and business corporations desired and came to possess.

Far from being perfect ecologists, the Hasinai nevertheless used the land in ways that made them the most productive, advanced, and populous peoples of Texas. What Mexican General Terán called "the eternal forests of Tejas" and the Spanish earlier called "Provincia de los Tejas," was simply home to the Hasinai Caddos; it had been that way for a long time. When a Caddo chief went to visit General Terán at Nacogdoches in 1828, Terán asked him whether he resided in the land of Mexico or in the land of the United States. Terán said that, when the chief "fully understood what was being asked, he replied that he was not in Mexican territory nor in that of the North Americans, but in his own land, which was nothing else but his."[106]

The Caddo chief soon experienced, however, what the history of Boggy Slough reveals—that human relations with the land are dynamic and always changing.

CHAPTER 3

A Land of Production

The charming landscape which I saw this morning is indubitably made up of some twenty or thirty farms. Miller owns this field, Locke that, and Manning the woodland beyond. But none of them owns the landscape.

—**RALPH WALDO EMERSON** (1836)

"We have a beautiful place, Mrs. Foster. It is on a high hill. We have beautiful flowers and roses and all kinds of fruit, and two large oak trees at the front of our gate. Red elms are all around our place. Our yard is just lovely, with all kinds of flowers. Oh, Mrs. Foster, you just ought to see our place. The redbirds are building in our vines. Mamma has a good many little chickens. The little martins have come to see us now, and we have made them a little house." With much pride, young Jessie Christie wrote these bucolic words from Sullivan's Bluff, now in the north end of the Boggy Slough Conservation Area, in the spring of 1912. Published in the *Houston Post's* "Our Young Folks" regular Sunday column, this letter was one of many dozens received weekly by the celebrated journalist and librarian Margaret Hadley Foster, who for many years encouraged the children of Texas to write her concerning a variety of topics, teaching them especially to observe and think about the world around them.[1]

Jessie Christie was one of sixteen Christie children born and raised at Sullivan's Bluff, where fifty-nine years earlier her maternal grandparents had settled a 320-acre preemption homestead grant that now includes the North Boggy Slough clubhouse. On an adjoining homestead grant, on cleared hills and terraces above Franklin Slough (named for one of Jessie's uncles), Jessie and her siblings, along with their parents and a number of aunts, uncles, cousins, nieces, and nephews, lived all around the Sullivan homesteads, which were divided by elm-shaded creeks and branches. From hilltops cleared by her forebears and grazed by sheep and cattle, Jessie could see eastward across the mayhaw-lined slough and the Neches River into Angelina County. From her Aunt Beulah Rushing's home, located on an even higher hill to the south, she could gaze for miles southward across Cochino Bayou and the pine-covered hills of South Boggy and beyond.[2]

Three of Jessie's younger sisters—Evie, Eunice, and Lara—also wrote letters to Mrs. Foster, sharing with readers of the Sunday *Post* the joys of "gathering pretty flowers on the hillside," of hearing "the pretty little birds singing," and being "glad it is springtime."[3] The Christie girls were members of Mrs. Foster's Happyhammers Club, whose mission was "to hammer happiness when and wherever possible." The club tree was the live oak, and the club pet was the mockingbird. Birds and birdsongs were important to Happyhammers, and the Christie sisters were especially perceptive of them. Their father, Henry Lafayette Christie, a native of Louisiana, named their oldest brother

Boggy Slough natives Jessie Dell Christie, seated, with her sisters, from the left, Evie Ora, Mary Alma, and Lottie Estelle, at Sullivan's Bluff, ca. 1910. Letters written by Jessie, Evie, and two other sisters describing the landscape around their rural home and school in 1912 and 1913 were published in the *Houston Post*'s long-running Sunday column, "Our Young Folks." *Author's collections.*

John Audubon—who went by "Audie"—for the noted naturalist and ornithologist John James Audubon.[4]

In addition to sharing the beauty of birds, hillsides, trees, and flowers, which were very much a part of the Christies' home and "place," the girls also wrote fondly of their male and female teachers at nearby Mount Pisgah School and of good times with family at Christmas, as well as to share a favorite verse. Evie wrote once to explain why she felt "girls are more useful than boys," saying it was because "they can cook, scrub, set the table, wash dishes, sew, clean the yard, make up beds, sweep, attend to the little baby, milk, hoe, and plow," while boys "just work in the field."[5]

The letters of the Christie girls reveal much about their world and their places in it. Primarily they show that the girls and their siblings were the inheritors of a land dynamically refashioned by generations of human endeavor. The girls' physical awareness and appreciation of trees, flowers, and birds contrasted with a landscape that now included fences, gates, bare-earth yards, rosebushes, birdhouses, schoolhouses, and domesticated livestock. Much of the nature that Jessie and her sisters wrote about was in fact produced. At their heart, the letters illustrate the inseparability of Boggy Slough's natural and social history, which, even through the eyes of children, was evident everywhere one looked.[6]

The Christie parents and grandparents located their homes and nearby fields in much the same way as had the Hasinai peoples before them. They followed natural patterns of the land—topographic relief, soils, vegetation, availability of water—and observed the types and populations of wildlife they found. All these things offered vital clues about where and how to settle and best make a living. They selected features they preferred, gave names to them, such as Sullivan's Bluff, and established their homes and "places" among the gentle mesic slopes and stream terraces, under the sun-dappled shade of elm-lined spring branches, and on the wooded and open hills within a mixed pine and hardwood forest already shaped by centuries of natural as well as cultural influences.[7] It was no coincidence that the Christie home and fields were located in the same land survey where Caddo ceramic pottery sherds are still being found today.[8] Such sites were not too much unlike the places the Christie girls' ancestors had left behind in South Carolina, Georgia, Alabama, Mississippi, and Louisiana.[9] Soon old as well as new pathways, trails, and roads connected them with their neighbors and with towns. Such a landscape, a refashioned environment of forest edges, provided families of all centuries their most basic needs of provision and protection. But such places were not only practical, they could be—as the Christie girls saw them—also "beautiful," and possibly idyllic.[10]

Like the Hasinai people before them, nineteenth-century Boggy Slough settlers worked the forested land by clearing it for agricultural crops.

A red-tailed hawk watches over a clearing that was once the old Sullivan home place, March 2018. *Photo by the author.*

They knew that the presence of certain hardwoods, such as lowland hickories and oaks, walnuts, elms, ashes, and sycamores, could be indicators of fertile soil, knowing that the trees had done as much to enrich the soil as the soil did to nurture the trees. Also like the Caddo, settlers procured nearby wood, plant, stone, and animal resources for their livelihoods.[11] Each culture modified their environment and sought to manipulate it by mimicking natural processes in similar ways, but to different purposes. The Hasinai altered their ecosystems by burning and otherwise shaping the land to promote a mosaic of habitats wherein a great variety of flora and fauna thrived. Such ecological diversity, whether natural or artificial, meant an increase in the things that kept them alive. Their use of fire was very different from that of American settlers, who burned and chopped to create a uniformity of ecosystems. Whereas Indians added to nature's seeming randomness by enhancing

forest edges in a broad patchwork pattern across a vast expanse, settlers with domesticated livestock sought to control nature as much as possible within smaller, fixed land units and sites. The different cultures produced meaningfully different outcomes. It was not that the Hasinai were model ecologists and American settlers were great despoilers of nature, but wildlife did not overgraze, whereas cattle, sheep, goats, and hogs did.[12]

Driven to accommodate their livestock—supplying it with year-round food and eliminating its predators—settlers came to see the land no longer for what it could provide but for what it could produce. Land became something to be "improved" and "developed." As much as was possible, forests were to be cut, swamps reclaimed, and farms brought "under the plow." As settlement advanced across the land under ax, fire, hoof, and plow, biological diversity declined. Plants and animals that hindered "improvements" were eliminated, and ones believed to be more useful and productive were introduced in their places. In such ways, the land was to be "gladdened," Texas governor Oran M. Roberts wrote in 1881, while another pastoralist proclaimed it was his "ambition to see a drove of sheep on every hill, a herd of cattle in every valley, and hear the grunt of the hog from every swamp."[13]

East Texas settlers, including Boggy Slough's Anglo-American families, used fire as their most powerful tool in shaping their environment. Throughout the 1840s, Adolphus Sterne of Nacogdoches recorded in his diary during the last week of each February that "the whole country [was] on fire." "Every farmer," he observed, was "burning logs or brush" and smoking up the countryside. At nights, "the whole world look[ed] to be on fire," he wrote, while during the days—because of abundant smoke—the sun "ha[d] not, nor could not, make her appearance."[14] Forestland burning was so prevalent across the United States during the nineteenth century that in 1880 the US Census Bureau, in cooperation with the US Department of Agriculture, attempted to quantify its extent. The findings conservatively estimated that at least 10,274,089 acres of forestland had burned dur-

The red dirt road that leads to the old Christie home place, August 2018. *Photo by the author.*

ing the twelve-month study period. Burned forest acreage in twelve southern states accounted for 60 percent of the total, with Texas contributing at least 599,359 acres to the number, mostly attributed to farm clearing and improving pasturage beneath high forest canopies.[15]

Late winter and early spring cycles of burning persisted in East Texas throughout the nineteenth century and well into the 1930s, much to the dismay of early-twentieth-century "second crop" pine-tree-protecting lumbermen, who sought to control the fires, as well as their human starters. State forester J. H. Foster and his colleagues' May 1917 publication, *Forest Resources of Eastern Texas*, recorded that "woodland fires" were "serious problems" throughout the region, but especially in Houston and Trinity Counties, where Boggy Slough was situated. They wrote that in Houston County, "probably two-thirds of the timbered area burns annually, largely to improve the grazing,"

while in Trinity County, "practically the entire area, outside of improved farm lands, burns over annually."[16] A few months later, Foster revealed in a Lufkin newspaper article that between September 1916 and November 1917 at least 1,304 wildfires had burned some 1,248,674 acres of forest within eighteen East Texas counties, representing 16 percent of approximately eight million acres that were under state protection.[17]

Whenever the fires of farmers and stockmen escaped into the surrounding countryside, Southern Pine Lumber Company's Diboll mill manager Watson Walker Jr. mentioned them in his regular reports to T. L. L. Temple in Texarkana. For example, in a March 9, 1925, letter, writing from the mills at Diboll, Walker reported that "very bad" wildfires in Houston County made him "uneasy all the time, both here and in the woods." Although such runaway fires seemed inevitable, Walker lamented, he was sure to inform his cousin and employer that his logging crews were "very careful" to prevent additional fires that might result from the sparks of steam log loaders and locomotives.[18]

Firing the woods annually for reasons of grazing and cultivation was once so common that fire historian Stephen Pyne concluded the customary practice was basically "the fabric of the rural South."[19] The practices of Boggy Slough's settlers were little different. Land surveys of tracts within today's Boggy Slough Conservation Area, which were made prior to Southern Pine Lumber Company purchasing the land, routinely mentioned the occasional "pine stump . . . burnt out."[20] By combining knowledge of centuries of the collective experiences of the southern Indian tribes with those of their own ancestors in land reclamation efforts back in Europe, Boggy Slough's families knew that the landscapes most productive of berries, nuts, honey, and wildlife and most conducive to livestock grazing existed because of periodic broadcast fire. In addition to burning logs from girdled trees to clear "new ground" for their expanding agricultural fields, they customarily burned the woods and other unenclosed land to shape the vegetation to their liking and comforts, taking great care to protect the split-rail "field fences" and "fence rows" that protected their corn, sugarcane, fruit trees, and sweet potato patches from free-ranging livestock. Descended from Scottish and Irish livestock-herding traditions, settlers set fires to improve pasturage and control brush in pineland savannahs; to control ticks, chiggers, and fleas—and, after 1901, the cotton boll weevil; and to cause rattlesnakes, copperheads, and cottonmouths to be seen and at least avoided. Burning to limit broadleaf brush in the understory not only promoted grass and forbs for their livestock but also allowed breezes to flow freely through the forest and across creeks and hills to cool their residences. They burned annually around their homes so their children in bare feet could roam and play, and they surrounded their houses, picket fences, and other wooden buildings with cleared, bare-earth yards, which served as firebreaks against the escaped fires of neighbors and as a point at which to ignite protective backfires when needed. In such intensively burned areas nearest their homes and fields, pine did not regenerate, nor was it necessarily desired. Such use of fire, combined with brush-eating goats, served Boggy Slough's herdsmen and farmers well.[21] The shift in the use of natural resources from "Indian fashion" to the purposes of homesteading was both a cause and a result of the scope of each culture's footprints on the land. Boggy Slough's earlier societies believed in possession by communities, whereas the nineteenth-century society adhered to a standard of possession by individuals. Primarily of English heritage, these people believed that when free men and women mixed their labor with the earth it imparted to them a right to own that "improved" land and to establish their "places" on it. In turn they assigned property boundaries between their lands and the lands of others. Indians moved their villages from time to time, which allowed cultivated fields to return to forests and regain fertility, but nineteenth-century settlers became bounded on fixed sites by their own property systems. Their continuous cropping depleted the soils of nutrients after a time, and likewise, their domesticated livestock placed stress on the native plants, which had earlier supported wildlife on the move. Soon the most palatable native forage and browse species declined, and settlers cleared more and more land to plant more and more corn and nonnative "improved" feed crops simply to feed their domesticated animals. To keep their livestock out of their expanding fields, on which the people also depended, settlers erected split-rail fences, something also new to the landscape, as were the later picket fences that surrounded their houses and bare-earth yards of chickens. Mast-bearing trees such as oaks, hickories, and chinquapins provided abundant food most years for their foraging hogs in the woods, but the occasional unpredictability of this resource led even Oran M. Roberts to write, while he served as the state's governor in 1881, that the "good farmers" of East Texas knew well that "the best mast falls in the [corn] crib."[22]

The imprints of Boggy Slough's settlers were also noticeably deeper in their cultivation practices. Whereas Indians used hoes made from stone and bone, scratching their fields no deeper than a few inches, settlers used iron plows pulled by the much larger muscles of draft animals, turning the soil more deeply and more frequently. Also, settlers continuously planted cotton, a commodified cash crop, whereby an expanding agricultural market economy became another feature of the altered landscape.

Many of Boggy Slough's early Anglo-American families prospered and increased during their first few generations, especially those homesteaders north of Cochino Bayou, as a new world of fences, gates, pastures, corncribs, barns, and enlarged fields of single crops quickly reflected their advancing labors. But the increased pressure on the land also produced a social competition among and within the generations. Neighbors and kin certainly helped one another, and they usually married among themselves, but all community assistance was essentially for individual gain. Not all lands were equal, and even the best lands were unable to serve the growing numbers of peoples and ambitions. As families grew through the generations, at a time when it was not uncommon to raise nine or more children, who each raised nine or more children themselves, the bounded land became further divided and exploited. Clannish rivalries and jealousies erupted at the same time that economic and social change from elsewhere arrived in the form of railroad and lumber corporations, which first came for the land's newly commodified pine trees and then, to have greater control of a renewable resource, acquired the land itself. Soon a rural population born to the land found it increasingly difficult to earn a living directly from it. Within a relatively short time, during one generation's experience, corporations displaced the settlers, who had earlier dispossessed the Indians. With each change in culture, the land also changed, as did society's demands on it.

The nineteenth-century settlement of Boggy Slough by American farmers and pastoralists was in many ways similar to the settlement of much of East Texas. Bounding the land began under Mexican colonization laws of the 1820s, which intended to settle the country with industrious people who would work the soil by grazing it with livestock and cultivating it in annual crops. The succeeding land policies of the Republic of Texas and State of Texas had similar intentions through homestead preemption grants, which required both residency and cultivation for several years prior to a settler actually owning the lands. The government grants classified land as best suited either for grazing or for farming, which affected the land's selling and taxing values, with farmland being the more valuable of the two. Although the presence of timber held local and practical value, forests were usually seen as a liability to agricultural clearance.[23]

Boggy Slough's first land grant surveys occurred along Cochino Bayou and Cedar Creek, where grantees saw alluvial soils and wetland meadows, believing they promised good land for growing crops and grazing livestock. In time settlers realized that the bottomland soils along those streams, which were near the river, were too poorly drained for most agricultural endeavors. Even cultivated sugarcane on those lands proved unprofitable because of the resulting syrup's salty flavor caused by the saline nature of the poorly drained soils.[24] As it happened, the original owners of those large Mexican and Republic of Texas surveys did not reside on them, and instead they sold the land as absentee owners. The actual settlers of those lands typically came and went throughout the nineteenth century, leaving for better opportunities elsewhere. Smaller-sized homestead grants north of Cochino Bayou proved to contain lands better suited to long-term settlement.

Along with individuals, railroad companies also acquired unappropriated lands through internal improvement grants made at various times by the state government. In South Boggy, the Buffalo Bayou, Brazos and Colorado Railroad Company (BBB&C) acquired two small sections of fewer than 200 acres each, first surveyed in 1860, which are now partly inundated under the waters of Black Cat Lake; in North Boggy, the International-Great Northern Railroad (I&GN) Company obtained larger grants in 1875, totaling some 4,500 acres still inside Boggy Slough Conservation Area, which included the drier and steeper sloped uplands of pine and hickory northwest of Cochino Bayou. One grant in North Boggy along the Neches River went to famous early Texas financiers and merchants Thomas F. McKinney and Samuel May Williams in 1857.[25] Lands deemed the poorest—those that flooded frequently for long durations, such as at the mouth of Cochino Bayou and parts of Boggy Slough Island—went last, the proceeds from their sale going to the state's Permanent School Fund.[26]

The earliest land surveys in Boggy Slough were Mexican government colonization grants made to settlers in the colony of empresario José Vehlein, a German merchant of Mexico City and partner with David G. Burnet and Lorenzo De Zavala in the Galveston Bay and Texas Land Company. In 1835 Candido Sanchez and Juan José de los Reyes, declaring themselves natives of Mexico, married

The tiny gravestone of the infant Annie Mae Johnson, who was born and died on August 21, 1904. She was buried on a hill that later became the site of the Boggy Slough Hunting Club's second clubhouse. In the 1950s, Southern Pine Lumber Company placed a heavy barrier of railroad rails to protect the grave from cattle and hogs. *Photo by the author, June 2014.*

with children, and being farmers and stock raisers, located their leagues of land (4,428 acres each) to contain the evergreen switch cane and hardwood bottomlands and wet prairies along Cedar Creek and Cochino Bayou. Both surveys were near the Neches River but far enough away to avoid lengthy overflows. Sanchez located his Cedar Creek survey to include the confluence of Elm Creek, which became later known as the South Fork of Cedar Creek. Reyes located his Cochino Bayou survey to include the confluence of a stream flowing from the north, later named Bristow Creek. By the Mexican standard of valuing and classifying land, these grants were primarily cattle and sheep grazing lands. The classification of Sanchez's Cedar Creek grant was 60 percent grazing and 40 percent farming lands.[27] Reyes's Cochino Bayou league was classified as 75 percent grazing and 25 percent farming lands.[28]

Today the Sanchez league constitutes a large part of what is considered South Boggy Slough and includes the former 640-acre Rayville calf pasture, the northern portion of Cedar Brake Saline Prairie, the far western end of the Bluff Prairie Saline, a portion of the old railroad wye and station known as Vair, and the ruins of Southern Pine Lumber Company's hunting club lodge of 1941–1966.[29] Near the site of the clubhouse ruins, protected by a fence made of steel railroad rails, is a small white stone

grave marker commemorating the little-known Johnson family, who, on August 21, 1904, buried their infant daughter Annie Mae on the hillside.[30]

This hillside is part of a one-mile-wide ridge of high ground situated between the Neches River bottomlands to the north and the Cedar Creek bottoms to the south. The ridge leads eastward to a bluff on the Neches River, where a portion of the old Bidai Trail crossed the river at Rocky Crossing, near what is today the Denman clubhouse.[31] The trail once connected the Bidai tribes west of the Trinity River, in the Bedias Creek region in present-day Walker and Madison Counties, to the Hasinai tribes and Spanish manufactured goods at Nacogdoches.[32] The extreme southern base of this ridge later served as high ground for wagon and postal delivery roads, becoming the early location of State Highway 94, before the highway's route was straightened and elevated across the floodplain of the Neches River and Cedar Creek in 1937, becoming today's southern boundary of the Boggy Slough Conservation Area.[33] The ridge also served the tracks of the Texas Southeastern Railroad, beginning in 1906, and the ridge continues to provide high ground for South Boggy's main road today, which leads northwestward, often using or paralleling the old Texas Southeastern Railroad grade. Most of the diagonally positioned Reyes league along Cochino Bayou is now outside of the Boggy Slough Conservation Area, but the southeastern portion, which contained the rail station of Neff, where the Texas Southeastern and Eastern Texas railroads crossed, remains inside the Boggy Slough boundaries, near a road that connects with US Forest Service Road 511 at what early pasture riders named "Whiskey Gate."[34]

How long Candido Sanchez lived on his Cedar Creek land grant, if at all, is uncertain. In August 1839 he sold it to H. L. Wiggins of Shelby County for thirteen cents an acre, and with his six children he began living in Sabine Parish, Louisiana. What became of his wife Encarnacion Flores is also uncertain.[35] It is likely Sanchez fled the newly formed Republic of Texas during the tumultuous Córdova Rebellion of August 1838 and its aftermath, when racial and ethnic distrust ran rampant after the discovery of a Mexican conspiracy to incite Indian violence against white settlers in East Texas as part of Mexico's effort to regain Texas. Meanwhile, Wiggins sold the Sanchez league in 1866 to W. H. Cunningham of Lafayette Parish, Louisiana, for eleven cents an acre, during the economic depression following the Civil War.[36] Local tax rolls declared ownership of the Sanchez league unknown as early as 1838, and for a while the famous land speculator Frost Thorn, said to be Texas' first millionaire, was a claimant, as he was in many Mexican grants across East Texas. Later claims to the Sanchez lands were those made by actual settlers, including the Turner, Moore, Hutson, and Clegg families.[37]

Juan José de los Reyes probably never intended to live on his Cochino Bayou grant. Known to Mexican officials as a *prestanombre*, or name-lender, he essentially lent his name to another man, Juan de los Santos Coy, who officially received Reyes's land title in December 1835. Santos Coy paid Reyes $100 (just a little more than two cents an acre) for right to the title in January 1836.[38] The land eventually divided into smaller parcels and transferred to other owners, including the Luce, Anderson, Morgan, Moore, Womack, Durham, and Kenley families, among others, before being acquired by Southern Pine Lumber Company.[39]

The largest single grant and survey of land in the Boggy Slough Conservation Area was a Republic of Texas first class headright of 4,605 acres made to John M. Walker of Chappell Hill, Washington County, in 1845. Located directly above the Sanchez league, with Cochino Bayou and the Neches River as its northern and eastern boundaries, much of the land seasonally flooded, as it does today, with more than half of it being flat and below 175 feet in elevation. Early boundary and stream meandering surveys within the tract revealed that post oak (*Quercus stellata*), red oak (*Quercus falcata*), and pine (*Pinus echinata*) dominated the uplands, while giant cane and switch cane (*Arundinaria gigantea* and *A. tecta*), overcup and water oaks (*Quercus lyrata* and *Q. nigra*), water hickory (*Carya aquatica*), and ash (*Fraxinus* spp.) filled much of the flat lowlands. The original grant classified the land as only 20 percent farmland quality, with 80 percent valued as grazing lands.[40] A native of Kentucky, Walker came to Texas in 1829. He never resided on his Neches River land, and with his wife Rebecca parceled it out in transfers to a number of individuals, including their own children. In time, titles were owned by the Houston East & West Texas Railway Company and by the Joyce family of Iowa, owners of lumber businesses across the country, including the Trinity County Lumber Company, which began operating a large mill at Groveton, Texas, in 1882.[41] Smaller tracts were owned by the Womack, Franklin, Vance, and Tiner families just prior to being acquired by Southern Pine Lumber Company.[42]

By far the most interesting settlers of the Walker survey, as well as of any lands in South Boggy, were the Britton and Rose families of Ohio, who settled together during the 1850s, near the slough that still bears the Britton name. The Britton and Rose women—Letitia, better known as "Lidia," and Jane—were sisters and pioneer natives of Ohio, the children of Timothy Sharrock and his wife Ellen Cronk. Lidia and Jane were born in Guernsey County, Ohio, and they married and gave birth to all of their children there—Lidia Britton having nine children and Jane Rose fourteen. Lidia's husband, James Britton, was born in Ireland in

1798 and Jane's husband, John Rose, was born the same year in Virginia. At the time, before the creation of West Virginia in 1863, Ohio and Virginia were divided only by the Ohio River, and Guernsey County was near the river. The Brittons and Roses left Ohio and moved to East Texas sometime after 1853. They settled first in Cherokee County, where James Britton died in 1856. By 1857 they were living in Trinity County, where they settled on the low meadows and creek flatlands near what is now called Britton Slough in the north end of the John M. Walker survey.[43] The 1860 Trinity County census recorded Lidia Britton, age forty-nine, as the widowed head of the Britton family living with five of her sons and two of her daughters, all between the ages of eleven and twenty-three. Enumerated in the census next to Lidia's household was her sister Jane, age fifty-five, along with Jane's husband John, age sixty-two, living with five of their sons and five of their daughters, all between the ages of eight and twenty-seven. The two oldest Britton and four oldest Rose children had already left home by this time. Living with the Roses were James and Delilah Allen, natives of Alabama and Louisiana, ages twenty-seven and eighteen, as well as twenty-eight-year old Dred Barker, identified as a free mulatto born in North Carolina, the only free mulatto in Trinity County, Texas, at the time.[44]

What compelled these middle-aged sisters and their families to leave the Ohio valley and start new lives on the Neches River more than a thousand miles from their former homes remains a mystery. By 1860 they had chopped, burned, cleared, plowed, and planted 120 acres of a 320-acre tract of land, first as tenants, then as owners, purchasing the title directly from Walker and his wife in 1863 for only fifty-five cents an acre.[45] The families planted corn, potatoes, peas, beans, and cotton, enclosing the fields with wooden-rail fences, and they released their herds and droves of livestock into the surrounding unenclosed upland and bottomland forests, where evergreen switch cane and various mast-producing trees occupied the hardwood bottoms; sedges (especially *Carex cherokeensis*), maidencane and switchgrass (*Panicum hemitomon* and

P. virgatum), and eastern gamagrass (*Tripsacum dactyloides*) likely filled the slough meadows and marshes as they do today; and pinehill and other bluestem grasses (*Andropogon* and *Schizachyrium* spp.) occupied the uplands.[46]

These families were something more than simple herdsmen and yeoman farmers. The four oldest Rose boys—James Hanson (better known as "Hanse"), John, George, and Sandy—gave their occupations to the enumerator of the 1860 census as "cow drover." The agricultural census further recorded that the Brittons, Roses, and Allens owned 64 beef cows, 50 milch cows, 122 hogs, 91 sheep, 37 oxen, 17 horses, and 9 mules. In addition, the food crops the families planted and harvested during the previous year's growing season included 830 bushels of corn, 162 bushels of Irish potatoes, 175 bushels of sweet potatoes, and 28 bushels of peas and beans. They also grew and ginned 21 bales of cotton weighing more than four and a half tons.[47] In addition they produced 248 pounds of wool, 400 pounds of butter, $235 worth of home manufactures, and slaughtered $610 worth of livestock during the year.[48] This production came from the free labor of twenty-three people, seven of them children, although the families may have hired additional laborers as well. This extensive agricultural activity of land clearing, planting, and herding went beyond subsistence farming and indicates a level of commercial enterprise, including dairying and wool production.

The lives of these hardworking, predominantly Ohioan families living in Trinity County, Texas, during the sectional divisiveness of the Civil War must have seemed extraordinary to their neighbors, predominantly Southern, who did not work the land quite as aggressively. Beginning in 1861, the Britton and Rose boys married three Alabama-born daughters of James P. Henderson of Cherokee County, whose wife Sarah had died sometime before 1860.[49] The first to marry were twenty-four year olds Timothy P. Britton and Frances C. Henderson, to whom three children were born at Britton Slough, although two died in infancy.[50] In 1865 James "Hanse" Rose married Frances's sister Nancy, and several years later Timothy Britton's brother Charles married the sister Louisa. There was at least one other wedding, when the widow Lidia Britton remarried in about 1865, nine years after her first husband's death. We know only her new husband's last name, being revealed in local public land records many years later: in 1909, longtime Trinity County resident W. H. Womack testified before Southern Pine Lumber Company attorney Robert E. Minton, saying he was once a neighbor to the Britton family, knowing them beginning in 1857. Womack stated that Lidia "married a man by the name of Jackson" at the close of the Civil War, but soon afterward, "both died and were buried in the same grave." Womack further testified that he was personally "present at their burial."[51]

What exactly happened is uncertain, but it is clear that before the close of the tumultuous decade of the 1860s, during which Trinity County was an especially chaotic and lawless region, all of the Britton, Rose, and related family members moved away.[52] Brothers John, George, and Sandy Rose returned to Ohio, joined the Union army, and died during the war. Most everyone else, however, remained in Texas, and settled in DeWitt and Lavaca Counties, perhaps seeking better land, politics, and opportunities there.[53] Timothy Britton died shortly after he arrived in South Texas, leaving his wife Frances alone to raise their one surviving daughter, Nancy. In 1871 Timothy Britton's youngest brother Charles returned to East Texas briefly to marry Louisa Henderson, who was already his sister-in-law. Charles and Louisa then moved to Erath County, taking along and providing for Frances and Nancy as well as Frances and Louisa's younger unmarried sister, Romisha.[54] Nancy Britton, born in 1865, married J. M. Steel of Erath County in 1888, and they, along with Frances, sold the Britton lands in Boggy Slough to A. C. Harrison of Cherokee County in 1891, for forty-seven cents an acre. Harrison's purchase paid big dividends when he sold the same land to Southern Pine Lumber Company fourteen years later for $5 an acre, 950 percent more than he had paid for it.[55]

Little else is known of these early Boggy Slough Conservation Area families. Even the locations of their graves—that of Lidia and her second husband and those of her infant grandchildren—are lost. A possible location is the high ground about 700 yards south of Britton Slough, where the peak of a ridge rises some 45 feet above the banks of the slough and a feeder stream to the west. Vegetation on the ridge was relatively sparse in 1933, according to aerial photographs, but a mature pine and hardwood forest with a thick undergrowth of yaupon, vines, and holly now covers it, with indications that the hilltop is the home and bedding grounds of countless feral hogs, perhaps the descendants of Britton free-range hogs of 160 years earlier.[56] Even less is known about the fates of James and Delilah Allen and Dred Barker, who seem to have disappeared from the historical record after the 1860 census. For natural as well as cultural reasons the Britton, Rose, Allen, and Barker families came and went, leaving little else besides the Britton name to identify the slough.

Such a coming and going represents a general pattern of settlement in South Boggy, whereby few people stayed long enough to share multigenerational attachments to the land such as the Christie girls held for the North Boggy lands during the early 1910s. Both early and modern soil surveys indicated slightly better soils north of Cochino Bayou, rather than south of the stream, and Cochino Bayou remains a distinct dividing line between the better hill country to the north and the flatter, slower drained lands to the south. But soils, topography, and geography do not fully explain the differences between settlement patterns of north and south; only culture and history can do that.[57] None of the original surveys in South Boggy were homestead grants, whereas at least eleven surveys in North Boggy were actually settled by homesteaders. Homestead grants were smaller than the earlier colonization grants, either 160 or 320 acres in size. And since the preemption laws that established them required the land to be "actually settled upon and cultivated" for three years, there was almost an obligation for the grantees to select the sites of their homesteads carefully, for they knew their selection of land would influence their family's ability to stay alive.[58] Once they mixed their labor with the soil—clearing fields and building houses and fences—there was a connection to those places on the earth that now bore their surnames on official maps as well as in public records filed at the local courthouse and at the state land office. Earlier large surveys in South Boggy that were made to individuals also bore the surnames of those grantees, but those lands were provided to people who never seriously intended to reside there. The homestead grants in North Boggy were made mostly during the 1850s and early 1870s, well after the wildly speculative activities that characterized much of East Texas' early land history had concluded, in which acquiring land seemed more important than settling on it.[59] Although there were a few exceptions, homesteaders in North Boggy tended to remain on their preemption lands, whereas people who moved onto the lands of absentee owners in South Boggy often moved away. A correspondent for the journal *Sunny South*, published in Atlanta, Georgia, visited East Texas in 1887 and wrote of these peripatetic people—many of whom simply squatted—saying, "The consequence of this way of living is that they are always moving, and their children grow up without knowing the pleasures and comforts of a home that could be made comfortable and beautiful if the land was their own."[60] Most true homesteaders not only owned the land, but they stayed put long enough to fashion their homes in such a way to realize the beauty of "place," such as the Christie girls wrote about. This sense of place was not shared by most of South Boggy's residents, even if they did purchase more manageably sized tracts within the large absentee surveys like the Brittons did.

Most of North Boggy was settled predominantly by natives of Alabama and Mississippi, whose parents hailed from South Carolina and Georgia.

They shared a mostly Scots-Irish heritage, clannish tendencies, and Celtic traditions. Their surnames originated in Scotland, Wales, northern Ireland, and the English highlands. Besides Sullivan and Christie, the names of the more prominent families included Oliver, Brock, Franklin, English, Luce, Tier, DeBruhl, Durham, Moore, Saxton, McLean, Carrigan, McConnell, Price, Rushing, Campbell, McKinney, Carlisle, Conner, and Anderson.[61] Unlike the settlers south of Cochino Bayou, these more upland farmers and herdsmen families firmly planted themselves on the land and established post offices, stores, cemeteries, and a school, and they participated in public service at the county level. Most settled during brief windows of time just before and after the Civil War. Although a few of the earliest families did leave after suffering hardships caused by the war, most remained to welcome a new wave of Southern immigrants following the war.

Federal population and agricultural census records along with county tax rolls reveal that these families were large, consisting of from five to more than a dozen children. Many families lived on tracts of land between 80 and 200 acres, which they owned. Nearly all families rendered for taxes at least two dozen hogs, several beef cows, at least two milch cows, a horse or two, several goats, two to three dozen chickens, a stock dog or two, an ox or two, and at least one mule. Some families owned more than one hundred hogs and more than fifty head of cattle. Several families also raised sheep, such as the Sullivans, who rendered seventy-seven head for taxation in 1870, and the Olivers, who continued to render up to thirty head in 1900. Some families kept bees, especially those who held good-sized fruit orchards. Most families cultivated between 10 and 40 acres of land, about 60 percent of which they planted in corn, 30 percent in cotton, and the balance in sweet potatoes, Irish potatoes, peas, beans, and other garden vegetables. Many families also grew sugarcane along the creek bottoms, usually in fields of one-half to one acre in size, which yielded between fifteen and thirty gallons of molasses and cane syrup annually. They also

The postal community of Sullivan's Bluff, indicated by a large circle in this 1875 *Cram's Rail Road and Township Map of Texas*, was located north of Cochino Bayou in what is now the Boggy Slough Conservation Area. *Author's collections.*

grew on average an acre of apple trees and an acre of peach trees, with each orchard yielding about twenty bushels of fruit annually. Some families also cultivated pears, plums, several varieties of grapes, strawberries, raspberries, dewberries, and blackberries. Most families consumed at least fifteen cords of wood per year for fuel, as well as for home manufactures, such as in making furniture, implements, fencing, and wagon maintenance.[62] Fencing, especially before the general use of barbed wire at the end of the nineteenth century, consumed the majority of forest resources, whereby each 10-acre field required some five thousand split rails. In making the rail fences, the farmers may have preferred some species, such as cedar and post oak for bottom rails and posts (especially in a staked-rail fence), but whatever suitable trees were most convenient to the site—pine, oak, or ash—usually sufficed.[63]

Settlers of North Boggy testified for one another in their preemption claims and served as chain carriers for the county surveyor in marking and establishing each other's property boundaries. They assisted one another in land clearing (known as log-rollings), house and barn raisings, and fence building and mending. They hunted and fished and herded livestock together. Their children and grandchildren played and attended school

together and frequently married one another. By 1900, census enumerators filled whole pages, fifty lines each, with the names of people related in one way or another. Multigenerational kinship was not uncommon, especially among the Sullivan, Christie, Durham, Franklin, Tiner, Moore, Rushing, Luce, Oliver, Hutson, and Vance families.[64]

Among the earliest settlers of North Boggy were the Christie sisters' grandparents: Samuel Doxie Sullivan and his wife Lucinda, who along with their four young boys moved to Texas from Mississippi in 1849. After unsuccessfully attempting to settle lands in Cherokee County, they moved in November 1853 across the Neches River, southward, to vacant public land in southeastern Houston County that today contains the big curve in the highway and the North Boggy Slough clubhouse. The tract contained a creek, several branches that were probably spring fed at the time, a number of gently rolling hills and sloping terraces, and well-drained and fine-textured soils, including some that contained sandstone fragments known locally as "red lands." Such soil was generally considered excellent farmland, and a 1905 Houston County soil survey called it "the most highly prized soil in the county," showing the Sullivan community situated within the soil type boundaries. Later, in the twentieth century, the USDA classified several of the soil types within and immediately surrounding the Sullivan survey as "prime farmland."[65]

The Sullivans, with the oldest of their sons and one male slave, marked the land as a claim, intending to preempt 320 acres under Texas homestead laws.[66] Just weeks later, and probably unknown to the Sullivans, the state of Texas reserved certain lands from settlement, including where the Sullivans located, to incentivize construction of a transcontinental railroad through the state, known as the Mississippi and Pacific Railroad. The act called for setting aside public lands to provide as grants to builders of a railroad of some 800 miles, from the state's eastern boundary to a point at or near El Paso. The state's efforts failed when Governors Bell and Pease found no acceptable construction contractors, and late in 1856 the legislature reopened the reserved lands to settlement, effective January 1, 1857.[67] In the meantime, the Sullivans had spent three years chopping, burning, and clearing some 60 acres of the land, producing crops by which they fed themselves and their livestock, without an official survey. Eventually state officials informed Sullivan he had right to only 160 acres, not the 320 acres he claimed, because of a change in the preemption law in 1854. Since Sullivan began to settle before the new law's passing, he filed a petition to the state legislature in August 1857, pleading his case. He claimed he settled and began cultivating and grazing 320 acres of Houston County land on or about November 7, 1853, believing in good faith he was authorized to do so under the 320-acre allowance. He claimed that had he been able to locate and secure the services of the county surveyor in a timely manner, there would not have been the confusion. He testified that he rode to Crockett in December 1853, but the surveyor was nowhere to be found. Sullivan returned to Crockett in the spring of 1854, again to engage the surveyor, but once more found him absent. Sullivan then rode a "considerable distance," he said, to find the deputy surveyor, John W. Bodenhamer, only to learn that Bodenhamer's "sore eyes" prevented him from making a survey. Sullivan later located Absalom Gibson, another surveyor in the district, "and obtained a promise from him to come in a few days," but the promise went unfulfilled. Such was

life in rural Houston County during the 1850s, and a sympathetic legislature ruled in Sullivan's favor and granted him the 320 acres of land, which was surveyed in 1858 and patented in 1861, some eight years following the Sullivan family's initial settlement.[68]

Already living in North Boggy when Sullivan and his family moved there were the families of Curtis W. Tier and his daughter and son-in-law, Lucinda Margaret and Lazarus Price, none of whom had yet received their own official land grants. When they did, their surveys adjoined Sullivan's land on the northwest and southeast sides. Tier's survey was northwest of Sullivan's and was also part of the Mississippi and Pacific Railroad Reservation, but Tier chose to accept the lesser grant of only 160 acres (according to the 1854 law), receiving it some twenty months earlier than Sullivan received his larger, but delayed, grant from the state legislature. Price's land adjoined Sullivan's on the southeast side, and it, like Sullivan's, was a survey of 320 acres, which also required a petition to the state legislature and a favorable ruling. The three men served as witnesses for one another in fulfilling the homestead residency and cultivation requirements, and they also assisted the government surveyors in making one another's boundary surveys by carrying the survey chains and witnessing the measurements.[69]

Lazarus Price was born in South Carolina but grew up along the Neches River in present-day Angelina County, where his father Elisha moved their family in January 1840, when Lazarus was six years old. Lazarus's father obtained a 484-acre grant of land just west of today's Boggy Slough Conservation Area, which included the alluvial flatlands along Bodan Creek, as well as a ridge over which Highway 103 now stretches, including the junction with Highway 7. A natural river crossing near the Price home became known as Price's Crossing and later as Price's Ferry, eventually becoming Texas Highway 7.[70] Lazarus Price was still a boy during the late 1840s when his eventual in-laws, Curtis and Dolly Tier, moved across the Neches River into Houston County with their daughter Lucinda Margaret, who was about the same age as Lazarus. The Tiers, like the Prices, were natives of South Carolina, but the Tiers moved to Texas after brief stays in Mississippi and Arkansas, while the Prices moved directly to Texas.[71]

In 1851, while in their late teens, Lazarus and Lucinda married and settled on the land that became the Lazarus Price 320-acre homestead tract in North Boggy, which was positioned in both Houston and Trinity Counties, mostly below the newly established Trinity County line.[72] The Price survey had the Neches River as its eastern boundary and included gently rolling red soil uplands and switch cane bottomlands, as well as a "river swamp" and the headwaters of a slough below a bluff where Caddo pottery sherds are still being found. In 1858 Lazarus Price helped survey another 160-acre homestead tract adjoining his land to the south for his wife's brother James, who married Price's sister Easter Adeline, but further changes to the preemption law and the coming of the Civil War interrupted completion of Tier's grant application.[73]

As many Boggy Slough men did in 1862, Lazarus Price left his wife and four children, his land, fields, and livestock, and enlisted in the Confederate Army. Price served in the 17th (Moore's) Texas Cavalry (dismounted), and in time became sergeant of Company J. Union soldiers captured him at the Battle of Arkansas Post in January 1863 and took him as a prisoner of war to Camp Chase, Ohio. He was exchanged for the release of Union soldiers in April and soon fought with the Army of Tennessee in battles at Chickamauga, Chattanooga, Lookout Mountain, and Missionary Ridge. In December 1864, Union soldiers again captured him, at Franklin, Tennessee, and placed him in a prisoner of war camp near Nashville. Price died there, succumbing to chronic diarrhea on April 9, 1865, the same day that General Lee surrendered to General Grant. Buried in Nashville, Price left behind his wife and children and his Neches valley lands. His widow Lucinda, whose brother James

also died while serving in the Confederate Army, returned to the home of her parents just east of the Sullivan place and followed them as they moved to Hopkins County some time before 1870.[74]

Members of the Luce and Oliver families, who after the war settled homestead preemption surveys of their own, just west of Tier's land, eventually owned the Tier land, while one of the Sullivan daughters, Laura Alice, and her husband Henry Lafayette Christie—whose family emigrated from Natchitoches, Louisiana—came to own the Price land after their marriage in 1881.[75] The Christies established their home and fields on red land soils at the southwest corner of the Price survey on a slight knoll above a creek that divided the Christie and Sullivan homes (possibly at the same site as the Price home place). There, above the creek, and below stately red elms, the Christie girls were born and raised and wrote their nature letters published by the *Houston Post*. The slough that originated in the Price survey, less than a mile east of the Christie place, became known as Franklin Slough, named for Doc Franklin, who in 1876 married as his second wife Josephine "Ginnie" Christie, who was a sister of the Christie girls' father.[76] While the Franklin home place was southwest of the Christie place, Franklin established his agricultural fields a mile southeast of there, just above the west bank of the slough on a tract of I&GN Railroad land. As for Price's Ferry, Samuel Sullivan and his son John Calvin, who each also served in the Confederate Army, returned home from the war and operated it as Sullivan's Ferry, by which it was known until a bridge replaced the service early in the 1930s as part of State Highway 7/103.[77]

Most of the remaining unsettled lands in North Boggy were apportioned and surveyed in the decade following the close of the Civil War. Although other families besides the Tiers moved away, many more moved in. Besides the Christies and Franklins, the families of Moore, Rushing, Luce, Oliver, and Durham came to call Boggy Slough home. While Trinity County's population actually decreased after the war and grew only modestly

View looking up a hillside of hickories where Beulah Christie and her husband Charles R. Rushing lived before the 1910s. *Photo by the author, March 2018.*

during the 1870s, Houston County maintained its population following the war and became one of the fastest-growing counties in the region during the decade that followed. A similar pattern existed between North and South Boggy, whereby the settlement and population of North Boggy grew at a much greater rate than did those of South Boggy.

Although all of Boggy Slough Conservation Area, north and south, remained a rural area, it was by no means isolated and was economically and socially connected to other settlements in the four-county region of Houston, Trinity, Cherokee, and Angelina. With an increasing commercialization of farming, merchants moved in and purchased locally grown cotton on credit. Soon, the prewar post office communities of Coltharp and Hager in Houston County, Cheeseland in Angelina County, Centralia and Nogalus in Trinity County, and Shook's Bluff in Cherokee County were revitalized.[78] Coltharp and Hager were about eight miles west of North Boggy, in the upper valley of Cochino Bayou (commonly called a creek outside of Boggy Slough), and at various times those settlements offered churches, general stores, cotton gins, and grist mills to a wide region. Beginning in the 1870s, Coltharp also had a small pine saw and shingle mill, owned by Henry Payne, which supplied pine plank, boards, and cedar shin-

gles directly to area farmers and herdsmen.[79] At the same time, a similar-sized pine sawmill at Bonner's Mills, in Angelina County, located directly across the river from South Boggy, just north of present-day Highway 94, served settlers of that area; it was owned by William H. Bonner, who also owned lands in South Boggy. Boggy Slough's settlers, north and south, utilized the products of those mills to build new board homes, install wood plank floors and new cedar shingle roofs, and occasionally cover over existing log houses. Nogalus, Centralia, and Apple Springs, located ten miles southwest of North Boggy and between five and eight miles west of South Boggy, were settled during the 1860s but grew to prominence after 1870, providing stores, grist and sawmills, and a cotton gin that served an expanding local market. Cheeseland, six miles to the northeast, and Shook's Bluff, five miles to the north (seven miles by river), offered general stores, as well as saloons.[80]

Shook's Bluff also had a cotton gin and was an infrequent river port and cotton-shipping point. Although steamboats occasionally paddled the Neches River as far north as Shook's Bluff, they did so at great risk and only during the wettest of seasons. Because of numerous shallow rocky shoals, the Neches was rarely navigable above the confluence of the Angelina River, some 120 river miles downstream of Boggy Slough, and by the late nineteenth century the United States Army declared the upper Neches was "in no sense a navigable stream." Since navigation that far upriver was utterly impossible most of the year and was

As the communities north of Cochino Bayou steadily recovered following the war, Samuel Doxie Sullivan and his sons Charles Benjamin, John Calvin, and William Luther—all former Confederate soldiers—returned home and quickly assumed places of leadership in the region. Samuel Doxie served as county judge of Houston County's Precinct 3, until his death in 1874, and Charles Benjamin served as a county road overseer through the 1890s. True to his namesake, John Calvin became a minister of the gospel, as did his nephew William Rufus Sullivan, one of Charles Benjamin's sons. During the taking of the 1870 federal census, John Calvin served as the assistant marshal for all of Houston County, signing some 163 pages of large census sheets that enumerated 8,147 citizens. In 1872 the federal government established Sullivan's Bluff as one of only ten post offices in Houston County, and the Sullivans ran a general store in connection with the post office while John Calvin operated the nearby river ferry.[82]

Also after the war, Samuel Sullivan's son Leonidas obtained a homestead grant just south of his father's land, while one of Charles Benjamin's sons, Samuel T. Sullivan, obtained a homestead grant that adjoined his grandfather's land on the northeast side, stretching to the river. Members of the Luce, Key, and Oliver families obtained their own preemption surveys nearby early in the 1870s, all of them west of the Sullivans.

County, state, and federal maps beginning in the 1870s and continuing through the 1920s showed various roads with "Sullivan's Ferry" in their names passing through "Sullivan" or "Sullivan's Bluff," which connected towns throughout the four-county

Butterflies enjoy the blooms of Texas groundsel (*Senecio ampullaceus*), which grows in abundance on the hickory hillside where the Rushings and Christies lived. *Photo by the author, March 2018.*

risky at best during a very short season, insurers offered no protection above Boon's Ferry, 80 miles downstream from Shook's Bluff. Steamboat service ended completely when even the crudest of narrow-gauge railroads reached central Cherokee County from the north in the middle 1870s, and the Shook's Bluff post office closed permanently in 1876.[81]

region. Portions of some of those roads still exist today in North Boggy and serve as primary forest access roads. Although the region continued to be known as Sullivan's Bluff, a new post office named Tesla opened in the community in 1894, with three Sullivans—Edward, Susan, and William—serving as postmasters until the office closed in 1910.[83] The post office was named for Nikola Tesla, the scientist who pioneered the practical use of electrical alternating current during the 1880s.[84]

In 1875, the state apportioned several large tracts above Cochino Bayou, comprising some 4,500 acres still inside the Boggy Slough Conservation Area, to the International & Great Northern Railroad Company, which transferred them to the New York and Texas Land Company, owners of around 5.5 million acres of land in Texas. Since they were unoccupied, some of the I&GN lands around Sullivan's Bluff were already being squatted on or otherwise utilized by the neighboring farmers and stockmen-herders, including the Sullivans, Luces, Rushings, Franklins, Christies, Durhams, Olivers, and Moores. The families established a cemetery that straddles the boundary line between two of the I&GN tracts, naming it Mount Pisgah, a common name for cemeteries across the South, named for the mountain peak east of the Dead Sea from which Moses could see the Promised Land but could not enter, as recorded in Deuteronomy 3. In Houston County, Mount Pisgah was, and remains, pronounced more times than not as "piz'-ghe," and death certificates sometimes phonetically spelled it as P-i-s-g-y. David Crockett Moore and his wife Elizabeth, who emigrated from Georgia just after the war, made the first recorded burial at Mount Pisgah, in November 1876, for their seven-year-old son Henry Lawrence. Today the cemetery contains some seventy-five marked graves, although only about two-thirds of these have inscribed names that are still legible. Nearly half of the stones with legible inscriptions mark the graves of children under the age of ten.[85]

The area's residents also established the Mount Pisgah School District and erected school buildings near the cemetery, which served the children of both Houston and Trinity Counties within at least a three-mile radius. The Neches River and Cochino Bayou served as the district's eastern and southern boundaries, with Houston County's Hagerville and Conner Creek districts bordering to the west and north. Mount Pisgah's early school trustees included members of the Brock, Moore, and Sullivan families. Some graduating students returned to Mount Pisgah School to teach their younger siblings, cousins, nieces, and nephews. Since the schoolhouses were right beside the cemetery, teachers let their students stand quietly at the schoolroom windows to watch the occasional funeral procession, as remembered later by Viola Harber, a student during the 1910s. A much-dilapidated structure remains near the cemetery today, a remnant of the school's earlier buildings, although the largest school building was moved off the property a few years after Mount Pisgah's consolidation with the Kennard schools in 1934.[86] A little more than a mile west-northwest of Mount Pisgah is another cemetery, named for the Luce family, containing about two dozen hand-poured concrete grave markers as well as about two dozen unmarked graves.[87]

Although most Boggy Slough families never approached the level of pastoral and agricultural ambitions of the antebellum Britton and related families, all of them depended in varying degrees on the raising of livestock for home consumption as well as occasional market sales. In addition, some families maintained a few goats to control the emergent hardwood brush that generally accompanied farm clearing, while a few families, such as the Olivers and the Moores, each rendered annually for taxes between eighty and a hundred goats through at least 1900.[88] While the Brittons in South Boggy and the Sullivans in North Boggy raised sizable flocks of sheep for wool production during the initial decades of settlement, sheep ranching rarely, if ever, prospered, primarily because of the specialized range conditions and intensive protective care that flocks required.[89] Cattle and hogs, which required less care and attention, proved to be the livestock of choice.

Before the arrival of railroads late in the 1870s, cattle in East Texas were driven over various "beef roads" to markets in Louisiana, where they fetched prices more than double their value in Texas.[90] The Opelousas Cattle Trail was one early route, or series of paths, through and from various points in East Texas to Louisiana, and was probably utilized by some of Boggy Slough's earliest stock raisers. In 1936 the Texas Highway Department published a map of "historical interests" as part of the state's centennial commemorations, which showed the conceptualized trail crossing central Houston County into northeastern Trinity County, crossing Cedar Creek and Highway 94 between Apple Springs and the Boggy Slough Conservation Area. From there the trail entered and passed through southern Angelina County, crossing Highway 59 between Diboll and Burke, on its way to Louisiana at a crossing of the Sabine River in northern Newton County.[91] Today, at least in name, a few "beef roads" survive in some localities, including one in Trinity County, about six miles north of Groveton, perhaps a remnant of a feeder route.

Boggy Slough has a long history of livestock raising. The name Cochino Bayou, which appears in Boggy Slough's earliest land records as Arroyo de los Cochinos—meaning literally "stream of pigs"—suggests a ranching tradition dating back to the Spanish and French colonial period.[92] As seen in chapter 2, wild hogs, descendants from escaped pigs from the De Soto-Moscoso Expedition of 1542, were plentiful in the Neches valley by the late seventeenth century, and efforts by immigrant Indian tribes to raise them for commercial profit were well under way by the 1820s. Although beef was an important food on the American frontier, pork was the most widely consumed meat in America throughout most of the nineteenth century, and in much of East Texas its primary status persisted well

into the twentieth century. While most East Texans preferred their beef fresh, they salted their pork and conveniently packed it in barrels for preservation. Salted pork was so prevalent in nineteenth-century East Texas that immigrant's guides cautioned newcomers against eating too much of it, for health reasons.[93] So pervasive was the hog and its salted meat that a number of early catchphrases still endure, including, "root hog, or die," to express self-reliance during difficult circumstances; "going hog wild," to convey frenzied excitement; and "eating high on the hog," to mean times of plenty, when prosperous families selectively ate cuts of meat above the belly, instead of the less desirable feet, hocks, and jowls. Similarly, the "full pork barrel" also meant prosperity; and conversely, "scraping the bottom of the barrel," meant times of want, when the last supply of salted pork was at hand.[94]

Hogs were the ideal stock in rural economies such as Boggy Slough. Turned loose in the woods to feed and fend for themselves, they roamed in herds for mutual protection against bears, wolves, and panthers. They required little care beyond occasional human contact—usually corn feedings from horseback to prevent them from going totally wild. They were highly efficient at converting almost any landscape into a valuable source of protein, being at least twice as efficient as cattle and sheep and containing more usable meat and fat as a proportion of body weight than even a steer.[95] They would eat almost anything. With their strong teeth and jaws they readily ate hard nuts and roots and even small animals, and their thick skins protected them from most threats. Nineteenth-century observers wrote that hogs readily consumed even rattlesnakes by using their hooves to hold the reptiles to the ground as they shredded them with their sharp teeth and tusks.[96] Furthermore, a sow could begin reproducing when only a year old, whereas a cow required another year or two to become fertile. Pigs also multiplied at a far greater rate than cows, producing an average-sized litter of six piglets after only four months of gestation, whereas a cow took nine months to produce only a single calf, and rarely two.[97]

Essential to the raising of both cattle and hogs was the customary practice of permitting livestock to roam freely on unenclosed land, regardless of its "owner." From earliest memory, Boggy Slough as well as much of the US South had been open range, an everyman's common. Having free access to bottomland forests, meadows, fish, and game resources was critical to most families' existence. Custom as well as law required that fences keep livestock *out*, rather than *in*, and it was the farmer's responsibility to enclose his crops. One Texas law in 1859 required that "every gardener, farmer, or planter" provide around their cultivated fields a fence at least five feet high, sufficient to keep cattle and horses out and "prevent hogs from passing through." Later, even railroad companies were responsible for fencing their tracks and were liable for damages to livestock injured or killed by trains.[98]

As settlement populations increased, many Boggy Slough families probably relied more on livestock herding than on farming—at times to the detriment of their well-being. As one early-twentieth-century observer wrote of the region's open range razorback hogs and piney woods cattle, "These denizens of the pine lands have evolved from generations which were obliged to rustle far and wide for food, and one must be strong of jaw and vigorous of digestion to relish their meat." Even children recognized the distinction. When eight-year-old Lara Christie of Sullivan's Bluff wrote to readers of the *Houston Post*'s "Young Folks" column in the spring of 1913, she revealed, "My papa is going to farm this year. I am sure glad," probably implying that her father did not farm the previous year.[99]

To assist in rounding up free-ranging cattle and hogs, Boggy Slough families by necessity owned at least one good stock dog, usually several. Beginning in 1900, some counties began taxing these valuable animals, and many of Boggy Slough's stock dogs rendered a tax value of fifty dollars, the same as the best horses and about six times the value of an adult cow.[100] Assessors for Trinity County valued a few Boggy Slough stock dogs even higher. For example, in 1910 Z. T. Franklin rendered 102 acres of land in the J. M. Walker survey, just twenty hogs valued at one dollar each, and a single dog valued at $100. Because hog populations and tax renderings were notoriously underestimated, Franklin may have gotten away with rendering only twenty hogs, but tax collectors equalized any differences with a high valuation of his dog.[101]

Stock dogs were no mere pets and were essential to rural families. They could round up any free-ranging cow or calf and even the fiercest hog, in uplands or swamps. Rural herdsmen used the same aggressive dogs to run and hunt deer and bear, a practice that severely diminished those once-plentiful animal populations.[102] In one early Republic of Texas promotional publication, Mary Austin Holley wrote that deer at that time were "so plentiful and tame" that they freely approached farms and grazed and browsed "in company with the cattle." Concerning black bear, they frequented the forests, swamps, and canebrakes, she said, and were "a favorite object of the hunt."[103] Within three generations of settlement, however, populations of both deer and bear were in sharp decline, just as Mexican general Terán had predicted some three-quarters of a century earlier. Deer, which were prized game animals, were overhunted, while bear, seen as predators to livestock, especially to hogs, were simply killed out. Boggy Slough's Sullivan family tradition tells that during the first year of their settlement at Sullivan's Bluff, "a big bear gathered under the house," causing terror among the children while their father was away. When Sam Sullivan returned home, he saved the day by shooting and killing the frightening creature, which was quite possibly merely after the family's chickens, lambs, or pigs. The story, nevertheless, illustrates how cultural accommodations to domestic livestock adversely affected wildlife.[104]

While Boggy Slough settlement patterns of the nineteenth century seem to have shaped the land at a noticeably faster rate than those of earlier peoples, the appearance during the early twentieth century of railroads, with their accompanying stations, temporary tent camps of track workers, and logging camps of lumber companies, brought even quicker changes. While nature was not conducive to consistent and reliable steamboat transportation along the upper Neches, railroads—much more than a technology—had become by 1900 part of a complex cultural system of human relations that facilitated dependable connections between both natural resources and manufacturing facilities and between manufactured products and distant market economies. To the people of Boggy Slough, the railroads brought change that was permanent and caused not only the arrival of strangers and the departure of family, but also the buying of their forest trees and then the purchase of their farms and houses. Most importantly, the land that was their home transformed suddenly into a financial asset of corporations run by people whose own homes were many miles distant.

Up until the late nineteenth century, the manufacture of shingles and sawn lumber at nearby mills was simply incidental to Boggy Slough's settlement activities, which in many ways merely expanded agricultural and pastoral lifeways, rather than altered them. The local needs for white oak, elm, red gum, and black gum in barrel making and other local manufactures was also an adjunct to settlement.[105] Economic change elsewhere, however, turned lumbermen and timber buyers to the southern yellow pine forests in Texas for softwood building materials as a market replacement to the depleted white pine forests of the Great Lakes states. Once railroads from St. Louis and Houston reached Angelina County early in the 1880s, timber and land buyers followed close behind. When news broke of the planned construction of a 30-mile railroad from Lufkin across the Neches River into Houston County, timber buyers descended on Sullivan's Bluff, offering cash to farmers for their otherwise nearly valueless large pine trees.

In 1899 lumber mogul Richard H. Keith of Kansas City, who was backing construction of the new rail line known as the Eastern Texas Railroad, began acquiring 120,000 acres of land in support of a new Houston County sawmill he planned to build just north of Coltharp, near the new town of Ratcliff. Inside what is now Boggy Slough Conservation Area, Keith purchased lands along Cochino Bayou, which he utilized to provide his railroad with a right-of-way as well as hardwood crossties, including a tract that today contains the state's grand champion loblolly pine tree.[106] At the same time, a mercantile and sawmilling business firm known as Abe Harris & Company, composed of brothers-in-law Abraham Harris and Louis Lipsitz, leaders of the Jewish community in Tyler, purchased North Boggy's I&GN Railroad survey lands, some 4,500 acres, at the price of only $2.38 an acre. Abe Harris & Company also bought the timber rights to most of the remaining Boggy Slough lands north of Cochino Bayou, whose owners consented to sell their timber but not their land, from which they still earned their livings, accepting prices as low as forty cents an acre.[107] Since Abe Harris & Company owned sawmills and logging railroads in both Cherokee and Angelina Counties, the firm obtained the North Boggy timber in support of those operations.[108]

Bordering today's Boggy Slough Conservation Area, a short distance from the west fence and less than two miles west-southwest of Mount Pisgah School and Cemetery, the Eastern Texas Railroad Company established a station known as Druso in 1902. Almost overnight, the station became a small town that included a post office and general store, a small cotton gin and sawmill, saloons, and even a steam-powered syrup mill. The entrepreneurial Moore family of Sullivan's Bluff embraced the changes wrought by the railroad and played a noticeable role in the development of the new town, aspiring to a new middle-class status and obtaining an Auburn automobile as one of the earliest registered motor vehicles in Houston County. Elizabeth "Fannie" Moore served the last ten years of her life as the town's postmistress, while her husband David Crockett assisted as mail carrier. Their sons Albert, Crockett, and Charlie ran the steam saw and syrup mills and engaged in a host of other businesses, including barrel stave and crosstie making and commercial sugarcane farming. For a while Albert Moore advertised his "pure ribbon cane syrup, in buckets or barrels" within the daily pages of the *Houston Post*. Regrettably for him, most of his sugarcane fields were in the poorly drained bottoms of Cedar Creek and Cochino Bayou, and the soil's salinity caused an unsavory flavor to the syrup, which soon put him out of the syrup business. All of the Moore boys worked for Southern Pine Lumber Company at one time or another, and Crockett operated a Southern Pine steam log loader during the earliest logging operations at Boggy Slough.[109]

Druso was a typical rural railroad town at the beginning of the twentieth century. Rough by nature, it catered to transient railroad and sawmill workers, logging crews, job hunters, traveling salesmen, and general adventurers. As some remembered the place, it was a "gouge eye town," known more for brawls and bad news than for anything good. The town's name appeared frequently in newspapers across the state, usually concerning knife fights and shoot-outs, but also for several train accidents. Several derailments, some of them deadly, occurred on the Eastern Texas Railroad in the soft Cochino Bayou bottoms near Druso. One particularly tragic wreck happened in July 1904, when heavy rains severely softened the track bed two miles east of Druso, inside the Boggy Slough Conservation Area. When the rails sank and spread under the weight of a regular passenger train bound for Lufkin, two coaches left the track, toppled over, and injured nearly everyone on board. Those who flew through windows or who could otherwise free themselves from the shattered cars used axes to rescue those trapped beneath the wreckage. The railroad company sent physicians to the scene from both ends of the line. After caring for the injured, doctors listed two children, ages two and three, among the dead. Then, on the following day, the road's track foreman died when the flanged-wheeled tricycle he rode derailed near the scene of the previous day's wreck, tossing him off a trestle.[110] A few years later, near the same Cochino

bottomland location, a railroad motor car wrecked in the night and killed the Kennard sawmill town company doctor and badly injured the mill's superintendent and another employee.[111]

When the state's newspapers were not mourning the people of Druso, it seemed they were ridiculing them. Many farmers in and around Druso believed the shipping facilities provided by the railroad company were insufficient. Whenever they petitioned the state railroad commission for better service, E. J. Mantooth of Lufkin, the railroad company's attorney, successfully argued against the appeals, usually deriding the community in the process. One such time was in 1911, when Mantooth declared to the state commissioners that Druso's small size did not justify any additional expenses than those already made. The *Austin American-Statesman* reported that the commissioners erupted in laughter when Mantooth dramatically presented a single photograph that showed "the entire town." More laughter came when Mantooth read aloud one particular petitioner's letter, which begged him "to prevent the town being fenced up."[112] Fences, real as well as figurative, were no laughing matter to Boggy Slough's rural communities. Nevertheless, it seemed that rural folk lost to the corporations every time.

Construction of the Eastern Texas Railroad drew many Sullivan's Bluff sons away from their family farms to public work. Some labored on the railroad, such as John Audubon "Audie" Christie, the Christie girls' oldest brother, who remained a regular employee of the Eastern Texas line after the road's initial construction. Others worked at the large sawmill near Ratcliff, which employed nearly a thousand men.[113] Still more, including sons of the Sullivan, Roach, Tiner, Moore, Oliver, Rushing, Christie, and Durham families, would work for Southern Pine Lumber Company and the Texas Southeastern Railroad Company when those operations reached the area in 1907. In 1916, Texas Southeastern Railroad general manager E. C. Durham recognized the commendable work of such men in a letter he wrote to T. L. L. Temple. Although his sincerity was stained by common prejudice, even as he referenced his men's own prejudices, Durham nevertheless praised his employees' services and accomplishments, saying, "These men are nearly all home-made products, the raw material having been secured from the forks of the crik [sic], Cracker's Bend, and other localities where the climate favors the propagation of the hill-billy species. Considering their originating points and early environments, I think they are entitled to a good round measure of credit for the energy and ambition they have displayed."[114]

Durham's use of the term Cracker's Bend was both general and specific. Commonly used, "crackers" and "hillbillies" were derogatory expressions for poor rural whites across the South. Specifically, even before the arrival of the railroads, W. W. Aiken, editor of the *Crockett Courier*, had called the North Boggy community of Sullivan's Bluff, "Cracker's Bend," explaining in 1913 that his reason was because, "it used to be that no negroes were allowed there."[115] Such racial prejudices became especially evident once the sons of Sullivan's Bluff farmers and stockmen were joined in the new industrial work by laborers that the railroad and lumber companies brought with them, including persons of color. Such people were not often welcomed or accepted by the rural communities whose inhabitants still owned much of the land, as evidenced in an October 1908 news article that appeared in the *Southern Industrial & Lumber Review*. The article described the "race troubles" that often resulted in East Texas between what the journalist called "the farmers owning the land" and "the sawmill companies." "In most cases," the writer observed, "the trouble seems to be purely malicious on the part of the farmers. They sell the timber on their lands to the sawmill companies, and when these concerns send their crews to cut the timber, the farmers refuse to allow the negro laborers of the company to venture on the land to cut the timber. They generally give no reasons except that they do not want them on their land. In many cases the forces of the company and the farmers come to blows."[116]

At Boggy Slough, when Southern Pine Lumber Company began logging there in 1907, about 3,000 acres of the land north of Cochino Bayou was still owned by rural white families who had sold only their timber to the lumber companies. As was true all across East Texas, when migrant black and Mexican workers came to logging and railroad camps at Sullivan's Bluff, racial tensions among the rural white communities became heightened.[117]

Economic changes brought the people of Sullivan's Bluff social changes that many were unprepared for, especially in 1910, when Southern Pine Lumber Company moved its Logging Camp No. 1 from below Cochino Bayou to a new site barely a mile from the Mount Pisgah School and then built a logging railroad along the wagon road that ran right beside the schoolhouse. Suddenly, the sights and sounds of steam locomotive whistles, chuffing cylinders, barking exhaust stacks, and scraping iron wheels rolling on steel rails became part of the school children's daily experiences. Sadie Estes Woods, who later taught public school in Diboll, remembered that as a child during the 1910s she regularly walked with her brother Lee along the new railroad tracks, going to and from the Mount Pisgah School. During a 1984 interview she recalled meeting men speaking an unfamiliar language, saying that Southern Pine Lumber Company "would bring Mexicans out there, and my brother was scared to death. We would see them working on the tracks, and we would go way out in the woods and come back to keep from going by them, he was so afraid."[118] The rural woods children were so unfamiliar with people from Mexico and with the Spanish language that even innocent encounters were frightening.

Although newspaper correspondents called the new Southern Pine Lumber Company camp "Diboll Front," just as they had done for other camp locations that had served the Diboll sawmills, T. L. L. Temple wanted to name the new site near the school Walkerton, after his second cousin and the Diboll mill manager, Watson Walker. Regardless of the camp's name, however, it was an unpleasant place, known for public drunkenness, stabbings, and shootings. The *Crockett Courier* reported that a "drunken row" by "three white men" at the camp during the spring of 1913 resulted in the death of one of the revelers, but no one was brought to justice because the only witness in the case reportedly "left the country."[119] In February 1914, the *Courier* reported that George Smith, "a negro," was accused of using a tent stake to murder Walkerton's superintendent, Lewis Glass, "a white man," who had supposedly "incurred the displeasure of the negro." The article further reported that Smith had escaped law officials for the moment, but Governor Colquitt was offering a $300 reward for his capture.[120]

Editor Aiken's "Cracker's Bend" was known also for a number of family feuds, which seemed to only intensify in violence once the railroads arrived, no doubt influenced by the social unrest that railroad tracks brought to rural communities, revealing a passionate backcountry code of justice. One area feud that involved the English and Wilburn families carried on for more than a decade and resulted in a "six-shooter" shooting spree at the Stubblefield Schoolhouse near Hagerville in 1914, which left one man dead and two wounded.[121]

By far the most notorious and violent feud of the region, however, occurred within the boundaries of today's Boggy Slough Conservation Area. It involved the Christie and Durham children, whose fathers had married daughters of Samuel Doxie Sullivan, the patriarch of Sullivan's Bluff.[122] The resulting bloodbath would take the lives of the Christie girls' father, their twin brothers, and one of their uncles.

Henry Lafayette Christie and Laura Alice Sullivan, who married in 1880, had sixteen children born to them (three sons and thirteen daughters), including three sets of twins.[123] Dorchester "Doc" Starnes Durham married Ella Doxie Sullivan in 1891 and they had seven sons and one daughter born to them. Each family at least partly farmed and grazed their livestock on the former lands of the Sullivans, which by 1900 had expanded well beyond the three Sullivan homestead surveys to include the adjoining surveys of Price, Winter, Tier, Johnson, as well as those of the I&GN Railroad,

encompassing some 1,500 acres among the extended families, which by this time also included the Franklin, Rushing, Tiner, Vance, and James families, among others. Legendary rivalries grew between the Durham and Christie boys, whose fathers played no passive roles. It was well known that the Christies accused the Durhams of borrowing excessively from Christie lands in cutting and hewing hardwood crossties for the railroads, while the Durhams accused the Christies of intentionally marking Durham hogs as their own. Fights erupted often among the boys at community gatherings, especially at frequent night dances, where alcohol flowed freely. At one of the bigger dances in December 1911, which brought crowds of people from miles around, cousins Jewel Christie and Sollie Durham competed for the charms of a certain young lady whose name has since become lost to history. One version of the story holds that one of the boys may have said something insulting about the other boy's dance partner. Details of what occurred vary, depending on the source, but it is clear that alcohol and boasting made up no small parts in the affair. After indulging in whiskey, Jewel and Sollie began to brawl on the dance floor. Since Sollie was younger and smaller than Jewel, Sollie's younger brothers Carr and Little Doc came to his assistance, followed by Jewel's twin brother DeWitt coming to Jewel's aid. As the five cousins fought, suddenly one of the Durhams began flailing a knife. Jewel Christie was cut severely, almost to the point of death. One of the boys' uncles—one of the Sullivans—carried Jewel to a doctor who sewed many stitches to save his life. The Christies believed Doc Durham, the Durham boys' father, instigated the use of the knife, although some witnesses believed Doc actually tried to stop the fight. Whatever the case, the Christies were determined to exact revenge.

In immediate retaliation, the Christies shot Durham hogs on the open range and left them to rot, but this was only the beginning of more sinister acts. Soon the eldest Christie brother, Audie, who was married and already a father himself and was apparently not even present at the knife fight, planned an execution of his uncle. At another big dance just a few weeks after the knife fight, on February 10, 1912, a chair was placed inside the host home at a strategic location near an open window. The Christies arranged for their Uncle Doc to sit in the chair so that Audie could shoot him from outside the house while hiding in the dark. At the appointed time, as Uncle Doc sat in the chair holding a bottle of whiskey, "laughing and enjoying himself," said witnesses, two gunshots rang out over the music of guitars and fiddles. Uncle Doc fell to the floor dead. Two local lawmen were at the dance (some accounts claim they had been tipped off to the suspected assassination), and they chased what they believed to be at least one unidentified figure through the dark of night to the patriarch Christie's home, which was located about 400 yards west of today's North Boggy deer stand 102. Audie was found in the house, but he did not allow the lawmen peaceful entry. After fighting their way in and conducting a thorough search, the lawmen found a pair of shoes under one of the beds. The sole of one of the shoes, which had a distinctive crack, matched shoeprints near the open window where Doc was shot.

Audie Christie was apprehended and was later tried for his uncle's murder in November 1912 at Crockett. A jury found him guilty and convicted him to a life sentence in the state penitentiary. Audie appealed, but a higher court upheld the conviction and sentence. Audie's brother, Jewel, was tried as an accomplice in the crime, but he was acquitted.[124] Carr Durham, still stewing about the dance fight with Jewel eleven months earlier and now further enraged by Jewel's acquittal in the murder of his father, vowed to take Jewel's life, as well as the life of Jewel's father. "You killed my father, so I'm gonna kill you and your father," Carr was heard to say, witnesses later testified.

A year after the murder trials, on the afternoon of November 18, 1913, as Henry Christie and his twins Jewel and DeWitt rode home from Ratcliff, they received the full measure of Carr Durham's brand of justice. Newspaper accounts, which were based on initial sheriff reports as well as later court testimony, stated that the men were returning home in a two-horse wagon, after purchasing supplies for their farm and various family members. Some versions said a wedding suit for one of the Christie boys was among the items purchased. Uncle Henry and Jewel sat on the spring seat, while DeWitt sat behind them in the bed of the wagon, strumming a guitar. All were singing songs and drinking whiskey, when suddenly Carr Durham appeared in the middle of the road. Carr was riding a mule and was armed with a pump shotgun and a .32 Winchester repeating rifle. Carr blocked the road and exchanged heated words with his uncle and cousins. When Carr thought that one of the Christies reached for a gun, he emptied the pump shotgun into his kin. Uncle Henry, hit by loads of buckshot, fell backward into the wagon, while Jewel, also hit by buckshot, fell out of the wagon and into the road. As DeWitt jumped off the back of the wagon and ran away, Carr chased him for nearly a hundred yards, firing his lever action rifle until four bullets finally dropped DeWitt dead to the ground. Carr then returned to Jewel lying in the road, and shot him twice more with the .32 rifle. In all the shooting, the horses had bolted away with Uncle Henry laid out inside the wagon. After making sure the twins were dead, Carr chased the wagon on his mule. The shootings occurred no more than a mile from Walkerton, the Southern Pine Lumber Company logging camp, and the horses did not stop until the wagon hit a stump near the camp, within sight of Deputy Sheriff Walter Crow, who was visiting the camp at the time. Crow ran to the wagon to find the dead body of Henry Christie, just as Carr rushed upon the scene, still clutching the cocked Winchester in an aiming fashion. Carr lowered the rifle only after Crow convinced him that Henry Christie was dead. Carr then surrendered to Crow, claiming he killed all three men in self-defense, even though it was uncertain whether the Christies had been armed or not.[125] Later, after Carr's arrest, the Houston County sheriff also arrested Carr's brother Sollie, in addition to Carr, claiming he "could not understand how [only] one man could do so much shooting."

Pale purple coneflowers bloom around the joined tombstones of twins DeWitt and Jewell Christie at the Mount Pisgah Cemetery, summer 2015. The twin boys were killed, along with their father, by their cousin Carr Durham during a feud in November 1913. *Photo by the author.*

The November 20, 1913, issue of the *Crockett Courier* carried the story at the top of the front page, with the bold headline, "Another Tragedy in a Houston County Feud." Editor Aiken reported that the incident occurred in a "typical section for the scenario of a feudal story . . . that remote corner of Houston County known as Cracker's Bend." The tragedy was reminiscent of the melodramas portrayed in the new media of "moving pictures," the editor stated, except "in the latest act of the real feud," fiction was "outdone."[126] The Durham brothers spent three weeks together in jail, until their release on bail bond. Eventually, only Carr stood trial, which occurred in November 1914. The *Courier* reported that at least one hundred witnesses were examined over the course of several days, as spectators filled the courthouse and

courtyard daily.[127] Most witnesses testified to the feuding tendencies of the Christies and Durhams. Carr pleaded self-defense, and his jury found him not guilty of murder.

Some people later said that Carr was haunted by his actions—of so violently taking the life of his uncle and cousins—at least until he was gunned down himself, at Alazan, in Nacogdoches County, in May 1916, supposedly by someone testing his newly acquired, tough reputation. He was buried beside his murdered father, at Mount Vernon Cemetery, about four miles west of the North Boggy property.

At Mount Pisgah Cemetery, where Carr's uncles and cousins were buried, memorial tombstones for Henry Lafayette Christie and his twin sons Jewel and DeWitt now stand beside one another, near a row of cedar stumps among pale purple coneflowers. A decorative arch joins the headstones of the twins, inscribed with identical birth and death dates. Visitors to the burials rarely miss noticing the breath and sighing sound of wind passing through pine boughs all around. Noted Texas journalist Leon Hale visited the graveyard in 1977 and wrote of sensing melancholy. The feud, he said, was "a very sad story indeed." He especially lamented the cemetery's forlorn name, Mount Pisgah—the mountain peak from which Moses could see the Promised Land, but from which he could not enter.[128]

After the death of her husband and twin sons, while her eldest son remained in the state penitentiary at Huntsville, Laura Christie fell behind in the payment of taxes on 148 acres of Christie land in the southwest corner of the Lazarus Price survey. Earlier, her husband had sold the fee title to the survey's other 172 acres. Laura's remaining daughters, who were still at home at the time of the killings, married soon after and had mostly moved away, including the four girls who wrote their nature letters to the *Houston Post.* After cutting the merchantable trees on the Christie land, as well as the trees on tens of thousands of acres of surrounding forests, Southern Pine Lumber Company began in 1913 to operate a 32,000-acre fenced cattle ranch on the cutover lands. Not want-

Laura Alice Sullivan Christie, the Christie girls' mother, ca. 1929. One of sixteen Sullivan children who grew up at Sullivan's Bluff during the nineteenth century, Laura gave birth to sixteen children of her own there. One of her sons killed her brother-in-law in a feud and one of her nephews killed her husband and her twin sons in retribution. *Author's collections.*

ing the Christie tract within the enclosed ranch to revert to a sheriff auction, Southern Pine officials convinced Laura and her heirs to sell the home place at $9.12 an acre in 1918, withholding from the payment the amount of back taxes owed. Late in October, during the season in which trees let go of life aboveground, Dave Kenley, Southern Pine's timber and lands manager, arranged for Ratcliff State Bank to handle the deed transaction, which required the signatures of twenty-one people, including Laura and her ten surviving children and their spouses.[129]

Laura Sullivan Christie spent her remaining years living with her daughters and sons-in-laws away from Sullivan's Bluff, where she was born and

gave birth to her sixteen children. She lived first with her daughter Jessie and son-in-law Simon Smith—who briefly worked for the Southern Pine Lumber Company Ranch, at Rayville—until Simon took a railroad job in the sawmill town of Carmona in Polk County. Laura then moved to live with her daughter Maude and son-in-law B. Roach, who had taken a sawmill job at Trinity.[130] Just about all of Laura's sons-in-law worked for railroad and lumber companies, as her son Audie had done. Laura died in Trinity in January 1939, and her body returned to Mount Pisgah Cemetery ("Mt. Pisgy," according to her death certificate), where she was buried next to her husband, twin sons, and other family members.[131] Her son Audie received one of Governor Miriam Ferguson's numerous pardons during the 1920s. After a divorce from his first wife, he remarried and lived out his remaining days in Oklahoma and later in the city of Houston.[132] The Christies' kin—among them, the Franklins, Moores, Olivers, and Rushings— left Boggy Slough at about the same time that Laura Christie moved away, although a few remained a short time more.[133] Southern Pine Lumber Company bought their land, improvements, and hog claims, and placed tenants in their former homes, requiring the new residents to grow food crops for the company's cattle and serve as forest fire watchmen.

Today, a few of Jessie Christie's red elms, or at least their seedlings, remain at the former site of the Christie home place, not far from where a land surveyor cited a large one in his field notes during the summer of 1858.[134] Although probably not as abundant as they were during the spring of 1912, when Jessie wrote of them being "all around our place," they now grow on the roadsides at the curving juncture of two red dirt roads, near a dry branch, where the house used to stand in a clearing that is now forested. Although notoriously despised by lumbermen more than a century ago and by some foresters today as "the most useless pieces of vegetation in our forests," elms once made up for their lack of merchantable utility with their elegance and grace and their value to birds, especially to small, vocal, and insectivorous warblers—the "pretty little birds singing" that Jessie and her sisters wrote about.[135] Boggy Slough's first settlers believed that the presence of elms indicated fertile soil, but it was the vase-shaped tree's stately beauty and the special qualities of elm shade that made them worthy of sparing when homestead clearing often razed most other trees.[136]

No other tree but the elm, said nineteenth-century botanist Charles Sargent, was so closely associated "with the idea of home."[137] The elm's typical fountain shape of skyward springing boughs, lofty showers and sprays of branches, and hundreds of thousands of small, tooth-edged alternating oval leaves made it a noble tree, whose matchless shade displayed a unique dappling quality of shadow and light. The botanist Donald Culross Peattie imagined that "the play of light and shade from elm leaves [was] like music without sound, a dance without dancers." Elms were dooryard and household "friends," he said, whose lofty branches hung above a home "like a blessing." An elm was a "living monument," he declared, which could "scarcely grow to old age without collecting rich human associations around it."[138] Even the often society-scorning naturalist Henry David Thoreau praised human affections for elms, concluding that homes graced by them exhibited "a surer indication of old family distinction and worth than any evidence of wealth."[139]

Both the red elm (*Ulmus rubra*) and white elm (*Ulmus americana*) displayed similar ornamental traits. The white elm, whose limbs tended to droop more at the ends, generally grew taller. The red elm, also known as Indian elm and slippery elm, was hardier, however, and inhabited a broader range of soils and sites, especially across North Boggy. The red elm also provided medicinal qualities utilized by Indians, who taught them to white pioneers. The Christies and other Boggy Slough settlers may not have revered their elms quite as much as

A stately red elm, one of several that grows at the former Christie home place, where Jessie Christie lived and wrote about them in the *Houston Post* in 1912. *Photo by the author, August 2018.*

New Englanders did, who famously planted them in rows along village and city streets to form outdoor "cathedrals," but they nonetheless appreciated their graceful presence and their value to songbirds among their homes.[140]

Jessie also wrote of blooming plants, roses, and vines in her mother's yard. The roses and most of the vines are absent now, but an ancient row of crape myrtles (*Lagerstroemia indica*) still persist, along with ornamental chinaberry (*Melia azedarach*) trees. Repeatedly burned back by prescribed forest burnings, both plants continue to root sprout, with the numerous crape myrtle shoots forming an almost impenetrable thicket row. The shoots reveal themselves each summer by stretching skyward bouquets of pink blossoms, protruding above resprouting American beautyberry shrubs and scrubby sweetgums that resemble bushes more than trees. The clearing that once surrounded the house site is settled now mostly by tall, naturally seeded pine trees, although a young pine plantation occupies the northern end of the homestead, between the main road and one of the creeks. Beginning early in the 1950s, company foresters utilized several of the North Boggy settlers' abandoned fields as pine plantations or as sites for food plots for deer. In more recent years they placed a hog-proof deer feeder at the site of the old Christie house, right beside the crape myrtles.

Occasionally, a disturbance caused by road maintenance or logging activities will unearth remnants of the lives once lived at the Christie place, revealing such artifacts as broken china plates and cups, cast iron children's toys, a wagon wheel iron tire, and various patent medicine bottles. Among the items found recently, a wholly intact bottle of Groves Tasteless Chill Tonic—once a common drug to prevent and treat malaria and its accompanying fevers and chills—serves as a reminder that life experiences at Sullivan's Bluff were not always idyl-lic. Malaria was once known as "the scourge of the South," and outbreaks were likely each summer following the spring flooding of sloughs and swamps, which created stagnant pools for breeding mosquitoes.[141] The presence of trees such as elms and sycamores, which settlers believed were indications of fertile soil, also warned of malarial low grounds. Living in such places posed a risk taken by every settler near a river. The Christie place, among its hills of red elms, was not river bottom land, but it was only half a mile from the swampy bottoms of Franklin Slough, which bordered the fields and farms of the Christies, Franklins, and Rushings.

Jessie and her sisters did not mention malaria in their letters to the *Houston Post*. Nor did the letters contain notice of sawmills, railroads, and distant market economies, although these things had changed their lives forever. The girls' letters also belied the grim details that their innocent and bucolic springs of birdsong and flowers ended in a cemetery with tombstones next to their beloved school. Human conflict had stained the ground, as Boggy Slough's history, and future, changed once again.

CHAPTER 4

T. L. L. Temple and the Humble Beginnings of a Legacy

For there is hope of a tree, if it be cut down,
it might sprout again.

—JOB 14:7

While the first generations of English-speaking settlers were establishing their homesteads in Boggy Slough, Thomas Lewis Latane Temple, the man whose legacy would shape the land more than any other, was born in Virginia, more than a thousand miles away. Orphaned at the age of eleven, he was raised by older cousins, and although never poor, he saw and recognized the comforts of privileged living from a distance, catching a glimpse of wealth's liberating power when his two oldest brothers received an inheritance from a prosperous uncle who was a cotton planter in Arkansas. Upon completing his formal education after the Civil War, Temple left Virginia, followed his brothers to Arkansas, and there sought to create his own fortune—not in cotton fields, but in southern yellow pine forests.[1]

Southern yellow pine trees, which had grown straight and tall in the energy flows from the sun, became commodities—something priced, bought, and sold—when the already commoditized white pine forests of the northeastern and Great Lakes states dwindled and failed to satisfy the expanding nation's insatiable demand for softwood building material. For centuries, America's seemingly inexhaustible forests of white pines, filled with trees that reached heights of more than 150 feet and girths of more than six feet, were unrivaled in supplying the timber needs of a colonial empire and in birthing a vibrant, new nation.[2] Largely as a result of wasteful harvesting practices in the northeast and Great Lakes regions and the rapid expansion of railroad construction across the South after the Civil War, the expanding web of markets of exchange quickly entangled yellow pine forests within their far-reaching urban-rural system of economic connections. Southern farmers and homesteaders, including those at Boggy Slough, found money indispensable as local industries grew to become giant factories supplying world markets. Whether they wanted it or not, Boggy Slough's residents soon discovered that a new order of industrialized commercialization was replacing their long-held agrarian ideals of self-containment.[3]

When Temple moved to southwestern Arkansas in 1876, he found much of the region covered with an almost continuous forest of yellow pine, extending over many hundreds of miles. The short-leaved species (*Pinus echinata*) occupied the high, dry ridges, while the loblolly species (*Pinus taeda*) thrived in the wetter soils just above the bottoms.[4] Writing during the last quarter of the nineteenth century on behalf of the US Department of Agriculture, Dr. Charles Mohr said short-leaf pine, the most widely distributed pine species across the United States, was "most abundant and in fullest perfection" west of the Mississippi River, while in southwestern Arkansas, northwestern Louisiana, and northeastern Texas, it found "its best development," often in "pure stands, scarcely surpassed in . . . timber wealth."[5] Temple learned the economy of southern yellow pine trees in such forests, and with pride he formed multiple corporations that bore "Southern Pine" in their names.

In Texas, where Temple ultimately made his fortune, the rise of yellow pine production—and consumption—was dramatic. The annual value of the state's lumber mill products rose from less than $2 million in 1870 to nearly $18 million by 1900.[6] The manufacture of lumber became the most important industry in the state during the 1880s, ranking first in number of wage earners, wages paid, capital invested, and value of manufactured products.[7] From the late 1870s through the rest of the century, lumber also ranked first in tonnage moved annually by Texas railroads. Lumber and other forest products from East Texas were carried to treeless West Texas and to virtually every state and territory in the Union. Lumber was also shipped through Sabine Pass to ports in the United States, Mexico, Central and South America, and Europe.[8]

───── ◆·◆·◆ ─────

Thomas Lewis Latane Temple was born on the eighteenth day of March in 1859 at Wayland in Essex County, Virginia, to Episcopal clergyman Henry Waring Latane Temple and Susan Jones, each descendants of pioneer Virginia families. T. L. L., or Tom, as he came to be known, was the ninth child and the fifth son born to the union. He was five years old when his mother died in 1864, and he was eleven years old when his father died early in 1871.[9] Another death affected the family profoundly in 1865, when Tom's two oldest

brothers, John Newton Temple (1847–99) and Charles H. T. Temple (1855–81) inherited a fortune upon the passing of their mother's affluent bachelor uncle, Dr. Orlando Scott Jones. Born in 1809, Dr. Jones descended from a wealthy Virginia family and received his education at Rumford Academy, in King William County, graduating from William and Mary College in 1829. He later earned an MD from the Medical College of Philadelphia, although he never fully entered medical practice. Instead, he took the proceeds from the sale of lands his father gifted him and moved in 1837 to the newly organized state of Arkansas, settling in Franklin Township, Sevier County. From there he acquired land and developed plantations along the bottomlands of the Little and Red Rivers in Arkansas and Louisiana. He never married and provided in his will of 1861 for much of his property and all of his Arkansas lands to go to T. L. L. Temple's two oldest brothers, in the event of their mother's earlier death.[10] The oldest brother, John Newton Temple, moved to Arkansas before 1870 to claim the inheritance, followed later by his brother and co-heir Charles.[11]

After the death of his mother, young Tom Temple moved a short distance from his father's home to live with his older cousin Lucy and her husband Watson Walker of Chatham Hill. Family tradition tells that Tom and his father never did "get along," so while receiving his education at Aberdeen Academy, in King and Queen County, he yearned to go west, as many of his kinsmen had done.[12] In September 1876, at the age of seventeen, he bade farewell to Virginia and moved to Little River County, Arkansas, to be near his brothers John and Charles, bringing their youngest brother, William, age fifteen, with him. Tom tried farming upon reaching the lands of his brothers, but according to one of his grandsons, he soon "left his mule in the field" and walked to the nearest town, his mind and temperament unsuited to farm labor.[13] At Ashdown he tried railroading, but he had no interest in that line of work either. He next took a job in the Little River County courts, becoming a deputy clerk, where he witnessed numerous land

and timber transactions, which piqued his interest and appealed to the entrepreneurial spirit of an orphan seeking his own way in life. Recognizing the relationships between far-reaching markets and local natural resources, he soon moved to Texarkana, where he found his life's calling while working as a bookkeeper for one of the growing number of lumber manufacturing and sales firms headquartered there.[14] As southern yellow pine began to replace the diminishing resources of northern white pine in satisfying the growing nation's increasing needs for softwood building material, Temple found himself at the fore of a burgeoning lumberman's frontier, where profit margins were among the highest in American business at the time.[15] As expressed famously in 1902 by lumberman Robert A. Long of Kansas City, who would later purchase one of T. L. L. Temple's sawmills at Lufkin, Texas, "I believe that I can truthfully and correctly say that no great body of timber has ever made or promises to make as good a per cent of profit for its investors as has yellow pine. As to beauty of growth, in my opinion, there is no other forest under the canopy of heaven that can compare with it."[16] T. L. L. Temple could not have agreed more.

At Texarkana, Temple met a number of up-and-coming lumbermen and railroad builders. Among them were Texarkana pioneers the Whitaker brothers, William Lowndes Jr. and Benjamin, who had taken what remained of their father's sizable antebellum wealth accumulated in a Cass County, Texas, cotton plantation (their father Willis Whitaker Sr. was one of the largest slave owners in Texas in 1860) and invested it in timberlands and railroad construction ventures after the war. The influential Whitakers organized and built a number of businesses in Texas, Arkansas, Louisiana, and Oklahoma, including the Texarkana and Fort Smith Railway, which was a part of the Kansas City Southern Railway system, and Benjamin Whitaker served two terms in the Texas senate during the 1890s.[17] Temple, young and ambitious, moved fluently among the Whitakers and others like them in Texarkana's business and social circles. In December 1880, Temple married Georgie Derrick Fowlkes, who was the younger sister of Benjamin Whitaker's wife, Anna Patterson Fowlkes. Georgie and Anna were natives of Arkansas, whose paternal grandfather had left Virginia four decades earlier to develop a cotton plantation on the Red River, at Spring Hill, in Hempstead County, southeast of Fulton, amassing a considerable fortune before the Civil War. Like Temple, Georgie was born in 1859, and her father also died just after the war, when she was only eight years old.[18]

Late in 1881, T. L. L. and Georgie, along with their newborn daughter Gertrude, moved to the new postal community of Hoxie, Texas, in Cass County, 30 miles southwest of Texarkana, in the heart of Texas' shortleaf pine country. There, T. L. L. operated a sawmill prior to the town's name changing to Wayne in 1883.[19] The mill work was demanding, and Georgie and Gertrude returned often to Texarkana during T. L. L.'s busy labors. "I hardly know when I am to be seated long enough to write a letter," he apologized in a belated communication to his sister Mary back in Virginia in August 1882. Temple confided that "some men seem to enjoy the absence of their wives, but it is not so with me," adding, "I do think a sawmill is a great deal of trouble."[20]

Realizing that his strength was in managing markets and men, rather than machinery, Temple soon hired a contractor to run the Hoxie mill. Then, in partnership with his brother-in-law, Benjamin Whitaker, he purchased interests in other milling operations up and down the tracks of the Texas & Pacific railroad, mostly in Cass County, which Whitaker knew well. Temple occasionally leased small tracts of land, near the railroad, on which he and his partners operated small sawmills and paid for nearby pine timber as they cut it, often for as low as fifty cents per 1,000 feet, board measure. Owners of the land actually preferred that it be cleared of timber because they believed the soil held more value if it were put under the plow and converted to agricultural fields.[21]

In 1887 Temple joined a partnership with other Texarkana businessmen, including E. A. Rand, Frank Grigsby, and Ab Scott, known as Atlanta

Lumber Mills, of Atlanta, Texas. Temple served as the partnership's general manager, supervising the work of more than one hundred employees.[22] Temple soon joined other enterprises. With railroad builders D. J. Grigsby and G. M. D. Grigsby, he formed Union Mills Lumber Company. With his brother-in-law Benjamin Whitaker again, along with lumbermen C. M. Putman and Sanford H. Bolinger, he formed Southern Pine Lumber Company, which operated a planing mill at Kingsland, Arkansas, in 1889.[23] Within only a few years, Temple's business ventures included operating lumber mills in Texas and Arkansas, lumber wholesaling across the Gulf Southwest and Kansas, and real estate speculating in the Oklahoma Territory. He enjoyed some early success, but hardship was never far away. By 1890 his Southern Pine Lumber Company had reached too far, too fast. It fell behind in meeting contractual obligations, sank into debt, and altogether failed in 1891. Union Mills Lumber Company, of which Temple owned one-fifth interest, also experienced financial and legal difficulties. Temple found himself a defendant in numerous lawsuits; one legal fight advanced all the way to the United States Supreme Court. Eager for independence, Temple divested himself from the partnerships and reorganized Southern Pine Lumber Company as an Arkansas corporation in September 1892, with himself as president and majority stockholder. This new venture, however, fared no better than the one it replaced, and Temple soon liquidated its assets to pay off his debts and settle more lawsuits. By 1893, most of the once-abundant pine timber in Cass, Bowie, and Harrison Counties, where most of Temple's mills had operated, was nearing exhaustion, and a timber shortage was added to Temple's difficulties.[24] Doggedly persistent, Temple once again, for the third time, reorganized his Southern Pine Lumber Company late in 1893, and he looked for new opportunities in other forests. This time he made his Southern Pine Lumber Company a Texas corporation and included for the first time his younger brother William, who had in the meantime become a successful merchant at Fulton, Arkansas.[25]

It is unclear how much financial assistance T. L. L. Temple and his brother William may have received from their older brothers who inherited the lands of their mother's uncle. Charles, the younger brother of the inheritance, died a bachelor in 1881. Since it was after Charles's death that T. L. L. began his lumber partnerships and that William entered the mercantile business on his own account, it seems likely that Charles's portion of the inheritance was sold and the proceeds distributed among the six surviving Temple siblings.[26] It is also uncertain how much assistance, if any, Temple may have received from his wife's family, which held more antebellum wealth than even Temple's wealthy uncle, Orlando Jones.[27]

Regardless of what happened, biographical sketches of T. L. L. Temple written and published during his lifetime, based on information he provided, did not mention financial support from anyone. Instead, the accounts stressed the "loneliness" and "unhappiness" of his "orphan state." Biographies in journals and books published by *American Lumberman* maintained that T. L. L.'s father provided "nothing for his heir" and left him "to face the world unassisted." Another observed, "From a lowly position he made his way up in the world by sheer force of ability and energy. No helping hand was extended to guide and encourage him."[28] Whatever the case, it is certain that Temple held enough wealth early in the 1880s to start out in the burgeoning yellow pine lumber business, although in a relatively small way at first, and as a junior partner in larger ventures. In the process he learned valuable lessons, but the experiences also left him vulnerable and in a poor financial standing. So it was in such a state of mind and financial insecurity that, late in 1893, from his office in Texarkana, Temple turned his gaze and cast his faith to the forests in Angelina County, Texas, 180 miles to the southwest. As a trade journal later framed the moment, T. L. L. Temple held "only his personality" as "total capital and surplus."[29]

Temple's choice of Angelina County, Texas, as the beginning of what would later become a Fortune 200 company late in the twentieth century,

above the Beaumont mills, were reported.[31]

Change seemed to come when Angelina County received two railroads in the 1880s. One line passed north and south through the eastern middle of the county in 1881–82, eventually connecting Houston to Shreveport, Louisiana. The road's official name was the Houston, East & West Texas Railway Company (HE&WT), but East Texans jokingly knew it as "Hell Either Way Taken," for its meager construction and the convenient acronym. More seriously, the railroad company's corporate seal contained the image of a lone, tall, straight pine tree, with no low branches, which signified the intended traffic of the road: clear, first-class pine lumber.[32] The other road, originating in Tyler, and backed by several of the HE&WT's investors, connected to the HE&WT tracks, in 1885, in the center of the county at Lufkin, soon to be the new county seat. This second railroad was the Kansas & Gulf Short Line, which became part of the St. Louis Southwestern Railway of Texas (SSW) system in 1899. Although known simply by the SSW's nickname, the Cotton Belt, the railroad's primary business in central East Texas, by far, was forest products.[33]

The construction of two railroads into and across a county usually produced an impetus for immediate and significant economic and population growth. Such did not happen in Angelina County. The primary reason was that both railroads were of narrow-gauge construction, meaning their rails were closer together than those of standard-gauge roads. As the name suggests, standard gauge, a measurement of 56.5 inches between the rails, was a

was interesting. Before 1900, Angelina was one of East Texas' least populated counties. Although the 1880 census and the 1882 Texas Commission on Insurance, Statistics, and History reported that the county held immense stands of all three native yellow pines—longleaf, shortleaf, and loblolly—and thick stands of walnut, ash, hickory, magnolia, elm, and oaks in the bottomlands along the Neches and Angelina Rivers, major lumber companies were slow to tap those resources. Experienced lumbermen knew that without adequate railroad transportation, Angelina's natural bounty could never reach markets abroad profitably. In the meantime, much of the county's pine timber was being harvested and floated down the Neches River to nationally rail-connected sawmills at Beaumont, in Jefferson County, more than 300 river miles away.[30] Those engaged in floating logs down the Neches River were so numerous by 1879 that the state enacted a log brand act that spring, which required all logs transported on rivers to be "stamped," "chopped," or "gouged" with identifying marks of ownership on their ends. During the law's first year of enforcement, ninety-four separate marks were registered for the Neches River alone, where log jams as high as 20 feet above the surface of the water, more than 100 miles national standard for railroad construction generally adopted after the Civil War. In theory, narrow-gauge roads were cheaper to build and operate, as long as the road's freight both originated and terminated on the line. In practice, they were often unsuccessful because the interchange of heavy, bulky freight, such as forest products, between different-gauged roads was costly and essentially prohibitive. Although small sawmills emerged along Angelina's 36-inch-gauge tracks soon after construction, they were incapable of maximizing profits, and larger mills did not appear until the railroad companies converted their lines to standard gauge in 1894 and 1895. When that happened, economic conditions transformed in a hurry.[34]

To understand both the uneventful influence of the narrow-gauge roads and the transforming impact of the gauge conversions, the federal census records help to tell the story. Angelina's population grew from 5,239 in 1880, when there were no railroads, to 6,306 in 1890, when there were two narrow-gauge roads, a 20 percent increase. This rate of growth was far lower than the state average, however, which was 40 percent. By contrast, Angelina's population grew from 6,306 in 1890 to 13,481 in 1900, after the two railroads converted to standard gauge—a hefty 114 percent increase—while the state average lagged far behind at 36 percent growth. Contributing to this increase was the construction of new sawmills in the southern part of the county along the widened tracks of the Houston, East & West Texas Railway, including T. L. L. Temple's new Southern Pine Lumber Company mills at Diboll.[35]

News that the two railroads would widen their tracks reached lumbermen in spring 1893. When T. L. L. Temple began to consider Angelina County as the manufacturing base of his new business ventures, land and timber acquisitions there were already occurring. Several firms, such as Tyler Car and Lumber Company, A. Harris and Company, and Angelina County Lumber Company, acquired timber and established mills along the Cotton Belt railroad, northwest of Lufkin. Local landowners, Charles L. Kelty, W. H. Bonner &

Sons, W. J. Townsend, and E. J. Mantooth—some of whom also owned mills—increased their land and timber holdings in the central region of the county.[36] In the southern part of the county, within Mexican land grant surveys south of Bradley Prairie, speculation there had occurred even earlier. To these lands along the HE&WT Railway, T. L. L. Temple cast his fortunes at an opportune time.

Whereas the lands included hardwood bottoms along White Oak Creek, where the Keen, Courtney, and Ashworth families had settled before 1880, it was the pine timber that attracted the speculators.[37] Among them was the noted land agent and mayor of Marshall, Texas, Amory R. Starr, who owned a few tracts.[38] The most important portions, however, were owned by two out-of-state men: Dr. Joseph Slemons Copes, a native of Delaware, and Greenwood LeFlore, the prominent Choctaw chief and Mississippi state senator. As a physician to the Choctaws who remained in Mississippi following passage of the federal Indian Removal Act of 1830, Dr. Copes had befriended the wealthy planter LeFlore during the 1830s and served as his agent and attorney in acquiring many thousands of acres of land across the South, especially after becoming a traveling life insurance salesman based in New Orleans late in the 1840s.[39] Copes began acquiring lands in Angelina County in 1860, at times in his own name, sometimes in LeFlore's name. Occasionally land transferred back and forth among them and their family members, including Copes's son-in-law, Jason T. Diboll. Some lands were acquired through tax forfeiture and estate sales, while others were obtained, and some lost, through court judgements.[40] In about 1877 Copes gave one of his nephews, Henry Francis Copes, lands in Stovall Prairie, east of Diboll, on which to live, in exchange for managing the Copes lands in Texas. This Copes family would remain in Angelina County, even after the death of Joseph Slemons Copes a few years later, which effectively ended Henry Francis Copes's overseer responsibilities, although parts of the later town of Diboll still bear the name Copestown today.[41]

Chief LeFlore died in 1865, and Joseph Slemons Copes died in 1885, leaving to their heirs about 12,000 acres of land in southern Angelina County. Two decisions of the US Circuit Court of the Eastern District of Texas at Tyler settled claims between the LeFlore and Copes heirs in January and May 1892, whereby the LeFlore heirs received a quarter of the lands and the Copes heirs received three-quarters.[42] The lands were divided so that each parcel would benefit from access to the rails of the HE&WT railroad.

Five months after the second court decision, the LeFlore heirs sold their land—2,943 acres—to local lumberman Charles L. Kelty for $6,900.[43] Three weeks later Kelty sold the same land for $7,806 to southeast Texas lumbermen Samuel Fain Carter and Martin T. Jones.[44] Carter and Jones had enjoyed earlier success in the sawmills at Beaumont and Orange, and upon moving to the city of Houston, they further engaged in banking and lumber retail yard businesses. They formed Emporia Lumber Company in 1892 and quickly acquired thousands of additional acres of land and timber in Angelina County and constructed a sawmill on the HE&WT railroad at a station known as Emporia, one mile south of where T. L. L. Temple would later build his own mill at the station known as Diboll.

By 1893, the Copes heirs' lands resided in the hands of two women: Joseph Slemons Copes's daughter, Asenath A. Phelps of Los Angeles, California, and his granddaughter, Rosa Louise Diboll of New Orleans, Louisiana. Rosa's brothers, Collins Cerré Diboll and Joseph Copes Diboll, had transferred their interest in the lands to their sister in 1890 and 1891, respectively, before the land split with the LeFlore heirs.[45] With Joseph's assistance, the two women negotiated a business plan with T. L. L. Temple that provided not only Southern Pine Lumber Company's humble beginning but profoundly influenced the first thirty years of the company's history in remarkable ways. The details of this plan reveal the Copes heirs' business savvy as well as their early recognition of forestlands as renewable natural resources.

Rosa Louise Diboll Bres of New Orleans, ca. 1930. Rosa, along with her aunt, Asenath Phelps of California, held the mortgage on Temple's first sawmill in the Angelina County town he named for the Diboll family in 1894. *Courtesy of The History Center, Diboll.*

On January 13, 1894, Temple contracted with Phelps and Diboll to construct a pine sawmill on their land, very near the HE&WT railroad tracks, for which their father and grandfather had provided a right-of-way thirteen years earlier. For the name of the sawmill's rail station and the town that would develop around it, they chose Diboll. No one knows for certain who chose the name, but there were already towns in Texas with the names of Temple and Phelps, in Bell and Walker Counties, respectively. Exactly six months later, on July 13, after completion of the mill's construction—a relatively small 50,000 board feet per day single circular sawmill—Phelps and Diboll transferred fee title to 20.5 acres of land, on which the mill stood, to Southern Pine Lumber Company. On the same day, in a separate transaction, Temple mortgaged the land and everything standing on it to the women as surety that Southern Pine Lumber Company would fulfill its obligation to cut the merchantable pine timber on 6,845 acres of surrounding Copes estate land, paying the women seventy-five cents for every 1,000 board feet of timber cut.[46]

This mortgage agreement, based on a "stumpage" contract, was vastly different from the common timber deed of the day. There were several important distinctions: Timber deeds were a matter of public record, much like a land deed, wherein a person or company paid a landowner, usually *in cash*, a certain price per acre for rights to the timber standing on the land, with little regard for the exact amount of timber. Any consideration for the volume of timber was simply reflected in the price per acre, but many sellers never bothered with such details and were eager simply to accept the quick cash. Besides, such sellers were generally resident farmers who desired the land cleared anyway, so that land conversion to cultivation or grazing could occur more rapidly. At the time, many timber deeds in Angelina and surrounding counties sold for one dollar or less per acre. It is important to consider that, whereas timber deeds focused on the amount of *acreage*, stumpage contracts concentrated on the amount of *timber*. This was a major difference. For example, by the first method, a person owning 320 acres of timberland might make $320 by selling the timber in a common timber deed but, by the second method, could make far more by selling the timber by the foot, as in the Copes-Temple deal, which was seventy-five cents per 1,000 feet cut. This is especially revealing when considering East Texas forestland at the time held on average between 6,000 and 12,000 board feet of merchantable pine per acre.[47] When comparing a $320 timber deed to a stumpage contract worth between $1,440 and $2,880, it is not difficult to see why the timber deed was generally the preferred instrument of the lumberman, while a stumpage contract was usually favored by the savvy landowner. Thus, the latter method prevailed with the Copes heirs, who became in a sense Temple's contractual business partners. Did Temple not have sufficient cash, capital, and credit to build a new mill and purchase enough timber to support its operation, especially considering his recently failed Southern Pine

Lumber Company of Arkansas? Did he truly need outside assistance from those willing to gamble on his "personality?" Or were the Copes heirs simply unwilling to cash out, since they recognized the sustainable income potential of forests as a renewable resource? Perhaps it was a combination of all three. Whatever the case, Temple entered into an essentially pay-as-you-go financial arrangement, something avoided or not needed by many of his competitors, including Emporia Lumber Company, whose larger mill one mile south of Diboll operated on *purchased* lands that were once owned by the Copes-LeFlore partnership.

Despite a seeming handicap, the Temple mill at Diboll met and perhaps exceeded all expectations. Realizing steady profit margins from the beginning, Temple not only repaid his former debts but reinvested in expanding his Diboll operation, and he soon began purchasing additional timber and lands as well as investing in other lumber companies and railroads inside and outside Angelina County. All the while his business plan with Asenath Phelps and her niece, Rosa Diboll, who would marry and take the name Bres, continued until 1924, long past the four to five years it took to cut the initial merchantable timber on the original 6,845 acres. For three decades the two women and their families benefited from Temple's success by continuing to own the lands immediately surrounding his Diboll mills, conspicuously influencing the manner in which Southern Pine Lumber Company and the town of Diboll grew.[48] Through the years their willing assistance was necessary in all plant expansions, and they sparingly sold Temple only the minimum amount of land and rights-of-way he required, reserving additional land uses and mineral rights for their own benefit.

An early reporter once detailed the extremely high lumber stacks at Diboll and the extensive efforts required to use them, saying "high piling" was necessary because of the "economy of space."[49] Utilizing elevated boardwalk dolly ways, which were higher than those of other mills, crews of workers stacked boards "down and up" to great heights, necessitated by the mill's relatively small footprint. The limited space also prevented Temple from building adequately sized millponds for storing his pine logs. Whereas the ponds of most other mill owners varied in size between seven and twelve acres, the first Diboll millpond was barely one acre, severely limiting the amount of logs that could be stored, which affected logging operations all the way back to the woods. Most sawmilling operations made "hay"—that is, timber—while the sun shone, storing up large reserves of logs at the mills during the dry season to limit potential log shortages during the difficult wet season. Temple could not do that. The small ponds at Diboll in the early days meant Temple's logging railroads had to be kept in excellent shape year-round to facilitate continuous logging. As one early writer said of Temple's railroads at Diboll, "They have to be good all the time, wet or dry, winter or summer, so as to submit to the daily haul."[50] Diboll's ponds were so small and limiting that when Temple built another sawmill at Lufkin in 1899 for the Lufkin Land and Lumber Company, the *Houston Post* reported the millpond there was going to be "the largest in East Texas."[51]

For lands the women retained, Temple had to negotiate, and purchase, utility and transportation rights-of-way, easements, and leases with every plant and railroad expansion. Each grant, too, was usually conditional. When the company expanded in 1903 by erecting a larger first-class double-band sawmill, requiring the purchase of more land and rights-of-way, the Copes heirs set the minimum valuation of the improvements at $75,000.[52] They placed similar stipulations and restrictions on an easement for a vital water pipeline the company built from a pumping station at Ryan's Lake on the Neches River to the mills in 1908 and 1909. The pipe had to be sufficiently buried belowground and maintained so as to not interfere with any other land uses.[53] Likewise, all Temple's logging railroads across the Copes lands could not restrict the further use of those lands "for other purposes for which they may be adapted."[54] By keeping their options open, they limited Temple's.

The more improvements Temple made to his Diboll mill and railroad operations, the more valuable the surrounding Copes heirs' land, timber, and rights-of-way became. For example, when the company purchased from Phelps and Diboll-Bres a little over 200 acres surrounding the mills in 1909, the price was $50 per acre, significantly more than the $2.34 per acre the LeFlore heirs had received for adjoining lands just a few years earlier.[55] And in 1917, Southern Pine Lumber Company paid the women $65,000 for the rights to a *second cutting* of merchantable timber from the remaining Diboll lands, this time in the form of a timber deed, which now included hardwoods as well as pine. Furthermore, the company chose to pay the property taxes on the lands until the mills were ready to cut the timber, fearing a lapse in tax payments might prevent the eventual harvest of the trees.[56] Temple still did not own the land, but he had more invested in it than its owners did.

Seeing his way past the Copes heirs would take considerable time. Until then, Temple steadily reinvested his earnings in additional lands and timber reserves. "Buy timber, buy timber, buy timber" was not only Southern Pine Lumber Company's "guiding principle," wrote one lumber trade journalist in 1908, it was "the main portion of its success."[57] Temple's opportunity to purchase more than 25,000 additional acres of timberlands in Angelina and San Augustine Counties presented itself in June 1898, upon the death of lumberman Martin T. Jones, a founding partner of the Emporia Lumber Company mill just south of Diboll.[58] Driven by an entrepreneurial spirit, yet still affected by limited financial resources and the peculiar arrangements with the Copes heirs, Temple sought the assistance of fellow Texarkana lumberman Enoch W. Frost. Temple fashioned a land-buying partnership between his Southern Pine Lumber Company and Frost, whereby Frost contributed 60 percent and Southern Pine 40 percent of the funds to purchase the lands at $5.58 an acre. Signing the deed to the lands was Jones's young nephew, Jesse H. Jones, the famous real estate developer and financier who several decades later served as the powerful chairman of President Franklin Roosevelt's Reconstruction Finance Corporation.[59]

Frost and Temple acquired additional lands, bringing their partnership total to 35,000 acres. Temple next formed a three-way milling partnership early in 1899 with Frost and Canadian George A. Kelley to incorporate the Lufkin Land and Lumber Company and the Texas and Louisiana Railroad Company.[60] Temple planned for the land and lumber company to manage the lands, manufacture pine lumber, and then sell the cutover lands as farms, with "their magnificent growths of hard woods left intact," said one contemporary account. Temple planned for the railroad company, of which he served as president, to haul timber from the forests, carry lumber from the mills, and later transport the cleared lands' agricultural products. The 25-mile-long railroad would therefore provide increased selling value to the cutover lands while the converted farms would provide ready-made traffic revenue for the railroad company. Time proved the venture a tremendous success.

While Temple assembled his new Lufkin partnerships, he also bought out Southern Pine Lumber Company's logging contractor, J. J. Bonner Timber Company of Diboll, in November 1898. The transaction included two locomotives; seventeen logging cars; several miles of railroad with additional rails, spikes, fish plates, ties, and bridge material; and the timber on an additional 4,000 acres of land owned by the Angelina County Lumber Company to which Bonner was indebted.[61] Temple certainly understood debt, and now he was a buyer rather than a seller. He also bought an additional 338 tons of used steel rails from the HE&WT railway, which he used to expand the logging railroad's reach.[62] In 1900 he incorporated the railroad as a common carrier known as the Texas Southeastern (TSE) Railroad Company, and he directed its construction northeastward from Diboll to connect with his Texas and Louisiana Railroad several miles due east of Lufkin at Diboll Junction. The move was strategic, since the junction gave his Diboll mill a connection to the Cotton Belt rail lines at Lufkin, which meant not only competitive options for shipping his Diboll lumber but also a share in rate divisions. Interestingly, Temple did not plan for the TSE Railroad to be long-lived, since the company's original charter called for a corporate life of only seven years.[63]

The Lufkin Land company venture was never intended to be a sustained operation either. With an initial cutting capacity of 40 million board feet of lumber per year, the state-of-the-art double-band sawmill was a "cut out and get out" deal from the beginning. Even the logging was done by contract, which, T. L. L. Temple said, "relieves you of a great deal of trouble and investment." Crews cut only pines and left the hardwoods for later farmland development by others.[64] A full-page advertisement in the December 11, 1902, special issue of the *Lufkin Weekly Tribune* stated that "all" of Lufkin Land and Lumber Company's 35,000 acres were "splendidly watered by the Angelina River and numbers of creeks and springs." Once the lands were cleared of pine, the advertisement claimed, they were sure to be "the finest lands for general farming purposes and for truck growing, especially, to be found in East Texas."[65]

The Lufkin Land company mill proved a financial success from its beginning, paying a reported 12 percent profit every month. Decades later many lumbermen still considered it during its early days as "the most successfully operated sawmill plant in the South."[66] Cashing in on the ventures' success, Temple and his partners transferred the Texas and Louisiana Railroad Company to the Cotton Belt railroad conglomerate of lines in 1903 and sold the Lufkin Land and Lumber Company to the giant Long-Bell Lumber Company in 1905. With the profits, Frost invested in land, timber, and sawmills in Nacogdoches County, while George A. Kelley, who later became a Lufkin mayor, joined Polk County lumberman W. T. Carter to obtain forestlands in southeastern Angelina County, forming the Carter-Kelley Lumber Company and building a large sawmill at Manning, 16 miles east of Diboll. Temple used his proceeds from the sale of the Texas and Louisiana Railroad to reinvest in more lands and timber in support of his Diboll operation, which he also expanded by adding a new double-band sawmill in 1903. With the proceeds from the sale of the Lufkin Land sawmill and lands in 1905, Temple entered yet another partnership, this time with Garrison-Norton Lumber Company, which operated a sawmill at Pineland in Sabine County. Temple quickly bought out those partners and organized Temple Lumber Company as a new Texas corporation in 1908.[67]

It seemed Temple was finally overcoming some of the odds that were earlier against him, but understandably he was also finding available land and timber purchases for continuance of his Diboll mill increasingly difficult to come by. Most of the best, more profitable lands—those containing a greater concentration of pine—were already secured by other mill operators and speculative timber buyers, and Temple had even played a peculiar role in their acquisition by others. In the process, Temple found his land and timber agents buying more and more tracts situated in and along the middle Neches River valley, west and northwest of Diboll, including the Boggy Slough lands. These lands did not contain as heavy a concentration of pines as did the more upland tracts. Instead, a large percentage of Temple's lands contained extensive bottomland hardwoods, which had been earlier rejected by lumbermen because there was not yet a market for them. Finding himself a pine sawmiller owning substantial acreage that contained hardwoods, Temple again faced new challenges. In typical fashion, Temple welcomed the hardship as yet another opportunity for achievement. If there was no market for Texas hardwoods, then Temple would make one. As one industry writer summarized early in 1904, Southern Pine Lumber Company was "not a business which was deliberately created in all its parts or worked out in well perfected plan," yet it nevertheless succeeded.[68]

As late as 1899, not a single sawmill in Texas was devoted exclusively to milling hardwood lumber. Hardwoods were still seen primarily as mere indications of good farmland and were thus regarded as a hindrance to agricultural conversion; even the

US Department of Commerce considered them an "encumbrance on the land."[69] Since large milling operations initially targeted pure pine stands along uplands, from which the highest profits could be made, mill owners and operators settled for lands containing hardwoods mixed with the pines only as the stands containing the highest concentrations of pine became scarce. Even then they generally left the hardwoods standing, as Temple's own Lufkin Land and Lumber Company did. Bottomland hardwood forests in Texas were the last to receive the attention of lumbermen. In the meantime, long-established settlement patterns continued to steadily clear the hardwoods for land conversion to farms. Writing for the US Forest Service in 1903, botanist William L. Bray of Austin lamented the absence of hardwood mills in Texas, saying the alluvial soils of the hardwood bottoms in the state were so rich "that clearing for settlement is outstripping the lumberman. Field after field of unsurpassed forest is being deadened and destroyed merely to get rid of the trees."[70] The loose bottom soils of East Texas, Bray said, had produced oaks up to six feet in diameter, ash up to four feet, and hickories up to three feet. He felt that if such trees were going to be "wasted" in agricultural development, then at least the best interests of the general public as well as the private landowners would be better served by developing hardwood markets. Others, including economists, agreed with Bray. In the *Texas Almanac for 1904*, the author of an article titled "The Hardwood Wealth of Texas" lamented over the best white oaks in the state being "gutted" by stave makers, whom he called "devastators of the forests," because the practice of barrel making was "exceedingly wasteful" of large trees, which held more value as millwork material, whereby the whole trunk of the tree was utilized, not just a small lower portion of the butt log, as in stave making. He called on the lumbermen of Texas to "awaken" to the hardwood resources surrounding them and construct mills specifically designed for hardwood timber before the best resources were otherwise squandered.[71]

Having significant hardwood forests and a business drive to convert them to liquid capital,

T. L. L. Temple was one of the first lumbermen in Texas to manufacture and market large quantities of hardwood lumber products. Yet, like some of his earlier pine ventures, the beginning of his hardwood operations was not without trials either. In the April 16, 1904, issue of Chicago's *American Lumberman*, Temple announced a "great opportunity" existed in East Texas, where his Southern Pine Lumber Company owned 100 million board feet of "valuable hardwoods." The Diboll lumber company was "extremely anxious," the advertisement stated, for "a hardwood concern to establish a mill on its lands."[72] The A. J. Oliver Lumber Company of Chicago answered Temple's call, and in June 1905—the same month Temple sold his Lufkin Land company assets—began construction of a hardwood sawmill at Diboll, with Henderson Brick and Construction Company erecting a two-story, 60-foot-by-120-foot building using construction materials supplied by Southern Pine Lumber Company. By November, however, hardship ensued when Oliver Lumber Company failed financially, mill construction at Diboll ceased, and courts seized the property. Numerous liens were filed in the Angelina County courthouse, including those made by Southern Pine, which supplied, among other things, lumber, roofing, cement, iron, oil, telephone and telegram services, and an overdrawn store account. Even Watson Walker Jr., Southern Pine's Diboll manager, suffered personal losses.[73] In May 1906, court-appointed trustees sold the Oliver hardwood mill to the Blount Family of Nacogdoches, who moved the equipment and machinery out of Angelina County.[74]

Although unsuccessful in partnering with an outside hardwood company, Temple was unshaken. Setbacks were nothing new, and he remained focused on succeeding one way or another. In December 1906 he began building his own hardwood mill at Diboll, erecting it right beside his pine mill this time. Designed for manufacturing lumber from both hardwoods and pine, with little downtime between the two different operations, the new mill began cutting "high grade hardwoods" in April 1907 and was quickly touted

a success in the trade journals.[75] In January 1908, while the mill was cutting hardwoods from Boggy Slough, *American Lumberman* praised Southern Pine Lumber Company nationally as "one of the few pine manufacturing institutions which have successfully engaged in the manufacture of hardwood lumber at the same time, and this fact alone makes the institution an extraordinary one."[76]

The Diboll hardwood mill that was built in 1907 operated until 1954. Although it occasionally cut pine—utilizing a pond for handling pine logs, which floated, and a crane for hardwood logs, which did not—hardwood trees from the Neches, Angelina, and Trinity River bottoms, mostly oak, gum, and ash, made up the bulk of its more than four decades of operation. Another hardwood lumber mill at Diboll, which had no millpond for pine logs because it cut hardwoods exclusively, operated beside the combination mill during the early 1910s. Journals publicized it as "one of the best hardwood mills on earth," until fire destroyed it in 1915. During the time that Diboll operated the three mills together, the journal *Southern Industrial and Lumber Review* declared that Diboll was "the largest sawmill plant in the state of Texas."[77] Although the words "Southern Pine" were in its corporate name, Southern Pine Lumber Company was nevertheless a pioneer of large-scale hardwood sawmilling in Texas, and the bottomland hardwoods of Boggy Slough were among the first trees cut by its mills.[78]

Whether they cut pine or hardwoods, Temple and his managers learned a valuable lesson about renewable natural resources at Diboll. Evidence literally surrounded the Diboll mills. More than once Southern Pine officials tried to buy out the Copes heirs, and they even enlisted assistance from Lufkin real estate agents E. J. Conn and P. M. Albritton in their efforts. Not until 1924, however, when Asenath Phelps was eighty-six years old, did persistent efforts prevail, and Southern Pine purchased fee title to the remaining Copes lands for $37,260. This was after purchasing the timber on those lands a second time for $75,000.[79] The Copes women did very well for themselves. By retaining the land, they were able to sell the title at a significantly higher valuation than if they had sold out earlier, and in the meantime, they also realized the profits from two timber sales. If anything, their more than three decades of managing the land demonstrated the remarkable ability of East Texas shortleaf pine lands to replenish timber, if responsibly managed.

Temple's managers found that the Copes forests they cut during the 1890s regenerated rapidly. Trees that were eight to ten inches in diameter and deemed unmerchantable during the first harvest had grown to more than twice that size by the 1920s.[80] When Southern Pine eventually cut the Copes lands the second time in 1926, Edwin C. Durham, president of the Texas Southeastern Railroad, wrote to T. L. L. Temple and declared that the second-growth timber was so "fine" that it was "hard to believe these tracts were cut over once." Durham told Temple he was convinced that, if East Texas timberlands were conservatively harvested, "a crop can be taken every fifteen or twenty years."[81]

Temple may have begun small in the East Texas lumber industry, but his experience and conservative market approach allowed his businesses to prosper in the fullness of time. He had come a long way since August 1882, when he wrote to his sister Mary, saying he thought a sawmill was "a great deal of trouble."[82] A tradition of the Walker family of Chatham Hill, Virginia, who raised young Temple after the death of his mother, holds that Temple had always told them he "would make one million dollars and retire."[83] Although Temple had fulfilled his financial ambitions by the time he reached his early forties, he never fully retired, serving as president of his many businesses until his death at the age of seventy-six. He did withdraw quickly from daily business operations, however, which allowed him time to serve on the boards of numerous trade and business organizations both regionally and nationally, as well as to engage in philanthropic work in East Texas, southwestern Arkansas, and abroad. He gave to various "aged and orphans" homes across the country, including those for African Americans. During World War I, he regularly sent Victrola records to army personnel overseas, and after the war he supported the work of state committees for "the Fatherless Children of France." He also served internationally on the boards of European benevolence funds to relieve the widespread devastation and suffering caused by the war.[84]

Displaying a trait not uncommon among the best of Texas lumber company presidents during the early twentieth century, Temple took a benevolent interest in his employees and their families, which was continued by his descendants. Through more than three-quarters of a century of family ownership, the basic Temple business philosophy was, "whatever is good for the employees is good for business." During Diboll's formative years, newspapers and trade journals across the Southwest reported that T. L. L. Temple sought to "make of Diboll a model lumber town in every way." As one early reporter expressed, Temple believed that while growing the wealth of his businesses, he should not "overlook the welfare of his employees."[85]

"He was always planning to do something for his people," Fannie Farrington, an early and long-time Diboll resident, said in a 1954 interview with John Larson of the Forest History Foundation. Sharing Temple's devotion to Christian Science, Fannie and her husband Franklin left St. Louis and moved to Diboll on Temple's personal invitation in 1903. Franklin served as the town's postmaster and Fannie worked in the commissary. Together they labored alongside the people, "regardless of denomination, race, creed, or color," Fannie said. She and her husband organized Chautauqua meetings, served as Sunday school teachers and Red Cross workers, and were often the intercessors between the community's needs and Temple's philanthropy. Temple sent personal funds to the Farringtons and to other selected persons in Diboll so they could assist those in need, including less fortunate employees and their children who could not afford

Southern Pine Lumber Company employees pose at Diboll, November 1907. *Courtesy of The History Center, Diboll.*

proper clothing or special health-care services, at times providing wedding clothes and home furnishings to some employees.[86]

In 1908 Temple constructed a special building for his Diboll employees and their families so they would have what he called "a comfortable place in which to spend their evenings socially and educationally." He placed Fannie Farrington over the use of much of the building, including what one journalist called, "a magnificent library, well stocked with good literature." Most journalists were unsure what to call the structure, exactly, because as one *Houston Post* columnist wrote, it was "something new in a lumber camp." T. L. L. Temple called it "the Library," while others called it "the club house," probably because the two-story structure also contained a billiard and pool

room and "a suite of bath rooms."[87] One journalist reported that the main hall, billiard room, and stairway were to be "finished entirely in red gum manufactured by the hardwood mill of Southern Pine Lumber Company." At the time, Southern Pine Lumber Company was logging Boggy Slough, where red gum (*Liquidambar styraciflua*) made up about 30 percent of the merchantable timber. Red gum, which was simply the market name of lumber manufactured from old-growth, bottomland sweetgum, developed pink or ruddy heartwood, which was highly prized in paneling and veneer work, because of its tendency to show handsome figuring on quartersawn cuts and its ability to take a high polish.[88] The public building with a library, according to one journalist, was intended to be "the crowning glory of Diboll."[89] Throughout the following years, the Temple family continued to support public libraries in Diboll and throughout the state, receiving the Texas Library Association's very first Philanthropic Award for statewide support of public libraries in 1973. Thirteen years later, the T. L. L. Temple Foundation received the same award.[90]

Although Temple owned limited real estate in Diboll in the beginning, he still provided public buildings to be utilized as the meeting places for churches of the Baptist and Methodist denominations and for fraternal organizations such as the Knights of Pythias, the Odd Fellows, and the Woodmen of the World. He also provided a community meeting room with a stage for public lectures and an "electric theater" for entertainments. At both Diboll and Pineland he established community gardens and dairy and poultry farms that were stocked with animals from his Riverside Farm just north of Texarkana, Texas.[91] He took a special interest in the Diboll and Pineland schools, encouraging his kinsman E. C. Durham, who had married his daughter Gertrude's sister-in-law, to serve as longtime chairman of the Diboll school board, requesting of him close involvement in school affairs and activities, as well as regular, detailed reports.[92] Temple also gave scholarships to mill town student graduates who wished to obtain continuing education and teaching certification.[93] His Pineland and Diboll schools often stood ahead of the schools of other mill towns. When inspectors from the high school division of the State Department of Education examined the Diboll high school in 1926, they filed their report by closing with the summary, "The school is to be congratulated in that it has such loyal friends in the Lumber Company who in every way possible advances the interest of the school even to the extent of most generous contributions when the school funds are inadequate. The Company at Diboll has given ample evidence that one corporation at least has a soul."[94]

At the time of his death, in 1935, Temple requested that his children establish a trust fund from his estate so that the special needs of his aged and injured employees and their families would

Georgie Temple Munz, one of T. L. L. Temple's five children. She gave her family fortune to the T. L. L. Temple Foundation, which has given more than half a billion dollars to philanthropic causes in East Texas, mostly during the past two decades. *Courtesy of The History Center, Diboll.*

continue to be met. His family complied, establishing what they called the Temple Foundation, which assisted employees and their families well into the 1960s. In 1962, Temple's daughter Georgie, with assistance from other family members, established a new foundation, known as the T. L. L. Temple Foundation, which expanded the philanthropic mission of the earlier organization to include a number of new community initiatives. By 2018, the T. L. L. Temple Foundation had given away more than $480 million, most of that amount since 2000.[95]

Temple also took time for leisurely pursuits. He loved playing as well as watching tennis and golf, and he was a founder and prominent member of the Texarkana Country Club. For many years he sponsored the Temple Cup, a trophy given to the best doubles tennis players that the states of Texas and Arkansas could produce. Challenge cup matches were hosted in Austin by the University of Texas and in Dallas by Southern Methodist University. Temple's son, Arthur, helped organize the competitions.[96] Temple's daughter Georgie, a talented athlete herself, married the Texarkana regional tennis star Harry Munz, who successfully competed in various state and tristate (Arkansas, Texas, and Oklahoma) finals annually. Many of Temple's other family members also excelled at tennis, including Henry Gresham Temple and several members of the Webber family. Temple's Texarkana managers and business associates, such as L. Daniel Gilbert, John E. Hintz, and Hershel Payne, were also noted tennis athletes. Even Temple's Riverside Farm manager, Harvey MacQuiston, and Harvey's brother Paul, won a number of US titles and were the national doubles champions of Mexico.[97] Years later, T. L. L.'s grandson Arthur Temple Jr. married Harvey MacQuiston's daughter Mary, who was also a tennis champion. After her father moved to Dallas and formed the Oak Lawn Tennis Club, she began winning titles by the age of fourteen, winning state junior doubles titles in 1933 and 1934, state singles in 1936, and once even an Olympic match in Dallas. Mary's older sister Charlotte also won a number of tennis titles.[98]

T. L. L. Temple especially relished playing the card game bridge, hosting and attending large bridge parties wherever he found himself during his long journeys, and he tried to teach the game to his Diboll executives. He once wrote to his grandson T. L. L. Temple III, cautioning him against gambling in games of marbles, fearing the lad would lose self-control, which would have been "economically wrong and morally wrong." Temple shared that he never bet more than one-tenth of a cent per point in his bridge games, and then he did so only for sporting reasons to make the game "interesting" and never for "trying to make money."[99]

Temple traveled often, taking advantage of free rail transportation across the country given as a

T. L. L. Temple and his son Arthur Temple Sr. pose with their tennis rackets, ca. 1907. *Courtesy of The History Center, Diboll.*

courtesy among railroad company officers and directors. As the president of the Texas Southeastern Railroad Company and of the Lufkin, Hemphill & Gulf Railway Company, Temple and his immediate family rode the nation's rails free of charge practically anywhere they wished to go. Two of his daughters' weddings were at Asbury Park, New Jersey, and at Los Angeles, California. Temple regularly attended professional and semi-professional tennis and golf championships across the country and asked that his subscriptions to sporting magazines be forwarded to him at various hotels. He constructed clay tennis courts at his Diboll and Pineland company towns, where mill managers worked diligently to prepare the courts before his visits and then made the improvements

The tennis court at Diboll, November 1907. Nearly all of T. L. L. Temple's family members and managers were avid tennis players and some were state, tristate, and national champions. *Courtesy of The History Center, Diboll.*

that he suggested after he left. Temple encouraged all his top executives to take up the sports of tennis and golf, even purchasing memberships to the Lake Myriad Country Club at Lufkin for some of his Diboll officers, encouraging them to put down their shotguns long enough to learn to swing a golf club.[100] At the same time, his Diboll officials encouraged him to bird hunt instead.[101] Although Temple did attempt to breed bird dogs as a hobby, he rarely hunted. E. C. Durham wrote him once, saying, "If you will go out with Dave [Kenley] and me or with Arthur [T. L. L.'s son] and quail hunt a few times, you will lay the golf bag aside until the hunting season is over."[102]

Temple's many travels were recorded regularly by the country's newspapers. By May 1907, readers of the *Dallas Morning News* and the *Daily Arkansas Gazette* knew him as "the millionaire lumber dealer of Texarkana," who visited "his country place near Diboll" aboard friend and fellow lumberman William Buchanan's private rail car, described as "one of the finest in the South . . . a veritable palace on wheels."[103] Temple's goings and comings were extensive enough that some news reporters were unsure of his home, describing him as "the millionaire lumberman of St. Louis."[104] Much earlier, in 1900, Temple had become affluent enough to begin spending his summers at Quogue, in

Southampton, Long Island, New York, eventually owning a home there as well as stock in the Quogue Beach Club. After his wife Georgie died in St. Louis in November 1900, Temple regularly spent between five and seven months of the year at the oceanside resort village, usually from April through September, enjoying the soothing ocean waters, milder summer temperatures, cabarets, plays, concerts, parades, and daily games of golf and other sporting recreations.[105] New York City was sufficiently near for visits, and Temple became connected in Manhattan social circles enough that he would occasionally return there for the Thanksgiving and Christmas holidays, with his stays at the Hotel Astor publicized by the New York and Brooklyn newspapers.[106] Temple especially enjoyed having his children join him at Quogue during the summers, and some of them continued to visit Quogue well after his death.[107] In 1916, his son Arthur Temple Sr. married Katherine Robson Sage of New York City, whose aristocratic Manhattan family also owned a home at Quogue, known as The Maples.[108] T. L. L. Temple served with William and Amelia Sage on many of Quogue's social and civic committees, and his grandson Arthur Temple Jr. spent his youthful summers at Quogue with the Sage family. T. L. L. Temple thoroughly enjoyed his time at Quogue, right up until his death, leaving there just days before dying of a heart attack at Texarkana on October 2, 1935.[109]

Temple spent so much time at Quogue and elsewhere that he was exempted from paying income taxes to the state of Arkansas, where he owned a substantial home, since he did not reside there at least six months out of the year.[110] Having multiple places of residency, located in three states, Temple began to vote in the elections of Angelina County, Texas, in 1932, claiming Diboll as his domicile, which later helped to save his heirs from paying the higher inheritance taxes of Arkansas, which were, according to one Texarkana attorney in 1935, "the highest of any State in the Union."[111]

During Temple's lengthy absences from Texarkana, he left the operations of his businesses to a talented young man named Lewis Daniel Gilbert, who served many years as secretary, vice president, and general manager of most of the Temple businesses.[112] Gilbert and his wife Mary moved into T. L. L. Temple's house in Texarkana by 1908, and until Gilbert's death in 1931, Temple entrusted his businesses as well as his home to them, as Mary Gilbert served as Temple's longtime housekeeper.[113] T. L. L. Temple's grandson Arthur Temple Jr. said in a 1985 interview that he remembered Gilbert well, considering him a "modern day chief operating officer."[114] Others who knew Gilbert, and who actually worked under him, called him "the absolute general manager," indicating the power Temple entrusted to him. With few exceptions, Temple expected Gilbert to handle the majority of business matters as well as family affairs, even when they involved communicating with Temple's sons—T. L. L. Temple Jr. and Arthur Temple Sr.—which was often a disappointment to them.[115] In a 1985 interview, Gresham Temple said that his great-uncle hired Gilbert simply "to take things over," since T. L. L. was living on Long Island "six to seven months out of the year."[116] With Temple's abiding trust, Gilbert had risen rapidly through the ranks of Southern Pine Lumber Company. Beginning as a salesman, he promoted quickly to secretary and treasurer, and within a couple more years to vice president and general manager, also becoming a board director. Perhaps T. L. L. saw in Gilbert similarities to his own childhood experiences, as well as those of his wife Georgie's, since Gilbert's father died before Gilbert was old enough for school, leaving Gilbert and his brother Lucius, who

Lewis Daniel Gilbert served as T. L. L. Temple's powerful general manager from 1909 until he died of a heart attack while deer hunting at Boggy Slough in 1931. *Courtesy of The History Center, Diboll.*

also made a career in the lumber business, in Louisiana, to be raised by their widowed mother and maternal grandmother at Port Sullivan, Texas.[117]

During his last days, T. L. L. Temple had no way to know the future. When he died in October 1935—during the season when nature prepares for the approaching winter—his lumber companies had just a few months earlier sold more than 80,000 acres of cutover forestland to the national government for only $2.50 an acre, far lower than the amount Temple had paid for the land a couple of decades earlier. Retrenchment at home and abroad was the order of the day, as the world continued to suffer under a major economic depression that had begun six years earlier; even Boggy Slough was for sale when he died. While the season was tough, T. L. L. Temple's life had demonstrated to his family and to all who knew him, the value of hope, tenacity, and an indomitable will. Temple had built a business and a business model rooted in market research and a conservative adherence to those markets, a love of enterprise, and a raw determination to succeed against all odds. Like a top-killed shortleaf pine seedling that resprouts following fire, Temple was resilient. He had shown how to reemerge from the ashes, time and time again, following the fires of life. Not unlike a tree itself, which grows both downward into the earth and upward into the heavens, Temple had grown a family business that in time learned the value of putting down deep roots and patiently stretching upward. The steady regenerating forests, and their thoughtful management through seasons of growth and dormancy, droughts and floods, would be the future of his businesses and his family. His lumber businesses would flourish for twelve decades, while his family's philanthropic foundation that carried his name would prosper even longer.

CHAPTER 5

A Land of Industry

Railroads, Logging, and Land Acquisition

What's the railroad to me?
I never go to see
Where it ends.
It fills a few hollows,
And makes banks for the swallows,
It sets the sand a-blowing,
And the blackberries a-growing.

—HENRY DAVID THOREAU (1854)

T. L. L. Temple was late to arrive in Angelina County, but he was especially delayed in purchasing lands and timber in Trinity and Houston Counties, west of the Neches River. By the time he began acquiring the lands that make up today's Boggy Slough Conservation Area, he faced not only significantly higher prices, but also a meager selection of what remained. Both Trinity and Houston Counties received a standard-gauge railroad in 1872, well ahead of Angelina County, and lumbermen from near and far relocated their mills to the new rail line or began new mills from scratch, focusing their operations in Trinity County. The central and southern portions of Trinity County held an especially high concentration of pine timber, which attracted not only the rails of another railroad in 1881 but

the mills of some of the largest lumber firms in the state, including Cameron & Company, Josserand Brothers, and Thompson Brothers, as well as the Joyce family of Iowa and Chicago. At the new railroad and mill town of Groveton, which quickly became the county seat, the Joyce family's Trinity County Lumber Company operated what was reportedly "the largest sawmill west of the Mississippi River" for twenty years before T. L. L. Temple purchased his first Boggy Slough tract of land.[1] By 1900, even more lumbermen had entered the region. Two of them purchased land and timber inside what is now Boggy Slough Conservation Area, and one of them built a railroad straight through the middle of it from east to west, also erecting, in 1902, at a site 11 miles west of the river in Houston County, a sawmill that was even larger than the Groveton mill. Not only would purchasing Boggy Slough–area timber and lands be difficult for Temple—paying inflated prices to experienced sellers for lands containing lesser concentrations of pine timber, while relying on the integrity and loyalty of purchasing agents doing business in an especially unruly region—but logging the lands, which consisted of sizable hardwood bottoms, and marketing their products would be equally challenging.

As seen in chapter 3, the industrial utilization of nature came to Boggy Slough first in the form of a steam railroad that was conceived by men who lived much farther away than Temple's home office in Texarkana. Constructed between 1900 and 1901 and known as the Eastern Texas Railroad, this 30-mile short line stretched across the Boggy Slough lands from east to west, carrying the commercial ambitions of Kansas City businessmen over its rails. With plenty of cash and capital, these men, led by coal and lumber mogul Richard H. Keith, purchased in 1899 and 1900 more than 120,000 acres of timberlands, mostly in Houston County, at the price of a little more than $2 an acre.[2] Boosters of the day claimed that the mill Keith and his partners built at a strategic site near the center of their holdings, one mile west of present-day Ratcliff, was "the largest in the world." Although the claim was an exaggeration, the mill was in fact one of the largest in the nation at the time. Equipped with a sawing capacity of 300,000 board feet of lumber per eleven hour shift, the triple-band and gang sawmill was six times the size of Temple's initial Diboll sawmill. The roofed mill buildings were so large, news reporters said, that electric lighting was required during even the brightest parts of the day. The mill's builders were owners of the large Central Coal and Coke Company of Kansas City (better known as 4-C), capitalized at $7 million, whose subsidiary firm, Louisiana and Texas Lumber Company, operated the Houston County mill, which employed more than a thousand men, some of whom came from the Boggy Slough farms.[3]

When the industrial land acquisition of Boggy Slough began, T. L. L. Temple was busy purchasing the lands, timber, railroads, and sawmill machinery for his Lufkin Land and Lumber Company operations in Angelina County. As Temple worked to build that operation with the financial assistance of Texarkana lumbermen, A. Harris and Company of Tyler purchased most of the Boggy Slough lands and timber north of Cochino Bayou. Composed of Abraham Harris, a native of England; his father-in-law, Joseph Lipsitz, a native of Poland; and Harris's brother-in-law, Louis Lipsitz, A. Harris and Company was a large, nationally successful mercantile business, which many

years later became the Sanger-Harris Department Stores. Although A. Harris and Company's business activities were based mostly in Dallas and New York, the three men of the partnership called Tyler home, where they were influential leaders in that city's Jewish community. They also owned extensive lands, timber, railroads, and sawmills located on the Cotton Belt railway, north of Lufkin, in Angelina and Cherokee Counties. Their holdings included the mills of Chronister Lumber Company at Wildhurst, and Bodan Lumber Company at Pollok. Connected with their mills, they also owned the short line railroads Pollok & Angelina Valley Transportation Company and Durham Transportation Company.[4] Anticipating the construction of the Eastern Texas Railroad, A. Harris and Company hoped to expand their sawmilling operations from the east side of the Neches River to the west side. In 1899 Abraham Harris purchased 7,041 acres of I&GN Railroad lands from the New York and Texas Land Company, situated mostly in what is now Boggy Slough Conservation Area, excluding from the surveys about 331 acres that had been fenced by squatters and converted to agricultural fields.[5] Between 1899 and 1902, A. Harris and Company also bought some 1,830 acres of additional Boggy Slough Conservation Area lands that surrounded the I&GN tracts. These purchases included the homestead surveys of W. T. English, Curtis Tier, and parts of the S. D. Sullivan, S. T. Sullivan, and L. A. Sullivan grants, as well as the McKinney and Williams grant. Abraham Harris also purchased rights to the pine timber on another 1,546 acres, mostly from Sullivan's Bluff farmers, including the Sullivans, Christies, Franklins, Rushings, and Luces. Abraham Harris and A. Harris and Company purchased the more than 8,500 acres of combined lands for prices between $1.87 and $2.50 per acre, while for timber-only transactions they paid between forty cents and $1.49 an acre.[6] When Southern Pine Lumber Company bought the same properties from A. Harris and Company in 1905, T. L. L. Temple paid $125,000, representing an average price of $14 an acre for land titles and more than $3 an acre for just the timber.[7] By paying a price that had inflated by some 500 percent during only six years, Temple learned the hard way that arriving late to the party had its consequences. But he also knew that if his Diboll milling operation was going to have any future at all, acquiring the less commercially desirable timber along the Neches River valley was his only option.

Paying higher prices for land and timber was only part of the challenge. Temple not only had to work with experienced men on the make, so typical of the time, but he also had to place considerable trust in a number of hired local entrepreneurs, whose loyalties and personal ambitions were often questionable. Although Temple played active roles in forming large ventures such as Southern Pine Lumber Company, Lufkin Land and Lumber Company, and Temple Lumber Company, he left the acquisition of Boggy Slough lands mostly to the discernment and actions of others. By 1902, the year of the first Boggy Slough land transactions, Temple had begun relying on less-experienced family members, friends, and employees, as well as hired agents—who were perhaps too experienced—to purchase lands and timber for his Diboll operation. He initially assigned such tasks to his second cousin and Diboll's mill manager Watson Walker Jr. and to his personal friend and Diboll's planing mill foreman William Ashford. John Massingill, Diboll's early timber and lands manager, also participated briefly.[8]

William Ashford was the most active of Temple's land agents at the beginning of Boggy Slough's acquisition, transacting no fewer than eighty-nine deeds to lands in Trinity County during only a few months of 1902, some transactions involving up to $25,000 in cash. Ashford purchased what timber and uncut lands he could find, buying the land with its timber usually for less than if he had purchased just the timber. Ashford then transferred most of the purchases to Southern Pine Lumber Company, but occasionally he resold them to Trinity County Lumber Company at Groveton. Although uncut timberlands that were not already held by speculators had become increasingly scarce, it

William Ashford, an early business partner of T. L. L. Temple, served as Temple's land agent in purchasing most of the land that now constitutes the Boggy Slough Conservation Area. *Courtesy of The History Center, Diboll.*

remained a buyer's market. Ashford bought all the lands in and around Boggy Slough that he could, using Temple's money, even if those lands were nearer to a competitor's mill. He knew he most likely could sell those lands later to that competitor for at least a nominal profit or use them to trade for different lands nearer and more conveniently situated to Diboll's operations.[9]

As Trinity County land acquisitions progressed and contiguous tracts along the river began to accumulate, Ashford became known as a Southern Pine Lumber Company agent, which resulted in stalled transactions. At the same time, willing sellers of strategically located lands became more difficult to locate. Seeking help that was more local and specialized, Temple hired Nathan Dawson Wright, an independent surveyor and self-advertised "land lawyer," who had offices in both Groveton and Lufkin. Although Wright bought and surveyed land and timber in early

John Massingill, shown riding his horse through an open forest along a Southern Pine Lumber Company logging railroad, was Temple's early timber buyer for the Diboll sawmill. *Courtesy of The History Center, Diboll.*

Boggy Slough tracts and assisted John Massingill in estimating the pine and hardwood timber on all of Southern Pine's lands late in 1907, his tenure with the Temple companies was brief. He once identified himself in a public deed as "a friend of Southern Pine Lumber Company," but his bosses soon suspected otherwise.[10] Buying and selling land for others came with temptations to the middleman, whose own interests often entangled with those of their employers. In time, Wright, as well as Massingill, left Southern Pine's employ. Afterward, company records reveal Wright was "causing trouble" and "causing trouble again" for the Temple family of lumber and railroad businesses, as Wright represented injured employees in lawsuits against the Temple companies and strategically bought lands, timber, and rights-of-way that interfered with Southern Pine's objectives.[11]

Acquiring the Boggy Slough lands was a lengthy process, requiring many hundreds of deed transactions and numerous court rulings over the course of decades. Initially, Walker, Ashford, Massingill, and Wright spent nearly six years acquiring timber, often "with the land thrown in," but they found that a number of sellers—such as the Sullivans, Christies, Luces, Moores, Olivers, Franklins, and Rushings, among others—were multigenerational

resident farmers, and at first they chose to sell only their timber and retain title to their homesteads, believing the land would provide them additional fields for farming and better pasturage once the forests were cleared. Although Southern Pine Lumber Company secured enough timber to begin logging in 1907, later it was the job of others to obtain the fee title to all the lands. That job fell mostly to Trinity County brothers-in-law David Crockett "Dave" Kenley, a surveyor and cattleman hired in 1908 to succeed Massingill as timber and lands manager, and Robert Elmer Minton, an attorney and Southern Pine's longtime chief counsel. At times the two were controversial men on the make themselves, but they and their shrewd talents became nonetheless essential to an absentee lumberman's hopes for success in the Neches River valley at such a late stage in the commercialization of forest lands.[12]

The Kenley family, of which Dave was one of five brothers, was well established in Trinity County before the advent of Southern Pine Lumber Company. The boys' father, George Kenley, was an early county treasurer. The oldest Kenley boy, Carrol H., served at various times as Trinity County's county clerk, tax collector, and county judge, and was a Groveton city mayor. Carrol also owned an influential abstract of title company at Groveton, where he was also the president of Guaranty State Bank and a vice president of the Groveton First National Bank.[13] The second-oldest son, Sam F., was a merchant and postmaster at Nogalus. The third son, Richard Oscar, was an attorney and a law partner with brother-in-law Robert Elmer Minton, who married Richard's sister, Lucy Kenley. The fourth-eldest son was David Crockett, better known as "Dave," who was the land surveyor and cattleman who was often assisted by his youngest brother, Polk, in surveying newly purchased lands, including those in Boggy Slough. All of the brothers were involved with Southern Pine Lumber Company and Boggy Slough in various ways, including owning some Boggy Slough lands before Southern Pine's acquisition of them.[14] Most important, for nearly six decades, R. E. Minton and Dave Kenley served as influential employees and stockholders of the Temple companies. Minton served the various Temple lumber and railroad companies for fifty-four years as their chief counsel, remaining on the payroll until he was eighty-nine years old, while Dave Kenley was employed by the Temple family for fifty-nine years, most of that time as head of Southern Pine Lumber Company's Timber and Land Department.[15] It would be hard to find two more influential persons and personalities during the early history of Southern Pine Lumber Company and of Boggy Slough.

Very little happened in Trinity County land dealings without Minton's and the Kenley brothers' involvement. Three of the Kenley brothers were notaries public and witnessed numerous land and timber sales transactions, including the deeds that transferred Boggy Slough lands to Southern Pine Lumber Company. All of them speculated in land and timber, including buying land directly from the General Land Office and at sheriffs sales.[16] As a notary public and land title abstractor, as well as county clerk and tax assessor, C. H. Kenley knew land values and the identity of landowners probably better than anyone else in the county.[17] Between 1900 and 1903, C. H. Kenley even owned a major part of the Lazarus Price survey, where the Christie family lived.[18] Almost immediately after the discovery of commercial quantities of oil at Spindletop in Jefferson County early in January 1901, Oscar Kenley began speculatively buying mineral rights to lands all across Trinity County.[19]

The Kenley-Minton family knew most everyone and everything in Trinity County, and they were well known themselves. One of the most remarkable events contributing to their renown, if not their ignominy, occurred late in April 1907, when Carrol and Oscar Kenley and brother-in-law R. E. Minton were arrested for gunning down Texas Ranger James D. Dunaway and the former county attorney of Trinity County, Howard L. Robb, on the streets of Groveton in broad daylight. An examining physician and the Texas assistant adjutant general reported projectiles from an automatic shotgun, a rifle, and a pistol inflicted the wounds in the men's riddled bodies, the shots having been fired from the upstairs window of the Kenley & Minton law office, where witnesses saw the figures of three men and a number of protruding gun muzzles at the time of the shooting. Miraculously, the Texas Ranger survived his wounds, but the former county attorney, who most unfortunately was not the intended target, died five days later. Charges of murder and assault with intent to kill were levied against all three men, but only Oscar Kenley stood trial, and then only for aggravated assault and assault with intent to kill Ranger Dunaway, who had publicly quarreled with Oscar Kenley for several years over the politics and misunderstandings of a local Law and Order League at Groveton.[20] Just days before the shooting, Ranger Dunaway had confronted Kenley on the streets of Trinity, pulled him aside, severely beat him, and threatened his life if he ever reported the intimidation. In retaliation, Kenley promptly informed Governor Campbell, despite Ranger Dunaway's warnings. The governor recalled Dunaway to Austin and personally rebuked him, since Dunaway was well known for aggressively settling personal scores and for placing the Rangers often in a negative public light. Governor Campbell ordered Dunaway to move at once from the town of Trinity, where he was stationed, and to keep away from Oscar Kenley. Dunaway left the governor's office and took the earliest train back to Trinity. But instead of packing his bags to leave, Dunaway took a connecting train to Groveton, where he publicly announced his intentions of revenge, which prompted the preemptive shooting from the upstairs window of the Kenley & Minton law firm office.[21]

Throughout the country, from Los Angeles to New York City, newspapers had a field day with the sensational story. Immediately following the shooting, the *New York Times* carried the front-page headline, "Texas Lawyer Wires Governor Campbell That He Had to Shoot a Ranger," and then, after the state moved the much publicized trial to the city of Houston, the headline, "Disarmed of 100 Pistols: Spectators and Witnesses Searched as They Entered Texas Courtroom."[22] The trial was lengthy; the court summoned some 250 witnesses from across the state—and later sent the bill for transportation costs to the citizens of Trinity County. After many prolonged days and nights of hearing testimony, a Harris County jury found Kenley acted in self-defense against the overzealous and abusive Texas Ranger, acquitting him after deliberating less than ten minutes.[23] Kenley later claimed the deliberation was "exactly four minutes."[24]

Well before the trial, Trinity County's reputation as one of the rowdiest and most lawless places in East Texas was no secret. The region had been unusually violent during the Civil War and Reconstruction, producing a number of notorious outlaws, including the legendary vigilante John Wesley Hardin, who during his life killed more than thirty men and infamously declared he never killed anyone who did not deserve killing. The violence and the breakdown of law and order in Trinity County only intensified with the coming of the railroads, sawmills, and an increasing number of saloons during the last quarter of the nineteenth century. More than once, outlaws torched the Trinity County courthouse to destroy the criminal records against them. One Trinity County sheriff died in the line of duty, while others simply quit.[25]

In 1902, when T. L. L. Temple's land agents began filing their many dozens of Boggy Slough deeds at the Trinity County courthouse, Groveton was in a state of near anarchy, overwhelmed by what local historian Flora Bowles called "a reign of lawlessness that was appalling."[26] In August that year the county's citizens voted to prohibit intoxicating liquors, but the many saloon operators in Groveton defied the law and kept their saloons open. Most elected officials turned a blind eye to the illegal activities, and, according to Bowles, many citizens believed some of them were actually elected to office "with a clear understanding that they should cater to the wishes of the law breakers, who were their creators as officers."[27] Men described as "drunken desperados" routinely rode their horses through the streets of town while discharging their guns into storefronts, and some were so bold that they rode into saloons and drank their whiskey while seated in the saddle. Store owners usually closed early on Saturdays, and women and children were rarely seen in town.

Between 1903 and 1906, while Southern Pine Lumber Company agents continued to file Boggy Slough deeds at the courthouse, thirteen murders occurred in Trinity County; ten of them were assassinations, including the deaths of two private investigators hired by Groveton citizens in their own attempt to prosecute bootleggers. It was a time when Groveton was home not only to a resident Texas Ranger force but also to a deputized Methodist minister who openly carried a pistol to defend himself against bootleggers who had burned his church and parsonage.[28] Convictions rarely occurred, and no one knew for certain whether the presence of the Rangers helped or hurt matters, especially when an especially violent one with a short temper seemed only to add to the unruliness. There was such a state of chaos in Groveton during Southern Pine Lumber Company's acquisition of Boggy Slough that Texas Ranger captain Bill McDonald's biographer famously quoted him as saying Trinity County was "a hopeless field for reform . . . [and] if a whole community has no use for law and order, it's not worthwhile to try to enforce such things."[29] It is no wonder that T. L. L. Temple left the Trinity County land acquisitions to others.

In such a disorderly social environment, Boggy Slough Conservation Area had its stormy beginnings as a Temple property. It seemed no person or corporation could do business in the region without becoming tarnished in some way, or possibly worse. After his acquittal, Oscar Kenley continued to legally represent Temple's lumber and railroad businesses for several more years. He might have continued to serve as one of Temple's attorneys for many more years, had he not gotten himself into another wildly publicized altercation with Ranger Dunaway at a lunch counter in a downtown Houston drugstore in November 1912, which resulted in Kenley's fleeing to California to escape what he considered "continued harassment and hounding by the Rangers." Kenley eventually returned to Texas—and resided in Wichita Falls briefly and then in Houston, where he lived most of the rest of his life. His leaving East Texas, however, allowed his brother-in-law R. E. Minton to become Temple's longtime attorney for the Diboll operations. Minton was originally from Sabine County, where his attorney brother, John W., remained to also serve the Temples for many years, but on behalf of their Pineland and Hemphill operations.[30]

Besides confronting inflated prices, uncertain business associations, and general lawlessness and blemished reputations peculiar to Trinity County, Temple's Southern Pine Lumber Company faced many other, more common, difficulties in acquiring Boggy Slough at the beginning of the twentieth century. Nineteenth-century homestead families often had eight to twelve children, and some Boggy Slough families, such as the Sullivans and Christies, had sixteen. Often these children married young and raised comparably sized families themselves. It was not uncommon, then, for there to be multiple dozens of heirs within only a couple of generations. Although some descendants moved on, many remained on the land and married their neighbors. The resulting claims of the many heirs produced a number of quitclaim deeds that trickled into Minton's and Kenley's offices for decades. The discovery of large oil reserves in southeast Texas during 1901 only compounded the issue, as land and minerals were divided and subdivided in various proportions, with new claims surfacing even when the oil and gas did not. In addition, there were several squatters,

or adverse possession, claims to handle, since many Boggy Slough families had gradually begun to clear and fence the neighboring I&GN lands that were owned by the absentee New York & Texas Land Company.[31]

Many East Texas land surveys, especially the earliest ones, had problems inherent from the beginning. Three governments granted titles to the lands that now make up Boggy Slough: Mexico, the Republic of Texas, and the State of Texas. All of them inherited a colonial Spanish metes and bounds survey system, which utilized natural boundary markers such as trees and streams. This survey system, combined with the fact that the governments essentially relied on the grantees to locate and survey the lands, created irregular and unsystematic ownership patterns on the land. Not only did some of the early surveys have boundary discrepancies and conflicts within themselves, their boundaries also often conflicted later with adjoining surveys. Southern Pine Lumber Company's litigation to clear the titles lasted decades, often involving actions from the district courts and from various state officers.

In a 1954 interview with a Forest History Society interviewer, Dave Kenley told of Southern Pine's efforts and expenses in defending title to lands and timber within the Sepúlveda survey (Trinity County Abstract 40) between 1906 and 1920.[32] Watson Walker, William Ashford, and Nathan Wright had purchased the properties between 1902 and 1905. Although Oscar Kenley had found some discrepancies in 1906, serious trouble with the titles was not evident until after Southern Pine cut the timber in 1908. In that year a plaintiff from Nacogdoches County filed a law suit against the company, claiming that the original Mexican grant, which was made in 1826 for two leagues of land along "el Arroyo del Cochino," was illegitimate. Kenley said that, as part of the court proceedings, he and Tom Vansau Sr., the father of one of Kenley's cattle hands, walked across more than 4,000 acres of cutover lands for seven months, marking and counting every stump as well as tree-top. Together, the two men accounted for some

155,000 trees that had been cut. In addition, Kenley said the company spent "thousands of dollars trying to find records in Mexico City. We traced so far as to find that the original grantee, José Antonio Sepúlveda, was kicked by a mule in Nacogdoches and was killed."[33] T. L. L. Temple hired the Beaumont law firm of Greer, Minor, and Miller to assist Oscar Kenley, and later R. E. Minton, in the legal battle, which required several visits to Austin for meetings with the land commissioner, the attorney general, the governor, and members of the legislature. In 1911, a court in Tyler ruled against Southern Pine in the amount of $16,000, which the company refused to pay. Instead, they appealed the decision and filed countersuits.[34] Finally, in 1920, an act by the Texas legislature validated Southern Pine's title.[35] Although Southern Pine Lumber Company sold most of the Sepúlveda lands to Southland Paper Mills of Lufkin during the late 1930s, a small portion of the northern league, just south of Cochino Bayou, bordering North Cedar Road, remains part of Boggy Slough Conservation Area today.[36]

The 4,428-acre Sanchez league, granted by Mexico in 1835, and the 4,605-acre Walker survey, made by the Republic of Texas in 1845, also contained conflicts, mainly through speculative activities that occurred well before 1902, when Southern Pine Lumber Company began purchasing the lands. In the company's earliest purchase of land that now makes up Boggy Slough Conservation Area, Southern Pine paid $13,000 in cash to W. E. Johnson of Leon County in February 1902 for his claims and interests in 5,759 acres of land, which included all of the Walker survey and 1,107 acres of the Sanchez league, which adjoined the Walker survey to the south, together constituting more than 30 percent of what is now Boggy Slough Conservation Area.[37] As a single transaction, the price paid was a little more than $2 per acre, but that in no way represented the full price paid for the land. As Southern Pine officials later discovered, there were exceptions, conflicts, and prior inholdings within these lands that they were able to clear only through various rulings of local courts and the purchases of numerous quitclaim

deeds.[38] For instance, the Houston, East & West Texas Railway claimed some 3,150 acres within the Walker survey, which had to be purchased additionally, and, as seen in chapter 3, the Britton lands were also located there, and those were purchased separately as well. To settle additional claims within the Walker survey, Southern Pine purchased no fewer than fourteen deeds to other tracts there, between 1906 and 1921. Sellers included the Franklin, Tiner, Wells, Oliver, Gibson, Milligan, Womack, Place, and Vance families.[39] To clear titles to additional tracts within the Sanchez survey, Southern Pine purchased no fewer than twenty-seven additional deeds between 1902 and 1953 and also received favorable court decisions.[40]

Further confusion with the Walker survey included attempts by the General Land Office to allocate Confederate Scrip and Permanent School Fund lands within the east end of the survey during the late nineteenth century, all of which the General Land Office eventually invalidated or corrected in Southern Pine's favor.[41] Part of the misunderstanding concerned doubt as to whether or not the intermittent stream known as "Boggy Slough" or "Old River" was actually the Neches River in 1845, when the Republic of Texas accepted the boundaries of the Walker survey, which identified the river as its northern and eastern limits. In 1886 and again in 1908, some surveyors suggested that Boggy Slough, not the Neches River, was the southeastern boundary of the Walker survey, which placed into dispute some 423 acres of land. The surveys that resulted from efforts to resolve the controversy provided some of the earliest preindustrial descriptions of Boggy Slough Island and the forests around it. In 1886 a surveyor recorded that the island was "covered with large cane" and described the ridge northwest of the slough as containing "upland oak and pine timber." The same surveyor noted an extensive "river swamp" north of the ridge and west of the slough, as well as "ponds of water in edge of swamp" southwest of the island.[42] In November 1910, Dave Kenley surveyed the meanderings of the slough and recorded stream depths and widths. He found growing in the center of the stream channel what he called ironwood trees (possibly *Ostrya virginiana* or *Carpinus caroliniana*) up to 12 inches in diameter and post oak trees (possibly *Quercus lyrata*, also known as swamp post oak) up to 20 inches in diameter. By cutting some of the largest of the stream channel trees, he counted growth rings as evidence against the stream being the river sixty-five years earlier. He also surveyed the meanderings of the Neches River on the east side of the island, making records of its depth and width at various points, and personally interviewed the earliest settlers familiar with the streams since the time of their childhoods. He placed copies of his surveys and findings in the public records at Groveton and at the General Land Office at Austin. Eventually, courts determined that Boggy Slough was not the Neches River in 1845.[43]

Although timber was the primary natural resource sought by Temple's natural resource managers and agents, oil was at least an incidental objective. Early on, the most noteworthy oil reserve tracts in Boggy Slough were those that included Bluff Prairie, a large saline prairie that was noted in the earliest land surveys and is now partially inundated under the dammed waters of Black Cat Lake and A.T. Lake, just north of Highway 94. Early in the twentieth century, various "oil experts" investigated the prairie and reported that surface indications of white sands and salt-encrusted formations, interspersed with low elliptical mounds, signified economic potential. Oil at Bluff Prairie "might not flow over the top of the ground," said one early topographical engineer with the US Geological Survey, but under the surface there was "good oil . . . in abundancy." The *Houston Post* enthusiastically reported in 1904 that Bluff Prairie's oil prospects "could not be any better [than] to strike a gusher."[44]

Before Southern Pine acquired the prairie, much of it was owned by the Bonner family of Angelina County, whose patriarch W. H. Bonner Jr. in 1872 settled a homestead just across the river

from Boggy Slough, where he operated Bonner's Ferry (on the site of the former Gann's Ferry) and Bonner's Mills, a steam saw and gristmill. He also served as an Angelina County county clerk and state representative, raised cattle, and sold land and timber to several large sawmill operations in the region, including sales to Southern Pine Lumber Company and Emporia Lumber Company.[45] In 1902 the Bonners sold the pine timber on their Trinity County lands, which included portions of Bluff Prairie, to Southern Pine Lumber Company.[46] In 1903 the Bonners, along with a number of Lufkin families, including the Mantooths, Abneys, Abrams, and Denmans, formed the unincorporated Bluff Prairie Oil Company and contracted with several oil producers from Houston and Beaumont to drill two wells on the Harding survey, near a later clubhouse known as "Little Boggy." One well was planned to be at least 800 feet deep and the other at least 1,000 feet. Also making up the Bluff Prairie Oil Company were George A. Kelley and E. A. Frost, who were business partners with T. L. L. Temple in his Lufkin Land and Lumber Company.[47]

Wildcat drilling at Bluff Prairie began late in August 1904. About six weeks later, at a depth of 300 feet, one well hit a pocket of gas, which spewed mud and slush thirty feet into the air. The *Houston Post* described the occurrence as a "pyrotechnic disturbance . . . a tremendous gas blowout."[48] Before the end of the year, T. L. L. Temple announced his plan to relocate his Texas Southeastern Railroad from Diboll toward the northwest, bridge the Neches River, and tap what was then known as the "Bluff Prairie Oil Field." Although excitement lingered for several months, Bluff Prairie did not produce oil or gas in commercial quantities, and the Bluff Prairie Oil Company ceased drilling. Between 1905 and 1916, Southern Pine Lumber Company gradually obtained ownership of the Bluff Prairie lands, which became part of its cattle ranching operation in 1913, but the Bonner family retained portions of the mineral rights.[49]

Bluff Prairie again became the focus of oil exploration beginning in January 1922, when Lufkin real estate agent P. M. Albritton located several "reliable oil men" who were interested in paying $5,000 for the right to drill there down to a depth of 3,500 feet. Kenley replied to say that Southern Pine was interested, but he wanted "a good many limitations," including the right to select "the character of the men" allowed on the property, which by that time had become a fenced game preserve, in addition to a cattle ranch.[50] L. Daniel Gilbert expressed leasing concerns also, urging Kenley to proceed cautiously, if at all, since leases generally involved a minimum of 5,000 acres, and Gilbert feared such a relatively large amount of land might include some tracts whose titles were not yet perfected. Gilbert said that wherever oil was found, "it opens up the way for every shyster lawyer in the country to begin looking for flaws in titles, and we do not want any land litigation at all where it can be avoided."[51] Southern Pine Lumber Company again considered mineral development at Bluff Prairie in 1938, when company officials drew up plans for what they called, the "Bluff Prairie Saline Prospect," which, like earlier efforts, failed to succeed commercially.[52]

Additional title concerns emerged when Southern Pine officials drew up an oil and gas lease to Humble Oil Company in 1923. New discrepancies concerning a portion of Boggy Slough Island arose in July that year when Minton discovered that a man by the name of Joseph A. Martin had applied to purchase 156 acres of Permanent School Fund land in Trinity County more than a decade earlier. The purchase happened to include the southeastern part of the frequently flooded island, which had been included in the earlier conflicts over whether or not Boggy Slough was the Neches River in 1845 and the state's efforts to locate Confederate Scrip land grants along the river, inside the Walker survey. Minton learned that Martin had begun paying the state $2.55 an acre, on a forty-year term, for title to the land in 1912. This was unknown to

Southern Pine officials at the time, because the company's ranch foreman fenced the land in 1913. Furthermore, having acted in good faith, believing the bottomland acreage was included in the many earlier Walker survey purchases, Southern Pine Lumber Company loggers had cut the timber sometime between 1908 and 1910, probably during the first dry period that was available to them.

When Minton discovered that Martin had not made an interest payment since 1918, and he was believed to be dead, Minton went to Austin to meet with the land commissioner, James T. Robison. To prevent the forfeiture of Martin's acquisition of title, which might have placed the 156 acres back on the open market, subject to competitive bidding, Robison allowed Minton to complete Martin's acquisition of title and patent process by personally paying the remainder of Martin's debt along with back interest. The commissioner also agreed to delay any actions of the state until Minton obtained a local court's ruling against Martin, citing him by publication as a nonresident of the state, since state law required School Lands to be sold only to residents of the county where the land was located. To initiate the lawsuit, Minton instructed Kenley to issue a deed to the 156 acres of land, with Southern Pine Lumber Company as the grantor and the name of a "locally unknown individual" as the grantee. This person would then bring the lawsuit against Martin. Minton explained that a suit brought by Southern Pine Lumber Company would surely draw the attention of "enterprising persons," but a lawsuit initiated by someone unknown might escape notice. In August 1923, a deed transferred the company's claim to John E. Hintz, an executive of the Oil Field Lumber Company at Mexia, who was also a Temple family friend, former Temple Lumber Company salesman at Texarkana, and one of Dave Kenley's absentee cattle partners. In September, Hintz filed the lawsuit in the Trinity County district court. The court declared Martin deceased with no heirs, and awarded Hintz title to the land in October of that year. Upon receiving the court ruling, the General Land Office ordered a new official survey in January 1924, in the name of patentee Joseph A. Martin, and J. J. Ray Jr., the Southern Pine Lumber Company Ranch foreman's son, served as a chain carrier. Hintz then transferred the title to Southern Pine Lumber Company in July of that year.[53] Interestingly, Minton himself purchased and patented 118 acres of other Permanent School Fund land near the mouth of Cochino Bayou much earlier, in 1910, and did not transfer the title to Southern Pine Lumber Company for another forty-six years. His reasons for doing so would not be revealed until a third-generation Temple ascended to managing the company.[54]

———— ◆—◆—◆ ————

In 1917 Southern Pine Lumber Company acquired most of the 1,476 acre William Hampton survey, a mostly bayou bottom tract of land that today contains the state grand champion loblolly pine (declared in 2017). Since Southern Pine did not acquire the land or the timber until after the early logging camps had moved out, most of the timber was not logged until 1948, when certain pine and sweetgum trees contained more than 4,000 board feet of lumber each. In 1924 the Eastern Texas Railroad, which ran through the Hampton survey, was abandoned, and in the same year Southern Pine Lumber Company purchased from Ernest L. Kurth of Lufkin the 22 acres of land that made up the right-of-way, which today serves as the dividing line between North Boggy and South Boggy.[55]

More than 2,000 acres of homesteader's lands remained in the possession of more than a dozen farming and stock-herding families until after Southern Pine Lumber Company cut the timber on the tracts and fenced the surrounding lands as part of its cattle ranch. A. Harris and Company had purchased the timber rights from the settlers between 1899 and 1903 and sold them to Southern Pine Lumber Company between 1905 and 1907. After Southern Pine logged the lands of merchantable timber between 1907 and about 1914, it obtained from those families at least seventy-nine

tracts—all within today's Boggy Slough Conservation Area—after the ranch began, mostly between 1918 and 1924. Prominent among the families that sold their titles, and the years they did so, were the Sullivans, between 1916 and 1921; the Gibsons, mostly between 1913 and 1916; the Christies, Waltons, and most of the Durhams, in 1918; the Rushings, Womacks, Adams, and Wells, in 1919; and the Olivers, between 1918 and 1928; while other families, such as some members of the Andersons, Franklins, Gibsons, and Luces, did not sell until the late 1920s and early 1930s, with a few claims not settled until the 1950s. Additionally, there were a few small tracts that Southern Pine purchased from several of the Kenleys during the 1910s, 1920s, and 1950s.[56]

Logging the Land

Railroads were essential for logging Boggy Slough's forests more than a century ago. While it is perhaps not obvious upon first consideration, the railroads were directly linked to nature. Not only did Boggy Slough's railroads owe their existence to the land's newly commoditized pine trees, their constructions were fundamental encounters with the earth's soil, water, and topography. Beginning with Boggy Slough's first railroad, the Eastern Texas, its east-to-west construction through and across the Neches River bottomlands employed hundreds of men armed with shovels, hoes, wheelbarrows, axes, and saws. For more than twelve months during 1900 and 1901, these men labored alongside dozens of teams of draft animals, as the muscles of men and horseflesh worked together on behalf of the thermodynamic energies of the "iron horse." Advancing through 100-foot-wide rights-of-way—obtained by the railroad company's stockholders mostly by paying eager landowners a mere one dollar each—workers cut through forested hills and across prairies and fields. For a few miles out of Lufkin, they followed along the north side of the wagon road between Lufkin and Sullivan's Ferry, crossing the Lufkin and Alto road at Caruthers Station for four miles before crossing the Lufkin and Sullivan's Ferry road at Chancey and veering southwestward toward Pine Island.[57] They borrowed wood and earth resources readily at hand—using trees for crossties and bridge timbers, and dirt for fills—and both adapted and conformed to topography.[58] Railroad and lumber company directors, surveyors, and laborers may have decided the way by modifying the ground—excavating cuts, shoveling fills, and building wooden culverts and bridges—but the natural lay of the land determined the route. Since natural contours, watercourses, and gentle gradients enticed railroad builders, the flat plains of Cochino Bayou in today's Boggy Slough Conservation Area invited the path of least resistance.[59]

After the crews of men and teams of mules reached and crossed the two-and-a-quarter-mile wide Pine Island in Angelina County, they bridged the main channel of the Neches River just upstream of the mouth of Cochino Bayou in Trinity County. Braving alligators and water moccasins in the wide bottoms, men drove pilings; secured bridge timbers and bracings; grubbed and cleared the ground of trees, stumps, and endless roots; and graded the road straight across the Boggy Slough property for nearly four miles, passing alongside and sometimes partially through the jutting points of slopes and ridges north of the bayou. The river bridge was 18 feet high and 1,764 feet long and included the stream channel of Franklin Slough under its span.[60] Men and animals dug borrow pits and ditches (known as "bar ditches," slang for borrow) alongside the roadbed, and used the dirt fill to elevate the road's track bed at least eight feet above the frequently flooded bottoms. Still evident today, the borrow ditches connect with the maze of bottomland stream channels of Franklin Slough and Cochino Bayou near the river. For a half-mile stretch, just east of Neff, the roadbed skirted the north bank of Cochino's main stream channel, and workers built several bridges within the fills between the ravines of three sloping ridges on the north side of the bayou. West of the Boggy Slough property, the railroad builders crossed a number of Cochino feeder streams, requiring the construction of many wooden trestles and bridges, as the line progressed west-northwestward to the planned site of the big 4-C sawmill complex just north of Coltharp, between the new towns of Kennard and Ratcliff.[61]

While nature and a market economy lured the Eastern Texas Railroad to Boggy Slough, since the road was essential for connecting the commodities of the forest to railyards at Lufkin and markets beyond, the road's construction invited skilled professionals from afar. The general contractor was L. J. Smith of Kansas City, whose résumé already included the extensive Santa Fe and Katy railway systems. The chief engineer was Frank W. Valliant, namesake of the town of Valliant, Oklahoma, a rail station near a cottonseed oil mill that T. L. L. Temple would own some twenty years later.[62]

The Eastern Texas' assistant engineer was P. A. McCarthy, who left employment with the Chicago, Indiana & Eastern Railroad in 1900 for new opportunities in East Texas. Smith and Valliant left the region after completing the Eastern Texas' construction, but McCarthy remained in Lufkin, serving as that city's civil engineer before relocating to the city of Houston in 1909. While in Lufkin, McCarthy also became chief engineer for two other Boggy Slough railroads: T. L. L. Temple's Texas Southeastern Railroad (TSE) and Trinity County Lumber Company's Groveton, Lufkin & Northern Railway (GL&N). McCarthy joined the rails of those two lines together at Vair Junction, in Bluff Prairie, just north of today's Highway 94, to the mutual benefit of both of those roads' owners.[63] From Vair, GL&N trains, which carried manufactured lumber from the Groveton sawmill, rolled over TSE's rails southwestward across the Neches River to Blix, then turned east onto TSE's Lufkin branch to reach important connections with the Cotton Belt system at Lufkin. By reaching Lufkin in this way, the GL&N obtained competitive Cotton Belt shipping rates and divisions of rates for Trinity County Lumber Company's products, and TSE benefited through profit sharing by leasing its tracks in Trinity and Angelina Counties.

surveys in preparation of potentially building another branch line to Palestine and Waco.[65]

Although Temple railroads to Crockett, Palestine, and Waco never developed, mainline rails of the Texas Southeastern Railroad stretched rapidly northwestward from Diboll, followed Morgan branch northward from Neff, and ran parallel to the Neches River some 60 miles, passing through Boggy Slough and past what is today's US Highway 84, which runs between Rusk and Palestine.[66] Under joint operation by Southern Pine Lumber Company and TSE Railroad Company, the rail line—known as the "Neches Valley Route"—was for many decades one of the longest logging railroads in the state. The mainline crossed the Neches River twice and at least one spur track also crossed the river near the Southern Pine Lumber Company logging camp of Fastrill, named by combining the surnames of Diboll executives Frank Farrington, P. A. Strauss, and Will Hill. The mainline crossed the rails of the Eastern Texas Railroad in Boggy Slough at Neff, named for a Cotton Belt railway manager, and crossed as well as joined the rails of the Texas State Railroad 10 miles north of Fastrill, allowing log trains to use the Texas State Railroad trestle over the river to access timber tracts in Anderson County toward Palestine.[67]

To log the newly acquired Trinity County lands, Southern Pine Lumber Company established in 1907 two logging camps, where laborers—many of them with their wives and children—lived near the areas to be logged. Camp No. 1 was located inside what is now the Boggy Slough Conservation Area, in the area known as Rayville, on high

Construction of the GL&N and TSE railroads in Boggy Slough followed the same pattern of land utilization and building practices that the Eastern Texas had employed just a few years earlier. Topography influenced the routes as much as economic considerations, as lumber company owners sought the most economical way to capitalize nature's timbered bounty. Flush with new funds following the profitable sale of Lufkin Land and Lumber Company in 1905, T. L. L. Temple amended the charter of his Texas Southeastern Railroad Company multiple times between 1906 and 1909, including extending its chartered life from seven years to fifty-seven years, and invested in a Bucyrus steam shovel, the same type as those being used to dig the Panama Canal.[64] Temple's construction crews used the steam shovel to excavate cuts in uplands and to form massive fills through the extensive river and creek bottoms, which were prominent features of Temple's timber holdings. Temple also increased the TSE's capitalization from $100,000 to $250,000 and received authorization from the state to construct a rail line across the Neches River through Trinity and Houston Counties to the city of Crockett and southward into Polk and San Jacinto Counties. Additionally, the state authorized him to build a 10-mile branch line from Blix, near the Neches River, into Lufkin, as well as perform ground just northeast of the North Fork of Cedar Creek, in the Sanchez survey. Camp No. 2 was situated about two miles southwest of Camp 1, in the heart of the rural school community known as Iris, which today is just outside of the Boggy Slough Conservation Area. Children of both camps attended the Iris School until 1910, when Southern Pine consolidated both Trinity County camps at Walkerton, in Houston County, and then the camp children attended the Mount Pisgah School in the Sullivan's Bluff community.

Camp 2 was the larger of the Trinity County camps, comprising seventy-five portable houses for a hundred men and their wives and children, while Camp 1 consisted of fifty-four portable houses for seventy-five men and their wives and children. The houses of both camps were rectangular-shaped, about 30 feet long by 8 feet wide, sized and built to be lifted by steam log loaders and transported on flatbed and skeleton-style railroad log cars. Since their appearance resembled railroad box cars, although without wheels, the portable dwellings were often called "box car houses." Camp 2's water came from shallow surface wells, while Camp 1's water came from both a nearby spring and the Neches River, two miles distant.[68] Each camp contained a "box car" commissary—an extension of the larger company store at Diboll—that provided basic domestic supplies to the logging-camp families. The portable commissaries also contained a party line telephone receiver, which connected the logging camps to each other, to Diboll, to the Vair railroad station, and to the camps for the railroad steam shovel and bridge-building crews, which worked several miles ahead of the logging fronts.[69]

The numbers and types of working livestock and steam-powered equipment at each camp indicated the different environments and site conditions of each location. Camp 2 was located farther from the river than Camp 1, in a more upland setting, and its crews used forty-two mules, sixteen oxen, four slip-tongue high-wheeled log carts, nine eight-wheel wagons, and one steam self-loader. Camp 1, situated nearest to the river bottoms,

used twenty mules, eighty oxen, four slip-tongue high-wheeled log carts, ten eight-wheel wagons, and two steam self-loaders. Camp 2 contained a greater concentration of open upland pine, while Camp 1's wetter bottomland logging terrain necessitated significantly greater numbers of oxen (a five-to-one ratio compared with Camp 2) and the addition of a second steam loader that was dedicated to hardwood logging.[70] Oxen, although not as efficient as mules in upland-type terrain, excelled at logging in wet, boggy ground, where they could draw heavier loads than mules, because their cloven hooves afforded better footing in the bottoms and on swampy ground. Oxen held other advantages over mules: they cost less, were less excitable and withstood rougher treatment in the bottoms, lived on coarser feed, and required a less expensive harness, or yoke, that could be made in camp from natural resources at hand.[71]

Also assigned to Camp 1's hardwood operations in Boggy Slough's bottoms was Southern Pine Lumber Company's only Shay-type locomotive. Named for its designer, Ephraim Shay of Michigan, this unique locomotive was developed specifically for negotiating tight curves and operating on a softer track bed. The Shay utilized a telescoping drive shaft, rather than rigid rods, to power small-diameter geared flanged wheels, which bore the entire weight of the locomotive as well as the tender. The engine was ideal at providing efficient tractive effort and maneuverability under the least amount of weight—something needed in bottomland site conditions, where a heavier, more rigid, and less efficient rod-type locomotive would have been more likely to sink the track and jump the rails.[72]

The Boggy Slough logging camps during initial industrial logging were self-contained temporary places of habitation, typical of labor camps throughout the southern forests at the time. For the most part, camp residents lived in relative solitude, deep in the forests, owning very little personal property. Their only direct connection to the outside world was the mainline railroad that led back to the sawmill and the parent company town of Diboll. Most other community connections came through the

A Shay geared locomotive pulls a train of hardwood logs from Boggy Slough's bottomlands, November 1907. *Courtesy of The History Center, Diboll.*

Some boys assisted the mule and oxen keepers at nearby corrals, caring for the animals' feed and water requirements in the evenings and preparing and assembling yokes, harnesses, and tack in the mornings by lantern light. Older boys soon transitioned into working alongside their fathers at "the front," first as roustabouts, then graduating to more strenuous work.[74]

camp family's children, who attended the local schools with the area's farming children, where camp children were often seen as socially inferior. Few rural schoolteachers, already overworked, could afford to invest quality time in a camp child's education, primarily because of the transient nature of the child's upbringing. Logging camps rarely existed more than five years in a single location, and employment turnovers were frequent. Conditions at Boggy Slough's camps were similar.[73]

Men, women, and children at the camps worked long days. Everyone awoke well before sunrise and assisted in preparing breakfasts and lunches, and making other provisions for the day. The men left camp before sunup, riding the log trains to and from the logging work sites, hanging on to empty log cars going and grasping at logs and chains returning. They carried their lunches in repurposed syrup buckets, which usually contained the previous night's leftovers. Women stayed at camp, where they cooked, washed, cleaned, raised their children, and fashioned the best home possible under temporary conditions. When school-age children were not attending school, they helped around camp, scavenging for pine knots and other fuelwood and performing a host of other tasks necessary to assist a family trying to eke out a living in woods camps.

Labor at the logging fronts was divided into several occupations, including sawyers, mule skinners, bull punchers, and crews of steam loader and skidder men. Railroad grading crews worked ahead of the sawyers, clearing paths for the tracks that would haul the timber to Diboll. Sawyers worked in pairs of two and typically cut about 10,000 to 17,000 board feet of logs per day per two-man crew, depending on site conditions, such as topography, soil type, weather, amount of underbrush, and the type and size of timber cut. Boggy Slough's first industrial forest averaged about 8,000 board feet of merchantable timber per acre, so each two-man saw crew cut about one-and-a-half acres, or about five railcar loads, per day. The sawyers used crosscut saws, usually six to seven feet long, kept sharp by each camp's skilled saw filer. Each pair of sawyers also carried hickory wedges and a single-bit ax, as well as a double-bit ax and a bottle filled with kerosene and plugged with pine needles, which was used to clean the sawblade of sap accumulation. After the sawyers felled the trees by crosscut saws, they chopped off limbs and knots and sawed the trunks to specific log lengths, a practice known as bucking. They cut the logs into varying lengths, but sixteen

An early Southern Pine Lumber Company upland logging crew poses for the camera. *Courtesy of The History Center, Diboll.*

Women and children pose for the camera at Logging Camp No. 1 in November 1907. In 1913 the site was cleared and became Rayville, the headquarters of the Southern Pine Lumber Company cattle ranch. *Courtesy of The History Center, Diboll.*

and bottomland gums, before bucking reached the limbs in the tops, which were left behind to be carefully burned later as slash or allowed to otherwise decay. Much of the timber cut during this time yielded clear, straight, heartwood milled products, free of the knots and sapwood that are now common in lumber, because today's markets rarely wait long enough for trees to grow to maturity.[75] After sawyers cut the logs to length, the logs were transported to railroad trackside loading banks, known as skidways, pulled by animal teams using carts and wagons. Teamsters positioned the logs parallel to the tracks' rights-of-way, sometimes ahead of track-laying gangs. Workers typically skidded long pine logs trackside

feet eight inches was the most preferred length. The approximately half a foot allowance beyond sixteen feet was important, so that finished mill products could be sixteen feet long, or two sets of eight-foot products could be manufactured from each log. Virtually all the pines, oaks, gums, and hickories that were cut between 1907 and about 1914 were long-bodied and free of low-hanging limbs, and each tree provided three or more logs, especially the pines

Southern Pine Lumber Company used these teams of oxen to log hardwoods at Boggy Slough. *Courtesy of The History Center, Diboll.*

A Southern Pine Lumber Company mule team and slip-tongue logging cart in pine uplands. *Courtesy of The History Center, Diboll.*

ingenious log-moving tools. The primary working mechanism of the cart was a long pole, up to 30 feet long, which served as a slipping, or sliding, tongue that was attached by a chain to a vertical beam lever positioned over the axle and a horizontal roller. Attached to the roller on the backside of the axle were two chains and grab irons that hung below the axle. A teamster rolled the cart, straddled a log, moving the axle a few feet past halfway of the log's length, then ordered the mules to halt and back up a step. As the teams moved back, the tongue slipped, or slid, backward, releasing tension on the lever. A helper on the ground then threw back the lever to lower the chains and grapples, secured the grapples to the log, and repositioned the beam

individually, using slip-tongue high-wheeled carts pulled by teams of four mules, over distances of no more than 400 yards, while shorter logs, especially those that traveled longer distances, including most hardwood logs, came on the eight-wheeled wagons pulled mostly by yokes of oxen.[76]

The wheels of the single-axle high-wheeled carts were seven feet in diameter, and they were

A Southern Pine Lumber Company McGiffert log loader at Boggy Slough, 1907. *Courtesy of The History Center, Diboll.*

A Southern Pine Lumber Company crew demonstrates their McGiffert log loader's retractable motorized wheels, which made it self-propelled and provided a way to pass empty cars underneath. *Courtesy of The History Center, Diboll.*

to take up the slack of the chains. As the mule team moved forward again, the tongue slipped forward before catching in a locked position, in the process lifting the front of the log about a foot above the ground. The log then skidded along the ground to the trackside skidways, with only the back end slightly dragging the ground.[77]

Eight-wheeled wagons were used in Boggy Slough mostly to haul loads of multiple hardwood logs over longer distances than the carts that carried individual pine logs from much denser forested uplands. The eight wheels also spread the weight of the load, which was needed in the boggy bottoms. Crews loaded and unloaded the wagons by cross-hauling the logs over skid poles. Initially, Southern Pine Lumber Company used Lindsey wagons, which were manufactured in Laurel, Mississippi, before using locally made Martin wagons, which were manufactured in Lufkin.[78]

While animal powered high-quality carts and wagons did yeoman service in Southern Pine Lumber Company's Boggy Slough forests, Temple also purchased state-of-the-art steam-powered logging

equipment. Foremost were the McGiffert steam loaders, manufactured by the Clyde Iron Works of Duluth, Minnesota. Built to run on railroad tracks under their own steam, these nifty machines could stop and support themselves on frames outside of the tracks, while mechanically raising their chain-driven flanged wheels high enough to allow the passage of empty log cars rolling underneath, practically eliminating the need for rail sidings. The McGiffert self-propelled steam loaders also had powered drums that pulled cables through large booms that easily lifted logs from the assembled piles at the trackside skidways onto the railcars. The McGiffert loader could also be used as a short-haul skidder, pulling logs directly from where they fell to the bunks of the railcars.[79]

At some point before the logs were loaded onto railcars, a trained technician "scaled" them by measuring and recording the amount of merchantable timber in each log. The information was used later to pay the crews and to monitor the volume of the timber shipped. At times, crews cut hardwood logs alongside the pine, separating the two types onto different cars and assembling separate trains for delivery to the Diboll mills. Once loaded, the railcars held about 2,700 board feet of logs each, depending on the type and length of logs. Each

assembled train contained from nine to eighteen loaded cars, and crews sent from one to two trains per day from each camp to the mills.[80]

After the sawyers left a logging site in Boggy Slough, a large tie-making crew of sixty men arrived on the scene and cut remaining oaks and gums that were deemed too small for making lumber but large enough to provide crossties. Such trees were usually about eight to eleven inches in diameter. After sawing down the trees, men used flat-sided hewing broadaxes to chop and hew thousands of hardwood crossties for use on the ever expanding TSE mainline and Southern Pine Lumber Company logging railroads, since more than three thousand crossties supported each mile of railroad, and ties deteriorated and had to be replaced every five to seven years. Management sold the surplus ties to other railroad operations, since it was "the policy of the [Diboll] company to utilize all of its timber and lumber resources," according to an *American Lumberman* article of January 1908. At the time, railroad companies used ties that were eight feet long, hewed to dimensions between six-by-seven inches and seven-by-nine inches, hewed at least on the top and bottom surfaces.[81]

In addition to the state-of-the-art forty-five-ton Shay locomotive, which Southern Pine Lumber Company used specifically in Boggy Slough's hardwood bottoms, company officials used seven other locomotives—all rod-type engines—which varied between thirty and fifty tons each. Between 1911 and 1913, Southern Pine added four more rod locomotives to the operations, each one

Texas Southeastern Railroad Engine 7 pulls a train of Boggy Slough pine logs toward Diboll, November 1907. *Courtesy of The History Center, Diboll.*

A train of hardwood logs from Boggy Slough at the Diboll sawmills, November 1907. *Courtesy of The History Center, Diboll.*

weighing between sixty and sixty-seven tons, all of them new from the Baldwin Locomotive Works factories in Pennsylvania. Thus twelve locomotives, which operated under Southern Pine Lumber Company and Texas Southeastern Railroad Company liveries, served to bring the logs from the forests to the Diboll mills and transport the products of the mills to the Cotton Belt railyards at Lufkin.[82]

As logging operations in Boggy Slough progressed from south to north, Southern Pine Lumber Company purchased two new Clyde four-line steam cable skidders, which shipped from Duluth,

Minnesota, to Neff Station, in North Boggy, in 1914. At about the same time, Temple Lumber Company purchased two additional nearly identical Clyde four-line skidders for use in the Pineland mill's logging operations.[83] These massive double-boomed machines operated on railroads under their own power like the McGiffert loaders, but their primary purpose was to replace the animal-drawn log carts and wagons. By eliminating carts and wagons, along with dozens of mules and oxen and a host of related expenses, skidders were simply more economically efficient, but their use came with long-lasting consequences. They were dangerous to man, beast, and plants alike, negatively affecting the forests. The skidder's four cables, pulled by large steam-powered drums through blocks at the ends of giant booms, forcefully snagged logs from all directions at once, from distances of 600

or more feet away. The process, called cable "snaking," was extremely destructive to all vegetation situated between the skidder and the farthest stump, as log after log came walloping through the woods, destroying all in its path. Conservationists decried the industry's widespread use of steam skidders, because dozens of smaller trees were either snapped or uprooted, which severely hindered and at times prevented natural pine forest regeneration.[84] W. Goodrich Jones, "the Father of Texas Forestry," spoke against the steam skidder for decades, describing it once as "an octopus of steel," whose four long grappling arms became "enormous battering rams" that laid low "everything in their way." Even an occasional tree that somehow survived the mauling, he said, was "skinned so badly as to become worthless."[85]

T. L. L. Temple and his managers knew the destructive nature of steam cable skidders, but they also knew their use was necessary to compete in the markets. General manager Gilbert once wrote to the US Forest Service to acknowledge that the skidder's damage to young timber was "much greater" than by wagons and carts, but market realities dictated that a manager should be more concerned with reducing short-

term logging expenses than with conserving young timber.[86] Henry Gresham Temple, T. L. L. Temple's nephew and once an enthusiastic proponent of steam skidders, lived long enough to regret their use. In 1940, while rethinking the Temple companies' forestry objectives, he determined that the destruction skidders had caused company lands along the Neches River during the previous quarter of a century had rendered many acres of ground as "practically waste land," and he urged Arthur Temple Sr. to hire professional foresters "to cut our timber more intelligently" in the future.[87]

More than 25 percent of Boggy Slough's forest in 1907 was, and remains today, bottomland hardwoods. When staff from the trade journal *American Lumberman* visited Boggy Slough in November 1907, they published the estimated merchantable hardwood timber as consisting of 60 percent oak, 30 percent gum, and 10 percent hickory. Many other hardwood species, such as ash, elm, walnut, and sycamore, were also present, but apparently not of sufficient quantity to be included in the merchantable timber estimate.[88] A large part of the oak forest was overcup oak (*Quercus lyrata*), also known as swamp post oak. Capable of enduring several months of flooding, overcups were regarded as among the wettest of the timber species in Boggy Slough's bottomland forest. When not hollow, overcup yielded sawn wood with similar characteristics to the common white oak (*Quercus alba*) and was marketed as such.[89] Photographs in the January 18, 1908, issue of *American Lumberman*

heartwood exhibited a ruddy color, highly prized as decorative lumber when quartersawn and polished.[91] Photographs also showed large shagbark hickories growing among switch cane. Today, much of Boggy Slough's bottomlands resemble the forest scenes in those November 1907 photos, since the merchantable forests cut there more than a century ago have returned. To log the timber on Boggy Slough Island, railroad crews bridged the slough in July 1909, and later an earthen dam was made at the bridge site, which today serves as a road crossing onto the island, retaining river water within the slough throughout the year, benefiting wildlife.[92]

The 1907 *American Lumberman* photographs also showed the Diboll lumberyards, which contained exhibits of clear hardwood lumber manufactured from Boggy Slough's forests, including displays of white oak boards that were 22 inches wide and 18 feet long. Displays of red oak (*Quercus falcata* and *Q. pagodifolia*) showed boards 25 inches wide and 14 feet long. A board of black gum (*Nyssa sylvatica*), which the journal called bay poplar, was 32 inches wide and 14 feet long. A red gum board was 30 inches wide and 14 feet long, exhibiting its ruddy colors, which were planned to

showed large buttressed overcup oaks with trunks wider than the spread legs of a horseman mounted high in the saddle. Waterline marks and stains from past floods were as high as the horses' heads. The photographs, made late in November, also showed open bottomland understories with mostly fallen limbs and leaves on the ground. Other photographs showed giant sweetgum trees (*Liquidambar styraciflua*)—one that was four feet wide—growing among water oaks and switch cane.[90] Old-growth bottomland sweetgums, which were often 120 feet tall or more, featured trunks that were wide, tall, and straight. They were the "true red gums of the lumberman," according to early botany publications, because at old age the sweetgum's

A large red gum (old growth sweetgum) tree among other gums and water oaks in the Cochino Bayou bottoms, November 1907. Note the presence of switch cane in the foreground. *Courtesy of The History Center, Diboll.*

be a highlight feature within Diboll's new library building.[93]

Boggy Slough hardwood logging operations included many difficulties and challenges. Because of regular and frequent flooding, bottomland logging was seasonal, at best. Even after floodwaters subsided, the ground remained wet and soft for days or weeks. Bottomland logging was almost impossible during winter and spring, sometimes from as early as October to as late as June. Many letters from Watson Walker at Diboll to T. L. L. Temple in Texarkana expressed that he was "very blue" and "afraid" that the river would for many months "put us out of the bottoms" or "knock us

out of the hardwood." Walker often warned Temple and Gilbert of anticipated poor milling reports, repeatedly blaming the rising waters of the Neches for placing hardwood operations "in mighty bad shape."[94] The best that Walker could do, his bosses advised him, was to make great efforts to stockpile as many hardwood logs as he could during the dry season.[95]

When the bottoms flooded, so did the logging railroads, sometimes to the point of severely washing out, which left rails suspended in the air once the floodwaters subsided.[96] Railroad steam skidders and log loaders also flooded, as heavy rains caused considerable grief for the logging crews. Rising waters in the feeder streams nearest the river flooded crews almost while they worked. Walker once wrote to T. L. L. Temple to report that one of the steam cable skidders had to be abandoned in Houston County, since the floodwaters rose 12 feet before anything could be done to move it to higher ground. Once the rains subsided, floodwaters remained at least seven feet deep between the skidder and the mainline railroad, and it was several weeks more before men could begin to salvage the flooded equipment.[97]

The lumber quality of middle Neches River bottomland hardwood logs was occasionally poor. For one thing, trunks were often hollow. Sawyers

Large shagbark hickory trees in the Cochino Bayou bottoms, November 1907. *Courtesy of The History Center, Diboll.*

Wide and clear hardwood lumber at Diboll, manufactured from Boggy Slough forest trees, 1907. *Courtesy of The History Center, Diboll.*

left trees that were obviously hollow standing, and they abandoned the defective ones they had cut down before discovering otherwise hidden imperfections. Another issue concerned logs that mill managers found to be too small and crooked once they arrived at Diboll. Ownership and management were regularly at odds with logging foremen, who seemed to bring way too many inferior hardwood logs to the mills. Concerning low-quality oak and gum logs that he had observed at the mills, T. L. L. Temple once instructed Watson Walker to "correct" the problem of bringing in a large number of "crooked logs." It was simply best to leave those logs in the woods, Temple explained. Temple also disliked discovering that at times more than half of the oak lumber graded no better than No. 3 quality. Milling oak at such a low grade "will not pay," Temple reminded Walker, and he recommended making instead crossties out of such poor logs.[98] But, most important, he

stressed that such decisions needed to be made in the woods. It was too late once the inferior logs reached the mill.[99]

By 1918, some merchantable Neches valley hardwoods, especially black walnut (*Juglans nigra*), were nearly depleted.[100] In March of that year, with the nation's supplies of walnut gun stocks and airplane propeller blades at emergency levels, because of the world war, native East Texan US senator Morris Sheppard wrote to T. L. L. Temple, asking him for black walnut timber. Temple forwarded the letter to his Diboll hardwood mill manager, George W. Cleveland, who replied to Sheppard, saying that, "the best walnut [had been] cut out years ago when walnut lumber was in heavy demand." Cleveland explained that the Diboll mill was still logging walnut timber from the Neches River bottoms, but that during the two previous years it made up only 1 percent of its productions. Besides, Cleveland said, the quality of the walnut had been "inferior," since the logs were mostly "small and crooked, running

Another view of clear hardwood lumber—red gum, oaks, and bay poplar (black gum) up to 32 inches wide—manufactured from Boggy Slough timber in 1907. *Courtesy of The History Center, Diboll.*

tree today, one might ask what became of all the walnut trees? Any answer to the question should consider the possibility that many of the trees the Spanish called walnuts were actually hickories instead, since several of the Neches River hickories resembled walnuts in appearance. Also, since hickories were not native to Spain, it is likely that most Spanish observers were not experienced enough to distinguish the difference between hickory and black walnut.[103] Another consideration influencing an answer is that black walnut trees are especially sensitive to site conditions, requiring moist, well-drained, well-protected sites rich in soil nutrients—soil that is not too wet, too dry, nor too shallow—and they simply failed to regenerate abundantly after the disturbances caused by agricultural clearing during the nineteenth century and industrial logging and commercial cattle ranching during the early twentieth century. Interestingly, since walnut trees have such sensitive requirements, their seeds, like those of most hickories as well, are heavy, which ensures they will reach the ground under the tree and not be blown away by the wind to unfavorable soil conditions. Squirrels and other animals may disperse the seeds to sites away from the parent tree, but generally they do not travel too far distant and remain where the soil conditions are relatively unchanged. To further ensure the walnut's regeneration, there is also a peculiar antagonism that exists between a black walnut tree and many other plants growing within its root zone. Black walnuts produce juglone, a substance toxic to other plants found in the leaves, bark, nut husks, and roots of the tree, which serves to protect seedlings from competition for sunlight and soil fertility.[104] Also, site-sensitive black walnuts usually grew individually or in small groups. Considering all these factors, it would seem that there are fewer black walnut trees in Boggy Slough today than there were four hundred years ago. But it is also probably true there never were as many as the Spanish records might suggest.

With one of the few hardwood operations in the region during the time of Boggy Slough's first industrial logging, Southern Pine Lumber Company

largely to sap." What little amount of walnut lumber the Diboll mill had been able to make from such logs had graded mostly "common or worse.". Cleveland regretted that he had no better walnut timber to offer the government, but he suggested that Senator Sheppard try the Canadian and Grand River territories in Oklahoma and the Boston Mountain area in Northwest Arkansas.[101]

Black walnut trees remain along Boggy Slough's stream bottoms today, but just how abundant or rare the trees were before industrial logging may never be known. Nearly all Spanish-speaking observers of the Neches valley during the seventeenth and eighteenth centuries wrote extensively of walnut trees, using the word *nogal*. Even as recently as 1827, during his inspection tour of East Texas, Mexican general Manuel Mier y Terán recorded riding through an "endless forest of oak and walnut."[102] So prevalent were mentions of walnut in the early written records, and so scarce is the cut hardwoods not only from its own lands but also those growing on the lands of others as well, including the holdings of the Pine Island Lumber Company in Angelina County and the Central Coal and Coke Company's (4-C) lands in Houston and Trinity Counties. In the bottoms in Angelina County, Southern Pine built a tram road directly opposite Boggy Slough, in 1915. The road left the TSE mainline south of present-day Highway 94 and traversed ten miles northward, spanning all of Pine Island. This spur railroad and several others up and down the Neches, on both sides of the river, established a monopoly on the middle and upper Neches for the Temple hardwood milling businesses. When the owners of the Eastern Texas Railroad sought abandonment of that line of railway in 1920, commissioners of the Interstate Commerce Commission inquired about the availability of hardwood traffic that would justify keeping the railroad operational. The Eastern Texas' attorney, E. J. Mantooth of Lufkin, scoffed at even the suggestion of hardwood traffic, declaring at a public hearing in Washington, DC, that, "there is not a stick of hardwood that you can find on that whole [Neches] river that is marketable, that has not been cut out and hauled away by the Southern Pine Lumber Company. It has two mills at Diboll, one a pine mill that saws pine timber exclusively, and another large mill that saws nothing in the world but hardwood; and they have cut the timber clean from one end to the other of the hardwood. There is nothing left in there but cutover lands."[105] Mantooth, representing a client who wished to close the railroad, was dramatic in his argument, but he was not far from the truth in his assessment. Just a couple months earlier, Mantooth had received his facts directly from Dave Kenley, who had reported that the Diboll mills had already "cut and removed all the merchantable timber, both pine and hardwoods" from Southern Pine's lands, as well as "practically all" of the adjoining lands within at least ten miles of the railroad.[106]

Anticipating the inevitable abandonment of the Eastern Texas Railroad, Dave Kenley saw one last opportunity to conveniently monetize the re-

maining Cochino Bayou oaks that had survived previous mill harvests and crosstie procurements a decade earlier. In the fall of 1920, Kenley hired more than a dozen crosstie hackers to chop, hew, and stack ties along the Eastern Texas Railroad right-of-way between mileposts 16 and 17, west of Franklin Slough, on what is today the North Boggy Boundary Road. Several of the men he hired were former landowners of what is now Boggy Slough Conservation Area or were tenants of the Southern Pine Lumber Company ranch, including members of the Sullivan, Oliver, Rushing, Anderson, and Harber families. Kenley also hired a man to run a small crosstie sawmill on Pine Island. Southern Pine Lumber Company contracted with Cotton Belt railroad officials, who acquired the Eastern Texas line in 1906, to provide for them as many hewn and sawed oak crossties as possible from the river and stream bottoms, receiving from eighty cents to $1.05 for each tie made from walnut and the various white oaks (overcup, swamp chestnut, bur, and post) and from sixty cents to ninety cents for each tie made from red oaks (cherrybark, water, and willow) and gums (sweet and black).[107]

Although hardwoods made up much of Boggy Slough's forests, as they did all of Temple's forests that were located along more than 80 miles of the Neches River, most of the timber volume cut in Boggy Slough a century ago was, and has always been, pine. In addition to photographing Boggy Slough's hardwood forests and their milled products in November 1907, staff from *American Lumberman* also documented the pines and their milled products. They recorded that most of the pines were shortleaf, although at least one notable grove of longleaf was located north of Cochino Bayou in one of the I&GN Railroad surveys purchased from A. Harris and Company. Within that stand, there was at least one longleaf that measured 48 inches in diameter. There is today a longleaf pine in the Boggy Slough Conservation Area just south of Cochino Bayou that is a state co-champion tree at only 38 inches in diameter, but Boggy Slough's four-foot longleaf was apparently so common during 1907 that its measurement was

A grove of longleaf pines in the uplands of one of the International & Great Northern Railroad surveys north of Cochino Bayou. The *American Lumberman* photographer who took this picture noted that the largest tree measured 48 inches in diameter. *Courtesy of The History Center, Diboll.*

From a pure timber perspective, Boggy Slough's lands were not as photographically impressive as those of some of its nearest competitors, including the Thompson Brothers Lumber Company lands in Trinity and Polk Counties, which *American Lumberman* photographers featured only a few months later, in the summer of 1908. While at least one of Boggy Slough's longleaf pines equaled Thompson's 48 inchers, the Thompson lands held shortleaf pines up to five feet in diameter, as well as five-foot-wide cherry bark oaks, six-foot-wide white oaks, and ash trees up to six and a half feet wide. Southern Pine's timberlands averaged about 8,000 board feet of pine per acre, but Thompson's lands averaged much more. At least one of their 640-acre tracts in Trinity County averaged 25,000 board feet of longleaf pine per acre, and some of their shortleaf stands contained up to 30,000 board feet per acre.[110]

Ironically, it was Southern Pine Lumber Company's ownership of lands that contained a relatively low volume of merchantable pine that led to Temple's beginning of sustained-yield operations. Conservation came naturally. Boggy Slough's mixed pine and hardwood forests, which were essentially unwanted by earlier lumbermen, held many pine trees that were less than 12 inches in

not even mentioned in the published article, only in the photographer's unpublished notes.[108]

The shortleaf pines that were photographed near the early logging camps were shown growing among relatively open understories inhabited mostly by stands of American beautyberry (*Callicarpa americana*), but several photographs revealed a good bit of understory brush as well. At the Diboll lumberyards, the photography crew captured displays of 30-inch-wide pine boards, 16 feet long, completely clear of knots. Unfortunately, no *American Lumberman* photos showed any of the land's homesteads, which were still occupied at the time, perhaps because there was very little timber there to show.[109]

Wide and clear pine lumber at the Diboll yard, manufactured from Boggy Slough forest trees, 1907. *Courtesy of The History Center, Diboll.*

diameter, the minimum that Temple had determined could be responsibly cut on lands that he owned.[111] While Temple's sawyers at Boggy Slough left pines smaller than 12 inches standing, many of his competitors cut all or most of their pine timber because all or most of their trees were already a merchantable size. Pine timber stand volumes that measured more than 20,000 board feet per acre in 1908 were almost pure stands of mature pine, something Temple's Diboll operators knew little about. Temple did know, however, that the margin of profit in manufacturing lumber from small trees was low, just as he also knew that those same trees would bring significantly greater value if given another couple of decades to mature, especially with the competition of the larger trees removed.[112] Temple's milling and logging operations a quarter of a century earlier in Cass County had been unsustainable, resulting in his exodus to the Neches River valley. Now

owning the land, rather than only the timber, he sought a conservative approach. In a way, his experiences resembled an analogy that forester and ecologist Aldo Leopold would articulate many years later, but in reverse order: "If our system of land-use happens to be self-perpetuating, we stay. If it happens to be self-destructive, we move, like Abraham, to pastures new." And while it would be a future generation who would embrace Leopold's land ethic—a concept of land as a community to which we all belong, rather than as mere commodity—Temple nonetheless planted a small seed at Boggy Slough.[113]

Temple's fundamental conservatism, which he worked out as essentially a sense of intergenerational responsibility, is probably best understood when considering that Boggy Slough's first industrial timber harvest coincided with one of the nation's worst financial panics in history. Already in a recession, the national economy fell into crisis in October 1907, when the stock market fell nearly 50 percent in only nine months. The resulting panic caused businesses to fail and banks to default across the country. Financier J. P. Morgan used personal funds to stabilize the national economy and restore a semblance of public confidence during what became known as the Panic of 1907, which led directly to the creation of a national monetary commission and the Federal Reserve System.[114] Some economists felt that the lumber industry was hit worst of all. Several sawmill owners in Texas shut down, while many more reduced production, but only temporarily. T. L. L. Temple was interviewed in Houston in January 1908, and he told a *Houston Post* reporter that he had no intention of logging heavily until better markets returned. He said his managers would "continue the policy of curtailing production" by keeping the operation of the Diboll mills at half capacity or lower for as long as necessary. "We are going to be conservative," he said, "and are in no hurry to get back to running at full capacity."[115]

Besides being the year that industrial logging began at Boggy Slough, 1907 was eventful also for another reason. Despite the depressed economy,

Upland shortleaf pine growing a half mile north of the Eastern Texas Railroad at Boggy Slough, November 1907. Note the sapling stobs in the foreground, chopped to better reveal the pine timber. *Courtesy of The History Center, Diboll.*

Shortleaf pine timber at Boggy Slough, November 1907. *Courtesy of The History Center, Diboll.*

Texas still manufactured more than 2.2 billion board feet of lumber that year, a production mark that would stand as the state record for decades, until after the Great Depression of the 1930s. Texas was the third highest lumber-producing state in the nation in 1907, behind only the states of Washington and Louisiana. Nationally, the lumber cut was more than 40 billion board feet, with Southern yellow pine making up 33 percent of the total, much more than any other species.[116] National and state conservationists, who had called for production constraints for decades, were now more alarmed than ever. Their cries prompted President Theodore Roosevelt to call a Governor's Conference on Conservation of Natural Resources at the White House in May 1908. Although governor's conferences seem rather common occurrences today, Roosevelt's conference was the first gathering of

state governors to discuss national matters. It was also one of the most distinguished gatherings ever to assemble. The president, vice president, members of the cabinet, all of the Supreme Court justices, many members of Congress, the nation's brightest scientists, numerous special guests, and members of the press all attended. Texas governor Thomas M. Campbell did not attend, sending in his place Lieutenant Governor Asbury B. Davidson and the well-respected conservationist W. Goodrich Jones, who each made well-received speeches.[117]

The three-day conference was an overwhelming success, resulting in a number of recommendations to the president in full support of natural resource conservation, especially concerning forests and water resources. Throughout the summer of 1908, lumber industry publications were abuzz with speculation about what reforms might actually occur. The trade journal *Southern Industrial and Lumber Review*, which referred to the public's concern over the nation's timber supply as a "craze," queried forest owners across the South to see what, if any, conservation and reforestation efforts they were making on their lands. While most respondents declared to be in favor of conservation, only three Texas operations stated they were actually practicing any form of it: the Lutcher & Moore Lumber Company mills at Orange, the Thompson Brothers mills in several East Texas counties, and the Southern Pine Lumber Company mills at Diboll. Overall, lumber company responses were grim, as stiff market competition, penalizing tax structures, and forest fires were repeatedly cited as serious impediments to both conservation and proactive reforestation.[118]

The journal published Southern Pine Lumber Company's reply in their August 1908 issue while Boggy Slough logging operations were ongoing. Company officials stated that "so far" they had "only adopted the method of leaving all timber twelve inches and under, standing, and protect[ing] as far

as possible the young growth in the felling of trees, endeavoring to keep the rights-of-ways along our [rail]roads clean so that the danger of woods fires from the sparks of the locomotive may be reduced as much as possible." The response also admitted that the issue of forest conservation deserved "more attention," and it expressed a measure of hope that market conditions would soon allow the company "to take this work up along scientific lines and accomplish much more than has been in the past."[119] The response was diplomatic and apologetic, but also optimistic. While simple, it was nonetheless praised by the journal as a step in the right direction; most companies simply didn't care. Such expressions of conservative good will and faith in the future summarized T. L. L. Temple's business philosophy in a nutshell: the wise and thoughtful use of natural resources would support the present and provide continued opportunities for the future—perhaps even unlikely and extraordinary opportunities undreamed of at the time.

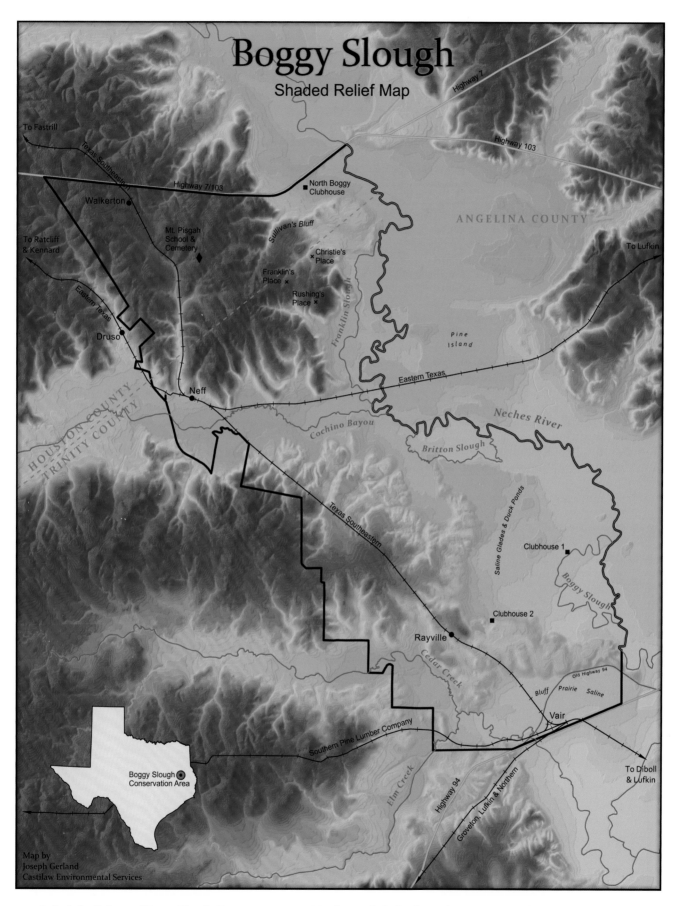

Boggy Slough
Shaded Relief Map

To Fastrill

Highway 7

Highway 103

Texas Southeastern

Highway 7/103

North Boggy Clubhouse

ANGELINA COUNTY

Walkerton

To Ratcliff & Kennard

Mt. Pisgah School & Cemetery

Sullivan's Bluff

Christie's Place ×

Franklin's Place ×

Rushing's Place ×

To Lufkin

Eastern Texas

Druso

Franklin Slough

Pine Island

Neff

Eastern Texas

HOUSTON COUNTY
TRINITY COUNTY

Cochino Bayou

Neches River

Britton Slough

Texas Southeastern

Saline Glades & Duck Ponds

Clubhouse 1

Boggy Slough

Clubhouse 2

Rayville

Cedar Creek

Old Highway 94

Bluff Prairie Saline

Vair

Southern Pine Lumber Company

Elm Creek

Highway 94

Groveton, Lufkin & Northern

To Diboll & Lufkin

Boggy Slough
Conservation Area

Map by
Joseph Gerland
Castilaw Environmental Services

A shaded relief map of Boggy Slough Conservation Area. *Map by Joseph Gerland, Castilaw Environmental Services, Nacogdoches.*

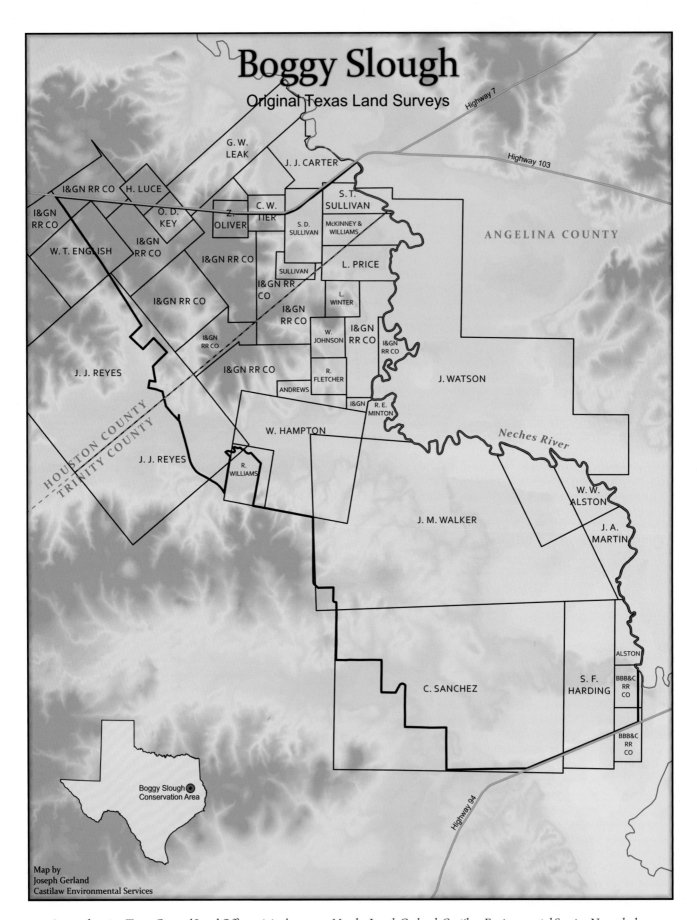

Boggy Slough
Original Texas Land Surveys

Highway 7

Highway 103

G. W. LEAK

J. J. CARTER

I&GN RR CO   H. LUCE

I&GN RR CO

O. D. KEY

Z. OLIVER

C. W. ITER

S. T. SULLIVAN

S. D. SULLIVAN

McKINNEY & WILLIAMS

ANGELINA COUNTY

W. T. ENGLISH

I&GN RR CO

I&GN RR CO

SULLIVAN

L. PRICE

I&GN RR CO

I&GN RR CO

L. WINTER

I&GN RR CO

W. JOHNSON

I&GN RR CO

I&GN RR CO

J. J. REYES

I&GN RR CO

I&GN RR CO

R. FLETCHER

ANDREWS

J. WATSON

HOUSTON COUNTY
TRINITY COUNTY

J. J. REYES

I&GN

R. E. MINTON

W. HAMPTON

Neches River

R. WILLIAMS

W. W. ALSTON

J. M. WALKER

J. A. MARTIN

ALSTON

C. SANCHEZ

S. F. HARDING

BBB&C RR CO

BBB&C RR CO

Boggy Slough
Conservation Area

Highway 94

Map by
Joseph Gerland
Castilaw Environmental Services

A map showing Texas General Land Office original surveys. *Map by Joseph Gerland, Castilaw Environmental Service, Nacogdoches.*

A dogwood tree scraped by a white-tailed buck deer blooms beneath mixed shortleaf pine and hardwood trees in the Boggy Slough Conservation Area in March 2017. *Photo by the author.*

Black Cat Lake sunrise from a kayak, September 2016. *Photo by the author.*

Black Cat Lake sunrise, May 2015. *Photo by the author.*

A lone cardinal flower blooms in the light of a setting sun along the banks of the Neches River near Britton Slough in October 2017. *Photo by the author.*

A sampling of Indian artifacts found by a Temple-Inland forester during road work along a terrace at the south end of Franklin Slough during the 1990s. *Courtesy of The History Center, Diboll.*

The red dirt road that leads to the old Christie home place, August 2018. *Photo by the author.*

View looking up a hillside of hickories where Beulah Christie and her husband Charles R. Rushing lived before the 1910s. *Photo by the author, March 2018.*

A stately red elm, one of several that grows at the former Christie home place, where Jessie Christie lived and wrote about them in the *Houston Post* in 1912. *Photo by the author, August 2018.*

View looking down the hickory hill where the Rushings lived. *Photo by the author, March 2018.*

The joined tombstones of twins DeWitt and Jewell Christie at the Mount Pisgah Cemetery in summer 2015. The twin boys were killed, along with their father, by their cousin Carr Durham during a feud in November 1913. *Photo by the author.*

The postal community of Sullivan's Bluff, indicated by a red circle in this 1875 *Cram's Railroad and Township Map of Texas*, was located north of Cochino Bayou in what is now the Boggy Slough Conservation Area. *Author's collections.*

Butterflies enjoy the blooms of Texas groundsel (*Senecio ampullaceus*), which grows in abundance on the hickory hillside where the Rushings and Christies lived. *Photo by the author, March 2018.*

The tiny gravestone of the infant Annie Mae Johnson, who was born and died on August 21, 1904. She was buried on a hill that later became the site of the Boggy Slough Hunting Club's second clubhouse. In the 1950s, Southern Pine Lumber Company placed a heavy barrier of railroad rails to protect the grave from cattle and hogs. *Photo by the author, June 2014.*

Lifelong partners in conservation work across Texas, Buddy and Ellen Temple at Little Boggy, November 2014. *Courtesy of The History Center, Diboll.*

In 2018, trustees of the T. L. L. Temple Foundation posed with the Cochino loblolly, the largest loblolly pine tree in Texas, according to the Texas Forest Service. From the left: W. Temple Webber III, Secretary-Treasurer Jay Shands, Vice-Chair Hannah Temple, Ellen Temple, William "Spence" Spencer (kneeling), Tom Darmstadter, Chair Charlotte Temple, David Webber, and Jack Sweeny. *Photo by the author.*

A grove of young pines glow in the golden morning sunlight as the moon sets behind them, at Rayville in the Boggy Slough Conservation Area, September 2017. *Photo by the author.*

Southern Pine Lumber Company Engine 13, a former Texas Southeastern Railroad locomotive, pulls a log train from Boggy Slough to Diboll, ca. 1959. *Courtesy of The History Center, Diboll.*

A black-crowned night heron perches on the bank of Boggy Slough, October 2016. *Photo by the author.*

A view of the stream Boggy Slough from a kayak, September 2017. *Photo by the author.*

A modern forest road traverses an old Southern Pine Lumber Company railroad line that leads to Cedar Creek, November 2018. *Photo by the author.*

A view of one of Cochino Bayou's many stream channels near the Neches River, November 2018. *Photo by the author.*

View of an abandoned Texas Southeastern Railroad trestle at Vair from a kayak, August 2014. *Photo by the author.*

An abandoned Texas Southeastern Railroad trestle over a branch that drains into Cochino Bayou, August 2000. *Photo by the author.*

American beautyberries thrive below pine stands kept open through prescribed burning. *Photo by the author, 2014.*

View of a logging tract about eight months after a selective harvest. *Photo by the author, 2015.*

A prescribed fire in the north end of Boggy Slough Conservation Area, late January 2017. *Photo by the author.*

Results of a prescribed burn in the south end in March 2018 about six weeks after the fire. *Photo by the author.*

A view of new sprouts from the basal roots of burned shortleaf pine seedlings at Boggy Slough Conservation Area, 2017. Shortleaf pines are the only southern yellow pine species capable of resprouting in this way. *Photo by the author.*

Buddy Temple displays a deer he killed at Boggy Slough on November 20, 1953, posing in front of the Southern Pine Lumber Company offices at Diboll. *Courtesy of The History Center, Diboll.*

Clara Silvers, wife of rider John Silvers, on her horse at the Rayville corrals in the 1920s. *Courtesy of The History Center, Diboll.*

BOGGY SLOUGH
Hunting and Fishing Lodge
DIBOLL, TEXAS

A Boggy Slough Hunting and Fishing "Lodge" postcard from the early 1950s. *Photo courtesy of The History Center, Diboll.*

Two views of logging operations at "the old farm" near Lottie Temple Deer Stand 22 in 2014. The site was earlier farmed by Charlie Harber's family during the late 1920s and early 1930s and during the late 1850s and early 1860s by the Britton and Rose families of Guernsey County, Ohio. The pines being harvested here were planted during the late 1950s and early 1960s. *Photos by the author.*

Stretches of barbed wire, remnants of Boggy Slough's early cattle ranching heritage, still linger over much of the conservation area, especially in the minimally managed bottomlands, as here in March 2018. *Photo by the author.*

Spring flooding of the Neches River inundates much of the conservation area's bottomlands, like Boggy Slough Island here in March 2018. *Photo by the author.*

A red-tailed hawk watches over a clearing at the old Sullivan home place in March 2018. *Photo by the author.*

A white-tailed deer near Rayville in March 2018. *Photo by the author.*

One of several protected nesting sites for Red-cockaded Woodpecker colonies in the Boggy Slough Conservation Area, October 2014. *Photo by the author.*

A great blue heron (*Ardea herodias*) glides over one of the conservation area's many bottomland lakes in November 2016. *Photo by the author.*

Two views of budding petals of pale purple cone-flowers (*Echinacea sanguinea*) in May 2015 at the Mount Pisgah Cemetery. *Photo by the author.*

The rare Neches River rose mallow (*Hibiscus dasycalyx*) thrives in marshy areas within the Boggy Slough Conservation Area. These buds and blooms in the southern end of BSCA were photographed in August 2014. *Photo by the author.*

A great egret (*Ardea alba*) stands on the end of a laydown log and looks down the Neches River in November 2016. *Photo by the author.*

Timber rattlesnakes (*Crotalus horridus*), like this nearly six-footer photographed in the sandy uplands of North Boggy in August 2014, can be found throughout the Boggy Slough Conservation Area. *Photo by the author.*

The Land Fenced

Ranching, Tenant Farming, and the Birth of Forestry

Natural life in North America has been more profoundly affected by fencing than by any other of man's devices, ancient or modern, for it is the fence which has enabled him to multiply at will those species which minister to his wants, while suppressing plants and animals which do not.

—ROY BEDICHEK (1947)

One of the ironies of the Boggy Slough Conservation Area is that although it became a place famous for big trees and modern forest and wildlife management practices, it was something far different during the first several decades of Temple ownership. Boggy Slough was first a demonstration property, not for forestry, but for the conversion of cutover forestlands to grazing lands. After the initial industrial cutting of Boggy Slough's pine and hardwood forests between 1907 and about 1913, T. L. L. Temple and his managers hoped for a second cutting of pine at some point in the future. The early logging crews had encountered a number of small-diameter pine and hardwood trees that were considered unmerchantable at the time, so they left those trees standing for a later cutting when their market values would be higher. Initially, Temple's managers were unsure when the harvest of what they called a "second

crop" of the fast-growing pine species would occur, but they had witnessed encouraging, even surprising, growth of young shortleaf pine timber on the cutover Copes lands at Diboll more than a decade earlier, and they hoped the small pines they left standing at Boggy Slough would do the same. Gazing any further than a couple of decades into the future yielded only a blur, as they relied mostly on their own experience to guide them. In the meantime, Temple's managers needed some way for the Boggy Slough lands to provide income and earn their carrying costs, since Southern Pine Lumber Company now *owned* most of those tracts, unlike the Copes lands, which were essentially leased during limited periods of time.

Although what is now Boggy Slough Conservation Area accounted for only 13 percent of Southern Pine Lumber Company's land holdings in 1913, it had distinctive natural as well as man-made attributes that made it more appealing to Temple's managers than any other acreage they owned. Boggy Slough was not only a relatively large and contiguous block of cutover lands, but it featured more than two dozen miles of the Neches River as well as three railroads running through the property. Hopes for continued commercial opportunities seemed promising.

One of the earliest challenges to any long-range commercial plan for Boggy Slough, however, was the fact that within the company properties there remained a number of small inholdings—totaling nearly 3,000 acres—whose settlers were at first content to sell their timber but not the land from which they still received their livelihoods. Some of these lands were now into the third and fourth generation of family ownership, but those later generations who were born to the land now found it increasingly difficult to earn their livings from it within the new industrialized economy. Fearful that these inholdings would revert to public auction because of nonpayment of taxes by their owners, the company pressured the remaining families to sell their land titles, transfer their hog marks (unique identification markings, usually ear notches, that owners gave to their hogs and recorded them in county courthouses), and move away. This eventually happened, but only after a decade or more of reluctance and even resistance by the homesteaders and their extended families. Still others remained on the land into the 1930s, as contractual tenants of Southern Pine Lumber Company, as part of a legal exercise to perfect titles, as there was concern for ownership challenges through adverse possession by limitation if squatters and open range herdsmen lingered unchecked. Also, early-twentieth-century land titles were often circuitous even under the best of conditions, but they were especially thorny in rural Trinity County, where the courthouse had burned twice during the nineteenth century. Just sitting back and waiting for trees to grow, depending solely on the goodwill of neighbors, tenant farmers, and free-ranging stockmen and hunters to protect the cutover land and its second-growth pine timber from wildfire and theft was not an option. There needed to be a way to occupy the land while making it pay its way.

A fenced cattle ranch seemed a practical solution for several reasons. The sudden removal of the high forest canopy of upland pines and bottomland hardwoods opened the forest floor to vast amounts of sunlight, causing an explosion of early successional vegetation, especially grasses. E. C. Durham, the manager of Temple's Texas Southeastern Railroad, later recalled the dramatic event at Boggy Slough, remembering that during the first couple of springs following timber extractions and subsequent slash removal, "the grass grew luxuriantly" and "provided excellent pasturage."[1] Scientists were just beginning to observe and study the relatively new phenomena of forest succession in East Texas, and they made similar pronouncements, including University of Texas botanist Benjamin Carroll Tharp, who declared that, "upon the ruins of the forest" a veritable grassland "springs into existence."[2]

Constituting a large part of the grasses at Boggy Slough in 1900 were the various tall bunchgrass bluestems (*Andropogon* and *Schizachyrium* spp.). The shade-tolerant pinehill bluestem (*Schizachyrium scoparium*), also known as little bluestem, made up possibly 50 percent of the preindustrial forest floor, while other grasses that were opportunistic invaders of highly disturbed areas, such as slender bluestem (*Andropogon tener*) and broomsedge bluestem (*A. virginicus*) were also present and quickly increased at higher rates than pinehill bluestem once the ground was disturbed by logging activities and the forest canopy was opened. Many other grasses, including the *Panicum* and *Axonopus* species, also increased, but it was the slender bluestem and broomsedge bluestem, commonly called "sage grasses" by Boggy Slough's managers, that were the bane of lumbermen seeking a second cutting of pine, because of the tall grass's characteristic late summer and early fall accumulation of dead, dry, coarsely tangled and matted "rough," through which fire ran readily on any dry day during any season even with only a single year's worth of accumulation.[3] Focusing on individual trees as a commodity, and not on the larger forest as an ecosystem, early lumbermen who looked to a second cutting of pine viewed almost all fire as potential wildfire that might destroy their young timber, which was now many miles distant from their watchful presence after the logging camps had moved away to new territory. Most early lumbermen in Texas gave little thought to actively using controlled fire as

Captain J. J. Ray and his "pasture riders" at Rayville, the Southern Pine Lumber Company Ranch headquarters, ca. 1920, now the Boggy Slough Conservation Area. Left to right, Herman Midkiff, Emery Midkiff, Hugh Gibson, Walter Robinson, John J. Ray, and John Silvers. *Courtesy of The History Center, Diboll.*

a management tool. Instead, they believed cattle could limit the fire hazard by eating the grass and trampling out trails that would serve as crude firebreaks. At the same time, they believed cattle could graze the grasses profitably. Furthermore, since pasture-riding ranch hands could serve extra duty as timber patrolmen, managers believed the simultaneous protection of a "second crop" of pines and the raising of livestock could be compatible, even synergistic, businesses. Boggy Slough's early managers gave little thought to a possible "third crop" of pines, and instead they managed toward the best use of Boggy Slough as a demonstration property for the gradual conversion of cutover land to pastureland.

The important job of selecting the person to initiate and manage the Boggy Slough ranch fell to Lewis Daniel Gilbert, Southern Pine Lumber Company's general manager. Oral tradition says Gilbert once worked on a hay hauling crew near Fort Worth during his orphaned youth, and he remembered a tough, experienced cow man of the area named John Jones Ray, "J. J." for short, whose rough demeanor and rugged appearance, which had earned him the title of "Captain Ray," made him a likely

candidate for the ranch manager's position. When Gilbert approached Ray about the Trinity County job, Ray was managing a cattle ranch on cutover pine lands in Hot Spring County, Arkansas, near Malvern.

J. J. Ray was a native of Georgia, but he grew up in Texas, in Archer and Erath Counties, and was said to have been a veteran of the Chisolm Trail. Ray also was known as an associate of the celebrated Texas Ranger captain Bill McDonald, who earlier, in 1909, declared Trinity County a "hopeless field of reform," according to McDonald's biographer Albert Bigelow Paine, who was also a biographer of the famous author Mark Twain. Ironically, as Boggy Slough's ranch manager, Captain Ray would find himself working alongside Southern Pine Lumber Company employees R. E. Minton and the Kenley brothers, whose arrests for gunning down Texas Ranger James Dunaway and former County Attorney Howard Robb in 1907 were a major influence on Ranger McDonald's views of the region in the first place. "You've got to stand over a place like that with a gun to make it behave," McDonald warned, and the counsel was not lost on Ray, who, at the seasoned age of forty-five years, in spite of the challenges awaiting him, accepted Gilbert's offer to move to Boggy Slough and head up the Southern Pine Lumber Company Ranch in the spring of 1913. A few years later Gilbert reflected on his decision to hire Ray as the

The home of rancher J. J. Ray at Rayville in 1919. Left to right, J. J. Ray, unidentified, unidentified, Frank Rushing, Josie Freeman Rushing, Joseph S. Freeman, Amy Elizabeth Freeman Rushing holding one-year old Roscoe Paul Rushing, and Charles Ellis Rushing Jr. *Courtesy of The History Center, Diboll.*

ranch manager, and he wrote that Southern Pine Lumber Company was extremely fortunate to have found him, for he was foremost "a man who knew what he wanted to do and how to do it."[4]

In Trinity County, Ray selected the former site of logging Camp No. 1, near the mainline tracks of the TSE Railroad, and there constructed a house for himself and ranch hands and planted a number of pear trees inside a picket-fenced yard. Nearby he built corrals, barns, sheds, loading chutes, a concrete tick eradication dipping vat, and silos for storing corn and other silage crops. Surrounding this area, within a 640-acre tract, he cleared most of the remaining trees except the straightest culled pines, cleared stumps with mules and "stump puller" machines, and turned loose herds of goats to eat out any emergent brush, enclosing the area in hog-proof net wire fencing. This highly improved pasture, along with the corrals, feed lots, and the railroad station and siding, became known as Rayville and served as the ranch headquarters. Known as a calf pasture, Ray used the special 640-acre hog-proof fenced area to acclimatize newly purchased cattle to the range, wean calves, and condition cattle before shipping them to market.[5] Within plank-boarded pens, non-feral hogs were held here, too, where they were fed and fat-

ted before shipping. Additional fence construction during 1913 enclosed a total area of about 10,000 acres within barbed wire. Fencing the expanding boundaries of the ranch continued during the next three summers, as lands north of Cochino Bayou were logged of merchantable timber. Using the rail lines of the TSE and the Eastern Texas railroads, Southern Pine Lumber Company delivered wire and fence posts of both cedar and creosoted pine to Ray's fencing crews.[6] By the end of summer 1916 the ranch consisted of approximately 30,000 acres, all under barbed-wire-fenced enclosures, with multiple cross fences and interior pastures within the larger boundary, as well as fenced lanes and gates to the several homesteaders still remaining. Ray even fenced the east side of the Neches River, across the river from the Boggy Slough property, claiming full water rights to the river.[7] The 30,000 acres consisted of all the property that now makes up Boggy Slough Conservation Area as well as about two thousand acres south of present-day Highway 94 and approximately 8,000 acres north of present-day Highway 7. After Southern Pine Lumber Company abandoned the logging camp at Walkerton, nine miles northwest of Rayville, Ray established additional corrals, a railroad loading chute, and a concrete dipping vat there in about 1920.[8]

A veteran cow man, Ray brought purebred Brahman bulls to the ranch to cross with the best selections of local East Texas cows. From a

Two of J. J. Ray's Brahman bulls at Rayville, ca. 1920. *Courtesy of The History Center, Diboll.*

A Southern Pine Lumber Company feedlot at Rayville, ca. 1920. *Courtesy of The History Center, Diboll.*

1910s commercial ranching perspective, Brahman crossbred stock were ideal for Boggy Slough's climate and range conditions. A hardy and long-lived breed, the Brahman was a proven hustler of less-than-ideal forage and thrived in hot, humid climates, while maintaining good reproduction cycles. Importantly, Brahman crosses provided hybrid vigor and efficiency. Their offspring were capable of grazing at farther distances from water than most other breeds and they were more resistant to flies and ticks, being spared the usual maladies insects caused other breeds, especially Herefords and their "white-faced" offspring.[9] Among the earliest Brahman cattle brought to

East Texas, Ray's purebred Brahman bulls made lasting impressions on early travelers of Highway 94 during the days when the highway passed through the northern section of Bluff Prairie (now Black Cat Lake). Remembering family automobile trips between Apple Springs and Lufkin during the early 1920s, Trinity County native Harrell Odom recalled that the remarkable appearance of Southern Pine's bulls dwarfed his family's diminutive automobiles during rest stops at an artesian well in the prairie. Through childhood eyes, Odom said "the huge, well-fed, humpbacked bulls didn't appear friendly at all," he wrote. "This was a breed of cattle far different from the mix-bred, poorly fed, little knotty-looking cows I was used to being around."[10]

Stocking the pastures began in 1913, and within a couple of years the Rayville Ranch contained, annually, between fifteen hundred and two thousand adult cows, more than a thousand calves, about a

Pasture rider Frank Rushing with his dogs, Rough and Rowdy, ca. 1920. *Courtesy of The History Center, Diboll.*

with Ray in his house at Rayville. Myrtle Nolen Rushing of Angelina County, who visited Rayville often during the 1910s and 1920s, recalled during a 2000 interview that Ray's wife Mary divorced Ray, since "she didn't want to live out there at Rayville, 'cause it was the lonesome-est place in the world." Trinity County census records showed J. J. Ray as divorced in 1920 and widowed in 1930. J. J. Ray's and Mary's two sons, Gilbert and J. J. Jr., who were born in Oklahoma late in the 1890s, did not live with their father as children, although J. J. Jr. later joined his father and eventually settled in Lufkin, where he found occasional employment in railroad work, becoming friends with E. C. Durham and later Arthur Temple Jr.[13]

Much of the history of the Rayville Ranch survives in written sources, such as lumber and railroad company records, but it was perhaps most alive in the memories of Charlie Harber, who lived most of his life on or near the ranch. Charlie was born in 1920 on Bristow Creek, in Houston County, near the Trinity County line, just north of Cochino Bayou. Seven years earlier, his father, Ellis, a tenant farmer and tie-cutter for Southern Pine Lumber Company, worked in the early fencing crews that enclosed the Boggy Slough cutover lands. As a child, Charlie lived "on the old Franklin Place" in North Boggy, which was the former home of the Christie girls' Uncle Doc and Aunt Ginnie Franklin, which straddled the Trinity-Houston County line. He learned to swim at the Walkerton Pond, a reservoir that served to fill the tenders of lumber company steam locomotives and provide water for livestock at the Walkerton corrals. Charlie and his siblings attended school at the Mount Pisgah Schoolhouse, which stood beside the small cemetery where his older brother Lonnie was buried in 1904. Charlie remembered a great sense of community that was shared by all of the ranch's occupants during the 1920s and how Captain Ray regularly provided grand barbecue feasts for his ranch hands and tenant farmers. The day-long barbecues were hosted along Cochino Bayou, which was centrally located to all of the ranch's occupants.[14]

hundred bulls, and a few hundred feeder steers.[11] In addition, at least fifteen hundred hogs, many of which had turned feral following the departure of earlier homesteaders, ranged the ranch's lower slopes and bottoms or anywhere hog-proof net wire fencing did not restrict them.[12] To care for all this livestock, as well as provide protection for the young growing pine timber, Ray hired pasture riders from among the area's residents, including multiple members of the Rushing and Tiner families, who were descendants of early settlers north of Cochino Bayou. From other regions within the pastures as well as just outside of them, Ray hired members of the Oliver, Silvers, Robinson, Midkiff, Gibson, and Tarwaters families. John Silvers Sr. and Walter Robinson became Ray's most trusted hands, while members of the Rushing family lived

Charlie Harber stands at the Walkerton cattle dipping vat in 2000. He was born in 1920 on Bristow Creek, less than a quarter-mile from Boggy Slough's perimeter fences, and he learned to swim at the Walkerton Pond. His father Ellis worked on the Southern Pine Lumber Company fencing crews in 1913 and later sharecropped for the company in both North and South Boggy. Charlie worked many years at Boggy Slough as one of Dave Kenley's pasture riders from the 1930s through the 1950s. He later worked for the Eason Lake Hunting Club as a patrolman on Temple lands in Angelina County. *Photo by the author.*

As a child during the 1920s, Charlie Harber watched numerous log trains roll through Boggy Slough. The steam trains carried logs from the Fastrill log camp in Cherokee County, and Charlie recalled the nostalgic movements and sounds made by the chuffing and whistling locomotives. He also remembered that the locomotives sometimes collided with Captain Ray's cattle, goats, and sheep, as well as deer, especially when the animals found themselves in a high-banked "cut," where the level roadbed cut through the sides of steep hills. Once, Charlie said, Engine 13, now on display at The

History Center in Diboll, even took the life of his new colt that his father had gifted him.[15]

Early in the 1930s, Charlie Harber lived on one of Rayville's farms south of the western end of Britton Slough, where Lottie Temple's Deer Stand 22 was placed years later. Harber said that his family was the last "to farm for the company" there, growing corn and cotton. A few years later, in those same abandoned fields, Harber planted rye grass for the cattle of Dave Kenley, who employed him as a cowhand and timber and game patrolman for many years. In the middle 1930s, Harber lived in a house he helped to build near Morgan Branch, a feeder stream of Cochino Bayou, near the old railroad station of Neff, which was the home of pasture rider Ab Grumbles and his family. The Grumbles house, which still stands in a dilapidated state, guarded Whiskey Gate, named because of a long-gone saloon located just outside of Boggy Slough. Although Charlie himself was a pasture rider at Boggy Slough, working for Dave Kenley from the late 1930s through the 1950s, he considered the earlier Southern Pine Lumber Company riders, whom he called "the old Rayville cowboys," as the last true cowboys, remembering his brother-in-law Walter Robinson, who married Charlie's older sister Viola, as "the finest horseman" he ever knew.[16]

John O. Booker Jr., who lived in Groveton as a boy during the 1920s, while his father worked as an engineer for the state highway department, also had fond memories of the Rayville cowboys, which he said all wore high-top, lace-up boots. He recalled in one oral history interview that his father and mother were friends with Captain Ray, and the Booker family often visited the Ray house. Booker particularly remembered that one of Ray's cowboys "played a guitar and sang." "I was real impressed by that," he said, "because I had seen them in the movies, and [now here] was a real cowboy" that was playing and singing.[17]

Edd Kenley, one of Dave Kenley's sons, also remembered the early Rayville cowboys from his childhood. "They all wore leggings," he recalled in a 2000 interview, "and they all carried

Pasture rider John Silvers with his horse and dog at Rayville, ca. 1920. Note the scattered corn husks and the hog in the background. *Courtesy of The History Center, Diboll.*

Raymond Silvers, son of rider John Silvers, poses in front of the Ray house in the 1920s. *Courtesy of The History Center, Diboll.*

pistols and wore big spurs." They were "real working cowboys," he said, often riding 20 miles a day in driving cattle through the various pastures. He also remembered the Ray house, where Josie Rushing, wife of cowhand Frank Rushing, did all the cooking and housecleaning for Ray and several of his hands. Young Edd stayed there with his father during frequent ranch visits during the 1930s and 1940s. Like Charlie Harber, Edd also remembered the log trains that passed daily in front of the Ray house, some stopping to deliver ice from the ice plant at Diboll. Remembering "Captain Ray," Edd Kenley described a peculiar test the veteran cow man devised to determine a

new rider's abilities. Ray would "get the man a half-broke horse and send him over to the neighbors to get two dozen eggs with an old burlap bag to carry them in," he said. Ray had instructed the neighbor to send back two watermelons along with the eggs. The rider was to carry the eggs in the bag slung over his shoulder, tote the two melons, and "get down and open the gap, get his horse through and close it, then get back on that half-broke horse, and if he could make that and not break too many eggs, well he got the job."[18]

Ranch work included riding and mending fences, herding cattle between pastures, rounding up and penning hogs, marking and branding stock, dipping and shipping cattle, feeding in the winters, and many other ranch tasks, some of which were perhaps unique to a pine-hardwood forest with more than 20 miles of river front-

Clara Silvers, wife of rider John Silvers, on her horse at the Rayville corrals in the 1920s. *Courtesy of The History Center, Diboll.*

One of the Southern Pine Lumber Company pasture riders at the Rayville corral, ca. 1920. Note the stock dog climbing the fence. *Courtesy of The History Center, Diboll.*

The riders also enforced Captain Ray's wishes concerning trespassing and hunting restrictions. Because Ray feared the area's free-range stockmen's dogs, which were employed also to run and hunt deer, would harm his calves and goats, he occasionally instructed his riders to shoot any stock dog found on the ranch that was not one of their own. Keeping the peace under such conditions was no easy task for the riders, since not everyone accepted the large commercial ranch with its long perimeter and cross fences and fenced lanes and gates, especially those who still owned lands within the perimeter fences during the ranch's earliest years and were accustomed to deer hunting wherever they and their dogs chose to roam. Charlie Harber said when his father worked in the fencing crews during the 1910s that Southern Pine Lumber Company issued him a pistol, a .30-30 Winchester, and the instruction, "You are to

age. In the bottoms, alligators were threats to young calves as well as to young hogs. The large reptiles hid in the murky waters and waited for calves and pigs to reach down for a drink. Charlie Harber recalled seeing a thirsty hog totally disappear in muddy slough waters that quickly churned to blood caused by a thrashing alligator devouring his meal. Harber also recalled the challenges that riders faced in rescuing cattle from bogs and rising waters when the creeks and river flooded. He said his brother-in-law Walter Robinson carried scars over much of his body from one particularly bad alligator attack during one of the floods.[19]

protect this place," since fence cutting and woods arson were common retaliatory actions.[20]

Even L. D. Gilbert, Southern Pine Lumber Company's general manager in the Texarkana offices, indirectly engaged Boggy Slough's remnant stockmen farmers, whom he labeled "the native element." In an article appearing in a livestock publication in 1918, Gilbert wrote of Boggy Slough's settlers and area residents, saying, "they take the stand that the Lord gave them this country and the razorback hog, so they make trouble wherever they can, sometimes by cutting fences, but principally by leaving gates open and starting woods fires."[21]

Others who worked at the Rayville ranch recalled experiences similar to those of Charlie Harber's father. In interviews conducted during the 1980s, some, such as J. B. Rushing, reduced their memories of Boggy Slough pasture riding to having simply "worked cattle and fought outlaws."[22] Clyde Thompson, who became Diboll's first mayor in 1962, began his employment with Southern Pine Lumber Company as a bookkeeper at Diboll in 1916. He later recalled that even in that job he quickly learned that "fence cutting [at Boggy Slough] was almost as common as fence building." One of his first assignments was to intercept a northbound passenger train south of Diboll, locate "two men with large hats and boots," and accompany them to Lufkin, making certain that the men remained on the train when it routinely stopped at Diboll. At Lufkin, he was to detrain with the men, who happened to be Texas Rangers sent to investigate fence cutting at the ranch, and escort them to Captain Ray's house at Rayville. Thompson's clandestine assignment, he explained, was designed to hide the unwanted publicity that a Diboll visit by the Texas Rangers would have created.[23]

Partly to defend against local hostilities in ways the pasture riders could not, Southern Pine Lumber Company placed carefully selected tenants on the Boggy Slough farms as soon as the original homesteaders relinquished their claims and vacated the land. The tenants acknowledged no ownership rights, but they accepted a house to occupy and fields to cultivate for personal as well as company gain. They essentially leased the land for a relatively nominal fee and provided a large portion of their farm products—mostly corn and cotton—to the company. In signed agreements, they pledged their loyalty to the company, agreed to "diligently" look after the land and trees; protect the timber from unlawful cutting; prevent and report trespassers; and watch for, report, and fight "forest and grass fires at all times."[24] Thus, Boggy Slough's tenant farmers—like the pasture riders—became, in a very basic sense, early foresters and game wardens who guarded against timber loss and poaching of wildlife. Whether or not anyone recognized it at the time, the company's forest tenancy practice held a curious similarity to the old European custom of nobility and crown setting aside preserves—lands reserved from reclamation and traditional fire practices—in the hopes of ensuring a restocking of trees and a protected supply of wildlife for privileged classes to hunt.[25]

When the Boggy Slough ranch began, there were already a number of agricultural fields, especially in the north end, so Ray kept many of them under cultivation—more than a thousand acres—for tenants to grow cotton to sell and raise feed crops for the cattle.[26] In addition to managing the cattle and hogs, Ray's ranch hands also tended to the various needs of the tenant farmers, at times collecting rents and relaying messages concerning the planting and harvesting of crops.[27] Whenever cotton markets plunged, such as during the near-record market lows of the middle 1920s, T. L. L. Temple instructed Ray not to sell the ranch's cotton those years, but to store it "in a good dry place," until higher prices returned.[28] At other times, such as during anticipated boll weevil outbreaks, Temple and Gilbert directed that all company crop lands that were not intended for cattle feed to be planted "entirely with food stuff." Fear of the boll weevil was especially great in the spring of 1917, so Gilbert instructed tenants to plant only corn, peas, peanuts, and sweet potatoes that year, guaranteeing each tenant $1.00 per bushel for corn, $1.25 per bushel for peanuts, $2.50 per bushel for peas, and $1.00 per bushel for sweet potatoes, "with the privilege of selling for higher prices on the outside" if they chose.[29]

Tenants often obtained personal loans from local banks to finance their crops. When bankers sometimes wrote to Dave Kenley, asking him to endorse tenants' notes, Kenley usually replied by explaining that "the land we farm" was only "incidental to our business," and as a matter of policy, he preferred not to involve himself "closely" in the finances of tenants. Nevertheless, he occasionally vouched for those he knew the best.[30]

Although most of the Boggy Slough company farms were located north of Cochino Bayou, some of the last lands to be farmed for cotton and corn were in the south end, along a creek that feeds into Britton Slough. Here a field of more than 300 acres, in the center of which company officials later placed a deer stand that became known as Lottie Temple's Deer Stand 22, was farmed well into the 1930s. Charlie Harber recalled that when his family relocated there in the early 1930s, he "was the last person to stick a plow in the ground there." It was fertile soil, he said, "but you couldn't farm, due to the deer. Back then, they [deer] eat up stuff faster than you could plant it."[31] By the late 1920s, Boggy Slough also contained a number of resident state game wardens, and they too participated in the farming. In March 1931 Boggy Slough game warden M. E. Parker grew a giant turnip that measured 33 inches in circumference. News of "the monster vegetable" made state newspapers, with the *Lubbock Morning Avalanche* reporting that Parker carried the turnip to Lufkin, where it weighed twelve pounds, although Parker claimed it earlier weighed fifteen "when it was in full leafage."[32]

Harber, Kenley, and others who knew early Boggy Slough well, all stressed the fact that Rayville was "a big ranch for East Texas." As a commercial operation, Ray sold the company's calves, steers, and hogs through livestock commissions at Fort Worth and St. Louis, usually during the fall, moving the livestock by railroad over the rails of the TSE to Lufkin, then over the Cotton Belt lines beyond. Records of TSE Railroad for the rep-resentative year 1924 showed the ranch shipped 521 tons of cattle that year. Ray usually shipped between fifty and two hundred head of steers at a time, averaging between 700 and 1,000 pounds each. Depending on market conditions as well as sanitary board rulings to restrict the movement of the Texas cattle tick fever, occasionally steers were held until they averaged between 1,200 and 1,600 pounds a head, before selling them.[33] Hogs, also, were rounded up, at least 150 head at a time, depending on the particular year's acorn crop, and shipped to market.[34]

Shipping livestock by rail caused them considerable stress, and records revealed that "poor rail service" or other delays often resulted in the inability to adequately feed and water the animals. This caused weight loss, illness, and sometimes death. In October 1919 one carload of cows took nearly a week to reach the Fort Worth livestock yards, costing the ranch a financial loss equivalent to a hundred pounds per head, Ray figured.[35] Ray, always anxious at shipping time, usually accompanied the cattle to ensure their safety and vigor, and when damages occurred, he provided firsthand information to E. C. Durham and R. E. Minton, who filed the many livestock legal claims against the carriers.

Although Ray shipped most calves and steers by rail, he also butchered some at the Rayville slaughterhouse, which supplied fresh beef to the Diboll company store. When the State Sanitary Board placed bans on shipping cattle because of periodic outbreaks of cattle tick fever, the ranch provided steady supplies of beef to all of the Temple mills and logging camp stores. During such times, Dave Kenley felt the Temple companies realized about the same income by "eating the entire calf crop up," and not "saving any of it," than if they had been allowed to ship the calves to Fort Worth or St. Louis anyway. For example, Kenley's plan during a 1923 shipping ban was to slaughter all that season's calves, which averaged 150 pounds dressed, each, and transfer the meat by a one-ton truck to Diboll, Hemphill, and Pineland, taking 600 pounds of beef to each place twice a week.[36]

Brahman-crossed steers at the Rayville feedlots, ca. 1920. Captain Ray's house is in the right background, just past the railroad tracks, and a goat shed is in the left background. *Courtesy of The History Center, Diboll.*

A Rayville feedlot and calf pasture, ca. 1920. *Courtesy of The History Center, Diboll.*

various bluestems in the hills; the sedges, eastern gamagrass, and panic grasses in the meadows; and canes in the bottoms—had sustained animals on the move. Even the cattle of the nineteenth-century settlers largely roamed, free of enclosing fences, and the most nutritive grasses were essentially preserved. Now, under fenced enclosures, high-quality forage such as pinehill bluestem, giant cane, switch cane, Virginia wild rye, big bluestem, and Indian grass, which were relished by livestock, almost disappeared with heavy grazing. At the same time, other high-quality forage, such as eastern gamagrass and wood oats, also declined significantly. In their places, less palatable and less nutritive grasses, which also were generally prolific seed producers, such as broomsedge bluestem, slender bluestem, tumble windmill grass, longspike tridens, bushy bluestem, and pineland threeawn, actually increased on the deteriorating range, as cattle avoided them during all but the briefest

While livestock market conditions proved challenging, the largest burden facing the ranch as a money-making venture was maintaining sufficient year-round forage to support the large herds of cattle that Southern Pine Lumber Company's officials demanded. Although the initial disturbance effect of industrial logging and crosstie procurements, along with slash and brush removal, created what managers called "excellent pasture for two or three years," the once "luxuriant" forage grasses seemed to disappear overnight, as the most palatable and nutritive native grasses, all of which were sensitive to heavy grazing, receded.[37] For centuries Boggy Slough's native grasses—the

Captain Ray and his riders at the Rayville corrals and loading chutes, ca. 1920. *Courtesy of The History Center, Diboll.*

seasons of tender growth.[38] Broomsedge and bushy bluestems, for instance, prolific invaders of disturbed sites, had such fleeting palatability that one of their common names during the nineteenth and early twentieth centuries was "poverty grass," since cattle would literally starve to death before touching them. Much earlier, Spanish governor Don Domingo Terán de los Ríos noted the unpalatability of East Texas broomsedge and bushy bluestem grasses during the fall and winter months. As the governor traveled across East Texas during November and December of 1691, he noted in his journals that his mules and horses "did not like" the pasturage they encountered, "because it was so coarse." Instead, he said his livestock "much preferred the moss that [grew] on the trees." The lack of palatable grasses caused the governor's entire mission to be a dismal failure. He said he and his men proceeded "practically afoot," because they lost all of their spare horses to starvation, "in spite of the fact that not one of them had been ridden."[39] And so, ironically some of the very grasses that Boggy Slough's ranch managers most wanted to control by grazing tended to be the ones cattle most disliked and that most increased. Furthermore, plants that were not grazed at all by cattle, such as woolly croton, commonly known as goatweed, appeared as additional indicators of a range badly overgrazed and widely trampled under cattle hooves.[40]

The majority of the forage grasses that remained at Boggy Slough were most palatable and nutritious during narrower windows of time, mainly from spring into early summer. By late summer, however, the relish at which cattle grazed them

declined significantly, as the leaf growth and flower stalks became coarse and less palatable. Thus, sustaining some kind of nutritious forage during the long fall and winter months became critical. Switch cane and giant cane (*Arundinaria*), which once grew in abundance along the creek and river bottoms and plains, was excellent year-round forage. It was high in protein, phosphorus, and calcium, but it was already in relative decline because of earlier use by settlers, who, in addition to grazing their livestock in the cane, converted portions of the cane bottoms to agricultural fields, especially sugarcane crop lands. What native cane remained was simply not enough to support the sustenance needs of large herds of cattle during the critical winter months when it was needed most.

In place of cane, as well as most other grasses, common carpet grass (*Paspalum platycaule*, or *Axonopus compressus*), which grew in a variety of soils but thrived in moist bottom sites, especially moist sandy meadows, began to spread. Most important to Boggy Slough ranch officials, it was an aggressive sod-forming grass that withstood heavy grazing better than the native bunchgrasses. In fact, it actually increased under heavy grazing, which caused the bunchgrasses to recede, which in turn allowed more sunlight to reach the shorter carpet grass, which spread rapidly through stolons, or runners. Tramping by excessive numbers of hooves did not seem to harm it either, and it was considered at least equal to Bermuda grass in that characteristic. Carpet grass was fair to good in overall forage value throughout the year, but it came to be grazed most valuably by Boggy Slough cattle from fall into early spring, when most other grasses were dry and coarse.[41] While providing nowhere near the nutritive value of cane, carpet grass nevertheless became an important management species at the ranch. So much so that, by the early 1920s, foresters with the US Forest Service inquired about the extensive carpet grass composition of the Boggy Slough pastures. In response, Kenley advised them that he and his fellow managers had learned to "like" carpet grass "better" than the tall bunchgrasses, simply because it responded favorably to heavy grazing.[42] In other words, while the most nutritive tall grasses, such as pinehill or little bluestem, had been eaten to near extinction, Kenley believed the expanding range of carpet grass kept the spread of the coarsest "sage grasses," such as broomsedge and bushy bluestems, at least in check.

As most of the best native range grasses declined, ranch officials refused to accept the fact that the land could offer only so much bounty. Other than managing for carpet grass, they gave little consideration to conserving or fostering the great variety of native grasses, and instead actively introduced nonnative grasses and legumes, which were promoted as both "practical" and "improved." In an effort to grow green winter pastures for grazing as well as for silage, Gilbert more than once instructed Ray to plant bur clover, a cool-season legume from the Mediterranean region of Europe. It was palatable and nutritious during the cold months, and it provided fertilization to the summer pastures by fixing nitrogen in the soil. Often planted in combination with Bermuda grass, it was at the time a common management species for winter pasture development across the South. A Texas A&M University publication of the day claimed there was "no better plant" for Texas' winter pastures.[43] But when difficulties occurred in establishing fall plantings at Boggy Slough, Gilbert encouraged Ray to keep trying, saying he knew "for certain" that bur clover was "being successfully grown in soil and under climatic conditions such as we have."

Ranch managers also experimented with a variety of other plants. In 1918 Gilbert thought he had found the perfect forage solution. In April that year, with much anticipation, he sent one hundred plants of kudzu (*Pueraria montana*) by express delivery to

Diboll, instructing Southern Pine officials there to rush them to the ranch immediately upon receipt. Along with the plants, Gilbert sent an agricultural "catalogue" and directed Ray's attention to specific sections that touted kudzu as "a very prolific forage plant." Gilbert instructed Ray to plant the kudzu, "as a trial under the most favorable conditions possible." The plantings of kudzu, arguably the South's most infamous invasive weed, capable of killing trees and damaging forests beneath its "prolific" crawling rope-like vines, did not establish. Ray's cattle must have even overgrazed them, and the land's feral hogs probably took their share as well. Nevertheless, in spite of such failures to establish many of the exotic and "improved" grazing and forage species, Gilbert reminded Ray "it is up to us to experiment with improved grasses and forage crops until we can learn what kinds are best suited to our soil and climate, for in that lies the possibility of increasing the number of stock we can carry at the least cost."[44]

And so, instead of backing off stocking numbers, company officials charged managers to actually "increase" the land's carrying capacity for cattle, in spite of declining range conditions. As early as 1918, Ray was winter feeding much of the Boggy Slough cattle herd at least three months out of the year. Forced to supplement the more than 300 acres of silage crops of corn, sorghum, and cowpeas from the Southern Pine farms at Boggy Slough as well as from other resources, Southern Pine ran up costly winter feed bills by purchasing railroad carload shipments of cottonseed cake and meal.[45] Seeking to minimize this expense, T. L. L. Temple soon acquired a number of cottonseed mills in Arkansas and eastern Oklahoma. In 1921 he organized, as an ancillary business to his cattle operation, the Temple Cotton Oil Company, which owned and operated cottonseed mills at Hope, Little Rock, Arkadelphia, Ashdown, and Idabel. Thus, in addition to owning a winter feed supply that could be shipped to the Boggy Slough ranch, Temple had an option to ship Southern Pine Lumber Company's cattle to his cottonseed mills and feed them there, with the additional possibility of shipping them on to Kansas markets.[46]

Another environmental factor affecting the profitability of running large herds of cattle in a second-growth shortleaf pine-hardwood forest was the proliferation of hardwood "brush" that appeared following the initial harvesting of mature trees. The same disturbance effect that brought the initial lush grasses awakened woody competition as well. Yaupon and persimmon sprouts became especially aggressive following logging. Also, lowly shrubs of oaks—post oak, blackjack, sandjack, and red oak—as well as sweetgum, which had maintained juvenile statures of slender sterile shoots only a foot or two in height under the high forest canopy, were stirred to active competition once the sunlight flooded the forest floor following the soil and canopy disturbances caused by logging. In 1904, University of Texas botanist William L. Bray and others wrote of this emergent "scrub oak" characteristic of the commercially harvested shortleaf pine forests in Texas, identifying it as a major challenge to further land use.[47] United States forester Charles Mohr had written even earlier, saying in 1897 that the emergent hardwood growth in Texas' shortleaf forests soon shaded "the ground completely" after the "removal of the pine."[48]

The concept of advanced forest regeneration, which Boggy Slough's managers wrestled with for the first time, had been identified earlier in other parts of North America. During the 1850s, Henry David Thoreau, who probably pioneered the term "forest succession" while surveying woodlots in Massachusetts, wrote of "many little oaks" within mature white pine forests which sprung "immediately" to trees "once the pines [were] cleared off." In a way, pines were nurseries to oaks, he said.[49] But while Thoreau stressed that the "many little oaks" must have been planted earlier by squirrels that carried acorns into the pine groves "unnoticed," Bray and other Texas scientists emphasized the already well-established roots of oaks, which ran horizontally just beneath the ground's surface. Bray wrote that while the small oaks were almost imperceptible beneath tall shortleaf pines, their roots sent forth extensive shoots and sprouts immediately following removal of the pine canopy.

Whether from acorns planted by squirrels or from long-established roots, the result was the same: the removal of the southern yellow pine canopy released emergent hardwoods that lumbermen considered to be unworthy of succession since they believed them "incapable of attaining commercial size and quality," only "form[ing] a dense jungle that prevent[ed] the growth of valuable species"— meaning pine. Most annoying to Boggy Slough's early managers, the broad leaves and vigorous growth of shrubby emergent hardwoods shaded the grass and prevented its increase.[50]

Initially, Rayville's managers thought it would be a relatively simple matter to eradicate the emergent brush.[51] In an effort to encourage as well as maintain pastures under Boggy Slough's young pines, Ray and Kenley continued for several years to release extensive herds of goats to browse out the underbrush, similar to the way the homesteaders had done to control the brush that often accompanied farmland clearing, but at a much grander scale. Goats arrived at Boggy Slough by railroad from all over the state, including some in multiple carloads from "somewhere west of Houston," as Durham could not always recall the precise locations in his reports to T. L. L. Temple.[52] Locally, herds came from Angelina, Cherokee, and Sabine Counties.[53] Southern Pine Lumber Company imported so many goats that sheep and goat ranchers across the Southwest began to inquire of ranching prospects in the region. In April 1918 Kenley received interest from a man in Palacios, along Matagorda Bay, who said he recently sold his New Mexico sheep ranch and was thinking of relocating to East Texas. Kenley replied there was little hope for a thriving sheep business in East Texas, but he encouraged the rancher's interest in the goat business, explaining that Southern Pine Lumber Company held one thousand Spanish and three hundred Angora goats in Trinity County alone and many more were welcome.[54] By 1920 Rayville was home to some three thousand head of goats, and a later estimate, perhaps an exaggeration, placed the number as high as ten thousand.[55]

A migrant Mexican goatherder stands in a field of woolly croton (also known as goatweed) among a herd of Southern Pine Lumber Company brush-eating goats and a small stock dog at Rayville in 1918. *Courtesy of The History Center, Diboll.*

Spanish goats, long famous as brush eaters, were effective in controlling undesired vegetation in some Boggy Slough areas, especially immediately around the Rayville headquarters, where Ray built them a large, painted two-story goat house.[56] For the ranch overall, however, they ultimately failed to keep up with the emergent woody vegetation. "The cut over land everywhere," Kenley once conceded, was unrelenting in "springing up" more and more brush, regardless of the efforts they made to contain it. Gradually the goats simply died out. The most common blame was the damp and humid climate, which pasture riders believed caused hoof rot disease. As for the long haired, "wooly" Angora goats, Charlie Harber said the pasture riders often "found them hung up in briars, dead," since the brush, especially yaupon, was so thick in places.[57] Wolves too, undoubtedly took their share of the goats. Durham reported in November 1926 that packs of "timber wolves" were "destroying" Ray's goats and were boldly approaching Ray's house, becoming "a nuisance." No one in Texarkana needed to be alarmed, however, Durham wrote, for Ray had "a scheme for exterminating them."[58] Predator species such as wolves had no place in Rayville's highly managed agricultural and ranching economy. The details of Ray's extir-

pation plans remain unknown, but photographic evidence and oral histories confirm the company did employ a number of government trappers.[59]

Early pasture creation also consisted of work crews chopping and cutting vegetation, especially "in the hills," while occasionally they deadened, by girdling, "mature trees of the kinds which were valueless."[60] A real boon to the creation of pastures occurred between November 1916 and December 1918, when the company supplied cordwood to a federal government contractor as part of World War I mobilization and support efforts. Cordwood came from the Boggy Slough ranch as well as from the mills. Waste slabs from the hardwood mill at Diboll, including sweetgum, furnished some of the wood. Durham wrote to T. L. L. Temple in November 1916, saying, "I don't know what our Uncle Sam is going to say when he tries to burn some of Southern Pine Lumber Company's green gum slabs."[61] Although mill refuse made up some of the shipments, Rayville became the focus of what company officials called "the government wood business," whereby remaining and otherwise unmerchantable hardwood trees were cleared for handsome profit. In addition to Southern Pine Lumber Company receiving pay for the wood itself, TSE Railroad Company received one dollar per cord of wood carried "from any station on our line," E. C. Durham proudly reported to Temple. This was important because the primary logging operations for the Diboll mills had moved to San Augustine County in 1915, leaving the northern section of the TSE lines without any steady revenue freight business until after the war. Since T. L. L. Temple pressed Durham regularly to "dispose" of the TSE Railroad, or at least the portion in Trinity and Houston Counties, Durham was especially pleased to report by March 1917 that the TSE moved cordwood every day from Rayville and Diboll, some of it going to Fort Bliss. With Dave Kenley in charge of the wood-cutting crews, Durham reported with amazement the volume of wood produced. At times, five to ten carloads of cordwood a day shipped, which was remarkable considering that all otherwise "merchantable" timber had been removed just a few years earlier, including large pine and hardwoods for the Diboll mills and medium-sized hardwoods for crosstie manufacturing.[62]

The government cordwood operations cut everything large enough to make a stick of firewood. Pine was generally excluded, except occasionally it was thinned from thickets where the growth was determined too thick for optimum regeneration.[63] To increase both cordwood production and pasture development, Kenley hired what he called "a large force of Mexicans," late in 1917, and went to Laredo to make arrangements for wage payments to the men's families who remained in Mexico.[64] Kenley employed the men at cutting and hauling cordwood and also in deadening smaller hardwoods by girdling them. T. L. L. Temple soon received steady reports from Durham of Kenley "making daylight in the thickets around Rayville and . . . getting more Mexicans every day or so."[65] Durham also employed some of the men in railroad maintenance work on TSE Railroad's Lufkin branch, but the majority of them, between 100 and 165 men at a time, labored in the brush clearing at Boggy Slough.[66] Throughout the two years of government cordwood production, Durham said he was "glad to get the business" and was "anxious to move all the wood which [could] be cut," since the unexpected traffic was essentially paying the railroad's taxes and interest costs.[67]

As a result of such intensive clearing, Boggy Slough's aesthetic appearance improved so much

that both Santa Fe and Cotton Belt railroad officials considered purchasing the TSE railroad, mainly "from a stock raising and agricultural standpoint," Durham once told Temple. The hardwood that was "cut off to improve the range and help the young [pine] timber to grow," Durham told Temple in February 1918, encouraged the Santa Fe people especially. The clearing made the "long clean bodies of trees" appealing, he said, but the grass growing beneath the young shortleaf timber looked just as attractive. Early in June 1918, Durham proudly reported to Temple that Santa Fe's "industrial agent and a government man" spent a Sunday afternoon and all of the following day visiting "the ranch." Durham said he was almost certain that Santa Fe would own the TSE rail line "before the year [was] out."[68]

While behind the scenes there was concern about the ranch's sustained profitability, T. L. L. Temple and his managers made every effort to promote the extensive demonstration cattle operation. In 1917 the Southern Pine Association, of which Temple was a director, joined with general businessmen, railroad officials, and state agencies across the South to create a Committee on Cut-Over Lands, which in turn formed the Southern Cut-Over Land Association. This organization served as a clearinghouse to sponsor scientific studies on the utilization of cutover forestlands, which mostly favored their conversion to farms and ranches in order to increase the country's agricultural and livestock production during World War I. Temple made sure that the Boggy Slough ranch would serve the committee's interests by placing L. D. Gilbert as a member of the committee and the association.[69] For his part, Gilbert wrote an article about the Boggy Slough ranch, which appeared in the November 1918 issue of *Cut-Over Lands*, a fledgling St. Louis trade journal edited and published by James E. Gatewood, the longtime former editor of the publications *Age of Steel* and *St. Louis Lumberman*. Proudly printing his journal's mission statement at the top of each issue's front page—"Devoted to the conversion of cut-over timber lands to their most productive use for

Children of the pasture riders feeding hogs at Rayville, ca. 1920. *Courtesy of The History Center, Diboll.*

farming, stock raising, fruit growing and kindred purposes"—Gatewood introduced Gilbert's article as "the most practical and informative" contribution that had appeared in the eight-month history of the journal. Gatewood encouraged "every large land owner in the South" to read it.[70] In the article, Gilbert summarized the steps Southern Pine Lumber Company had taken to establish the ranch, including what he called "the land clearing scheme," and the various trials encountered and lessons still being learned in attempting to sustain high-quality pastures. The article was billed as "practical and informative," containing "facts and not theories." Gilbert presented the ranch's primary challenges as tick eradication, the destructiveness to grasslands caused by razorback hogs, and the opposition to a closed range by the area's residents, who left gates open and set what Gilbert believed to be retaliatory woods fires. Above all these, however, Gilbert stressed the detriments and challenges of emergent hardwood brush. "The soil will grow grass if the sun is permitted to shine on it," he concluded, warning that the brush had to be "destroyed" if there was to be any possibility of commercial success. At the end of the article, he almost forgot to mention that "a good stand of young pine, which doesn't shade the ground to any considerable extent" did remain at the ranch, and he expected the young pine trees to "make rapid

growth, with the other timber and brush removed."[71]

Not surprisingly, Gilbert's article attracted the attention of both the US Forest Service and the newly created Texas Forest Service, whose long-term forest values seemed to be at odds with those of Southern Pine Lumber Company and the Southern Pine Association's Committee on Cut-Over Lands.[72] Although in places at Boggy Slough the young, clean-bodied shortleaf timber indeed appeared impressive, especially in the absence of underbrush, closer inspection by the governments' new university-trained foresters—the title itself new—revealed serious concerns. Believing that small herds of cattle did no serious harm to pine seedlings, foresters knew very well that large herds of cattle, hogs, and goats certainly did, and they questioned the extensive ranching resolve of Southern Pine officials. They also suspected that grazing cattle intensely enough to promote and maintain densely sodded carpet grass adversely affected soil conditions to the point of inhibiting sustained pine regeneration as well.[73]

Whenever questioned by forestry officials, Gilbert responded by confessing that his knowledge of forestry was "only general, with very little in the way of tests and experiments to go by." In fact, as he wrote in 1921 to R. D. Forbes, director of the US Forest Service's Southern Forest Experiment Station at New Orleans, "you might say that all I know of the subject is just from observation from watching the growth of the young timber as well as some of the destructive elements," of which he included mechanical logging and hogs. All the while, Gilbert repeatedly explained that Southern

Pine Lumber Company did not necessarily share the state and federal forest agencies' long-term visions for cutover forest lands, at least not without assistance from the state and federal governments in the form of tax relief or outright government ownership of the land. His defense was simply that Southern Pine Lumber Company managed its lands with no forestry goals beyond a second cutting of pine. "We have not in any case counted on more than two crops of timber," he once wrote to Forbes. To state forester E. O. Siecke, he once explained that his companies remained "uninterested in a third crop, or in protecting the seedling pines for a third crop." Even fire prevention was given "little thought," he said he was "sorry to confess," because the "second crop" of timber was expected to come from logging crews' culled trees, which were about six to ten inches in diameter and whose tall crowns were believed to be "beyond the danger of fire damage."[74]

Yet while Gilbert explained that ranching might be Southern Pine Lumber Company's long-term goal for some of its cutover lands, especially at its "grazing proposition at Diboll," by which he meant Boggy Slough, he also shared personal doubts about its sustainability. As Gilbert saw it, the interests of ranching and growing pine timber shared a common adversary. The recurring hardwood brush, Gilbert once told Forbes, was the "the most serious handicap to the development of the cut-over land." If only there was a way to "successfully destroy" it, then there was every reason to expect "these cutover lands could be made the most valuable grazing lands in the country and at the same time we could be growing pine trees from the seedling."[75]

To learn more of Southern Pine's cutover forestland management, the US Forest Service sent a logging engineer, a native of Maine named Austin Cary, to Diboll early in 1923. After touring Boggy Slough and seeing the double-edged approach to cattle and tree farming, Cary, who would later become known within the forest service as the "father of southern forestry," saw nothing but a land of contradictions.[76] In a nine-page memo to

Southern Pine Lumber Company officials, Cary identified the obvious conflicts as "the interests on the one side of grass, and on the other side of timber," one "versus" the other. Cary acknowledged that high-quality pastures could indeed be established on cutover lands, as demonstrated in the large and highly managed calf pasture immediately surrounding Rayville, but he reminded Diboll officials that it was due only to the "obliteration of all timber, both hard and soft woods." Parts of Boggy Slough, in other words, had become pure pastureland, with no trees. As for other areas of the ranch—especially in pastures that did contain a "second crop" of pine—Cary questioned the persistent efforts to "stay in the [live] stock game." In those areas, especially where carpet grass had not yet taken hold, Cary believed that, "with the hardwoods obliterated and pine preserved, reproduction of the pine promises to obliterate the pasturage."[77] Cary challenged Boggy Slough's managers to choose which master they would serve: grass or trees, ranching or forestry. In Cary's mind there was no middle ground. While addressing an age-old truth—that regardless of a particular spot of earth's natural attributes, man tends to try to shape it into something of his own creation—Cary argued that Boggy Slough's best use was to encourage pine regeneration in the uplands and allow bottomland hardwoods to naturally regenerate in the often overflowed river bottoms. He told Diboll's officials he was confident they would decide correctly, since he knew that "timber growing on your lands is going to look better to you as time passes."[78]

Of course, Cary was right about Boggy Slough. But it would take another generation of Temples and their managers to finally accept, and embrace, the fact. Nevertheless, Gilbert's overall forestry views did change somewhat, and in short time he began to accept the state and federal foresters' recommendations for studies on company lands, writing to state forester E. O. Siecke once to say that he felt obliged "to cooperate" with the Texas Forest Service "in the matter of setting aside

A snowball fight in front of the Ray house following a December 21, 1929, snowstorm, when nearly ten inches of snow fell at the Groveton (Trinity County) weather station. On the far left, holding a giant snowball, is Clara Silvers; on the far right is Vera Crim. They were sisters.

some representative acres of second growth, and also stands of young seedlings and watching the results." He changed his mind, he said, because it was not "too long ago" that he believed "even a second crop" was unlikely."[79]

Thus humbly began Southern Pine's program of "practical forestry," as Gilbert, and later Kenley, called it, which initially entailed simply keeping the company's lands, especially the Boggy Slough ranch, open to state and federal government foresters for observation and study. Gilbert remained so cautious, however, that when the US Forest Service's Southern Forest Experiment Station released its investigative report for 1923, it stated that Southern Pine Lumber Company was "*quietly* investigating the possibility of a perpetual operation for at least one of its mills" (emphasis added).[80]

Throughout the rest of the 1920s, Gilbert instructed Kenley as well as Watson Walker to continue their cooperation with government forestry officials, especially Austin Cary, who introduced them to several progressive lumber companies across the South. Foremost was Crossett Lumber Company of Arkansas, which had begun in 1921 to develop a new "sustained yield" cutting practice modeled after Germany's forest management practices.[81] By 1926, Kenley was well on his way to developing his own version of a sustained-yield policy after investing several years of "studying and working on" what he called "this re-forestry

problem." With Cary's guidance, Kenley analyzed Southern Pine's timber-cutting practices and made extensive tree growth calculations. He wrote to university presses and state geological and economic surveys to request forestry and silvicultural publications, especially new manuals that encouraged the planting of faster-growing loblolly pine.[82] Occasionally, he sent Gilbert interesting publications as he discovered them, including US chief forester William B. Greeley's "Back to the Land" article, which appeared in the March 31, 1923, issue of the *Saturday Evening Post*. In that particular piece, Greeley equated the nation's cutover lands and the declining towns they once supported as being "one with Nineveh and Tyre . . . mostly barren and idle lands, without an industry and almost without a people."[83]

By 1924 Kenley was indeed thinking about a "third crop" of pines, at least from company lands outside of Boggy Slough. In that year he began lightly burning the forests after logging activities, explaining to Gilbert that by "singe[ing] the tops over" during the wet spring season he prevented "the heavy fires" which in the past had swept through their logging slash and destroyed young timber. From other southern forest managers, particularly those in Arkansas and Florida, Kenley learned to use "precautionary fire," when damp conditions allowed it, in order to prevent hotter general fires that destroyed all pines smaller than two inches in diameter and shorter than ten feet in height, especially during dry seasons within two years of logging, while dried pine needles remained on the fallen treetops. Preemptive low-temperature fires during wet times not only prevented a later conflagration, but they allowed saplings to compete against the emergent hardwood sprouts that otherwise prevented pine growth and reproduction. He once explained to Gilbert in 1926 that he thought he remembered T. L. L. Temple had nearly two decades earlier experimentally tried to protect seedlings and saplings on some of the Sepúlveda lands just west of today's Boggy Slough by advising crews to pile and burn the slash within a "cleared-off" area, but Temple thought the labor costs "proved too expensive" and he "abandoned" the practice. Kenley estimated that had Temple found "some practical method" of fully implementing a definite policy of slash control through prescribed burning from that time forward that the company's value "would have been worth a million dollars more" thanks to the resulting increase in production of commercial sawlogs. With such an incentive, Kenley reported that he would continue to "singe the tops" as weather and labor conditions allowed, and he would monitor the results.[84]

Although earlier denounced by such prominent federal foresters as Henry S. Graves, William B. Greeley, and Aldo Leopold as "propaganda," "a fallacy," and "the scourge of wildlife," light broadcast burning did have merit in the yellow pine forests of the South, where it had been advocated by Yale University forestry professor Herman Chapman since at least 1912, during his extensive work with Crossett Lumber Company on their shortleaf pine lands in Ashley County, Arkansas.[85] Chapman argued for many years that prescribed surface fires, if ignited under controlled conditions every six to eight years, not only safely removed the logging slash and debris from the bases of mature trees not yet merchantable—thus protecting them by removing fuel that would have otherwise produced subsequent hot fires—but it also prepared a suitable seedbed for seedlings from the preserved trees, which in turn provided third and fourth crops of pines.[86] Although it could be argued that Kenley and other industry leaders of the

1920s advocated controlled light burning merely to promote and manage monotypic stands of commercial pine sawlogs, the gradual acceptance of fire as a natural tool by industrial owners of timberland in time influenced the prescribed burning practices of today, which seek to broadly manage for natural diversity.

Also by this time, Dave Kenley had begun buying fee title to shortleaf pine lands where Southern Pine Lumber Company had earlier owned only timber rights. And Gilbert became fond of writing that both he and Kenley were "very much interested in watching the growth of long timber in the [cutover] shortleaf forests."[87] By simply cooperating with the state and federal forestry agencies early in the 1920s, Southern Pine Lumber Company earned a reputation as an industry leader in Texas conservation. In 1926 Gilbert became chairman of the East Texas Chamber of Commerce's Forestry Committee and later served as a vice president of the Texas Forestry Association. He was lauded in newspapers across Texas as "widely known as an authority on forestry matters." Until his death late in 1931, Gilbert traveled across the state, often with state forester Eric O. Siecke, Senator I. D. Fairchild of Lufkin, and fellow East Texas lumbermen O. M. Stone of Jasper, Paul Sanderson of Trinity, and Ernest L. Kurth of Lufkin. He delivered educational messages that forestry was a matter of "public welfare . . . equally important for all classes of citizens." He appealed to non-industry owners of what he called "non-agricultural soils"—lands whose soils were best suited for "timber crops"—to give up traditional farming and become tree farmers instead. He shared news that it was Southern Pine Lumber Company's goal to keep forests "continuously productive" and sawmills operating "on a permanent basis," just as any successful farmer would manage his agricultural fields. He delivered speeches with titles such as "The Timber Crop in East Texas" and "Timber Growing as an Industry," both of which borrowed from US chief forester Bernard Fernow's "Timber as a Crop" speech, which he had delivered at the World's Fair way back in 1893, three decades earlier. While highlighting the Temple companies' economic successes, he preached the "great need for missionary work along conservation lines in East Texas," cautioning that the "second crop" would not produce the private or public profits of the past, unless the public joined industry in providing tax relief as well as tax incentives to timberland owners. Still resounding with agricultural language, he said that industry and the public "must husband timber resources" to prevent both from becoming "crippled."[88]

While the beginnings of a true sustained-yield forestry policy took gradual root within Southern Pine Lumber Company, much like the slow but deep-growing taproot of a longleaf pine seedling, the mounting concerns of cattle ranching at Boggy Slough continued to consume ranch managers for much of the 1920s. Southern Pine did not finally practice sustained-yield forestry as an endorsed policy until 1940, and Boggy Slough retained its identity as simply "the ranch" until the 1960s. Although some managers, such as E. C. Durham and Watson Walker, had already surrendered their hopes for cattle-ranching success by 1926, Gilbert—with T. L. L. Temple's consent and support—sought to increase the company's efforts to make it profitable, in effect feeding a white elephant.[89]

To maintain large herds of high-quality cattle, Temple and his managers had purchased more than a thousand goats from all across the state, hired more than one hundred brush-chopping migrant workers from Mexico, and purchased five cottonseed oil mills in Arkansas and Oklahoma. And then, in 1927, Temple was persuaded to purchase nearly 27,000 acres of additional grazing lands in South Texas with the intention of wintering his Boggy Slough cattle there, a decision which negatively affected the Temple companies during the painful years of the Great Depression, when Arthur Temple Sr. was forced to sell the South Texas lands for 60 percent less than what his father had paid for them less than a decade earlier.[90]

At the center of nearly all the ranch decisions during the 1920s and 1930s was Dave Kenley, essentially a cow man himself, who was not the of-ficial Boggy Slough ranch manager, but, as head of Southern Pine's Timber and Land Department, he concerned himself in its affairs whether he was asked to do so or not. Furthermore, Kenley and Gilbert, Durham, Walker, and John E. Hintz were partners in their own cattle company, separate from Southern Pine Lumber Company, running at times some 1,500 head of cattle on thousands of acres of cutover lands in Houston and Angelina Counties, as well as lands in South Texas, all of which Kenley either owned or leased from other landowners, including Southern Pine Lumber Company.[91] Kenley headed up the cattle partnership, which began in 1918, and Gilbert allowed Kenley tremendous liberty in how he conducted its affairs. On one notable occasion in 1925, Gilbert allowed Kenley's partnership—this time including J. J. Ray but excluding Durham—to purchase certain lands and timber in Trinity County for just under $20,000 and then sell those properties to Southern Pine Lumber Company for nearly $93,000, generating profits to each individual in amounts of between $14,450 and $20,000, which each man carried as credits in personal accounts on the books of Southern Pine Lumber Company.[92] At the same time, Kenley ran hogs and cattle with the Midkiff family of Houston County (some of whom were Mr. Ray's riders at Boggy Slough), and later he would partner with other stockmen in the region, including Roy Treadwell of Angelina County and Grady Singletary of Cherokee County, to graze cattle in other locales.[93] Having these management experiences, Kenley was never shy in offering advice to Gilbert in the operations of the Boggy Slough ranch, and Gilbert usually accepted it. When at times Gilbert seemed reluctant, however, Kenley took Southern Pine's ranching matters directly to T. L. L. Temple, whom he believed enjoyed having a large ranch he could "call his own," regardless of its many troubles. In subtle and other ways, Kenley justified his own attachments to raising cattle by encouraging his employer's interests in the pastime as well.[94]

In April 1922, Kenley wrote Temple to say that he made a "research trip" to Fort Worth and found

Southern Pine was selling more than five hundred head of cattle there each fall. He said these cattle were "very fat in the fall," but so were nearly all the other cattle offered during the crowded fall market. Kenley felt Temple was not realizing the full value of his assets, and he explained the need to find a more economical way of feeding the cattle through the winter, and then selling them in the spring market, when profit margins would be greater. The missing component, however, was "winter grass," which Kenley reported he was seeking to locate, having earlier written to several ranchers south of Houston, including William Clayton of Rosenberg.[95] Temple, like Gilbert, did not initially share Kenley's passion for locating winter pastures so far away from Boggy Slough. Kenley remained unrelenting, however, reminding them throughout 1922 how much he disliked "giving away cattle," as he felt Temple and Gilbert were continuing to do.[96] In the meantime, closer to home, Kenley sought more local pasturage for Southern Pine cattle, and with his brother-in-law R. E. Minton negotiated with the Henderson family of Lufkin to lease grazing rights to some 3,700 acres of cutover lands on Pine Island, across the river from Boggy Slough, offering to pay the taxes during the duration of the lease.[97] Working through Lufkin real estate agent P. M. Albritton, Kenley also purchased for Southern Pine Lumber Company the John F. Renfro Ranch, some 9,239 acres of cutover lands in Angelina County, east of Diboll, for $73,026, adding even more grazing options, in addition to more second-growth pine timber reserves.[98]

Early in 1923, Kenley again pitched the South Texas grass idea, but with an additional incentive. Kenley advocated shipping the cattle from Rayville to South Texas grass in the fall and selling them there "ourselves" directly "off the grass" in April and May, saving at least $10 per head versus selling them through the Fort Worth commissions. Also, he reasoned that selling them directly would alleviate the additional expenses and delays associated with dipping the cattle for the control of ticks before transporting them to a distant market. Kenley suggested that Mr. Ray find and lease for

two to three years a South Texas pasture that could take a thousand head of cattle.[99] While Gilbert and Temple quietly mulled over this idea, Kenley offered another proposal later that summer, writing Gilbert to tell him of a visit he made to the Kenley-Gilbert-Durham-Hintz "partnership cattle" that were grazing pastures near Alice, west of Corpus Christi. While there, Kenley said he learned of a ranch for sale, and although he felt it was cheaper to lease grass than to own it, he wanted to mention the property to Gilbert nonetheless in case he was interested. Kenley felt prospects were good for the land purchase to be a "paying proposition" and that certainly "no money would be lost."[100] Gilbert declined the offer, saying he remained fundamentally opposed to "an investment in a ranch down there," but at the same time he acknowledged both Kenley's and Ray's "conclusion that if we are ever to make the Diboll ranch go, we are going to have to have some South Texas grass."[101] Until Gilbert himself could accept that conclusion, however, he urged Kenley and Ray to "make every feasible experiment in the way of brush killing" at Boggy Slough. He made several suggestions, including using crude oil and cutting the brush while it was "hot and dry to see if that will kill it," and he directed them to "work the goats to the best advantage possible." Then in the fall, when the grass was dead enough to burn, but before a desiccating frost, he wanted them "to burn the worst thickness." In summary, he said Kenley and Ray had the rest of the summer as well as the fall to kill the brush again. If those efforts proved unsuccessful during the following spring, Gilbert said he would give them one more year of trying, and if that failed, then he "might" be willing to "give it up as an impossible undertaking."[102]

But through several more seasons, and in spite of the cutover land's natural tendency to regenerate brush, Gilbert's ranching resolve at Boggy Slough remained steadfast. In July 1927, he finally consented to purchasing "South Texas grass." More precisely, he authorized the purchase of 26,899 acres of worn-out sheep grazing land, which straddled Dimmitt and Webb counties, in the northwest edge of the South Texas *brasada*, or "brush country," some 400 miles southwest of Boggy Slough. Known as the Valenzuela Ranch, the property was situated near the town of Catarina, south of Carrizo Springs and about 30 miles southwest of Cotulla, near where Dave Kenley held ranchlands.[103] Previous Valenzuela Ranch owners included prominent sheep ranchers Thomas Kearney and James A. Carr and wool merchant Edward Kotula of San Antonio. By 1927, however, very little palatable grass remained, and so what was conceived to be an adjunct to the "land clearing scheme" and cattle operation at Boggy Slough wound up being yet another money pit, but far from the East Texas pineywoods, just as the Temple Cotton Oil Company was becoming. Probably because Temple Lumber Company already owned considerable real estate through its extensive retail division operations, Gilbert arranged for that company to acquire the Valenzuela Ranch. Then, in January 1931, during the Great Depression, he transferred the ranch to Southern Pine Lumber Company to ease the excessive debts of Temple Lumber Company, which carried a number of other overvalued properties on its financial statements. But regardless which Temple business owned the South Texas ranch, Kenley, Gilbert, and, after 1931, Arthur Temple Sr., spent considerable time trying to lease the land, instead of using it themselves. In 1936, after less than a

decade of owning the property and barely using it, they sold it to San Antonio oil man George W. Lyles for less than half of what they paid for it.[104]

Gilbert died in November 1931, at Boggy Slough while deer hunting.[105] Arthur Temple Sr. ascended to Gilbert's position as secretary and general manager of the Temple companies, after serving as head of the retail lumber sales division. For the first time in a quarter of a century, a Temple was again running the day-to-day operations of the Temple businesses, beginning right in the middle of the Great Depression. The ranch at Boggy Slough would be one of Arthur Temple Sr.'s most unpleasant management experiences for much of the rest of his life, for he had no personal interest whatsoever in cattle. Temple's reorganization efforts during the 1930s placed the Boggy Slough ranch, and even the land, at the center of a retrenchment policy, where everything was reexamined and questioned. Through it all, the ranch illustrated some fundamental truths in environmental history—that nothing happens in a vacuum, that there are natural as well as social implications to every action taken on the land, that all things are connected across space and time, and that there are often unexpected and unintended associations and consequences. As time revealed, one of the ranch's unintended outcomes would dominate the management of Boggy Slough for decades to come, becoming both a blessing and a curse.

CHAPTER 7

The Fenced Land

Game and Wildlife Management

History shows that game management nearly always has its beginnings in the control of the hunting factor. Other controls are added later. The sequence seems to be about as follows: 1, restriction of hunting; 2, predator control; 3, reservation of game lands (as parks, forests, refuges, etc.); 4, artificial replenishment (restocking and game farming); 5, environmental controls (control of food, cover, special factors, and disease).

—ALDO LEOPOLD (1933)

The once-abundant white-tailed deer herds of East Texas, evidenced by Mexican general Terán's inspection of records documenting that some eighty thousand deerskins had traded annually through the Nacogdoches customs house during the 1820s, were—as Terán predicted—soon diminished.[1] Caddo trade of the land's natural resources to French, Spanish, and American agents had already placed heavy pressures on deer and other wildlife by the time settlers from the United States advanced across the land with ax, fire, hoof, and plow during the 1830s. At the same time that land-use patterns changed, which gradually decreased wildlife habitat, the game that remained was simply overhunted. The quest for

the last deer, bear, and turkey was relentless. For several generations the mere sighting of a game animal track brought hunters and their fierce stock dogs out in droves.[2] Boggy Slough tenant farmer and pasture rider Charlie Harber said in 1992 that early-twentieth-century farmers and stockmen "believed in killing whatever they could see. If they found a deer track, it may [have] take[n] them two days with three packs of hounds, but they killed it. That's what happened to the deer."[3]

Yet in spite of such hunting practices, white-tailed deer—which could survive civilization's impact perhaps better than any other animal—persisted in small herds within isolated sections of East Texas well into the 1910s, especially where at least a semblance of protection existed. Boggy Slough became such a place, where the same fences that kept the cattle in and the public out provided a haven for deer. By regularly patrolling and protecting the company's livestock and second-growth timber interests, Captain Ray's pasture riders kept in check not only game hunters but also predator species such as timber wolves and coyotes. Furthermore, some of the early successional, disturbance-induced woody brush and shrubs of the cutover pine-hardwood forest provided necessary browse and cover for deer and other wildlife species, despite the company's attempts to eradicate such vegetation with browsing goats in the promotion of pastures.[4]

Guy Burke, a government trapper, with a red wolf he trapped at the Boggy Slough ranch during the 1920s. *Courtesy of The History Center, Diboll.*

As early as 1915, within two years of fencing the Rayville pastures, E. C. Durham, general manager of T. L. L. Temple's Texas Southeastern Railroad (TSE), began entertaining Tyler and Texarkana officials of the Cotton Belt railroad "at the ranch," where deer hunting was already known as "good sport." Deer had become scarce not only in East Texas, but across the nation, so news of their presence traveled fast among privileged businessmen. By the summer of 1916, reports of "plentiful" deer at Boggy Slough reached the St. Louis offices of the Cotton Belt's top executives. Upon learning of their interest, Durham eagerly extended Boggy Slough hunting invitations to the Cotton Belt's president and his "friends," promising that "everything would be prepared for them."[5] Such "hunting parties," as they were called, became grand sporting entertainments, which allowed Durham to provide business executives with both exciting and relaxing times enjoying the East Texas outdoors: hunting, shooting, fishing, and fellowshipping around a warm campfire. The "parties" also provided excellent opportunities to showcase Boggy Slough's cattle and the adaptive uses of cutover forest lands. In such a setting, Durham garnered good business relations, at the minimum, and at best he hoped to work out a sale of the TSE Railroad.[6]

What began as goodwill extensions to railroad company officials in time became a whole new business model for the Temple businesses, as Southern Pine Lumber Company executives soon joined Durham in entertaining various persons and organizations whose favor would serve their own business interests. On printed identification cards, guests were informed by their hosts, "We have invited you to enjoy our hospitality on this occasion because we like you. We want to know you better and to cement the bonds of friendship now existing into stronger ones."[7] Only grave scheduling conflicts prevented invitees from accepting invitations. Some sacrificed the Thanksgiving holiday away from their families. Others set aside all personal responsibilities, replying, "You couldn't keep me away with a team of horses," or "I'll be there with bells on!"[8]

Besides transportation executives, those invited to partake in the hunting and fishing "privileges," quickly included lumber dealers, dry goods and general store suppliers, officials from various manufacturing and trade organizations, executives of oil and gas companies, bankers, lawyers, physicians, and, most importantly, influential officers of local governments and tax boards, representatives of workers' compensation insurance companies, and state and nationally elected officials. Although the wives of pasture riders and company executives did occasionally deer hunt, for several decades, only men were included in the official hunting "parties." As W. E. Merrem, a longtime official with Houston Oil Company, Southwestern Settlement and Development Company, and East Texas Pulp and Paper Company, wrote in his memoirs, Boggy Slough was known as much for "its abundance of deer" as it was for its boisterous drinking and "loud crap shooting sessions." Temple official Kenneth Nelson once wrote to Arthur Temple Jr. and enclosed a list of all county officials who had been invited to hunt that year, explaining that those counties "where they have women as [Tax] Collectors, of course, they were not invited."[9]

To better manage the outdoor activities and accommodate growing numbers of overnight guests, Southern Pine Lumber Company organized the Boggy Slough Hunting and Fishing Club in 1922 and built a clubhouse on the west bank of Boggy Slough on slightly elevated ground toward the middle-upper end of the slough.[10] At the back of the clubhouse, attorney R. E. Minton constructed an elaborate trolley system for a trot line that stretched the width of the slough, which allowed for baiting and fishing from the bank. The original club comprised eleven members, including T. L. L. Temple and L. D. Gilbert of Texarkana; Watson Walker, W. P. Rutland, Dave Kenley, E. C. Durham, J. J. O'Hara, P. H. Strauss, and J. F. Judd of Diboll; chief counsel R. E. Minton of Lufkin; and company ranch manager Captain J. J. Ray.[11] Among the stated purposes of the club were "the protection and propagation of fish and other game," "the cultivation of the arts of sportsmen with rod and gun," "erecting clubhouses," and "the mutual improvement of the social culture of its members." Importantly, club rules disallowed the use of dogs to hunt deer, which had been a common local practice for decades. Walker, Durham, and Rutland served as early officers, while Captain Ray, being already a resident on the property, served as the club's manager, supervisor, and the clubhouse caretaker.[12]

The clubhouse proved a success from the beginning. Planned deer hunts at Boggy Slough were relished by Diboll management and their appreciative guests, who often wrote that the Temple parties at Boggy Slough were "the most enjoyable times [they] ever experienced." An executive with the Texas Employers' Insurance Association once wrote, "Boggy Slough! What a place! I really did have the time of my life—never had so much fun since Heck was a pup."[13] The clubhouse provided Diboll officials intimate time with selected business associates and government officials, as well as with the Texarkana

BOGGY SLOUGH
Hunting and Fishing Lodge
DIBOLL, TEXAS

Interior and exterior views of the second clubhouse, from a Boggy Slough Hunting and Fishing "Lodge" postcard of the early 1950s. *Courtesy of The History Center, Diboll.*

bosses who occasionally participated in the hunts or at least visited the clubhouse to further advance the goodwill efforts. The hunts also offered the upper level employees a relaxed, rustic setting in which to see Gilbert and Temple family members in a less formal environment. Company correspondence reveals that executives often delayed tough business decisions for weeks, sometimes for months, until face-to-face meetings with Gilbert could be arranged during fall hunts at the clubhouse.

The Texarkana executives, who were not all deer hunters, enjoyed the retreats too. Although they visited Diboll and Pineland so rarely that Arthur Temple Jr. once described their East Texas outings as "sort of like going to India for the British," trips to Boggy Slough during the fall were exceptions.[14]

Charlotte Temple, daughter of Mary and Arthur Temple Jr. and now chair of the T. L. L. Temple Foundation, jumps rope outside the Boggy Slough clubhouse, ca. 1949. Barney Franklin and his daughter Jean hold the rope as Charlotte (wearing a striped shirt) and her cousin Carolyn Allen jump. *Courtesy of The History Center, Diboll.*

At one of the many weekend Temple family gatherings at the clubhouse, Charlotte "Chotsy" Temple, wearing a striped shirt in the foreground, enjoys time with her family and friends. Going counterclockwise around the table, beginning with Chotsy, are her mother Mary, her aunt Charlotte Barry, her aunt Ann Allen, Irma Franklin, Kester Denman (standing), and Jake Durham and his wife Ruth. Some of the children in the background are Jean Franklin, Suzanne Clement, Buddy Temple, Sonny Clement, Bim Franklin, and Carolyn Allen. *Courtesy of The History Center, Diboll.*

Gilbert especially liked deer hunting, and did so at every opportunity. T. L. L. Temple, who preferred golf and tennis over all other forms of outdoor recreation, was also fond of his visits to Boggy Slough because he said they afforded him the opportunity of simply "being with the boys." T. L. L.'s son, Arthur Temple Sr., who said more than once that he was "not at all interested in the [deer] hunting at Boggy Slough," still appreciated the camaraderie and relaxation he experienced at the Trinity County clubhouse.[15] While he did not own a deer rifle, Arthur Sr. did love to quail and duck hunt and he usually did so during his visits at the appropriate seasons. During much of his adult life he also took an active role in shaping Boggy Slough's lowland glades and bottomland forests to promote water retention to increase duck habitat. Arthur Sr.'s son, Arthur Jr., learned to deer hunt at Boggy Slough, as did his grandson Buddy, and both men eagerly anticipated the opening of the squirrel, deer, duck, and quail seasons at Boggy Slough. After the construction of a modern clubhouse in the early 1940s, Boggy Slough became even more special as a place for Temple family gatherings, a home away from home, and where several generations first learned to drive automobiles. Mary and Arthur Temple Jr.'s children, Chotsy and Buddy, recalled many weekends spent there during the late 1940s and early 1950s as "fun times" they enjoyed with their mother and father, aunts and uncles, cousins, friends, and the kitchen crews. The children ran and played inside and outside the clubhouse, rode horses, swam in ponds, played various games, and had plenty of good snacks, meals, and liquid refreshments. The children especially enjoyed the nighttime campfires, when Arthur Temple Jr. told ghost stories and passed around "the heart of a dove"—a wad of ground beef which the children timidly held with their eyes closed. Years later, Chotsy's and Buddy's own families continued many of those traditions, spending every Thanksgiving holiday there for more than half a century.[16]

Opening-day deer hunts at Boggy Slough during the 1920s were grand affairs and events not to be missed. Having to attend court proceedings in Crockett, Dave Kenley missed the opening day of the 1923 deer season, but Gilbert wrote him a letter about the big day as soon as he returned to Texarkana. Gilbert said that he was sorry Kenley missed the hunt "at the ranch," for he felt Kenley surely would have taken a deer, as several were killed that day. Adding a little sporting swagger, Gilbert said that lumber and oil man Frank Bonner of Houston, who attended the hunts, was spreading the rumor that the deer simply "gave up" when they heard that Gilbert and his friends had come.[17]

While all hunting parties were great fun, not all hunts were successful in bagging game, especially during the earliest days. Responding to disappointing news of opening-day results in 1925, T. L. L. Temple wrote from Texarkana to Diboll officials, saying he was "sorry the Kansas people didn't have better luck, and I don't understand why Mr. Minton, who is such a good shot, should have missed

two."[18] Yet, whether deer were killed or not, the fellowship at the camp was appreciated by all. Kenley described a November 1926 hunt at Boggy Slough to Gilbert, who this time was unable to attend. Kenley wrote that "everybody had an awfully good time," and many "distinguished guests," including Judge Stark from the Sabine District, were present. Unfortunately, the judge was unable to kill a deer, but he did "see a number of them," Kenley said, which was reward enough. The whole party was satisfied, Kenley said, especially since Ned Shands had shot "a small deer, which was very fine eating," and Watson Walker had "shot some ducks."[19] Later that season, Kenley invited Gilbert to come down and join another hunt that Watson Walker was planning, which included Durham, Rutland, and Kenley, as well as four or five of Walker's "Lufkin friends" and possibly two or three others "on the out-side." It would be a great opportunity for Gilbert to meet the new business associates, Kenley said, and in addition there were some important business matters that Kenley wished to "thrash out" with Gilbert during the hunt.[20] Through the years, Kenley and Gilbert developed strong business and personal relationships, which were only strengthened by their work managing the Boggy Slough ranch and by their love of deer hunting. When Gilbert died of a heart attack in November 1931, it was while he was deer hunting at Boggy Slough, wearing one of Kenley's hunting jackets.[21]

Although hosted hunts were highly successful for obtaining desired business results, Boggy Slough's barbed-wire fences and armed pasture riders did not sit well with many area neighbors who soon found themselves, "on the out-side"—outside of the fences as well as outside of the company club. Some, including the husbands of the Christie sisters, still claimed customary access rights to the river bottoms, where they, like their ancestors, had ranged their hogs and hunted and fished freely for as long as anyone remembered, regardless of who owned the land.[22] They and others like them were common people who believed in common law and simple traditions. They contested unnatural wire fences and opposed all attempts to exclude them from the bottomlands. By their thinking, Southern Pine Lumber Company, headquartered some 200 miles away in Texarkana, were the outsiders. By disrespecting fences and asserting the traditional hunting and herding rights of their people, they did not see themselves as outlaws at all. In fact, in the eyes of many, some were heroes, even martyrs.[23]

Until the 1920s, game laws in Texas were few, weak, and mostly unknown or ignored. In rural East Texas, trespassing laws were also unfamiliar because most of the region remained an open range, where the only fences enclosed cultivated lands. Livestock herding and deer hunting traditionally went hand in hand, and consequently, hunting on unenclosed lands continued virtually unrestrained as long as game remained.[24] Even after the creation of somewhat enforceable trespassing and game laws, poaching continued to be a thorny issue for Boggy Slough's early managers, especially when Captain Ray and his riders shot stock dogs that were not their own inside the fences, believing the dogs endangered their calves and goats. As a result, rural conflict akin to outright war often ensued.[25]

Although certain parts of Houston County and Angelina County were under limited local option laws that restricted the roving of hogs by the 1910s and early 1930s in the two counties, respectively, Trinity County, where most of Boggy Slough was situated, remained open range throughout the ranch's history.[26] Accordingly, in Trinity County, it was the fence builder's responsibility to prevent the passing of livestock into enclosed areas, and dozens of miles of non-net wire fences and the Neches River were no barriers to roving hogs. Serious misunderstandings resulted on both sides of the river and both sides of the barbed wires, especially when some of Ray's own hogs occasionally escaped into what Kenley called "hog law country" in Houston County and "hog law territory" in Angelina County.[27]

The complete closing of the open range did not occur until long after the conclusion of Southern Pine Lumber Company's ranching "experiment," but the hard-fought battles played out dramatically at Boggy Slough for several decades. Essentially, the matter was one of urban versus rural populations—large landowners (often absentee, such as Southern Pine Lumber Company) versus smallholders. Those who wished to control, and thus "improve" the range, by closing it, included livestock breeders, timber companies, railroad companies—of which Temple was all three—but also the US Forest Service, Texas Forest Service, Texas Fish & Game Commission, townspeople, newspaper editors, chambers of commerce, and civic clubs. Those who sought to keep the traditional range open were the rural stockmen and hunters, who depended on every meager resource of the land simply to survive. As public employers grew in economic prominence, and as the region's population progressed from rural to urban, the open range gradually, but certainly, dwindled with each passing decade through often heated local and, eventually, statewide elections.[28]

While the range wars and game battles continued, Southern Pine Lumber Company sought help from all who could provide it. Early in 1923, Watson Walker, who was T. L. L. Temple's second cousin, presented the matter of managing Boggy Slough's fish and game resources to US Forest Service forester Austin Cary, who was already assisting Kenley with his "re-forestry problem." Cary assured Walker that he fully understood the concern, adding that fish and game management for forest landowners was "contentious" throughout the United States, especially in New York, where he had personally witnessed unfortunate results. "The heart of the matter," he explained, was "that regardless of law and landownership, the residents of a region feel entitled to a share of these national products, and generally, by one means or another, manage to secure it. Attempts at rigid exclusion have often, and in ordinary law-abiding communities, resulted in bitter feelings, reprisal, and forest fires." Cary said the situation was the same all across the nation, and added that in his home state of Maine, "hunting and fishing cannot be lawfully excluded from uncultivated areas."[29]

Cary offered Walker one example of a successful southern forest operation, which he suggested that Diboll officials model. Cary explained how pioneer conservationist Evan Frank Allison and his Allison Lumber Company managers at Bellamy, Alabama, "started out some years ago to protect game and build up a good stock of deer on their timber property. They worked in the first place for observance of the fish and game laws, then by careful handling of the people, they further limited the hunting season. Now there is a big stock of deer in their woods, and each fall Mr. Allison invites to his hunting camp a party of the state's notables to enjoy a week's sport of the finest description. The people living about have their turn at it too, however, and though the time is limited, they are satisfied because the stock of game is such that they can now kill as much in a week as formerly in a whole season."[30]

Of course Cary's description of the Allison Lumber Company's conservation efforts was a management model Diboll officials were already trying to develop independently. Although a clear policy would take decades to mature at Boggy Slough, some similarities were shared between the two lumber companies' experiences. Cary's 1923 description of "the people living about" the Allison Lumber Company's woodlands and their feeling "entitled to a share" of "national products" such as deer was comparable to Gilbert's 1918 descriptions of Boggy Slough's "native element" and their views of the land. But a major difference was in Gilbert's characterization of the ranch's neighbors as "antagonistic to any development and especially . . . control of the range." It bears repeating that Gilbert published his opinions in a national magazine, writing that Boggy Slough's neighbors believed, "that the Lord gave them this country and the razorback hog, so they make trouble wherever they can, sometimes by cutting fences, but principally by leaving gates open and starting woods fires." Such a description articulated the distant views of an absentee corporation that was attempt-ing to convert 32,000 acres of former woodlands into pastures, while economically profiting from the wildlife that lived behind fences.[31] The relative disconnect between Southern Pine Lumber Company and the communities in which it operated—whether real or merely perceived—persisted for decades. Tensions did not begin to ease until long after Arthur Temple Jr. moved the company headquarters to Diboll during the 1950s and began to initiate a true ownership class of administration, eventually implementing Temple Industries' popular and highly successful, "We Want to Be a Good Neighbor," publicity campaign during the early 1970s, following the company's public offering of stock shares in 1969.[32]

Fences, nevertheless, played a constructive role in game conservation. Boggy Slough's ranch managers believed that the number of deer inside the fences remained relatively plentiful, while deer populations outside the fences fared poorly, because pasture riders simply protected the deer from public hunting at a critical time.[33] The protection was not completely intentional at first, but when managers realized the connection, they fervently sought to capitalize on and increase the positive effects. For many years in various media outlets—especially in newspaper articles published in the *Diboll News-Bulletin* during the 1950s and in the *Diboll Free Press* during the 1960s—company officials told how, decades earlier, Captain Ray and his hog-proof net wire fences excluded "nesters" and "hay seeders" and their vicious stock dogs, thereby providing a "sanctuary" for game that otherwise would have been freely chased and killed out.[34] Ray was usually portrayed as a tough man during a tough time that demanded strength. No one ever found him without his .45 revolver within reach. Some outlaw hunters made threats and curses against him, but no one dared to personally challenge him with a gun. On the other hand, Ray was compassionate toward wildlife. He was a proud gamekeeper and reported to Texarkana each season's "awfully good crop of fawns," which he gladly took under his attentive care.[35] For his devotion to game protection at Boggy Slough,

Captain J. J. Ray, Southern Pine Lumber Company's ranch foreman, with a deer he killed in front of the original Boggy Slough Hunting and Fishing Club's clubhouse on the banks of Boggy Slough, ca. 1930. *Courtesy of The History Center, Diboll.*

his obituary in the *Lufkin Daily News* in 1941 called him "the Father of Wild Game."[36]

The actual process of protecting and propagating wild game, however, was arduous. Ray and Diboll officials regularly informed Gilbert and Temple concerning trespassers, fence cutters, fire starters, and poachers, and they reported in detail their tireless efforts to eliminate such activities. In the

beginning, Ray and his armed men—always on swift horses—rounded up "intruders" and took them before the sheriff in Groveton, where they were given "a strong talk."[37] This method was effective in only a few instances, and soon there were enough trespassers as well as repeat offenders that other legal means became necessary. By 1917 attorney R. E. Minton, Dave Kenley's brother-in-law, who himself was earlier arrested and charged—but not prosecuted—for the murder of a Trinity County law official and for assault with intent to murder a Texas Ranger, became responsible for handling Boggy Slough's trespassers in the courts.[38] Minton prosecuted the cases so zealously that he acquired the unofficial title of "Judge" Minton. In the absence of adequate trespassing laws during the days of a mostly open range, Minton used court-imposed injunctions in an attempt to discourage and prosecute unwanted entries. The process sought first to apprehend anyone caught inside the barbed-wire fences and take them before a county judge, who would issue an injunction, forbidding reentry to the property. If caught again, the enjoined trespasser would face the penalty of a $100 fine and two to three days in jail. Minton's records reveal that he enjoined more than three hundred people caught inside Boggy Slough's fences between 1917 and 1929, with nearly 90 percent of the injunctions having occurred between 1921 and 1926, just before Southern Pine leased Boggy Slough to the state fish and game department as a game warden–patrolled wildlife preserve.[39]

Some of those caught inside the fenced pastures without authorization were former landowners, such as members of the Moore, Tiner, Wells, Womack, Luce, Brock, Oliver, Anderson, McClain, and Roach families. Minton enjoined most of them within three years of their selling land titles and hog claims, and some within just a few months. Besides the excuse to fish and to hunt for deer, ducks, and squirrels, one common reason they gave for crossing the perimeter fences was to round up the remnants and the offspring of their roving hogs. A typical incident occurred late in the summer of 1922, when J. J. Ray found

Lee Anderson "hunting his hogs" inside the Boggy Slough fences and apprehended him. Anderson and other members of his family had been caught trespassing earlier, back in 1919, and were already enjoined and ordered to remove their hogs and keep them out.[40] When Anderson appeared in court to avoid forfeiting his bond concerning the 1922 case, he pled that he had no more money to continue fighting legal proceedings and he vowed to "never again" reenter Boggy Slough "for any purpose" if Minton would relent his prosecution. Minton explained to Anderson that he had no "personal interest" in the matter and that he was only representing the interests of Southern Pine Lumber Company. In a show of good will, however, Minton told Anderson that he would convey Anderson's "proposition" to his employers. When Minton reported the status of the case to Ray, he sternly advised him, saying that since Anderson "now realizes he is thoroughly whipped," Ray should "demand a bill of sale to all hogs he may have in the pasture and thus cut him off from any excuse of re-entering."[41]

Other cases resulted in revenge, including the notorious fence cutting. So common was the practice of locals cutting the barbed-wire fences at Boggy Slough that Gilbert acknowledged it in his June 1918 cattle-grazing article in the St. Louis journal, *Cut-Over Lands*.[42] One person Gilbert must have identified, as "making trouble wherever they can," was John Wells, who had sold 140 acres of land to the company just north of Cochino Bayou, near Franklin Slough, in March 1919. Wells was enjoined by Minton just six months later, however, for returning to the land to round up his hogs.[43] As recorded by oral historian Thad Sitton in his 1996 book, *Backwoodsmen*, Wells believed he was not adequately compensated for his hogs, which he claimed were several hundred head. After being "filed on" for trying to gather them, Wells took some of his kin and together they spent the better part of a night cutting Boggy Slough's fences "between every post" for at least ten miles. Sitton wrote that when Ray's riders, who were described as "hard men," later mended the fences, at least

three of them retied the wires while another man stood guard with a .30-30 rifle.[44]

⎯⎯⎯ •◆• ⎯⎯⎯

Although Minton may have denied a "personal interest" in prosecuting trespassers who herded hogs, he seemed to relish going after anyone who would dare to hunt Boggy Slough's game species without an official invitation. In January 1923, Minton wrote Ray to correct an oversight in the injunction process. Minton was concerned that several enjoined trespassers were circulating claims that they had standing invitations from Ray's riders to hunt and fish in Ray's pasture. Two such enjoined persons were Lufkin automobile salesman Calvin Mantooth Jr. and Lufkin banker Jim Abney. Minton advised Ray to revoke all authority he might have delegated to his employees in granting permissions to "outside persons," explaining, "I think we have this Lufkin bunch pretty well whipped now, but if we try a case and one of them should escape on proving an invitation, even by one of your employees who in fact had no authority, we would lose a large part of what we have gained. If this bunch finds that they can defeat us in that way, they will be prepared to prove by some of their sympathizers that he was present on a certain occasion when someone 'invited' him to come over, and out of court we will go. Besides, we will be put to the necessity of having all of the ranch employees and Company officials present in court every time to show that none of them gave any such invitation."[45]

In spite of Minton's instructions and warnings, however, confusion within what he called "the family organization" concerning who did, or did not, have authority to invite guests, and even who those guests should be, continued for many decades. Especially aggravating to Minton was the fact that some Boggy Slough club members continually invited outlaw hunters who Minton had enjoined at least once before. Minton feared not only that such actions might be unlawful, but also that they made for awkward encounters. As Minton once explained

Shotgun-wielding hunters at Boggy Slough proudly display their kills of deer, squirrels, and a fox during the 1920s. Left to right, Hugh Gibson, unknown, Jack Sanders, and Benny Smith. *Courtesy of The History Center, Diboll.*

to his fellow club members, "It places me in a very embarrassing position when I must appear before a court and ask that someone who has violated the injunction be fined $100 and be placed in jail for three days when we are carrying other persons who were enjoined, maybe in the same case, as our guests." Put another way, as Minton explained further, "You can well imagine how some fellow, whom I am asking to have placed in jail for contempt of court, feels toward us when we are carrying some other fellow who was in the same crowd when they were caught. It certainly does not elevate us in public estimation to handle affairs this way."[46] But as with so many other hunting club matters, Minton rarely received the cooperation from his fellow club members that he felt he deserved.

For decades, several repeat law offenders and club rules breakers remained popular guests at Boggy Slough's hunting parties. Two of the most long-standing ones were Jean Shotwell, an executive with the Lufkin Telephone Company, and Ned Shands Jr., a Lufkin attorney. In 1922 Minton had enjoined Shotwell and his father for unlawfully hunting in Boggy Slough.[47] But, according to Minton, just two years later, "at Watson Walker's earnest solicitation and upon Jean's solemn promise to

conduct himself in a sportsman-like manner," Minton reluctantly dropped the injunction so that Shotwell could be a lawful guest of Walker, T. L. L. Temple's cousin. What frustrated Minton the most, as he later informed Arthur Temple Sr. in a long letter of December 9, 1936, was the fact that Shotwell had admitted to game warden Enoch Jones that he had "killed does and other unlawful game on the ranch" throughout the 1920s. Then, during the early 1930s, Shotwell began the practice of "carrying his friend," Ned Shands Jr., "dropping him off along the highway, unknown to anyone, without invitation and without a guest card or hunting license." Minton reminded Temple that when pasture rider Walter Robinson finally apprehended Shands, it had caused considerable "trouble and friction among us." Minton further recounted that, as recently as November 26, 1936, pasture rider Ab Grumbles had caught Shotwell "in the upper end of the hunting ground without any guest card and no member of the club with him." And then, only a few days later, upon "hearing a shot," Walter Robinson caught Shotwell again, this time with two of his sons, at the south end of the ranch "along the highway," where one of the boys "killed an unlawful deer." Robinson carried the boys before the justice of the peace, "but the justice said he could do nothing with them because they were minors less than 17 years old."[48] "It is apparent to me," Minton concluded in his letter to Temple, that after twelve years, "our efforts to make a good sportsman out of Mr. Shotwell are in vain and

I am of the opinion that we should again invoke the injunction and so advise him." Minton also again explained the many years of embarrassments and difficulties he had endured in trying to enforce both the game laws and the club rules, when there seemed to be so little assistance from many of the other club members.[49]

Regardless of Minton's pleas, however, both Shotwell and Shands continued to be invited guests of the Temples at Boggy Slough. From 1937 through 1950 Shotwell even served as Arthur Temple Sr.'s personal guide, escorting Temple's many guests between the clubhouse and the deer stands and duck ponds, since few people knew Boggy Slough better. Arthur Sr. often said that the successes of his sponsored hunts were in large part due to Shotwell, who, along with Shands, eventually became lifelong "woodsman friends" of Arthur Temple Jr.[50]

———◆·◆·◆———

Minton himself began still-hunting deer (without using dogs) inside the protective Boggy Slough fences by at least 1922, when he helped organize the Boggy Slough Hunting and Fishing Club, which prohibited the use of dogs in running deer. Although he held membership in other hunting clubs up and down the Neches valley, as did most Southern Pine Lumber Company department heads, Minton considered Boggy Slough Island his favorite hunting ground. Just south of the island, on slightly higher ground, he built a personal hunting lodge, which is still in use today.[51] In addition to his prosecutorial work, Judge Minton is remembered as a sportsman, a naturalist, a skillful hunter, and an excellent shot. He especially enjoyed hunting with a black powder muzzle-loading rifle and wearing a coonskin cap. Minton took Arthur Temple Jr. on his first deer hunting trip at Boggy Slough and instilled in him a love for hunting and the outdoors. Temple later claimed Minton's hunting grounds on Boggy Slough Island for himself and marked them as "A. T. Area," and they remain marked that way today.[52]

While Minton's role in protecting Boggy Slough's wildlife did much to earn local hostilities, Captain Ray also played a part in the bad relations, especially in how he placed Boggy Slough's fences. Not only did the company's fences enclose some 32,000 acres situated along more than 20 miles of the river, which denied public water access from the west, but by placing the ranch's east fence on the east side of the river, Ray restricted river access from Angelina County as well. Such fence placement caused Ray's riders to consider anyone found on or near the river to be a suspicious person at best. Many people in Trinity and Houston Counties sought practical solutions to the problem, and while risky, the most common way to fish in the river was to go by the public road (today's Forest Service Road 511) to the Eastern Texas Railroad right-of-way, then walk four miles east down the tracks, cross the high river bridge, and fish from the riverbank on Pine Island or from small boats that were kept hidden away in brush. In summarizing one contempt-of-court case that concerned the river late in 1922, Minton reported to Gilbert that a fisherman was caught by Ray's men and brought before the judge at Groveton. In spite of the man's pleas that his fishing trip to Pine Island only involved his walking along the railroad right-of-way, which he understood was lawful, and that he was simply exercising his right to fish a navigable stream, the judge ruled against him, and the man spent two days in jail. Minton was disappointed the penalty was not greater, but he agreed with the judge, who stated "the case had some mitigating circumstances in it" that prevented further punishment.[53]

Such misunderstandings about the river persisted for decades and were only complicated when seasonal floodwaters left the river's banks. Fishermen, squirrel hunters, and duck hunters alike preferred the river at such times, often partaking in all three sports at the same time. During the late 1950s and early 1960s, a few overzealous Boggy Slough pasture riders also seemed to relish such times, and their actions often resulted in further stress on public relations. On horseback, the riders often swam the sloughs and were upon boaters in a

Whereas women were rarely invited to company deer hunting parties during the 1920's, this photo from the family collections of pasture rider John Silvers showing an unidentified woman and child displaying their deer kills at Boggy Slough indicates that some women did participate in the sport at an early date. *Courtesy of The History Center, Diboll.*

hurry, threatening to shoot holes in the boats if the occupants did not come ashore. Boaters usually took their chances in the water, fearing that they surely would be trespassing if they landed their vessels on dry ground. Still, riders usually had ways of identifying such people, and they would be waiting for them at their places of employment the next business day to make arrests.[54] In 1963, fisherman Jerry Lee of Angelina County felt that he had been falsely accused by Boggy Slough's riders more than once, so he sued Southern Pine Lumber Company and rider Elmer Cutler for false arrest and false imprisonment, eventually accept-

ing a financial settlement out of court in 1966 and an invitation to a deer hunt at Boggy Slough.[55]

Not all visits to the river along Boggy Slough lands were so unpleasant, however. In his 1980 book, *Over on Cochino*, Harrell Odom told a delightful story about his family's fishing trips on the Neches that he enjoyed as a child during the 1920s. Odom recalled that his parents, grandparents, uncles, aunts, and cousins would travel by wagons through Boggy Slough's gates and through the Cochino bottoms, until they reached the Eastern Texas Railroad bridge at the river, where family friend Calvin Tiner worked for the railroad company as a bridge watchman and water pump station attendant. Tiner kept a railroad motor car nearby and used it to escort the women and children across the river to Pine Island, while the men and horses swam and floated the wagons across. Odom described the railroad motor car ride across the high bridge as "the most thrilling part" of the whole trip. Through the eyes of a boy, it was "more important than the fishing part." "As far as I was concerned, Calvin Tiner was about the most important person in the world," Odom explained, "and I resolved someday to be an operator of a river pump station and travel by motor car over railroads, including high river bridges." Although Odom did not mention it in his book, Calvin Tiner was "important" also for another reason. Having earlier been one of Boggy Slough's enjoined trespassers, Tiner had since become one of Ray's patrolmen, and he played no small part in Odom's fond memories of certain Boggy Slough excursions.[56]

In 1951, in an act of goodwill by Southern Pine Lumber Company, game wardens and company pasture riders Ab Grumbles and Lee Bishop cleared riverbank camp sites at Boggy Slough at four locations between Highways 94 and 7. "The public can now go there for a fishing paradise," the *Diboll Buzz Saw* reported in its July 1951 issue, while also cautioning that, "the destinations must be reached by boat rather than across the ranch." The campsites were identified as "Christie Bluff, Mount Cochino, Bill Evans' Island, and at the 94 crossing."[57]

Whether Ray's men patrolled the fences or the river, the job of catching deer hunters at night was especially difficult as well as dangerous. At times during the 1930s, Minton believed more than two dozen poachers were hunting regularly inside the Boggy Slough pastures at night. Pasture riders, some who held commissions with the state as game wardens, were instructed to locate the points of entrance, then stake out the area to catch the hunters in the act. Night hunters, or "fire hunters," as they were known—because they carried small fires in pans or in carbide lanterns to illuminate the glowing reflections of deer eyes—entered from all points, especially through the Cedar Creek pasture and by way of the river and Pine Island in Angelina County. Ray's men became familiar with the various places where poachers used logs and skiffs to cross the "old river" and the "new river" to reach the Boggy Slough lands. They often camped out "a night or two" near those access points and made their arrests by land as well as by water, at times capturing men dragging out deer overland and at other times finding them huddled in boats full of ducks.[58]

Enjoining trespassers before the district court of Trinity County had some success in deterring trespassing initially, but several notable persons continued to cause grief, even after being enjoined, fined, and sent to jail. It was not uncommon for a hunter caught in Boggy Slough to firmly declare that they would return and kill a deer for every single dollar of the fine they paid.[59] Correspondence during the 1920s and 1930s tells of many "perpetually enjoined" persons who continually gave "a great deal of trouble to the ranch men." Many repeat poachers simply went upriver from the Boggy Slough property, launched their boats,

and as Minton explained, they proceeded to "float down and shoot such game as could be found along its banks," causing Ray's men "to be constantly on the lookout along the river banks." Always an irritation to Minton, several repeat offenders fought with and engaged Ray's men in "cussing sprees" and escaped further prosecution through sundry technicalities, including Ray's men not having their state game warden commission papers on their persons at the time of the confrontations. Poachers utilized the public highways the same way as the river, despite Minton's special care to prevent such transgressions. In reluctantly giving public access through Boggy Slough for state Highways 94 and 7/103, Minton sought to give to the state only the rights-of-way through, rather than fee title to, company lands. Ever distrustful, Minton claimed later that "the local highway office was incensed over this limitation, probably because Mr. G. R. Abney, one of the engineers in its employ, was also under a perpetual injunction, and others of the employees thought to use the right of way for hunting purposes."[60] As it turned out, several of those persons Minton enjoined were indeed employees of the highway department, while others were employees of pipeline companies and telephone utility companies—all people who had legitimate reasons to be on the land at certain times, but who abused liberties and transgressed beyond their limits. Seeing large populations of deer was simply too much of a temptation for some.

Such an abundance of deer drew daring illegal hunters from not only Trinity, Houston, and Angelina Counties—not all of whom were hunting simply to put meat on the table—but also from places more than a hundred miles away. Pasture rider Charlie Harber said that during the 1940s he apprehended both the manager and the front desk clerk of Houston's William Penn Hotel, but not before they had killed "a nice 10-point buck." Harber said that he hid under a cattle guard near Cochino Bayou and surprised the men at close range, seizing their guns without incident. Most other times, however, Harber said that he used his swift horse to surprise and catch even the wariest of poachers. One horse in particular was especially adept at running down intruders by charging through brush and jumping fences with ease. She became spirited, he said, especially "when you got after somebody or an animal or something." Once, when poachers on the run crossed a fence near Cochino Bayou, Harber said his horse "jumped that fence with me on her [and] it scared the living fool out of them!" When asked how many people he had apprehended in Boggy Slough during the 1940s, he replied: "I don't know how many. There was a lot of them. They come through here often. I caught them out of Nacogdoches and everywhere else."[61]

———•◆•———

Notwithstanding the many poachers caught during the 1940s, illegal hunting at Boggy Slough was especially rampant during the first two decades of the company ranch's operations. According to Minton, some three dozen persons regularly poached during the 1920s, which led him to call on the state to employ full-time resident game wardens at Boggy Slough, in hopes they would bolster the efforts of the company's employees. Minton felt the state never did enough to assist, however, and he even believed several of the state wardens did more harm than good—like he had felt about some of the Texas Rangers at Groveton during the saloon wars a quarter of a century earlier.

Minton let his employers know of his distrust at every opportunity. Writing letters to Arthur Temple Sr. in December 1931, Minton reported that wardens up to that time had been "unscrupulous men" who themselves were "criminals." One of them was earlier indicted in Nacogdoches for bootlegging, Minton said, while others had "joined themselves with Ray's enemies," illegally hunting and then hiding out across the river at the camp of Nat Wright (the former Southern Pine Lumber Company land agent). Minton also claimed that the warden who was indicted for bootlegging had joined poachers in "cussing" Ray and making threats on

his life. Had it not been for Ray always having "his big pistol in his belt and so convenient [to his access]," Minton said, Ray surely would have been killed any number of times because the poachers felt they could "have their way" with Ray removed, for they felt "safe against all but Ray." Minton also complained that the wardens drank whiskey and played poker at the Boggy Slough clubhouse, even mingling with club members and their guests, while doing "nothing" to lend assistance to Ray.[62]

Surely Southern Pine Lumber Company's early relationship with the state wildlife department was not as bad as Minton believed. Durham admitted that some of the Boggy Slough wardens were "indifferent" at times, but they were never as deplorable as Minton made out.[63] In fact, the relationship began well enough in 1926, when Southern Pine Lumber Company led the way in game conservation efforts in East Texas by leasing some 47,000 acres of land, including Boggy Slough, to the Texas Game, Fish, and Oyster Commission as game preserves. In February of that year Southern Pine officials joined with fellow Angelina County landowners E. J. Conn, J. W. Hawkins, I. D. Fairchild, and John S. Redditt in establishing 26,652 acres along the Neches River between Diboll and Manning as State Game Preserve No. 23. Two months later, Southern Pine Lumber Company and R. E. Minton established another 20,000 acres of their lands along the Neches River in Trinity and Houston Counties (the land that is now Boggy Slough Conservation Area) as State Game Preserve No. 27.[64]

Authorized by legislation in 1925, state game preserves embodied the first major effort to conserve wildlife across the entire state.[65] The preserves were designed to set apart private lands for a period of ten years, place game wardens on them to prohibit public hunting, and use the protected land to restock deer, quail, and turkey, which would, it was hoped, spread by "overflowing" into adjacent territory. There, the game could then be hunted by the general public. The state's goals in the program were to obtain relatively inexpensive "game farms," justify increased funding for law enforcement, and garner statewide political support for wildlife conservation. Landowners received free patrol service of game lands and state prosecution of trespassers.[66]

Deer used in the restocking program came mostly from the Kerrville-Fredericksburg region, although commissioners originally planned to obtain herds from Northern Mexico. Quail and turkey came from South Texas, while fish came from state hatcheries.[67] Upon establishing the Angelina County preserve, E. J. Conn stressed the importance of the program to all East Texans. In the pages of the *Lufkin Daily News*, he claimed that the restockings would "offset" the statewide decrease in game and would soon "afford plenty of game for everybody." Conn predicted that within only a few years the "restocking of game of all kinds and fish for the lakes and streams" would "overflow" the bounds of the preserve, and the younger generation would again "know what game [wa]s without having to look at pictures in books on natural history."[68]

The state located most of the early game preserves on cattle ranches west and northwest of Fort Worth and in South Texas, where armed range riders were already prohibiting public hunting.[69] Such was the case with Boggy Slough, which had been a fenced ranch for thirteen years prior to the state lease. Southern Pine Lumber Company was the first lumber company in the state to join the preserve movement, while later in 1926 the Gibbs Brothers and Thompson Brothers offered some of their cutover forest lands in Trinity, San Jacinto, and Walker Counties along the Trinity River to the program, becoming Game Preserves No. 32 and No. 33.[70]

Newspapers published across the state reported that about three hundred deer per year were stocked on the game preserves during the program's first decade. Unfortunately, records of the state game commission prior to 1938 do not survive, and the newspaper accounts prior to that time gave very few details about the restockings, including those that might have occurred in Boggy Slough.[71] Arthur Temple Jr. told his game biologists in 1981 that some of Boggy Slough's deer had come from South Texas as well as from Kansas, but he offered no information about when the transfers occurred.[72]

Although they offered no clues about the origins of the stocked deer, oral history interviews provided first- and secondhand witness accounts of the restockings at Boggy Slough. In 1986 historian Thad Sitton interviewed Claude Welch Sr., whose father Tom was a TSE Railroad section foreman at Neff near Cochino Bayou during the 1920s. Welch recalled seeing deer released from railroad stock cars, but at first sight he did not recognize them. He explained that even though he had "roamed the woods like a squirrel" his whole life, he had to ask his uncle, "What is them things, Uncle Jim?" "Them's deer," the older man replied.[73] In 2000, former Boggy Slough pasture rider Charlie Harber, who lived as a child at Boggy Slough during the 1920s, said that he knew "those deer were shipped in here from somewhere." While it troubled him that he never discovered the origins of the stocked deer, he said he remembered "hearing my father [tell of] seeing those deer jump out of boxcars." It was unforgettable, he explained, because his father said that "some of them broke their legs when they came out."[74]

Although the details of Boggy Slough's early game restockings remain unclear, there is no doubt that deer increased substantially during the lease period when the state provided several game wardens as residents on the property. Charlie Harber recalled that the number of deer rose so high that it was a special day when Captain Ray let his father shoot one of them for meat on the family's table, a privilege earlier allowed only to hunting club members and their guests. Then, by the early 1930s, deer had become so plentiful, Harber said, that his family could no longer farm in South Boggy because deer "ate up stuff faster than you could plant it." Harber remembered seeing as many as 140 deer at a time in his family's fields (located where Lottie Temple Deer Stand 22 had been placed years later), and he said his father tried to control their numbers with arsenic.[75] Correspondence among Arthur Temple Sr., R. E. Minton, E. C. Durham, and J. J. Ray during 1932 corroborated Harber's memories. The men more than once acknowledged that "the deer are increasing very rapidly and are already so numerous as to be a nuisance."[76] In later years Judge Minton further confirmed the fact that deer had increased significantly during the lease period, in spite of hunting—both lawful and unlawful—"until the browse was exhausted and a great many of them died from starvation."[77]

During the 1930s, several individuals estimated the number of deer inside Boggy Slough's fences. In 1933, when Southern Pine Lumber Company sought to sell the game preserve, Dave Kenley estimated its deer population at more than one thousand, telling prospective buyer George Huffman of Houston that Boggy Slough was "one of the best game preserves in East Texas."[78] In 1937, in an article that appeared in the Dallas Morning News, E. C. Durham estimated the increasing herd at two thousand. In the same year, state wildlife biologist Dan Lay estimated the number to be "between 1,500 and 3,000."[79] Lay also claimed that the protected deer had "overflowed" into surrounding territories, citing eight new hunting clubs that adjoined Boggy Slough on both sides of the river as beneficiaries of the game migrations. In the pages of the state wildlife department's annual report for 1936–37, Lay wrote that Boggy Slough had become "the deer incubator of East Texas."[80]

Perhaps indicative of where the state's deer hunting prospects stood during the 1930s, as well as Boggy Slough's established reputation for deer, the Dallas Morning News in November 1939 carried the whimsical headline, "Logging Train Gets Credit for First Deer of Season at Lufkin." Sent as a special news item from Lufkin, the story told of Southern Pine Lumber Company Engine 13 striking and killing a seven-point buck at the break of dawn in the Cochino bottoms near Neff. The steam locomotive, now on display at The History Center in Diboll, was traveling northward, pulling empty log cars to the logging camp at Fastrill, when it struck the deer at 5:30 a.m. Bonnie Brown, who had succeeded Tom Welch as the Neff railroad

section foreman, found the deer, dressed it, and had it waiting for the locomotive crew later that morning upon their return run to Diboll with loaded cars.[81]

Such stories made for interesting conversation among readers of the Dallas Morning News, but there remained nevertheless a moral complexity concerning Boggy Slough's "abundant" deer, especially during the game preserve period. Although their very existence was due to a strict prohibition of public hunting, deer were seen by the rural populace as a public resource not to be hoarded behind fences, especially not by a nonresident lumber company. Many rural folk believed that the so-called game preserves of the 1920s and 1930s represented a corrupt connection between private wealth and state conservation, since hunting club members and their guests continued to hunt the deer that were protected at taxpayer expense. This was particularly true when state efforts at Boggy Slough resulted in a "nuisance" level of overstocked deer, many of which died from starvation.[82]

The line between law and lawlessness, while clear in attorney Minton's eyes, was at best blurred in the views of many of the area's rural whites, who suddenly became interlopers and "intruders" on the lands they were born and raised on. Although rightful property owners accepted money for their land titles and hog claims, Boggy Slough's rural populace experienced a complete culture shock within only a few years of Southern Pine Lumber Company's entrance into Trinity and Houston Counties. The company's 32,000 acres under fence redefined the long-established open range customs of hog herding as trespassing, hunting and fishing as poaching, and setting ecological fires as arson. Although the change occurred in less than a decade, societal adjustments to it required several generations.[83]

One person who especially challenged the changing order—and the game preserve in particular—was Walter Marion James, a cousin of the Christie girls of Sullivan's Bluff.[84] A World War I veteran and highway department employee, James had been enjoined by Minton for unlawfully hunting in 1926. Despite the injunction, James defiantly continued to hunt behind Boggy Slough's fences, especially at night, and became sort of a folk hero for successfully eluding and confounding the pasture riders and game wardens. One fateful night in August 1932, however, he met three state wardens at point blank range in the Cedar Creek bottoms near Vair. There, in the dark, James and the wardens exchanged gunfire, mostly buckshot loads from shotguns. When the shooting was over, James had been hit numerous times and bled to death near the railroad grade.[85] Robert James, one of Walter's brothers, served as the informant in completing his brother's death certificate. He made sure that the document contained the phrase, "killed while hunting in game preserve."[86]

Although the game preserves at Boggy Slough and in Angelina County were initially popular, public support for them eventually waned, especially after the James shooting. Although hunting clubs and conservation-minded politicians stepped up efforts to educate the public on the importance of conservation laws and their continued enforcement, the campaign was a struggle.[87] Even a legislative council later declared that the early game preserves of the 1920s, while implemented with the best of intentions, were in effect merely "deer preserves" that benefited only privileged classes of hunters while doing very little for actual wildlife conservation.[88] Never truly pleased with the state, Judge Minton had actually canceled both of Southern Pine Lumber Company's leases before their minimum terms, ending Boggy Slough's (State Preserve No. 27) in 1934 and Angelina County's (State Preserve No. 23) in 1935.[89] With or without the state's direct involvement, it seemed that deer on company lands, especially at Boggy Slough, were both a blessing and a curse.

This was perhaps most evident after the company ranch closed in 1933 and Captain Ray's best men left with him or joined E. C. Durham's own ranching operations at Shawnee Prairie. With Ray gone, the responsibility of protecting Boggy Slough's land, timber, and game fell solely on Dave

Kenley, who for many years experienced difficulties in hiring dependable patrolmen. It was partly for that reason that he was able to convince his own employers during the late 1930s to allow him cattle grazing rights at Boggy Slough, so that his personal cow hands could supplement the protection provided by the company's men.

While not all of Kenley's men held state commissions as game wardens, all of the company patrolmen did; at least one of them also held a "special ranger" commission. The company men, who were essentially hired guns, often came from the same woods-wise and violent stock as those who they guarded against, and some of them had tarnished pasts of their own.[90] They were often described as "hard," "arrogant," "overbearing," and "humiliating" men who practiced "winning by intimidation."[91] They at times ruthlessly enforced their interpretations of the law and in the process caused regrettable collateral damage. Their employment was nevertheless seen as a necessary evil, which even Arthur Temple Jr. later defended, saying that younger generations had no idea what it was like to live during an era of sawmill company towns, nor did they understand the difficulties of being an industrial landowner trying to keep the peace during such a time. "Back then you had to be tough or you simply wouldn't be in business," he said during one interview in 1999.[92]

Yet Temple was also concerned with the overall effectiveness and fairness of the riders, and because of this he had assumed direct supervision of them during the early 1950s.[93] One issue that continually irritated him was the fact that they often left Boggy Slough not only to pursue suspected trespassers but also to participate in the work of the area's other law enforcement officers. Temple once wrote to rider Jay Boren early in 1955, reprimanding him along with riders Claude Davenport and Elmer Cutler for spending "too much time . . . outside of our own lands." They needed to understand, he explained, that chasing after people outside of the fences created "a good many problems for me. It has got to be our official attitude that we keep our nose out of other people's business outside of our property, as I feel that we certainly have plenty to look after inside the fence."[94]

Seeking tighter control of the riders, Temple required them to sign a two-page document in February 1956 that contained a list of nine rules that governed their employment. Among the requirements were the confinement of their activities to the protection of company lands and their forbiddance of going "outside of this limitation." Among other constraints, they were also forbidden the "use of vulgar or abusive language" as well as "violence in any form" except in their self-defense during the execution of their duties. They were not allowed to discuss their activities with others "nor the manner in which [they] performed them," and "under no circumstances" were they permitted to "discuss local gossip" with anyone other than Temple or with persons he designated.[95]

Despite the rules and Temple's steady admonitions to the riders, troubles continued, mainly because the pasture riders had already developed unhealthy relationships with several of Boggy Slough's neighbors. Among the thorniest of dilemmas was an ongoing feud between Temple's riders and Trinity County constable Earl Smith, whose lands and family home place bordered a portion of Boggy Slough's west fence just south of Cochino Bayou. Smith, who was born in 1914—just a year after the Boggy Slough fences went up—had become a legendary deer hunter and deer dog breeder by the 1940s. According to his own family, he killed "well over a thousand deer in his lifetime" and his dogs were famous for giving "many a deer a violent shove into eternity."[96] That at least some of those deer may have come from nearby Southern Pine Lumber Company pastures never left the suspicious minds of the riders, who believed that Smith and his sons not only poached on company lands but also assisted and protected other poachers, many of whom were apprehended near Smith's land along Cochino Bayou.[97]

It was common knowledge that Boggy Slough rider and deputy game warden Claude Davenport's stops and searches of Earl Smith and his sons on public roadways had led Smith to run for the elected position of Trinity County constable in the first place, primarily so he could stop and search Davenport in retaliation.[98] One confrontation between the two lawmen on a Friday evening in August 1962 on the North Cedar Road near Smith's home ended with Davenport shooting Smith multiple times in the chest with a pistol and reportedly leaving him for dead. A member of Smith's family was with him at the time and rushed Smith to a Lufkin hospital, where he miraculously survived his wounds and lived another twenty-two years.[99] News of the shooting appeared on the front page of the Saturday edition of the *Lufkin Daily News,* and a United Press International story of the shooting appeared in the Sunday editions of newspapers from Dallas to Brownsville.[100] A later edition of the *Trinity Standard* only added that Davenport had been arrested and arraigned for assault with intent to murder, that he was released on bond, and that Smith remained in critical condition in a Lufkin hospital.[101]

Southern Pine Lumber Company attorney Ward Burke said later that the shooting was his worst experience in a long legal career.[102] Because Davenport had "disobeyed specific orders"—mainly leaving Boggy Slough to engage in outside activities—Burke terminated his employment, instructed him "to move as soon as possible," and encouraged him to "find a job away from here." Those measures were in Davenport's personal "best interests," he said, since they were intended to prevent retribution from the Smith family. With the company's assistance, Davenport took a job with the East Texas Wildlife Conservation Association in Hardin and Jasper Counties, working on lands that were leased from Southern Pine Lumber Company.[103] "Keeping the peace" with the people of Trinity County had always been difficult, Burke said, and while the Smith shooting was terrible, he believed that, in the end, it actually led to better relations between the company and the public, primarily because of a resulting tighter control of the riders, improved mutual respect between the company and local law enforcement agencies, and through the opening of increased public hunting and fishing op-

Henry Gresham Temple, wearing a white shirt in the foreground, stands with Clyde Thompson in front of the original Boggy Slough Hunting and Fishing Club's clubhouse on the banks of Boggy Slough during the 1930s. *Courtesy of The History Center, Diboll.*

portunities on company lands, including at times wider public access to Boggy Slough.[104]

Deer played a defining role in Boggy Slough's history, but they were not the land's only abundant game species. Ducks were also plentiful, as well as quail, especially during the 1910s, when Boggy Slough was a land of ecological "edges." The combined activities of early mechanical logging, cattle ranching, and tenant farming provided quail with the required interspersed woodland, brushland, grassland, and cultivated cropland land types.[105] In September 1916, E. C. Durham reported to T. L. L. Temple that the "quail crop" that year was "mighty fine," and he encouraged Temple to set a date for a quail hunting party immediately after December 1. Durham said that those of Temple's party who hunted would certainly "enjoy the sport," while those who did not hunt would nevertheless "have the pleasure of looking a nice brown bird in the face at the breakfast table each morning."[106]

While T. L. L. Temple only occasionally hunted quail and bred bird dogs, it was his son Arthur Temple Sr. who was the true bird and duck hunter

of the family.[107] T. L. L. Temple once shared with his cousin, Watson Walker, that "Arthur seems to enjoy bird hunting more than anything that he does. Golf has to take a back seat, which is hard on us [the Texarkana office staff], but I am glad that he enjoys it."[108]

For many years, Arthur Temple Sr. was a member of the Hempstead County Hunting Club in southwestern Arkansas. The highly exclusive club managed Grassy Lake, an old-growth cypress swamp near the confluence of the Little and Saline Rivers, just north of Fulton where the Little River joins the Red River. The swamp had been protected from logging by lumberman William Buchanan, the same man whose private railcar T. L. L. Temple had occasionally borrowed. Club members kept the lake, long known as "a biologists' paradise," in as nearly a natural condition as possible.[109] Arthur Temple especially liked Grassy Lake because, as he told his Diboll employees, it offered duck hunting at its finest and was so near to Texarkana that he could hunt in the mornings and still go to the office later in the day.[110]

Although Boggy Slough offered no cypress swamps, South Boggy—the land south of Cochino Bayou—did have swamps and flats of cutover overcup oaks, which were near the river and the sloughs, and of cedars and hawthorns along the Cedar Creek bottoms. Boggy Slough also contained a few shallow lakes, marshes, and "flag ponds" among the several saline prairies, which began to hold increased amounts of water during the late 1930s, a result of altered drainage patterns caused by the construction of Shell and Pan American crude oil pipelines through the Sanchez and Walker surveys and by the relocation and grade elevation of Highway 94.[111] Focusing on these natural features—already altered by outside disturbances—Temple drew from his hunting experiences at Grassy Lake to further manipulate Boggy Slough's wetlands to increase waterfowl habitat and hunting opportunities.

One of Temple's abiding concerns was how to "hold the ducks" for longer periods of time. With such excellent habitat existing all around the club's hunting ponds, he felt there was a need to concentrate the ducks' roosting and feeding requirements at designated ponds to maximize hunting proficiency. After a January 1938 hunt at Boggy Slough, Temple wrote to Kenley to share some of his thoughts. He said that he had been "thinking we might want to plant wild rice or something to hold the ducks in our ponds during the day, because it seems to me that while thousands of ducks roosted on our lakes, they were inclined to leave early in the morning for feeding grounds and did not return until late in the afternoon, after the expiration of the legal shooting period. If we could hold these ducks in the lakes during the day, or if we had feed there which would make them attractive to ducks, they would stay throughout the day and, not only would the ducks roost there but other ducks would come in from the river bottoms as well." Temple said that he had written to the biological survey office of the USDA and had received some literature concerning duck feed. Temple enclosed the papers in his letter and asked Kenley to investigate the costs involved and to return the literature to him because he also wanted to share it with the members of his Grassy Lake club.[112]

Another concern was water availability. Late summer and fall droughts were not uncommon, and many of Boggy Slough's artificial shallow ponds often dried out. Early in November 1939, Kenley reported to Temple that if it did not rain soon, the "only duck shooting" would be at "your private pond," where he believed the ducks were "too tame to shoot." Kenley said that he thought "a good many ducks" were "raised" there because during his last visit he "saw something like a hundred, but they would not fly."[113]

During the fall of 1940 ducks were abundant at Boggy Slough. This pleased everyone, but Kenley was concerned that hunting the waterfowl all day long would result in their quick departure. Late in October, Kenley wrote to club members Clyde Thompson, E. A. Farley, J. J. O'Hara, R. E. Minton, J. F. Judd, H. G. Temple, and Arthur Temple to share his concerns with "our duck hunting around Boggy Slough." He said that hunting should be limited to the mornings, so that "the ducks might stay with us awhile." He explained that there were "a good many ducks out there with us now," but he was "certain, when the season opens, if we shoot all hours of the day, they will leave in a short time."[114]

Clyde Thompson replied, saying that he agreed "heartily" to hunting time restrictions, but he also reminded Kenley that such restrictions had been the rule of the Boggy Slough Hunting and Fishing Club "for the past several years." In fact, as he also reminded Kenley, the restrictions had been plainly printed on the back of all guest cards: "Duck hunting 7 to 11 a.m. only."[115] After Arthur Temple was reminded of the time restriction that already existed, he said he was pleased that shooting hours had been limited because it was best "for those of us who love this sport." But at the same time, he also expressed his personal preference for a hunting time of "daylight until noon."[116]

Interested in improving hunting conditions at Boggy Slough, Arthur Temple met with Hilbert Siegler, a field biologist with the Game, Fish, and Oyster Commission, in November 1940. Upon learning of the state's renewed programs to increase waterfowl habitat, Temple proposed setting aside one of Boggy Slough's "lakes" as "a duck sanctuary" and "wild fowl refuge," if the state would assist in the cost. Siegler agreed, and the two men decided that one of the artificial lakes "through which the pipeline runs" would be an ideal location for the

Members of a fishing party at the original clubhouse on Boggy Slough pose for a flashlight photograph during the 1930s. *Courtesy of The History Center, Diboll.*

Boggy Slough cooks pose in front of the original hunting and fishing clubhouse during the 1930s. In the front row, left to right, are Contella Walker, Vessie Thomas, Oscar Jones, Macho Andrews, Temple DeBerry, and T. R. Fowler. Middle row, left to right, are Joe Diamond, Lloyd Hubbard, Fred Randolph, A. C. Scott, R. L. Covington, and Finnie Simmons. Back row, left to right, are lumber company managers Henry Gresham Temple and Wilbur D. Fogg, with president Arthur Temple Sr. *Courtesy of The History Center.*

preserve. In December Temple wrote to Kenley to share the good news, saying that the refuge would be "a fine thing for the ducks at Boggy Slough." He added that the government would "fence the lake, plant duck food, and perhaps do other things too for the promotion of more game." Other than desiring to revise the lease contract by reducing the term from ten years to five years, Temple said that he could see no objections, because "we have everything to gain and nothing to lose by cooperating with the State." Temple was so enthusiastic that he signed the contract in advance and sent it to Kenley for his final review, asking him to mail it to Austin afterward.[117]

Kenley replied, saying that he was "certainly proud" of Temple's actions. "There is nothing that pleases me more than to see us do this," he wrote. "In fact," Kenley said that he had earlier thought of suggesting just such a plan, because he knew it would "be very beneficial to us as hunters, as it will keep the ducks in this neighborhood, and [when] they go out to feed we will have a chance at them." "Besides," he continued, "it will add materially to our wild life as being where it can always be seen by our visitors." Kenley admitted that he was perhaps too enthusiastic, but he shared his hopes that the duck preserve would simply improve the "game proposition" progressively more as the years passed. He reminded Temple that abundant deer and ducks would be "very advantageous" to the company because "if we ever want to sell out, there is no doubt in my mind, if we have it well stocked with game, that we have added $5.00 per acre to the value of our land."[118]

During the next several weeks Temple and Kenley continued to think about the exciting new waterfowl preserve, but with different concerns. They exchanged many letters about the preserve, with Temple occasionally writing multiple times during the same day. What bothered Temple the most was deciding which particular pond on the pipeline should be "set aside." There were three of them. Initially he decided that the middle pond would be ideal since he thought the ducks would eventually fly from there and provide "good hunting" for the other two ponds. He questioned that selection, however, because he feared that the sanctuary ducks would be disturbed by hunters "passing by the middle pond" as they made their way to the other ponds. Upon further consideration, he believed that the pond closest to the river, the northernmost pond, would be the least disturbed by hunters and therefore it should be the sanctuary site. He soon feared, however, that the ducks there would fly to the nearby river and away from the hunters at the other ponds located to the south, which he did not like either. Out of frustration, Temple finally instructed Kenley to meet personally with the state game biologist "and work out whatever you and he think would be best to provide [the most] ducks to shoot at."[119]

Temple's worries with the new duck preserve concerned hunting, while Kenley's anxieties concerned what to name it. He wrote to Temple just before Christmas, suggesting a modification to the state contract that would change the name of the preserve from "Southern Pine Game Preserve" to "'Temple Game Preserve,' as a memorial to your father." T. L. L. Temple had died five years earlier, and Kenley said that he had thought about also including his given name of Thomas, but he decided against it since "so few people in this part of the country would know it." Nevertheless, Kenley explained that he thought it was important to at least use the Temple name because "we owe it to your father." Arthur Temple replied and said that while he "certainly appreciate[d]" Kenley's "thoughtful suggestion," he felt that his father "was himself so little interested in hunting and even perhaps in the propagation and preservation of game, that I wonder if it would be appropriate to call our game preserve 'Temple Game Preserve.'" Besides, Temple continued, his father's name was so "closely connected" with the name Southern Pine Lumber Company that the two names were essentially synonymous. Temple closed his letter by admitting that he could be "entirely wrong" in his assessment, but unless others in the company felt as Kenley did, he was content to leave the name as "Southern Pine Game Preserve," which had been the name of the earlier deer preserve.[120] In the meantime, Kenley's efforts were focused on "getting rid of the hogs" before the duck food was planted. Kenley vowed to do so, saying, "I will be sure and get them entirely cleaned out this year, or that is, as far as it is practical to do so."[121]

By the end of March 1941, upon learning that the state had not yet begun to work on the duck preserve, Temple became impatient. He questioned the delays, again explaining that the "big handicap to successful duck hunting" at Boggy Slough had always been "the lack of food. The ducks have used our ponds for roosting and resting, but after a little shooting they withdraw to quieter areas. If we had sufficient food, however, they would be drifting in, I think, all through the day."[122] Temple also shared with Kenley that he and one of the game commission's representatives had observed ducks eating "some kind of vegetation" several months earlier in two of the ponds along the pipeline, "the two which are separated by a levee," but neither of the men could identify the plant. The game commission's man thought it might be duck potato and he had collected samples and taken them "to headquarters to determine just what it was." Temple was especially disappointed that he had not heard back from the man. He said that, in addition to establishing the duck preserve along the pipeline and planting whatever vegetation the state recommended there, he had also wanted to transplant some of the unknown vegetation "to the big pond on the prairie [Bluff Prairie Lake, later Black Cat Lake]" to also improve the hunting there.[123]

Meanwhile, Kenley had also been thinking about Bluff Prairie, sharing with Temple that he was already planning to sow wild rice and "have a boy drive a bunch of cattle over it until they tracked it in." He told Temple he could fence the planted area for an expense of no more than fifteen dollars as "an experiment," since he had heard good results from similar efforts with wild rice along the coast.[124]

With Temple's urgings, work on the state duck preserve soon progressed, and by November it was nearly completed. But the earlier confusion over which pond to select had now turned to major dissatisfaction. Kenley explained to Temple that he had selected "the lower pond" and thought that the contract had specified it. Temple, however, said that after all the discussions, he had understood the preserve was going to be "the middle pond," which was his choice in the beginning. What actually happened, however, was that the state had taken "the two upper ponds on the pipeline." Work crews had removed trees, built two dams, constructed wire fences, and placed signs—all before Temple knew anything about it.[125] In personal visits to Diboll, as well as in letters, Temple shared with Kenley how "terribly disappointed" he was in the outcome. "The

best shooting we have ever had," Temple explained, had been in the two ponds that the state now protected from hunting. "If I had had any idea that they were going to take those two ponds, I would have suggested that they take the one farther down the pipeline, or even the one on the prairie [Bluff Prairie] next to the old highway," he explained.

Temple said that he wanted Kenley to see if he could modify and possibly even annul the contract. He realized that the state had accrued some expenses, but he said he disliked the outcome so much that he was willing to press the issue. If nothing along those lines could be done, he said he wanted Kenley to seek a reduction in the lease term, something shorter than five years. If the reduction couldn't be made, Temple said it would mean "that our best duck shooting will be lost to us for that length of time and we will simply be providing a refuge for the benefit of others and for the conservation of ducks to be sure."[126]

Unfortunately for Temple, the term of the contract was actually for a period of ten years, not the five years that he had wanted when he signed the incomplete document a year earlier in advance of anyone else reviewing it. Kenley told Temple that he figured the state had expended $469 on the project so far and suggested that he could make similar improvements somewhere else less expensively. If allowed to do so, Kenley said they could "work it out" to "replace" the state's expenses by swapping locations.[127] Temple consented to Kenley's "compromise," so long as "we might recover the best hunting spots we have and give in place the pond farther down the pipeline or perhaps the one on the prairie next to the old highway [Black Cat Lake]."[128] After Kenley built another dam and fences, the state agreed to swap locations and called the new preserve site "Cedar Brush," which was protected from hunting for ten years.[129]

Kenley made several levees and dams at Boggy Slough during the 1930s and 1940s, using tractors and other mechanized equipment. The earthen structures required constant maintenance and sometimes they completely blew out. In October 1944 Kenley reported to Arthur Temple Sr. that he had repaired the dams "at the main duck pond at Cedar Brush" and also the dam "at Arthur's camp," which became known later as "Little Boggy."[130] Lee Estes, an automobile mechanic and service station owner in Diboll, also participated in dam construction and repairs.[131] The early dams were the result of mostly trial-and-error engineering, evidenced by the fact that Kenley at times intentionally broke them so he could "cut the timber that [wa]s covered by the water, so as to not lose the timber."[132]

Boggy Slough, the stream itself, and also the other sloughs were dammed. Many of the slough dams, or rather weirs, remain today, although they also require constant maintenance. In 1948 a large dam was built at Rayville on the downward slopes to the north—just west of the pipeline and the 1941 company clubhouse—which impounded an 18-acre lake. Although Kenley called it *our* [livestock] tank," in his letters to Arthur Temple Sr. when it was built, it became commonly known as "Buddy's Pond," named for Buddy Temple, Arthur Temple Sr.'s grandson, who had grown up fishing in a much smaller stock pond nearby. Kenley fertilized the new pond in 1949 "to grow fish," and it became an instant popular fishing hole, which remains so today. The pond also provided abundant water for Kenley's cattle, which grazed Boggy Slough until the early 1960s.[133]

Boggy Slough's innumerable hogs were a constant threat to duck feeding sites. Although both Arthur Temple Sr. and Jr. instructed Kenley repeatedly, for decades, to "get them out of there," hogs still remain even in the twenty-first century.[134] Kenley certainly removed thousands of them. He rounded them up sixty to a hundred at a time throughout the 1940s, often on a monthly basis, and sold the ones from South Boggy to the Groveton Livestock Company and those from North Boggy to the Houston County Livestock Commission for ten cents a pound on the hoof and for twenty cents a pound dressed, making about $500 a month for the company. Since Kenley used his personal ranch employees to round up the hogs, he received half of the proceeds, which Southern Pine Lumber Company usually paid to his son Edd. Arthur Temple Sr. occasionally requested one of the hogs for his family's use, always insisting that he pay for it since it was "Company property."[135]

At the same time that Arthur Temple Sr. established the Cedar Brush duck preserve, he signed another agreement with the state game commission, in December 1941. This one allowed the state, in cooperation with the US Bureau of Biological Survey, to restock wild turkeys, which were once native to the region. Upon signing the lease document, Temple said that he was "reluctant" to enter into "the turkey experiment on the ranch" because it required "considerable expense" to provide a large pen and "to raise food" for the birds. Nevertheless, he consented, explaining that, "having turkeys on our preserve would be a tremendous asset."[136] Years later, Arthur Temple Jr. recalled the early 1940s restocking of turkeys, saying that between 100 and 150 "young turkeys" were placed at Rayville in a 50-acre pen, which had walls that were 12 feet high. Inside the pen, the birds were fed and protected, he said, and when they matured, they flew out. The stocking plan worked well, he thought, but only "for about two years." After that, the birds seemed to have disappeared. He did not provide a clear reason for the stocking failure, but he did say that he thought the birds were Rio Grande turkeys, and he believed eastern wild turkeys might have fared better. He also recalled that shortly after the early 1940s Boggy Slough restocking, he stocked eastern birds on the company's cutover longleaf pinelands in Newton County, in an area known as Scrappin' Valley, and there the program was more successful.[137] In Boggy Slough's cutover pine-oak-hickory woods, however, it is likely that at least thirty years of fire suppression and overgrazing by overstocked cattle and deer had seriously impaired turkey habitat.[138]

The wildlife protection that began behind the Southern Pine Lumber Company ranch's fences was undeniable. Whether Dave Kenley's claim that he "was the first one to have an idea to capitalize on [wildlife]" was true or not, the business benefits that deer and other game brought to the Temple companies was indisputable.[139] The great experiment that was first cattle, then wildlife, at Boggy Slough, continues to have ramifications in today's conservation area. Game hunting, particularly deer, remains a management focus, although today's managers must balance those needs within the higher goal of reestablishing and maintaining the broadest natural diversity possible, while also maintaining a working forest contributing financial income to the region.

One thing is certain, the mere presence of deer at Boggy Slough, as well as the natural and social conditions that supported them, shaped the land's management like nothing else. And this was no more evident than during the long and depressed years of the 1930s.

CHAPTER 8

The Land for Sale

The Great Depression and Difficult Decisions

E'en now, methinks, as pondering here I stand,
I see the rural Virtues leave the land.

—**OLIVER GOLDSMITH** (1770)

The decade of the 1930s was pivotal in Boggy Slough's history. It was an uncertain time when everything about the land as well as the future of the Temple businesses was carefully evaluated and reconsidered. For several years all of what is now the Boggy Slough Conservation Area was offered for sale on the open market. In various ways the ranch, the cows, the hogs, the deer and ducks, the land, the waters, and the minerals were commoditized and offered for purchase. Only the "hunting privileges" and the "second crop" of timber were to be retained. Arthur Temple Sr. figured that the value of the land, minus the timber and minerals, was worth only $2.50 an acre. The minerals and royalties he estimated at another $2 per acre, while he thought the deer and ducks might add between $1 and $2 more per acre. At times he was willing to sell out completely to an individual or to the state and federal governments for as little as $5 per acre if he could obtain the payment in cash.[1] For one reason or another, he as well as several prospective buyers wavered when it came time to make their final decisions. Perhaps the greatest achievement of the 1930s was that Boggy Slough simply remained a Temple property.

Two significant events occurred late in 1931 that would profoundly shape the history of Boggy Slough as well as the history of the Temple businesses and family for decades to come. The first was the death of Dan Gilbert, who died suddenly of a heart attack, ironically at Boggy Slough while deer hunting, on November 16.[2] The second was the immediate elevation of Arthur Temple Sr. to Gilbert's vacated position of vice president and general manager of all the Temple businesses. Arthur Temple became the first Temple-family vice president since his uncle William Temple briefly held the position in 1893 at Southern Pine Lumber Company's beginning, and he became the first Temple to serve officially as Southern Pine's general manager.

Gilbert had presided over a quarter century of tremendous growth by the Temple businesses. The scope of the companies expanded greatly, as Gilbert purchased and built new mills and railroads and acquired additional lands and timber to support them. His tenure also saw the expansion of the retail lumber business and a growth in real estate acquisitions obtained mostly through foreclosures. Much of the expansion, however, occurred during the inflated economy of the middle and late 1920s, which left the Temple companies ill prepared for the Great Depression. The over-

Arthur Temple Sr. gave the best years of his short life to holding together his family's lumber businesses during difficult times. *Courtesy of The History Center, Diboll.*

expansion of real estate investments through Temple Lumber Company's retail operations, the mounting ranching debts, and the accumulation of nearly a decade's worth of overpriced timber proved to be major problems. Under Gilbert's direction, Dave Kenley, as head of the Timber and Lands Department, had embarked on a timber buying spree in the 1920s that later crippled the company. Kenley bought hardwood and pine timber all across East Texas, from the coastal counties of Jefferson and Orange in the south to the Red River counties of Bowie and Red River in the north. Kenley became giddy at times during the buying frenzy, writing Gilbert from all across the state to say he "hate[d] to take time to eat or sleep" since he figured his waking hours were worth "at least $1,000 per hour" to the company (more than $14,000 per hour in 2016 dollars). Gilbert commended him. "I cannot say too much praise in

what you have accomplished," he once wrote, and even considered buying timber in Mexico.[3] Once the Depression hit, the Temple forest products businesses lost money simply by operating, even with lower labor expenses, because the cost that had been paid for the raw materials nearly rivaled the selling price of the manufactured products.

In later years, Arthur Temple Jr. blamed Gilbert's free spending and expansionist policies for his father's early death in 1951 at the age of only fifty-six. Arthur Jr. recalled his father's many restless nights and his moving a cot to the screened porch so he could stir and pace freely and not wake the family during the worrisome times of the Depression.[4] But Arthur Sr. always reminded his son that Gilbert's reason for attempting to grow the Temple companies had been "for little Arthur" and for the continued success of later generations. Arthur Sr. mentioned Gilbert's consideration whenever Arthur Jr. contemplated quitting the family businesses, which Jr. often did during the middle 1940s, after beginning his employment at the Temple Lumber Company lumberyard at Paris, Texas, in 1939.[5]

Gilbert had been a manager, an employee who was not of the ownership class. So while he did what he thought was right, he would not ultimately reap the benefits or failures of his actions. He also died in considerable personal indebtedness to the Temple companies, mainly through his investments in various speculative ventures, also during the 1920s.[6] Gilbert, like most of the top executives, freely speculated in side investments and carried personal accounts within the company's books. Gilbert allowed these activities, and participated in them himself, as long as they did not negatively interfere with the main Temple businesses, or at least did not seem to do so. Nevertheless, conflicts of interest regularly surfaced and were ultimately tolerated and simply brushed aside. Gilbert's cattle partnerships with Dave Kenley and with others within Southern Pine Lumber Company, as well as their buying and selling land and timber personally, were just two examples of speculative ventures that often conflicted with the company's interests.[7] Another example included Kenley and Texarkana office personnel buying four small sawmill operations in 1923 to limit Southern Pine Lumber Company's competition in cutting state-owned gum and oak timber in the creek and river bottoms along the Texas State Railroad, north of Boggy Slough, in Cherokee and Anderson Counties. With Gilbert's blessing, Kenley gave sawmilling "a whirl" by purchasing for his own account two of the "little mills," including one that was earlier owned by the state, and operating them for personal profit.[8] Other ventures of Temple's top executives included investments in oil and gas leases and royalty speculations, with Kenley once sending an urgent telegram to Arthur Temple Sr. in 1934, begging him to send money

David Crockett "Dave" Kenley, Judge Minton's brother-in-law, was a Temple employee from 1908 through 1967, served as Southern Pine Lumber Company's longtime head of the timber and lands department, and held cattle grazing leases to more than 20,000 acres of Boggy Slough from 1939 through 1962. *Courtesy of The History Center, Diboll.*

and execute an emergency deed signature on his and E. C. Durham's behalf, "to save our hides!"[9] One of Gilbert's largest debts in 1931 concerned his investments in John E. Hintz's Oil Field Lumber Company, which also involved several of the Temples and eventually reorganized and became Temple Builder's Supply.[10]

Arthur Temple Sr. inherited the management of the Temple businesses under just about the worst economic conditions possible. The nation's gross domestic product more than doubled between 1910 and 1920, and it maintained an upward trend throughout the 1920s. But after the stock market crashed in the fall of 1929, everything faltered and failed. The Dow Jones Industrial Average reached a low level that would be unmatched for another quarter of a century.[11] The Temple businesses struggled under a burden of debt, taxes, overvalued assets, and a number of labor and other social responsibilities. Arthur Temple's first line of defense was to encourage all his managers to liquidate "everything not directly connected with the manufacture of lumber and the retail distribution thereof." Cutover forest land was deemed a liability. Retrenchment policies encouraged Kenley to protest property tax valuations with such zeal that his fanatical tactics became notorious in some counties, especially in Trinity County, where most of the Boggy Slough lands were located. Balancing debts to federal and local governments (in the form of corporation and property taxes), to various creditors, and to payroll and other employee obligations became all-consuming. The companies borrowed money regularly from the Federal Reconstruction Finance Corporation and from numerous other sources, including even local citizens in Angelina County, to pay off rising debts to the banks and maintain basic credit.[12]

Increasingly, Arthur Temple came to rely on E. C. Durham, who was Arthur's sister Gertrude's brother-in-law, whose guidance he valued, especially as it related to Boggy Slough and to important labor issues. One of Durham's earliest recommendations to Temple was to raise wages and salaries

E. C. Durham, a Temple family member and general manager of Temple short line railroads, was probably the first person to entertain deer hunting business guests at the Boggy Slough ranch, beginning in 1913. *Courtesy of The History Center.*

immediately, even as debt rose, to offset efforts being made to unionize Temple's employees at Diboll. In a four-page letter, Durham revealed that other local industries, such as Lufkin Foundry & Machine Company, were paying wages and salaries nearly triple what Southern Pine was paying for the same class of labor. Durham also shared that Southern Pine employees were paying "higher average rents and other living costs" than the employees of other lumber companies. It was imperative, Durham advised, to raise wages and salaries voluntarily, without being "told to do so by the government," because preempting the government's possible creation of a minimum wage would go a long way toward retaining employee loyalty. Above all, Durham warned, if Temple ever lost "control of the labor, there [would] be little joy in living, and the loss to our businesses [would] be tremendous."[13]

The most pressing matter that came to Temple's attention within just days of Gilbert's death, however, was intensifying troubles at the Rayville Ranch concerning the Boggy Slough Hunting Club and with poachers whose confrontations with Captain Ray and his men were becoming violent. Ranch manager Ray was increasingly worried with the distractions caused by the game preserve and the hunting club's various "privileges" to hunt and entertain guests at the ranch. Company attorney R. E. Minton was especially anxious, believing that simply too many people were hunting, both legally and illegally, and no one seemed to know who was authorized to hunt and who was not. Minton's and Ray's strong resistance to the club caused many of the Diboll managers to fear that their hunting and fishing might cease altogether. Since no one wanted that to happen, Durham advised Temple to move ever so cautiously to temper the deluge of negative reports coming almost daily from Minton and Ray. But above all, Durham warned, nothing should be done to "antagonize Mr. Ray."[14]

Minton's written complaints to Arthur Temple Sr. were numerous. He wrote to him on December 12, 1931, to report that "fire hunters"—night hunters—were again giving J. J. Ray's riders "considerable trouble," and Ray and Minton feared that one or more deaths would soon occur. They felt this way because, two nights earlier, Ray and his men had caught five poachers who revealed sinister plans to harm company employees. The five men had together killed two does, Minton explained. Two of the men carried headlights, while in the darkness behind them the other men trailed, with guns raised, prepared to shoot and kill anyone who opposed them. Fortunately, Minton said, "three of our men were together and no shooting was done." Minton also reported that "some 15 or 20 more" poachers were "fire hunting under the same circumstances, with agreement among them that they will kill anyone who interferes." This was a most serious matter, Minton stressed, and he wanted Temple to know that he had immediately

"Judge" R. E. Minton, who zealously protected Boggy Slough's deer and taught Arthur Temple Jr. how to hunt them, was a longtime legal counsel for the Temple businesses. *Courtesy of The History Center, Diboll.*

telephoned Texarkana to convey the urgent news, but upon finding Temple out of town, he was forced instead to write the letter. Minton shared that Ray was already planning to hire additional help to "clean the situation up," but Ray and Minton both wanted clear direction from Temple, warning that "if our employees do the shooting, you will then probably be faced with prosecution for murder or assault to murder and our employees want to know whether in such event the Lumber Company would bear the expense of defense, and you are also liable to be faced with a damage suit by the injured party or surviving relative." Minton said Ray was waiting for Temple to call him by telephone immediately upon his receipt of the letter, or better yet,

for Temple to come to Lufkin as soon as possible to meet in person with Ray.[15]

Arthur Temple replied to Minton by letter on December 15, explaining that he was in New Orleans the first part of the week and then in Ohio the remainder of the week, thus his being unavailable to receive the urgent phone call. Temple said he was "very sorry" to hear of the recurring troubles at the ranch and he "hardly kn[e]w what to recommend to put an end to it." He suggested Ray and Minton get with Durham and Kenley and together they "work out some solution to the problem or some course to follow," adding, "I would hate like the dickens to see any of our men kill a poacher." If such was the case, however, Temple said Southern Pine Lumber Company would indeed "defend any man who is brought into court for any such act committed while on duty," for he felt that the Company had "every right to protect our property." Temple also expressed some concern for why Minton was not having better assistance from the state in "patrolling" the ranch. He closed by encouraging Minton to "get this matter adjusted satisfactorily" and to keep him advised in "what steps are taken," adding that while he was "pretty busy at the present time with other things," he would "be glad to meet Mr. Ray or any of you at any place at any time."[16]

Minton was displeased by what he considered to be a passive response, and he replied by another letter saying that during Temple's delay, he, Ray, and Durham had already met about the issues, agreeing to turn the matter over completely to Ray's "experience and judgment." Since Minton now believed the number of regular poachers was "as high as 40," Ray would employ "additional help," with or without the state's assistance. Since Temple specifically brought up the state's "help," or lack of it, Minton seized the opportunity to share again his many frustrations with certain "unfaithful wardens," writing several paragraphs detailing their offenses, in case Temple was not already aware of them. Minton cautioned, however, that while these "unscrupulous men" were recently "removed from this terri-

tory, we still face the Bolshevistic condition left in their wake." While Ray had "faced this situation for all these years," endeavoring constantly to avoid bloodshed, Minton warned he did not know how much longer the killing could be avoided.[17]

But that was only half of the story. Minton also wanted Temple to know that some of the Boggy Slough Hunting and Fishing Club's own hunting parties had simply gotten out of hand in recent years. While Ray was facing all the troubles "on the outside," Minton explained, "our club guests were overrunning the premises, 30 or 40 of them at a time, and Mr. Ray was not advised who they were, when they came or when they would leave." Furthermore, "interspersed with them" were many "local fellows Mr. Ray knew to be his enemies." And while there were definite "club rules designed to regulate the use of the premises, no one observed them." Minton informed Temple the situation was so "intolerable" that Minton and Ray had actually "persuaded Mr. Gilbert to dissolve the club" just before Gilbert's untimely death. Thinking the club was indeed closed, Ray was most surprised when someone later advised him of a scheduled party "without Mr. Ray's knowledge or consent." In several paragraphs Minton explained the con-

fusion and disagreement among the ranks at Diboll concerning Boggy Slough. In the aftermath of Gilbert's sudden death, Minton declared the situation dire: "This has created such friction in the 'family' that, apparently, your office is going to have to take the matter in hand and decide what is to be done, issue instructions and enforce them." If not, then Minton told Temple he should seriously consider "a profitable sale of the game crop."[18]

Temple disliked Minton's demands. Not only was Boggy Slough out of control, it seemed its primary protector was also. Temple delayed a couple of days before replying to Minton, during which time he received another letter from E. C. Durham advising him against upsetting Ray. Temple then wrote Minton cautiously and said he did "not want to assume the responsibility" of making policy decisions about the club. He said he and his father had discussed the matter and they decided that since Ray knew the "circumstances and conditions better than anyone else," that the local club members should work out all details to Mr. Ray's "entire satisfaction." Temple said he had "heard fragments of the plan" to sell Boggy Slough's "hunting privileges" before, but he needed to know more about the plan before making that decision. Until then, he wanted to keep the land as well as the game that was on it. He reminded Minton of "the tremendous assets we have in this ranch as a hunting preserve on which we can entertain our business friends and customers." Temple said he expected that as long as only "conservative parties" were allowed, Ray should have no problem. In fact, Temple thought that since the current deer hunting season was nearing its conclusion, the club members would have much of the following year to work out a plan "under which we can operate happily and without antagonizing and without injustice to anyone."[19]

Early in 1932, Temple finally met with both Ray and Minton, listened to their concerns, and reiterated his confidence in them to develop new rules for the hunting club, "entirely in accordance with Mr. Ray's wishes." All seemed well, until March, when Minton sent the proposed rule changes to Texarkana. There were objectionable restrictions in the rule changes that Temple did not expect. Among them was the elimination of all liquor and practically all guests. Temple shared with Durham that he felt the proposed regulations were "quite stringent, and in fact, considerably more so than I would like to see." Temple wondered if the company's "hunting privileges on the ranch" could continue "with any degree of satisfaction or profit from a business standpoint" if the proposed rules were adopted. Completely dissatisfied with the new rules, Temple wrote Durham and tried to persuade him to meet with Ray and work out something else. Ray was certainly "the man on the place" with the "responsibility of the ranch," Temple acknowledged, but Ray also had to be reasonable.[20] Durham answered that he did not think any set of rules could be framed that would completely please Ray or Minton while also allowing the company to continue its use of hunting privileges "with any degree of satisfaction or benefit." Short of discontinuing all hunting at Boggy Slough, Durham advised Temple to accept Minton's and Ray's proposed rules, regardless how distasteful, at least "until we can stop the dog's tail from wagging the dog."[21]

Temple then reconsidered the entire matter, and in a two-page letter to Minton, copying Durham, he outlined his objections, principally two of them. First, he wanted guests who represented the company's best interests to be allowed continued access to the ranch. In doing so, however, Temple was "okay" with eliminating "private parties," as suggested by Durham as a compromise to eliminating all guests, believing the guests at private parties composed the majority of Ray's displeasure. While most club members opposed this restriction, Temple was willing to relinquish the point, saying, "Ray's objections are valid objections." Besides, Temple cautioned, "the ranch" and its hunting privileges were "too valuable" to the company to let private interests interfere. As for the restriction of all liquor, Temple was unyielding. "Regardless of how we may feel about prohibition or the enforcement of the Eighteenth Amendment," he wrote, "I think that we should probably recognize the fact that we cannot control the acts of individuals, and particularly when those individuals are our guests." Temple suggested that "we simply have an understanding among ourselves, or even an agreement, that there should be no free liquor provided." Temple further explained his belief that such a course would eliminate "promiscuous drinking and confine it to small quantities which might be brought along by individuals. In other words, I think the trouble has been in the past in the quantity provided and the way it has been handled, rather than in liquor itself. I don't believe there would be any objection or criticism if it were handled just as a man might handle it in his own home. If we should have very strict rules and regulations on this point, I am afraid that we might hurt someone's feelings, with the result that we might suffer more than we would gain in good will." Temple suggested Minton and Ray seriously reconsider the objectionable points, for he really did not want to close the ranch to hunting altogether, especially since Minton and Ray were also telling him the deer population was increasing so fast "as to be a nuisance."[22]

The remainder of the year 1932 passed with no definite club policy changes occurring, other than the standing order to pacify Ray at all odds. Temple cautioned his managers about it regularly. All parties needed to be scrutinized for the best possible good will to the company, and the numbers of guests needed to be kept smaller than it had been in the past. By April, Dave Kenley was entertaining oil lease men and others in squirrel hunting and fishing at Boggy Slough and was making plans for the fall.[23] In October, Temple cautioned Kenley further. Inviting influential oil men to squirrel hunt and fish may have been okay during the spring and summer, when overall visitation was relatively low, but Kenley should be careful before including them unnecessarily during the busy fall deer hunting season, especially if one of the men were to be placed in Temple's own party he was planning for November.[24]

In time, Temple came to dislike more and more the Rayville Ranch, which, although it may have fostered the abundant deer herds, also interfered with capitalizing on those results. The compounding troubles caused by poachers, pasture riders, and the hunting club were bad enough, but the ranch's never-ending expenses called for drastic measures. As early as February 1932 Temple contemplated ridding himself of the operations, readily admitting a number of times that he did not "know a darn thing about the cattle business."[25] Preferably, he wanted out sooner rather than later. Besides, Ray's own health was declining, as he suffered increasingly from what doctors diagnosed as rheumatoid arthritis, stomach ulcers, and abdominal adhesions. A stomach operation in 1926 did little to ease Ray's suffering, and certainly the increasing poaching troubles added to his worsening condition.[26] The ranch itself was finally beginning to be recognized as the liability it had been for years. But the worst of it was still yet to come.

Eyeing more than two thousand head of cattle at the Rayville Ranch, Temple thought he saw between $40,000 and $50,000 in cash that could be used to help pay taxes and meet payroll at a critical time. In February 1932, Temple and Kenley devised a plan whereby Ray would leave Boggy Slough, move to Southern Pine's smaller 9,000-acre Renfro Ranch in Angelina County, lease it for six years, buy the 320 to 350 head of company cattle already there, and develop the property as a game preserve as he had done at Boggy Slough.[27] The Renfro Ranch had been acquired only recently by Southern Pine Lumber Company, in 1925, and was not near the showcase property that

was Boggy Slough. The second-growth timber, the grass, and the game were inferior, but Temple and Kenley thought the smaller scale of operations might appeal to the aging and ailing Ray.[28] As for the cattle left behind at Rayville, Kenley would find a buyer, beginning first with the wealthy lumber and oil man J. M. West of Houston, who showed initial interest, especially if he could also buy or lease Southern Pine Lumber Company's 27,000-acre Valenzuela Ranch in Dimmitt and Webb Counties.[29] West also was considering a purchase of several underperforming Temple Lumber Company retail yards in South Texas.

Of course this was shaping up to be the best possible outcome. But just when all seemed to be going so well, Ray began to push back against plans for his relocation and his new, independent status, and J. M. West suffered a terrible automobile accident that left him bedridden for months. Ray would need further convincing to vacate, while West's lengthy recovery effectively ended meaningful negotiations. The most surprising development, however, was the gradual revelation that Ray held $34,853 in notes owed to him in his open account with Southern Pine Lumber Company.[30] Ray demanded satisfaction in his disposition, especially since the company had persuaded him to relocate to East Texas in the first place, or else he would demand his money, which was cash the company could not afford to surrender, and at times it simply did not have. The company was in considerable debt already and was obtaining loans from numerous sources, including local citizens, such as the Oliver and Hyman families of Angelina County, which was never a pleasant experience, because the transactions required the signatures of Arthur Temple, Henry Gresham Temple, and T. L. L. Temple—all three—in order to keep the loans out of the public records.[31] Debt was piling up, as the company was essentially borrowing from one source to pay another, and just when Temple thought he could get out of the ranching business and realize some badly needed income in the process, he learned he would barely make it out crawling, if he came out at all.

Incredibly, negotiations with Ray languished in fits and starts for more than twelve months. Temple, Durham, and Kenley worked constantly at appeasing Ray.[32] Durham cautioned delicacy at all times, once writing that Ray was "a hard nut to crack."[33] More than once Ray agreed to leave Rayville and accept the Renfro proposition, but backed out over disagreements about timing of the move and whether or not he would take his money in whole or in part, or "leave it with us," as Temple so often pleaded. To sweeten the deal, a paid leave of absence for Ray was contemplated, and a paid vacation was offered. Ever present was the fear that Ray would immediately "sever his connection to the Company, expecting to be paid off."[34] Ray once counter-offered to accept the Renfro lease if he could also lease Rayville. That was annoying enough to Temple, because it wouldn't get rid of Ray or the cows. Yet Kenley, thinking as a cow man himself, readily jumped in to express his own interest in leasing Rayville, instead of Ray, and to accept some of the offers that Ray had declined. No one seemed to understand, however, that Temple was done with cows at Rayville. He did not want company cows there, nor did he want Ray's or Kenley's or anyone else's.

In the meantime, until Ray was out, convincing him to keep Rayville's operational costs as low as possible and disposing of the cattle as quickly as possible was also a challenge. Temple wanted to sell the cattle to have money to pay off Ray, while every day of delay the cows ate into the money Temple could not afford to lose. Ray held out for the best market conditions, and Kenley at times not only supported the decisions but probably thwarted and sabotaged several deals in the process, with Durham suggesting as much in his reports to Temple. This aggravated Temple to no end, yet he always caved in to Kenley, acknowledging he knew nothing of cows and he knew of nothing better to do than to trust Kenley.[35]

While the negotiations with Ray wore on, poaching conditions at Boggy Slough deteriorated from bad to worse, just as Minton had warned. On Friday evening, August 19, 1932, tragedy occurred

at the ranch, the scant details of which survive only in incomplete company records, paltry newspaper reports, and a few surviving oral history interviews. According to company records, on that night, just after dark, between the hours of eight and nine o'clock, three Trinity County men—Walter James, an unidentified nephew of James's, and an unidentified barber from Groveton—gathered in Groveton before traveling to Southern Pine Lumber Company's Cedar Creek pasture near Vair, about two miles southeast of Ray's house, where they crossed the fence and entered the pasture to "fire-hunt." Upon crossing the fence, James's gun accidentally discharged. The men proceeded a half mile beyond the fence, following an old logging railroad, when they were met by three lights that flashed on them. Shooting immediately followed, mostly buckshot at close range. James was hit at least twice and fell to the ground, while his companions ran and hid about 300 yards away. James, although injured, was able to make it to his nephew in the dark, but he was wounded too badly to move farther. His nephew and the barber left him for help, but upon returning, they found James had died. The next morning, the *Lufkin Daily News* ran a hastily assembled story that said "Jones," actually James, was a longtime state highway employee and that he had been "assassinated."[36] On Sunday, a story ran in the *Dallas Morning News* that stated James had been "hunting with a headlight" in the "Diboll State Game Preserve." That story also included mention that James had earlier shot to death his father-in-law in a domestic dispute, but James was exonerated by a jury in Conroe.[37] Then on Monday, another story ran in the *Lufkin Daily News* that reported charges for the murder of James were brought against three men, who were identified as Ink (Enoch) Jones, E. E. Ivy, and Emory Midkiff, who were state game wardens "very diligent in the discharge of their duties." The story further stated the men made their bonds of $5,000 each at Groveton and were represented by the prominent Lufkin attorney J. J. Collins.[38]

Durham reported news of the shooting to Arthur Temple by letter on August 22 and said that Ray was "advancing the theory that two parties of fire-hunters came in contact with each other and then the shooting ensued." Durham stated there was "no evidence as to who did the shooting." Only upon the insistence of the Trinity County sheriff were the three game wardens arrested and charged with murder, Durham explained, adding that the warden Midkiff, who was earlier one of Dave Kenley's personal ranch hands, was also one of Ray's employees at the ranch.[39] Temple replied to Durham, writing that he was sorry to hear the news and he certainly hoped none of the company's men were involved in the shooting, and if they were, that "they were fully justified in their actions."[40] Durham responded the following day to explain that, since the shooting occurred on company land that was leased to the "State Game Department," the whole matter was "a State affair and Southern Pine Lumber Company has nothing to do with it," other than "the interest which its officers and employees have in seeing the law enforced."[41]

Walter James's death certificate, containing information provided by one of James's brothers, gave the cause of death as "homicide" due to "gunshot wound of chest and left arm . . . killed while hunting in game preserve."[42] Understandably, the local populace was stirred by the news, and the shooting is still discussed today. Oral historian Thad Sitton wrote of the shooting in his 1995 book, *Backwoodsmen*, saying, "There was no middle ground in the interpretations. Depending on whom one spoke to, James was either "'a rough man, but a good man,' who was determined to assert the traditional hunting rights of his people, or, he was a sociopathic outlaw, a man who had killed his father-in-law and who was accustomed to beating his wife and bootlegging whiskey on the courthouse square in Groveton."[43] As for the three wardens who were arrested, and quickly released, records of the Trinity County District Court do not reveal that prosecutions were ever made concerning James's death. The records do verify, however, the 1929 change in venue to Montgomery County concerning James's trial for the killing of Sam Moore, James's father-in-law, "who had for many years," the records state, "been a peace officer in Trinity County."[44] It appears J. J. Collins—claimed by many, including Arthur Temple Jr., to have been "the greatest trial lawyer in East Texas history"—kept the murder charges from advancing further.[45] R. E. Minton had enjoined James, as well as other members of James's family, from reentering Boggy Slough as early as 1926, and James was well known to Southern Pine Lumber Company and others as a repeat offender, adept at eluding the law and the riders. Charlie Harber, who grew up in Boggy Slough, being twelve years old at the time of the shooting, said he heard many stories of Walter James told by veteran pasture riders over the years. According to Harber, James was one of "the old time outlaw hunters," who taunted Ray's men and the wardens as if it were a thrilling, yet dangerous, game, one that James eventually lost.[46]

The James killing at Boggy Slough and the generally depressed economy of the day made game protection a sour affair in East Texas. Fearing a public outcry that might influence the state game commission in Austin to give up the unpopular fight to fully enforce the few game laws that existed, Durham, who was active in the Angelina County, East Texas, and United States chambers of commerce, wrote a public affairs letter to sportsmen and others interested in the preservation of wildlife in East Texas within three weeks of the shooting. Sending the letter to "a number of prominent men," Durham reminded them of the "several preserves in Angelina and adjoining counties" upon which "deer and other game have increased very rapidly." Durham said "the overflow from the protected areas" had "restocked the surrounding territory and provided good hunting in many localities where game had been practically exterminated before the preserves were established." The effective protection of these "havens and breeding grounds," Durham argued, was essential to ensure a game supply for the future, so that "the boys and young men of today may enjoy the pleasures and benefits of hunting in future years." Durham urged the necessity of the game commission hearing from "the best element of the citizenry," and he asked sportsmen to seek from the commission "strict enforcement of the law" and the continued protection of the "breeding grounds located in this section of the State."[47] No doubt, there were many recipients of Durham's letter. The *Lufkin Daily News* reported just three years later, in a positive feature story on the area's hunting clubs, that "approximately 750 Angelina County men are either interested, or directly connected with, hunting and fishing clubs in the county." Located just nine miles from both the Neches and Angelina Rivers, Lufkin was then billing itself as "the perfect haven for hunters, fishermen, and campers who like to get out in the open air and enjoy the beauty of the winding rivers and wooded spots," which was an "outdoor life made possible by a heavily forested East Texas river bottom."[48]

A couple of months after the James shooting, Kenley delivered to Texarkana some sorely needed good news concerning "the ranch," writing in October to Arthur Temple as well as to T. L. L. Temple, who had just returned from his summer residence at Quogue, New York. Although Ray and the cattle remained firmly planted at Rayville, Kenley boasted that his efforts to fight property valuations on behalf of the two family lumber companies had resulted in an $813,045 reduction in valuations over the previous year. Kenley explained, "I went around and visited nearly every commissioner separate at his home and worked on him as hard as I could. I think we can credit at least $150,000 of the reduction to the Ranch. Had I not had these boys out there, I do not think I would have been able to have gone back and made the contact with them at their homes as I did. I know that the Ranch needs all the credit that we can give it."[49] Kenley said he was most proud of the significant savings he obtained in Sabine and Angelina Counties—$339,178 and $155,180, respectively—but he said he was still protesting the valuations in Anderson and Trinity Counties. He also conceded that he escorted the "Sabine County Board" to Laredo, where Kenley "let them see a little of Mexico, which they had never seen before." The trip was "appreciated very much," Kenley boasted, and he firmly believed it led to a $1 per acre reduction in the valuation of 93,000 acres of Sabine County cutover forestland. Kenley was especially proud to report that the entire trip to Laredo and Mexico cost no more than $150.[50]

At this time, making money in the lumber business was simply out of the question, and Arthur Temple Sr. was elated with such news as Kenley's tax savings. He congratulated Kenley for such "splendid" work on behalf of his family's businesses, saying, "I don't know of anything of greater importance to us right now than saving money," and "while the ranch may deserve some credit, it has only given you an opportunity or provided the background for your own effectiveness."[51] Temple said he and his father were in agreement that Kenley should "use the ranch to good advantage for the benefit of any of our companies" and encouraged Kenley "to use the hunting privileges" whenever he was so inclined. "In fact," Temple declared, "this ought to be the main purpose of the hunting preserve."[52]

Kenley took such encouragement to heart. After Ray finally moved out early in 1933, Kenley used the Boggy Slough hunting "privileges" more and more to entertain county courts, occasionally taking the commissioners from as many as six different counties at once, believing it necessary to keep tax values down, especially in Trinity County. He regularly stressed to Arthur Temple Sr. that he rarely enjoyed such duties, since he cared little for hunting personally. "It is merely business," he wanted Temple to know. As to why he took so many commissioners at the beginning of the deer season, he said it was merely "to get rid of the bunch" and to "shed some of these obligations." Admittedly, it was "a little difficult to handle these commissioners from the different counties together," Kenley acknowledged, because "sometimes you do not want them to compare notes on you." Nevertheless, Kenley managed.[53]

Kenley's "handling" methods for county commissioners were peculiar, to say the least, mostly because he did not always utilize the company clubhouse on the banks of Boggy Slough, thinking it best to keep "the Trinity County bunch," especially, out of the lower end and "away from the other courts." As he explained once to Arthur Temple, "I fixed up a log house on the North end of the ranch, about five miles from our ranch house, and I usually slip in there the first day of the season and let these boys have a little party. I took it on myself to limit them to two deer. However, they hardly ever kill but one. If we spend the night, I make the boys furnish their bedding with the exception of a bale or two of hay that I usually furnish."[54] Kenley kept Temple informed about his economy-class hunting parties to ensure that they would not interfere with Temple's own high-profile parties or any others occurring during the coveted opening day. There was rarely any conflict, however, since most of the company parties were conducted out of the clubhouse on Boggy Slough, and Kenley's "log house" parties were about seven miles north of that, five miles above the Rayville ranch house, and more than a mile above Cochino Bayou and the old Eastern Texas Railroad. Although it cannot be known for certain, Kenley's fixed-up log house was likely the former hilltop Rushing house, the former home of the Christie girls' Aunt Beulah and Uncle Charles. Arthur Temple Sr. regularly admitted that he knew very little about Boggy Slough north of Cochino Bayou, and so he consented to Kenley's irregular actions, confining his own parties to hunting south of there.[55]

Despite the economized entertainments for Trinity County commissioners, Kenley still struggled with the tax valuations in that county. It was not so much that he had a problem with Trinity County, but county officials certainly had difficulties with him. Beginning in 1932, Kenley, along with Minton and Durham, mounted a unified front against all county courts, agreeing to "withhold, in one way or another, the payment of taxes" to hold down the spending of the county commissioners. They believed that since lumber and railroad companies paid the majority of taxes, they could place the commissioners "under constant surveillance," thinking if the commissioners did not spend so much, they would not tax so much.[56] In addition, Kenley wrote patronizing letters to

the local courts, reminding them of millions of acres of cutover lands in the Great Lakes states that had reverted back to the states because of nonpayment of taxes and how the same was now happening in Louisiana. Kenley warned the same result would happen in Texas, "and there would be *no* taxes realized," if East Texas county commissioners did not embrace their "duty" and reduce the land values.[57]

Ever so shrewdly, Minton counseled Kenley's handling of Temple's taxes, saying "the fact that so many others have not paid" could be used "as a bluff to prevent a levy on your property by local officers and thus let you drag without payment." Furthermore, Minton advised Kenley to raise enough money in order to obtain a certified check and make a tender payment of taxes in just one county based on Kenley's own valuations, not the county's, "which check on that basis would not probably be accepted, and then by returning the check and having it cancelled, you could use the same deposit as a basis for the next county, and so on, until you have made a legal tender in every county, without ever having had to raise more money. Also this tender would enable you to avoid interest and penalty" for the actual nonpayment.[58] It seemed Minton and Kenley were getting perhaps too good at their jobs of holding down Temple's business expenses, although to the detriment of the local governments.[59]

Yet despite the clever tactics, continued nonpayment of taxes in Trinity County, where most of the Boggy Slough lands were located, eventually became an embarrassment to the Temple family. In February 1935, three Trinity County officials—the school board president, the superintendent of schools, and the tax assessor-collector—traveled to Texarkana to personally meet with Arthur and T. L. L. Temple. They came all the way to Texarkana, Arthur Temple wrote Kenley in a letter, "to explain to us the plight of the schools and to enlist our support," because a number of districts were "at the end of their rope and cannot go any longer unless they get some money from us." Temple said he and his father "explained the best we could the reason for our failure to pay taxes in Trinity

County for the past several years," but "the gentlemen" countered to say Southern Pine's lands were valued on the same basis as all the other lumber companies' lands, and those companies had paid their taxes, while Southern Pine had not. Temple stressed to Kenley several times his desire to "help the schools" by finally settling the four-year dispute and paying the taxes fully or even partially, if it could be done "without prejudicing our right in any suit which might be brought against us."[60] Temple mentioned a legal suit because this was not the first time Trinity County officials had visited him in Texarkana about the taxes. In August 1934 a special attorney representing Trinity County came to Temple's office, saying a suit was inevitable because they knew Temple paid taxes in other counties, but not in Trinity County.[61]

Kenley responded to Temple's concern in a letter, saying he had long ago learned to "fight down" the argument to "pay what the other fellow paid," claiming if he had not handled the Trinity County taxes as he was doing the valuations would be double the current amounts, which were still too high, Kenley believed. Furthermore, Kenley claimed, "I think we have accomplished a great deal of good for the counties in putting these fights on, since we have kept them from going further in debt." And Kenley's brand of benevolence did not stop there. At the same time, he explained, Temple's businesses were benefiting from "these fights we have put on in Trinity County," because by their "refusal" to pay taxes to Trinity County they were effectively "adjusting" the valuations most favorably in adjoining counties.[62]

Temple replied to say his understanding of the Trinity County valuations seemed "equitable, fair and reasonable." And he again stressed his desire to settle the tax dispute, especially since he understood the schools would be closing soon if Southern Pine did not pay at least part of their taxes. Temple continued to stress this desire a few days later during a personal visit to Diboll and in multiple letters to Kenley upon his return to Texarkana.[63] Eventually, Arthur Temple left the final decision in Kenley's hands, but only because his father insisted that he do so.[64] With T. L. L. Temple's direct support, Kenley fought Trinity County tax officials as hard as he knew how, refusing to pay the land taxes unless the county reduced their valuations. Early in April he made a trip to Austin concerning a Texas Forestry Association meeting with the governor and the US Forest Service, led by Texas lumbermen Ernest Kurth and Paul Sanderson. While there, Kenley learned from certain senators and representatives that there was more than $150 million in unpaid taxes across the state, and the amount was piling up "every year." With such news, Kenley believed landowners would "finally quit paying altogether," and tax revenues would have to come from other sources, possibly even a sales tax. He was strengthened in his resolve to continue fighting, and he wrote Arthur Temple to say he was "awfully glad" he went to Austin, for he had learned "we might not have done so badly by not paying our Trinity County taxes."[65]

Eventually both sides in the tax fight made concessions. Early in May 1935 Kenley and the Trinity County commissioners finally reached a settlement. A land valuation was accepted by both parties, one that was closer to Kenley's figures than to the commission's original numbers. As a consolation to Southern Pine Lumber Company for even a slight concession, Kenley felt he more than made up the land value difference by obtaining a reduced valuation for Temple's seven miles of mainline railroad that remained in the county.[66] Also, all valuations were retroactive without penalty or interest for the four years of delinquency. At Arthur Temple's request, since available cash remained tight, Southern Pine paid one-third of the back taxes in May and paid the balance in July at 6 percent interest for the sixty days of extension. Kenley's tax battles with Trinity County resulted in a savings of more than $10,000 in actual money, not merely in valuations. Upon the tax fight's conclusion, Arthur Temple told Kenley he was "very glad" the matter was finally resolved. It was "a good settlement," he said, "I think."[67]

Meanwhile, back at the Rayville Ranch, while Kenley and Durham were finally relocating Ray to the Renfro property in Angelina County early in 1933, they had found a buyer for the cattle Ray was leaving behind. Dr. George F. Middlebrook of Nacogdoches and his brother-in-law Luther Dean Hall purchased the remaining cattle in January that year. A native of Hope, Arkansas, and a graduate of Washington University School of Medicine at St. Louis, Dr. Middlebrook was a prominent Nacogdoches physician who had served as a sawmill company town doctor at Graysonia in Arkansas, at Lake Charles in Louisiana, and at Caro, Dunham, Mayotown, Cushing, and Haslam in Texas. He was also a cow man, like Kenley. Hall was Dr. Middlebrook's brother-in-law, being the husband of Middlebrook's wife Annie Lou Carter's younger sister Effie Mae. Hall was also one of Dave Kenley's employees in Southern Pine's Timber and Land Department, where he no doubt experienced firsthand Kenley's own cattle dealings, which may have helped him to convince Middlebrook to assist him in buying the Rayville cattle. In order to execute the sale of the cattle, however, Southern Pine had to sell a six-year grazing lease of Rayville lands to Middlebrook and Hall. Thus it seemed cattle were destined to remain at Boggy Slough for at least a while longer. The small consolation was that while Arthur Temple was still not rid of the cattle, he at least no longer owned them.[68] Upon drawing up the lease, Kenley was mindful of Arthur Temple's concern to reserve the hunting privileges for Southern Pine Lumber Company in order "to protect what game we have for our future use."[69]

At the same time, Kenley returned to seeking buyers of the lumber companies' extensive cutover lands, including the Rayville Ranch, which Middlebrook and Hall showed no interest in purchasing, only leasing. Kenley pitched the lands through the Houston, San Antonio, and Dallas real estate markets, considering the price of $5 an acre if he included the mineral rights, or $3 an acre if he retained them.[70] He presented Rayville as a premier ranch property with "no farms sold out of it," perimeter fenced and cross fenced with both net wire and three or four barbed wires, divided into a dozen pastures. Most fence posts were either cedar or creosoted. The ranch contained "many improvements," he advertised, including a dozen houses and two sets of loading pens and dipping vats. The land was good grazing land, he said, able to support 1,500 head of cattle as well as 1,500 hogs "in the woods." In addition, Kenley said in some advertisements that Rayville was "one of the best game preserves in East Texas," containing more than a thousand head of deer, while in other endorsements, he claimed it to be "the best preserve" anywhere in the state, "with the exception of the Kerrville district [where] you find more deer." Also, the property had many duck ponds, he advertised, including one of 200 acres in size, where Kenley said he had personally seen as many as six hundred ducks at a time. In addition, there were many sloughs that were also good for duck hunting, and squirrel hunting was good as well. Kenley said the creeks that ran through the property provided "extra good farm land," with 1,000 acres still under cultivation by tenants, who provided cotton and "rent corn" annually to sell.[71]

It was not long before Kenley began to consider the federal government as a potential buyer of the company's lands, something Gilbert had advocated early during the 1920s. In February 1933 Kenley shared with Arthur Temple that he was seeing definite and positive reforestation results through fire protection in cooperation with the Texas Forest Service and was beginning to see the possibility of even more advantages through a stronger relationship with the federal government. Kenley said that during a visit with E. O. Siecke of the Texas Forest Service, he was pleased to learn that President-elect Franklin Roosevelt had once owned cutover forest lands in Georgia and worked successfully for fire protection there. Then, as governor of New York, Roosevelt had appropriated some $4 million "to purchase worn out lands to grow forests on." Kenley said he believed there was a good chance the federal government, under Roosevelt's leadership, might soon buy cutover lands in Texas, perhaps using funds of the Reconstruction Finance Corporation, a relief program of outgoing President Hoover. Instead of trying to sell the cutover lands to private parties to be used as farms or ranches, as Temple had been advocating, especially with the Boggy Slough lands, Kenley suggested the cutover lands might actually, and finally, be able to regrow timber under federal ownership and management. Why not let the public fund the expense of reforestation and fire protection, Kenley asked. Then, without the burden of various land and timber carrying costs, Southern Pine Lumber Company and Temple Lumber Company could maintain their high position in the markets by focusing on manufacturing and sales while ensuring a constant outlet for Uncle Sam's growing timber. Kenley stressed to Temple that he thought it wise "to get busy and see" whether the state legislature would pass an enabling act to allow the federal government to purchase land in East Texas for the "purpose of growing timber."[72]

Temple initially replied by saying he doubted the federal government would be interested in any of their lands, but he quickly emphasized that if Kenley's hunches were correct, Kenley certainly should prepare to sell the government any and all cutover lands "for reforesting or for any other purpose if they want it." He added, "If a state law is necessary to permit the Federal Government to buy cut-over land, then I think by all means it would be advisable for us to take such steps to initiate this legislation." He advised Kenley to get with Durham and lawmakers in Austin. "You might even go so far as to prepare a bill, with Mr. Minton's assistance, to be submitted."[73]

Three months later Senator John S. Redditt of Lufkin sponsored just such a measure, which allowed the federal government to purchase lands, and in no time Kenley was meeting with federal land agents and showing them Southern Pine and Temple Lumber lands all over East Texas, using every angle he could imagine to interest them.[74] He especially highlighted the abundant game on the Trinity County lands. While many meetings were held at the Angelina Hotel in Lufkin, Kenley took the government men to Boggy Slough as much as possible. Once in November 1933, Kenley wrote to Arthur Temple to say he met a federal agent in Lufkin and took him to the Boggy Slough club-

house for dinner, "and I let him hear some deer stories the boys were coming in telling." Kenley said he told the agent "how much I would enjoy seeing the Federal Government own the ranch so it would be taken care of and let the State get the benefit of the work we had done protecting the game."[75] Kenley came to envision a multilevel partnership among federal and state governments and private corporations in the ownership and management of the land, game, and timber. He explained to Henry Gresham Temple in December 1933 that "through a little work at Washington in interesting the game department," a "good deal of our holdings, including the ranch," could be sold, because "if the Federal Government does purchase any land in East Texas, anything that is stocked with game will be more desirable to them."[76]

Kenley continued to push his federal game preserve idea into the spring of 1934, defending it in letters to Arthur and Henry Gresham Temple. While Arthur Temple at this time preferred to sell the lands of the Pineland and Hemphill operations more than Diboll's lands, Kenley reminded them one federal land agent was "more interested in our game preserve lands up and down the [Neches] river, than any [other lands] we had." "In fact," Kenley said, "I could not interest him enough in the Sabine and Newton County lands to get him to go over there." Concerning Boggy Slough's lands, Kenley said he worked to convince the federal agent of the "possibilities of the Federal Government using this land for the conservation of game, and tried to show him where ours was an ideal location, in the central part of East Texas, where game would spread all over East Texas from it." Kenley was especially pleased when he believed he had influenced the agent enough to return to Washington in early March, presumably to attend "a Game Conservation Department" meeting called by President Roosevelt. After several days of hearing nothing from the departed land agent, he advanced an idea to the Temples, "if it would not be worthwhile for us to have a strong man to go to Washington and see if we could not get it worked out to where we could sell our Southern Pine Lumber Company holdings for a Federal Government game preserve and let us retain the timber for a long time."[77]

While Kenley waited on news from Washington and further instructions from the Temples, he suddenly began to doubt the possibility of Boggy Slough's sale to the federal government. He worried that Trinity County's "entire citizenship" would be against Southern Pine's abrupt sale of 35,000 to 40,000 acres to the federal government, if they were not already against it, because of the tax revenues that would be lost (ironically, even though Kenley was already withholding the company's tax payments because he challenged their excessiveness). Kenley told Arthur Temple he feared Trinity County would soon petition the government and derail any deal. Kenley admitted that Trinity County would "finally get" 35% of future timber sales, but he knew the reality of cutting timber again at Boggy Slough was "so far off" that the uncertain prospect would be of no immediate consolation. Kenley also suddenly began to worry about a future in which Southern Pine Lumber Company did not own land—land he had worked hard to obtain and consolidate the holdings of for decades—and he worried about the company's diminished position in new markets that would certainly include pulp and paper, products of a new industry that would be favorable to young growing timber. Also, in March, a federal agent had shown Kenley what he later described to Temple as "a large map of East Texas" that showed blocks of lands "laid off" being considered for purchase. Included in an eastern block of lands was "most of ours," Kenley said—lands immediately around their Pineland and Hemphill mills. In a western block around Diboll was "the ranch property and a good deal of other property of ours." The marked map troubled Kenley. In April 1934 he cautioned Arthur Temple, who was still pressing land sales, that "giving up so much land" in Trinity County might "hurt our idea of perpetual cutting here [at Diboll] awfully bad." He added, "From a sawmill standpoint we probably would be doing the right thing, but if we give any consideration to the possibility of paper mills, we might be doing the wrong thing."[78]

By late spring 1934, Kenley's enthusiasm to sell Boggy Slough, especially to the federal government, had diminished significantly, while Arthur Temple's resolve to obtain cash from any and all sources remained constant. Although Temple sensed Kenley's waning desire to sell lands, he encouraged him to press on nevertheless. While both men worked tirelessly to hold the businesses together while ensuring an uncertain future, the physical distance between Texarkana and Diboll did not help matters and added to the stress. Each man found the other often indecisive, and usually in disagreement. It seemed when one was finally ready to act, the other held reservations and differing inclinations.

Earlier, during the summer of 1933, Arthur Temple himself had sold Southern Pine's extensive North Texas timber holdings in and around Clarksville to Joe Kurth of Lufkin, who was obligated to cut at least ten million board feet of pine timber per year and agreed to let Temple sell to another man all the gum, elm, sycamore, and hackberry logs for veneer.[79] This gave Temple badly needed cash inflow at a critical time. Of course Temple was elated with his timber deal, as was Kenley, but each man interpreted it differently. Writing from his office in Diboll to Temple in Texarkana, Kenley said Temple's transaction was "exactly what I have hoped we would be able to do—disposing of the North Texas timber to enable us to stay with every foot of timber we have down here."[80] While Kenley was hoping Temple's desire to "dispose" of land and timber would have been satisfied with the Kurth deal for the Clarksville timber, Temple ignored Kenley. Instead, Temple wrote to say he would "like mighty well" to sell not only more timber but as much land as possible, regardless of its location.[81] As he explained, "My idea has been, and is, that we have so much more land than we need, so much in fact that we are land poor," and "it behooves us to turn some of this land into cash."[82]

Another example of conflicting views concerned the federal government's interest in creating a subsistence homestead colony for at least a hundred families in Angelina County, which would have involved the purchase of between

2,000 and 3,000 acres of Southern Pine Lumber Company land south of Lufkin, along the Diboll-Lufkin highway (State Highway 35). The federally backed project, an effort of the Texas Rural Communities Corporation (TRCC), was driven largely by Helen Kerr Thompson. The resourceful daughter of the well-known horticulturalist John Steele Kerr and the wife of lumberman and legislator J. Lewis Thompson, Helen was the founder and resident manager of the philanthropic Woodlake agricultural community, which she established on several thousand acres of cutover Thompson Brothers Lumber Company lands in Trinity County during the early 1920s. The Angelina County project was designed to mimic the successes of her Woodlake project and sought to remove unemployed families from the relief rolls of urban regions and place them onto rural lands where they would work as communal farmers.[83]

When Kenley informed Arthur and Henry Temple of the Angelina County federal relief prospect in March 1934, Arthur Temple urged Kenley to hasten a deal, even though the land contained mature timber that would require "sacrificing" by removing it during severely depressed market conditions, something Kenley opposed. Temple said the housing project was "rather interesting" to him, "for two reasons." The first reason was the price of $20 per acre suggested by Ernest L. Kurth of Lufkin, who was "anxious" to secure the federal project for Angelina County and was also a TRCC board member, along with several of the state's university presidents. The second reason was Temple's enthusiasm "to sell a large quantity of lumber" to the government. Temple even offered to "come down" to facilitate the deal. But Kenley advised against the company's involvement. He thought that the land was not particularly good farmland in the first place, and he cautioned that a selling price of $20 an acre was too optimistic. He also pointed out that a sale, at whatever price, would involve a fifteen-year payment, which he doubted the government could sustain. The land was also near Lufkin, the populous county seat, Kenley explained, containing state highway frontage that

he hated to lose. All things considered, Kenley argued, Southern Pine would be better off holding the land, with its timber intact, until a day when better lumber markets returned. When that day arrived, Kenley contended, the company's "third cutting" of timber would be "by far the best." He argued that thanks to newly implemented wiser harvesting practices, as well as better management of the growing timber, the time between the second and third cuttings would be shorter than the time between the first and second cuttings, and the higher volume of regenerated timber would be advantageously noticeable also. But Southern Pine would have to forgo the temporal income to realize the anticipated higher yields in the future.[84] Eventually, Kenley stalled long enough so that the TRCC moved their interests to other potential community sites across the state. Importantly, Kenley's resistance to selling the land resulted in its later development by Arthur Temple Jr. and the Temple family into Angelina College, late in the 1960s, which included a free donation of 140 acres, and the Crown Colony Country Club and neighborhood late in the 1970s, which comprised some "750 acres of rolling hills and stately trees," according to promotional news accounts at the time.[85]

The federal agents charged with locating and purchasing cutover lands in Texas for the national forests soon returned to East Texas, and Temple was encouraged by the continuing news of their activities. He regularly wrote Kenley, even sending him clippings from the *Texarkana Daily News* concerning the lands to be purchased, urging him to make sure "some of ours" was included.[86] He was afraid of missing out, and his fear resulted in mixed messages to the already indecisive Kenley. At times Temple explained he most wanted to liquidate "cut-over land that is not growing any timber," but if those lands did not interest the federal agents, he wanted to sell land that was indeed growing timber, including "Diboll's cut-over lands," as long as "we would be given a certain length of time in which to remove the timber."[87] At other times Temple expressed a desire to sell only Pineland's and Hemphill's lands, "because we will be through at Pineland and Hemphill in a few years, while at Diboll we have a long cut ahead and are attempting to grow timber."[88]

On the morning of May 28, 1934, right after Temple finished writing another letter to Kenley urging him again to "devote our strongest efforts" to selling lands "without growing timber," one of the government land purchasing agents walked into Temple's Texarkana office. He discussed with Temple the affairs of other lumber company's sales, including prices, and Temple immediately called Kenley by telephone. Temple followed the phone call with urgent written instructions for Kenley to meet with Henry Temple so they could travel together to meet the purchasing agent in Houston the following day. Temple stressed it was time to finally "make up our minds" in the government land matter and "get in with ours" before it was too late. "I see no reason why we should not offer all of Pineland's and Hemphill's acreage," he stated, "reserving the mineral rights for a period of years and the timber for a sufficient length of time for us to remove it, both of which I understand will be entirely agreeable to the government. This land won't be worth much after we get it cleared of timber and after the Government has made its purchase, and I am firmly convinced that we ought to take advantage of this opportunity to dispose of Temple Lumber Company's land at least, for which we will have no need in a few years after Pineland and Hemphill are cut out."[89]

Believing the Pineland and Hemphill operations were nearing exhaustion, Temple saw no better opportunity than the present time to sell those lands. So within days of the government man's visit to Texarkana, Kenley renewed his connections with the purchasing agents and began to arrange lodging for the men to stay in Diboll, in rooms at Mrs. Estes's boarding house and elsewhere in town. When asked if some of the government men could lodge in the Temple family guest rooms in the library, next to the company offices, Arthur Temple replied, stressing that "by all means we ought to exert ourselves to provide quarters for these men" to "have them close at hand."[90]

Meanwhile, at Boggy Slough, after less than a year into the Middlebrook-Hall grazing lease, Middlebrook abandoned the project altogether and sold and shipped out the Rayville cattle at a reported loss of nearly 40 percent, and he dissolved the partnership with his brother-in-law Hall. Unknown at the time to Southern Pine officials, Hall subcontracted with N. S. Locke, an oil man from Gladewater, to take over the grazing lease and purchase from Hall the remaining horses, mules, feed, and implements at Rayville that were part of the original sale. When Durham learned of Hall's deal with Locke, Durham at first refused to permit the transfer of the lease, but upon his meeting Locke, who presented to Durham numerous letters of references from banks and businesses, Durham recommended that Southern Pine work directly with Locke, whom he described to Arthur Temple as "a man of some wealth." Durham felt Locke would certainly accept a new lease, if not an actual purchase, of Boggy Slough, and as a bonus Locke might even lease or buy the company ranch in Dimmitt and Webb Counties, which also remained unsold.[91] Temple replied that while he, his father, and Henry Temple were in agreement to either lease or sell Boggy Slough to Locke, they were "perfectly willing to leave" the final determination to Durham. But to help Durham in the decision, Temple shared his personal views by saying, "We are long on land and real estate and short on money, and I think therefore whenever we can make a lease or a sale of land which we do not need, or even land that is growing timber and we can reserve the timber, we ought to do it." It was nearly the same message he had been giving Kenley. Temple therefore encouraged Durham to "work out the best deal you can, reserving the timber of course."[92]

In essence, Kenley agreed with Temple. Since oil men at the time were among the few who had disposable income, Kenley said the next time anyone heard from Locke, they "should trade with him and get whatever" they could "out of him."

Kenley's only reluctance was how best to protect the reserved timber if they sold the land to a buyer who intended to use the land as a ranch, because "it would be more desirable to them to let it burn over and clean out as much timber as they could." But if any deal was made, Kenley thought an outright sale was preferable to a lease with the option to buy at the end, since Locke "would wake up by that time and find out that he did not want it."[93] If, however, a new lease of Rayville was the best deal to be had, Kenley and Durham both wanted Locke to "get rid of the hogs" and be prohibited from running them in the future.[94] As it turned out, leasing Boggy Slough to Locke proved the most expedient, if not the best, deal to be made at the time, with Locke agreeing to remove the hogs by the first of June 1934.[95] In the meantime Boggy Slough remained for sale to both private and public buyers.

Meanwhile the federal government continued to acquire cutover lands across East Texas. Feeling this pressure and knowing the purchasing agents were lodging at Diboll, Locke again expressed interest in purchasing Boggy Slough in January 1935. This time Arthur Temple expressed he was "not so anxious to dispose" of Boggy Slough as he was other cutover lands, especially those of Temple Lumber Company, but he continued to write Kenley, saying he saw "nothing to be gained by retaining land where we have a reservation of the timber for as long as we need to cut it at Diboll." Temple felt that a reservation of Boggy Slough's timber for ninety-nine years was ideal, and he stressed his desire to also reserve hunting privileges on the 32,000 acres, if at all possible, in the sale to Locke. He was perfectly willing to accept "in the neighborhood of $5 per acre" and let the mineral rights go, but if they were unable to reserve hunting privileges, he wondered whether Boggy Slough's close proximity to a paved highway as well as being "bordered by the Neches River" might bring added value. He felt sure this natural setting with easy access to man-made "duck ponds and other improvements" was worth more than $5 an acre, especially if Southern Pine could no longer enjoy Boggy Slough's outdoor sport "privileges."[96]

Late in January, while considering a sale to Locke, Temple received news from the Atlanta office of the US Forest Service, saying they had approved the purchase of 80,196 acres of his companies' lands in Sabine County and 5,187 acres in Trinity County at $2.50 an acre.[97] The price was low, in fact the lowest given to any of the eleven lumber companies selling land, but Temple knew these particular lands were severely cut over and they were not regenerating pines, since some tracts had no more than 500 feet of merchantable timber per acre after initial cuttings more than twenty years earlier had removed some 12,000 board feet or more per acre. Five hundred board feet of pine per acre, after more than a quarter of a century's worth of growth, in no way constituted the definition of timberlands.

Overall, Arthur Temple was pleased with the sale. Now that he was finally assured some of the badly needed income, he wanted more. Since the government had passed on Boggy Slough, Temple was now ready to sell it to Locke. After receiving news of the forest service purchases, Temple wrote Durham to say he was "ready and anxious" to meet and work out the details. Crossing in the mail, however, was news of a contempt of court case against Locke that was affirmed by the United States Circuit Court of Appeals at New Orleans. The suit involved Locke's oil wells, which had produced petroleum in excess of the federal limits of production, in violation of provisions in the National Industrial Recovery Act of 1933. Temple wrote to say he had "read in the Dallas News a Mr. Locke was headed for the federal penitentiary for contempt and wondered if he was our man." Durham replied he understood Locke would serve ninety days in a federal jail. Temple then instructed Durham to "communicate with Mr. Locke, find out what his plans are, or I might say what the Government's plans are for him," and arrange a meeting as soon as possible. Temple reiterated, "I am very anxious to put this deal through and think we ought to follow it up vigorously."[98]

Copied in the correspondence was Kenley, who later wrote to say he thought any deal with Locke was "mighty good," if they could indeed obtain the $5 per acre minimum that Temple was wanting. But while Kenley had seemed ready to sell to Locke just a few months earlier, he now raised old objections as well as new concerns about adequate fire protection on the reserved timber, as well as about the taxes they would have to pay on the unprotected trees—two issues that constantly "nagged" at him, he said. The threat of fire was on his mind "every time" he thought of selling Boggy Slough to a private party. "I would hate to see us get mixed up to where we could not control it and control the fires on it," he wrote. Kenley, still torn between the advantages and disadvantages of a private versus a government sale, also brought up the idea of selective logging, arguing that if Southern Pine did ever decide to implement fully a sustained-yield cutting practice, adequate fire protection would "surely pay us," as he felt the "third cutting" would realize more profit than the "second cutting" through wiser management.[99] In summary, Kenley pointed out the major differences, as he saw them, between a sale to the government and one to a private party. For one, selling to a private party, such as Locke, would include selling the mineral rights, while a sale to the federal government would allow for keeping them—a possible advantage to a government sale. For another, selling to a private party would allow a reservation of the timber for ninety-nine years, although with uncertain fire protection, while a sale to the government, which would include adequate fire protection, would probably not allow more than a five- or ten-year reservation of the timber—advantage to a private sale. After much hand-wringing, Kenley stated that the bottom line for Southern Pine Lumber Company, if they were going to sell Boggy Slough to the government, was, "it would just be on the theory that we were going to cut out and look forward to winding up altogether here [at Diboll] and abandon the idea of making a perpetual operation." Regardless of the pros and cons, Temple pressed Kenley to continue to seek the federal government's interest in Boggy Slough, for the primary reason that it might help them in their negotiations with Locke,

which Temple seemed to prefer over a government sale, primarily because he could reserve the timber for a longer period of time, and he did not share any of Kenley's grave concerns about fire.[100]

Before a serious meeting with Locke could be arranged, Durham too began to waver, illustrating again the dysfunctions between Diboll and Texarkana at critical times. Durham's indecisiveness stemmed from E. B. Hinkle, Temple's longtime oil lease man, who suddenly advised against the $5-per-acre price, believing Temple and his managers had undervalued the mineral rights and royalties. Because of recent leasing activity in the area, including some activity around Apple Springs as well as the installation of a new drilling rig on the Pine Island property across the Neches River from Boggy Slough, Hinkle felt certain he could obtain an advantageous lease if given time, and he advised against the sale.[101]

Durham thus delayed with Locke, to give Hinkle time to explore the possibility of leases. Temple, however, did not think Hinkle's reasons at the time merited such an action, saying that Hinkle was "always . . . more inclined to gamble on oil and hold for a price on account of the prospects than I am."[102] Kenley, too, who had initially invited Hinkle's assessment, now agreed with Temple. Southern Pine had explored oil leases of Boggy Slough numerous times before, even recently, so Temple expressed to Durham in a letter late in February, saying simply, "I want to sell the ranch." Surely, he wrote, "all the arguments in favor of and against a sale" were already "brought out," and unless there was a new objection that he was unaware of, then "personally, I think we ought to sell."[103]

While Temple did let Durham know that he was ready "to put over this deal" and offer his "warmest congratulations," he nevertheless consented to giving Hinkle time, since Durham felt it was wise, but only as long as it would not jeopardize a sale if and when it was ready to happen. Meanwhile, nothing developed with Hinkle, and Locke, too, began to defer, claiming he needed his unnamed partner "on the ranch deal" to inspect the property. Since the partner's travel schedule did not allow a convenient time to visit Boggy Slough, delays continued for several weeks beyond even Southern Pine's postponements. Kenley eventually determined that Locke was "just stalling with us," believing Locke was merely using the negotiations as a ruse to divert attention away from the fact that he had done nothing to remove the hogs as he had agreed to do under the lease.[104] In time, in the midst of delays on both sides, negotiations broke down completely, and Boggy Slough again escaped sale.

Boggy Slough remained available for purchase for at least a couple more years, but no other negotiation for its sale came as close to completion as the one with Locke during the early months of 1935. But while Boggy Slough was virtually off the auction block, its role in the federal government's purchase of lands in East Texas continued. As Kenley worked with federal agents to finalize the Temple Lumber Company land transactions with the US Forest Service, he offhandedly mentioned to one of them early in April 1935 that Southern Pine had another 100,000 acres of land north of Boggy Slough, in Houston, Anderson, and Cherokee Counties, that they were interested in selling, constituting a major portion of Diboll's operational forest. Kenley admitted later to Arthur Temple that he misrepresented the quality of the lands and timber, telling the agent they would accept nothing less than $12.50 an acre. Kenley said that at such a high valuation, however, the government man became "very interested," as Kenley had hoped, although the agent clarified the government could pay no more than $10 an acre.[105] Although Kenley was ready to drop the whimsical idea immediately upon sharing it with his boss, Temple wanted Kenley to keep the possibility open and actively pursue the government's interest, even if it was a long shot. "Any" prospect of $10 an acre was worth the effort, he said. In fact, after Temple considered the taxes and interest if Southern Pine continued to own the land, as well as calculating the growth rates of timber, he believed they could "buy the timber back ten or fifteen years from now at considerably less than it would cost us to carry

it." Besides, Temple continued, "it's not like [we are] selling this land and timber to some other manufacturer, but we will have an opportunity to buy it back when we are ready to cut it, and it can hardly bring to the Government more than fair market price or more than a mill could afford to pay." Seen in this light, T. L. L. Temple also expressed he was "not opposed" to selling the additional 100,000 acres, but since Henry Temple was unconvinced of its merit, T. L. L. preferred unanimous consent among the directors and officers. Although Arthur felt he could surely obtain Henry's blessing, he had great difficulty directing the actions of Kenley, who did not truly want to sell the 100,000 acres. In the end, the boastful pitch that Kenley had made to the federal agent was nothing more than an old habit of a seasoned horse trader.[106]

Early in May, Kenley planned to use the Boggy Slough clubhouse to host a barbecue for the federal purchasing agents during their visits of the purchased lands in the region, including the Trinity and Houston County lands sold by other lumber companies. Joining them would be a host of other industry and government men, including multiple officials of the US Forest Service and Texas Forest Service and members of the Society of American Foresters. At this gathering, Arthur Temple wanted Kenley to press the sale of the additional 100,000 acres of Southern Pine lands, and he expressed a desire to join the party as well to assist in making the deal. Kenley was now in another pickle. Again he had raised the idea of selling land to the federal government, stirred Temple's enthusiasm and consent, and then backtracked. Kenley did his best to persuade Temple against coming down, explaining that the large crowd of people would offer little opportunity for Temple to do the visiting he desired. Besides, the gathering was "practically" the US Forest Service's party, and those men would be "busy entertaining the other fellows," Kenley said. Furthermore, the river bottoms were flooded, and the party would have to travel from Lufkin to Boggy Slough "on our train." Temple did not really want to come, did he?

Despite Kenley's efforts to dissuade him from coming, Temple would not be kept away, especially since he knew Henry Temple also would be there, and he wanted to see Henry. It would be a "splendid opportunity," Arthur Temple said, for him to be with "everyone" and become "better acquainted." Temple may have had certain expectations about intimate meetings with the government men, but Kenley did his best to divert attention away from selling the 100,000 acres. In fact, he went so far as to come up with a whole different solution. His new idea: instead of the federal government buying the land and taking the timber away from the lumber companies and the taxes away from the county governments, the federal government should simply "pay the taxes and carrying charges on the land" on behalf of the private owners. The private owners, after all, could grow timber "cheaper than the Government could ever be able to grow it," he felt. Kenley believed the government was already doing something similar for cattlemen. Being a cow man, he explained to Temple how he had tracked the finances of a recent cattle transaction, specifically investigating the relationship between the National Finance Credit Corporation and the Federal Intermediate Credit Bank. He concluded the federal government's relief efforts were "carrying 75% of the investment of the livestock men." If the federal government "would do this same thing for the timber growers," Kenley posited, "there would be no need for the Federal Government to purchase land to grow timber on."[107]

After Kenley shared his revelation with the federal land agents, they became almost speechless. They finally asked him for letters "to carry to Washington," which Kenley gladly provided. Kenley also wrote the Southern Pine Association (SPA), seeking their support of his idea, and in doing so he took the concept a step further. Kenley explained to A. G. T. Moore of the SPA the necessity of the federal government advancing money to the lumber companies "for a long time and at a low rate of interest." The lumber companies would use this money to pay taxes on lands "they already

have," as well to purchase additional lands, "so they could get on a sustained yield basis." Kenley continued, describing how Southern Pine Lumber Company had "looked forward to getting on a sustained yield basis for many years and [we] had purchased any holdings that we could that were inside of ours for this purpose up until the depression hit us."[108] If only the federal government would use the relief money differently, Kenley said, there would be no need for the government to own land, and everyone's needs would be met more economically.

Clearly, Kenley did not want to sell any more land to the federal government than had already been approved, and he was serious about keeping "Diboll's lands" available for Diboll's future. Moreover, Kenley even withheld and managed to retain the 5,187 acres of Trinity County lands the government had accepted for purchase in January 1935. Kenley said later of his actions that he was "entitled to the credit" of keeping the land "from being delivered to the Government."[109]

Nothing of Kenley's government finance plan ever developed. The federal government's interest in obtaining Temple's additional 100,000 acres devolved into a weak effort by the Texas Forest Service to use federal funds to buy the land for its own purposes. Kenley disparaged the efforts, saying that state foresters merely wanted "to play with" the land anyway. Nevertheless, Arthur Temple made sure to keep the land selling prospect on Kenley's agenda for most of the rest of 1935. But Kenley never really tried again, nor did the federal government. As to why Kenley did not sell more lands to the government, Kenley once suggested that the federal government finally ran out of money or lost a desire to spend any more of it. If pressed, he claimed the real reason no further deals occurred was because the citizens disapproved of losing local tax dollars through government ownership of land, and politicians recognized that fact.[110]

Through many trials and tribulations and fantastic turns of events, Boggy Slough weathered some significant storms during the darkest days of the first half of the Great Depression. Company ranching efforts were finally eliminated, and a policy of timber growing began its gradual implementation. Major challenges remained, however. Although the Boggy Slough "ranch" was gone officially, cows owned by others would continue to graze Boggy's range for several more decades and remained the cause of endless headaches and heartaches. And the cutover forests and overgrazed pastures had much growing and healing still to do. The questions of what would become of the hunting club, and of all the deer, and who would make those decisions, also remained unsettled.

CHAPTER 9

Whose Land Is It?

Personality Factors in Shaping Boggy Slough

*Land is the only thing in the world worth workin'
for, worth fightin' for, worth dyin' for, because
it's the only thing that lasts.*

—MARGARET MITCHELL (1936)

While Boggy Slough weathered the darkest days of the Great Depression, serious questions about the land's future, and who would answer them, remained. Attempts to gradually convert 32,000 acres of cutover forests into quality pasturelands in support of a large cattle ranch ultimately failed, just as US Forest Service officials had predicted a decade earlier.[1] When Arthur Temple Sr. became Southern Pine Lumber Company's vice president and general manager late in 1931, he did his best to rid his family's lumber businesses of cattle and other unnecessary far-flung assets to pay down debts. He soon found himself leasing Boggy Slough to doctors and oil men, however, who were the only ones with enough cash to purchase the company's livestock.

Temple was able to secure the cattle sales only by granting grazing leases, because the buyers claimed they had no other place to move the cows. For six years the leases changed hands as each successive party learned what Temple already knew: the mixed pine and hardwood forestland was simply incapable of profitably supporting large herds of cattle, something even the early Spanish missionaries had foreseen two centuries earlier.[2]

Temple's managers believed that the protected game and wildlife was the best product of the experimental ranch, a result of natural processes as well as social realities. They found that white-tailed deer proliferated in an early successional, fire-suppressed, and brushy cutover forest where human and animal predators were controlled. Captain Ray and his armed pasture riders had prohibited not only free-range stockmen and hunters and their dogs and fires, but also timber wolves and coyotes.[3] By protecting the land's remaining pines as well as calves and goats, they also protected the deer. So safeguarded were the deer behind Boggy Slough's perimeter fences that their increasing numbers eventually became "a nuisance" to the company's tenant farmers, and they high-lined trees and woody shrubs (eating tender twigs on branches as high as deer could reach) to the point of starvation.[4]

Temple and his managers also learned that deer—and their management—could be good for business. Their favored status, as what environmental historian Donald Worster called "big game in an otherwise diminished world," kept property tax valuations in check and customers, business associates, and law makers and law enforcers loyal and friendly.[5] Such natural and social benefits came at great costs, however, none of which showed up accurately on the company's bottom line.

With the ranch gone, so were Captain Ray and his rangers and thus the game protection with them. Timber-watching tenant farmers also left when they were no longer needed to cultivate corn and other forage crops for Ray's cattle. Southern Pine would have to hire "strong men"—who were of the same rough stock and violent tendencies as those who they guarded against—to patrol the thickening, fire-suppressed woods. In time, such patrolmen alone proved inadequate, and Dave Kenley, head of the Timber and Land Department, convinced the Temples that cattle and their human keepers were necessary at Boggy Slough, which continued to be known for several more decades as simply, "the ranch land that we are protecting."[6]

Even before the grazing leases to Middlebrook, Hall, Locke, and their successors expired, Kenley had begun moving his own cattle into Boggy Slough, in June 1938, keeping them there through 1961. He argued that his herds of cattle, which he initially kept smaller than those of Captain Ray, reduced the fire danger by their grazing and browsing, while their networks of beaten trails served as convenient fire breaks.[7] At the same time, Kenley's brother-in-law and Southern Pine's chief counsel, R. E. Minton, continued to bring legal pressure against poachers and all others who would threaten game and its productive management, as well as against anyone who would retaliate by harming Kenley's cows.

Until the 1960s, cattle and deer, and Kenley and Minton, dominated Boggy Slough's administration, as each man treated the property as if it was his own. To Kenley, it was his "headquarters," from which he directed his personal cattle ventures. Whenever he offered management advice to the Temples, he said "the only way" he knew to give it was to consider Boggy Slough as "if it were mine." To Minton, Boggy Slough was his sporting playground, which he indeed partially owned until 1956. When Minton guided Arthur Temple Sr. and his son Arthur Jr. on Jr.'s first deer hunt at Boggy Slough in 1936, he reminded the Temples that they

"Judge" R. E. Minton, Southern Pine Lumber Company's longtime chief counsel, poses with a deer he killed with a muzzle-loading rifle at Boggy Slough, ca. 1929. *Courtesy of The History Center, Diboll.*

were hunting and visiting the company clubhouse as *his* "guests."[8] Although this was technically true at the time, since Arthur Temple Sr. had dropped his membership in the Boggy Slough Hunting Club three years earlier, it was hardly a detail to mention. Arthur Temple Sr. often felt compelled to remind Minton that he nevertheless remained a major stockholder and the chief executive officer of the company that allowed the hunting club's very existence, and for that reason alone he was at least "permitted to express an opinion" in matters concerning Boggy Slough and its wildlife.[9] Because of their strong personal attachments to the land during the physical absence of the first two generations of Temples, Kenley and Minton defined Boggy Slough more profoundly than anyone else for half a century.[10]

There were many examples of the two men's personal bonds to Boggy Slough; one of the most legendary instances concerned their protest against the construction of a state highway through the north end of the property in the late 1930s. Until he died in 2008, Charlie Harber, who worked cattle for Dave Kenley during the highway's construction, talked often of Kenley's and Minton's hostility to the public road. According to Harber, Kenley and Minton "hated that highway."[11] By the spring of 1937 their opposition reached the capital city of Austin, where the highway and Temple's hunting club became controversial subjects at public meetings of the state highway and game commissions.

Twenty years earlier, in 1917, at the very beginning of the state highway department, transportation commissioners designated State Highway 7 to connect Crockett and Lufkin, the county seats of Houston and Angelina Counties, as a portion of the Central Texas Highway.[12] Roads that passed through Sullivan's Ferry on the Neches River already connected the two cities, but they were merely remnants of local wagon roads, which were maintained by the counties, if at all. For decades they had served the communities through which they passed, but they were not a state highway, which was straighter, wider, higher, smoother, and, importantly, state-funded.

In 1925 the highway department considered using the recently abandoned Eastern Texas Railroad right-of-way for the portion of Highway 7's route between Kennard and Lufkin, a path that ran along Cochino Bayou, through the middle of the Boggy Slough ranch. Minton opposed the idea, not only because Southern Pine Lumber Company's interests were involved but also because Minton personally owned a 92-acre tract of land at the mouth of Cochino Bayou through which the highway was projected to cross. Even though this land was already surrounded by Southern Pine Lumber Company's holdings, Minton purchased the tract from the state in 1911, and he had employed his brother-in-law Sam Kenley to carry the surveyor's chain and his brother-in-law Carroll

Kenley to notarize the documents.[13] Although Minton later offered to sell the bottomland tract to Southern Pine Lumber Company, on time at 6 percent interest, giving his employers what he called "first opportunity before selling it to someone else," his preference was to trade it for a company tract located five miles to the southeast, on which his personal hunting clubhouse sat, on the banks of Boggy Slough (today's McClain Camp). Such a request was bold, even for Minton, and was not granted. As it happened, Minton retained the Cochino Bayou tract until eventually selling it to Southern Pine Lumber Company in 1956, when he retained "all mineral rights of every kind as well as an easement on, over and across" it.[14] So, throughout the 1920s and 1930s, with Minton and Southern Pine Lumber Company owning the land—and the former railroad right-of-way, which they had purchased from Ernest L. Kurth in 1924—the proposed highway route along the abandoned railroad was practically dead on arrival.[15]

In 1930, another projected route emerged, this one running well north of the current Boggy Slough Conservation Area. Minton himself drafted and proposed the course, which crossed the Neches River at Anderson's Crossing and connected with State Highway 40 at Wells, in Cherokee County, some 18 miles north of Lufkin. No action was taken until 1935, when state and local officials recognized the plan as totally inadequate because Lufkin, the Angelina County seat, was not directly served. Finally, in 1936 the state recommended and the federal government approved funds to construct the much-anticipated highway along a third and final route, which would cross the Neches River at Sullivan's Ferry over a new bridge.[16] At the time, the portion of the new state highway east of Crockett was redesignated as State Highway 103, although several years later the state changed the identifying number of the highway portion between Crockett and the Neches River back to Highway 7, as it remains today.

Southern Pine Lumber Company officials in Angelina County, armed with Arthur Temple Sr.'s initial blessings from Texarkana, resolutely opposed the new route, believing a state highway through Sullivan's Bluff would jeopardize their many years of work in protecting wildlife in the region. Since the Boggy Slough fenced ranch at that time included about 9,000 acres north of the highway's projected route (and today's Boggy Slough Conservation Area) and some 23,000 acres south of the route, Dave Kenley and R. E. Minton especially contested the plan. It was Minton, however, by most accounts "a great naturalist" and sportsman, who fought the road most visibly in the eyes of the public, expressing astonishment that the state would again consider building the highway through the fenced preserve after he had successfully defeated all earlier attempts during the previous decade.[17] After Minton obtained an injunction against condemnation of the company lands, the issue became embarrassing to the Temples when the commissioners courts of both Houston and Angelina Counties took to the press early in 1937. The courts claimed the route through the Company's ranchlands was "the only hope" of ever obtaining the much-needed highway since all the necessary rights-of-way through Houston and Angelina Counties had been obtained already, except for only the short five-mile stretch through Boggy Slough.

Responding to pressure from the local courts as well as from newspaper reporters, Will Tucker, the chief officer of the state game department, went on public record on April 14. While he acknowledged the new highway might make law enforcement on Temple lands more difficult "to some extent" because "accessibility of game from the road would provide more temptation for hunters to trespass," he believed that the highway would "not hurt the game," and he gave the department's full consent to the project.[18] Minton was already displeased with Tucker, having canceled the state's 1926 lease of Boggy Slough as a game preserve in 1934 because he believed the state failed to adequately protect the property from "intruders." And now Tucker's publicized endorsement of the state highway route placed Minton's opposition in an especially difficult position, because Minton had just leased the north half of the Southern Pine Lumber Company ranch as a hunting lease to J. W. Austin, an executive of the Humble Oil Company's lucrative East Texas Oil Field and organizer of the Malibu Hunting Club.[19]

Minton's early cancellation of the state game preserve lease and his grant of a private hunting lease to the Malibu Club was not only a criticism of the state game department, it was also a partial implementation of what he had earlier advocated as "a profitable sale" of Southern Pine Lumber Company's "game crop"—something he had suggested to Arthur Temple Sr. back in 1931.[20] Minton regarded such favored game species as deer as "crops" to be wisely cultivated, harvested, and managed, not much different from what his brother-in-law Dave Kenley was attempting to do with pine trees. Such a view of nature as "resources"—a world to be wisely managed to meet social demands—was nothing new. All Boggy Slough peoples had held such an outlook in one fashion or another. But Minton's mostly economic approach to nature was similar to what Gifford Pinchot had publicly advocated three decades earlier within the US Forest Service, and it differed little from what forester and ecologist Aldo Leopold had articulated throughout the 1920s in his conceptions of "game farming," especially in his 1933 book, *Game Management*.[21]

Leopold, who had visited East Texas in 1909 as a student of the Yale Forest School (performing his fieldwork for the Thompson Brothers Lumber Company in Tyler County, downriver from Boggy Slough), declared in *Game Management* that "effective conservation" required "a deliberate and purposeful manipulation of the environment—the same kind of manipulation as is employed in forestry." As an ardent naturalist himself, Minton surely was at least aware of Leopold's writings. And since Leopold defined game management as "the art of making land produce sustained annual crops of wild game for recreational use" and that its purpose was "to enhance the yield above what unguided nature would produce," Minton did not see how deer, which he and Kenley had diligently produced and managed for more than a quarter of a century, could survive with a state highway running through the middle of the protected grounds. Knowing that public highways were powerful spaces, Minton feared the new road would expose deer further to their primary predator, the unchecked hunter.[22]

Minton's agronomic approach to Boggy Slough's deer "crops" was shared by Kenley, who once thought that government ownership of game as well as forest preserves was in Southern Pine Lumber Company's—and the public's—best interests. By 1937, however, both men were distrustful of governments. Minton felt that private hunting clubs, particularly when backed by oil company money and influence, could better afford to provide the kind of game protection that Southern Pine Lumber Company's lands required and deserved, especially during lean times of economic depression. In Minton's mind, the state had not only failed to protect Boggy Slough's game during the state lease period, but was now betraying tenets of scientific management.

Since it was the new privately leased hunting club lands through which the new highway would pass, and because Minton's opposition to state development plans had become highly publicized, Humble Oil Company executives asked Minton to publicly disassociate their company's interest in the controversy. Minton did so grudgingly, but he, along with Kenley as head of Southern Pine's Timber and Land Department, also continued to refuse a grant of the necessary right-of-way to the state, and they used the courts to stymie the state's counter efforts. As an alternative solution, the two men offered again the right-of-way for the Anderson's Crossing route, north of the ranch, stating their belief that the river crossing there was the best geographic location for the new road. They insisted that the only way they would consent to the Sullivan's Ferry route, which would divide the ranch, would be if the government constructed on both sides of the highway what Arthur Temple Sr. called, "a game-proof fence to keep the game in and the poachers out"—something that the state and Houston County refused to do.[23]

Meanwhile, the local county commissioners courts, which had for years taken what Kenley called "whippings" from both him and Minton over taxes, property valuations, and other matters, found in the highway issue a fight they were sure to win.[24] In April 1937, Angelina County judge Butler Rolston declared in the *Lufkin Daily News* that it was "the height of absurdity for a private hunting club of small membership to stand in the way of a major highway project."[25] For one thing, Rolston explained, "the Southern Pine pasture is not a [state] game preserve, but a private hunting club maintained by the Southern Pine Lumber Company, its officials, and a few other citizens as a private club for their personal use. That is their privilege, and they are entitled to do so if they wish, but can we as citizens afford to subordinate what we believe to be the welfare of our community and county to the wishes of a few individuals who desire to have a good place to hunt and fish?" Adding further sarcasm, Rolston continued, "We regret exceedingly that the parties in question feel the construction of this state highway to be detrimental to their welfare, but such is the price of progress, and in a democratic country like ours, the minority must give way to the will of the majority, which in this instance is 99.9 percent of the affected people in Angelina and Houston counties. Of course we all appreciate the efforts of the Southern Pine Lumber Company to develop a fine hunting club for its officials and individuals who have leased the hunting grounds, and it is regretted that construction of a new and badly needed highway across East Texas should conflict with their pleasures, but hunting clubs do not of themselves build cities and they do not develop the trade territory of a city." Besides, Rolston continued, since federal aid for the highway's construction through the ranch was already in place, any change to the route at such a late date would "probably delay the project for years, if not block it forever."[26]

On April 19, all those involved in the controversy traveled to Austin, where the fight resumed in the form of hearings before the state highway commission. There, Minton was an unlikely partner with Cherokee County interests in arguing for a relocation of the highway to the town of Wells, instead of Lufkin.[27] Minton stood first and argued that the Wells route would be cheaper to build by crossing less river bottom land and would serve more people along the way than the direct route to Angelina's county seat. He quickly abandoned that contention, however, and presented instead a passionate plea for wildlife protection.

Minton explained: "My only [true] purpose in appearing on the matter is in the interest of those who cannot appear—our wildlife."[28] He then provided a history of Southern Pine Lumber Company's game protection efforts, beginning with their fencing the ranch in 1913. He explained how a part of the southern preserve—Captain Ray's old 640-acre hog-proof calf pasture—was a longtime designated "quiet section," where "the animals use it as a refuge when they are disturbed [and] consequently it serves as the source of game for the entire surrounding country." He claimed that a highway built anywhere through the preserve would ruin the "sanctuary" as well as more than two decades of diligent and dangerous work in policing and protecting it.

Lucy Kenley Minton, Judge Minton's wife, also appeared before the commission and joined her husband's public opposition. While her husband focused mostly on the animals themselves, Lucy stated that she was primarily looking after the "morals" of "the young people of East Texas." She explained she had "found in raising a family" that "planned trips among wildlife diverted their attention from harmful things." With a passionate sense of responsibility that rivaled her husband's, she declared it was "God" who "put our game here, and man dominion over it, not to kill it out but to protect it."[29]

Also appearing at the state hearing was Senator John S. Redditt of Lufkin, who served on the senate committees over both the highway and game departments. A decade earlier Redditt had joined some of his own lands with Minton's and Southern Pine Lumber Company's in Angelina and Trinity

Counties to establish the first state game preserves in East Texas. Redditt now, however, stood against Minton and Southern Pine Lumber Company, declaring, "The road will serve the best interests of all, while the Game Preserve interests only a few. I favor the preservation of game, but I do not believe this preserve should stand in the way of road progress which means much to the entire state." Angelina County's Judge Rolston also appeared before the state commissioners. He stated that, after having thought about the matter considerably, he now believed that the road through the hunting club would in fact "better protect" the game, because rangers and wardens would then have better access to the areas that needed enforcement of game laws the most.[30]

A few days after the hearing in Austin, as the tide of public opinion continued to rise against his Southern Pine Lumber Company, Arthur Temple wrote to Minton and expressed his uncertainty in the wisdom of continuing the Highway 103 fight. He was beginning to think that a prolonged contest would only make the fallout of an inevitable defeat worse, and he suggested that Minton drop his opposition completely. The next day, however, Minton wrote to Temple and shared news that only complicated matters more. Minton informed Temple of the state's plans for yet another projected highway, which would involve company lands in Trinity County. Minton reported that Senator Gordon Burns of Huntsville was especially in favor of this new project, since Burns had received some two hundred letters from constituents in support of it. Minton warned Temple that Senator Burns was well aware "that your keepers have pistol-whipped persons caught in the pasture" and any opposition to the new Trinity County project, "whether fought in Austin or in Groveton," was sure to "bring on you severe adverse public opinion in Trinity County"—as if the bad publicity from the company's opposition to the Houston County highway was not enough adversity already.[31] Minton said he earlier had tried to avoid giving advice to Gilbert and T. L. L. Temple in policy matters, but in this case he suggested that Temple resist a fight in Trinity County, especially "if we are to let Highway 103 go through in Houston County."[32]

By this time, Arthur Temple had had enough. It was bad enough that the relocation and widening of Highway 94, which had begun in 1935, had already disturbed South Boggy, and the construction of Highway 103 through North Boggy seemed inevitable, but now another possible road, what Minton called a new "river road," threatened to publicize again his employees' violent handling of poachers and trespassers. After consulting with Southern Pine's board of directors, Temple wrote Minton a long letter on May 5. He copied both of his lumber companies' department heads at Diboll and Pineland, as well as Senator John S. Reddit and Ernest L. Kurth of Lufkin. Temple wrote that he had been placed "in a very embarrassing position in connection with these highway matters," and he now wanted to express his full views directly so that everyone would know them firsthand. He conceded that he had given his initial support in opposing the roads, but he explained that "the good will of the people of Angelina, Houston and Trinity counties is so important to us, I do not think we ought to [now] take any stand with respect to either one or both of the proposed highways which would antagonize the citizenship of these counties." Yes, he agreed, "we value very highly our game preserve, to be sure, and I think most anyone who is interested in the preservation of wildlife would concede that we are doing a good thing in protecting the game on our preserve, a good thing not only for those of us who have access to the ranch and enjoy hunting, but also we are doing something for posterity." But, Temple emphatically insisted, "We cannot afford to antagonize the people of the several counties in which we operate and in which we own land and timber, and aside from incurring the ill will of our neighbors, we cannot afford to block progress or oppose the will of the majority."[33] Therefore, Temple said, he felt the best thing to do was to express only "mild opposition" to the various highway projects and then "give in without a determined fight." Temple told Minton that "when we do this, I think that possibly we should make some public announcement through you in order to overcome the ill feeling which has been generated." Temple also acknowledged Minton's unenviable position in the matter, saying "I realize full well that [this course of action] is probably a big disappointment to you because you have had such a vital interest in maintaining and protecting the wildlife which we have built up over a period of years in our preserve."[34]

To say that Minton might have been disappointed was a gross understatement. Particularly, Minton disliked Temple's "suggestion" that "we should make some public announcement through you in order to overcome the ill feeling which has been generated." In a return letter, Minton carefully quoted back to Temple his exact words and replied to them specifically: "I assume by this [suggestion] that someone in your organization will prepare the statement desired and send it to me for publication." Otherwise, Minton said, "when I so clearly stated my interest in the matter, I do not see that I should start [another] newspaper controversy as to the veracity over *my* position in the matter." In other words, if Temple would send him a statement written by someone else, Minton would "arrange for its publication," but he would play no other part in the matter. Minton had already made his personal views known, and he would not change or back down from them.[35]

Arthur Temple waited nearly two weeks before writing a response to Minton's defiance. When he did, he explained that he had been busy and did not have a good opportunity to write. Now, at such a late date, Temple decided that maybe it was best to simply "let the matter rest" and "take our medicine." He would not request further public statements from Minton about Highway 103. Temple also reiterated his regret in how "most unfortunate" the whole "controversy" had become, and he shared some of the blame for the poor outcome, saying he had completely underestimated how "dead set the people of Lufkin and Angelina County were on having this highway."[36]

While the tone of Temple's letter to Minton was conciliatory and graceful, Minton nevertheless disliked backing down from a fight, especially one involving Boggy Slough. A shrewd lawyer, Minton found plenty of wiggle room in Temple's words, and in spite of knowing the spirit of his employer's wishes, he stubbornly allowed his filings in the courts of appeals to run their due course anyway, which further delayed the highway for several more months.[37] But his heel-dragging fight was a lost cause, and he knew it. The highway went through as planned, and Minton resented it for the rest of his life.[38]

While the unpleasantness of the highway defeat remained fresh in everyone's minds, Minton urged Arthur Temple to establish the powerful Game Committee, which would provide unified management of the company's wildlife assets and hopefully avert future public embarrassments. It was another example of Minton's devotion to wildlife management generally and to Boggy Slough particularly. Organized in the fall of 1940, the committee included Minton, Dave Kenley, Arthur Temple Sr., Henry Temple, Clyde Thompson, and E. C. Durham. All were members of the Boggy Slough Hunting and Fishing Club, and Boggy Slough served as their model for game management.[39] Besides regulating hunting and fishing on all company lands, one of the committee's purposes was to cooperate "with State and Federal governments in their efforts to restore the wild animals and birds in this section of the State," which Boggy Slough had begun in 1926.[40] Dan Lay, the new state game biologist for East Texas, became a regularly invited guest at the early meetings of the committee.[41] Representatives from the hunting clubs who leased company lands, and all club and company pasture riders, were also included.

Minton's ideas permeated the early agendas. Foremost was determining the quantity of the game on the various lands and the means of increasing those species "in a reasonably limited time," and discovering the greatest populations of game that the lands could support—what Minton called the "saturation point" of restored game.

Also addressed were ways and means of increasing wildlife habitat, establishing "rest periods" from hunting, and creating "sanctuary areas" like those within Boggy Slough. Minton made sure that all club managers knew the importance of enforcing rules and regulations, protecting fences, defending against intruders from public roads "and the river banks," and preventing "trespassers [from] intermingling with guests."[42]

At its outset, the Game Committee's most troublesome concern remained the highway department's various road expansion projects. By 1940, Minton was particularly concerned about Boggy Slough's increased public exposure caused by the relocation of Highway 94 across Bluff Prairie. In August 1935, to facilitate the new construction, Minton had granted a 100 foot right-of-way to the state, along with the right to procure earth and other construction material nearby. To elevate the new roadway across the often flooded river and creek bottoms, the state dug a number of large borrow ditches along the new route, which filled with water the first time Cedar Creek flooded and remain filled even today. When the public immediately began to fish in the new ditches, Minton interpreted their actions as trespassing. To make matters worse, many bank fishermen along the ditches took advantage of new access to the abandoned roadbed of the Groveton, Lufkin & Northern Railway and its creek trestles at Vair to further encroach by fishing in the stream channels that connected to the highway ditches. Pasture rider Walter Robinson posted the area, but to no avail. Minton was particularly aggravated, because his agreement with the state had provided for proper fencing to be placed along the new road, at state expense, but nothing was done about it.

Although Minton acknowledged fears of another "public storm" of criticism if Southern Pine Lumber Company installed the fences, instead of the state, he nevertheless proceeded to do so, arguing that the company would "ultimately lose control of the situation" if the area remained unprotected. Minton notified the highway department of his intentions in August 1941, claiming the fences were necessary for the safety of the motoring public and for the protection of Southern Pine Lumber Company's property, as well as "the cattle and other livestock of its lessee." Of course, the lessee was Minton's brother-in-law, Dave Kenley.[43] Under the management of Minton and Kenley, Boggy Slough's land, water, deer, and cattle were inseparable from fences.

Minton demonstrated, in his opposition to the highway department and his creation of the Game Committee, his personal attachments to Boggy Slough, to its wildlife, and to his many years of trying to protect what he valued. From his relentless prosecution of trespassers and poachers beginning early in the 1910s through his highway challenges and game restoration efforts beginning in the 1920s, perhaps no one was more attached to Boggy Slough than Minton, except perhaps his brother-in-law Dave Kenley.

Ironically, Dave Kenley's whole career was linked to Boggy Slough. According to Kenley's 1954 oral history interview with John Larson of the Forest History Society, Southern Pine Lumber Company hired him as the result of a destined meeting during the spring of 1908, as he rode his horse through the Cedar Creek bottoms that continue to drain much of the Boggy Slough Conservation Area today. Kenley stated that he was going home from teaching school, and had 35 miles to ride on horseback. "I made all the shortcuts I could," he said, "and since I was on horseback and going the trail way, I ran into where Southern Pine Lumber Company was cutting timber in Trinity County just south of Cedar Creek. The [fallen tree] tops had stopped the trail, and being a cloudy day, I got lost, or turned around. I met the woods foreman, Mr. Massingill, and he asked me what I was doing there. I was ashamed of being lost, having been raised in the woods, so I told him I was hunting a job. So he immediately began to talk to me about a job with the Lumber Company."[44] From such an unlikely beginning, Kenley began his employment on May 1, 1908, and was employed for the next fifty-nine and a half years.[45]

At Boggy Slough, where he interviewed for his job, Kenley spent much of the rest of his life. As the young department head of Southern Pine Lumber Company's Timber and Lands, Kenley assisted in establishing the Boggy Slough ranch in 1913. He consolidated the ranch's properties by negotiating the purchase of the remaining homesteaders' lands and hog claims north of Cochino Bayou, whose owners were earlier content to sell only their timber. He directed and supervised the intensive land clearing efforts during World War I, located and purchased thousands of goats for the ranch, and assisted Captain Ray in managing the company's cattle for two decades. After Captain Ray vacated, Kenley managed the lessees of Boggy Slough for six years and then ran cattle there himself for another quarter of a century, vigilantly patrolling the woods and pastures. He helped organize the first Boggy Slough Hunting and Fishing Club in 1922 and assisted in its reorganization in 1933. Also, Kenley, along with Minton, maintained private hunting cabins near one another on high ground at the south end of the Boggy Slough stream—cabins that are still in use today by others.

Both men cared deeply for Boggy Slough's wildlife. Minton was responsible for creating the Game Committee and placing the outspoken Kenley as one of its members, while Kenley used the committee even more powerfully to advocate for Boggy Slough's deer, which he considered one of Southern Pine Lumber Company's greatest assets.

At the very beginning of the Game Committee's existence, Kenley asked its members to consider the serious question of who, exactly, should be allowed to hunt the company's best herds of deer. All agreed that the "best hunting" was in Trinity County, because of Boggy Slough, but not everyone agreed with Kenley's and Minton's desire to severely restrict hunting privileges there. The matter became contentious in December 1940, after Arthur Temple Sr. and Henry Temple had allowed the White brothers of the newly formed Temple-White Company at Diboll to organize the North Cedar Hunting Club, which adjoined Boggy Slough. Neither Kenley nor Minton accepted the White brothers into the original Temple "family organization" because the Whites, originally from

Indiana, had only recently moved from Bogalusa, Louisiana, and because their business, which was making broom and mop handles from sawmill waste materials, did not own any land. In Kenley's economy, the Whites and their guests, who were mostly personal friends and family members, brought no added value to the farther-flung Southern Pine Lumber and Temple Lumber companies. Most importantly to Kenley, when the Whites and their guests killed Boggy Slough's deer, which roamed freely into North Cedar, they were squandering valuable resources that should have been reserved instead for government officials who were in positions to do the most good for the Temples' landholding companies.[46]

Kenley boldly expressed his opposition about the North Cedar Club, telling Arthur Temple Sr. and Henry Temple that it was "extravagance" for their members and guests "to kill a deer that could be sold as high as we might sell them, if we [continue to] capitalize this just right." He reviewed a long history of how he had used "the ranch" at Boggy Slough as "good will" to "entertain out here, not in an expensive way in drinking or playing cards," but simply in making sure that tax officials had the opportunity to see and shoot a deer occasionally. He reminded them how deer hunting at Boggy Slough had saved the Temple companies $50,000 in taxes during the worst years of the Great Depression and that if those figures "were gotten up and used against us publicly we would be hurt very much." He explained that nonresident corporations like the four Temple lumber and railroad companies were at the "total mercy" of the local tax boards and that deer had been his most "persuasive power" in "working the courts," which otherwise would have found it very easy "to place excessive values on non-resident tax payers' property." He said that he had won "very few protests and tax suits in the courts," but at Boggy Slough he had done very well. He added that he felt he would have abused Southern Pine Lumber Company if he killed "a deer or two" every year like the Whites were talking of doing. In fact, he claimed that since 1915 he had killed only two deer himself, and one

of his sons had killed one. If Kenley had his way, he said that no Temple employee would ever be allowed to kill a deer, for they should be saved for high-profile guests, where their value would be much higher. He also reminded them that he was "the first one to have an idea to capitalize on the ranch," and while it had been "quite difficult" and "plenty of trouble," he felt that it was "the first of its kind that was ever organized in East Texas."[47]

Kenley's views were shared by Minton, and together the two men so jealously guarded Boggy Slough's deer that they imposed more restrictions on North Cedar's members than they did on any other Temple club, even clubs that were composed entirely of non-Temple employees. Arthur Temple Sr. challenged that brand of zeal, asking the brothers-in-law repeatedly why they would place such limitations on "our own people," when they did not require the same restrictions "from outsiders, [to] whom we are under no obligations whatsoever?"[48]

What Kenley and Minton often failed to realize was that Temple also valued Boggy Slough's deer, but his valuation differed from theirs. Kenley and Minton, who were employees with limited responsibilities, often saw deer and their "capitalization" only as they pertained to tax savings and lawsuits. Temple, who owned the company that owned the land, whose responsibilities were many, saw a larger picture. When Kenley and Minton tried to abolish the North Cedar Hunting Club during the spring and summer of 1941, Temple revealed yet another social value to Boggy Slough's deer.

Labor organizers had made significant inroads into East Texas sawmill towns earlier that year, and on May 27 representatives of the American Federation of Labor successfully organized the workers at the mills of the Kirby Lumber Company at Silsbee. One week later, representatives of the Congress of Industrial Organizations distributed "Be American: Organize!" pamphlets throughout Diboll, even gaining entrance inside the mills, unseen by night watchmen. Upon learning of the unionizing activities, Temple wrote to his Diboll officials, telling them that the North Cedar Hunting Club should by no means be abolished. There was simply no good reason to risk his employees' loyalty by removing or severely restricting their hunting privileges now or at any other time. In fact, as he told Minton, he not only wanted to prohibit further restrictions on the North Cedar Club, but he hoped that hunting privileges there and on other company lands might actually be expanded. "I have always been desirous of giving some of our key men and employees hunting privileges which would cultivate their goodwill and fortify us against any subversive activities," he said. Surely, whatever it was that Minton and Kenley were trying to impose through the Game Committee, they could "accomplish [that] purpose without sacrificing our own men."[49] Under such direction, the North Cedar Hunting Club not only escaped abolishment, but hunting privileges to employees there and on other Temple lands expanded throughout the 1940s, especially in 1948, when Arthur Temple Jr. became general manager. In that year, Temple gave a free company lease of 17,000 acres along the Neches River, south of Boggy Slough, to the Ryan's Lake Hunting and Fishing Club, which comprised Southern Pine Lumber Company employees. By 1951 some hunting clubs on Temple lands were indeed abolished, but not for the purpose of further restricting access. Instead, those lands and "pastures" were opened to hunting by the general public.[50]

Although deer at Boggy Slough played a significant role in Kenley's nearly six decades of forest and wildlife management, he always thought that cattle grazing made it all possible. He firmly believed that keeping cattle on cutover lands was good for the Temple lumber companies, and he began securing grazing leases on most large tracts of cutover lands during the 1910s, even leasing some of those tracts himself. He believed that cattle grazing and browsing kept fire hazards such as tall grasses and brush at bay, while they also "beat out trails," which he claimed served as convenient fire breaks when fires did occur.[51] Furthermore, since cattle required the active presence of men moving them from pasture to pasture, feeding them dur-

ing the winters, branding them, and rounding them up for shipping, the company's timber was further protected from fire and trespass while wildlife was sheltered from illegal hunting. Most of these reasons had contributed to the theory behind establishing the large Rayville Ranch in the first place.

After the company ranch closed, Kenley convinced Arthur Temple Sr. and Henry Temple that keeping cattle at Boggy Slough was the right thing to do, contrary to the US Forest Service's earlier pleadings against it. One of Kenley's primary arguments was that Boggy Slough, at 32,000 acres, was the largest company property under fence, yet it had no government fire protection. Although Kenley faithfully supported the fire-control efforts of the Texas Forest Service from its beginning and made sure that other lands of the Temple lumber companies received the agency's protection, he reserved the Boggy Slough ranch, since Captain Ray and his rangers effectively provided that service, which saved the company money that would have been paid to the agency. Likewise, when Kenley leased Boggy Slough to others, he required them to also provide fire protection. But he never completely trusted the lessees, believing they cared little for preventing forest fires—much less putting them out—since fire would only advance their personal interests by producing more forage for their cattle. Surely, he thought, he could devise some better way to protect the company's interests.[52]

Throughout 1938, as the last outside grazing lease on Boggy Slough neared its expiration, Kenley continued to stress the necessity of keeping cattle there. In May, Kenley shared with the Temples news of federal agricultural assistance programs that he was learning about through his cattle interests in West and South Texas, which could make cattle-raising in East Texas more successful than it had been a decade earlier. Kenley said that as long as the company could demonstrate an active "ranch program," there would be government assistance. Kenley even proposed an elaborate plan whereby Southern Pine Lumber Company and Kenley would form a "small corporation" of

$6,000 capitalization to handle a "cow business," which Kenley proposed to manage. Kenley offered $50 a month of his salary "to cover any time" he might give the joint venture, while "Southern Pine Lumber Company would get the advantage of the Government payments and the development of the pastures." Obviously, Kenley was thinking about cows and pastures at least as much as he was considering trees and deer.[53]

A couple of months earlier, Arthur Temple had already written to Kenley to express his reluctance "to get back into the cattle business, because of our previous experience."[54] He did not want the company to invest even one dollar more in cows, preferring that "someone else" had "the privilege of running cattle on our property." Tired of the recurring matter, he suggested that Kenley get with Henry Temple, and he would be content with letting them decide what was best for the land and the company. Acknowledging that "we [the company] are not interested at all in cattle," Kenley then presented himself as the perfect "someone else" to begin leasing Boggy Slough and protecting it better than it had been before. Who else would care more about the company's interests, he asked? And who else possessed enough cattle and other resources to adequately operate on so much land?[55]

On June 10, even though a grazing lease to others had not yet expired, Kenley moved fifty-nine of his cows, along with two bulls and twenty-one calves, into Boggy Slough. He reported his actions to Henry Temple, saying he placed them "on the North end of the ranch where Mr. Grumbles lives."[56] It was a relatively small herd, to begin with, but others would arrive later. Although Henry Temple questioned Kenley's "schemes," sharing his reservations with Arthur Temple that Kenley might somehow try to turn Boggy Slough back into a large cattle ranch, Kenley argued that such possibilities were long gone. While Captain Ray had stocked about one cow per 15 to 20 acres of land, "that was before the brush grew up so badly," Kenley explained. Realistically, he now planned to run no more than one adult cow per 60 acres. In time, however, his herd gradually increased until

a Texas Parks & Wildlife Department browse utilization study during the late 1950s found that South Boggy alone contained a stocking rate of one cow per 15 acres.[57]

Kenley's plan in running cattle at Boggy Slough was to combine his job as head of timber and lands directly with his personal cattle business. He saw mutual benefits to each party, while always claiming that "the Southern Pine Lumber Company received considerably more out of it than I [did]." Even though Kenley paid little or nothing to the company for his lease "privileges" in the beginning—and later not more than four cents an acre annually—Kenley felt he always handled the matter "in a business and successful way for Southern Pine Lumber Company, regardless of what it [was] for me [personally]."[58]

Kenley's leases of Boggy Slough in Trinity and Houston Counties, as well as his leases of company lands elsewhere, including the 9,000-acre Renfro pasture in Angelina County, were drawn up by Kenley, who, in addition to being the lessee, was also the lessor's representative. Kenley simply signed the contracts as the lessee and filed them in his office. The signature lines for Southern Pine Lumber Company were left blank. Kenley did send copies of the incomplete contracts to Texarkana, but apparently no one there paid them any attention. Not until 1950, after Arthur Temple Jr. became the Diboll manager and asked attorney J. J. Collins to look into the grazing agreements, did any understanding of the relationship begin to emerge. But by that time, various supporting letters from Henry Temple, who had died two years earlier, had granted extended concessions to Kenley, which only complicated matters for at least another decade. Collins found that several of the contracts, as well as some of the supporting letters, outlined conditions that were "very liberal" to Kenley's favor, "without very much protection of any kind by the Company."[59]

Although definite conflicts of interest emerged over the years, Kenley never saw them as such. Instead, he actually believed that by running his cattle at Boggy Slough he provided a personal favor

Arthur Temple Jr., left, listens intently to Lufkin attorney J. J. Collins at the Boggy Slough clubhouse in about 1949. Temple later described Collins as "the greatest trial lawyer in East Texas history." *Courtesy of The History Center, Diboll.*

to the company. Besides giving Boggy Slough protections from fire and "intruders," he claimed that during most years he netted for Southern Pine Lumber Company between $750 and $1,000 annually through what he called, "the Government ranch program."[60] Taking advantage of New Deal agricultural assistance programs, Kenley applied for and received monies from the federal government for several years' worth of converting old homesteads and tenant farms into pastures, claiming he channeled the funds to the company, "always handling it so as to get the biggest income I could out of it, and possibly do the least work."[61] He usually employed a combination of his own as well as company employees in such work. In a 2000 interview, Charlie Harber, one of Kenley's personal employees, recalled one planting project from 1939, whereby he and Kenneth Nelson, a Southern Pine employee who later succeeded Kenley as head of the land department, surveyed one 300-acre field, where Harber's family had lived

during the early 1930s. Three-quarters of a century earlier it had been part of the old Britton family land, where Deer Stand 22 is located today. After surveying the field and receiving seed, Harber then used a hand-crank spreader to sow five tons of rye grass seeds.[62] Late in the 1950s, under Arthur Temple Jr.'s direction, the company planted pine trees in the same field, and when those trees were harvested in 2014 they had grown too large for the Diboll sawmill, which had been rebuilt in 1999 to more efficiently handle the smaller-sized timber of modern markets.[63]

It did not take long for Kenley's grazing leases of Boggy Slough to cause serious misunderstandings. When Kenley pointed out that no money had been spent on fences in more than a decade and that some $3,000 was needed for repairs, Henry Temple objected, believing Kenley was personally liable for fences under "his lease privilege." But Kenley argued that the company should pay, using "the grazing program" funds. But even if those funds were not used, Kenley contended, he still felt the company should pay, because "good fences" benefited the company more than they did Kenley, because they protected the timber and game, which he argued were more valuable than his cows.[64] When other disagreements arose, Kenley quickly claimed that he made very little, if any, personal profit under the lease agreements. After leasing Boggy Slough for five years, Kenley explained that "East Texas [wa]s the hardest ranching country in the world," and Boggy Slough was especially difficult. The often-flooded river, creek, and slough bottoms, Kenley said, had caused him to lose several dozen cows to drowning, including twenty head during one particularly bad overflow. In addition, more than forty cows died as a result of falling limbs during the winter of 1943–44, while twenty-seven others had been shot and killed by poachers, mostly by night "fire hunters." He also lost several more cows each year to roadkill on Highway 103 and to thieves. Kenley claimed that had it not been for the fact that he never paid a salary to his hardworking son Edd, there would never have been even a hope for a profit.[65]

One of the greatest conflicts of interest with Kenley running his cattle at Boggy Slough concerned the fact that he was the boss of his own riders as well as the boss of the company riders, some of whom held state commissions as game wardens. Because Kenley supervised the work of all the men, and because Kenley's own riders provided the company with game and timber protection, Kenley often crossed the blurred lines that distinguished the men's duties. Since Kenley's men helped the company men do their jobs, Kenley reasoned, why not occasionally ask the company men to help his men do theirs?

By far the most experienced rider and cow hand of Boggy Slough during the company ranching days was Walter Robinson, Charlie Harber's brother-in-law. Robinson had left Boggy Slough with Captain Ray when Ray moved to the Renfro pasture in 1932, but Robinson returned to Boggy Slough and to Southern Pine Lumber Company's employment when Ray left East Texas a couple of years later. Kenley then placed Robinson as the primary protector of the entire 32,000 acres. All was well until January 1943, when Diboll manager E. C. Durham hired Robinson away from Southern Pine to work on Durham's own Shawnee Creek Ranch in Angelina County, paying him $90 a month and furnishing him a horse and feed. As a Southern Pine Lumber Company employee, Robinson had made only $78 a month, and Kenley had required him to provide his own horse and feed. Kenley wrote to Arthur Temple Sr. immediately upon learning of Robinson's departure, saying he was "very worried," because only the best of men could be trusted in the position of Boggy Slough's "keeper." Even if Kenley could find a suitable replacement for Robinson, which he felt was impossible during the wartime labor shortage, he said it would take "three or four months" for that person "to get acquainted out there."[66]

Arthur Temple replied, saying he was "nothing less than distressed" to learn of Robinson's leaving. He felt the company simply could not "afford to let him go." Temple said Robinson was "a very fine type of man, one in whom I have always had the

Ray pasture rider Walter Robinson with a lassoed buck deer believed to be injured, ca. 1930. *Courtesy of The History Center, Diboll.*

greatest confidence and respect, and I personally would be willing to do almost anything to retain him in our service." Temple suggested impressing on Durham how important Robinson was "to the ranch," believing that Durham could more easily find a man for his needs than it would be for the company to replace Robinson. Temple said he also wanted Kenley to match Durham's offer of the increased salary and provide him a horse and feed.[67]

Kenley quickly met with Robinson, but was unsuccessful in enticing him back to Boggy Slough. Kenley reported to Temple that Robinson preferred Durham's offer, since it would mean "a good many things" less "to contend with where Durham [wa]s located." Also, Robinson told him he would have to receive a good deal more than $90 a month for him to return. Kenley shared with Temple his belief that even if Robinson could be satisfied, Durham was unwilling to release him, and he would surely match or exceed any counteroffers that Kenley would make.[68] Clearly, the Temples seemed to have too many employees who were actually cattlemen. Durham by this time had even begun to call himself "the Country Squire," a title he exploited in the pages of the *Dallas Morning News* and that later appeared on his death certificate.[69]

With Robinson's departure from Boggy Slough, trouble came soon after, just as Kenley and Temple had feared. Word of Robinson's vacancy traveled quickly, and trespassing and poaching increased. Early in October Kenley wrote to Arthur Temple Sr., Arthur Temple Jr., Henry Temple, R. E. Minton, and Clyde Thompson to inform them of "considerable trouble down near the highway with trespassers on the ranch." Intruders were entering South Boggy at will through an unprotected gate on the "old highway," and some were even driving in automobiles. Most recently, Kenley said, two cars of hunters entered with "search lights." Kenley underscored the dire need of finding "a good man to break this up," but again he acknowledged the wartime labor shortage, which made the task difficult. In the meantime, Kenley recommended that the gate be locked to help prevent future incidents, even though he acknowledged the lock would be a considerable inconvenience to everyone, admittedly mostly to himself. Arthur Temple Sr. replied, saying that he wanted the "gate on the old highway locked day and night in season and out of season." He suggested Kenley devise a convenient detour for all those who had "legitimate business on the ranch." If such a detour was impractical, then Temple advised Kenley to make sufficient numbers of keys for everyone needing them, and Kenley would just have to make do with the inconvenience.[70]

Also in Robinson's absence, the company's riders began to complain to Diboll managers and to Temple family members, saying that Kenley was placing heavy demands on them to look after his cattle. After months of receiving detailed complaints, Arthur Temple Sr. wrote Kenley a stern letter in August 1944, copying his son Arthur Jr. and his cousin Henry Temple, saying that he was extremely displeased to learn of Kenley's behavior toward the company men and even more so that such behavior was the real reason Walter Robinson had left Boggy Slough for greener pastures in the first place. Policing Boggy Slough was a tough enough job, Temple said, and the company riders simply could not do all the things they were paid to do and act as state game wardens while also looking after Kenley's cattle and the many "personal jobs" he asked of them. "As a matter of fact," Temple wrote, "I think the old saying, 'A Man Cannot Serve Two Masters' applies." Temple said that all of Kenley's fellow Diboll managers had turned to him and convinced him he had to insist that Kenley's "personal interests at the ranch be divorced entirely from the Company interests of protecting the timber and game." Furthermore, Kenley needed to clearly define the duties of the company men so that all conflicts of interest would be "eliminated."[71]

Believing the matter settled, Temple then expressed in his letter the need for someone to better care for the new and modern company clubhouse, which had been constructed in 1941 along the new pipeline near the old Rayville feedlots. The clubhouse had been neglected and "abused," Temple said, and he wanted a company rider to live in the nearby Rayville house (Captain Ray's former home) and for that person "or his wife" to serve as the clubhouse's manager. Arthur Sr. shared that there had been some consideration for Arthur Jr. to manage the clubhouse, since he had recently taken a keen interest in Boggy Slough, especially after he moved to Lufkin to manage the retail lumber yard there. While admitting that he did not think his son should be the clubhouse manager, Temple said that someone, nevertheless, needed to oversee the clubhouse and live near it, and the Rayville house was ideal for that purpose. Temple asked Kenley if he might release the old house from the lease, if he did not need it, so that the company might use it instead.[72]

Kenley, who was described by those who knew him best as extremely short-tempered and "awfully quick to fly off the handle," did not receive Temple's letter well.[73] In response, Kenley wrote Temple three scathing letters totaling some 2,700 words, copying Henry Temple.[74] Kenley claimed Temple's information about Walter Robinson was "a mistake." Robinson did not leave the ranch because of Kenley's cattle work, Kenley said, for Robinson always "volunteered" his assistance and liked doing it. In fact, Kenley said that Robinson more than once told Kenley he especially enjoyed working with Kenley's son Edd and "how he hated to leave on that account."[75]

Concerning the company riders who had complained to Arthur Temple Jr. and to other managers, Kenley said that these were merely misunderstandings. Kenley said he may have occasionally asked company riders to accompany his cattle drives, but he said this was solely because he knew they would be learning the ranch grounds better. What better way to familiarize oneself with Boggy Slough than to herd cattle across the land, especially through the bottoms? Kenley pointed out that Temple needed to know that in several cases the company riders would have been completely unacquainted with parts of the pasture had it not been for their accompanying Kenley's own men in cattle work. Besides, Kenley believed the riders actually preferred to be around his personal men. "Almost every rider we have had enjoys being present when cattle are marked and branded or vaccinated," he wrote, "or enjoys being present when they are shipped."[76]

Furthermore, "the facts," Kenley said, were these: "My men [not the company's] have actually caught the last three men that have been caught in the ranch, hunting. My men have found the last two deer that intruders killed on the ranch, that were found, which likely would have never been found by the game wardens we [the company] have." Kenley reminded Temple that his own men also served as game wardens purely on behalf of the company, even though they were not paid to do so. Kenley explained that as recently as a week earlier his men "tracked up three fellows that had been going in there fire hunting," and they located

two of the men as far away as Dallas. "My men have been in the pasture a great deal," Kenley said, at least a third as much as the company's regular riders, and they did much good for the company. Furthermore, also during just the previous week, Kenley's own men "found a bad fire" and "got it out before it burned not more than 20 or 25 acres." Kenley also argued that since he was now providing hay and corn to the company pasture riders on his own account, the cost of that service far exceeded the value of any work the company riders ever provided him personally. "In addition," Kenley said, "I have furnished considerable feed for the [company's] milch cows [and] I have done everything I could to keep the [company] men satisfied, which has been a difficult job."[77]

Straying to an insubordinate and condescending tone, Kenley continued: "To follow your suggestion *exactly* as I understand it, would be that you want me to go out there and tell the riders, 'Now don't you have anything to do with the cattle—if my men come along driving the cattle here, you stay away,' or if I go out there to ship cattle, 'you stay away from the pens,' and tell my men, 'If you see an intruder, you pass him up,' or 'if you find fire, pass it up,' and 'if you see where anyone has killed a deer, or any sign of him, you go on and say nothing about it.' If you insist on doing that, I would suggest and advise that we hire another rider in the Cedar Creek pasture, down where we used to use the third man, at once. We have lots of intruding in there and for the man in the Robinson house to stay on the highway as much as he is asked to do, he cannot cover this part of it." "For some time," Kenley explained, the company had been able to employ only "very weak men on the South end of our work." Had it not been for Kenley's own men taking up the slack, he argued, "much more harm" would have occurred.[78]

Kenley also reminded Temple of the "Government program," which he had worked hard to secure, gaining the support of "the County Agent and the A&M College." Kenley said that receipts had occurred during most years and he had always "turned [the money] over to the Southern Pine

Lumber Company," even though he had used his own men as well as his own tractor in the work, including the work on the duck ponds. Kenley admitted that he did use two company men—Walter Robinson and Ab Grumbles—"on this work," but it was only for a few days.[79]

Concerning Temple's request for the company use of the Rayville house, which Kenley said he was indeed using, Kenley simply could not "spare" it. The house was his "headquarters," he said. He kept it furnished and supplied with saddles and horses "all of the time" and kept at least one man there five days a week during the summers and constantly during the winters. Kenley said he also stored all of his cattle and horse feed there and distributed it from there "over the entire holdings." No, Kenley said, Temple could not have use of Ray's old house, for Kenley could not "get along without it."[80]

In one of the three letters, Kenley requested a sit-down discussion with both Arthur and Henry Temple. Kenley wanted them to know that he had worked hard to deter intruders in a manner that kept fences from being cut, fires from spreading, and in the process no one being killed, as had occurred under Captain Ray's watch. Kenley readily admitted that Captain Ray was "a much smarter cow man" than himself, but he reminded the Temples that Ray was unsuccessful in turning a profit, while Kenley's personal operation of Boggy Slough brought the company cash each and every year. He said "the Company got nothing" from the "different fellows" who leased Boggy Slough after Captain Ray left, but Kenley had brought the company more than $12,000 so far—more than $2,000 annually—at least by his own calculation. Kenley also boldly declared that he was especially proud of buying a previously unsettled hog claim for "$50 or some small amount" and then "managed to sell the remnant of hogs that you did not own and got you $2,500 or $3,000." Kenley also reminded Temple that removing the hogs had improved the duck hunting, which Temple enjoyed.[81]

Kenley honestly felt that his personal cattle work and the company's interests of protecting timber and game were inseparable—that only through mutual cooperation could Southern Pine's best interests be met. He told Arthur Temple that he was surprised that anyone "in our own family" would make such "unjust" reports and "criticisms" about him, especially since "we have so much to contend with out there." Just the mere suggestion of disharmony, he told Temple, "could cause a little trouble from the outsiders, if they felt we [were] disorganized."[82] Already troublemakers were at work to challenge the company's long-standing fight against trespassers, he said in one of the three letters, because the lower courts were beginning to rule on behalf of some individuals who were claiming a right to enter the ranch under the old pretense of rounding up their hogs—swine that Kenley himself had been rounding up and selling. Kenley reasoned that as long as he "got the job done," that was all that mattered.[83]

To Kenley, his getting "the job done" meant mostly "protecting" the mature pine trees that were already there. Although still unrealized by Arthur Sr., Kenley gave little thought to what his cattle might be doing to a sustained regeneration of the forests at Boggy Slough. It would be Arthur Jr. who would discover later that pine trees grew most productively in the absence of cattle. But in the meantime, Arthur Temple Sr. demonstrated the patience of Job. He replied to Kenley's three letters with two letters of his own, again copying his son Arthur Jr. and his cousin Henry. Temple explained that he never doubted the advantages the company received through Kenley's cattle work and leasing Boggy Slough; he merely wanted Kenley to make "a very clear delineation" of the company men's work. "That is all in the world that I had in mind," he said. Surely, "clearly defining the riders' duties should be a very simple thing," he pleaded. Temple said that he could not help but think that since Kenley had hired the pasture riders on behalf of the company that they felt obligated to him in his personal cattle business as well. Temple admitted he was not there and had no "first-hand knowledge of the situation," but because he had "heard from so many different individuals," including his own son, he knew there was certain conflict, and he desired "complete harmony" instead. Temple also took great care to convince Kenley that the "criticisms," as Kenley called them, bore no "reflection on your work." Temple wrote, "As far as I know, there is no objection to your lease of the grazing privileges and certainly we know that you have done a darn good job in holding our taxes down and that you are just as much interested as Henry or I, or anyone else, in keeping our land in a productive condition." Thus, "under the circumstances," Temple said he "well appreciate[d]" Kenley's need for the Rayville house as his "headquarters," repeating Kenley's wording, and he was "perfectly willing" for Kenley "to keep it." Temple said he would simply "work out" some other "plan for the protection of the club house at Boggy Slough." But Temple also advised that should Kenley want to discuss such matters further, it had to be done "in a calm, dispassionate, and impersonal manner."[84]

This was not the first time Kenley had lashed out at Arthur Temple Sr., especially concerning Boggy Slough and cattle, nor would it be the last. For nearly a quarter century, Kenley and former general manager Dan Gilbert had been pals. With T. L. L. Temple's passive blessings from Quogue and elsewhere, Gilbert, from his office in Texarkana, had granted Kenley many liberties in managing the company's distant timber and land operations.[85] Gilbert also allowed Kenley to engage in extensive personal ventures involving land, timber, cattle, and sawmills. Gilbert even occasionally partnered with Kenley in some of those deals. In lumber company matters, Kenley was often offended. Whenever he had expressed that he felt slighted in some way, Gilbert had smoothed things over by sharing various assurances with him, writing that "Mr. Temple," who wanted "nothing but harmony and good feeling to exist," never "lack[ed] in appreciation of your able and conscientious work for the Company. . . . He is not only anxious to do everything within reason to satisfy you, but he does want to deal justly and liberally with you." Gilbert once wrote Kenley to say that Temple desired for "every department head to feel that he is

one of the family and that he is permanently established in the business." And even though Kenley was not a blood relation, Temple still considered him as family, "fully and completely, first, last, and always."[86]

After the deaths of Gilbert in 1931 and T. L. L. Temple in 1935, Kenley did not receive such coddling, at least not initially. Consequently he felt underappreciated by the new generation of Temples—Arthur and Henry Temple. Kenley became overly sensitive concerning all oversight, interpreting even basic supervision as a personal affront. When Kenley and Arthur Temple Sr. exchanged their letters concerning conflicts of interest at Boggy Slough in 1944, they each held unpleasant memories of a similar confrontation six years earlier.

In 1937 Arthur Temple Sr. hired an outside auditor to perform an efficiency evaluation on all the Temple businesses so that the financial troubles experienced during the Great Depression would be less likely to occur again. Kenley was outraged by the whole process. On one occasion Temple had to personally explain the matter to him as, "nothing more than an ordinary audit, which almost every large, well conducted business has from time to time."[87]

Still, Kenley considered the audit as a personal criticism, especially since much of it centered on the financial failure of the Rayville Ranch, the Valenzuela Ranch fiasco, the exposure of the controversial personal ventures of several of Temple's managers—including Kenley—and the timber and land department's purchase of large quantities of overpriced timber and cutover lands during the 1920s. While Kenley readily admitted he had purchased too much timber—much of it already cutover—at excessively inflated prices during the boom of the 1920s (especially hardwoods) he argued he was simply "meeting competition," since the Kurths and other lumbermen were doing the same. Besides, he claimed he did only what Gilbert had directed and T. L. L. Temple had approved. In fact, Kenley argued, no one "was any stronger on this [buying more land and timber] than

Mr. Temple himself," because the acquisitions were necessary to sustain the Diboll mill's operation. Furthermore, Kenley said he believed that one day a new paper mill industry would make all of his cutover land purchases pay off in the end, even at the high prices he paid and even "if we do want to abandon the idea of growing [sawlog-sized] timber on our lands." Arthur Temple Sr. never disputed those claims, but Kenley's "defense of criticisms," as Kenley called it, did not stop there.[88]

In several manifestations of overreactions to the audit—one from February 1938 included a memorandum of some 2,200 words—Kenley enumerated the many "credits" he felt he was "due."[89] Kenley had always worked hard for the Temple companies, he said, having lost ten pounds in body weight because of worries concerning land titles and oil leases, and at times having to travel out of state. He recounted numerous specific instances where he had saved the companies money, many of them because he was a cattleman. He reminded Temple of one case involving a large timber purchase for Temple Lumber Company. Kenley said he "bought it on an estimate of about 3,000 or 4,000 feet per acre, when it actually cut 6,000 feet or 7,000 feet per acre." Making this lucrative deal possible, Kenley boasted, was his personal "knowledge of stock" and of stockmen. "The old man was always trading livestock, mules, cattle, etc.," Kenley explained, "and I was able to talk his language."[90] Kenley claimed that both of Temple's lumber companies as well as his railroad operations benefited from his ability to considerably reduce taxes and appraisals, often by more than 50 percent, especially in every county where fellow cowmen composed the county courts. Kenley said he once took a thousand dollar personal loss in a cattle deal with a Sabine County commissioner to gain the commissioner's friendship for Temple Lumber Company, which was worth tens of thousands of dollars more to the company.[91] Kenley said he was even partners with some county commissioners in cattle ventures, and he used those personal relationships to the benefit of the companies. "What I knew about cattle was a great deal of

help to me in Houston County," Kenley explained, "as this was a one man's court, and he was a cowman, and the lumber company has furnished him a nice Hereford bull through me."[92]

As for criticism of the Rayville Ranch, Kenley claimed the experiment "was not an entire loss," because the timber and game had been protected in the process. He reminded Temple that the presence of game had "enhanced the value of the land at least $1.00 per acre," and repeatedly maintained that the increasing value of the game would one day recover all of the losses endured by the ranch. (By 1941, Kenley claimed the game had added $5 in valuation to every acre at Boggy Slough.) Kenley argued that his personal knowledge of cattle markets in South Texas prevented further losses by the Rayville Ranch, and he desired "credit" for shipping the Rayville cattle and feeding them in South Texas at strategic times.[93]

Kenley's long memoranda from February 1938 contained many more instances of how much he felt he was worth to the companies. Kenley reminded Temple of the bleakest years of the Depression when the banks demanded "to have some reputable people make up an estimate of our timber." Kenley said Gilbert was ready to pay professional timber estimators up to $60,000, until Kenley convinced Gilbert to let him make the estimate himself. Kenley said he "made it as showy as I could," which was accepted by the banks, at no additional cost to the companies. Kenley said his personal handling of purchasing the railroad rails for the Fastrill logging camp early in the 1920s saved Southern Pine another $50,000. He claimed he saved Southern Pine another $21,000 in an oil lease deal in Cherokee County by "traveling around over two or three states and seeing about fifteen different people" and "underwent considerable strain" doing it.[94] Kenley claimed that through his relentless efforts he was able to place loyal occupants on company lands and obtain some 350 tenant contracts, which helped clear "many defects" in company land titles involving more than 90,000 acres. Kenley also wanted "credit" for being the one to suggest that Southern Pine Lumber Company return to an earlier policy of logging only trees that were at least 12 inches in diameter, which had saved a fortune, he claimed, because the policy had gradually become as small as 8 inches, which was wasteful. He also thought he was "entitled to the credit" for "saving the 5,000 acres in Trinity County from being delivered to the Government," referring to his last-minute withdrawal of certain lands the US Forest Service had agreed to purchase in 1935. Kenley also reminded Temple how he stood his ground, with T. L. L. Temple's backing, during the withholding of taxes to Trinity County during the middle 1930s, which saved Southern Pine many thousands of dollars, which Arthur Temple had wanted to pay to keep the schools open.[95]

Other disagreements between Kenley and Arthur Temple Sr. occurred throughout the 1940s, including disparities over even trivial matters, such as who "deserved credit" for having implemented a sustained-yield, selective cut forestry program for Southern Pine Lumber Company in October 1940.[96] In placating Kenley, Temple had once considered the policy as one of Kenley's "outstanding achievements," but Kenley mentioned the matter so often and proudly in later years that Temple reminded him that he, too, was one of its earliest proponents. Kenley did have much to do with developing the program for Southern Pine, but it was only after years of steady urgings from both federal and state foresters, who had consistently explained to him that the practice was "no longer an experiment." "Many companies" had successfully practiced sustained-yield forestry, State Forester E. O. Siecke told Kenley once in April 1939. If Kenley doubted it, Siecke told him to look no farther than the Angelina County Lumber Company, which had been "doing a fine job of it."[97]

Kenley saw all new ideas that were not his own as threats to what he called his "practical" knowledge and experience, which he proudly defended. This was perhaps no more evident than in the important decision to hire, or not hire, a full-time college graduate forester. Henry Temple pushed for hiring one in 1940, arguing that the timber on company-owned lands needed to be cut

"more intelligently" than it had been in the past. During the 1920s and 1930s, Kenley had hired a few trained foresters for specific project work with much success, but he quickly let each of them go, seeing no need to employ them permanently. The Angelina County Lumber Company had retained a full-time professional forester since 1937, and the Long-Bell Lumber Company's Texas operations had hired graduates of the New York State College of Forestry even earlier.[98] It was not long before Arthur Temple Sr. wondered why his lumber companies had not done the same.

In July 1944 Arthur Sr. encouraged Kenley to hire a graduate forester, "as your assistant," stressing that management of the fledgling sustained-yield policy was "too vital to let a few dollars stand in the way." Specifically, Temple wanted Kenley to pursue New York State College forestry school graduate B. Koontz, who recently had left the Texas Forest Service for private practice as a pulpwood contractor. Temple also wanted Kenley to "approach the Louisiana School of Forestry at Baton Rouge."[99]

Kenley routinely provided several reasons against hiring a college-trained professional forester. One excuse throughout the early 1940s was that the war had made hiring quality men "impossible." In July 1944, Kenley cautioned Temple, saying that he should "bear in mind during these times" that "it is not what we know is best, but we have to do the best that we can."[100] Kenley said hiring a forester anytime soon was "out of the question" because any man worth hiring was also worth keeping, and that man's present employer would certainly pay to retain him. It went without saying that Kenley would never have considered hiring a man straight out of college. Another of Kenley's reasons—and one Arthur Temple Sr. especially doubted—was that Kenley argued that a forester could actually "hurt us, if he is not practical, and if we should turn him loose." Kenley contended that for decades he had "accomplished a great deal in our practical work," which was never criticized by federal or state foresters, and someone inexperienced "from outside" would only

Semi-mechanized tree planting at the Rayville pastures in January 1950. Bill Nichols, graduate forester, plants the trees behind a tractor driven by W. A. Neal. According to company records, most of these seedlings were soon "destroyed" by overpopulated herds of hogs and deer. *Courtesy of The History Center, Diboll.*

jeopardize it. Kenley further argued that much of the work performed by the state and federal agencies remained "in an experimental stage," and he doubted the universal application of such efforts to the Temple companies' lands.[101]

Although its revelation would not surface for several more years, the primary reason that Kenley opposed hiring a graduate forester full-time was that he feared his grazing leases of Boggy Slough might come to an end. Although properly managed pine woods grazing had become an important wartime industry across the southern forests, Kenley did not want a resurfacing of the old argument that USFS forester Austin Cary had raised back in 1923, what Cary identified as "the interests on the one side of grass, and on the other side of timber," one "versus" the other, and Cary's belief that timber, not grass, was best for Boggy Slough. After all, Kenley was first a cattleman, and second a forester.[102]

Ignoring Kenley's obstructions, Arthur Sr. and Henry Temple finally created a new position of forester early in 1946 and elevated one of Kenley's land and timber department employees, Kenneth Nelson, to fill it. Although Nelson did not have a degree in forestry, he had impressed the Temples

in his fifteen years of diligently working under Kenley and specifically in his eagerness to execute the sustained-yield initiative and ensure its success.[103] In some ways, Nelson was a compromise, but he proved to be the right man at the right time to modernize Southern Pine Lumber Company. If nothing else, Nelson was at least "practical" in Kenley's mind, and he was someone Kenley could accept, if not endorse. Importantly, when Arthur Temple Jr. succeeded Henry Temple as general manager of the Temple lumber companies early in 1948, Nelson was already in place to implement the progressive ideas of the third generation of Temples. Southern Pine Lumber Company established a Forestry School Scholarship to Stephen F. Austin State Teachers College in June 1948, and Nelson began hiring college-graduate foresters from there and other colleges and universities the following June.[104] Not surprisingly, Nelson and Arthur Jr. began the new foresters' jobs at Boggy Slough, where they planted pine trees and built roads, cattle guards (because of Kenley's cows), and dams, the last mostly to increase wildlife habitat and recreational hunting and fishing opportunities.[105] By February 1951, Nelson had hired seven graduate foresters, whom he supervised to grow and manage the regenerating Temple forests.

After giving Nelson new job responsibilities, Arthur Sr. and Henry Temple retained Kenley to continue his handling of the two lumber companies' tax affairs, utility rights-of-way, and ongoing negotiations for major timber acquisitions. Two years later, when Arthur Jr. came to Diboll and discovered that Kenley occupied a large majority of his time managing his personal cattle businesses, he reported it to his father, who questioned Kenley's salary of $10,000 a year.[106] Although he expressed his disapproval of Kenley "getting far and above what he should be getting," Arthur Sr. did little to rectify the situation until September 1949, when a postwar recession hit. At that time, Arthur Sr. finally wrote to Kenley and asked him to "voluntarily resign" his positions with the Temple companies. Doing so would save them considerable money, he said, and besides, Kenley was doing "so little" work anyway. Temple explained that Kenley was "in a much better position than most men," since he had "built up a very substantial business in cattle," and he would experience no "hardship" by leaving and devoting his full attention to his "private affairs." Why not finally retire, Temple asked? "As a matter of fact," Temple wrote, he was disappointed Kenley had not already resigned on his "own initiative." Temple closed his letter by saying that there was "nothing unfriendly" in his suggestion; in fact, he wanted their personal relationship to "continue on, but from a business standpoint," Kenley's continued employment was no longer "justified."[107]

For four decades—through historic periods of economic growth, decline, and recovery, and two world wars—Kenley had done much good for the Temple companies, building up timber and land reserves, perfecting titles, keeping taxes low, preventing forest arson, and contributing to the future success of the Temple businesses, and especially Boggy Slough. But markets, business practices, management philosophies, and society had changed tremendously during those four decades, and Kenley had stayed essentially the same, while becoming increasingly difficult to supervise. Oil men and even other lumbermen, such as Ernest L. Kurth of Lufkin, complained of Kenley's "endless disagreements" and "continuous squabbles," despite Arthur Sr.'s pleas for Kenley to handle himself so as to not "offend others" or "embarrass me."[108]

From Kenley's perspective, he had resented the management changes following the death of general manager Dan Gilbert some eighteen years earlier. He now challenged Arthur Jr.'s supervision just as he had earlier challenged Arthur Sr.'s management. There was one major difference, however. Arthur Jr. now resided in Angelina County and maintained his office at Diboll, whereas his father and grandfather had resided and held offices in Texarkana and elsewhere. Arthur Jr. brought the hands-on approach of the ownership class to management, which was now always near to Kenley and ever watchful of him. Kenley's activities were more closely monitored. His unending quarrelling would be tolerated less. And his numerous grazing leases of company lands, especially of Boggy Slough, were increasingly questioned.[109]

Not surprisingly, Kenley pushed against a voluntary resignation in the fall of 1949. Kenley contended that his services, even though he admitted he was giving "not more than 15%" of his time to the Temple businesses, were too valuable to the companies for him to leave. Arthur Sr. insisted that $10,000 a year for only 15 percent of Kenley's time was simply "out of line"; that is why he had asked Kenley to resign in the first place. Arthur Sr. traveled to Diboll and met with Kenley more than once about the matter. They also exchanged several letters. Eventually the two men agreed that Kenley would not resign, but he would take a reduction in pay instead.[110]

In defining his limited work and negotiating what he should be paid for it, Kenley wanted at least $5,000 a year, stating again how much money he had saved the companies in his shrewd handling of property taxes for decades. He also claimed that many of his timber deals had made profits for the companies that exceeded his annual salary many times over, and he expected to be able to do the same in the future. Temple acknowledged that no one could have "done as good a job" as Kenley in "saving us a lot of money," but he challenged Kenley's bargaining claim of possibly making the lumber companies his annual salary through timber negotiations as "reasoning that would probably apply to many jobs in our organizations."[111] In other words, Temple said that saving and making money for the companies *was* Kenley's job, and to pay him $5,000 a year for only 15 percent of his time would have been equivalent to a rate of pay "of almost $35,000 per year for full time." Surely, Temple contended, Kenley did not expect such compensation. Temple countered with an offer of $3,000 a year, later raised it to $3,600, and finally went as high as $4,000, which Kenley accepted. Although Arthur Sr. considered the pay arrangement as "a retainer," rather than a salary, he quickly regretted the agreement, believing that the companies received "very little out" of Kenley for the amount of money they paid him. Furthermore, they also retained his negativity. Although Arthur Sr. advised his son often to "dispense with [Kenley's] services altogether at some appropriate time," Kenley kept his position and his $4,000 annual rate of pay through the end of 1967, sixteen years after the death of Arthur Sr.[112]

The Temples had similar experiences in reducing R. E. Minton's salary. Back in March 1933, when Arthur Sr. asked Minton to consider a salary reduction because the Temple companies were in a financial crisis, Minton had resisted. Temple explained that other employees had taken reductions "down to rock bottom," and even at a reduced salary Minton would remain "the highest man on the payroll with one exception." Temple said that many men were "working for less than they [were] really worth," and he considered their doing so as "evidence of their loyalty." He asked Minton to do likewise.[113] In typical fashion, Minton argued that, unlike "other employees," he bore many personal expenses, such as a stenographer's salary, office rent in Lufkin, the depreciation expense of his personal automobile, new books for his law library, and stamps, stationary, and other sundry items that no one else bore. Also, Minton said that while the Depression may have caused other employees to receive less pay for less work, their reduced hours had created more "leisure" time for them to "engage in other undertakings," while the Depression actually "increased the matters going

thru my office."[114] According to Minton, Temple was fortunate that Minton did not ask for a pay *increase*. Only many years later did Minton finally accept a pay decrease similar to Kenley's, but not until after Arthur Jr. had begun to rely increasingly on other attorneys, such as J. J. Collins and Martin Dies, to provide for the companies' legal needs.[115] Minton, like Kenley, remained on the Company payroll through the end of 1967, when Minton was eighty-nine years old.

But there were other difficulties with Kenley and Minton, two men whose personal and professional interests were so closely bound to Boggy Slough. Early in November 1949, less than two weeks after Arthur Temple Sr. settled Kenley's new pay arrangement, Arthur Jr. wrote to his father, complaining about $75,000 he was paying to Kenley and Minton for timber they personally owned in Trinity County.[116] Arthur Jr. said that Kenley "has really held our feet to the fire, and this is especially bad since this land was bought when he was supposed to be buying stuff for Southern Pine." Arthur Sr. replied that he did not "like this timber deal at all." While reserving his final judgement and hoping there was a misunderstanding somewhere, Arthur Sr. agreed that "it just does not look right to me for us to be buying timber from one who has been employed by us on a salary to buy timber for the Company and one who has been retained by us to pass on titles. I don't blame Mr. Minton as much as I do Dave Kenley."[117]

Of course there was no misunderstanding, at least not the kind Arthur Sr. might have hoped for. Unknown to Arthur Jr. at the time, and at least partially forgotten by Arthur Sr., was Kenley's and Minton's long-standing practice of buying certain timberlands in East Texas for themselves, especially in Trinity County, even including certain tracts within the Boggy Slough Conservation Area, claiming they did so in the best interests of their employers. Their three primary motives in doing so arose when, one, the titles were in question and they chose to bear the liabilities instead of exposing the corporations; two, it was advantageous to keep the lumber companies' names out of the public records to keep selling prices low and lawsuits to a minimum; and three, the properties were State School Fund lands that contained timber, because a direct transfer of those lands to a corporation presented legal complications.[118] Furthermore, included in some of their transactions during the 1910s were "old home places," some of them abandoned and many of them fewer than 100 acres in size. Minton and Kenley often believed that perfecting the titles to such homestead tracts was simply too risky for a lumber corporation to assume, so they bought the tracts personally and routinely sold the timber to the Temple companies. After the timber was removed by the company's logging crews, Kenley fenced the tracts and grazed them. Dan Gilbert had agreed to these activities, sometimes even participating in them himself. Also, Gilbert had allowed both men to work closely with Dave Kenley's oldest brother, Carroll H. Kenley, who owned the only title abstract company in Trinity County. For several years Minton and the Kenleys customarily bought lands privately and then profitably sold the timber to Southern Pine Lumber Company, keeping the amounts paid out of the public records. So intertwined were the land-buying activities that the men on occasion used the letterheads of the Kenley & Minton Law Firm, the C. H. Kenley Abstract of Title Company, and the Guaranty State Bank of Groveton (of which Carroll Kenley was president) to transact Southern Pine Lumber Company business, and Dave Kenley employed his brothers Sam and Polk to assist in surveying the lands, both personal and those owned by Southern Pine.[119]

The problem with such land-purchasing practices was that the arrangement—and certainly the regenerating timber—looked vastly different four decades later. What was once a condoned business practice became almost unbearable two generations later and was especially distasteful to Arthur Temple Jr. "Arthur and old man Dave Kenley never did get along," Charlie Harber often recalled. Harber, who witnessed many interactions between Temple and Kenley, was fond of telling the story of when Arthur Jr. became so angry once about

paying Kenley an exorbitant amount of money for timber on one 1,400-acre tract in Trinity County that he told Kenley he was "going to cut everything off that was large enough to make a 2x4," essentially leaving Kenley a clear-cut wasteland. Harber said that Kenley replied, "Good. That's exactly what I want you to do, because I'm going to make a pasture out of it."[120]

As unsavory as such timber deals were to later generations of Temples, the main source of contention between Arthur Jr. and Kenley, however, continued to be Kenley's cows at Boggy Slough. This was especially true after Arthur Jr. began using aerial photography as a forest management tool during the 1950s, something his father had suggested doing as early as July 1948, during Arthur Jr.'s first year as general manager.[121] By the late 1950s, Temple's foresters began noticing large numbers of openings throughout the forests—what Temple later referred to as "grassy plots" and "fields"—which only became larger from one year to the next. Temple later revealed during oral history interviews that his foresters explained to him that Kenley's cows were enlarging the openings through their congregating and bedding-down. Temple said that he instructed Kenley to plant pines in those places, since "that's the business we are in," but he said Kenley resisted and claimed the soil would not grow pines on those sites. Temple said that he ordered pines to be planted anyway, and those former openings proved to be "some of the best pine-growing land" the company ever owned—but only after the browsing and trampling cattle were removed.[122]

But regenerating timber was not the only natural resource that Kenley's cows competed against. In 1957, Arthur Temple authorized a plant composition and vegetative alteration study at Boggy Slough. The research considered the ecological consequences of heavy grazing and browsing pressures from both cattle and deer.[123] With a long history of carrying large populations of both herbivores, Boggy Slough was an ideal location for such an experiment. Using various combinations of inclusion and exclusion plots located in upland, creek bottom land, and river bottom land sites, the three-year-long study found that Kenley's cattle negatively competed with deer for forbs and browse at critical times during spring and fall. In plots where cattle were not excluded, tall grasses disappeared, desirable forbs declined, and the most palatable woody browse deteriorated. The result was undeniable: cattle not only prevented natural pine regeneration, but they also caused a proliferation of short grasses, "weedy invaders," and a declining deer range, where even hardwood regeneration was absent.[124] US Forest Service forester Austin Cary had hinted at such a conclusion thirty-seven years earlier, but now science had proven it. The days of Kenley's cows remaining at Boggy Slough were numbered.

Telling Kenley that he had to remove his cows from Boggy Slough early in 1961 was "the hardest thing I ever did," Temple said in a 1985 interview. Setting aside his past differences with Kenley and Minton, Temple had come to appreciate the "great personal cost" the two men had paid to protect and defend Boggy Slough. Through more than half a century, the two men had shaped the land and the Temple businesses unlike anyone else, and there might not be a Boggy Slough Conservation Area today without them. But Temple also knew that

what his foresters had told him was true. One from Duke University had told him plainly, "You are making a terrible mistake running cattle on your land."[125] With that, Temple finally accepted the realization that timber and wildlife at Boggy Slough should be managed without the presence of cattle, and he finally asserted a landowner's right to evict a tenant.

Through nearly six decades, Arthur Temple Jr.'s father and grandfather had allowed most decisions about land management to be made by their employees—local men who were essentially sportsmen and cattlemen at heart. Although Arthur Temple Jr. became a great sportsman himself and even dabbled in the cattle business with Kenley's help, upon the death of his father in 1951 he immediately asserted an ownership class of management that brought definite, although gradual, changes to land stewardship and to Boggy Slough. For half a century, Boggy Slough's management had been mostly reactionary, defined by Kenley as "practical work." Now was the beginning of proactive scientific management. And the question of who owned Boggy Slough was no longer in dispute. Arthur Temple Jr. asserted his inherited ownership and management rights of Boggy Slough, and his larger-than-life personality would shape its future.

CHAPTER 10

The Ranch Becomes Boggy Slough

It is axiomatic that as the natural production of a desired natural resource fails, it is supplemented by semi-artificial means of production. This is the long and short of game farming. This is the long and short of Forestry.

—ALDO LEOPOLD (1919)

Arthur Temple Jr.'s love for Boggy Slough began during his youth with a deer hunt over the Thanksgiving weekend of 1936. Receiving the hunting trip required some begging, however, for although his father was an avid duck hunter, he cared little for hunting deer. In fact, Arthur Sr. did not even own a deer rifle, and he usually borrowed one from a Texarkana friend the few times that he did hunt. Unable to delay the inevitable hunting trip any longer, Arthur Sr. finally wrote to R. E. Minton early in November, saying that his son was "very anxious to go down for a deer hunt on Thanksgiving, and I suppose I will have to take him." He asked that Minton make all the arrangements, including buying a Texas hunting license for himself, borrowing a rifle "for the boy," and, if it was not too inconvenient, Minton was requested to "go out with us." Arthur Sr. said that they planned to leave Texarkana early on the afternoon of Thanksgiving Day so they could arrive at the clubhouse before dark and begin hunting Friday morning. Minton replied that he

was "delighted to have" them, but he encouraged Arthur Sr. to come down Wednesday afternoon instead, informing him that the duck hunting season at Boggy Slough opened on Thursday morning. If they arrived a day earlier, Minton said that they would have plenty of time to hunt both deer and ducks and also a "large crop of squirrels." The squirrels were especially abundant that season, he said, and he felt "sure that Arthur Jr. would enjoy squirrel hunting also."[1]

The invitation of an extra day brought excitement to both of the Temples. Arthur Sr. even asked his Texarkana friend James Dawson to join them for the extended hunt. He wrote to Minton and informed him that Dawson would be coming and bringing his shotgun and rifle. Temple explained that since he had earlier planned to borrow Dawson's rifle for himself, he now needed Minton to provide two rifles and ammunition, since he thought he might also "attempt to get a deer," although he admitted he would spend the majority of his time "on the duck pond." Temple closed his letter expressing, "Needless to say, we are all looking forward with a great deal of pleasure to this trip, and I want you to know that I appreciate very much you having us down, and particularly your interest in Arthur Jr."[2]

Many years later, Arthur Jr. credited Minton as well as E. C. Durham with teaching him how to hunt that day at Boggy Slough. His continued trips there during his youth instilled in him a love of the outdoors at an early age and also renewed his father's interests in the Boggy Slough Hunting Club, which had waned during the difficult days of the Depression and the slow liquidation of the cattle ranch. After 1936, Boggy Slough became a place where father and son bonded over duck hunts and deer hunting parties.

T. L. L. Temple and Arthur Temple Sr. had directed the family's East Texas interests from afar, but Arthur Temple Jr. had come to call Angelina County, Texas, his home by the age of twenty. Born at Texarkana, Arkansas, in 1920, as a boy he summered with his mother's and father's families along the beaches at Quogue, Long Island, and spent parts of the winter with his aristocratic Sage and Whitney relatives in New York City.[3] Early on, he cultivated a natural talent for moving assuredly in many different social circles. He began his career in the Temple family businesses upon leaving the University of Texas at the age of eighteen to work as a bookkeeper at Temple Lumber Company's retail lumberyard in Paris, Texas. He quickly transferred to the Lufkin lumberyard, became its manager by 1941, and made it the most profitable building products center of the thirty-three retail yards owned by his family—"from the Red River to the Rio Grande," as the popular advertising slogan proclaimed.[4]

His business acumen and boundless energy were legendary. He became executive vice president and general manager of Southern Pine Lumber Company at the age of only twenty-seven, following the death of his cousin Henry Gresham Temple in February 1948. By the age of twenty-nine, Arthur Jr. was president of five businesses, vice president of five more, a director in ten others, and held active leadership roles in countless additional enterprises big and small, local as well as regional. In all of them he wielded a Midas touch.

Arthur Jr. became president of Southern Pine Lumber Company at the age of thirty-one, upon the death of his father in 1951. Living by the motto, "Do it right, but do it right now," he soon became a larger-than-life figure in East Texas and wherever his business interests took him. His over-six-foot frame, love of East Texas and the outdoors, and

his tenacity inside and outside boardrooms from Texas to New York endeared him to many East Texans and made him a force to be reckoned with for others.[5]

By the time Arthur Temple Jr. moved to Lufkin, he was a regular visitor to Boggy Slough, taking every opportunity to become involved in its management. To be nearer the action in 1941, he built a personal clubhouse beside a duck pond dam at the edge of Bluff Prairie and called it Little Boggy. Whereas his father favored spending time at Grassy Lake, in Arkansas, because it was convenient to his Texarkana office, Arthur Jr. preferred Boggy Slough because it was convenient to his Lufkin and, later, Diboll offices. Because both men loved to hunt ducks, and fish for largemouth bass, they bonded over such activities during Arthur Sr.'s periodic visits to East Texas, which became more frequent and increasingly enjoyable, especially after the births of Arthur Sr.'s grandchildren: Charlotte, better known as "Chotsy," in 1940, and Arthur Temple III, better known as "Buddy," in 1942.

During the two men's hunts at Boggy Slough during the 1940s, the young and ambitious Arthur Jr., still in his twenties, impetuous, and even reckless at times, received steady doses of fatherly advice and correction, along with equal amounts of praise. Arthur Jr.'s intense lifestyle and breakneck pace were often questioned. His father especially worried about his high blood pressure and recurring "severe headaches." His "wading after ducks without rubber boots" was another concern of his father. The practice was "very apt to affect your heart in later years," his father warned, saying he knew it to be true because he consulted a trusted doctor about it. Even his older cousin W. Temple Webber, whose Diboll office was across the hall from Arthur Jr.'s, shared concerns for his health and fast pace of life.[6]

Arthur Jr.'s vigor and passion for the outdoors, as well as for everything else in life, was admirable, his father told him, but not at the expense of his health. For years his father chided him to "slow down and take time to enjoy life . . . get more relaxation at home and not go out socially so much

Arthur Temple Sr., center, sitting on the barstool footrail at the Boggy Slough clubhouse, ca. 1950. To his left is his son Arthur Temple Jr. and manager E. A. Farley; to his right is his nephew W. Temple Webber and family member Harry Walker. *Courtesy of The History Center, Diboll.*

and keep late hours." He was instructed to "take more time to engage in cultural pursuits," read more, and take "an active interest in the church." His father admonished him to live his life "for other things than making money," especially immediately after World War II, when high taxes gave little incentive "to accumulate" it.[7]

While his father adored him for his outstanding business achievements, he also sought to make him an even better man, for the present as well as for a long future ahead of him. He encouraged Arthur Jr. to be a "worthy" heir to "the empire" that his grandfather had "built up through great labor and sacrifice." His father more than once reminded him that he was proud to have also "held together" the family's businesses with an equal amount of dedication during a most difficult time that had destroyed many other family businesses, and he desired more than anything that his son would continue that legacy. Particularly, his father disapproved of his coarse language, telling him that all he wanted for Christmas in 1946 was, "a resolution on your part to elevate your conversation. It is just a little rough at times. . . . You have had too good a background and have too fine a character to let yourself be brought down to a common level."[8]

That such admonishment was given during or just after time spent together at Boggy Slough never affected the ability of the place to continue to unite the two men. Arthur Jr. was never shy in sharing advice of his own, as demonstrated once when his father considered withdrawing as a sponsor of a Boggy Slough hunt because he felt that he "would do very little sleeping with all the noise that attends a Boggy Slough party" and would be embarrassed, "as sponsor of the party, to go to Lufkin or Diboll to sleep." Besides, his father also feared that he could no longer "eat the things that I used to eat."[9] Arthur Jr. rebuked him, writing, "You are a relatively young man, and you take absolutely no interest in anything other than your job, the radio, and your home. I think that's the best way to die of dry rot that I ever heard of. It isn't normal for a man to give up everything on the pretense of getting old at the age of fifty-two. I think you are on the wrong track in your attempt at taking care of yourself. The record shows that people who have lots of outside interests have lived a good bit longer and get a good bit more out of life than those that withdraw to themselves. I think you are just getting lazy, and are just using your age as an excuse to justify your laziness."[10] Although bold, such banter proved effective, because Arthur Sr. sponsored his Boggy Slough hunting party that year, and all other years afterward.

⁂

Arthur Jr. first loved Boggy Slough because of his personal interests in hunting and fishing, but he quickly recognized the place's historical role in developing and strengthening his family's business relationships. Bringing the hands-on approach of the ownership class, he came to love and understand Boggy Slough even more intimately than Minton and Kenley had, and he envisioned it as accomplishing even greater goodwill for his family's businesses.

One of the first things Arthur Jr. questioned was the outdated accommodation provided by the original company clubhouse, which later he derided as "the little shack on the slough."[11] It had been built in 1922 on the west bank of Boggy Slough, across from the island. Long before the Temples arrived, the slough had been named Boggy for a reason. Arthur Jr. especially disliked the fact that poor bottomland roads naturally limited access to and from the old clubhouse. "There would always be some guy that couldn't handle the muddy road, and he'd get stuck," he explained in a 2000 interview, "then everybody behind him would be stuck, and they'd have to walk up to the clubhouse, and then walk back out and try to get their cars out." Too many times wet conditions caused more cold overnight stays than high-profile visitors had planned, he recalled, and without telephones, plumbing, or electricity, conditions were "pretty rough."[12] Years later, John Booker, who built truck logging roads during the early 1950s, said that whoever built the first clubhouse "couldn't have picked a worse spot. . . . When I was there [after the original clubhouse had been abandoned], a flood came and tore it all up and floated most of it away."[13]

Arthur Temple Sr. agreed with his son, but while he felt that a new clubhouse was needed, he did not necessarily dislike the slough location.

Throughout 1940 he wrote to Dave Kenley, saying that while he enjoyed the "fellowship" offered by the clubhouse on the slough, he felt that the house itself was always lacking. In one of his letters he said that he wanted "something nicer than what we have at present, because we have a wonderful place for hunting, a very attractive site for a clubhouse—really a big asset for the cultivation and maintaining of good will, but we discount all that with a very unattractive and overcrowded clubhouse, lacking many of the facilities which make life pleasant."[14] Temple also shared that although he had never seen the Trinity County clubhouse of the Cameron family of Waco, he understood that it was "very nice and very much more in keeping with the prestige and standing of its owner and sponsor than is ours." Temple said that he had given the matter considerable thought, and he wanted a "more comfortable and attractive" clubhouse, one that "would be a lodge built out of logs with a large combination living room and dining room with a big open fireplace at one end and then perhaps two large rooms to serve as dormitories or sleeping quarters." He stressed that he wanted the sleeping rooms apart so that "the snorers and the non-snorers may be separated." Temple closed one of his letters, quipping, "While I do not like to encourage extravagance or the spending of unnecessary money, I cannot overlook the fact that Uncle Sam would pay $24 out of every $100 we might put into such a project, because the present tax on corporation profits is 24%."[15]

Arthur Temple Jr. later said that he drew most of the plans for the new clubhouse himself, receiving the approval of his father and his cousin Henry Temple. He selected a new construction site near Rayville, which was about a mile and a half southwest of the slough clubhouse, and most importantly, it offered access without traversing river bottom lands. Shell Pipeline Company had placed a pipeline running north–south through the eastern portion of the Sanchez survey in 1937, and the Pan American Pipeline Company placed another pipeline beside it in 1940.[16] The cleared pipeline right-of-way through the ridge near Rayville

Arthur Temple Sr., foreground, relaxes in a rocking chair and visits with Harry Walker at the Boggy Slough clubhouse, ca. 1950. *Courtesy of The History Center, Diboll.*

View of the second Boggy Slough clubhouse, ca. 1950. *Courtesy of The History Center, Diboll.*

the oldest and most prized deer mounts were two large bucks killed by Judge Minton's son, Robert Elmer Jr., and daughter, Marjorie, in 1925 and 1928, respectively. It was said that each deer had weighed more than two hundred pounds.[17]

After the opening-day weekend at the new clubhouse, longtime guests lauded the Temples for their new accommodations, writing appreciative letters expressing gratitude for "the most enjoyable times . . . ever experienced."[18] Even the ultraconservative Dave Kenley expressed approval for the new accommodations. Arthur Sr. wrote him on December 20, saying that he was "glad" Kenley approved because he was concerned he might have thought it was "a little too nice or too fancy for a hunting lodge."[19] Kenley liked the new clubhouse so well, in fact, that he asked to reserve

offered a prime all-weather-access location at the top of a hill, which was about 35 feet higher in elevation than the slough clubhouse site.

Arthur Jr. supervised construction of the new clubhouse, which opened just in time to host the fall 1941 deer hunts. The trophy wildlife mounts from the old clubhouse—deer heads, stuffed ducks, bobcats, alligators, and trophy fish—were hurriedly moved to the new lodge and placed so that new trophies could be added later. Among

View of the Boggy Slough clubhouse, ca. 1956. A fire destroyed it in 1966. *Courtesy of The History Center, Diboll.*

A group of Stephen F. Austin State College forestry students at the Boggy Slough clubhouse, ca. 1949.

it over the Christmas holiday for his own family to enjoy.

From the new clubhouse's beginning, Arthur Temple Sr. and Jr. encouraged its use by "our people at Diboll." It was more than a hunting lodge, they said, because it was intended to be a place for civic gatherings and where department heads could take their families "on weekends and get a great deal out of it as a recreation center."[20] Many Diboll families did enjoy the new club-

house, and others throughout East Texas did as well. A number of area citizens and families were invited there before their children entered service during World War II, and organizations such as the East Texas Area Council of Boy Scouts and Cub Scouts became regular guests. The Scouts frequently held large Explorers' Sport Camps, where campers enjoyed several days of archery, rifle, skeet, bait-casting, and fly-casting contests, with pow-wows held nightly around the clubhouse's large fireplace.[21] In time the clubhouse was used throughout most of the year by numerous families and civic and educational groups and organizations.

By August 1944 the clubhouse was used so much that Arthur Temple Sr. became concerned that it was actually "badly used and even abused." Since he had always "thought well of the idea of having someone directly responsible," he wrote that he wanted someone to care for the clubhouse's maintenance full time. It was at this time, during one his disputes with Kenley over his lease of Boggy Slough, that he suggested a company pasture rider live in the former house of J. J. Ray and that "he or his wife should be given the responsibility of the care of the club house."[22] There was too much investment in the new clubhouse, he said, "to let it go to rack and ruin." When Henry Temple suggested that Arthur Temple Jr. serve as the clubhouse's manager, Arthur Sr. disagreed, believing that his son was already overextended in his responsibilities. He felt that, since the clubhouse was meant to be "used all the year around, and to a large extent by the people of Diboll," John O'Hara of Diboll would make "the best custodian."[23] As it turned out, although he did not live on the property, Arthur Jr. took the job of clubhouse manager, serving until he accepted the general manager's job at Diboll early in 1948. At that time he placed Ben Anthony, a family relative through his Webber cousins, in the position of clubhouse manager, which Anthony held until the lodge burned in December 1966.[24]

Ben Anthony and his staff of cooks and waiters contributed immensely to the success of every entertainment at Boggy Slough. Guests liked the simple but hearty and well-prepared southern-style meals and the country hospitality. They especially relished the famous cornbread and fried chicken dinners.[25] Most of the clubhouse employees were black mill and railroad workers from Diboll, who were also excellent musicians and church choir members. For many years their musical leader was "Professor" Will Jackson, who traveled during the 1920s with the Christy Brothers Circus, which wintered in Beaumont, Texas. Jackson played trumpet in one of the circus bands led by Everett James, the father of Harry James, who became one the most famous trumpet players in jazz and pop music history and credited Jackson's flamboyant "hot" jazz trumpet style as an early influence.[26]

Sometime during the mid-1930s, Jackson moved to Diboll, took a job at the Texas Southeastern Rail-

Ben Anthony, longtime manager of the Boggy Slough clubhouse, wearing a hat and holding a largemouth bass, stands with Martin Dies Jr. during the 1950s. *Courtesy of The History Center, Diboll.*

road Company, and became a Boggy Slough waiter and entertainer, first at the old clubhouse and later at the new lodge. Guests thoroughly enjoyed Jackson's playing and the stirring vocal and musical numbers performed by his "colored choir," as guests knew them. Some guests were so impressed that they extended invitations through the Temples asking the choir to perform at their hometown civic club meetings, some as far away as Texarkana. In such ways even a choir fulfilled Boggy Slough's ambassadorial mission well beyond the property's boundaries.[27]

Yet for all the goodwill that the clubhouse staff provided, social customs of the day meant that the choir members were lodged in separate buildings nearby and also hosted other black visitors. For example, in November 1949, Senator Howard A. Carney, suffering from rheumatism, wrote to Arthur Temple Jr. from Austin and apologized

Cooks pose at the bar at the Boggy Slough clubhouse, ca. 1950. *Courtesy of The History Center, Diboll.*

Boggy Slough cooks, 1948, left to right, Percy W. Garrett, Charlie Billy Runnels, A. C. Phillips, and Q. T. Bussey. *Courtesy of The History Center, Diboll.*

for his need "to get the negro boy who works here to drive me down during the hunt." If not too much trouble, Carney asked, "I thought perhaps he could stay in the shack with the cooks while we were there."[28] Many years later, Buddy Temple lamented the cook shack's separate, but unequal, accommodations during a site visit in 2014. He regretted the lack of running water, especially since the clubhouse water well was so conveniently situated to the shack. "In those days," he said, managers "weren't too concerned about the creature comforts of the people who worked out here."[29]

⸺⸺◆⸺⸺

In the new clubhouse built in 1941, hunting parties were held on every weekend of the deer hunting season, and oftentimes additional parties were squeezed in during times earlier in the week to accommodate the demand. Overnight guests typically arrived on the afternoon of their first day, usually a Friday, and if they arrived early enough, they hunted that evening. They also hunted in the morning and evening of their second day, and then departed on the morning or the afternoon of their third day. Some guests occasionally hunted again on the morning of their third day, but during World War II, hunting was not allowed on Sundays.[30]

Although the state game department had invested heavily in restocking deer in the region—releasing some five thousand deer in thirty-two East Texas counties during the 1940s and 1950s—Boggy Slough remained one of the few places where deer could be consistently killed each season.[31] The place's fame advanced through numerous photographs, published in newspapers across the state, that showed smiling hunters holding up the heads of large antlered deer with headlines and captions such as, "Didn't Get Away." Some photographs showed bucks with antlered racks of more than twenty-six points.[32]

Yet in spite of the trophies that appeared in the newspapers and hung on the clubhouse walls, Boggy Slough's overall deer herd suffered little from the club's hunting pressure. The state game commission reported during the 1960s that Boggy Slough's hunter success rate during the 1950s was no higher than 15 percent—much too low for the sustained health of the herd, which suffered occasional die-offs. This showed that the hunting club's guests were not real hunters, but were instead influential businessmen and government officials whose friendships the company courted because they were simply good for business. The state's findings were probably no surprise to Kenley, who had argued for decades that it was not as important for clients to kill a deer as it was for them merely "to see a few."[33]

In addition to bringing their shotguns for ducks and squirrels and their rifles (and sometimes bows and arrows) for deer, many guests also brought their fishing tackle to fish in the artificial lakes that were stocked with bass. Invitations often included wording such as, "We hear a number of lunkers have been caught lately." And through the 1950s, guests were also encouraged to hunt quail. Although the company allowed guests to bring their own dogs—for bird hunting only—staff provided "capable dogs" if needed.[34]

The new clubhouse accommodated up to twenty-four overnight guests, and was always at capacity during the deer season. If there was a last-minute cancellation, plenty of willing hunters were standing by on a waiting list. Equally important to the success of each hunting party were the additional day guests, sixty to seventy of whom joined the hunters for lunch and supper on each party's second day, always filling to capacity the large dining room. Most day guests stayed for at least some of the after-meal "fellowships," which included drinking and card playing in the game room and relaxing in high-backed rocking chairs around the big fireplace in the huge center room. Group singing was also popular, and was one of Arthur Temple Sr.'s favorite pastimes.

Among those who attended the meals and fellowships were members of the who's who of Texas businessmen and community leaders. They included newspaper publishers and editors, automobile dealers, politicians, lawyers, bankers, realtors, oil men, highway department and utility company officials, hardware store owners, hotel owners and managers, and trucking company officials. In addition, the officers of many of the larger local businesses, such as Lufkin Foundry & Machine Company, Texas Foundries, Lufkin Coca-Cola Bottling, and Perry Brothers Department Store, also came routinely. Throughout the 1940s, Ernest L. Kurth, one of the most influential industrialists in East Texas, was a regular Boggy Slough guest, as was the powerful US congressman Martin Dies.[35] Of course numerous other lumber and paper mill company executives rounded out the dinner guest lists. By the 1950s, such notables as Charles Stillwell of Time Inc. and R. M. Buckley of Eastex Pulp and Paper Company, along with the executives of International Paper Company and Champion Paper and Fibre Company, annually attended the Boggy Slough hunting parties.[36]

The parties sponsored by Arthur Temple Jr. during the 1940s were usually reserved for the first two weekends closest to the opening day of the deer season in Trinity County. The dates of Arthur Sr.'s parties fluctuated each year depending on the opening day of the duck season in southwestern Arkansas, because Arthur Sr. rarely missed opening day at his Grassy Lake duck preserve. In some years, the Temple family parties were held around the Thanksgiving weekend. Arthur Sr. routinely put off sponsoring a Boggy Slough party until the last minute, explaining that his guests were merely his poker playing pals from the Texarkana Country Club and his duck hunting friends from Grassy Lake. Since no one in his circle really cared to hunt deer, and they gave no "direct benefit to Southern Pine Lumber Company," he usually hesitated to reserve the clubhouse for two nights during the deer season, which he felt deprived others of opportunities to hunt. Another reason was that he felt a Boggy Slough party was "quite expensive for the pleasure to be derived," as he often wrote to his son each fall.[37] But Arthur Jr. always encouraged him to sponsor a party anyway. Arthur Sr. obliged him, and he never regretted it. After every party, he wrote appreciative letters to his son thanking him for having insisted that he "put on a party," saying that each year became more enjoyable. Typical was his letter of November 17, 1950, in which he thanked his son for his part in making the party "a complete success . . . as always." It was probably "the best party I have yet sponsored," he told him. "Everyone seemed to have an awfully good time, and there was nothing unpleasant except the unfortunate incident Wednesday night when Henry Lewis got his rib broken."[38]

Under Arthur Temple Jr.'s localized leadership following World War II, Texas state congressmen and senators became regular visitors to Boggy Slough, and occasionally governors, such as Lufkin native Allan Shivers, and lieutenant governors, such as San Augustine native Ben Ramsey, also visited.

In rolled-up sleeves, Arthur Temple Jr. visits with Senator Jimmy Phillips of Angleton at Southern Pine Lumber Company's July 4 barbecue in 1950. *Courtesy of The History Center, Diboll.*

Although Arthur Temple Sr. identified more with Arkansas politicians than with those from Texas, he especially approved of his son's political activities in the state where most of the family's business interests lay.[39] He once wrote to him, saying it was "a fine thing that you are entertaining these men [Texas government officials]: I don't know of any better way to get close to a group of men than on a party at Boggy Slough, and I am confident that much good will result to our companies and other industrial organizations in our area."[40]

In November 1949, after Arthur Temple Jr. entertained seven of the state's most influential senators at Boggy Slough, he wrote to his father: "We did a good job, and I think that our efforts may pay off next session when there is a very real threat of a severance tax [on timber]. We hit some awfully good licks with them and I know they all enjoyed it." He added that Senator Carney of Atlanta, who had hunted at Boggy Slough "in the old days with Bud Rutland and others, had a wonderful time. Although he was on crutches, we put him out in a flat by the road in a chair with a blanket around him and he got a very large buck. He was really thrilled over it."[41]

Although it was not his first deer hunted and killed at Boggy Slough, Buddy Temple displays one that he shot there on November 20, 1953, posing in front of the Southern Pine Lumber Company offices at Diboll with his gifted .30-30 Winchester. *Courtesy of The History Center, Diboll.*

Just a few days before Senator Carney and his fellow senators arrived, seven-year-old Buddy Temple, who later became a Texas politician himself, killed his first deer at Boggy Slough during an evening hunt in a palmetto flat not far from Judge Minton's old clubhouse near Boggy Slough Island. Buddy had just been gifted a new .30-30 caliber Winchester Model 94 by attorney J. J. Collins, and he used it proudly to bring down the small buck.[42] Both Buddy's father and grandfather were there for the special occasion, and each of them later expressed in letters that they "got a big kick" out of "Buddy's deer," although neither one of them photographed the special occasion. Arthur Sr., an avid photographer, regretted that while he had his camera with him he did not have his "flashlight equipment" and therefore was unable to even attempt to obtain the much desired "picture of Buddy with his deer." He was further disappointed to learn that "the locker plant had skinned out" the deer

before any photograph at all was made, for he had hoped that "someone" might have taken a photograph "of Buddy standing by the deer . . . rigged up in his hunting regalia just as he was the night he came in from his stand." Also regretting that no photograph was made, Arthur Jr. later consoled his father, telling him that he planned "to have the little head mounted for Buddy's room."[43]

News of the Texas senatorial parties at Boggy Slough occasionally made the newspapers, for all the wrong reasons. One such occasion was in December 1954, when local game wardens—acting "on a tip"—cited Senator Warren McDonald of Tyler for hunting outside his home county without a license. When the wardens arrived at the Boggy Slough clubhouse and found McDonald with a deer and without a license, about thirty state officials were present. Among them were Senators Ottis Lock of Lufkin and Doyle Willis of Fort Worth, along with Lt. Governor Ben Ramsey. Newspapers from as far away as Clovis, New Mexico, carried the story over the course of several days. The *El Paso Times* reported that while the game wardens from Lufkin and Groveton made "a call to their Austin headquarters," Clyde Thompson, "the newly elected president of the Angelina County Chamber of Commerce," arrived with a license for McDonald, who promptly "tagged the deer . . . and ran off with him" before the wardens were finished with their business.[44] Senator McDonald later returned to appear before a Groveton justice of the peace, and, according to an Associated Press article in the *Dallas Morning News*, he declared that he had "shot my first and last deer." He pled that he had informed his hosts upon arrival at the clubhouse that he did not have a license and that, although someone had arranged for his license by telephone, they "forgot to pick it up when they went into town."[45]

Many members of the Texas legislature visited Boggy Slough primarily for the fellowship and did not necessarily hunt. Texas representative

US Senator Price Daniel at the Boggy Slough clubhouse in September 1954. To his right is state representative and secretary-treasurer of the Texas Lumber Manufacturers Association, A. E. Cudlipp, of Lufkin Foundry & Machine Company. To Senator Daniel's left is Clyde Thompson of Southern Pine Lumber Company, a longtime Temple employee and Boggy Slough Hunting Club member who hosted Texas senators at the clubhouse annually. *Courtesy of The History Center, Diboll.*

Charles Wilson of Trinity—who later became a US congressman—was elected to the Texas House in 1961 and became a regular guest at the Boggy Slough clubhouse, often hosted by his good friend Buddy Temple. In later years, Buddy recalled that several political campaigns during the mid-1960s were thrashed out over poker games at the clubhouse during legislative parties held there. One in particular occurred during the fall of 1965, when representatives Rayford Price of Palestine and Wilson were each considering a race for the Texas Senate. Buddy remembered that he, Wilson, Price, and a young man named Fred Head, who was not yet a state representative but who would later be an infamous opponent of Price's in the House, were well into a lengthy poker game, when an "unbelievable" hand was dealt at about five a.m. "Everybody was dealt a good hand," he said. Head kept "bumping the pot, bumping the pot, bumping the pot," until only he and Price remained in the game. Finally, at about 6 a.m., Head won, and Buddy said that Price owed Head the amount of "probably $5,000, or something like that . . . [and] he had no way of paying the debt." Then, as the day was dawning, Wilson and Price stepped onto the back porch alone and talked for about fifteen minutes. When they returned, Wilson informed Buddy that

Price would not run for the Texas Senate and that Wilson would pay Price's debt to Head.[46]

Outside of the deer hunting season, the clubhouse also hosted meetings of area county agricultural agents and organizations such as the Texas Lumber Manufacturers Association, the National Lumber Manufacturers Association, the Southern Pine Association, the Texas Forestry Association, the Hoo-Hoo Club, and the Texas Municipal League.[47] These events usually included notable speakers, such as US congressman Martin Dies during the 1940s and Texas secretary of state and attorney general John Ben Shepperd, US congressman Lloyd Bentsen, and US senator Price Daniel during the 1950s. Audiences of up to two hundred people usually attended.[48] The clubhouse also hosted regular gatherings of law enforcement officials and civic groups, as well as forestry students from Stephen F. Austin State College. During most of the "off-season" gatherings that occurred during the spring and fall months, Ben Anthony set up dinner and meeting tables outdoors under the shade of young pine trees.[49] Arthur Temple was quoted often in the *Diboll Free Press* during this time, saying he was "happy that we can make Boggy Slough available to worthy groups and organizations for their meetings and conventions

US Congressman Martin Dies, a regular visitor to Boggy Slough during the 1940s, gestures outside the clubhouse in about 1948. *Courtesy of The History Center, Diboll.*

Members of the Texas Lumber Manufacturers Association meet outside the Boggy Slough clubhouse during one of their annual meetings held there during the 1950s. *Courtesy of The History Center, Diboll.*

KTRE radio, of Lufkin, advertised as the "nation's forestry station," broadcast the annual meetings of the TLMA at the Boggy Slough clubhouse during the 1950s. Ernest Kurth, of Southland Paper Mills and owner of the radio station, stands at the far left. Others identified are Al Cudlipp, T. Gilette Tilford, Jim Edens, and Russ Eagle. *Courtesy of The History Center, Diboll.*

each year. We feel that it is this kind of public service which makes industries such as ours 'good citizens' of our county and community."[50]

During the 1950s, the clubhouse also hosted meetings of an organization known as the East Texas Federated Hunting Clubs. This group was composed of representatives from nineteen hunting clubs, all located near Boggy Slough, mostly along the Neches River. Heavily influenced by Arthur Temple Jr., who usually hosted the semiannual meetings, the centralized group passed rules for each club in accordance with Boggy Slough's management experiences. The rules concerned game as well as timber resources. Among other things, each club was to require its members to sign "fire prevention pledges," post lists of "persons filed on" at each clubhouse, and agree to help police the club's lands, especially against the use of dogs in running deer. For several years, the organization hired what they called a "freelance patrolman" to spend time at each hunting club during the month of November, camping out at least thirty nights "in the pastures," "in the woods," and "on the river."[51] The group also considered the occasional financial request to assist an injured pasture rider's family, such as in 1954 when Dave Kenley sought

to provide Christmas presents to the children of one of the Pine Island Hunting Club's riders, who was badly beaten by poachers who were chased across the river and into the Boggy Slough club, where the beating occurred.[52]

By 1950, some of Boggy Slough's guests were flying into the new Angelina County Airport, where Southern Pine officials provided automobile transportation to and from the clubhouse. After the death of Arthur Temple Sr., Arthur Temple Jr. and W. Temple Webber usually combined their hunting parties, which consisted of the closest friends and associates of the Temple companies and family. These parties were followed by those of Latane Temple, who hosted hunts for the retail and wholesale sales departments. Next were Clyde Thompson's hunts for state government officials, especially members of the legislature. Following these were parties for Temple Lumber Company, Temple-White Company, the Diboll Treating Plant, and then all company foremen. Lastly, Arthur Temple Jr. always squeezed in at least one hunting party for the area's state game wardens, making the warden hunts part of the club's rules in 1954.[53] By this time, Temple had made arrangements for Dave Kenley to handle most of his county commissioner hunts on lands north of Cochino Bayou, using the clubhouses of the Malibu Club and the Collins, Dies, Williams,

an abundant supply of game, as well as the state's continued cooperation in protecting it. Guests were encouraged to act responsibly so that the club would particularly "merit the good will of those whom we are not able to entertain." Guests and members alike were also reminded to pick up trash anywhere they might find it. Finally, the cards stated the club's hopes that each guest would enjoy the club's hospitality

and Garrison Law Firm Club during the first two weeks of each hunting season.[54]

and that their acceptance of the invitation would "aid in making missionaries out of men like you for conservation of game and wild life."[55]

By the early 1950s, club rules permitted each member to build and own private clubhouses, subject to the wishes of an executive committee controlled by Arthur Temple Jr. Earlier, Judge Minton, Dave Kenley, and Arthur Temple Jr. had built private clubhouses, but now the other nine members—W. Temple Webber, Latane Temple, Clyde Thompson, E. A. Farley, Ben Anthony, Carroll Allen, Joe Denman, Kenneth Nelson, and R. L. Farley—were allowed to do the same if they desired. Members were reminded that they had been "selected" for membership because of their "responsible positions held in the Company organization and their interest in its successful operation." Accordingly, they were allowed to invite their immediate family as guests, so long as it did not "interfere with parties sponsored for the Company." After all, the main objective of the club was "to promote Company business and good will," and all other uses of Boggy Slough were "subordinate to this primary purpose." Also during the early 1950s, the club began to recognize the importance of the region's "patrolmen, the game

From its beginning in 1922, the Boggy Slough Hunting and Fishing Club sought to reward key personnel within the Temple family of businesses— originally Southern Pine Lumber Company and Texas Southeastern Railroad Company—with individual recreational "privileges," while also providing them a means of advancing their department's business interests. Members rewrote the club's rules about once every decade. Early on, all guests were required to possess a personalized guest card and invitation, signed by a club member, which authorized their presence on the property on specific dates. Guests were to present the card when requested by game wardens and patrolmen. The cards let the guests know that their invitation was an exclusive privilege and that they had been selected by the club "to cement the bonds of friendship now existing into stronger ones." Also included were at least eleven rules and regulations, which were necessary, the card explained, to maintain wardens, and peace officers" by sponsoring at least one hunting party annually for them. At such a time the wardens were permitted "to kill game and fish," but they were reminded that at all other times their presence was "as officers only."[56]

By 1963, the name Boggy Slough Hunting and Fishing Club had changed to Boggy Slough Game Preserve Committee. The committee's membership remained the same as the club's membership a decade earlier, except that the Farleys were replaced by Ward Burke and H. J. Shands Jr., and Herb C. White Jr. was added late in 1963. Committee members were still reminded that the purpose of the preserve was "for the benefit of Southern Pine Lumber Company and its affiliated companies and not for personal benefit." Rules remained essentially the same as earlier, except that fishing by guests became more restricted. A guest could fish only by receiving a printed day permit signed by certain committee members and could not receive more than two such permits during any one month. Also, fishing was allowed only from January 1 to August 31 so that it would not interfere with the various hunting seasons.[57]

Throughout the years, most of the club membership remained company department heads, who were responsible for sponsoring the various hunting parties on behalf of their departments. They were also responsible for the party expenses, which were charged against their departmental budgets. By 1960 the rising costs of entertaining at the clubhouse had risen higher than Arthur Temple was willing to continue supporting without some kind of cost restructuring. In later years he always stressed the fact that the company had provided between five thousand and six thousand meals a year at the clubhouse, which he felt was extravagant. On December 30, 1960, he wrote to all department heads, instructing them to "not make any plans for a party at Boggy Slough next year or do anything that would indicate to your customers that there may be one this next year." He explained that he was considering "drastically reducing the volume of traffic at Boggy Slough," and he did not want any commitments to be made

until further notice. Three days later he wrote to everyone again and clarified that "the annual carrying costs for expenses *not including* such things as the rider, taxes, et cetera," amounted to "about $9,000 per year." He explained that the expense figure did not include "Ben Anthony's time," nor "numerous other items which probably could accurately be charged to the operation of the hunting club." Since there had been eleven hunting parties during 1960, Temple said that he wanted to begin charging each future hunting party a "use fee" of $900 in addition to "actual party expenses" because "the money [was] being spent," and it was "costing that much to have the facilities." He stated that while he felt that everyone could continue to "get a great deal of good" out of the entertainments if they were "properly handled," he remained unsure that such expenses were actually "worthwhile."[58]

Even after charging the use fee, Temple remained dissatisfied with the costs of entertaining at Boggy Slough because it was still the company's money, regardless of how it was accounted for. Also, Temple had grown tired of "the crowds," saying in December 1962 that, as much as he liked to hunt, he had not "bothered" to go that year because "it is no fun to go hunting when the place is about as crowded as New York City."[59] While it seemed that nearly everyone was suddenly hunting at Boggy Slough in late 1962, what affected Temple most, however, was lingering worries over pasture rider Claude Davenport's near-fatal shooting of Earl Smith that August, and he would attempt drastic measures to calm the concerns.

In an attempt to finally eliminate the financial costs as well as the social responsibilities of operating the hunting club, and perhaps also eliminate the burdens of its occasional negative publicity, Temple sought to lease the property to someone else in the spring of 1963. He first considered the Austin-based Sportsmen's Clubs of Texas, Inc. (SCOT), the recognized state affiliate of the National Wildlife Federation. Temple worked with the organization's president, Henry J. LeBlanc Sr. of Port Arthur, to explore Boggy Slough's possible role in SCOT's new nonprofit, public hunting initiative, known as "Operation Whitetail-East Texas." The Caesar Kleberg Foundation for Wildlife Preservation had pledged $200,000 to finance the effort, King Ranch manager Richard Kleberg Jr. was intending to play a role in its management, and SCOT needed only an ideal location in East Texas to operate. After making an "on-the-spot inspection of the Boggy Slough area," LeBlanc explained to Temple in a four-page letter, on March 8, that he was sure a lease of Boggy Slough to SCOT could be worked out to their mutual satisfaction, thereby providing quality "low-cost hunting and fishing to the people of East Texas." LeBlanc detailed all the particular shared benefits that a lease of the clubhouse, hunting grounds, and fishing waters might include and closed by saying, "In this way you could be relieved of the many worries connected with the public use of your lands. You can refer them to SCOT and let us do the worrying."[60]

Before Temple made his final decision, he asked longtime employee and Boggy Slough club member Clyde Thompson what he thought. Thompson replied in writing, stating that he supposed a lease to SCOT would be the "next best" option, "if we are going to discontinue operating Boggy Slough," but, to be honest, he stressed, "I am opposed to letting Boggy Slough go to anyone or any organization." He argued that, despite the obvious challenges that always accompanied operating Boggy Slough as a hunting club, no one could have done a better "public relations job for us" than "we have done ourselves." Because he also believed that no organization now or in the future could continue to do as well, Thompson advised against Boggy Slough's lease and proposed instead, "perhaps some tightening of restrictions in its use."[61]

In time, Temple decided against SCOT leasing his Trinity County hunting preserve. Instead, he gave a lease of nearly 10,000 acres of company land in Sabine County, near Bronson, to the Operation Whitetail-East Texas project and became a vice president of SCOT to closely monitor its work in the region. The East Texas operation began in the fall of 1964 and became so popular that deer hunt-

ing there was restricted to the use of bows and arrows only by 1974.[62]

Still unhappy with Boggy Slough's operations, however, Temple next sought a lease to a more local organization and set his sights on Lufkin Foundry & Machine Company, which was already using the clubhouse during the spring off-seasons to entertain its ever-growing customer base, particularly its customers from Canada and California. Temple offered Boggy Slough on a five-year lease in the spring of 1964.[63]

The formal agreement included a two-page inventory of all property contained in each room of the clubhouse, thoroughly itemized down to even the number of spoons, bed sheets, ashtrays, poker chips, and bottles of lighter fluid. Walter Trout, the president of Lufkin Foundry, wrote to Temple in April, saying that he and his directors were "anxious to have Boggy Slough," and they were nearly set to execute the legal documents. By the terms of the lease, Lufkin Foundry agreed to pay $20,000 per year to Temple Industries for use of the clubhouse and all of the land south of Cochino Bayou—about 10,000 acres—"for hunting, fishing, camping, and recreational purposes." Temple employees were explicitly excluded from those activities during the five-year lease period. Temple did reserve rights to harvest and manage the timber and to drill for oil and gas, as well as the right to cancel the lease if Temple Industries obtained the financial funding and government permits to build a paper mill at Boggy Slough or if Temple sold or merged its assets "to or with some other persons, firms, or corporation." If any of those events occurred, Temple agreed to release Lufkin Foundry from "further payment of rent" and to refund "a pro rata portion" of the lease monies already paid for that year. Also, since Temple had just recently ended Kenley's three decades of grazing cattle at Boggy Slough, he reminded Trout that "grazing [was] prohibited, as we do not like livestock on the premises with the exception of the keeper's horse and [milch] cow."[64]

One peculiar condition of the lease concerned the pasture rider. He was to remain an employee of Temple Industries because Temple "wanted control of [him]," but his salary, unemployment taxes, social security taxes, and health, accident, hospital, and pension benefits were to be "repaid" by Lufkin Foundry "to Temple Industries." This proved a deal breaker, because, as Walter Trout later explained to Temple, he was able to obtain unanimous board approval of only $100,000 for the five-year lease, which he initially thought included the rider's compensation, since it had been included in earlier negotiations when Lufkin Foundry considered leasing the Malibu Club. Trout explained that one member of his board disliked spending more than $100,000 to lease someone else's property, since that money could be spent instead to build their own facilities. Trout said that since his company had "never made a move that was not unanimously agreed upon" by its directors, he unfortunately would "have to pass up Boggy Slough and start looking for a second best place."[65]

⁕

After 1964, with ideas of leasing Boggy Slough behind him, Temple continued the club's operations as usual until late 1966, when the clubhouse burned to the ground during the early morning hours of December 8. The story made the front page of that afternoon's edition of the *Lufkin Daily News*, with bold headlines that stretched across the entire width of the sheet: "Historic Boggy Slough Clubhouse Burns; Loss to Exceed $100,000." Along with the clubhouse, called "an East Texas landmark," some 200 acres of surrounding land burned, although "little timber damage was done." The suspected cause of the blaze, as reported to the public, was "a renewal of a fire that was started Wednesday to burn brush or by faulty wiring." Although never officially endorsed, rumors circulated that arson might have played a role.[66]

The weekly *Diboll Free Press* also carried news of the fire on the front page of its December 15 issue. Editor Paul Durham wrote that the clubhouse had been "a landmark embedded in the hearts of thousands of people" and that "the smoking ruins held

the loss of more than money—precious, friendly memories, and irreplaceable trophies, pictures and mementos of thousands of hunting trips." Most lamented, he said, was the loss of "some of East Texas' most unusual deer heads," including "one 39-point freak, several with more than 30 points, and all with enough large antlers to make them conversation pieces." More than fifty such deer heads were lost, including Boggy Slough's earliest trophies that had been moved from the earlier clubhouse. They, along with many other game and fish mounts, had been itemized two years earlier in the Lufkin Foundry lease proposal. Among the trophies lost were a dozen mounted fish, several mounted ducks, three stuffed alligators, several bear skins, one full mount of a bear (which had been recently killed by Charlie Harber and his son at the nearby Eason Lake Club), and an "8-point goat head felled by the sure shot of the Company's Executive Vice President, Joe Denman" (the result of a practical joke).[67] On the front page of the *Diboll Free Press* was a photograph of a grim-looking Ben Anthony, the clubhouse caretaker, standing among the smoldering ruins with his head hung down. The clubhouse had been a second home to him for nearly two decades, and the game trophies, it was said, were his "proudest possessions." He especially lamented the loss of two mounted buck deer heads, which had been famously mounted in a corner of the large game room, on separate walls, with their antlers "locked together in mortal combat, unable to untangle themselves," just as they had been found by a game warden many years earlier, the newspaper reported.[68]

⁕

Arthur Temple first considered rebuilding the clubhouse on the hill overlooking Black Cat Lake. Temple Lumber Company provided him a building materials and basic labor cost estimate for a new, two-story clubhouse in June 1967.[69] The projected cost was $112,900, which included air conditioning units of 7.5-ton and 10-ton capacities;

floors, cabinets, and stairways made of oak; cypress paneling; and cedar shake roofing. The cost did not include, however, any appliances, water lines, driveways, sidewalks, soil retaining walls, or yard and grade finishing. At the July 1967 special meeting of Temple Industries' board of directors, which was held in Austin, Temple announced that he was then considering "the possibility of rebuilding the Boggy Slough clubhouse on Sam Rayburn Lake," instead of at Boggy Slough. He stated that he wanted to "await developments in the Toledo Bend Dam area" before making his final decision, explaining that "if the Boggy Slough clubhouse were rebuilt near Pineland," then the company's Scrappin' Valley lodge and property would be "leased to some large company, possibly an oil company."[70]

The connection between the Boggy Slough clubhouse and the new Sam Rayburn and Toledo Bend Lakes illustrated the significance of land and water development projects that had occurred across East Texas during the 1950s and early 1960s. Nearly all of them affected Temple Industries' interests, especially the two reservoirs, which became the two largest freshwater lakes in the state. Temple owned lands surrounding both of the large reservoirs, whose dams were generally contested by the timber companies because they erased more than 200,000 acres of timber-producing lands. Arthur Temple, however, saw the dams as inevitable, given the historical droughts (he had canceled the 1952 deer hunting parties at South Boggy because the forest was so dry and he feared wildfires) and the political landscape of the time. Instead of fighting the lakes, as the Kurth interests had done, he embraced them as opportunities for real estate development projects, the proceeds from which he used to buy additional timberland elsewhere and still made a profit.[71]

In the end, Temple chose not to rebuild the Boggy Slough clubhouse—at Boggy Slough or anywhere else. "The estimate was a good bit more than I wanted to spend at the time," he later recalled, adding that he occasionally regretted the decision.[72] Instead, he ended the lease of the Boggy Slough lands between Cochino Bayou and High-

way 7, which had been given to the old J. J. Collins law firm, and he seized the firm's "ram-shackled clubhouse," as he called it, in retaliation for the firm's opposition to him over country club matters in Lufkin.[73] He eventually reimbursed the law firm for their improvements in 1969, settling with Pitser Garrison, who expressed much gratitude for the amount of time that he and his fellow law partners were allowed use of the lands.[74]

After obtaining the Collins clubhouse, business entertainments at Boggy Slough were held mostly north of the old Eastern Texas Railroad line, using the law firm clubhouse, which the Temple companies constantly improved and enlarged over the years, and South Boggy—the area south of the railroad line—became an even more exclusive club, managed by the Sportsmen of Boggy Slough (SOBS), which was chartered as a nonprofit organization in 1979.[75] The SOBS was an organization similar to the former company hunting and fishing clubs. Its purpose was to advance "the protection, harvesting, and propagation of game and fish" and to cultivate "the art of sportsmanship" among its members—but its charter and bylaws also contained modern language that encouraged "multiple use of forest lands." Also included were provisions to comply with the state's new shooting preserve license act, which, among other things, required the keeping and reporting of record books pertaining to hunters and dates and the types of game animals and birds killed. The incorporators were Joe C. Denman Jr., Ward R. Burke, and Henry H. Holubec Jr., Arthur Temple joined Denman and Burke to make up the first board of directors, and Burke served as the records keeper.[76]

Also in 1979, Chotsy Temple wrote the "SOBS Anthem," a six-verse song with a repeating chorus in the key of C, which paid tribute to the group's members from near and far and their enthusiastic gatherings around Boggy Slough chili making, a tradition every February going back at least to the early 1960s. Arthur Temple, who crowned himself the "Exalted Great Chili Maker," helped design the SOBS membership patch, and he encouraged all members to wear it on the "official uniform" of jumpsuits or coveralls, on which "a few stains and a torn place or two added a great deal of class." In a memo to the longtime aide to President Lyndon and first lady, Lady Bird Johnson, Temple described the patch: "You will note that the crest shows a winking deer in a bed of pine boughs superimposed above a shield which displays a poker hand, beer cans, a target, and rifles whose ends have been exploded, and a chili pot consuming a human body. I know you will wear this proudly." During some years, the SOBS actually met at the Scrappin' Valley clubhouse, which was a favorite place of Time Inc. executives, who thoroughly enjoyed the "chili makings from Boggy Slough deer" and the numerous skits written and performed by SOBS members.[77]

When Temple considered building a new Boggy Slough clubhouse overlooking Black Cat Lake early in 1967, the waters of that off-channel impoundment were already well established. Earlier identified as the Bluff Prairie Saline by the Texas Bureau of Economic Geology in 1918, the seasonally flooded prairie began to hold increased amounts of water during the 1930s, following the state's relocation of Highway 94 and Southern Pine Lumber Company's construction of duck pond dams around the pooled waters, which were further influenced by at least one artesian well—the result of Bluff Prairie Oil Company's abandoned well holes in 1904.[78]

The lake became further established in 1951 when Arthur Temple Jr. assigned one of his engineers, John O. Booker Jr., to construct a new access road into South Boggy. In a 2014 interview, Booker recalled that Temple never liked passing through other people's property to access South Boggy, which became necessary after the old highway ceased being a public road. Booker remembered that the company had "a dispute with these people [along the old highway], which included the beer joints there." To alleviate matters and provide a less

unsightly entrance, Temple ordered Booker to create a new entrance road, straight off the new highway, which would be located wholly on company property. This meant coming across Bluff Prairie and through one of the duck ponds then known as Prairie Lake. Using a dragline, Booker said that he and his small crew scooped up buckets of mud and dirt from the wet prairie and built a causeway, which connected the new highway to the old highway at the base of the bluff on the company's east boundary line. "It was a mess," he said, "but [we dug] a big deep ditch all the way around the left side of that." Using a bulldozer and graders, his crew packed and smoothed out the elevated roadway, "and leveled it all up nice and pretty," he said. He added that "there wasn't much water in there [at the time], but it was wet, and when it rained, and we stopped it up of course, then it started holding water."

The causeway was constructed in time to at least partially appear on the US Geological Survey maps for 1951, and the name Black Cat Lake also appeared, with no one truly knowing the origin of the name. An earlier Davy Crockett National Forest map also contained the name Black Cat Lake, but for many years Temple family members went on calling the dammed waters Prairie Lake, regardless of what the maps showed.[79] The *Diboll Buzz Saw* reported in its November 1951 issue that the new road served "the purpose of good transportation into the premises and at the same time keeps plenty of water in the duck pond. The road is some twenty feet high and is remindful of the famous seawall at Galveston." The paper added that the causeway and connecting road were graded, drained, "and packed so well that a Ford rides like a Cadillac on them."[80] Several years later the company obtained water rights to 500 acre-feet (163 million gallons) of water per year from the Neches River, which the company pumped into the impoundment as needed during dry periods.[81]

Assured of a steady supply of water, Arthur Temple instructed Kenneth Nelson in May 1966 to plant "several thousand Cypress seedlings next winter on the north side of Black Cat Lake,"

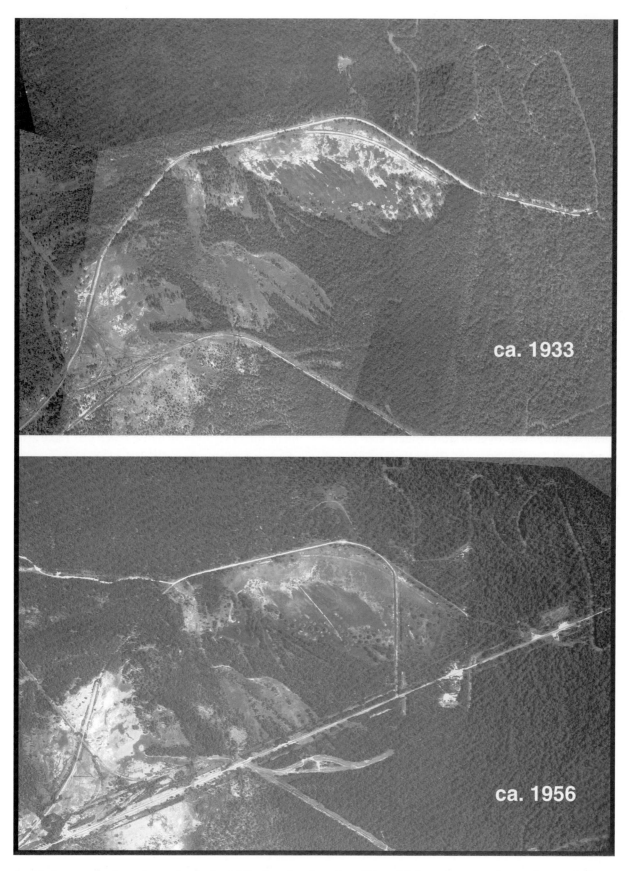

Aerial photographs show changes to the land following the relocation of Texas Highway 94 across the southern end of Bluff Prairie during the late 1930s. *Author's collection.*

especially in "the big shallow area" along "the old highway." Temple said that he thought the cypress trees "might be something pretty attractive and also probably commercially valuable eventually."[82] During the 1980s Temple directed his new professional wildlife managers to plant more cypress trees, this time along the Black Cat Lake causeway as well as "wherever we could find water," as one of the managers later recalled.[83] Although Temple's hope that the trees would be "commercially valuable" never came to fruition, the trees have proven aesthetically pleasing and their roots prevent erosion.

John Booker had actually begun grading and building modern roads in Boggy Slough in 1950, to better facilitate logging activities and deer stand access. Before that time, until the 1930s, logging had been done by railroad, and company logging crews and ranch hands had maintained the old wagon roads mostly with animal-drawn graders. Booker's job, as he explained in later interviews, was to build all-weather roads so that the company "could log with trucks" on a permanent basis. In a 2011 interview Booker described how he rode on horseback to locate abandoned railroad grades, flagging between six and seven miles of projected roads a day. As he did so, he made notes of the locations and sizes of new culverts that would be needed. He was already supervising the operations of a concrete plant in Diboll, so he made all the culverts there. Proper drainage was critical, he said, because "you can't build roads without draining them." His road-building equipment consisted of one small dragline excavator, four dump trucks, one Caterpillar D8 bulldozer, two road graders, one horse trailer, one service truck equipped with an air compressor and a winch, and a bus to transport crewmen. He said the bulldozer was often too small for removing stumps, so they mostly used dynamite for that purpose. For building the bridges over Cochino and Cedar Creeks, he said his crew made their own

pile driver by salvaging a large pile-driving weight and simply attaching it to their dragline. "We just got above the [piling] and hammered, and we got pretty darn good at it," he said.[84]

Booker recalled that during the early 1950s he and his crews built well over 100 miles of modern roads, which included a main road that led north from Boggy Slough through the company's lands along the river all the way up past the Texas State Railroad between Rusk and Palestine. He said they encountered "a good many snakes" as they went along, but remarkably no laborer was ever bit. "You sure had to watch your step" with copperheads and water moccasins, he added, for they "didn't back up and run" like other snakes. He said that many men, especially those in the logging crews who worked just ahead of Booker's crews, killed "a lot of snakes [and] most of them, the big ones, were timber rattlers." "I don't know why we killed them [the timber rattlers]; they don't present much of a threat," he later lamented.[85]

After building roads and bridges, Booker said his next Boggy Slough "assignment" included locating and building deer stands. He said many early stands were simply board seats nailed to the bases of trees. Hunters were shown the way to the particular trees by flagging, and they were instructed to sit and face the wind. Booker said that he began erecting board-braced platform stands at the height of about six feet, selecting "a cull tree of some kind, an oak or something, not a good merchantable tree" into which he nailed his boards. While the elevated stands were intended to improve the hunter success rate over the early ground seats, he said that he did not build stands much higher than six feet because "you didn't want to use too much lumber [since] you had to tote everything into the woods manually."[86]

Of course deer management, which had defined Boggy Slough since the 1910s, remained a challenge throughout the twentieth century. As the

Kenneth Nelson, on the far right, was one of Dave Kenley's early timber and land department employees who Arthur Temple Sr. elevated to the new position of forester in 1946. Nelson stands with logging and milling managers Richie Wells and E. A. Farley, and with Arthur Temple Jr., wearing chaps, ca. 1950. *Courtesy of The History Center, Diboll.*

ever-abundant deer population continued to increase, often approaching and at times even surpassing the carrying capacity of the land, protecting the young pine trees that Arthur Temple had ordered to be planted during the 1950s became a new concern, especially since the evergreens were planted during the winter months—the time of year that the overbrowsed and overgrazed land lacked food the most. This was especially true while cattle continued to graze and browse the range before 1962. But even after Kenley's cows were removed, the tree plantings usually fared poorly, especially if the previous year had seen low acorn production and little summer rainfall. For two decades, Kenneth Nelson reported to Arthur Temple that most planted pine seedlings did not survive. In 1966 he reported that "the deer destroyed" fifty thousand seedlings at one site alone "in less than three weeks."[87] This was distressing news because the company had already begun stepping up deer hunting pressure and harvest success rates in order to reduce the deer population. These efforts had even included the lawful killing of doe deer, which began in 1961.

The state legislature had only recently, in December 1953, opened the first antlerless deer season within some Hill Country counties, where visibly stunted animals and die-offs were common and

well publicized. Game biologist Dan Lay wrote in a 1954 *Texas Game and Fish* article that a doe season for the restocked deer herds in East Texas would one day "become necessary"— but not anytime soon—although Southern Pine Lumber Company officials begged to differ when considering Boggy Slough.[88]

Deer were so plentiful and tame at Boggy Slough during the 1950s that longtime road maintenance employee Bill Oaks recalled in a 1978 interview with Ellen Temple that he would see forty to eighty of them at a time near Rayville and "down around the old farms." Whenever Oaks would stop his grader, "deer would be there looking at me . . . and I would talk to 'em," he said. Perhaps most memorable to Oaks were the work breaks he took, often surrounded by deer. "I'd sit there on the road and have that grader running, sitting up there eating my dinner," he recalled, and "some deer would come up as close as that door right there and I would throw them something to eat, and they would eat out there with me. I would throw them a piece of bread or something or other."[89]

Deer hunting guests also remembered large herds of deer that seemed unafraid of humans. In 1975 W. E. Merrem, longtime official with Houston Oil Company, Southwestern Settlement and Development Company, and East Texas Pulp and Paper Company, recalled one of his many hunting trips during the 1950s, when deer stands were simply board seats nailed to the bases of trees.

Embarrassingly, he remembered, "One time I took a stand in what was called the hog pen. I went sound asleep. A deer woke me by blowing loudly, almost in my face. I sat up and deer were all around me. I was so flustered I never got a shot."[90] And in October 1956 Arthur Temple wrote to friends and family telling them that he "almost couldn't hunt squirrel for all the deer around me [at Boggy Slough].... I never saw so many." To obtain more solitude, he told them he planned to do his future squirrel hunting in the Dollarhide Club, downriver from Boggy Slough, in Angelina County.[91]

It was the following year, in 1957, that Temple had authorized the three-year vegetative alteration analysis of Boggy Slough, which he had used to justify the eventual cancellation of Kenley's longstanding grazing lease and to begin planting "deer food" in hopes of protecting the planted timber. Conducted by the leading wildlife biologists and silviculturists of that day, including Charles A. McLeod, Dan Lay, C. E. Boyd, P. D. Goodrum, E. E. McDonald, and T. H. Silker, among others, the study and its findings were amazing. Dan Lay later summarized the revealing study at a wildlife symposium in College Station in 1966, saying, "The range was bare and obviously overstocked. Openings that should have had pine seedlings and saplings did not. The understory in 1957 was so open that deer could be seen more than a quarter of a mile. Most shrubs were hedged. Some were dead. There was little regeneration of hardwoods, except unpalatable persimmon (Diospyros virginiana). The herbaceous plants present were the species of early stages of plant succession: especially carpet grass (Axonopus compressus) and Bermuda (Cynodon dactylon) and unpalatable weeds such as goatweed (Croton capitatus) and poorjoe (Diodia teres)." Lay also reported that "pine browsing by deer was extensive" and warned that "a deer herd which makes use of pine is approaching trouble."[92] Lay's assessment of poor timber regeneration and the proliferation of carpet grass made it clear that little had changed at Boggy Slough since Austin Cary of the US Forest Service first studied Temple's "grazing proposition" there more than forty years earlier.

Throughout the late 1950s, as the vegetative utilization study advanced, Arthur Temple and Kenneth Nelson regularly equated the needs of simultaneously ridding the land of cattle, "planting enough food for the deer to carry them through the winter without causing their pressure on the young [planted pine] seedlings," and "get[ting] the legislature to allow the killing of a limited number of does."[93] Judge Minton also joined the deer herd improvement campaign, publishing an article in the Diboll News-Bulletin in 1957 advocating the need to reduce Boggy Slough's deer population. In his usual commoditized market approach, he claimed that some does had become "a total economic loss by reason of old age."[94]

Finally, in 1961, the state legislature allowed permits for the killing of antlerless deer at Boggy Slough.[95] The hunting club's guest cards for that year's hunting season stated, "Our premises are thought to be saturated with deer, and you are urged to take the maximum limit prescribed to help in preventing over population and damage to the herd and the premises, taking mature doe, where possible."[96] In issuing the permits to his department heads, Temple instructed them to "encourage your hunters to kill the big and old doe if possible. This will mean that we will have young vigorous doe left. I will appreciate it and the bucks will appreciate it."[97]

The majority of East Texas sportsmen at the time, however, saw the killing of does as controversial at best. Some were particularly displeased when they realized that Temple received the doe permits during the first legislative session of newly elected Representative Charles Wilson of Trinity, who was a Temple Lumber Company employee. W. C. Roach of Lufkin, a descendant of an early Boggy Slough homesteading family, wrote a disapproving letter to the editor of the Lufkin News in April 1962. He shared that as a longtime hunter in East Texas he was "very unhappy last deer season when Mr. Temple was given 300 special permits to shoot doe deer on his private property," which Roach alleged was merely a "special favor" that Representative Wilson had made for his employer.

Arthur Temple wrote a defensive letter to the editor the following day, stating that "Mr. Wilson had nothing whatever to do with the State Game Department's experiment in reducing the deer population on our land." In fact, he argued that it was "certainly ridiculous to suggest that Southern Pine Lumber Company sought this special privilege of killing doe contrary to the welfare of game population, after a thirty year history of outstanding work in protecting and propagating game in East Texas."[98] Although Temple did not mention it, Boggy Slough had just suffered another massive deer die-off during the winter of 1960–61, and this factor probably influenced the legislature's decision more than any other.[99]

While the legal killing of does remained a contentious issue at Boggy Slough as well as across the state for years to come, Boggy Slough's club members experienced great difficulty in using all of their doe permits. This was because few hunters, especially guests, wanted to shoot a doe at the famed hunting grounds, preferring to wait for a trophy buck instead. In 1962, during the second year of receiving the annual doe permits, Temple ended up giving half of them away to the Trinity County Game Protective Association to use during the last six days of the season, just four months after the Davenport-Smith shooting. The *Diboll Free Press* reported that Temple's "unprecedented public hunt" at South Boggy was expected "to add significantly to the good relations between the large land owner and the citizens of Trinity County."[100]

In spite of the doe permits and the extra efforts made to use them, the deer population remained overabundant, and die-offs continued into the 1970s. According to Dr. James C. Kroll of Stephen F. Austin State University, who began to study Boggy Slough's deer during that decade, Boggy Slough experienced a die-off of some six hundred deer during one year thanks to decades of what he called "overprotection." Kroll, who later became known as "Dr. Deer" and "the father of modern deer management," said that the Boggy Slough deer herd was "one of the best *worst* examples I could find in Texas" of overpopulation.[101]

When professional wildlife biologists Don Dietz and Bill Goodrum began their employment at Boggy Slough in 1981, hired on Kroll's recommendation some twenty years after the doe harvest permitting began, Dietz said, "There was [still] a browse line six feet tall. You could literally see a hundred yards under yaupon." He said he admonished hunting club members to "harvest more doe or Mother Nature would do it for them," adding that Arthur Temple even required hunting club members to pay in advance up to $100 for each doe permit they were assigned, telling them that they would be refunded their money upon their and their guests' using the permits. "I was amazed at how hard millionaires worked to get $500 back," he said.[102] Still, in spite of incentives as well as penalties to club members, many hunting seasons ended without hunters killing the number of does prescribed by wildlife managers. During the summer of 1985, another deer die-off occurred.[103]

———❖———

Keeping the lavish deer herds at Boggy Slough well fed was always a challenge. Managers felt that since the natural range—an oxymoron by the 1950s—had been unsuccessful in obtaining desired results, then nature needed assistance. Planting food for deer was never an option as long as Kenley's grazing lease was in effect, but when the lease ended in 1961, "deer food" planting efforts began in earnest. In 1962 managers planted oats and rye grass in various "openings" and along roads throughout South Boggy. Hogs took a heavy toll on the plantings almost immediately, which added another management obstacle, especially as the size and the number of food plots increased. At least 50 acres were planted that first year, and each successive year's plantings increased, at times up to 25 percent. By 1966, the company had begun spending $3,000 a year in its wildlife program at Boggy Slough, most of it used in planting food for deer.[104]

In 1963, several wetland areas were cleared and drained in order to plant summer and winter food plots, including a 33-acre flat along the north branch of Cedar Creek known as "Haw Prairie." Here, soil samples were analyzed by labs in Nacogdoches, and workers treated the ground with lime and various fertilizers including ammonium nitrate. They used a grassland drill to plant sorghum and cowpeas for summer feedings and singletary peas and fescue for winter food.[105]

During the late 1970s, as deer plantings expanded all across the property, the former Haw Prairie was dammed as a shallow, drainable duck pond. Grains such as browntop and Japanese millet and elbon rye were planted, and the prairie was flooded in the fall after the grains had produced seed heads to provide winter duck habitat. The site soon became known as "Aggie Land" because, according to one of Dave Kenley's grandsons, the flooded waters unintentionally backed up outside of Boggy Slough's fences and flooded Kenley land as well. The jest was aimed at Temple's engineers, many who had graduated from Texas A&M University and were important Boggy Slough club members.[106] Also during the 1970s, other wetland areas and green tree reservoirs were developed, coordinated by Temple's logging engineer Spencer Knutson, who received guidance from the Soil Conservation Service's Nacogdoches office and the US Forest Service's Lufkin office.[107]

In other places during the 1960s, especially around Rayville, workers planted dwarf live oak, Japanese honeysuckle, and even the ubiquitous yaupon. Those three species were planted mostly experimentally, but because of their relative success at the intensively browsed Boggy Slough, Temple-Eastex later used them during the middle and late 1970s as desired deer food plantings on company lands that had been clear-cut.[108]

In 1966, the Davy Crockett-Trinity Soil Conservation District nominated Arthur Temple for a statewide Wildlife Conservation Award as part of the Save the Soil and Save Texas awards program. He was nominated for the Individual Award, which was to be given to "the farmer or rancher who has done the best job of conserving wildlife native to his area." The nomination cited Temple's "dedicated work" on the 10,064 acres that was then South Boggy. The nomination cited extensive plantings of rye grass, crimson clover, oats, vetch, browntop millet, and sesame, making up numerous food plots for deer, ducks, and birds. Yaupon that had been planted "for cover and food" was also mentioned. "His place" had done much for protecting and raising wildlife, the nomination claimed, going back to at least the 1930s. The nomination also noted a logging practice of saving "den and food trees" for wildlife "as much as possible." Also included were mentions of three "fish pond-managed" lakes for fishing and duck hunting and the use of a water pump on the Neches River to keep the largest lake, Black Cat, filled to a desired level year round. "Had it not been for a few places like this one," the nomination concluded, "we would not have the wildlife we enjoy today."[109]

Throughout the 1950s and 1960s, many of the state's wildlife managers regularly visited Boggy Slough, including Dan Lay, who had declared it "the deer incubator of East Texas" as early as 1937. Lay, whose early field office was at Lufkin, strongly encouraged the restocking of turkeys in Angelina and surrounding counties early during the 1940s, and he was probably involved in Boggy Slough's turkey restoration efforts during that time, which were ultimately unsuccessful. He certainly participated in a number of wildlife studies at Boggy Slough, developing an early southern forest whitetail deer browse study technique still in use today. He also conducted quail research.[110] Such studies, especially the three-year vegetative alteration analysis, influenced Temple's final decision against cattle grazing and his adoption of a more scientific approach to both timber and wildlife management.[111]

During this time Dan Lay published a number of articles in wildlife and forestry journals and often cited his work at Boggy Slough. Lay also photographically documented some of the early 1960s wildlife food plantings at Rayville, noting such things as "plots of yaupon and honeysuckle" and "old yaupon and honeysuckle plantings." He also photographed areas that he identified as "croton in heavy Bermuda—little value to quail," which he noted were being mechanically disked to make way for more preferred wildlife vegetation. By 1966, Lay was pleased to report that the management changes being made at Boggy Slough, particularly the removal of cattle, were showing how quickly the land could recover from "excessive utilization." He wrote that "the rapid recovery of browse plants" had demonstrated "the speed at which old roots will grow new tops," especially "when it rains"—referring to recent rainfall rates that were significantly higher than during the drought years of the 1950s.[112]

"Deer food" plantings in South Boggy increased throughout the 1970s because Arthur Temple desired spacious plots of rye grass and crimson clover at as many deer stands as possible in order to improve hunter success and protect the health of the herd and the survivability of his pine seedlings. At other planting sites, including along the pipelines, new plants were regularly added, including "peas, peanuts, lespedeza, and other legumes." In 1979 sunflowers were planted at South Boggy with hopes of benefiting "all wildlife," but the deer quickly devoured them before any other species benefited from the plants.[113] Overall, however, Arthur Temple was pleased with the results of the food plots, and in 1976 he began to assign personal names to many of the improved deer stands, or "blinds," as he began to call them, to show affection for certain people who had "some past association" to a particular hunting location. In a way, just as Boggy Slough peoples of the past had assigned names to the land to signify a sense of belonging, Temple now assigned names to hunting locations as his own exercise in belonging. In his "preliminary list," he gave sixteen names to some sixty deer stands in South Boggy. Among them, he assigned the name of his good friend, Horace "Stubby" Stubblefield to Stand 1 and Stubby's son,

Gandy, to Stand 47. Arthur's own son, Buddy, was assigned to 31, and his grandson, Spence Spencer, to 45. Others included Henry Holubec, 2; Clifford Grum, 5; Jack Sweeny, 8; Joe Denman and his son, Trey, 9 and 50; John Booker, 11; Arch Hollinsworth, 12; Clyde Thompson, 16; Herb White, 27; Spencer Knutson, 30; Jim Shepley, 44; and David Wimp, 51. Temple later assigned the name of his second wife, Lottie, to Stand 22, and "A.T. Area" to Boggy Slough Island.[114]

John Booker carried out most of Temple's hunting and wildlife management plans for Boggy Slough and other company lands during the 1960s and early 1970s, but beginning in 1974 those duties were given to Gene Samford. This was one year after Time Inc. had acquired Temple Industries and merged it with its subsidiary Eastex Pulp and Paper Company to form Temple-Eastex. Samford was the former deer lease manager for Southwestern Timber Company, an Eastex subsidiary, and was by all accounts, "a gifted publicist." Under Temple-Eastex management, Samford often reported directly to Arthur Temple, who placed him over "special projects," which quickly developed into the company's fledgling wildlife department. Samford worked with Temple and others, including Spencer Knutson, to develop wildlife goals and objectives that included, according to a mission statement, "working with foresters to manipulate the forest environment to produce a mix of products, both timber and wildlife, and to manage wildlife habitat for "species richness" on all company lands."[115]

Samford continued earlier considerations for the habitat needs of nongame animals at Boggy Slough, including songbirds. He also increased the company's awareness for and attention given to the habitat needs of the red-cockaded woodpecker (RCW), one of the first birds listed as endangered under the Endangered Species Preservation Acts of the late 1960s and early 1970s. By 1970 Temple Industries had already begun working with state and federal wildlife biologists to isolate and protect RCW nesting areas, and within a few years Samford was also working with Stephen F. Austin State

University in performing RCW understory work at North Boggy, which would later continue for South Boggy colonies as well.[116] Samford hosted various chapter meetings of the Audubon Society at Boggy Slough, as well as wildlife and forestry students from Stephen F. Austin State University and Texas A&M University. In 1978, Samford proudly reported to Arthur Temple that American bald eagles had again "returned to Black Cat Lake, as in the past," in addition to two golden eagles, which had also made their return "to the prairie."[117]

Working with Dr. Kroll of Stephen F. Austin State University, Samford began to employ the relatively new technology of radio telemetry to trace the movement of Boggy Slough's deer. In 1978, he reported that the summer movements of ten deer had revealed that habitat containing French mulberry was most preferred.[118] Dr. Kroll's body of wildlife and environmental research at Boggy Slough during the late 1970s through the 1990s—made possible by Temple funding and which included more than just deer—contributed significantly to a wealth of knowledge that was shared within and across the entire natural resource discipline.[119] One multiyear white-tailed deer study alone, conducted during the early 1990s, cost in excess of $1 million.[120]

In 1975, Samford personally released into Black Cat Lake five alligators, which had been trapped near Beaumont. In a press release, Samford said that the transfers resulted from a desire to restock alligators because their numbers had been severely depleted because of "overhunting" and "the reclamation of their natural habitat for other uses." Samford cautioned that the alligators might initially wreak havoc on the wood duck population, but he said the ducks would adapt quickly to their new neighbors as they had in the past.[121] At the same time, he continued to maintain wood duck nesting boxes along the shores of Black Cat Lake and the other artificial lakes, a practice that had begun earlier in 1970.[122]

In 1976, Samford and Temple stocked Black Cat Lake with tilapia to control unwanted algae and "bushy pond weed." The shallow-water lake had become highly managed by this time, and had already been regularly sprayed with herbicide from airplanes to control water lilies, hydrilla, and other unwanted aquatic vegetation. Releases of nutria had also been tried, beginning in 1953, but they began to eat only the desired aquatic vegetation. Worse, they also debarked and girdled valuable pine trees by the hundreds in spite of great efforts to hunt and trap them out.[123] After managers had spent nearly twenty years in unsuccessfully eradicating nutria at Boggy Slough, Samford began allowing researchers to study their behaviors and diet to better understand their impact on the forest environment.[124]

Jonathan Hurst of the Sabine Fish Hatchery personally stocked Black Cat Lake with tilapia in April 1976 and wrote to Arthur Temple afterward explaining that tilapia were excellent at controlling bushy pond weed, algae, and "pond scums." Upon learning that Black Cat Lake might still be influenced by artesian springs, Hurst said he was hopeful that the warm-water fish would survive the winter and not need restocking every year if the spring flow rate was great enough to maintain the water temperature above 50 degrees. The tilapia did not survive, however, so management returned to the use of herbicides at least through 1982. Tilapia were stocked again during the middle 1980s, with one Temple-Inland wildlife biologist reporting that the "vegetative eaters" also provided "forage for the bass" and were "an asset to any lake or pond."[125] Buddy's Pond, which had been fertilized for fish pond management since its construction in 1949, also received stockings of tilapia during the 1980s.[126]

— ⋅•⋅ —

Throughout the 1970s, Booker and Samford routinely transported wildlife animals into and out of Boggy Slough, especially early during the decade, when Jack R. Stone of Wells, in neighboring

Cherokee County, served as chairman of the Texas Parks & Wildlife Commission. Stone had become a good friend of Arthur Temple during the 1960s through their mutual efforts to restock wild turkeys in East Texas and in building public support for the restocking of black bear.[127]

In 1969 Arthur Temple instructed Booker to locate some pen-raised turkeys and consider the possibility of raising them at South Boggy, where at the time there were no turkeys, as well as at Temple's other wildlife management area, Scrappin' Valley, where a few birds from earlier wild-trapped restockings still remained. After visiting a turkey farm, Booker reported that he could not "see any reason why we could not raise turkeys . . . at both places easy enough," but he suggested trying the pen-raised project only at South Boggy, from which brood stock or eggs could be gathered later and taken to Scrappin' Valley "to supplement our flock" there. Booker explained how a holding pen could be placed "in an isolated spot" where four- to six-week-old birds would be released and "fed within sight of the pen," first "on mash and then gradually introduced to maize." At the place he visited, the original brood stock of birds "still roost[ed] in the pine trees at the pens," he said. While they seemed to be "quite gentle," he explained that "the young ones raised naturally were very wild." By early August, Temple had already selected a pen site at South Boggy, "just below the burned clubhouse," and Booker had drawn plans for the construction of a 15-foot-by-32-foot holding pen and a 55-gallon-drum turkey feeder on a five-foot-tall platform.[128] Just before the opening of that year's deer season, Joe Denman instructed all hunting club members to plainly write on all guest cards, "Do Not Shoot the Wild Turkeys." By the following year and throughout the decade, those words were boldly printed in red on the guest cards and on signs placed throughout the property.[129]

It is not clear where the 1969 pen-raised birds came from, nor is their species definitively known. Company public relations news releases during the 1970s claimed they were eastern wild turkeys, but later the company's university-degreed

wildlife biologists believed they were Florida/Rio Grande cross birds. Those same Temple-Eastex and Temple-Inland wildlife biologists, the first ones assigned full time to South and North Boggy, also stated that raising turkeys in pens proved "to be a very, very bad approach," which was never officially sponsored by the parks and wildlife department.[130] By the late 1970s, however, South Boggy turkeys were at least numerous enough that Samford occasionally trapped and transferred some of them to other company lands. Nine that were trapped in January 1979 were moved to Jasper County.[131]

In the mid-1980s, after Samford hired professional wildlife biologists, eastern wild turkeys at Scrappin' Valley were trapped and transferred to South Boggy, where they were released near Lottie Temple's Deer Stand 22.[132] By spring 1987, South Boggy wildlife manager Don Dietz reported that he was hopeful for the possibility of a spring turkey hunt at South Boggy in 1988, "providing we have a good hatch this year and the state opens the season in our area. One gobbler per membership would not hurt the population at all."[133] Despite such hopes, however, and even with an open season, a turkey hunt by South Boggy members never occurred, Dietz said later.[134] Club members simply "showed no interest," he recalled, although he said he himself "heavily hunted" them. Regular intervals of prescribed burning during the 1980s and 1990s was key to managing the wild turkeys, Dietz later said, adding that when diminished budgets ended prescribed burning in the early 2000s, the turkeys suffered.

——— ·•· ———

Deer also continued to be moved around during the 1970s, based on wildlife census work. In 1974, Samford trapped seventy-five deer at Boggy Slough after discovering that the herd was eating "undesirable plants." After conducting tests to confirm that the deer were not diseased, Samford transferred them to other Temple lands in Newton, Jasper, and Sabine Counties, including Scrappin'

Valley.[135] In 1976, more of Boggy Slough's surplus does were trapped and released at Scrappin' Valley.[136] In 1978, Samford trapped another sixty "surplus deer" at South Boggy and transferred them to other company lands.[137] Also that year Arthur Temple approved Samford placing a "Grade A trophy whitetail buck from South Texas" in a five-acre enclosure at South Boggy to breed with the does already there. The following year Samford transferred two bucks and twenty does of "high genetic quality from South Texas" to equally distribute among Boggy Slough's and Scrappin' Valley's deer breeding pens.[138]

After so much attention had been given to feeding, as well as improving the deer herd through genetic breeding and disease control, the construction of high "deer-proof" perimeter fences began in 1975 and was completed in the middle 1980s.[139] Predator-control efforts also stepped up whenever needed, such as when the coyote population grew during the late 1970s, at least partially a result of the abundant deer. Samford wrote to Joe Denman in May 1980, saying that he had trapped more than one hundred coyotes the previous fall, which was "not even a dent in the population."[140]

Samford also brought to Boggy Slough during the 1970s a number of wild mustangs and burros from Bureau of Land Management lands in California. Although a well-intentioned public relations move—Samford told Temple that the public would approve of Temple-Eastex's saving the animals "from the glue factory"—the experiment was ultimately a mistake. Samford attempted to build on Temple's earlier stockings at Scrappin' Valley of American elk, nilgai antelope, black buck antelope, axis deer, and sika deer, begun in 1969, which were for a time interesting public curiosities. Perhaps the greatest drawback at Boggy Slough was that the mustangs and burros regularly escaped from their pens and contributed significantly to overbrowsing of the range. Soon, even Samford acknowledged that "a real horse problem" existed. By 1981 Temple said that he wanted the "jackasses" removed. They began to trap the mares in June that year, followed by the stallions in August 1982. Oscar Rodgers, a

longtime contract trapper, directed the operations, assisted by Temple's new wildlife managers Don Dietz and Bill Goodrum.[141]

———•◦•———

In 1982, Temple-Eastex adopted the first written wildlife management plan for Boggy Slough. A milestone in the history of the property, the document resulted from the company's hiring of its first university-trained wildlife managers: Darryl Stanley in 1978 and Don Dietz and Bill Goodrum in 1981. Not surprisingly, the plan was deer-centric. The document's first page stated, "Although all game animals are taken into consideration in the plan, our primary concern is with the deer herd. Our ultimate goal is to increase the number and availability of trophy bucks. This can be done primarily by increasing their nutrition and by obtaining a Buck/Doe ratio of 1:2."[142] Clearly, Boggy Slough had now progressed from "the deer incubator of East Texas"—Dan Lay's words in 1937—to trophy buck "factory"—Darryl Stanley's later abridgment.[143]

The management plan gave a high priority to food plots, which would consume more than 85 percent of the budgeted $8,875. The acreage and numbers of plots were to be increased to supplement the winter forage and "to sustain the size and quality of animals desired." The plots would no longer be prepared and planted by contractors—whose effectiveness Arthur Temple had always questioned—but would now be performed "by the [company] managers." Clover, vetch, and fescue were cited as the primary food plot plantings, and Japanese honeysuckle was selected as the primary vegetation for "other food plantings."[144]

Soon, browntop millet, lespedeza, soybeans, sorghum, iron clay pea, and chufa were also planted, separately and in combination, to benefit "deer, turkey, quail, dove, and hogs." At South Boggy, manager Don Dietz mixed squash and watermelon seeds into spring plantings "to provide a bonus," he said, "to any [SOBS club] member willing to come

Although the lumber company performed a prescribed burn on this particular cow pasture at Rayville during hand-planting of pine trees in January 1950, fire was generally excluded as a management tool in the timbered sections of Boggy Slough until the early 1980s. Efforts to actually plant pines in the many "open places" at Boggy Slough came about only after the ascension of the third generation of Temple ownership. *Courtesy of The History Center, Diboll.*

out ... during the 'off' season." He also planted sweet and field corn at Rayville, to provide "a bumper crop for both wildlife and members alike." The corn would be left standing, he informed club members in a newsletter, to provide "an aesthetic as well as nutritive value to the deer."[145]

The 1982 wildlife plan also called for the timber and wildlife departments to work together in accomplishing complementary goals. Foremost was the need for establishing prescribed fire practices "to promote the growth of natural browse." Importantly, the plan stated that regular prescribed fires would "do more over a greater number of acres to provide food to support more and larger deer than all other practices together." Since 1954, Dan Lay had been reporting the beneficial effects for wildlife that controlled burning in pine forests brought, citing significant gains in protein and phosphoric acid when compared to adjacent unburned forests, and now Boggy Slough, which had been a fire-suppressed land for the previous sixty-nine years, finally began to embrace fire in ways similar to those of the Hasinai peoples centuries earlier.[146] For the pure pine plantations in North Boggy (where clear-cutting had begun in 1975), the plan called for easing that practice's eventual loss of wildlife habitat by establishing "environ-

mental strips" to maximize the edge effect and the production of greater plant diversity, "leaving a few mast trees," and "planting portions of clear cuts in winter forage crops when they are not being planted in pine seedlings until the following year." It further recommended "over-seeding annuals in portions of pine seedling plantations," which would be "very beneficial to deer and quail."[147] The plan also required the wildlife managers to attend law enforcement schools and perform all patrolling of the property, thereby eliminating the old positions of "pasture riders," which had caused much grief in the past.

Although feral hogs were well-known threats to successful deer management, the 1982 plan treated them as game animals. Up until nearly this time, the hogs still held an agricultural market value, as evidenced by Arthur Temple's letters to district attorneys during the 1950s, thanking and congratulating them for their prosecution of Boggy Slough hog thieves. Even earlier, and throughout the 1950s, Dave Kenley had tried to "get rid" of the omnivores by trapping them and taking them to livestock auctions at Crockett and Groveton on a regular basis.[148] The 1982 wildlife plan called for Boggy Slough's hogs, which came and went across the river at will, to be trapped continually, with the males castrated, marked, and released, and the sows "released unharmed." At the same time, the plan stated that "intensive hunting of hogs" was necessary to relieve their "competition with wildlife for food." The plan encouraged "public hog hunts" at North Boggy, stating that they would be good "for public relations" since there were "many [hunters] who prefer shooting hogs rather than deer."[149]

In about 1985, managers at North Boggy, in an effort to grow a larger game animal with longer trophy tusks, released Russian genetic boars from South Texas to produce hybrid hogs for the company's guest hunters. Bill Goodrum later said that the effort was quickly deemed a mistake, since the hybrids became a more difficult animal to trap and manage. Today, managers claim that much of the Russian genetics have been bred out of the Boggy Slough herd, which at a sustained population of about sixteen hundred, remains a significant nuisance species despite constant hunting and trapping pressure, which removes about a thousand hogs annually.[150]

Record keeping and census taking were also key components of the plan. Methods developed by Texas Parks & Wildlife were to be employed, along with comparable work by Stephen F. Austin State University. Spotlight counts, track counts, incidental sightings, harvest statistics, lactation status, and reproductive tract analysis were to be meticulously recorded and compared to preceding years. Harvest recommendations of the managers were to incorporate the ongoing research work of Dr. James Kroll, as well as input from Arthur Temple. New deer stands were to be regularly placed, and old stands were to be relocated to maximize hunter success. Within three years of implementing the plan's repositioning of the stands, 67 percent of North Boggy's guests killed a deer, a major improvement over the 5 to 15 percent rate that Dan Lay had observed at South Boggy during the 1950s. And the success rate only increased. By 1988, Dr. Kroll declared that Boggy Slough "sported one of the best hunter success rates I have ever seen."[151] Soon, the successes of Boggy Slough's wildlife manage-

ment was providing technical assistance to some 385 hunting clubs throughout the company's more than one million acres of forestlands in Texas.

"Species richness" also included quail research. An extensive three-year project began at South Boggy in 1990, in which wildlife manager Don Dietz and land services manager Darwin Foster worked with Stephen F. Austin State University professor Montague Whiting and quail consultant Brad Mueller in considering all facets of quail management. Quail populations across East Texas had steadily declined after World War II, caused by the reduction and eventual elimination of widely disbursed row crop farming and the adoption of more narrowly focused land management activities, including maximum pine timber production. Quail, like most wildlife species, required many intersections of various landscapes: open woods, brush, grass, and fields, which provided necessary food and cover.[152] By 1990, experiences with clear-cutting had shown that excellent quail habitat existed during a pine plantation's first few years, when abundant sunlight produced a proliferation of green briars, dewberry, and blackberry vines under which the quail thrived. After about eight years of growth, however, the rows of planted pines formed a canopy of shade, robbing the protective plants of necessary sunlight. In other forested places, the long-standing practice of fire exclusion had created understory and canopy problems as well. The quail study considered how "habitat manipulation" could offset the eventual ill effects of pine plantations while further studying the use of prescribed fire in providing greater species diversity within all of the forest.[153]

Of course prescribed burning had been the primary tool in "habitat manipulation" centuries earlier when it was employed by the Hasinai people. When prescribed burning of Boggy Slough's industrial forest first began in 1982—initially driven by deer and turkey management goals—Samford proudly reported to Arthur Temple how quickly wildlife began "using the burned areas."[154] By the early 1990s the ongoing burning, when combined with the quail study, only added to the understanding of beneficial fires. Throughout the decade, burning efforts increased, which greatly benefited all wildlife, including RCW colonies. It was also a time when Texas Parks & Wildlife stocked additional turkeys at Boggy Slough, which mostly prospered as long as the burning practices continued. By the early 2000s, however, as Temple-Inland prepared to divest its timberlands, burning practically ceased and wildlife suffered, Dietz later recalled.[155] Not until after the T. L. L. Temple Foundation acquired Boggy Slough in 2013 would the use of prescribed fire return to a level desired by wildlife and forest managers. But by then, even the high brick chimney of the former company clubhouse, which managers had previously kept clear, became completely hidden from view by vines and brush.[156]

⸻

During the second half of the twentieth century, Boggy Slough experienced a complete turnaround in administration, progressing from a management class to an ownership class. Arthur Temple Jr. ensured that important decisions concerning the land would no longer be made by well-meaning managers who were essentially cow men at heart. He hired college-trained foresters to begin managing his timber resources late in the 1940s, and he hired university-trained environmental and wildlife managers during the 1970s and 1980s. In each case, these people often reported directly to

him. Considerations for wildlife advanced from simply capitalizing on the importance of "seeing" and "shooting at" game animals, and lots of them, to managing for successful trophy-hunting experiences while also providing healthy habitat for as many different wildlife species as possible. Decades earlier, in 1919, wildlife biologist Aldo Leopold had identified an important difference between what he called "game farmers," defined as those who sought "to produce merely something to shoot," and "wild-lifers," those who sought to produce a diversity of animals, both "game and non-game," for the greater benefit of the whole ecosystem.[157] Boggy Slough's advancement from game farming to true wildlife management may have been delayed, but there was now no doubt about its new direction.

Reestablishing vegetation diversity became central in understanding the larger environment, which in time revealed a vision of the full forest instead of only "crops" of timber and deer. Fire, which had been mostly excluded from Boggy Slough for nearly seven decades, became an important management tool again. And birds, all birds, were seen as indicator species of the health of the forest. As Buddy Temple would say upon the foundation's acquisition of Boggy Slough in 2013: "We are going to manage for the birds. As long as we provide the habitat that they need, we will be doing all right."[158] The Christie girls, who had written of Boggy Slough's birds exactly a century earlier, would have been pleased.

CHAPTER 11

Conservation Land

Boggy Slough is legacy land for our family;
it is legacy land for all of East Texas.

—BUDDY TEMPLE (2013)

Over a Thanksgiving holiday during the early 1960s, Buddy Temple came home from the army and went squirrel hunting in one of his favorite places at Boggy Slough. Seeking solitude under a high canopy of large oaks, he was disappointed when he discovered that Temple Industries, which was still family-owned at the time, had recently executed what he called "a real heavy hardwood cut in one of the bottomland areas." In recalling the event, which he said "took out many" of the largest trees, he said, "It was heartbreaking. I swore if I ever had anything to do with it, *that* would never happen again."[1]

Arthur Temple III, better known as Buddy, was born in 1942 and began to visit Boggy Slough with his father, mother, and older sister from almost the time he first learned to walk. His father kept a palomino Shetland pony for him, named Trigger, which he rode during horseback forest tours, often having to run his pony just to keep up with his father's "big black Tennessee Walker." Soon, Buddy began to ride the larger horses of the foresters, and by the time he was a teenager he said he was "turned loose" to roam the woods and fields, camp out at night, fish for lunker bass in the stocked lakes and

ponds, and float the river in a canoe. "Our friends and I would load up with cokes and sandwiches and cheese crackers and spend the whole day" on the river, he said, knowing well that family-owned company land embraced one or both riverbanks for dozens of miles upstream as well as down. At Boggy Slough, Buddy also learned to shoot rifles and shotguns, and he studied how to hunt, killing his first deer at the age of only seven.[2]

Having experienced "such a wonderful opportunity" to grow up as he did, Buddy considered it a privilege that shaped his lifelong environmental consciousness. "I realized at a very early age how important the natural world was to all of us," he said. "As I grew up, I just naturally gravitated toward conservation issues. I remember when I first went to the legislature in 1972, people thought it was odd, but the first bill I introduced was a bill to prohibit the dredging of the oyster beds in the bays along the Texas coast." Although the bill "went nowhere," he said, it nevertheless led to developing a good working relationship with the noted conservationist and Dallas attorney Ned Fritz, who Buddy would later join in efforts to regulate strip mining in the state.[3]

Buddy also attributed a reason for his personal connection to the natural world to his father's influence. "He was a great naturalist," Buddy recalled, crediting a Boy Scout leader in Texarkana who taught his father to "identify nearly every plant in the forest." Buddy said that his father also recognized early on that land had played a "critical" role

Buddy Temple with his father Arthur Temple Jr. and his new Winchester Model 94 carbine, which J. J. Collins gave him as a gift, ca. 1948. *Courtesy of The History Center, Diboll.*

Buddy Temple on his Shetland palomino pony named "Trigger" at the Boggy Slough clubhouse, ca. 1949. *Courtesy of The History Center, Diboll.*

in the family's businesses. This abiding appreciation of land and its history, passed down through the generations, inspired Buddy and the trustees of the T. L. L. Temple Foundation to purchase Boggy Slough as conservation land in 2013, prompted by the death of Buddy's father in 2006 and Temple-Inland's sudden divestiture of some 2.2 million acres of forestlands in four states, including 1.25 million acres in Texas. Upon completing the acquisition, Buddy turned and quietly said to his friend, fellow foundation trustee and retired multigenerational Temple executive Jack Sweeny, "We didn't lose it all, did we Jack? We saved the best part. And now we can protect it."[4]

———◆———

By 2013 Boggy Slough had experienced significant changes. Through the centuries, many generations of people had lived there and learned how to balance their cultural wants with caring for the natural environment that had made their lives possible. The balance became increasingly fragile as new and often distant economies began to place fresh demands on the land in the form of game animal markets during the eighteenth century and by farmstead agricultural practices and industrial tree-based economies during the nineteenth century. Something completely different developed during the first half of the twentieth century, when T. L. L. Temple's managers fenced the land, gradually depopulated it, and stocked it with thousands of cows and thousands more of goats. Their failure to make commercially successful pastures out of cutover forests resulted in the eventual adoption of modern forestry practices during the second half of the century. Then during the last third of the century, foresters began doing their jobs not only in the woods but also in the public marketplace of ideas, as a whole new environmentally conscious generation, of which Buddy and his sister Chotsy were a part, placed new demands not only on the land but on its owners as well.

Much of this new consciousness focused on logging. Although Boggy Slough had been mostly selectively harvested, there was nevertheless that

Mary Temple, first wife of Arthur Temple Jr., shoots skeet at Boggy Slough, ca. 1949. Barney Franklin pulls the lever, and those looking on include Arch Hollingsworth, Carroll Allen, Charlotte and Susan Barry, and possibly Rosalie Tucker. *Courtesy of The History Center, Diboll.*

were placed just prior to the foundation's acquisition and were strengthened afterward. Buddy's concern to "protect" the land was as much about preventing land fragmentation as it was about stopping unnecessarily heavy harvesting practices.[6]

By continuing to log the forest, the foundation carries on a tradition that has been part of Boggy Slough's history since Buddy's great-grandfather first selectively cut the pine and hardwood forests there some twelve decades earlier.

one particular heavy bottomland hardwood cutting during the early 1960s that made such an indelible impression on Buddy. Temple-Inland's later efforts at "hardwood management" during the 1990s, which resulted in cutting 194,000 tons of hardwood annually from the company's 141,000 acres of Neches River bottomlands in the form of 30-acre clear-cuts, including several at Boggy Slough, also factored into Buddy's desire to "save" and "protect" the land of his childhood.[5]

Yet today the Boggy Slough Conservation Area remains a "working forest," because Buddy and the foundation's trustees wanted to continue providing jobs and financial income to the region while also managing the land as a demonstration of modern conservation forestry practices and scientific research. Although the foundation, unlike for-profit corporations, is not bound to shareholder demands and market fluctuations, trustees nevertheless see wisely managed timber sales as supporting the needs of an operational expense budget, which includes control of nonnative invasive species while promoting overall forest health. Portions of the uplands are carefully harvested annually, while the bottomland hardwoods are protected under conservation easements that

It took some thirty to forty years for Boggy Slough's "second crop" of trees to mature. Following the closure of the company ranch, Southern Pine Lumber Company established the last logging camp on the property in 1938, on a hill near Cedar Creek at the southwestern corner of the property. Named Redgate, for the nearby red gate at Highway 94, the camp existed only a couple of years, to harvest second-growth saw-grade pine timber from lands west and south of today's conservation area, which had been sold to Southland Paper Mills for pulpwood plantation lands. Redgate was the last logging camp at Boggy Slough, because the company began to transition to truck logging at about that time, and to contract logging in 1941. After the discontinuation of the camps, logging employees rode in company labor buses over improved public highways to and from the work sites. Logging by company-owned railroads, which began to be phased out during the 1930s, ended altogether in 1962, with some of the last logs to move by rail coming from Boggy Slough.[7]

In 1948, during Arthur Temple Jr.'s first year of managing Diboll's operations, company loggers returned to Boggy Slough once again—since contract loggers were not yet allowed on the property—to log about a four-mile stretch of mostly uplands between Rayville and Cochino Bayou. It was the first time that those lands had been harvested since they had been first industrially cut forty years earlier. Included in the operations was a tract in the Hampton survey along Cochino Bayou. Much of it had yet to be logged for saw timber because the early logging camps had left the area before the company acquired the tract in 1917.[8] Charlie Harber, who served as one of Dave Kenley's pasture riders in 1948, remembered seeing massive pine and sweetgum logs coming out of the woods along the bayou, pulled individually by caterpillar tractors and "cat wagons." It was "virgin stuff," he recalled during a site visit in 2002. "Those trees were enormous. Some of them logs were six foot through or better," he remembered.[9] Three logs from one of the sweetgum trees, 16 feet each in length, were placed on a truck trailer and entered into the 1948 Texas Forest Festival Parade in Lufkin that October. According to the *Diboll Buzz Saw*, the three logs measured 4,084 board feet and "were by far the largest logs in the parade."[10] Most likely standing in the Hampton tract at the time were today's state grand champion loblolly pine and the state co-champion longleaf pine. The trees were either too small for the quality of sawlogs desired at the time or the loggers simply overlooked them. Either way, their actions turned into gifts to future generations.[11]

After 1948, Boggy Slough was not logged as often as were the company's other lands. The Temples came to know the value of conserving a few big trees, seeing a day in the future when the majority of people would prefer to see them growing in the forest rather than paraded down the highways and downtown city streets. When Boggy Slough's forests were harvested after 1948, they were mostly selectively logged according to the sustained-yield policy that Southern Pine Lumber Company had applied to 239,000 acres of its forestlands in 1941. Typically this meant logging mature and merchantable trees periodically, leaving the smaller ones for later cuttings, deadening emergent hardwoods in the dominant pine-type areas, and planting pine seedlings in the upland openings (although very few of the planted pines at Boggy Slough survived before 1961 because of the severely overstocked populations of both cattle and deer). After Diboll's hardwood lumber mill closed in 1954 and the flooring plant closed in 1956, very little hardwood logging occurred at Boggy Slough, although the practice continued on the company's other bottomlands until 1971.[12]

In April of that year, Temple Industries implemented a "new policy" to "hold" its bottomland hardwood timber and to restrict all sales of hardwoods to the "low grade trees" in "the pine and pine-hardwood stands."[13] As Arthur Temple Jr. explained the new policy to wildlife biologist Dan Lay of the Texas Parks & Wildlife Department in November of that year, Temple Industries would "take out old weed trees on the hills and in otherwise pure pine stands in order to make room for

A news clipping photo of Jean Shotwell displaying a set of large, irregular antlers containing thirty-eight points, found by young Buddy Temple in the Cochino Bayou bottoms, ca. 1950. *Courtesy of The History Center, Diboll.*

more pines in those pine-type stands," but they would preserve "ecological values" by managing the pine uplands as "all-age stands" and by not cutting "any hardwoods in the creek bottoms or river bottom areas."[14]

Temple's stances against bottomland hardwood logging and clear-cutting were significant, because many other timber companies had by the 1950s turned their hardwood bottoms over to indiscriminate railroad crosstie millers and pulpwood loggers while they clear-cut their pine lands and introduced loblolly pine plantations as far into the heavily cutover stream bottoms as possible. By the 1990s, evidence of the different approaches was written all over the land. Norman Davis, hired in 1990 as Temple-Inland's first "hardwood forester," recalled during a 2017 interview that he and his staff "were always marveling about how we could tell the previous owner simply by what had been done to the hardwood bottoms." At that time, the Temple-Inland forest comprised some five or six different prior ownerships and histories, Davis clarified, "and we could just about tell you who the [previous] owner was without looking at deeds." In some of the old Temple forests, he said, "you just couldn't see any cutting."[15]

Back in 1950, Arthur Temple Jr. also thought of planting fast-growing loblolly pine in the many thousands of acres of cutover river bottom lands that his family's lumber companies owned. After his predecessors had waited nearly forty years, only to find that much of the bottomland was "really not producing anything [merchantable]," Temple felt that nature needed some help. Longtime timber and land department head Dave Kenley, who knew the bottoms as well as anyone, especially Boggy Slough, persuaded Temple against trying to plant pine in the most overflowed areas, arguing that pine "couldn't stand the water for the long time it stays there." Instead, Kenley suggested planting fast-growing sweetgum, for poles that could be treated at Diboll's new creosote plant, or mechanically clearing the ground to establish rice fields. Arthur Sr. advised his son against both ideas, saying he seriously doubted either one of them would "pan out" economically. Short of selling the unproductive land, Arthur Sr. said he did not "know what to do with it."[16] Eventually, Arthur Jr. decided to continue doing nothing. While he kept seeking ways of making his other lands as financially productive as possible—"since that's the business we are in," he often said—he was also learning that in the natural world sometimes patiently doing nothing was actually the best thing to do. It was also the same advice that US forester Austin Cary had given Diboll manager Watson Walker specifically concerning Boggy Slough's bottomlands, back in 1923.[17]

Nevertheless, it seemed that each generation had to learn the lesson of "doing nothing" the hard way. Buddy Temple reflected on this during a 2014 tour of a Boggy Slough bottomland area that had been clear-cut and replanted during the 1990s, saying that managers eventually admitted to him that "the best thing to do with these bottomlands is nothing, don't touch them." "Exactly," Buddy said he reminded them, "that is what we [Buddy and his father] tried to tell y'all back then."[18]

As Arthur Temple Jr.'s conservative views of hardwood bottomlands continued to mature during the 1950s and 1960s, they became public during 1967, when Temple joined with the top executives of Kirby Lumber Corporation, W. T. Carter & Brother Lumber Company, International Paper, and the Eastex Corporation in pledging a logging moratorium on a combined ownership of 35,500 acres in southeast Texas. The move was a public goodwill show of support, to establish a Big Thicket National Monument while waiting for the federal government to finalize plans and secure compensation for the land's owners.[19] Temple's lands in the proposed monument consisted of 9,143 acres adjacent to the Neches River north of Evadale, in what was known as the "Neches Bottom Unit." It contained what forester Kenneth Nelson described in May 1967 as 3,040 acres in "the north end," which included "all of the uncut"—later clarified as "virtually untouched"—"acreage that we have in there."[20] Earlier, in 1963, the Society of American Foresters had shared their belief that Temple's lands north of Evadale held the last "as near [to] virgin timber left in the State, so far as hardwood is concerned."[21] Temple's committing of the old-growth bottomlands to the moratorium effectively shuttered his Pineland hardwood mill, which at the time was running only three days a week thanks to already diminished old-growth timber resources.[22]

Supporters of the Big Thicket National Monument, and of the later and much larger preserve, praised Temple for his leadership among the timber corporations, and especially for his decision to close his last hardwood mill.[23] They instantly identified him as a vital and necessary ally, and even friend, during nearly every major land conservation effort in East Texas for the rest of his life, whether he agreed wholeheartedly with their projects or not.[24] "The world was a better place" because of Temple, notable conservationist Geraldine Watson once wrote to him, acknowledging that she was certainly "no flatterer." His was a responsible company, one that would work with conservationists, not directly against them. Temple's leadership, and what Watson called his "concern, demonstrated by action," had given her "hope that environmentalists, scientists and the forest products industries [could] work together after all."[25] This was further evidenced in 1975, when Temple decided against cutting the timber on a 410-acre tract in the Lance Rosier Unit of the Big Thicket National Preserve, which his company had purchased for $34,200 in 1974, only to learn from the federal government, several months later, that the tract was inside the newly declared preserve boundaries.[26] Knowing that the timber contract's short time limit would expire before the federal government secured the money to purchase his timber rights, and after unsuccessfully receiving redress from the timber seller and from several conservation organizations, Temple chose to lose the money rather than cut the trees.[27] As some would say later, despite his hard-nosed business approach, Temple "really did care what people thought about him, his family, and his businesses." It was the essence of his "we want to be a good neighbor" environmental policy.[28]

Behind the scenes, Temple proved that he honestly did care. In 1973, he reminded his foresters that it was vital to "do all we can to be sensitive and responsive to the desires of the ecologists and naturalists," to work with them, he said, "to prevent the careless destruction of unique biological and botanical specimens." He also urged them not to interpret his instructions as a "publicity gimmick" or "as an extra burden on our field people, but rather as an opportunity for Temple to do something really very exciting." "As you know," he once wrote to his director of silviculture, Garland Bridges, "our company has always prided itself on its responsible stewardship of our lands, although perhaps our methods have been somewhat imperfect."[29]

To improve the Big Thicket's diversity of plant communities, Temple urged Temple-Eastex to donate some 2,100 acres of "arid sandlands" to The Nature Conservancy in 1977, naming the tract the Roy E. Larsen Sandyland Sanctuary, in honor of Time Inc.'s longtime executive and leading land conservationist. Located along Village Creek, a tributary of the Neches River, the tract contained sand deposits up to 300 feet deep and was the one type of ecosystem the Big Thicket Preserve did not yet contain. Over the next couple of decades, Temple-Inland and others would add lands and conservation easements to the Larsen Sanctuary, which grew to some 5,600 acres of protected lands by 1994.[30] Later, under Buddy Temple's chairmanship of the T. L. L. Temple Foundation (2000–2015), the Temples gave more than $11 million to The Conservation Fund, mostly between 2006 and 2009, which was used to purchase additional lands that further enhanced the Big Thicket National Preserve, to purchase conservation easements on surrounding tracts, to establish mitigation bottomlands along the Neches River south of Diboll, and to purchase the first tract of land in the newly established Neches River National Wildlife Refuge upstream from Boggy Slough, in Anderson and Cherokee Counties.[31] All of the initiatives, like the Boggy Slough Conservation Area itself, focused on further protecting the Neches River from dams and land fragmentation.

The Temple family's views on clear-cutting were no less significant than their seasoned beliefs on hardwood bottomlands. By 1972 Temple Industries, which had absorbed all the family's forest products, real estate, and banking businesses as a new publicly traded corporation in 1969, owned some 460,000 acres of forestlands. Temple promoted them as "perpetual forests," managed to sustain more than two billion board feet of growing timber despite a harvesting rate that had doubled during the previous decade. Unlike the operations of many of Temple's competitors, where trees were planted and harvested like rows of corn, Temple's forestlands were selectively harvested and naturally regenerated so that "the forest" was always there.[32]

When the US Senate conducted hearings on clear-cutting in May 1971, Arthur Temple Jr. obtained transcripts of the testimonies and had his foresters evaluate them. He quickly decided against clear-cutting as a single-tool management practice. While he admitted that some isolated areas that had experienced irreparable disturbance caused by nature or man might benefit from clear-cutting and plantation establishment, he believed that an uneven-aged forest provided the best ecological balance between the desires of commercial markets and the needs of nature. In a much-publicized address to a meeting of the Southern Forest Products Association in New Orleans in April 1972, Temple said that clear-cutting was merely "one string in our bow. Properly used, I think it's great. But I object violently to the pat answers that say it is the concept of the future. I think that's ridiculous!" He went on to explain that the regenerative growth of forest trees and plants had "covered up a lot of ignorance on our part over the years, fantastic mistakes that Mother Nature has recouped for us. No other resource-oriented industry can make that statement." But he warned that if the industry persisted in advancing the dangerous "fad" of clear-cutting, there might not be a similar redemption for future generations.[33]

Forestland and its wise and patient management were indeed important to the Temples.[34] In company annual reports to stockholders during the late 1960s and early 1970s, color photographs of people and wildlife enjoying healthy all-aged forests graced the covers and pages. The 1971 report informed the many new public shareholders of the forest's importance to their investment, stating that while the land's true value was "not reflected on the balance sheet" it was nevertheless their "greatest asset." The 1972 report equated ownership of thirteen shares of stock to indirect ownership of one acre of Temple-managed forestland.[35] Furthermore, it was company policy to use the proceeds from the sale of forestlands, whether to real estate development projects or to the federal government, to purchase replacement forestlands elsewhere, usually buying more land and timber than was sold.[36]

Although Temple's views on clear-cutting were clear, after Time Inc. acquired Temple Industries in August 1973—merging it with its subsidiaries, Eastex Pulp and Paper Company and Southwestern Timber Company to form Temple-Eastex—the tide of even-aged management quickly drowned his opposition to it. Conversion to pine plantations on the Eastex/Southwestern lands had begun during the 1950s, at rates of between 5,000 and 20,000 acres per year. New genetically superior loblolly pines, ironically developed at the Texas Forest Service's Arthur Temple Sr. Research Area in Cherokee County and produced at Eastex's nursery in Newton County—said to grow up to 25 percent faster than the common loblolly—made up the new even-aged timber stands.[37] Not long after the merger, even the oldest of the Temple lands began to be converted to plantations, including carefully selected portions of Boggy Slough—North Boggy during the middle 1970s and South Boggy during the 1980s.[38]

By 1976 some 250,000 acres of the combined 1.1 million acres of the Temple-Eastex forests were even-aged plantations. By 1983, the first year of Temple-Inland, more than 350,000 acres of the company's lands had been converted to planted rows of genetically engineered pine trees. Annual reports, which once touted the advantages of uneven-aged "perpetual forests," now explained to stockholders that "growth rates in many plantations are twice that which is historically experienced in the natural timber stands, and we plan to continue to convert additional acres to plantations each year." The stated goal was to convert at least 23,000 acres of forestland annually into "fast growing pine plantations," which would be managed on thirty-five-year rotations.[39] By 1990, half a million acres of Temple-Inland's forestlands in Texas had become plantations.[40] Although Temple resisted the land conversions, he later explained that "the demands of the stock market, not personal views," ultimately drove the decisions of public corporations.[41]

Until the foundation acquired Boggy Slough in 2013, the fate of the land was often unsettled, and not just because Wall Street began to exert management influence in 1969, which, regardless of the Temple family's wishes, led to the clear-cutting of both pines and hardwoods. Not only was Boggy Slough managed as a cattle ranch during the 1910s and 1920s, and almost sold to the federal government during the 1930s, it nearly became the site of a paper mill during the 1960s. In fact, it was Temple's lack of capital to build the much-desired mill that ultimately drove him to take his family-owned company public in the first place and secure the merger with Eastex Pulp and Paper Company, which already owned a paper mill, at Evadale.

Timber and lands manager Dave Kenley had corresponded with outside parties interested in developing paper mills in East Texas as early as 1931. By 1934 he had come to see a paper mill in the region as not only inevitable but as essential for "insur[ing] us a market for our cut-over land" and establishing what he called "a true perpetual cutting operation." Because pulpwood markets operated on young pine timber as small as five to ten inches in diameter, Kenley knew that a paper mill would mean faster harvesting rotations—roughly every fifteen to eighteen years rather than the forty years or more required by that era's saw timber markets—which meant quicker returns on investments. After much indecision about whether to

join Ernest Kurth and other investors in building a paper mill at Lufkin during the mid-1930s, Kenley finally whittled the issue down to the mill's fundamental need for timberland. "If the paper mill is ever built," he once counseled Arthur Temple Sr., then "someone has got to make a sacrifice to get it." By this he meant that at least one major timberland owner in the region would have to make a long-term investment of land.[42]

In 1938, Arthur Temple Sr. made that precious investment by trading some 47,000 acres of cutover lands in Trinity, Houston, Angelina, and Polk Counties for stock in Southland Paper Mills, which successfully began newsprint manufacturing operations in 1940. Ironically, at least part of Boggy Slough might have been included in these land sales had it not been for the existence of the cattle ranch, the various grazing leases, and Dave Kenley's personal plans to graze his cattle there. Although Southern Pine Lumber Company was the largest single shareholder in Southland at its beginning (because of the value of the invested lands), Arthur Temple Sr. served as its vice president while Ernest Kurth, who spearheaded the overall design and operations, served as president.[43]

After his father died in 1951, young Arthur Temple Jr. served on Southland's board, where he often clashed with Kurth and the other senior board members. Principally, Temple wanted his Texas Southeastern Railroad to handle all southbound shipments of paper, and he wanted to supply more wood chips from his Diboll operations than what had been agreed to earlier. Kurth maintained that his own railroad company, the Angelina & Neches River Railroad, on which the paper mill had been built and which was also a shareholder in Southland, had contractual obligations to the Southern Pacific Lines at Lufkin that dated from the paper mill's beginning. Kurth also maintained that the Diboll mills simply produced more chips than the paper mill could handle, and Temple knew it as true. In retaliation, Temple thwarted Kurth in land and timber deals at every opportunity, and he supported the Sam Rayburn lake project when Kurth, who had more land to lose under the impounded waters of the largest reservoir in Texas, opposed it. Eventually Temple obtained a stock buyout from Southland, whereby the 47,000 acres of cutover lands, which were worth about half a million dollars in 1938, had become stock certificates worth nearly $7 million twenty-three years later.[44]

After selling his Southland stock, Temple used the proceeds to further invest in Diboll's new fiberboard operations and to begin a partnership with US Plywood Corporation, which opened a plywood plant at Diboll in 1964, while he sought to construct a paper mill of his own. His grandfather had made a fortune in manufacturing building products, but profits from sawmills in no way matched those of paper mills. Temple hired engineers to study his lands, design a paper mill, and select a mill site. Because of the tremendous amount of water that paper mills required, his engineers selected Cochino Bayou as the reservoir site, Rayville as the plant site, and the Neches River to carry away the mill's effluent. Temple assigned land managers and lawyers to establish a local water control board of friendly appointees and charged them with obtaining all necessary environmental permits.[45]

Despite the extensive plans, two obstacles prevented the mill's construction. First, because the planned levee on Cochino Bayou would have flooded several thousand acres of US Forest Service lands, in addition to Temple's lands, the forest supervisor, John Courtenay, explained that he could not approve the project because the new Sam Rayburn and Toledo Bend Lakes had recently erased 60 percent of his agency's bottomland holdings. "With these bottomlands have gone the best of the deer and the bulk of the squirrel habitat," he clarified in a 1971 letter. Furthermore, he said he simply could not justify losing any more prime "multiple use resources," which would further reduce the monies the local counties received through timber sales, and the Cochino reservoir would require the relocation of Forest Service Road 511 as well as several other lesser roads. While Courtenay said he could not consent to the project as submitted, he did offer a possible exchange of "the inundated

lands" for "other lands of similar kind, amount, and value in an equally easy to administer area."[46] The second obstacle, and the one most decisive, however, was Temple's inability to secure adequate funding.[47] That paper mills required such a large amount of capital is what had prompted Kurth to partner with other investors, including the Temples, and to obtain a large government loan from the Reconstruction Finance Corporation a quarter of a century earlier. Once again, Boggy Slough was spared through a combination of natural as well as social factors.

⸻

There also would have been no Boggy Slough Conservation Area if the breakup of Temple-Inland between 2007 and 2013 had gone differently. During the early 1980s, market investors known as "corporate raiders" began to realize that US forest products companies held millions of acres of timberlands that were grossly undervalued. In many cases, acreage remained on their books valued as low as one dollar per acre. Under the governance of the United States Generally Accepted Accounting Principles (USGAAP), which applied to all publicly traded corporations, these timberland values remained stable, while trees grew and increased the fair market values of the lands. In efforts to unlock the real value of stock shares and seize the increasing asset value of the forest itself, corporate raiders initiated leveraged buyouts of forest products companies and sold off the pieces at significant profits. Raiders first acquired companies such as Diamond International and Crown Zellerbach, which no longer exist. Other companies, hoping to avoid similar fates, took preemptive actions and sold their forestlands themselves. Soon, large companies such as Georgia-Pacific, Kimberly-Clark, International Paper, and Boise Cascade had sold some 18 million acres of forestlands, mostly between 1999 and 2006.[48]

Further contributing to the decisions of forest products companies to divest their timberlands—

before allowing outside raiders to acquire them for free—was the Internal Revenue Code of 1986. Under a provision of this act, landowners who did not manufacture forest products would pay 15 percent capital gains tax on timber sales, while forestland owners who manufactured their timber would be taxed at the corporate rate of 40 percent. Under such a rule, shareholders claimed that forest products companies that owned forestlands essentially gave away a quarter of their profits to the federal government. Such implications gave rise to a new class of private forest owner: the timber investment management organization (TIMO), which was not industry and not owned by families or individuals, but was more tax efficient than any of them.[49]

Temple-Inland advertised in their first annual report to shareholders that most of their land carried "a book value of less than $100 per acre."[50] While not specifically mentioned in the report, parts of Boggy Slough were on the company's books for as little as two dollars an acre. Soon corporate raiders, including Carl Icahn, sought to acquire sufficient shares of Temple-Inland stock to influence board actions. In the fall of 2007, just a little more than a year following the death of Arthur Temple Jr. and after a record year for revenues, which had reached $5.56 billion annually, Temple-Inland sold more than 1.15 million acres of its forestlands in Texas to a TIMO for more than $2 billion and spun off another 57,000 acres to a real estate group. It was a 180-degree turn for the forest products company, which for more than a century had sought to acquire land, not just the timber growing on it. The forest was "an invaluable reserve," "a critical hedge against future market fluctuations," and "our greatest asset," according to persistent declarations in early stockholders' annual reports. One report during the 1950s affirmed that the forest would "ensure faith in the future of our company and its ultimate destiny." Words no more meaningful, nor inversely prophetic, ever appeared in a business statement. Within five years of divesting its forestlands, Temple-Inland ceased to exist.[51]

Significantly, Temple-Inland held on to Boggy Slough during the land sell-offs in 2007. After International Paper acquired what remained of Temple-Inland in 2012 for $4.4 billion, its leadership worked with the T. L. L. Temple Foundation and The Conservation Fund to ensure that Boggy Slough became a true conservation area in 2013. At the same time, International Paper, desiring only Temple-Inland's paper products division, sold the building products assets to Georgia-Pacific for $710 million. What was once one of the oldest and most successful forest products corporations in the United States was no more.[52]

———— ◆◆◆ ————

Under Buddy Temple's leadership, the Temple family saw their acquisition of Boggy Slough as a unique opportunity to preserve the last and most significant remnant of the old Temple forest and to continue the legacy of land stewardship that T. L. L. Temple had begun in East Texas more than a century earlier. Ironically, because of its extensive bottomlands, Boggy Slough had been overlooked by earlier industrialists, but now, for the same reason, it was being preserved as a critical central link between other important conservation lands up and down the Neches River—lands that the Temple family had also worked to preserve.[53]

Boggy Slough would be preserved also for scientific research and knowledge sharing. Buddy's and his family's earlier commitment to the Forest Research Institute at Stephen F. Austin State University was based on a conviction that the forest needed independent research—removed from industry—that would develop best-management practices for the land, not just for its owners, who were all too often driven by preferences for one resource over all others.[54] Buddy and the foundation saw Boggy Slough as an opportunity to do the independent research necessary, which could benefit the environmental health of the entire region, historically one of the richest areas of biodiversity in the country. All the while, Boggy Slough would

In 2018, trustees of the T. L. L. Temple Foundation posed with the Cochino loblolly, the largest loblolly pine tree in Texas, according to the Texas Forest Service. From the left: W. Temple Webber III, Secretary-Treasurer Jay Shands, Vice-Chair Hannah Temple, Ellen Temple, William "Spence" Spencer (kneeling), Tom Darmstadter, Chair Charlotte "Chotsy" Temple, David Webber, and Jack Sweeny. *Photo by the author.*

be what Buddy called "a Friend of the Forest," managed by "conservation forestry" practices designed to maintain the productivity of a working forest while also caring for the important ecological values unique to the region.[55]

During the process of acquiring the land, Buddy and his wife Ellen were each diagnosed with cancer. Buddy's illness was the more serious of the two, and it gave him a sense of urgency. As his strength steadily faded, he directed all of his remaining energy to loving his family and to caring for the land's own health and well-being. Until he passed away in April 2015, he threw himself completely into the work of restoring Boggy Slough's diverse ecosystems. In a fundamental way, the land gave him a kind of healing and restoration as well. The Boggy Slough Conservation Area brought Buddy's life full circle.[56]

By this time, Buddy and Ellen had already worked as partners in land conservation efforts across the state, and their several decades of shared experiences in leaving the land better than they found it would guide the foundation's work at Boggy Slough from the beginning. During the 1990s and early 2000s, while Buddy served on the advisory board of Texas A&M University at Kingsville's Caesar Kleberg Wildlife Research Institute, including more than a decade as its chairman, Ellen served on the governing board of the Lady Bird Johnson Wildflower Center, also for a decade, including three years as its president, and she helped lead its later affiliation with the University of Texas at Austin. Through those organizations, Buddy and Ellen implemented important native landscape and ecosystem restoration initiatives, which continue statewide today.[57] Additionally, as president of the Philosophical Society of Texas in 2001, Ellen assembled the annual meeting's program and titled it "The Land." She chose the topic because she and Buddy believed that the care of land was "the most critical issue" of the twenty-first century. Land was the one thing that all people shared, yet issues related to soil, water, plants, and animals often divided society. There needed to be common ground, Ellen said, "a place where we can agree enough to act and to create public policies" that would "get it right." The multiday symposium included notable biologists, ecologists, geologists, and land conservation professionals from across the country, including, among others, Patrick F. Noonan, Lawrence A. Selzer, Robert Breunig, Laura L. Jackson, Camille Parmesan, David J. Schmidly, Libby Stern, William R. Jordan III, Jessica Catto, Melinda E. Taylor, and Andrew Sansom.[58]

At the same time, Buddy and Ellen worked to restore 11,200 acres of an overgrazed and overhunted South Texas ranch in Duval County into a haven for native wildlife. The Temple Ranch also

Lifelong partners in land conservation work across Texas, Buddy and Ellen Temple at their family's Boggy Slough clubhouse known as Little Boggy November 2014. *Courtesy of The History Center, Diboll.*

the earliest sponsors of the Kleberg Wildlife Institute's South Texas Native Seeds Project, which they endowed. The wildly successful project developed commercially available, locally adapted native seed sources; conducted research to develop practical restoration methods; and led educational activities in support of restoration and conservation of native plant communities. The project's accomplishments soon spread to five other regions, enabling native plant restoration across the entire state by developing and providing certified native seeds to private as well as public landowners, including oil and gas pipeline companies and the highway department. After Buddy's death, Ellen provided multiyear support for the East Texas Natives Project in memory of Buddy and his love of the land, and the Boggy Slough Conservation Area became an important native plant evaluation site.[59]

To guide the Temple Foundation's initial restoration work at Boggy Slough in 2014, Buddy assembled a diverse corps of land and water authorities from across the country, including organizations such as The Conservation Fund, US Fish and Wildlife, Texas Parks & Wildlife Department (TP&WD), the Arthur Temple College of Forestry at Stephen F. Austin State University, and renowned private-sector environmental firms. From his earlier restoration work, Buddy knew that being a good steward of the land required incredible effort as well as patience. He knew that land could not be hurried, so at the advisory committee's first meeting he asked its members to provide a management plan that would "make Boggy Slough a truly unique place fifty years from now."[60]

Everyone agreed that Boggy Slough had an excellent start already. To build on what was already present, the committee recommended strategic harvesting of loblolly pines in the naturally regenerated areas to promote greater regeneration of the once-dominant shortleaf pines, since the general exclusion of ecological fires a century earlier had

became a valuable research and education venue, earning the Texas Parks & Wildlife Department's Lone Star Land Steward Award and the prestigious Leopold Conservation Award given by the Sand County Foundation in 2011. Access to commercially available certified native plant seeds was critical to their success in reestablishing native prairies and bringing back whole ecosystems. Buddy and Ellen learned that seeds of native grasses and forbs already in the ground sprang to life once overgrown woody brush and prickly pear cactus were controlled through mechanical clearing and prescribed fire, but areas with land disturbances such as pipelines and new highways needed additional assistance. Foremost was the need for ecotypic native seed sources, and Buddy and Ellen were among

View of a logging tract about eight months after a selective harvest. *Photo by the author, 2015.*

American beautyberries thrive below pine stands kept open through prescribed burning, 2014. *Photo by the author.*

portions of the land to shortleaf and longleaf pine savannahs was important to Buddy, since it would benefit all wildlife, including even reptiles and amphibians and especially birds, nongame and game species alike. Related to this ecosystem restoration was concern to further protect, foster, and study the rare and endangered red-cockaded woodpecker colonies. Another unanimous recommendation called for intensively protecting the several remnant and little understood saline prairies and their unique ecosystems from rooting feral hogs, thereby fostering the globally rare Texas prairie dawn-flower (*Hymenoxys texana*) and Neches River rose mallow (*Hibiscus dasycalyx*), which already grew in those areas.[61]

Besides the ubiquitous feral hog, another identified invasive species in need of control was the Chinese tallow tree (*Triadica sebifera*). Able to withstand long periods of standing water and readily

allowed loblollies to spread beyond the lower elevations and establish themselves in the uplands. The committee also recommended continuing the practice of cool-season prescribed upland burning, which had been implemented during the 1980s, and possibly expanding the practice into the warm growing season for more meaningful impact. In coordination with fires, managers would underplant fire-dependent shortleaf as well as longleaf pine species where necessary to further reestablish them. Doing these things would not only restore those two tree species to levels of historical presence, but would also reestablish an entire ecosystem with greater species richness. Restoring

Results of a prescribed burn in the south end of the conservation area in March 2018, about six weeks after the fire. *Photo by the author.*

A prescribed fire in the north end of the Boggy Slough Conservation Area, late January 2017. *Photo by the author.*

acres.[63] Cliff Shackelford, the TP&WD's statewide nongame ornithologist, recommended wise pineland savannah restoration and invasive plant controls, which would make the entire property a "natural food plot" and eliminate the need for artificial feeding stations. He also advised against building new roads, which would further encourage nonnative plants. Additionally, he asked management to consider allowing beavers—instead of man—to once again manage the wetlands, because, as he said, "beavers can do it best."[64]

Greg Grant, a horticulturist with Stephen F. Austin State University, reminded everyone of Boggy Slough's earlier industrial history, when timber, followed by cattle, then deer hunting were single-use purposes that drove most management decisions. He said that there were already "plenty of well managed forests, ranches, and hunting preserves, but very few well managed ecosystems."

resprouting when cut, this fast-growing invader remains arguably the most troublesome tree ever introduced to Texas. It began establishing itself in Boggy Slough's bottomlands following hurricanes and other wind events, which opened the forest canopy to their widely disbursed seeds, and remains a threat for displacing native tree and plant species. Early on, the foundation knew that Chinese tallow control would be a major expense, but a process that would also be studied scientifically.[62]

Some in the committee suggested phasing out the extensive array of wildlife food plots scattered across the landscape, which totaled some 452

The Boggy Slough Conservation Area, he said, not only had the potential but also the resources to be just such a land, and he thanked the Temples for their willingness and commitment to make it so.[65]

———————

Today, 30 percent of the Boggy Slough Conservation Area's 19,055 acres remain forested in mature bottomland hardwoods, with many trees well over one hundred years old. This is increasingly rare across the region. Although several 30-acre clear-cuts did occur in Boggy Slough's bottoms during the 1990s, they made up only 3 percent of that ecosystem and less than 1 percent of the total property. Many large trees remain. For example, in just one small area along Cochino Bayou, shagbark hickories (*Carya ovata*) up to 36 inches in diameter, black gum (*Nyssa sylvatica*) up to 61 inches, and red mulberry (*Morus rubra*) up to 30 inches, to name just a few examples, grow tall and healthy. They, along with all the other nearby bottomland plants and trees, are reminders of a heritage going back at least a millennium, when the great Caddo people called Boggy Slough home.[66]

Boggy Slough's uplands are likewise rare and diverse. Although about 17 percent of the 19,055 acres was converted to pine plantations decades earlier, more than 47 percent of the property (or about 74 percent of the upland areas) remains in naturally regenerated pine and mixed pine-hardwood forests. Many trees in these natural areas are also in excess of one hundred years old. The uplands are also home to sylvan champions. The state champion loblolly pine grows near the bottoms along Cochino Bayou, and the co-champion longleaf pine grows on a bluff south of Cochino Bayou. A plant community assessment performed in 2015 found that the diversity of Boggy Slough's forty-eight plant associations, twenty-one plant alliances, and twelve habitat series were believed to be the most diverse of any individual property in the state except for only the much larger and more geographically distributed four units of the national forests in Texas.[67]

———————

When Buddy Temple asked land advisers to assemble a management plan that would make the conservation area "a truly unique place fifty years from now," his love of Boggy Slough was similar to earlier peoples' pride in the land—from the Caddo people, who told Fray Damian Mazanet in the late seventeenth century that their central Neches valley land was "the best in the world," to the Christie sisters of Sullivan's Bluff, who wrote to readers of the *Houston Post* during the early 1910s: "Oh, you just ought to see our place."[68]

Boggy Slough has been many things to many people—home, hunting grounds, industrial forest, cattle ranch, game preserve, conservation area, and a place of spiritual comfort and renewal. Through the centuries, the land shaped people as much as people shaped the land. The story of Boggy Slough has not ended. History continues to show that the land is not static, nor are the societies that nurture it. The full resolve of present and future generations will be required to continue doing the hard work of caring for it, day in and day out. With each rising and setting sun and through seasons of want and plenty, they will continue to write its history.

Appendix

An Ecological Analysis From Boggy Slough Conservation Area's Original Texas Land Surveys

ALTHOUGH LIMITED IN SCOPE, THE original boundary survey records of the Texas General Land Office provide an important guide to understanding the nature of Boggy Slough's pre-industrial forests.[1] Performed mostly between 1835 and 1876, early metes and bounds land surveys identified the types and sizes of trees at precise points on the land, well before disturbances of railroad construction, industrial tree removal, drainage alterations, and reforestation occurred during the twentieth century. Importantly, the boundary surveys were not forest inventories, but because they included observations of topography and vegetational features in addition to documenting specific trees as corners, witnesses, and compass bearings, the records nevertheless offer a unique ecological sampling of the land.[2]

Boggy Slough's early surveyors utilized at least twenty-eight tree species. Perhaps not surprisingly, they cited pine more than any other tree, utilizing it in nearly all the upland tracts, but rarely, if at all, in bottomland surveys. Overall, surveyors utilized pine for their purposes 19 percent of the time, not distinguishing between the three different species—shortleaf, longleaf, and loblolly. After pine, surveyors marked post oak, hickory, and red oak at nearly equal frequencies, and together those species made up 40 percent of the survey trees recorded. Notably, pine, post oak, hickory, and red oak made up 59 percent of the survey trees, which were species highly driven by disturbance, required lots of sunlight to grow, and were unable to regenerate under shade, including their own. Next, surveyors cited sweet gum 8 percent of the time, while elms, pin oak, ash, blackjack oak, ironwood, white oak, and mayhaw, in descending

order, were noted between 5 percent and 2 percent each. Black gum, river birch, bitter pecan (bitternut hickory), overcup oak, holly, and persimmon were used between 2 percent and 1 percent of the time. And the remaining trees, used less than 1 percent each, were cedar, cherry, dogwood, linn (basswood or linden), maple, mulberry, water oak, willow oak, and button willow.

Surveyors frequently cited ash (probably green ash) and ironwood in bottomland surveys, especially surveys that included the sloughs, where field notes recorded that both trees grew within the stream channels. Holly "on the river bank" was common in all the surveys bounded by the river. Elm was commonly utilized in survey lines along the creeks and Boggy Slough, while river birch, a true streambank tree, was cited frequently along portions of Cedar Creek. In a swampy area along Cedar Creek, known as Cedar Brake Prairie, cedars were utilized.[3] Three-inch- and four-inch-diameter mayhaw trees were used in surveys that embraced Franklin Slough, while upland hickories were most frequently cited in the dry, steeper-sloped uplands north of Cochino Bayou, especially in the several International & Great Northern Railroad surveys. In some of those surveys, hickories were the most frequently cited species.[4]

Although most of Boggy Slough Conservation Area's early land surveyors used trees as much as possible in establishing boundary corners, in some cases, particularly when no trees were nearby, their field notes revealed that they "set [a] post in prairie." This was particularly true in the surveys involving Bluff Prairie (now partially inundated under the impounded waters of Black Cat Lake) and the northern portion of Cedar Brake Prairie along Cedar Creek.[5] Also, one surveyor set a post on Boggy Slough Island in 1886, when he also drew a map that noted the island was "covered in giant cane." The map also recorded a natural terrace located north and northwest of the island, over which the modern "Longleaf Road" now traverses. The surveyor labeled the terrace "upland oak and pine," well before the creation of longleaf and loblolly pine plantations there during the middle and late twentieth century.[6] A surveyor of Boggy Slough Island in 1908 cited elm, ash, black gum, post oak, white oak, and water oak trees in determining the island's size—423 acres—and stated that the often overflowed land was "worthless only to grow timber."[7] Surveyors also noted other bottomland features, such as "river swamps," within surveys involving the three sloughs: Franklin, Britton, and Boggy; and a "lake in swamp" in the Sanchez survey along Cedar Creek and another lake in the Harding survey near Boggy Slough Island.[8]

A number of different surveyors measured the conservation area's lands in thirty-five original surveys, which varied in size from 160 to 4,605 acres each. The two largest surveys were recorded south of Cochino Bayou, consisting of an 1835 Mexican grant (to Candido Sanchez of Nacogdoches) and an 1845 Republic of Texas grant (to John M. Walker of Chappell Hill), totaling 9,033 acres. Most of the surveys recorded north of Cochino Bayou were State of Texas homestead grants of 160 and 320 acres. Because the surveys north of Cochino Bayou were smaller and more numerous than the original surveys made south of the stream, the northern lands were better represented in the tree analysis. When considering later deed surveys of smaller tracts within the large Sanchez and Walker original surveys, a more detailed picture emerges for those lands. Of the trees that later surveyors noted in marking the smaller tracts, those cited most frequently inside the John M. Walker survey were post oak (32 percent), red oak (27 percent), and pine (18 percent). For tracts within the Candido Sanchez survey, those trees cited most were pine (16 percent), red oak (11 percent), river birch (11 percent), elm (10 percent), and post oak (9 percent).[9]

Of course, bias factors into any such analysis of survey records since individual surveyors may have preferred certain trees over others. Generally, though, surveyors sought trees of a middle age and size, most conveniently situated to their purposes, and at times they used whatever trees were available.[10] For instance, while one Boggy Slough surveyor utilized mayhaw trees of three and four inches in diameter along Franklin Slough, another surveyor on the opposite side of the river (on Pine Island), used a six-foot-diameter black gum and a five-foot-diameter red oak.[11] Certainly, when considering the differences between mayhaws and giant black gums and red oaks, other factors, such as differences in elevation and drainage patterns, influenced what trees were present, or not, and therefore original survey records still hold value in helping us understand what constituted a pre-industrial forest.

Notes

Chapter 1. A Story of the Land

1. Influencing the opening paragraphs of this chapter is Stewart, *Names on the Land*, first published in 1945 and still the best overall source on place naming in the United States.

2. For an example of instructions to Spanish explorers to name the land features and record them in diaries, see instruction numbers 12 and 13 given Governor Don Domingo Terán de los Ríos in 1692, in Mattie Austin Hatcher, trans., and Paul J. Foik, ed., "The Expedition of Don Domingo Terán de los Ríos Into Texas (1691–1692)," *Preliminary Studies of the Texas Catholic Historical Society* 2, no. 1 (1932): 8–9. For the name Tejas, or Texas, see Bolton, *The Hasinais*, 53–69. See also, Jonathan Gerland, "Living in the Land of the Tejas: An East Texas Twenty-First Century Re-Discovery of the Beginnings of a Place Called Texas," *Pine Bough* 17 (2012): 2–11. Among the earliest Spanish maps that show "Provincia de los Tejas" are Francisco Álvarez Barreiro's *Plano Corografico é Hydrographico de las Provincias de el Nuevo Mexico . . . Provincia de los Tejas . . . de la Nuebla España* (Mexico: Don Luis de Surville, July 4, 1770, copied from Barreiro's 1728 map), Cartographic Item, MS. 17,650.b at the British Library, London; and Nicolás Lafora and Joseph de Urrutia, *Mapa de toda la Frontera de los Dominios del Rey en la America Septentriol (ca. 1770)*, Library of Congress Geography and Map Division, Digital ID: g4410 ct000553, LOC Call Number G4410 1769. U7 TIL.

3. For the decline of Indian populations in Texas, see Smith, *From Dominance to Disappearance*, and J. E. Pearce, "Indian Mounds and Other Relics of Indian Life in Texas," *American Anthropologist* 21, no. 3 (1919): 223–34.

4. Swanton, *Source Material*, 10, 16; Norris, *General Alonso de Leon's Expeditions*, 181; in Bolton, *Spanish Exploration in the Southwest*, see "Itinerary of De León, 1690," 417, and "Letter of Fray Damián Massanet to Don Carlos de Siguenza, 1690," 353. For recent histories of the Neches River, see Sitton, *Backwoodsmen*, and Donovan, *Paddling the Wild Neches*.

5. Robert C. West, "The Term 'Bayou' in the United States: A Study in the Geography of Place Names," *Annals of the Association of American Geographers* 44, no. 1 (1954): 63–74. The name Arroyo de los Cochinos appears in early maps and field notes pertaining to the Juan Jose de los Reyes survey in Houston and Trinity Counties, within the records of the General Land Office at Austin.

6. Deuteronomy 3:23–28; Leon Hale, "A Sad Story in an Old Graveyard," *Houston Post*, June 24, 1977, p. 3-E.

7. *Records of Appointments of Post Masters, 1832–1971*, NARA Microfilm Publication M841, 145 rolls, Records of the Post Office, Record Group Number 28 (Washington, DC: National Archives). Tesla, Houston County, is found in volume 71-A (1890–1904): 431–32. Edmund J. Sullivan was appointed postmaster of Tesla in 1894, Susan L. Sullivan in 1900, and William R. Sullivan in 1902. See also Schmidt, *Encyclopedia of Texas Post Offices*, 203, 207, and *Texas Almanac for 1873*, 65. Sullivan's Bluff appears at its correct location on an 1875 map published by the Cram Atlas Company. See Cram, *Cram's Rail Road and Township Map of Texas*.

8. Dumble, *Geology of East Texas*, 313.

9. "A Big Gas Blowout," *Houston Post*, October 8, 1904, p. 7; "To Drill near Lufkin," *Houston Post*, August 24, 1904, p. 3; "Oil Abounds near Lufkin, Government Expert Making Topographic Survey of Section," *Houston Post*, July 12, 1907, p. 15.

10. Black Cat Lake appeared on the Wells SW Quadrangle of the 1951 edition of the United States Geological Survey 7.5 Minute Map. Observations of dark, long-tailed and long-legged, lean cats in the area have

been reported by several witnesses, including one by the author in 2014, who saw the cat-like figure west of the lake, near Vair, swiftly trotting away along the track of a road for about twenty yards before it exited out of sight into high marsh grass. Buddy Temple, in conversations with the author at the time, said he grew up knowing the lake as Prairie Lake, not Black Cat.

11. Neff was a rail station at the crossing of the Eastern Texas Railroad and Texas Southeastern Railroad (TSE) lines, named for W. N. Neff, a Cotton Belt railroad official. Walkerton was a TSE rail station and logging camp named for Watson Walker, the Diboll sawmill superintendent for Southern Pine Lumber Company. Rayville was a TSE station named for John Jones Ray, the ranch manager of Southern Pine Lumber Company.

12. Thoreau wrote of the Fitchburg Railroad and its relationship to nature in the chapter "Sounds" (Thoreau, *Walden*, quote on 139). The definitive history of Walden Pond is Maynard, *Walden Pond*. Over the past twenty years, the author has seen forest products company and hunting club maps that label Walkerton Pond variably as Walden and Walton.

13. A line from Oliver Goldsmith's 1770 poem "The Deserted Village" comes to mind: "E'en now, methinks, as pondering here I stand, I see the rural Virtues leave the land." Kenneth R. Olwig considers the poem when interpreting meanings of "Nature" in his essay, "Reinventing Common Nature: Yosemite and Mount Rushmore—A Meandering Tale of Double Nature," in Cronon, *Uncommon Ground*, 387–98.

14. Rhonda Oaks, "Temple Foundation Buys Boggy Slough," *Lufkin Daily News*, December 24, 2013; International Paper Press Release, "T. L. L. Temple Foundation, International Paper and The Conservation Fund Announce Landmark Forest Conservation Effort to Protect More Than 19,000 Acres in East Texas," copy in the records of the T. L. L. Temple Foundation offices, Lufkin. The deed for 693 acres of land (generally referred to as "family land") granted to Arthur Temple Jr., which includes Black Cat Lake and the sites of Vair and several private clubhouses, was executed by W. Temple Webber of Temple Industries on December 17, 1971, filed at the Trinity County Clerk's Office on September 5, 2013, Trinity County Deed Records, Trinity County Courthouse Annex, Volume 917, p. 38.

15. Henry David Thoreau, "Autumnal Tints," *Atlantic Monthly*, October 1862. These interpretations are influenced by the works of William Cronon, including "A Place for Stories: Nature, History, and Narrative," *Journal of American History* 78, no. 4 (1992): 1347–76; "Caretaking Tales," 87–93; *Nature's Metropolis*; and *Changes in the Land*; of Williams, including *The Country and the City* and "Ideas of Nature," 67–85; and of Worster, especially *Nature's Economy*.

16. Runte, *Allies of the Earth*; Fiege, *Republic of Nature*, 228–64; Steinberg, *Down to Earth*, x–xi, 63–68.

17. The authority on this subject for the entire Neches River valley is Sitton, *Backwoodsmen*.

18. William Cronon, "The Trouble with Wilderness," in Cronon, *Uncommon Ground*, 89.

19. Quoted in Jonathan K. Gerland, "A Brief History of Temple Land Ownership and Management in East Texas, 1893–2007," *Pine Bough* 12, no. 1 (2007): 21–22.

20. Rutkow, *American Canopy*.

21. These ideas were influenced by Thomas Gray's poem, "Elegy Written in a Country Churchyard" (1751); Schama, *Landscape and Memory*, 14, 577; and site visits with Larry Shelton of Nacogdoches.

Chapter 2. A Land of Provision

1. Among the major histories of the Caddo Indians of Texas are Bolton, *The Hasinais*; Swanton, *Source Material*; and Smith, *The Caddo Indians*. For Caddo archeology, see Perttula, *Caddo Landscapes*; Timothy K. Perttula, "How Texas Historians Write about the Pre-A.D. 1685 Caddo Peoples of Texas," *Southwestern Historical Quarterly* 115, no. 4 (2012): 364–76; and John E. Keller, "The Subsistence Paleoecology of the Middle Neches Region of Eastern Texas" (PhD diss., University of Texas at Austin, 1974). This chapter was also influenced by Williams, *Americans and Their Forests*, 32–49; Marc. D Abrams and Gregory J. Nowacki, "Native Americans as Active and Passive Promoters of Mast and Fruit Trees in the Eastern USA," *The Holocene* 18, no. 7 (2008): 1123–37; and Abrams, "Ecological and Ecophysical Attributes," 74–89.

2. Fray Francisco Casañas De Jesús María to the Viceroy of Mexico, August 15, 1691, in Mattie Austin Hatcher, trans., "Descriptions of the Tejas or Asinai

Indians, 1691–1722, Part 1," *Southwestern Historical Quarterly* 30, no. 3 (January 1927): 209. For a similar French description, see Foster and Warren, *La Salle Expedition to Texas*, 220.

3. Other descriptions included "clear forests," "a light forest," "woods somewhat clear," "clearings with open woods," and "a sparsely wooded land" with "clear groves." The quotes were made by Fray Isidro Felix De Espinosa in 1716, Fray Francisco Céliz in October 1718, and Juan Antonio De La Peña in July 1721. Isidro Felix De Espinosa, "The Ramon Expedition: Espinosa's Diary of 1716," *Preliminary Studies of the Texas Catholic Historical Society* 1, no. 4, trans. Gabriel Tous (Texas Knights of Columbus Historical Commission, April 1930): 19–21, 23; Céliz, *Diary of the Alarcon Expedition*, 72–73; Hadley, Naylor, and Schuetz-Miller, *Presidio and Militia*, 415, 449; and Santos, *Aguayo Expedition*, 55–56. See also Keller, "Subsistence Paleoecology," 32–49; Williams, *Americans and Their Forests*, 32–33, 38.

4. Studies on the cultural use of fire are extensive. Perhaps foremost is Pyne, *Fire in America*, 6–180. See also Keller, "Subsistence Paleoecology," 32–49; David H. Jurney, John Ippolito, and Velicia Bergstrom, "The Frequency of Fire in East Texas Forests," *Journal of Northeast Texas Archaeology* 13 (2000): 40–49; Bruce M. Albert, "Climate, Fire, and Land-Use History in the Oak-Pine-Hickory Forests of Northeast Texas during the Past 3500 Years," *Castanea* 72, no. 2 (2007): 82–91; Tharp, *Structure of Texas Vegetation*, 56; Jurney et al., "Role of Wildland Fire," 95–116; Abrams and Nowacki, "Native Americans as Active and Passive Promoters," 1123–37; Williams, *Deforesting the Earth*; Jeff S. Glitzenstein, Paul A. Harcombe, and Donna R. Streng, "Disturbance, Succession, and Maintenance of Species Diversity in an East Texas Forest," *Ecological Monographs* 56, no. 3 (1986): 243–58; Shepard Krech III, "Reflections on Conservation, Sustainability, and Environmentalism in Indigenous North America," *American Anthropologist* 107, no. 1 (2005): 78–86; Bruce D. Smith, "A Comparison of Niche Construction Theory and Diet Breadth Models as Explanatory Frameworks for the Initial Domestication of Plants and Animals," *Journal of Archaeological Research* 23, no. 3 (2015): 215–62; Marc D. Abrams, "Fire and the Development of Oak Forests," *BioScience* 42, no. 5 (1992): 346–53. One of the first to write extensively of human use of

surface fire to alter the North American environment was George P. Marsh in his *Man and Nature*, 133–36. See also Gordon M. Day, "The Indian as an Ecological Factor in the Northeastern Forest," *Ecology* 43, no. 2 (1953): 329–46; Omer C. Stewart, "Burning and Natural Vegetation in the United States," *Geographical Review* 41, no. 2 (1951): 317–20; Hu Maxwell, "The Use and Abuse of Forests by the Virginia Indians," *William and Mary Quarterly* 19, no. 2 (1910): 73–103.

5. Julianna Barr, "Geographies of Power: Mapping Indian Borders in the 'Borderlands' of the Early Southwest," *William and Mary Quarterly* 68, no. 1 (2011): 21–29.

6. Before investigations by an archaeological steward began in 2018, foresters, road crews, hunters, and various other visitors found artifacts widely, especially along the river, sloughs, prairies, and in the creeks as well as along roadway ditches. Most of the points and tools were petrified wood, while most of the pottery was a sandy-paste composition typical of Woodland peoples. During walking explorations during the 2010s, the author found numerous pieces of flaked chert in various stages of development in most of the intermittent and ephemeral stream beds.

7. Former Temple-Inland forester Stan Cook donated several dozen Indian artifacts to The History Center in Diboll in 2016, accession number 2016:005. George Avery personally inspected the artifacts in 2017, and Timothy Perttula and Tom Middlebrook examined photographs of them in 2016 and 2018, communicating their assessments through emails and telephone conversations with the author.

8. The author and Stan Cook guided Texas Historical Commission archaeological steward Tom Middlebrook to various sites in Boggy Slough on February 9, 2018. Shovel tests were performed at six sites, recovering thirty-nine artifacts, including a Caddo pottery sherd at the north end of Franklin Slough. Middlebrook wrote a thirteen-page report of the findings in early June and presented it to the author, who forwarded it to the staff and trustees of the T. L. L. Temple Foundation. A copy of the report was retained by the author.

9. Perttula, *Caddo Landscapes*, 130; Tim Perttula, "41AG22: An Historic Caddo Allen Phase Caddo Site in the Neches River Basin, Angelina County, Texas,"

TARL Newsletter (March 2018); email communications with Dr. Tom Middlebrook of Nacogdoches concerning site 41AG22, January 19, 2018, author's possession.

10. Hidalgo, in Hatcher, "Descriptions of the Tejas," part 3 (July 1927): 55; Manzanet, in Lilia M. Casis, translator, "Carta de Don Damian Manzanet á Don Carlos Sobre el Descubrimiento de la Bahía del Espíruto / Letter of Don Damian Manzanet to Don Carlos de Siguenza Relative to the Discovery of the Bay of Espiritu Santo," *Quarterly of the Texas State Historical Association* 2, no. 4 (1899): 305; J. M. Row and W. A. Geyer, *Plant Fact Sheet for Chickasaw Plum*, https://www.nrcs.usda.gov /Internet/FSE_PLANTMATERIALS/publications /kspmcfs10101.pdf.

11. See the maps in Barr, "Geographies of Power," 23, and Herbert E. Bolton, "The Native Tribes about the East Texas Missions," *Quarterly of the Texas State Historical Association* 11, no. 4 (1908): 256. See also Peña's mention of the Nacono's home being five leagues (13 miles) from the Spanish camp near the Neches in 1721, in Forrestal, "Peña's Diary," 41; Perttula, "41AG22."

12. Many of Boggy Slough Conservation Area's land features are recorded in the nineteenth century land grant survey records for Trinity County at the General Land Office in Austin. See especially the records for surveys (grants) along the Neches River, including L. Price, L. Winter, W. Hampton, J. M. Walker, J. A. Martin, W. W. Alston, S. F. Harding, I&GN (International-Great Northern) Railroad (two surveys), and BBB&C (Buffalo Bayou, Brazos, and Colorado) Railroad (two surveys). A saline prairie (now Black Cat Lake) in the S. F. Harding and BBB&C Railroad surveys is identified and described in Dumble, *Geology of East Texas*, 313. USGS 7.5 Minute Topographical maps that include Boggy Slough are Wells SW, Wells, Centralia, and Kennard NE quadrants. See also Julianna Barr and Edward Countryman, "Maps and Spaces, Paths to Connect, and Lines to Divide," in *Contested Spaces of Early America*, 1–28.

13. Bolton, "Native Tribes," 249–76; Pyne, *Fire in America*, 34–44, 71–83.

14. Casañas, in Hatcher, "Descriptions of the Tejas," part 1 (January 1927): 210. See also Marsh, *Man and Nature*, 133–36.

15. Hidalgo quoted in Hatcher, "Descriptions of the Tejas," part 3 (July 1927): 55.

16. Espinosa, "Ramón Expedition," 20. Espinosa here described the area just west of the San Pedro villages. He described the area northeast of the villages, toward the Neches River, on pages 21 and 23.

17. Domingo Ramón, "The Domingo Ramón Diary of the 1716 Expedition into the Province of the Tejas Indians: An Annotated Translation," ed. Debbie S. Cunningham, *Southwestern Historical Quarterly* 110, no. 1 (2006): 63–64. Ramón described the lands immediately around the San Pedro villages and northeastward to the banks of the Neches River.

18. Céliz, *Diary of the Alarcon Expedition*, 72–73.

19. Hatcher, "Descriptions of the Tejas," part 4 (October 1927): 152.

20. Ibid., 153.

21. Abrams and Nowacki, "Native Americans as Active and Passive Promoters," 1123–37.

22. Barr, "Geographies of Power," 22.

23. Gaspar José De Solís, "Diary of a Visit of Inspection of the Texas Missions Made by Fray Gaspar José De Solís in the Year 1767–1767. Translated by Margaret Kenney Kress with Introductory Note by Mattie Austin Hatcher," *Southwestern Historical Quarterly* 35, no. 1 (1931): 61; Gaspar José de Solís, "The Solís Diary of 1767," *Preliminary Studies of the Texas Catholic Historical Society* 1, no. 6 (1931): 382, trans. Peter P. Forrestal and ed. Paul J. Foik. The author corresponded with Jorge L. Garciá Ruiz in April 2018 about the differences in the two published English translations, specifically the English words "orchards" and "gardens" and the Spanish words *huertos* and *jardín*. A Spanish version of the diary was not located, but Professor Garciá believed the context was *huertos*, or orchards. Solís was writing of the same area as Casañas—the San Pedro Creek area west of the Neches River.

24. Bartram, *Travels of William Bartram*, 56–57; Abrams and Nowacki, "Native Americans as Active and Passive Promoters," 1123–37; see also individual species entries in Stahl and McElvaney, *Trees of Texas*.

25. Marsh, *Man and Nature*, 133–36; Glitzenstein, Harcombe, and Streng, "Disturbance, Succession, and Maintenance," 243–58; G. Loyd Collier, "The Evolving East Texas Woodland" (PhD diss., University of Nebraska, Lincoln, Department of Geography,

April 1964): 45, 51–52, and 63–68; Albert, "Climate, Fire, and Land-Use History," 88; Williams, *Americans and Their Forests*, 38; Norman L. Christensen, "Landscape History and Ecological Change," *Journal of Forest History* 33, no. 3 (1989): 116–25; Cronon, *Changes in the Land*, 49–51; Spurr and Barnes, *Forest Ecology*, 421–22; Pyne, *Fire in America*, 38. For an assessment of Boggy Slough's pre-settlement vegetation, see the Appendix, "An Ecological Analysis from Boggy Slough Conservation Area's Original Texas Land Surveys."

26. Spurr, *Forest Ecology*, 197.

27. Stanturf et al., "Fire in Southern Forest Landscapes," 613; H. H. Chapman, "Fire and Pines," *American Forests* 50 (February 1944): 62–64, 91–93; J. C. Bradley, et al., "Post-Fire Resprouting of Shortleaf Pine is Facilitated by a Morphological Trait But Fire Eliminates Shortleaf-Loblolly Pine Hybrid Seedlings," *Forest Ecology and Management* 379 (2016): 146–52; H. H. Chapman, "Is the Longleaf Type a Climax?" *Ecology* 13, no. 4 (1932): 328–34; H. L. Stoddard, "Use of Fire," 31–42; Albert, "Climate, Fire, and Land-Use History," 82–91; Cronon, *Changes in the Land*, 49–51.

28. Foster and Warren, *La Salle Expedition to Texas*, 204.

29. Letter, E. C. Durham to Arthur Temple, February 12, 1923, and Arthur Temple to E. C. Durham, February 14, 1923, in Temple Lumber Company Records at the East Texas Research Center, Nacogdoches (hereafter ETRC), box 29, folder 4.

30. See photographer J. D. Cress's notes for image numbers 311 through 315 from November 1907 in *American Lumberman* Photographs 1907 (1994:004), The History Center, Diboll.

31. Cronon, *Changes in the Land*, 49–51; Peattie, *Natural History of Trees*, 24–5; Zon, *Loblolly Pine*, 7–27, published in 1905, examines loblolly pine ecology in eastern Texas.

32. See the Appendix: An Ecological Analysis from Boggy Slough Conservation Area's Original Texas Land Surveys.

33. Williams, *Americans and Their Forests*, 32–38; Cronon, *Changes in the Land*, 49–51.

34. Foster and Warren, *LaSalle Expedition to Texas*, 206, 209.

35. Pyne, *Fire in America*.

36. Olmsted, *Journey through Texas*, 233.

37. Cronon, *Changes in the Land*, 51.

38. Ibid.; Marsh, *Man and Nature*, 133–36.

39. For example, despite its title, J. Ned Woodall, "Cultural Ecology of the Caddo" (PhD diss., Southern Methodist University, 1969) does not consider the Caddo use of ecological fire.

40. Espinosa's fire stories are told in Hatcher, "Descriptions of the Tejas," part 4 (October 1927): 160–61 (quote on 161); Bolton, *The Hasinais*, 150–52; and Swanton, *Source Material*, 213–17.

41. Foster and Warren, *LaSalle Expedition to Texas*, 208; Douay, "Narrative of La Salle's Attempt," 232.

42. See the Field Notes for Trinity County Abstract 477 (Lazarus Price Survey), General Land Office (hereafter GLO) files, Austin Texas. See also resurvey records from the 1910s for Trinity County abstracts 331 (I&GN #24), 477 (L. Price), and 730 (L. Winters) in Southern Pine Lumber Company Land Records (1993:015), The History Center, Diboll. The resurveys reveal the locations of "Dock Franklin's field," "Christie's field," and "Charles Rushing's" "fence row" along terraces just above Franklin Slough.

43. Pyne, *Fire in America*, 69–83; Spurr and Barnes, *Forest Ecology*, 3d ed., 275–94; Jurney, Ippolito, and Bergstrom, "Frequency of Fire," 40–49; Cronon, *Changes in the Land*, 47–58; Sitton, *Backwoodsmen*, 240–41.

44. Pyne, *Fire in America*, 69–83; Perttula, *Caddo Landscapes*, 87–89, 130–39, and 215; Cronon, *Changes in the Land*, 45, 53–55.

45. Cox, *Journeys of Rene Robert Cavelier*, vol. 1, p. 232 (quote); Barr, "Geographies of Power," 22–25.

46. Barr, "Geographies of Power," 22–25.

47. Delanglez, *Journal of Jean Cavelier*, 105. Jean Cavelier's account of his Texas journeys, especially as it relates to the circumstances of his brother's murder, is often suspect, but his observations of the landscape, while possibly exaggerated, are in essence substantiated when compared with other European observations of the time.

48. Barreiro, quoted in Jackson and Foster, *Imaginary Kingdom*, 58.

49. Ibid., as well as the author's personal experiences in open pine forests as well as brushy "woods."

50. Roberts, *Description of Texas*, 117.

51. Stephen F. Austin, "Journal of Stephen F. Austin on His First Trip to Texas, 1821," *Quarterly of the Texas State Historical Association* 7, no. 4 (1904): 289–90.

52. Parker, *Trip to the West and Texas*, 153–54, see also 149–59.

53. Ibid., 158.

54. Katherine Bridges and Winston DeVille, "Natchitoches and the Trail to the Rio Grande: Two Early Eighteenth-Century Accounts by the Sieur Derbanne," *Louisiana History* 8, no. 3 (1967): 245–47; Jackson and Foster, *Imaginary Kingdom*, 132. Rubi crossed the Neches near the mouth of Shawnee Creek in southeastern Angelina County, near the Jasper County line, not near the Highway 59 crossing as Foster claims. Rubi called the land south of the Neches River, with its dense undergrowth, "Purgatory."

55. The best source on the Bidai remains Andrée F. Sjoberg, "The Bidai Indians of Southeastern Texas," *Southwestern Journal of Anthropology* 7, no. 4 (1951): 391–400. The Bidai were related to the Orcoquiza tribes nearer the coast, along Galveston Bay and the lower Trinity and San Jacinto Rivers, and they were less settled than the Hasinai. The many branches of Bedias Creek, a western tributary of the Trinity River, are named for the Bidai people.

56. For Spanish efforts in traveling to and from the Bidai peoples in the middle eighteenth century, see Bolton, "Spanish Activities on the Lower Trinity River, 1746–1771," *Southwestern Historical Quarterly* 16, no. 4 (1913): 342, 348; and "Investigation of a French Settlement Conducted by Don Joaquin de Orobio Bazterra, Captain of La Bahia," in Bexar Archives Transcriptions, vol. 30, pp. 65–71. For the relationship between canoe travel and land management, see Gregory J. Nowacki and Marc D. Abrams, "The Demise of Fire and 'Mesophication' of Forests in the Eastern United States," *BioScience* 58, no. 2 (2008): 123–38; and Cronon, *Changes in the Land*, 50. Peña mentions using a canoe to cross the Angelina River in 1721, saying the

Indians kept the vessel for that purpose. See Forrestal, "Pena's Diary," 45. See also Swanton, *Source Material*, 158–59.

57. Marsh, *Man and Nature*, 133–34.

58. Jurney, Ippolito, and Bergstrom, "Frequency of Fire," 40–48; David H. Jurney, "Presettlement Vegetation Seen through Land Surveyors' Eyes and Notes," a thirty-nine-page manuscript in the possession of the author, provided by Dan K. Utley in July 2018; Joutel, in Foster and Warren, *LaSalle Expedition to Texas*, 204, 234, and 236.

59. Joutel, in Foster and Warren, *LaSalle Expedition to Texas*, 236.

60. "Letter from Fray Mazanet to the Cone de Galve, informing him of his trip to Tejas and relating his ideas about the settlements and growth of the missions, Mexico, September 1690," in Hadley, Naylor, and Schuetz-Miller, *Presidio and Militia*, 334.

61. Casañas, in Hatcher, "Descriptions of the Tejas," part 1 (January 1927): 209.

62. Hidalgo, in Hatcher, "Descriptions of the Tejas," part 3 (July 1927): 56–57.

63. Forrestal, "Pena's Diary," 38–46; Charles W. Hackett, "The Marquis of San Miguel de Aguayo and His Recovery of Texas from the French, 1719–1723," *Southwestern Historical Quarterly* 49, no. 2 (1945): 193–214.

64. Juan Antonio de la Peña and Peter P. Forrestal, trans., "Peña's Diary of the Aguayo Expedition," *Preliminary Studies of the Texas Catholic Historical Society* 2, no. 7 (1935): 39–41, 45, 49.

65. An argument for a dense forest interpretation of the Hasinai landscape is Daniel A. Hickerson, "Historical Processes, Epidemic Disease, and the Formation of the Hasinai Confederacy," *Ethnohistory* 44, no. 1 (1997): 40–42.

66. Sánchez, quoted in Keller, "Subsistence Paleoecology," 98; See also Jose Maria Sánchez and Carlos E. Castaneda, "A Trip to Texas, in 1828," *Southwestern Historical Quarterly* 29, no. 4 (1926): 249–88.

67. Jackson and Wheat, *Texas by Terán*, 91, 139.

68. Melinda Brakie, *American beautyberry Plant Fact Sheet.* USDA Natural Resources Conservation Service at Nacogdoches, TX, 2010. https://www.nrcs.usda.gov

/Internet/FSE_PLANTMATERIALS/publications/etpmcfs10015.pdf.

69. The Spanish visitors to the Neches valley were instructed by their political and religious leaders to record such observations. For example, see instruction 12 to Terán in Hatcher and Foik, "Expedition of Don Domingo Terán," 8–9.

70. Keller, "Subsistence Paleoecology," 146–56; Stahl and McElvaney, *Trees of Texas*, 44; Nowacki and Abrams, "Demise of Fire," 123–38; Swanton, *Source Material*, 132–34.

71. Bolton, *The Hasinais*, 122–23.

72. Swanton, *Source Material*, 154–56; Bolton, *The Hasinais*, 104–6.

73. Swanton, *Source Material*, 135–36.

74. Ibid., 137–38.

75. Ibid., 137.

76. Hidalgo, in Hatcher, "Descriptions of the Tejas," part 3 (July 1927): 56; Bolton, *The Hasinais*, 104; Weddle, *La Salle*, 232–33 and 280–87; Griffith, *Hasinai Indians of East Texas*.

77. Swanton, *Source Material*, 135–36, 154; Bolton, *The Hasinais*, 103.

78. Jackson and Foster, *Imaginary Kingdom*, 42; Joutel, in Foster and Warren, *LaSalle Expedition to Texas*, 203.

79. Newkumet and Meredith, *Hasinai*, 16. Solís said that Hasinai indeed "raise[d] chickens and turkeys," in Solís, "The Solís Diary of 1767," 382.

80. Hatcher, "Descriptions of the Tejas," part 1 (January 1927): 210; Bolton, *The Hasinais*, 100; Swanton, *Source Material*, 138.

81. Odom, *Over on Cochino*, 61–63.

82. Newell and Krieger, *George C. Davis Site*, 3; Weddle, *La Salle*, 232–33 and 280–87.

83. Bolton, *The Hasinais*, 111–19.

84. Swanton, *Source Material*, 157; Bolton, *The Hasinais*, 126; Hidalgo to the Viceroy, in Hatcher, "Descriptions of the Tejas," part 3 (July 1927): 56; Anderson and Oakes, *Giant Cane, Arundinaria gigantea* Muhl., https://www.nrcs.usda.gov/Internet/FSE_DOCUMENTS/nrcs144p2_002413.pdf.

85. Espinosa, in Hatcher, "Descriptions of the Tejas," part 4 (October 1927): 154–55.

86. Smith, *Caddo Indians*, 13; Bolton, *The Hasinais*, 128–37.

87. Mazanet, "Mazanet Seeks Aid for the Tejas Mission, 1693," in Hadley, Naylor, and Schuetz-Miller, *Presidio and Militia*, 346. By this time, Mazanet had given up nearly all hope in settling the land. A few years earlier he thought prospects exceedingly high, but now felt the land was not nearly as fertile as earlier believed, although the Indians still felt it so. Other factors, besides the land, were definitely at work.

88. Perttula, *Caddo Landscapes*, 17; Smith, *Caddo Indians*, 11; Williams, *Americans and Their Forests*, 58.

89. Espinosa, in Hatcher, "Descriptions of the Tejas," part 4 (October 1927): 156; Swanton, *Source Material*, 129–30; Bolton, *The Hasinais*, 119.

90. Dumble, *Geology of East Texas*, 313; Field Notes for Trinity County Abstract 118, GLO files; Jackson and Wheat, *Texas by Terán*, 80; "Texas prairie dawnflower (*Hymenoxys texana*) 5-Year Review: Summary and Evaluation," by U.S. Fish and Wildlife Service Texas Coastal Ecological Services Field Office Houston, Texas, https://www.fws.gov/southwest/es/Documents/R2ES/TexasPrairieDawn_5YrReview_Aug2015.pdf. Author's correspondence with Eric Keith and Larry Shelton, August 2018.

91. H. W. Pennington, "Sketch of W. W. Alston Survey in Trinity County, October 1886," Texas General Land Office Trinity County Scrip File 593 (W. W. Alston), Austin, Texas; Jonathan Gerland, "Boggy Slough Island, 1886," *Pine Bough Magazine* (December 2016): 30–31.

92. Anderson and Oakes, *Giant Cane*.

93. Swanton, *Source Material*, 156–57; Bolton, *The Hasinais*, 126; Stahl and McElvaney, *Trees of Texas*, 44.

94. Douay, "Narrative of La Salle's Attempt," 222–47; Swanton, *Source Material*, 39.

95. Swanton, *Source Material*, 10, 16; Stahl and McElvaney, *Trees of Texas*, 40.

96. Perttula, *Caddo Landscapes*, 22, 208–15; Smith, *Caddo Indians*, 8.

97. Smith, *Caddo Indians*, 8.

98. La Vere, *Caddo Chiefdoms*, 40–73; Douay, "Narrative of La Salle's Attempt," 222–47. Among the earliest transactions between the Hasinai and the French was LaSalle's trading of ax heads for Hasinai horses, which the Hasinai had obtained indirectly from the Spanish. Although the Hasinai tribes possessed few horses by the late seventeenth century, they willingly traded one for a couple of hatchets.

99. Letter, General Terán to the president of Mexico, June 30, 1828, in Jackson and Wheat, *Texas by Terán*, 101.

100. Diary entry of June 3, 1828, in Jackson and Wheat, *Texas by Terán*, 75–76. See also Ewers and Leclerq, *Indians of Texas*, 103–6.

101. The Talon brothers are quoted in Weddle, *LaSalle: Three Primary Sources*, 232–33 and 280–87. Casañas is quoted in Hatcher, "Descriptions of the Tejas," part 1 (January 1927): 211.

102. Olmsted, *Journey through Texas*, 86.

103. See the Spanish language survey field notes for the Juan Jose De Los Reyes grant (Trinity County Abstract 33 and Houston County Abstract 73) in the GLO files. Jordan, *Trails to Texas*, 108–9.

104. Jackson and Wheat, *Texas by Terán*, 128.

105. Three Neches River creeks just downstream from Boggy Slough are named Alabama, Biloxi, and Shawnee. There is also Shawnee Prairie in Angelina County, and several creeks across Texas are named Kickapoo. Cherokee County is named for the Cherokees. Pophers Creek, a tributary of the Angelina River, is named for a Shawnee chief. Effie Boon, "The History of Angelina County" (master's thesis, University of Texas, 1937), 36–38. The Pophers Series and the Ozias-Pophers Complex make up 26 percent of the BSCA.

106. Jackson and Wheat, *Texas by Terán*, 80.

Chapter 3. A Land of Production

1. "The Hap's Page, Club Talk," *Houston Post*, April 28, 1912, p. 43; Audrey Barrett Cook, "Margaret Hadley Foster," *Handbook of Texas Online*, https://www.tshaonline.org/handbook/entries/foster-margaret-hadley accessed March 30, 2018.

2. Former Temple-Inland forester Stan Cook met one of the Christie daughters in the 1980s at a Mount Pisgah Cemetery homecoming. She showed him the site of her family's homestead, "the Christie Place," and told him of the open hills and views across the slough and river. Charlie Harber, whose family lived as tenants of Southern Pine Lumber Company in the former house of Doc Franklin (an uncle of the Christie girls, who lived just west of the Christie home) during the 1920s, also told of the once-open views from the hilltops, during site visits with Jonathan Gerland in 2000. The location of the Christie family home, as shown to Stan Cook, is verified by Trinity County Deed Records, Trinity County Courthouse Annex, Groveton (hereafter TCCA), vol. 36, pp. 578–81. Crape myrtles, ornamental chinaberry trees, and several red elms remained at the home place site in 2018. Nineteenth-century land surveyors cited several three-inch- and four-inch-diameter mayhaws along Franklin Slough.

3. "The Hap's Page," *Houston Post*, September 15, 1912, p. 45; March 9, 1913, p. 66; and April 13, p. 64.

4. The author's correspondence with Christie family members during 2019, author's collection.

5. Evie's letter was published in the *Houston Post*, September 15, 1912, p. 45; two of Eunice's letters were published on March 9 (p. 66) and April 13, 1913 (p. 64). Lara's letter also appeared on April 13, 1913, p. 64. Two of the Mount Pisgah teachers named were Miss Dot Payne and Sam Russell. Information about membership in the Happyhammers Club was provided regularly in the long-running column. For instance see "Our Young Folks: The Club," *Houston Post*, November 3, 1901, p. 33, and "The Hap's Page: The Club," *Houston Post*, April 7, 1907, p. 41.

6. Williams, "Ideas of Nature," 76; Williams, *Country and the City*, 3; Doughty, *At Home in Texas*, 9.

7. The Sullivan and Christie home places were in the following surveys: the south end of S. D. Sullivan (Houston County Abstract 949), L. A. Sullivan (Houston Abstract 1007), eastern L. Price (Houston Abstract 840 and Trinity Abstract 477), and parts of IGN (Houston Abstract 614 and Trinity Abstract 869). Several spring branches were noted in these and surrounding tracts, in Southern Pine Lumber Company resurveys recorded in Southern Pine Lumber Company Land Rec-

ords, Houston County and Trinity County volumes (1993:015), The History Center, Diboll.

8. The Christie place was located at the southwest corner of the Lazarus Price survey; Caddo pottery in a single shovel test was found at the eastern end of the survey on a slight bluff at the head of Franklin Slough. Tom Middlebrook, Stan Cook, and Jonathan Gerland made the shovel test on February 9, 2018.

9. US Census population schedules, 1850–1920. Tippah County Historical and Genealogical Society, *History of Tippah County*, 8–13.

10. Odum, *Ecology*, 286.

11. Several stone footings remain at some of the old homesites, such as a large rectangular stone at the Franklin place and several stones around the Christie place and along nearby creeks, but modern mechanical forestry work, including road maintenance activities, have disturbed all of these sites, based on the author's observations and experiences.

12. Robin W. Doughty, "Settlement and Environmental Change in Texas, 1820–1900," *Southwestern Historical Quarterly* 89, no. 4 (1986): 423–42; Cronon, *Changes in the Land*, 33, 51–53.

13. Doughty, "Settlement and Environmental Change, 423–42; Cronon, *Changes in the Land*, 19–33, 51–53; Roberts, *A Description of Texas,* i, 21–22 ("gladdened" quote on 22), 37–38, 60, 122; Rankin, *Texas in 1850*, 23–24; J. B. Brosius, "Cut-Over Problems That Must Be Solved," *Cut-Over Lands*, October 1918, p. 6 ("ambition" quote).

14. For example, see entries for February 27 and 28, 1841, and February 23 and 27, 1843, in Sterne and McDonald, *Hurrah for Texas*, 30, 143–44.

15. Sargent, *Report on the Forests*, 492.

16. Foster, Krausz, and Johnson, *Forest Resources of Eastern Texas*, 25, 52.

17. "Grazing and Forest Fires," *Lufkin Daily News*, December 5, 1917.

18. Letter, Watson Walker to T. L. L. Temple, March 9, 1925, in Temple Lumber Company Records at the East Texas Research Center, Nacogdoches (hereafter ETRC), box 42, folder 7.

19. Pyne, *Fire in America*, 151. Pyne's chapter on fire history of the South is on pages 143–60.

20. For instance, see the surveys to seven tracts in Trinity County Deed Records, TCCA, vol. 32, pp. 229–32. One "burnt out" pine stump was ten feet high and 24 inches in diameter. Sixteen "field fences" were also mentioned.

21. Stoddard, "Use of Fire," 33–35; Pyne, *Fire in America*, 71–83, 131–49; Sitton, *Backwoodsmen*, 240–41; Stanturf et al., "Fire in Southern Forest Landscapes," 609–10. The boll weevil, from Mexico, had reached Trinity and Houston Counties in 1901. See "Distribution of Boll Weevil," *Galveston Daily News*, July 26, 1904, p. 10; "Condition of Crop," July 26, 1904, pp. 10–11; Albert E. Cowdrey, *This Land, This South*, 110–11, 127–31.

22. Roberts, *Description of Texas*, 76–77.

23. McKitrick, *Public Land System of Texas*. For Mexican views toward land usage during colonization, see article 6 of the Imperial Colonization Law of 1823, article 12 of the 1824 National Colonization Law, article 12 of the 1825 State Colonization Law, and article 10 of the 1825 Instructions to Land Commissioners, in Kimball, *Laws and Decrees*.

24. Mexican surveys were Reyes (Trinity A-33/Houston A-73) and Sanchez (Trinity A-39). Republic of Texas grants included Walker (Trinity A-640), Williams (Trinity A-438), and Hampton (A-259). The saline prairies were documented in Dumble, *Geology of East Texas*, 313. See also Odom, *Over on Cochino*, 23.

25. The survey name is McKinney & Williams (Trinity A-450/Houston A-770). Scrip was authorized in 1857 and the survey was made in 1860.

26. These were Minton (Trinity A-934) and Martin (Trinity A-953), General Land Office (hereafter GLO) files, Austin Texas. See also Alston (Scrip 593 and School Land Files 118590 and 131493), GLO.

27. Candido Sanchez survey, Trinity County A-39, GLO, box 51, folder 4, no. 3436, English translation. For Sanchez' league, surveyors set one post and utilized three post oaks, three pines, and two cedars in marking corners, witness, and bearing trees.

28. Jose De Los Reyes Survey Notes, Trinity County Abstract 33 and Houston County Abstract 73, GLO. For Reyes's Cochino Bayou league, surveyors set two

posts and used four red oaks, two blackjacks, one post oak, and one hickory for corners, witness, and bearing trees. The Reyes survey conflicted with the overlapping Sepulveda survey, which included the confluence of Bristow Creek with Cochino Bayou.

29. Dumble, *Geology of East Texas*, 313.

30. In the 1950s, Southern Pine Lumber Company erected a protective fence made from the heavy-gauge railroad T-rails. Memories persist of seeing other burials near the marked Johnson gravesite, but efforts by the author and Charlie Harber to locate them in 2000 were unsuccessful. See "Boggy Slough Burial Plot," at www.rootsweb.ancestry.com/~txtrinit/cemetery/boggy.html, accessed December 21, 2016.

31. Rocky Crossing is identified in surveys and testimonies recorded between 1910 and 1929 contained within Trinity County School File 118590 at the General Land Office archives in Austin, accessed by the author in 2016. One of the surveys is also recorded in Southern Pine Lumber Company Land Records, The History Center, Diboll, (1993:015), Trinity County volume, under the "A" tab for Alston. Since the 1960s, a diesel-powered water pump just below Rocky Crossing transfers water seasonally from the river up and over the land ridge to Black Cat Lake. A permit from the Texas Water Rights Commission, dated July 5, 1966, is contained in Trinity County Deed Records, TCCA, vol. 177, p. 254.

32. See the map by Florencio Galli, titled *Texas*, published in Mexico by Claudio Linati in 1826, known as the "Galli Map of Texas," at the Dolph Briscoe Center for American History, Austin, Texas. The map shows the road, or trail, crossing through the Bidai tribes on the west side of the Trinity River in a more or less direct line from Nacogdoches to La Bahia on the San Antonio River. In early Angelina County deed records, the road is known as "King's Highway," not to be confused with the better known El Camino Real, to the north, which State Highway 21 generally follows in places. A map that shows "King's Highway" in about 1900 is identified as "Exhibit A, Plat of Portion of Vicente Michelli Grant in Angelina County, Texas, Showing Land Owned by Tyler Building and Loan Association," in Angelina County Deed Records, Angelina County Courthouse (hereafter ACC), vol. G, pp. 366–67. A map from 1868, in the General Land Office at Austin, shows the trail passing through the Sanchez survey in Trinity County. See C. O. Stremme, *Houston County* (Austin: General Land Office, 1868).

33. The different routes of the road are shown in Texas Highway Department engineering division maps made during the 1920s and 1930s (accessed by the author at the TxDOT engineering offices at Lufkin in 2014), in a US Geological Survey 7.5 Minute map made in 1951 (Wells SW Quadrant), and in photographs made by the Tobin Aerial Survey Company in 1933 (access provided to the author by Acorn Forestry Services, of Lufkin, in 2014).

34. "Map of Yard at Neff, November 1909," in Texas Southeastern Railroad Records (1993:022) box 1, folder 19, at The History Center, Diboll.

35. Sanchez's wife was Encarnacion Flores. Land Deed from Candido Sanchez to H. L. Wiggins, Shelby County, Republic of Texas, August 13, 1839, copy on file in Trinity County Deed Records, TCCA, vol. A, p. 258; 1850 US Federal Census, Sabine Parish, Louisiana, Roll M432_239, page 116B, line 15.

36. Land Deed from H. L. Wiggins to W. H. Cunningham, Lafayette Parish, Louisiana, November 13, 1866, copy on file in Trinity County Deed Records, TCCA, vol. A, p. 259.

37. *Map of the Candido Sanchez, Guadalupe Ricardo, and Jose M. Gomez Leagues, Trinity County*, Henry Raguet Map Collection, box 1207/5, Briscoe Center for American History, Austin; Trinity County Deed Records, TCCA, vol. A, 316–19; vol. L, 166–67. See early tax rolls of Houston County concerning Cedar Creek preemptions.

38. Juan Jose de los Reyes to Juan de los Santos Coy, Trinity County Deed Records, TCCA, vol. Z, 602–7; see also 599–600. Author's emailed communications with Brian Stauffer of the Texas General Land Office, March 2018, author's possession.

39. See especially the deed from Juan de los Santos Coy to H. B. Fall, dated October 13, 1902, in Trinity County Deed vol. Z, 599–600, and Trinity County District Court Minutes L, 168. Liz Holcomb of Trinity County Abstract Company graciously granted the author full access to the abstract of title card files for all of the Trinity County lands, including the Reyes survey, during 2016 and 2017.

40. Walker's grant was a Houston First Class Headright, filed as Trinity County A-640. The GLO records for Trinity A-640 contain survey field notes for the Walker survey, as does GLO Houston County (later Trinity) Scrip File 593 (W. W. Alston), which contains an October 1886 map that shows land features such as swamps, upland oak and pine timber, and Boggy Slough Island. See also Trinity County Deed Records, TCCA, vol. 125, pp. 471–73.

41. See especially affidavits and title transfers in Trinity County Deed Records, TCCA, vol. D, 464–65; vol. G, 322–23; vol. R, 402–3; vol. U, 596; vol. 27, pp. 105–9; vol. 42, pp. 355–56; vol. 44, pp. 306–11; vol. 66, pp. 106–7, vol. 78, pp. 332–33. Liz Holcomb of Trinity County Abstract Company in Groveton maintains abstract of title card files for the Walker survey, which were used by the author.

42. Trinity County Deed Records, TCCA, vol. 41, pp. 54–57; vol. 45, pp. 179–81; vol. 46, pp. 341–46.

43. Affidavit of W. H. Womack, no. 679, April 2, 1909, in Trinity County Deed Records, TCCA, vol. 125, pp. 475–81; James Britton family tree at Ancestry.com.

44. Britton, Allen, and Rose families in the 1860 Trinity County, Texas, US Population Census, stamped page 318, lines 13–35.

45. The April 1863 deed from the Walkers to Timothy Britton mentions an adjoining tract was earlier sold to Lidia Britton, but no other details can be found. See Trinity County Deed Records, TCCA, vol. 27, pp. 105–9. In the Trinity County tax rolls for 1866, T. P. Britton rendered 320 acres of the J. M. Walker survey, presumably the tract he purchased in 1863.

46. US Federal Census, 1860, Agricultural Schedule, Trinity County, Texas, names of Lidia Britton, James Allen, and John Rose, T1134, roll 6, page 5, lines 31–33. Some of the wetland prairies, meadows, and natural marshes along the pipeline near Britton Slough were converted to flood-controlled duck hunting marshes in the 1930s and remain so today, with extensive earthen dams and connecting ditches and canals. Cherokee sedge, maidencane, and eastern gamagrass, still abundant today, probably dominated the area 160 years ago. Keith, *Plant Community and Fuel Model Assessment*.

47. US Federal Census, 1860, Population and Agricultural Schedules, Trinity County, Texas.

48. US Federal Census, 1860, Agricultural Schedule, Trinity County, Texas, names of Lidia Britton, James Allen, and John Rose, T1134, roll 6, page 5, lines 31–33.

49. See the James P. Henderson family in the Cherokee County Census for the years 1850 and 1860. He and his wife Sarah were natives of Tennessee; most of their children were born in Alabama.

50. Affadavit No. 683, J. M. Steel in the heirship of Timothy P. Britton, April 2, 1909, Trinity County Deed Records, TCCA, vol. 125, pp. 481–82.

51. Affadavit No. 679, W. H. Womack to the Public, April 2, 1909, taken before R. E. Minton, Trinity County Deed Records, TCCA, vol. 125, pp. 475–76.

52. Bowles, *History of Trinity County*, 32–36.

53. Owen, *Portrait and Biographical Record*, 336–37. The other Britton and Rose family members can be found in the 1870 census for DeWitt and Lavaca Counties, Texas, National Archives, Washington, DC.

54. Household of Charles W. Britton in Erath County, Texas, US Census for 1880, ED 153, stamped page 75A, lines 40–48.

55. Affadavit No. 683, J. M. Steel in the heirship of Timothy P. Britton, April 2, 1909, Trinity County Deed Records, TCCA, vol. 125, pp. 481–82; Trinity County Deed Records, TCCA, vol. 27, pp. 107–9 and vol. 33, p. 318.

56. The peak is shown on USGS topographic maps as having an elevation of 215 feet at approximately 31 degrees, 19.545 minutes north, and 94 degrees, 56.463 minutes west. The author last made observations of the hill in February 2018. Tobin Aerial Photography of all the Boggy Slough property was provided by Acorn Forestry Services, Lufkin, Texas, in 2016.

57. Land resurveys made by Southern Pine Lumber Company in the early 1910s as well as aerial photography from 1933 identify the "places" of the settlers and their cleared fields. By overlaying this imagery with modern soil surveys of the USDA, it is clear that most areas settled in North Boggy are identified today as "prime farmland."

58. De Cordova, *Texas*, 8.

59. Roberts, *Description of Texas*, 21.

60. "Camp Big Thicket, Life in the Piney Woods in Eastern Texas: A Graphically Written and Interesting Letter," *Sunny South*, November 5, 1887, p. 1. This article is perhaps most easily accessed in Francis E. Abernethy, *Tales from the Big Thicket*.

61. US Census population records for Houston and Trinity Counties, 1850–1940; GLO records of Trinity and Houston Counties; deed records of Houston and Trinity Counties; Southern Pine Lumber Company Land Record, volumes for Houston and Trinity Counties (1993:015), The History Center, Diboll; John Solomon Otto, "The Migration of the Southern Plain Folk: An Interdisciplinary Synthesis," *Journal of Southern History* 51, no. 2 (1985): 183–200.

62. Tax rolls of Houston and Trinity Counties, 1846–1910 and 1920, microfilm at the Texas State Library & Archives Genealogy Section, Austin, and at The History Center, Diboll; US Census Records, Population Schedules, 1850–1940; Agriculture Schedules, 1860–1880; Products of Industry and Manufactures Schedules, 1850–1880; Spaight, *Resources, Soil, and Climate*, 153–55, 311–12; Foster and Rozek, *Forgotten Texas Census*, 110–12, 217–18; Jeffrey Abt and Leabeth Abt, "Documents: The Gardening Sentiments of an Early Texas Pioneer," *East Texas Historical Journal* 29, no. 1 (1991): 63–70. Some pear trees still survived at some of Boggy Slough's old home places early in the 2000s.

63. A good explanation and description of split rail fencing is Todd Waterman, "Rail Fences: Their History and Construction," *Bittersweet* 9, no. 1 (1981): 4–15.

64. See especially the population schedules in the census records for Trinity County, precinct 4, in 1900 and 1910, including the names of Henry L. Christie, Doc Durham, Charlie Rushing, multiple Luces and Tiners. Dock Franklin, namesake of Franklin Slough, had for immediate neighbors the families of Henry Lafayette Christie, Charlie E. Rushing Sr., Thomas Luce, and William H. Tiner. Franklin's daughter Sarintha Ella (by his first wife, Altamira Hutson), married Samuel T. Sullivan, and another daughter, Mary Eliza, married Albert L. Moore, whose mother, Elizabeth Fannie, served as Druso's postmistress. After the death of Altamira, Franklin married Josephine Christie, and one of their sons married Lula Mae Tiner. See "Franklin, D. R., 'Uncle Doc'" in Hensley, Hensley, and Trinity County Book Committee, *Trinity County*

Beginnings, 358. The Tiner, Luce, Rushing, Franklin, and Christie families can be found in the 1900 Trinity County Census, Precinct 4, Enumeration District 98, page 17B.

65. Carter and Kocher, "Soil Survey of Houston County," 537–65. The author compared the 1905 soil survey with historic and recent topographical maps and imagery provided by Acorn Forestry Services of Lufkin and Raven Environmental Services of Huntsville.

66. The 1860 census "slave schedule" shows S. D. Sullivan owned one mulatto slave, age thirty. A Sullivan family history says Sullivan owned "slaves" at the time he moved to Texas, but sold them before moving to Houston County. See Slave Schedules, 1860 Census, Texas, Houston County, beat 3, page 17, column 2, line 39, and "John Calvin Sullivan," in Houston County Historical Commission, *History of Houston County*, 593–94.

67. "Mississippi and Pacific Railroad," in *Handbook of Texas Online*, https://www.tshaonline.org/handbook/entries/mississippi-and-pacific-railroad, accessed May 29, 2019.

68. S. D. Sullivan family in the 1850 Cherokee County Census and the 1860 Houston County Census; "John Calvin Sullivan," in Houston County Historical Commission, *History of Houston County*, 593–94; Affidavit of Samuel D. Sullivan, August 6, 1857, in Memorials and Petitions, Texas State Archives, Austin.

69. The preemption claim and surveyor's notes files are found in GLO. See Samuel D. Sullivan (Houston County A-949), C. W. Tier (Houston County A-1041), and L. Price (Houston County A-840 and Trinity County A-477).

70. The name Price's Crossing appeared in early land records, including field notes for Samuel Cheatham's 1848 survey that actually embraced the crossing. See GLO survey records, Elisha Price (Angelina A-503) and Samuel Cheatham (Angelina A-155). See also John Watson survey (Angelina A-648), which mentions Price's Ferry in 1859.

71. Curtis W. Tier family in the 1860 US Census population schedule, Houston County, Texas.

72. Lazarus Price genealogy on Ancestry.com, accessed in 2018; Lazarus Price survey (Trinity County A-477 and Houston County A-840), GLO.

73. Louis Winters Abstract A-730 Trinity County was originally surveyed for James Tier, who as a Confederate soldier died during the Civil War. Winters began occupying the land in 1875 and adopted the preemption in 1881. See files for L. Winters, Trinity County survey A-730, GLO.

74. Lazarus Price's military record in *Compiled Service Records of Confederate Soldiers Who Served in Organizations from the State of Texas,* National Archives Record Group 109, National Archives, Washington, DC. Lazarus's widow Lucinda was found residing in the household of her father Curtis Tier in the 1870 Hopkins County Census, Population Schedule, on stamped page 113, in the Black Oak post office region.

75. GLO files for Zebulon Oliver (Houston County A-803) and Hiram Luce (Houston County A-703); Southern Pine Lumber Company Land Records (1993:015), Volume Houston County, pages for C. W. Tier and Z. Oliver; Houston County Deed Records, Houston County Courthouse (hereafter HCC), vol. 39, p. 634; vol. 97, p. 10; vol. 96, p. 429; vol. 100, p. 22; and vol. 103, p. 71. The Tier survey was cited for delinquent taxes and unknown ownership in the *Crockett Courier,* March 3, 1893, p. 2.

76. Doc Franklin married Josephine "Ginnie" Christie as his second wife, a sister of Henry Lafayette Christie. Hensley, *Trinity County Beginnings,* 358.

77. Bonnie Smith Gayle, "John Calvin Sullivan," in Houston County Historical Commission, *History of Houston County,* 593–94.

78. Cravens, *History of Three Ghost Towns;* Cravens, *Between Two Rivers;* entries for each community in the *Handbook of Texas Online,* https://www.tshaonline.org/handbook.

79. Henry W. Payne's twenty-horsepower steam sawmill was located on Cochino Bayou, according to the 1880 Special Census, Schedules 5 and 6, Manufactures, Lumber Mills and Saw-Mills, Houston County, Texas, Microfilm T1134, roll 48, line 1.

80. William H. Bonner's sawmill was enumerated in the 1880 Special Census, Schedules 5 and 6, Manufactures, Lumber Mills and Saw-Mills, Angelina County, Texas, Microfilm T1134, roll 47, line 1, and it appeared in the Angelina County tax rolls for 1877, along with timberlands in the Sarah Underwood, J. B. Hardin, and J. Benton surveys. According to the 1880 census, the mill operation then employed seven workers. The place of Bonner's Mills appeared on *Gray's New Map of Texas and Indian Territory* (Philadelphia: O. W. Gray & Son, 1876). See also Haltom, *History and Description.*

81. "Examination from the Mouth of the Neches River, Texas, to Shooks Bluff," in *Annual Report of the Chief of Engineers, United States Army, to the Secretary of War, for the Year 1893, in Six Parts, Part 3, House of Representatives, 53rd Congress, 2nd Session, Ex. Doc. 1, Part 2, Vol. 2* (Washington: Government Printing Office, 1893): 1853–55. Insurance rates for shipping on the Neches River were given regularly by Beaumont newspapers of the day. See the holdings of Tyrrell Historical Library, Beaumont, especially the *Neches Valley News* and *Beaumont News-Beacon* issues from 1872 and 1873.

82. S. D. Sullivan is buried in a small neglected cemetery in the Davy Crockett National Forest, about one and one-quarter miles northwest of the North Boggy northwest boundary, about 75 yards east of a grove of large cedars near the end of Forest Road 561, just north of Highway 7 and south of Conner Creek and west of Forest Road 511. The cemetery is located in the Wm. Conner survey (Abstract 238), near a small stream channel that flows into Conner Creek, and is known as Kilgore Cemetery for the several Kilgore family burials also there. The author located the Sullivan and Kilgore graves in June 2018. *Crockett Courier,* February 21, 1890, p. 3, and February 12, 1892, p. 3; *Texas Almanac for 1873,* p. 65; Bonnie Smith Gayle, "John Calvin Sullivan," in Houston County Historical Commission, *History of Houston County,* 593–94; Aldrich, *History of Houston County,* 35–36.

83. After the establishment of Lufkin in 1882, the "Lufkin & Sullivan Ferry Road" in Angelina County, the "Sullivan Ferry & Crockett Road" in Houston County, and the "Sullivan Ferry & Centralia Road" in Trinity County connected the county seats of Lufkin, Crockett, and Groveton. These roads and communities are shown in Cram, *Cram's Railroad and Township Map; Texas Almanac for 1873,* 65; Charles W. Pressler and A. B. Langermann, *Map of the State of Texas* (Austin: General Land Office, 1879), map number 16973, General Land Office; P. A. McCarthy, *Angelina County, Texas, Good Road System No. 233 (1919) Revised,* reprinted on p. 44 of Lufkin Genealogical and Historical

Society, *History of Angelina County*; *Angelina County [Map Showing School District and Commissioner Precinct Boundaries], Drawn By J. F. Davis, Lufkin, Tex., February 28, 1924*, Accession No. 2001:006, Map No. 384, The History Center, Diboll; *McCarthy's Map of Angelina County, Texas* (Lufkin: P. A. McCarthy & Son, 1904), Accession No. 2001:030, Map No. 385, The History Center, Diboll; I&GN Railroad Survey Sections 22, 23, 24, 25, 26, 47, and 59 in Southern Pine Lumber Company Land Records, volumes for Houston and Trinity Counties (1993:015), The History Center, Diboll; "Observations from the Saddle," *Dallas Morning News*, August 15, 1899, p. 5; Carter and Kocher, "Soil Survey of Houston County," 537–65.

84. Although a few map producers of the time incorrectly labeled the Houston County post office as "Texla," the manuscript records of the US Post Office confirm the name as "Tesla." Texla, located in northern Orange County, Texas, near Louisiana, was the name of a post office and sawmill town there, beginning in 1906. The Tesla post office closed in 1910, while the Texla post office closed in 1929.

85. For example, see the death certificate of Laura Alice (Sullivan) Christie, January 28, 1939, Trinity County No. 70190. "Pisgah Cemetery," *Houston County Cemeteries*, 3d ed., 688–90; J. W. Wilkins, "Pisgah Cemetery," *Records of East Texas* 6, no. 1 (1971): 16–17.

86. Ainsworth and Rudloff, *Crossing over Cochino*, 180.

87. The author recorded the location of the Luce Cemetery on June 18, 2014, as north 31 degrees, 22 minutes, 49.8 seconds, and west 95 degrees, 1 minute, and 44.7 seconds.

88. Trinity County tax rolls, 1900; Roberts, *Description of Texas*, 117.

89. Carlson, in *Texas Woollybacks* (68) states that the sheep raised in East Texas during this time "were of a mean quality when compared to those of New England. They were of several varieties and mixed. Most of them had a little Merino blood." S. D. Sullivan rendered sixty sheep, and his son C. B. Sullivan rendered seventeen sheep for taxation in Houston County in 1870. A few persons raised sheep into the 1900s, such as the Brocks, who rendered eighteen sheep on the Reyes survey in 1900. See Trinity and Houston County tax rolls, 1860–1910.

90. Terry G. Jordan, "The Origin of Anglo-American Cattle Ranching in Texas: A Documentation of Diffusion from the Lower South," *Economic Geography* 45, no. 1 (1969): 76–77; Jordan, *Trails to Texas*.

91. *Texas State Highway Department Points of General and Historical Interest in Division No. 11* (Lufkin: Texas Highway Department, 1936).

92. See records pertaining to the Reyes survey and surveys of Cochino Bayou in the General Land Office archives, Austin. Jordan, *Trails to Texas*, 108–9.

93. De Cordova, *Texas*, 27–28.

94. Williams, *Americans and Their Forests*, 67–68; McWhiney, *Cracker Culture*, 52–53.

95. Roberts, *Description of Texas*, 120–21; Cronon, *Changes in the Land*, 129; Cronon, *Nature's Metropolis*, 226–27; Williams, *Americans and Their Forests*, 67–68; McWhiney, *Cracker Culture*, 52–53.

96. "Rattlesnake and Its Congeners," *Harper's New Monthly Magazine* 10, no. 58 (1855): 470–83.

97. Cronon, *Nature's Metropolis*, 226–27.

98. "Fences," in Williamson S. Oldham and George W. White, *A Digest of the General Statute Laws of the State of Texas* (Austin: State Gazette, 1859), 217–18; Steven Hahn, "Hunting, Fishing, and Foraging: Common Rights and Class Relations in the Postbellum South," *Radical History Review* 26 (1982): 37–64.

99. F. V. Emerson, "The Southern Long-Leaf Pine Belt," *Geographical Review* 7, no. 2 (1919): 89; Lara Christie, "Druso, Texas—Dear Happyhammers," *Houston Post*, April 13, 1913, p. 64.

100. Tax rolls for Trinity and Houston Counties, 1900–1920, microfilm, Texas State Archives, Austin.

101. Trinity County tax rolls, 1910, microfilm, Texas State Archives, Austin.

102. Truett and Lay, *Land of Bears and Honey*.

103. Holley, *Texas*, 95, 99.

104. Houston County Historical Commission, *History of Houston County*, 593–94; Lay, "Bottomland Hardwoods in East Texas," 20–21.

105. Williams, *American and Their Forests*, 94–95; Brown, *Timber Products and Industries*, 199–217.

106. Block, *East Texas Mill Towns*, 135–50; "Western Coal and Lumber Resources, as Exemplified by the Coal Mining and Lumber Manufacturing Departments of the Central Coal and Coke Company of Kansas City, Mo.," *American Lumberman*, November 1, 1902, copy at the Texas Forestry Museum, Lufkin; Thomas D. Isern and Raymond Wilson, "Lone Star: The Thompson Timber Interests of Texas," *Red River Valley Historical Review* 6, no. 4 (1981): 31.

107. C. B. Sullivan and his wife Lizzie accepted forty cents per acre for their timber. See Houston County Deed Records, HCC, vol. 34, pp. 116. For other timber deed transactions between Abe Harris & Company and North Boggy families, see Houston County Deed Records, HCC, vol. 31, p. 380, and vol. 34, pp. 112–15; and Trinity County Deed Records, TCCA, vol. 27, pp. 102–3; vol. 28, pp. 446–47; vol. 36, pp. 578–81.

108. For the firm of Abe Harris & Company, see "Abraham Harris Dies at Home in New York," *Jewish Monitor* (Dallas, Texas), November 14, 1919, p. 3. See also Abraham Harris in the census records for Cherokee County 1880 and Smith County 1900; his wife Fannie Lipsitz and her father Joseph and brother Louis in the 1880 Smith County census; and other genealogical information in "Declarations of Intentions to Become Citizens," in *East Texas Family Records* 10, no. 3 (Tyler: East Texas Genealogical Society, 1986): 29. See also entries for Durham Transportation Company and Pollok & Angelina Valley Transportation Company in *The Official Guide of the Railways* (New York: National Railway Publication Co., January 1907).

109. "Automobiles in Houston County," *Crockett Courier*, April 23, 1914; Ainsworth and Rudloff, *Crossing over Cochino*, 180. Odom, *Over on Cochino*, 21–29, devotes a whole chapter to Albert Moore, some of it speculation.

110. The train wreck occurred 17 miles from Lufkin, between the Pine Island and Druso stations. One of the children who died was named Marrs. The track foreman's name was Kramer. See "Disastrous Wreck on the Eastern Texas," *Austin American-Statesman*, July 17, 1904, p. 1; "Fatality in Train Wreck," *Dallas Morning News*, July 17, 1904, p. 2; "Two Killed" and "Another Fatality," *Shiner Gazette*, July 20, 1904, p. 2; Eastern Texas Railroad Time Table, May 14, 1907.

111. "Kennard Doctor Killed," *Houston Post*, July 5, 1918, p. 11. The doctor was identified as Dr. Smith, the mill superintendent as Mr. Rudd, and the other person as Mr. Ferris.

112. Classified ads, *Houston Post*, April 9, 1909, p. 12; "Finishes Docket: Railroad Commission Completes Hearings and Adjourns," *Austin American-Statesman*, June 14, 1911, p. 4.

113. US Census Population Schedules, Trinity and Houston counties, 1900 and 1910.

114. Four-page letter, E. C. Durham to T. L. L. Temple, September 4, 1916, ETRC, box 18a, folder 6. To Durham, "Cracker's Bend" was a generic place name as well as a specific reference to North Boggy's Sullivan's Bluff community, which had been earlier identified as Cracker's Bend by the editor of the *Crockett Courier*. Even one of the Rushing family members, who came from Boggy Slough to work on the ranch, called his neighbors "hay seeders." See interview of Jim Rushing (90a), January 13, 1986, at The History Center, Diboll.

115. Forrest McDonald and Grady McWhiney, "The Antebellum Southern Herdsman: A Reinterpretation," *Journal of Southern History* 41, no. 2 (1975): 153. One of Aiken's earliest mentions of "Cracker's Bend" was in 1897, when the *Courier* reported that three members of the Sullivan family, along with representatives of the Durham, Oliver, and Jordan families, "rode 32 miles from Cracker's Bend to appear before the grand jury and found it had been adjourned." See a transcript of *Crockett Courier*, October 22, 1897, in Crook and Brem, *Houston County, Texas*, vol. 2, p. 234. For editor Aiken's explanation of the name, see "Another Tragedy in a Houston County Feud," *Crockett Courier*, November 20, 1913, p. 1. Aiken also included the community of Hagerville in his definition of "Crackers' Bend."

116. "Sawmill Race Troubles—A Fighting Mill Man," *Southern Industrial and Lumber Review*, October 1908, p. 40. The article further told of law officers who stood by black woods workers of the Carter-Kelley Lumber Company, protecting them near the town of Manning in Angelina County, and of an armed R. W. Wier Lumber Company official who protected black workers logging a mill in Orange County.

117. Oral histories of Charlie Harber, as told to Thad Sitton in 1992, tell of black railroad workers being

murdered in the Cochino Creek bottoms in about 1900 or 1901, but the stories cannot be substantiated. The audio cassette interviews are at the East Texas Research Center, Stephen F. Austin State University. Charlie Harber told Jonathan Gerland similar stories in 2000.

118. Sadie Estes Woods, Interview 40a, July 18, 1984, with Megan Lambert and Marie Davis, The History Center, Diboll. The interview confuses Anderson Crossing with Walkerton. The distance between Walkerton and Mount Pisgah was about a mile and a half, the same distance that Woods verifies she walked to school. The sites of Walkerton and Mount Pisgah remain within the northwestern corner of the BSCA today. Modern roads follow the former railroad and wagon roads between Walkerton and Mount Pisgah, which would have been the approximate routes traveled between the two places.

119. "District Court," *Crockett Courier*, November 6, 1913.

120. "Killing at Diboll Front," *Crockett Courier*, February 12, 1914.

121. "Stubblefield Schoolhouse Killing," *Crockett Courier*, August 27, 1914, p. 1; Hyde, "Backcountry Justice," 228–49.

122. The traditional tales of the feud are Odom, *Over on Cochino*, 87–88; Mary Means Sullivan, "The Sullivan Family Feud," in Abernethy, Lincecum, and Vick, *Family Saga*, 170–72; Leon Hale, "A Sad Story in an Old Graveyard," *Houston Post*, June 24, 1977, p. 3E; and Ainsworth and Rudloff, *Crossing over Cochino*, 181.

123. Jessie and her sister Bessie were one set of twins.

124. *Crockett Courier*, November 21, 1912, p. 1, and November 28, 1912, p. 1; "State of Texas vs. Audie and Jewel Christie, Case No. 7512," in *Houston County District Court Records, Criminal Minutes*, vol. 6, pp. 87, 99; vol. 2, p. 189; vol. 5, p. 490; and vol. D, 260.

125. Accounts of the shooting and court proceedings are in several issues of the *Crockett Courier*. See especially the issues of November 20, 27, and December 11, 1913; and March 28, April 4, 23, October 15, and November 5, 12, and 19, 1914. Newspapers across the state carried similar stories, for example, see "Boy Admits to Killing Man and Two Sons," *Austin American-Statesman*, November 20, 1913, p. 1; also, in the *Lufkin Daily News*, "The Tragedy," November 12, 1913, p. 1, and "Still in Jail," December 2, 1913, p. 1. Issues of the Crockett Courier during 1913 incorrectly printed Carr Durham's name as Coll.

126. "Another Tragedy in a Houston County Feud," *Crockett Courier*, November 20, 1913, p. 1.

127. *Crockett Courier*, November 12 and 19, 1914, p. 1.

128. Hale, "Sad Story," *Houston Post*, 3E.

129. Trinity County Deed Records, TCCA, vol. 94, pp. 573–75; Two letters, Kenley to Ratcliff State Bank, October 1 and December 16, 1918, both copied to Laura Christie, in ETRC, box 20, folder 10.

130. US Census Population Schedules, Trinity, Houston, and Polk Counties, 1920 and 1930. Simon Jackson Smith's World War I draft registration card showed that he was employed by Southern Pine Lumber Company at Rayville in 1917. US Selective Service System, World War I Draft Cards, National Archives, M1509, Roll 1983696, Trinity County, Texas.

131. Texas Death Certificate, Trinity County No. 70190, Laura Alice Christie, January 28, 1939, Texas Department of Health, Bureau of Vital Statistics, Austin.

132. US Census Records Population Schedules, Texas and Oklahoma, 1910–1940, National Archives, Washington, DC; Audie Christie Family Charts on Ancestry.com, accessed in 2017 and 2018, and author's correspondence with family members, author's possession.

133. Deed Records, Trinity and Houston Counties, 1910–1930; Southern Pine Lumber Company Land Records (1993:015), volumes for Trinity and Houston Counties, The History Center, Diboll.

134. The 1858 red elm, 16 inches in diameter, was mentioned near the southwest corner of the Lazarus Price survey and the northwest corner of the Louis Winters survey, which was originally surveyed for James Tier, Lazarus Price's brother-in-law. See the L. Winters (Trinity A-730) survey field notes of George Gibson, on June 3, 1858, at the General Land Office, Austin.

135. Peattie, *Natural History of Trees*, 243; Rutkow, *American Canopy*, 218. The quote is from a publication cited by Peattie, although similar expressions were shared with the author during 2018 by Greg Grant, Stan Cook, and Larry Shelton, all of Nacogdoches

County. In emails exchanged with Greg Grant during June 2018, Grant said he was raised to call elms, "piss ellums."

136. Stahl and McElvaney, *Trees of Texas*, 51–52; American Forestry Association, *American Elm*, 3–7.

137. Charles S. Sargent, "The American Elm," *Garden and Forest*, June 11, 1890, p. 281.

138. Peattie, *Natural History of Trees*, 238–39.

139. Higgins, *Thoreau*, 135. Thoreau also wrote of elms in his diaries and in his essay, "Autumnal Tints," published in the October 1862 issue of *Atlantic Monthly*, 385–402.

140. American Forestry Association, *American Elm*, 4; Stahl, *Trees of Texas*, 51–52; Robert A. Vines, *Trees, Shrubs and Woody Vines*, 208–10.

141. Spaight, *Resources, Soil, and Climate*, 311–12.

Chapter 4. T. L. L. Temple and the Humble Beginnings of a Legacy

1. "Thomas Lewis Latane Temple," in American Lumberman, *American Lumbermen*.

2. Peattie, *Natural History of Trees*, 3–14.

3. Spratt, *Road to Spindletop*, 4, 64, 251, 284–85; Vera Lea Dugas, "Texas Industry, 1860–1880," *Southwestern Historical Quarterly* 59, no. 2 (1955): 151–83; Maxwell and Baker, *Sawdust Empire*, 20–22; *Eleventh Census of the United States (1890), Volume 13, Manufacturing Industries, Part 3* (Washington: Government Printing Office, 1895), 606.

4. Sargent, *Report on the Forests*, 543–44.

5. Mohr, *Timber Pines*, 96.

6. *Ninth Census of the United States (1870), Volume 3, Statistics of Wealth and Industry* (Washington: Government Printing Office, 1872), 453–54; *Twelfth Census of the United States (1900), Volume 8, Manufactures, Part 2* (Washington: United States Census Office, 1902), 864, 872–75; Defebaugh, *History of the Lumber Industry*, 500. "Lumber and timber products" were valued at $16,296,473 in 1900, enough to rank first in the state in value of manufactured products. When the value of the census classification of "lumber, planing mill products, including sash, doors, and blinds" is added,

the total figure increases to $17,901,770, or 15 percent of the total value of products of the state.

7. *Eleventh Census of the United State (1890), Volume 11, Manufacturing Industries, Part I* (Washington: Government Printing Office, 1895), 596–600. The identity of the southern lumber industry has yet to be adequately explained. Clark, in *Greening of the South* (19), published in 1984, argued that the southern lumberman has been too long overlooked and suggests that "historians have been cotton-blinded, seeing mostly staple agriculture, slavery, sectional politics, and 'wasted' southern society." Ayers, in *Promise of the New South*, published in 1992 (p. 123), declared that the "South's largest industry has remained virtually ignored" and that "lumbering more than any other industry, captures the full scope of economic change in the New South, its limitations as well as its impact." These statements remain relevant today. Texas produced more than 2.1 billion board feet of lumber in 1907, ranking third in the nation, behind only the states of Washington and Louisiana.

8. Raines, *Year Book for Texas*, vol. 1, p. 242; Spratt, *Road to Spindletop*, 257–59; Reed, *History of Texas Railroads*, 746. For the year ended June 30, 1901, lumber accounted for 4,889,467 tons moved by Texas railroads, or 19.8 percent of the total tonnage. Ranking second, at 3,699,704 tons, was coal, coke and lignite, or 15 percent of the total. At least an additional 1,105,545 tons, identified as "other and unclassified forest products" was also moved by Texas railroads during the year. Total forest products moved by Texas railroads during the year amounted to at least 24.3 percent of the total tonnage.

9. "A Sturdy Tree Has Fallen: Death Takes T. L. L. Temple Sr. of Texarkana," *Gulf Coast Lumberman*, October 15, 1935, pp. 14–15; "Thomas Lewis Latane Temple," in American Lumberman, *American Lumbermen*.

10. Biographical information for Orlando Jones can be found in box 5, folders 2–14, in the Carolyn Alevra Genealogical Collection (2000:027) at The History Center, Diboll. See especially typescripts and photostatic copies of "Last Will and Testament of Orlando S. Jones," Sevier County, Arkansas, Wills and Probate Records, vol. E, 202–7, 226–27, 234–49 in folder 8; "Jones Family Typescripts, 1896," p. 2, in folder 2; "A Jones Family of Essex County, No. 5," pp. 8–12, in

folder 4; "Jones, Dr. Orlando" in folder 12. See also "Dr. O. S. Jones," in Bagur, *Captain W. W. Withenbury's Reminiscences*, 260–70; manuscript returns of US Census of 1850, Franklin Township, Sevier County, Arkansas, dwelling house number 131, and US Census of 1860, Franklin Township, Sevier County, Arkansas, dwelling number 248.

11. John Newton Temple is enumerated in Arkansas' Little River County, Johnson Township, Richmond Post Office, in the US Census of 1870, page 5, line 31, National Archives, Washington DC.

12. Family Group Record for Thomas Lewis Latane Temple and note, Carolyn Alevra Genealogical Collection, The History Center, Diboll, box 4, folder 7; Biesele, *Cornbread Whistle*, 2. Watson Walker (1834–1900) and his wife Lucy Temple Walker (1838–1919) are buried at Saint Paul's Episcopal Church Cemetery in Millers Tavern, Essex County, Virginia.

13. Biesele, *Cornbread Whistle*, 1–2 (quote on 2); "A Sturdy Tree Has Fallen," *Gulf Coast Lumberman*, 14–15.

14. T. L. L. Temple is enumerated in the 1880 US Census as residing in Miller County, Arkansas, Texarkana Garland Township, Enumeration District 194, page 62, line 3. His occupation is "Book Keeper." "A Type of Texan Worth," *American Lumberman*, November 16, 1901, p. 1.

15. According to the July 2, 1880, federal population census, T. L. L. Temple resided alone as a bookkeeper in the Garland Township of Texarkana in Miller County, Arkansas, enumeration district 194, page 62. See also "Southern Pine from Forest to Retailer," *American Lumberman*, April 16, 1904, p. 36; Cox, *Lumberman's Frontier*, 235–62.

16. Quoted in chapter 11 of Hickman, *Mississippi Harvest*, 94; *Lumber Trade Journal*, March 15, 1902, p. 23.

17. "Black Eagle of Texas Senate Dead at Ripe Age," *Victoria Daily Advocate*, June 12, 1916, p. 2; "Senator Benjamin Whitaker of Texarkana," *Galveston Daily News*, June 19, 1893, p. 7; "Texarkana and Fort Smith," *Little Rock Arkansas Democrat*, October 11, 1887, p. 4; "Texas Progress," *Fort Worth Daily Gazette*, February 12, 1892, p. 5; "Texarkana and Fort Smith Railway," *Austin American-Statesman*, July 4, 1889, p. 1; "Prescott and Northwestern," *Little Rock Daily Arkansas Gazette*, January 21, 1892, p. 4; "Dragged to Death," *Marshall News Messenger*, June 29, 1894, p. 1; 1860 census, Cass County, Texas, Linden Post Office, p. 30, stamped page 360b; 1880 census, Bowie County, Texas, Texarkana, p. 16, stamped page 40b. For information on Willis Whitaker, see Campbell, *Empire for Slavery*, 274, and Christopher Long, "Whitaker, Willis Sr.," *Handbook of Texas Online*, accessed March 11, 2020, https://tshaonline.org/handbook/online/articles/fwh50.

18. Georgie Derrick Fowlkes and Anna Patterson Fowlkes were the daughters of Josephine Derrick and Abner D. Fowlkes. The Fowlkes family was enumerated in the 1850 and 1860 census, living in Hempstead County, Spring Hill Township, Arkansas. See also Fowlkes family information in the Carolyn Alevra Genealogy Collection, The History Center, Diboll, and Abner Fowlkes family trees in Ancestry.com.

19. Cecil Harper Jr., "Wayne, Texas," *Handbook of Texas Online*, accessed September 25, 2019, http://www.tshaonline.org/handbook/online/articles/hrw08; Bray, *Forest Resources of Texas*, 24–25, 52.

20. T. L. L. Temple to "My Dear Sister," August 20, 1882, photocopy of original, in Carolyn Alevra Collection, box 2, folder 3, and transcript in box 2, folder 4, The History Center, Diboll.

21. Cass County Deed Records, Cass County Courthouse, vol. D2, pp. 467–68 (October 6, 1882); vol. G2, pp. 287–88 (December 6, 1884); vol. H2, pp. 430–31 (June 15, 1886, Abner Fowlkes, bill of sale); vol. 12, pp. 78–79 (July 20, 1886); vol. I2, pp. 616–17 (June 9, 1887, bill of sale); vol. J2, pp. 595–97 (February 10, 1888, contract record); vol. T2, pp. 38–39 (August 29, 1893); and vol. S2, pp. 281–82 (October 22, 1894); "T. L. L. Temple" in Jennings, *Texarkana Pioneer Family Histories*; entries for "Whitaker & Galloway," "T. L. L. Temple Lumber Company," and "Atlanta Lumber Mills Company" in the Texas Forestry Museum's East Texas Sawmill Database and Research Files, Lufkin, Texas. Bray, *Forest Resources of Texas*, 25; Foster, Krausz, and Leidigh, *General Survey of Texas Woodlands*, 21–22 and 27.

22. "A Type of Texan Worth," *American Lumberman*, November 16, 1901, pp. 1, 27; "Timbered Texas," *Dallas Morning News*, July 20, 1893, special edition, p. 3.

23. "Neches Valley Pine," *American Lumberman*, January 18, 1908; American Lumberman, *American Lumbermen*, 3d series, 277–80.

24. "Timbered Texas," *Dallas Morning News*, July 20, 1893, special edition, p. 3; Bray, *Forest Resources of Texas*, 25.

25. Testimonies of T. L. L. Temple and his business filings, 108–16, and Testimonies of D. J. Grigsby, 126–31, both in *Transcript of Record, Supreme Court of the United States, October Term 1906, No. 365, Southern Pine Lumber Company, T. L. L. Temple, G. W. R. Chinn, et al., Plaintiffs in Error and Appellants vs. W. B. Ward, et al*; Case No. 82, in *The Supreme Court Reporter, Vol. 28, Cases Argued and Determined in the United States Supreme Court, October Term 190*, 240–47 (St. Paul: West Publishing Company, 1908). See also "Legal Notice, Cowley County, Kansas, Arkansas City Lumber Company vs. Benjamin Whitaker and T. L. L. Temple," *Arkansas Valley Democrat* (Arkansas City, Kansas), September 16, 1892, p. 3.

26. During visits with the author in 1999 and 2000, Bill Temple of Lufkin, one of Henry Waring Latane Temple's great-grandsons, suggested this possibility. Some of his reasons for believing such a possibility are contained in a letter he wrote to Carolyn Alevra on September 3, 1996, and within three pages of his notes dated August 22, 1996, all in the Carolyn Alevra Collection at The History Center, Diboll, box 5, folder 4.

27. For the wealth of the Fowlkes Family, see the population, agricultural, and slave schedules in the 1860 manuscript US Census returns for Spring Hill, Hempstead County.

28. "Thomas Lewis Latane Temple," in American Lumberman, *American Lumbermen*, 361–64; "A Type of Texan Worth," *American Lumberman*, November 16, 1901, p. 1.

29. "Neches Valley Pine," *American Lumberman*, January 18, 1908; "Southern Forest from Forest to Retailer," *American Lumberman*, April 16, 1904, p. 35.

30. Sargent, *Report on the Forests of North America*, 540–43; Spaight, *Resources, Soil, and Climate*, 4; Jonathan K. Gerland, "Sawdust City: Beaumont, Texas, on the Eve of the Petroleum Age," *Texas Gulf Historical & Biographical Record* 32 (November 1996): 26–27.

31. Gerland, "Sawdust City: Beaumont, Texas," 26–28; "Sawmills and Lumber," *Galveston Daily News*, December 24, 1890, p. 3.

32. The railroad company's corporate seal is imprinted on pages of the Houston East and West Texas Railway Company Directors' Record, 1889–1891 (2014:016), at The History Center, Diboll.

33. For the history of the HE&WT Railway, see Maxwell, *Whistle in the Piney Woods*; for the Cotton Belt history, see Joseph A. Strapac, *Cotton Belt Locomotives* (Huntington Beach: Shade Tree Books, 1977).

34. Jonathan Gerland, "Widening of Railroad Tracks in 1894 Put Diboll on the Map," *Pine Bough* 4 (December 1999): 2–3.

35. Ibid.

36. Angelina County Deed Records at the Angelina County Courthouse in Lufkin during this time recorded the numerous transactions by these firms and individuals. See also "Lufkin Literature: The Sawmill of T. R. Bonner & Co.," *Galveston Daily News*, March 22, 1891, p. 5; Haltom, *History and Description*; "Timbered Texas," *Dallas Morning News*, July 20, 1893, special edition, p. 3.

37. "Antonio Chevano League in Angelina County, Showing Subdivisions, Made by W. W. Davis, July 6th to 9th, 1881," manuscript map in Henry Raguet Map Collection, HR 1202/6, Briscoe Center for American History, Austin. Family sizes are found in the 1880 US Census for Angelina County.

38. "Land for Sale in Angelina County, Antonio Chevano League Grant, by Amory R. Starr, Land Agent, Marshall," Henry Raguet Map Collection, box 2F423, Briscoe Center for American History, Austin.

39. A copy of Greenwood LeFlore's July 9, 1835, power of attorney to Joseph S. Copes is in Angelina County Deed Records, Angelina County Courthouse (hereafter ACC), book D, 145. A copy of Greenwood LeFlore's last will, May 30, 1860, can be found in Angelina County Deed Records, ACC, book T, 74–78. Biesele, *Cornbread Whistle*, 5–6, is useful here but should be used cautiously.

40. The various transactions can be found in the Angelina County Deed Records, ACC; see the index pages for Copes, LeFlore, Phelps, and Diboll as grantees and grantors. Some of the more pertinent transactions are found in book D, 145 and 348; book F, 91–93, 101; book H, 72–73; book I, 422–23, 436–37; book M, 204;

book 11, p. 445. The will of Joseph S. Copes can be found in book N, 376–81.

41. Margaret Rogers Bullock typescript, Copes family notes, January 1986, in accession 1993:007, small collections box 1, The History Center, Diboll. This source claims the amount of land in Texas once owned by Joseph Slemons Copes was 300,000 acres.

42. Copies of the court decisions are in Angelina County Deed Records, ACC, vol. T, 274–86. David C. Bryant and John B. Rector were the judges. E. J. Mantooth and W. J. Townsend of Angelina County were the LeFlore heirs' attorneys.

43. Angelina County Deed Records, ACC, book T, 405–10.

44. Angelina County Deed Records, ACC, book T, 411–12.

45. Collins C. Diboll to Rosa Louise Diboll, June 3, 1890, and Joseph C. Diboll to Rosa Louise Diboll, August 11, 1891, in Angelina County Deed Records, ACC, book V, 248–49, and book S, 330–31. Joseph and his sister Rosa resided in homes next to each other according to the 1900 US Census for New Orleans, enumeration district 142, sheet 4-B. In 1900 Joseph's occupation was "builder"; in 1910 it was "architect."

46. The entire contract no longer survives, but details of the arrangement endure in other records. See Angelina County Mortgage Records, book C, 211–13. The stumpage contract of January 13, 1894, is referenced on pp. 211–12. The July 13, 1894, deed to the 20.5 acres of land is contained in Angelina County Deed Records, ACC, book U, 544–45. Details of the mill's capacity is contained in "Southern Pine from Forest to Retailer," *American Lumberman*, April 16, 1904, p. 37. Other details of the stumpage contract are found in *American Lumberman*, January 18, 1908. The Copes Estate rendered 6,845 acres in Angelina County for taxes in 1893, located in the A. Chevano, J. R. Chevano, J. Morine, and J. A. Prado surveys. See Angelina County Tax Rolls, 1893 (microfilm, The History Center, Diboll).

47. No records survive to indicate the exact timber "stand," or volume of timber, per acre for the Diboll lands at their initial industrial cutting. Estimates of timber volume varied greatly at the time, and overall numbers would have been lower then because very little if any of the tree tops were included in the bo-

nanza days of lumbering. Nelson Courtlandt Brown's *Logging—Principles and Practices* (1934) stated short-leaf pine stands of the Gulf Coast region varied between an average maximum volume of 12,000 board feet and an absolute maximum of 25,000 board feet. A rough inventory of Southern Pine Lumber Company's timber holdings in January 1908 showed an average of about 8,000 board feet of merchantable pine per acre and about 1,200 board feet of merchantable hardwoods per acre. See "Neches Valley Pine," *American Lumberman*, January 18, 1908, p. 84. Williams, in *Americans and Their Forests* (241), suggests nineteenth-century timberlands in the South held between 6,000 and 12,000 board feet per acre on average.

48. For instance, it was the Copes heirs, not Southern Pine Lumber Company, who gave most of the land for the early churches and civic buildings in town.

49. *American Lumberman*, April 16, 1904, p. 38.

50. "Neches Valley Pine," *American Lumberman*, January 18, 1908, pp. 86, 92. Public relations once feebly explained that the small millpond size was more by design rather than necessity.

51. "Short Texas Specials, Lufkin," *Houston Post*, May 6, 1899, p. 5.

52. Angelina County Deed Records, ACC, book 9, 569–71, contains the contract reference for the valuation of the new sawmill in 1903. See also Angelina County Deed Records, ACC, book 27, pp. 597–98, 609–11.

53. Angelina County Deed Records, ACC, book 27, pp. 597–98; "Long Pipe Line for Water at Diboll," *Southern Industrial and Lumber Review*, October 1909. It seems Southern Pine Lumber Company constructed the pipeline first, then paid for the easement after the fact. The Copes heirs released the company from damages caused to the timber in laying the line, but they required the pipeline to be buried so as not to prohibit cultivation or other uses of the land.

54. Rights-of-way restrictions were included in all the various transactions. This quote is from Angelina County Deed Record vol. 41, p. 238.

55. The acreage of the three tracts purchased in 1909 is explained in Angelina County Deed Records, ACC, book 27, pp. 609–11. A map of the tracts and their relation to the HE&WT and TSE railroads is included

on page 611. Parts of these lands were covered in an earlier deed from 1903. See Angelina County Deed Records, ACC, book 12, pp. 12–13. The tracts concerning the mill and related properties were situated on the A. Chevano, J. R. Chevano, and J. A. Prado surveys.

56. Angelina County Deed Records, ACC, book 41, pp. 235–39. Kenley made sure taxes were paid on 6,191 acres of the Phelps land and receipts sent to Mable Phelps (Asenath's daughter) in 1919 and 1920. See letters, SPLCo to A. E. Mantooth, March 27 and 28, 1919, and February 3, 1920, in Temple Lumber Company Records at East Texas Research Center, Nacogdoches (hereafter ETRC), box 19, folder 5. There was a "Mable Phelps" account with SPLCo at Lufkin National Bank in 1920. See letter, Lufkin National Bank to SPLCo, June 4, 1920, ETRC, box 19, folder 1.

57. "Neches Valley Pine," *American Lumberman*, January 18, 1908.

58. "Death of M. T. Jones," *Houston Post*, June 23, 1898, p. 1; *American Lumberman*, April 16, 1904, p. 36.

59. Various business transactions are recorded in the Angelina County Deed Records, ACC. See especially book 1, pp. 416–25, and book 3, pp. 5–16.

60. Charter of Lufkin Land and Lumber Company, May 31, 1899, no. 8774, and Charter of the Texas and Louisiana Railroad Company, July 24, 1900, Records of the Secretary of State's Office, Corporations Section, Austin; "Southern Pine From Forest to Retailer," *American Lumberman*, April 16, 1904, p. 36.

61. Angelina County Deed Records, ACC, November 7, 1898, book Z, 603–5. See also book 1, pp. 74–76, 135–37. The railroad was originally owned by William M. Atwood, of Bowie County, who sold it to J. J. Bonner in 1896. See *American Lumberman*, April 16, 1904, pp. 37–38. After selling the logging equipment, Bonner stayed on in Diboll as logging foreman. Tragically, his "little daughter" was "instantly killed" by the evening freight train on the Houston East and West Texas railway on December 2, 1898. See "Little Girl Killed by a Train," *Dallas Morning News*, December 3, 1898.

62. HE&WT Railway Company to Southern Pine Lumber Company, December 10, 1897, Angelina County Deed Records, ACC, book 1, pp. 206–8. Emporia Lumber Company also bought rails from the HE&WT. See Deed book 1, pp. 209–12. "Local and

Personal," *American Lumberman*, October 21, 1899, p. 36.

63. Charter and Articles of Incorporation, Texas Southeastern Railroad, September 22, 1900, in Records of the Secretary of State, vol. 1900, pp. 336–37. Southern Pine Lumber Company had earlier bought several miles of rails from the HE&WT railway in December 1897. See Angelina County Deed Records, ACC, book 1, pp. 206–8.

64. "Local and Personal," *American Lumberman*, October 21, 1899, p. 36; Letter, T. L. L. Temple to T. L. L. Temple Jr., July 6, 1917, ETRC, box 18, folder 2.

65. "35,000 Acres of Fine Farming Land for Sale," *Lufkin Weekly Tribune*, special edition, December 11, 1902, original at The History Center, Diboll. The practice of selling cutover lands for farmlands was not uncommon. For instance, the Angelina County Lumber Company had sold some 20,000 acres of cutover lands in more than two hundred tracts ranging from 25 to 100 acres each by 1916. See "Sawmills in Texas Fifty Years from Now?" *Dallas Morning News*, August 6, 1916, p. 4. Kirby Lumber Company also sought to sell even more cutover land for farms. See "Richter Pushes Development of Cut-Over Lands: Promises Made to East Texas Folk Are Kept," *Beaumont Enterprise*, February 16, 1930; "H. M. Richter Is Making Good on Tough Assignment: Common Sense Methods Used in Selling Land," *Beaumont Enterprise*, February 23, 1930; and "Cut-Over Timber Land Being Turned into Rich Farms," *Houston Post-Dispatch*, December 31, 1930, clippings in Temple-Inland Public Affairs Collection (1993:001), box 46, folders 11 and 12, The History Center, Diboll.

66. "G. A. Kelley, Capitalist, Financier, Beloved Citizen of Lufkin, Dies in Houston," *Lufkin Daily News*, December 11, 1931, p. 2; three-page typescript memo from H. W. Walker to Arthur Temple Jr., December 20, 1955, collection 1993:001, box 1, folder 16, The History Center, Diboll. The details of some of Walker's memories are incorrect, but other sources verify the profitability of the mill. T. L. L. Temple later said the mill was logged by contractors. Letter, T. L. L. Temple to T. L. L. Temple Jr., July 6, 1917, ETRC, box 18, folder 2.

67. An index to the transactions are in the Angelina County Deed Records, ACC, Southern Pine Lumber Company as grantee.

68. "Southern Pine from Forest to Retailer," *American Lumberman*, April 16, 1904, p. 35.

69. "Timbered Texas," *Dallas Morning News*, July 20, 1893, special edition, p. 3; US Department of Commerce, US Bureau of Corporations, *The Lumber Industry, Part 1, Standing Timber* (Washington: Government Printing Office, 1913): 118; Maxwell and Martin, *Short History*, 47.

70. Bray, *Forest Resources of Texas*, 19.

71. D. Woodhead, "The Hardwood Wealth of Texas," in *Texas Almanac and State Industrial Guide for 1904*, 146–147 (Galveston: A. H. Belo & Co., 1904).

72. *American Lumberman*, April 16, 1904, p. 37.

73. Southern Pine Lumber Company's claims are in Angelina County Mechanics Lien Record book 2 (1905), 111–15. Claims from others are in Mechanics Lien Record book 1 (1905), 16–39, Angelina County, County Clerk's Office, Lufkin.

74. "A. J. Oliver Lumber Company," East Texas Sawmill Database, Texas Forestry Museum, Lufkin.

75. "Saw Mill No. 2," *American Lumberman*, January 18, 1908, p. 93.

76. "A Successful Campaign of Conquest in Yellow Pine," *American Lumberman*, January 18, 1908, p. 34.

77. "The Three Southern Pine Lumber Company Mills," *Southern Industrial and Lumber Review*, July 1912, p. 45; Jonathan Gerland, "Diboll: Historic Home to Large Sawmills," *Diboll Free Press*, May 13, 1999, p. 3A.

78. Sitton, *Backwoodsman*, 113.

79. The land deed is found in Angelina County Deed Records, ACC, book 59, 628–29. Earlier efforts to buy out Phelps and Diboll can be found at ETRC, in letters: E. J. Conn to Dave Kenley, February 1, 1916, box 5, folder 4; R. E. Minton to Dave Kenley, October 10, 1922, box 19, folder 10; P. M. Albritton to Dave Kenley, April 5 and 14, 1923, box 2, folder 12. Time was urgent in 1923–24, for Southern Pine held the timber rights to the lands but had not yet cut the timber. The time allowed for doing so was running out, but if the company cut at present market conditions, the harvest would be at a loss. A plan to purchase fee title to the lands was entrusted to P. M. Albritton, who met with C. C. Diboll in New Orleans, who helped communicate with his sister and aunt.

80. Letter, Dave Kenley to L. D. Gilbert, February 26, 1923, ETRC, box 26, folder 9. Kenley had visited with representatives of the state and federal forestry agencies in determining rates and volumes of second-growth pine on Southern Pine Lumber Company lands. Kenley thought three inches growth per decade was a good estimate, while representatives of the forestry agencies said to count on four to five inches growth every ten years.

81. Letter, E. C. Durham to T. L. L. Temple, October 2, 1926, ETRC, box 44, folder 3.

82. Letter, T. L. L. Temple to "My Dear Sister," August 20, 1882, photocopy of original in Carolyn Alevra Collection, box 2, folder 3, and transcript in box 2, folder 4, The History Center, Diboll.

83. H. W. Walker memo to Arthur Temple Jr., December 20, 1955, in collection 1993:001, box 1, folder 16, The History Center, Diboll.

84. Many of Temple's philanthropic contributions during the 1910s are found in ETRC, box 15, folders 3 and 8; box 16, folders 7, 8, and 11; box 17, folders 4 and 11; box 18, folder 1; and box 18a, folders 1–6 and 8. For the 1920s, see ETRC, box 38, folders 2 and 3; box 41, folder 2; and box 42, folder 7.

85. "Gossip of the Corridors," *Houston Post*, January 9, 1908, p. 6; "Neches Valley Pine," *American Lumberman*, January 18, 1908, pp. 102, 104; T. L. L. Temple correspondence in ETRC, box 42, folder 7.

86. Fannie Farrington, Oral History Interview 11a, December 1954, The History Center, Diboll; Biesele, *Cornbread Whistle*, 4–5; Jonathan Gerland, "Fannie Farrington: Diboll's First Lady," *Pine Bough Magazine*, December 1999, pp. 10–13.

87. "Neches Valley Pine," *American Lumberman*, January 18, 1908, pp. 102, 104; T. L. L. Temple correspondence in ETRC, box 42, folder 7.

88. Peattie, *Natural History of Trees*, 310–11; "Neches Valley Pine," *American Lumberman*, January 18, 1908, p. 84.

89. "Neches Valley Pine," *American Lumberman*, January 18, 1908, p. 104; Fannie Farrington, Oral History Interview 11a, December 1954, The History Center, Diboll.

90. "Temple Family Receives State Library Award," *Diboll Free Press*, April 5, 1973, p. 1; "T. L. L. Temple

Foundation Receives Texas Library Association's Philanthropic Award," *Diboll Free Press*, April 10 and 17, 1986, p. 1. State Representative Buddy Temple accepted the 1973 award in Fort Worth; his wife Ellen accepted the 1986 award.

91. "Neches Valley Pine," *American Lumberman*, January 18, 1908, pp. 102, 104. Temple's Riverside Farm was in Bowie County, Texas, on McKinney Bayou, just off Summerhill Road, about seven miles north of Texarkana. A map of the farm is in Temple Family Collection 1986:003, oversize box 2, folder 6, The History Center, Diboll. See also Estate Papers of T. L. L. Temple, Angelina County Probate Records, file X-1989, number 0226, January 11, 1936, Angelina County County Clerk's Office, Lufkin, Texas, and T. L. L. Temple's correspondence with E. C. Durham and L. D. Gilbert in ETRC, boxes 17, 18, 18a, 30, 38, 41, 42, 44, and 45.

92. Correspondence between Durham and Temple between 1915 and 1920 is contained, often in reverse chronological order, in ETRC, box 17, folder 3; and box 18a, folders 2 through 6. Their correspondence during the 1920s is contained in boxes 20 through 50. See also Durham's writing contributions in issues of Diboll's *Pine Leaf* school newspaper during the 1920s, available at The History Center, Diboll. Before coming to Diboll in 1908, Durham had served at least six years as the ticket agent at Texarkana's Union Station for the Texas & Pacific and Iron Mountain railways. "New Ticket Agent Named," *Dallas Morning News*, April 11, 1908; "Durham to Leave Texarkana," *Dallas Morning News*, March 22, 1908, p. 4.

93. T. L. L. Temple and Fannie Farrington Correspondence, 1919–1926, ETRC, box 18a, folder 8; box 41, folder 2; and box 42, folder 7; Elodie Miles Edwards Collection, The History Center, Diboll.

94. "Department of Education, High School Division, Report on School Supervision on Diboll High School, January 19, 1926," ETRC, box 44, folder 4.

95. Angelina County Probate Records, Estate of T. L. L. Temple, file X-1989, number 0226, January 11, 1936, Angelina County Office of County Clerk, Lufkin, Texas; "Estate of T. L. L. Temple," collection 1986:004, box 1, folder 6, The History Center, Diboll; Temple Foundation Records, 1993:016, The History Center, Diboll; T. L. L. Temple Foundation Records, Lufkin, Texas.

96. Letter, L. D. Gilbert to T. L. L. Temple, September 24, 1917, ETRC, box 18, folder 2; "Challenge Cup Back to Dallas," *Arkansas Democrat*, September 27, 1917, p. 7; "Texarkana to Play Austin for the Temple Cup," *Austin American-Statesman*, June 14, 1918; "Texarkana Wins the Temple Cup," *Austin American-Statesman*, June 17, 1918, p. 3; "University to Meet Dallas at Tennis," *Bryan Eagle*, April 21, 1921, p. 4; "Texas University Sends Team against Oklahoma, En Route Tennis Would-Be Champions Will Play Team at Texarkana for Temple Cup," *Austin American-Statesman*, May 16, 1919, p. 9; "Wilmer Allison Offers to Denfend Net Cup," *Amarillo Daily News*, November 12, 1940, p. 7; "A Sturdy Tree Has Fallen," *Gulf Coast Lumberman*, 14–15; "Texarkana Pioneer Family Histories, compiled by Nancy Moore Watts Jennings, Secretary, 1916," at http://genealogytrails.com/ark/miller/pioneerfamilies3.html, accessed August 8, 2019.

97. H. H. Shelton, "Texas Sporting Gossip on Baseball, Football, Tennis," *El Paso Herald*, September 20, 1910, p. 5. Eight of the Munz tennis trophies between the years 1909 and 1922 are contained in the Mary Munz Collection (2005:009) at The History Center, Diboll.

98. "Dallas Winner of Three Net Crowns, Miss Mac-Quiston Takes Girls' Singles," *Austin American-Statesman*, May 5, 1929, p. 8; "Dallas Netters Hog Honors in Meet," *Lubbock Avalanche-Journal*, May 5, 1929, p. 4; Obituary for Mary MacQuiston Denman, Press Release from Carroway Funeral Home, March 26, 2019, copy in office of Ellen Temple, Lufkin. Birth Certificate of Mary Helen MacQuiston, Bowie County, Texas, no. 21993, November 15, 1918, Ellen Temple office files, Lufkin.

99. Letter, T. L. L. Temple to Latane Temple, March 29, 1926, ETRC, box 43, folder 1.

100. T. L. L. Temple correspondence with various family members and employees in ETRC, box 14, folders 1, 2, and 5; box 15, folders 1–8; box 16, folders 2–5; box 18, folders 1–3; and with E. C. Durham in ETRC, boxes 17, 18, 18a, 30, 38 (especially folders 2 and 13), 41, 42 (esp. folders 1, 2, and 7), 43 (esp. folders 1 and 2), 44, and 45. As the general manager of the Texas Southeastern Railroad Company, Durham

wrote to the various railroad companies to obtain annual and other passes for Temple and his family members. Gertrude Temple married George Webber at Asbury Park in August 1901 and Georgie Temple married Harry Munz at Los Angeles in July 1917. "Married at Asbury Park," *Daily Arkansas Gazette*, August 31, 1901, p. 2; "Two Surprise Weddings," *Arkansas Democrat*, July 18, 1917, p. 2.

101. Four-page letter, E. C. Durham to T. L. L. Temple, September 4, 1916, ETRC, box 18a, folder 6.

102. Three-page letter, E. C. Durham to T. L. L. Temple, November 9, 1925, ETRC, box 41, folder 9; four-page letter, Durham to Temple, September 4, 1916, ETRC, box 18a, folder 6; letter, Dave Kenley to T. L. L. Temple, June 14, 1918, ETRC, box 15, folder 5.

103. "Temple Entertains Party, Texarkana Lumber Man Takes His Friends to Country Home," *Dallas Morning News*, May 25, 1907, p. 8; "Jaunt in Private Car," *Daily Arkansas Gazette* (Little Rock), May 25, 1907, p. 2.

104. "Former Houston Lumberman Leaves Hospital," *Houston Post*, February 6, 1919, p. 5.

105. Georgie Derrick Fowlkes Temple died in St. Louis of colloid cancer of the ovary on November 30, 1900, and was buried in Texarkana on December 2, the twentieth anniversary of her and T. L. L.'s wedding. City of St. Louis Certificate of Death, number 9005, November 30, 1900, Missouri State Archives. "Quogue Rentals Heavy," *Brooklyn Daily Eagle*, April 28, 1912, p. 51; "Quogue Cottagers," *Brooklyn Times Union*, May 1, 1914, p. 9; "Rentals at Quogue," *Brooklyn Daily Eagle*, March 24, 1912, p. 11; Estate Papers of T. L. L. Temple, Angelina County Probate Records, file X-1989, number 0226, January 11, 1936, Angelina County, County Clerk's Office, Lufkin, Texas.

106. Letter, Arthur Temple Sr. to E. C. Durham, October 1, 1935, ETRC, box 98, folder 8; letters between T. L. L. Temple and H. G. Temple, October 19 and November 16, 1926, ETRC, box 42, folder 2; T. L. L. Temple Correspondence in ETRC, box 45, folders 1 and 2; letter, A. L. Burford to R. E. Minton, "Estate of T. L. L. Temple, Deceased," October 14, 1935, ETRC, box 97, folder 6; Estate Papers of T. L. L. Temple, Angelina County Probate Records, file X-1989, number 0226, January 11, 1936, County Clerk's Office, Lufkin, Texas; "Distinctively a Lumberman," *American Lum-*

berman, January 18, 1908, p. 80; "Gay Weekend at Quogue," *Brooklyn Daily Eagle*, September 2, 1934, p. 16; "Large Parties Precede Quogue Field Club Monte Carlo Party," *Brooklyn Daily Eagle*, August 18, 1935, p. 15; "Quogue Is Very Gay," *Brooklyn Life*, August 4, 1923, p. 10; "Southamptonites," *Brooklyn Daily Eagle*, July 8, 1934, p. 18; Richard H. Post, *Notes on Quogue, 1659–1959* (Quogue: Quogue Tercentenary Committee, 1959), 73–75.

107. "Gay Weekend at Quogue," *Brooklyn Daily Eagle*, September 2, 1934, p. 16; "Large Parties Precede Quogue Field Club Monte Carlo Party," *Brooklyn Daily Eagle*, August 18, 1935, p. 15; "Quogue Is Very Gay," *Brooklyn Life*, August 4, 1923, p. 10; "Southamptonites," *Brooklyn Daily Eagle*, July 8, 1934, p. 18. Correspondence of Arthur Temple Sr. and T. L. L. Temple in ETRC, boxes 42, 97, and 98.

108. "William H. Sage Died Yesterday," obituary clipping from an unknown newspaper, dated February 13, 1942, in Carolyn Alevra Collection (2000:007), box 8, folder 2, The History Center, Diboll; "Gay Weekend at Quogue," *Brooklyn Daily Eagle*, September 2, 1934, p. 16; "Large Parties Precede Quogue Field Club Monte Carlo Party," *Brooklyn Daily Eagle*, August 18, 1935, p. 15; "Quogue Is Very Gay," *Brooklyn Life*, August 4, 1923, p. 10; "Southamptonites," *Brooklyn Daily Eagle*, July 8, 1934, p. 18.

109. Letter, Arthur Temple Sr. to E. C. Durham. October 1, 1935, ETRC, box 98, folder 8.

110. Letter, A. L. Burford to R. E. Minton, "Estate of T. L. L. Temple, Deceased," October 14, 1935, ETRC, box 97, folder 6.

111. Ibid., "highest of any State" quote; letter, R. E. Minton to A. L. Burford, October 16, 1935, ETRC, box 97, folder 6; letters, R. E. Minton to A. L. Burford, September 11, 1936; and R. E. Minton to Arthur Temple, September 16, 1936, ETRC, box 104, folder 6.

112. "Neches Valley Pine," *American Lumberman*, January 18, 1908, p. 80; letter, Arthur Temple Sr. to E. C. Durham, October 1, 1935, ETRC, box 98, folder 8; letter, A. L. Burford to R. E. Minton, October 14, 1935, ETRC, box 97, folder 6.

113. L. D. and Mary Gilbert appear in the 1910 and 1920 census records as boarders in T. L. L. Temple's Texarkana, Arkansas, home, with Mrs. Gilbert iden-

tified as housekeeper. By the time of the 1930 census, Gilbert was married to Irma, and they no longer lived with T. L. L. Temple. In the 1920 census, Arthur Temple Sr., his wife Katherine, their daughter Ann, and their mulatto servant Henrietta Buchanan also resided in the T. L. L. Temple home. See also Death Certificate of L. D. Gilbert, number 49675, Angelina County, Texas, filed November 30, 1931, State Department of Health, Bureau of Vital Statistics, Austin, Texas; and Gilbert's military service registration card, serial number 2526, Bowie County, Texas, September 12, 1918, United States Selective Service, World War I Draft Registration Cards, 1917–1918, National Archives, Washington, DC.

114. Megan Lambert interview with Arthur Temple Jr., July 11, 1985, Interview 56b, The History Center, Diboll.

115. Correspondence among T. L. L. Temple Sr., T. L. L. Temple Jr., Arthur Temple Sr., L. D. Gilbert, and C. M. McWilliams concerning Temple's relationship with his sons is found in ETRC, boxes 14 (esp. folder 1), 15 (esp. folder 5), 16 (esp. folder 8), 17 (esp. folder 3), 18 (esp. folder 3), and 43. See especially letters of C. M. McWilliams to L. D. Gilbert, September 21, 1916, in ETRC, box 15, folder 5; and September 26, 1916, in ETRC, box 16, folder 8; and those of Arthur Temple to his father in 1916 in ETRC, box 18, folder 3; and in 1919 in ETRC, box 17, folder 3.

116. Gresham Temple, Interview 74a, August 16, 1985, pp. 16–17, The History Center, Diboll.

117. "Deer Hunter Drops Dead," *Taylor Daily Press*, November 17, 1931; Death Certificate of L. D. Gilbert, Angelina County no. 49675, November 16, 1931. Lewis Daniel Gilbert, appeared in the US Census Population Schedule for Milam County, Texas, Port Sullivan Beat 2 in 1880; for Miller County, Arkansas, Texarkana Ward 2 in 1910 and 1920; and Miller County, Arkansas, Texarkana, Garland Township, in 1930. Gilbert's mother did remarry, to S. W. Wallace, in 1883. Lucius W. Gilbert was the general manager at a sawmill in Donner, Louisiana, during the 1910s and 1920s. See United States Census Records, Population Schedules, Terrebonne Parish, Louisiana, and letters from L. D. Gilbert and Dave Kenley to Lucius Gilbert, dated February 11 and 12, 1923, in ETRC, box 19, folder 10; and box 26, folder 9.

Chapter 5. A Land of Industry

1. Bowles, *History of Trinity County*, 46–53; Robert S. Maxwell, "Lumbermen of the East Texas Frontier," *Forest History Newsletter* 9, no. 1 (1965): 15–16; East Texas Sawmill Data Base research files for the sawmill towns of Saron, Groveton, Josserand, and Willard and for the corporations headed by the Cameron, Josserand, and Thompson families, Texas Forestry Museum, Lufkin.

2. Eastern Texas Railroad Company, Finance Docket No. 4, Testimonies and Hearings before the Interstate Commerce Commission Pertaining to the Construction, History, and Abandonment of the Eastern Texas Railroad, National Archives II, College Park, Maryland; "Western Coal and Lumber Resources, as Exemplified by the Coal Mining and Lumber Manufacturing Departments of the Central Coal & Coke Company of Kansas City, Mo.," *American Lumberman*, November 1, 1902; "The Kennard Mills," *Southern Industrial and Lumber Review*, October 1908, p. 40; notes and vertical files pertaining to the history of the Central Coal and Coke Company 4-C Sawmill at Kennard, Texas Forestry Museum, Lufkin. While the amount of land owned by the Kansas City operation was stated variously to have been between 120,000 to 170,000 acres, surveys of the tax rolls for Houston and Trinity Counties reveal the actual amount was closer to 120,000. See also Trinity County Deed Records, Trinity County Courthouse Annex (hereafter TCCA), vol. T, 82–90.

3. "Lumber," *American Lumberman*, November 1, 1902, pp. 62–65; "The Four-C Mill," *Beaumont Enterprise*, April 16, 1905; "Coltharp News Notes," *Houston Post*, March 3, 1901, p. 7.

4. "Abraham Harris Dies at Home in New York," *Jewish Monitor* (Dallas, Texas), November 14, 1919, p. 3. Time tables and a list of officers of the two railroad companies can be found in the January 1907 issue of *The Official Guide of the Railways of the United States* (New York: National Railway Publication Company, 1907). Entries for the lumber companies can be found in the East Texas Sawmill Data Base, Texas Forestry Museum.

5. Trinity County Deed Records, TCCA, vol. T, 190–99 and 122–23; vol. 32, pp. 227–47.

6. Houston County Deed Records, Houston County Courthouse (hereafter HCC), vol. 22, pp. 60–61; vol. 23, p. 401; vol. 31, p. 380; vol. 33, p. 328; vol. 34, pp. 112–15; vol. 40, p. 117. Further details are contained in Trinity County Deed Records, TCCA, vol. 27, pp. 102–4; vol. 28, pp. 446–47; vol. 32, pp. 227–47; and vol. 36, pp. 578–81.

7. Trinity County Deed Records, TCCA, vol. 32, pp. 227–47.

8. According to Ashford family tradition, William Ashford and T. L. L. Temple were friends or associates before the Diboll association. This is based on the author's conversations with Susan Schinke of Diboll, granddaughter of William Ashford, between 1999 and 2017. William Ashford and Julia Bond Thompson received their marriage license in Cass County in 1885, while T. L. L. Temple was sawmilling there.

9. See Ashford as a Grantor and as a Grantee in Trinity County Deed Records, TCCA, 1902–1910, Trinity County, county clerk's office, Groveton.

10. "N. D. Wright, Surveyor and Land Lawyer," *Trinity County Star*, March 3, 1905; "Nathan Dawson Wright," in *East Texas: Its History and Its Makers*, vol. 4, edited by Dabney White, 392–93 (New York: Lewis Historical Publishing Company, 1940); Mrs. L. T. Jordan, "Wright, Nathan Dawson," in Lufkin Genealogical and Historical Society, *History of Angelina County*, pp. 870–71. See various deeds in Trinity County Deed Records, TCCA, 1895–1920, especially vol. 38, pp. 253–54. See also timber estimates found in Southern Pine Lumber Company Land Record Ledgers (1993:015), The History Center, Diboll.

11. See for example Cause No. 2381, Angelina County District Court, R. M. Maberry versus Texas Southeastern Railroad, 1911; R. M. Maberry Accident File 1911 (accident date of July 24, 1909) in Texas Southeastern Railroad Company Records (1993:022), The History Center, Diboll; and letters from E. C. Durham to T. L. L. Temple, July 8 and 19, 1916, in Temple Industries Records at the East Texas Research Center in Nacogdoches (hereafter ETRC), box 18a, folders 4 and 6; also letters between Dave Kenley and L. D. Gilbert, October 24 and 26, 1922, ETRC, box 19, folder 10. There are also charges of dishonesty that remain in oral histories. See Charlie Harber interviews with Jon-

athan Gerland, dated May 4, 2000 (interview 157a), and March 27, 2002 (interview 157d), The History Center, Diboll.

12. Land transactions of the agents are on file at the Trinity County, county clerk's office. See also Southern Pine Lumber Company land records for Houston and Trinity Counties at The History Center, Diboll (Land Record vols. 6 and 11 in accession 1993:015) and in boxes 3, 4, and 44 of Temple Industries Records, ETRC. R. D. Forbes, *Timber Growing and Logging*, 14.

13. "Elected and Appointed Officials of Trinity County between 1850 and 1985," unpublished manuscript at Trinity County Museum, Groveton (hereafter TCM); "R. O. Kenley," *Trinity County Star*, March 3, 1905; "Carrol H. Kenley," in Bell, *Journey to Jubilee*; Kenley Correspondence and Family Files, TCM.

14. For the land acquisition activities of the Kenley brothers and Minton in Trinity County, see Trinity County Deed Records, TCCA, 1890s through 1910s, and correspondence between the men during the 1910s in ETRC, box 3, folder 8; and box 4, folder 6.

15. Memo, Vernon Burkhalter to Arthur Temple, November 14, 1967, Arthur Temple Jr. Business Papers (2004:014a), box 101, folder 6, The History Center, Diboll.

16. Sam and Richard Kenley bought lands in North Boggy, especially following the construction of the Eastern Texas Railroad. For instance, Sam Kenley purchased better than 100 acres in the S. D. Sullivan survey in April 1903 and October 1905, selling the tracts to Southern Pine Lumber Company in November 1905 for $6 an acre. Tom Welch lived on the land, cultivating 51 acres. Southern Pine Lumber Company Land Record Volumes (1993:015), Trinity County Volume 11, The History Center, Diboll.

17. Carrol Kenley is included throughout Dave Kenley's correspondence in the Southern Pine Lumber Company (Temple Industries) Records at the East Texas Research Center (ETRC); see especially boxes 4, 19, 20, 22, 26, 30, 48, 50, 55, 65, 71, 75, 81, 90, 95.

18. See sheriffs deed and tax judgement in Trinity County Deed Records, TCCA, vol. V, 262; vol. 1, p. 24; and vol. 29, p. 219; as recorded in files at Trinity County Abstract Company, Groveton (hereafter TCAC, accessed in July 2017.

19. The many transactions can be found in the Trinity County Deed Records, TCCA, R. O. Kenley as Grantee.

20. "H. L. Robb Is Dead: Three Men Are Charged," *Houston Post*, May 3, 1907, p. 4. The bonds for the release of the three men were in the amounts of $1,000 each for C. H. Kenley and R. E. Minton and $2,500 for R. O. Kenley. See also Alexander, *Bad Company and Burnt Powder*, 235–43; three-page letter, R. O. Kenley to W. L. Hill of Huntsville, August 7, 1912, in correspondence of R. O. Kenley, TCM; "Want Officials," *Houston Post*, June 13, 1908, p. 5; "Bars Rangers," *Houston Post*, June 14, 1908, p. 11; "A Plea of Justification," *Houston Post*, June 16, 1908, p. 9; "Is Not Guilty," *Houston Post*, June 17, 1908, p. 5; "Statement of Tull H. Robb," *Houston Post*, November 20, 1912, p. 9.

21. "Badly Wounded, Ranger Dunaway and Attorney Robb Shot at Groveton, Kenley Admits He Fired," *Houston Post*, April 27, 1907, p. 4; Alexander, *Bad Company and Burnt Powder*, 239. For one of Dunaway's earlier assault cases, see "Dunaway Case Dismissed," *Houston Post*, September 19, 1905, p. 7.

22. "Lawyer Shoots Two Officials," *Los Angeles Herald*, April 27, 1907; "County Attorney Slain," *New York Times*, April 27, 1927, p. 1; "Disarmed of 100 Pistols," *New York Times*, June 12, 1908, p. 1. The *Times* reported Robb's death prematurely. He did not die until May 2. See "Death of H. L. Robb," *Dallas Morning News*, May 3, 1907, p. 4.

23. The trial was extraordinary. Newspapers reported that a number of Texas Rangers came from across the state to attend the trial as both witnesses and spectators, but after some refused to surrender their weapons at the courthouse doors during one particular day of the trial, the Harris County judge denied their entrance into his courtroom. Also, the *Houston Post* reported the trial cost some $6,000, mainly comprising the transportation costs of 250 witnesses, and the bill was sent to the taxpayers of Trinity County. See "To Attend Trial in Houston," *Houston Post*, June 11, 1908, p. 9; "Bars Rangers," *Houston Post*, June 14, 1908, p. 11; "A Plea of Justification," *Houston Post*, June 16, 1908, p. 9; and "Is Not Guilty," *Houston Post*, June 17, 1908, p. 5.

24. Letters, especially R. O. Kenley to Judge Berry of Madisonville, August 13, 1912, in the R. O. Kenley Correspondence Files at the Trinity County Historical Commission Archives, in Groveton. Newspaper accounts reported the jury deliberated less than half an hour. See also Alexander, *Bad Company and Burnt Powder*, 238–39; two articles, "Ranger Shot Down" and "Rangers Ordered to Groveton," both in *Dallas Morning News*, April 27, 1907, p. 3; "Situation at Groveton," *Dallas Morning News*, April 28, 1907, 2d ed., p. 11; "Dunaway Recovering," *Dallas Morning News*, May 17, 1907, p. 3.

25. Bowles, *History of Trinity County*, 31–38, 78, and 81.

26. Ibid., 78 and 81.

27. Ibid., 31–38, 78–81; Sitton and Conrad, *Nameless Towns*, 101–3. The vote was 909 for prohibition and 720 against prohibition. See Order No. 1, August 13, 1902, Trinity County Commissioners' Court, Minutes of Meetings, vol. E, 325–27.

28. Bowles, *History of Trinity County*, 89–91; "Evidence Is In, Arguments of Groveton Murder Case Will Be Made Today," *Houston Post*, June 1, 1907, p. 7; "Verdict of Not Guilty, Winslow and Parks Acquitted," *Abilene Semi Weekly Farm Reporter*, June 3, 1907, p. 1.

29. For McDonald's full remarks about Trinity County, see Paine, *Captain Bill McDonald*, 265–72, 433–36 (quote 266).

30. For much of what happened after the 1908 trial, see at least eight letters between R. O. Kenley and judges in Harris, Anderson, and Walker Counties in 1912 and 1913, among other Kenley papers, in the R. O. Kenley Correspondence files at the Trinity County Historical Commission's archives at Groveton. For the November 1912 assault by Dunaway on Kenley at Rouse's Drug Store in Houston, see "Attorney Victim of an Assault," *Houston Post*, November 19, 1912, p. 9; "Statement by Tull H. Robb," *Houston Post*, November 20, 1912, p. 9; and "Dunaway Will Appeal," *Lufkin Daily News*, September 12, 1913. For a sampling of legal cases R. O. Kenley handled for Southern Pine Lumber Company and Texas Southeastern Railroad, see several personal injury and accidental death files in box 1 of Texas Southeastern Railroad Records (1993:022) at The History Center, Diboll. See also "R. O. Kenley Sr., Former ACC Board Member, Succumbs," *Abilene Reporter-News*, April 16, 1960, p. 3; McDaniel, *Sabine County, Texas*, 16–17, 192, 210.

Brothers Robert E. Minton and John W. Minton are in the 1880 Sabine County Census, stamped page 247, E.D. 86, page 21, lines 45 and 46.

31. Among the settlers of I&GN lands were Dock Franklin, S. T. Sullivan, C. B Sullivan, Charles Rushing, and the Hutson, Luce, Walton, and Wells families. See Southern Pine Lumber Company Land Records, Trinity County Volume, I&GN survey pages; Trinity County Deed Records, TCCA, vol. 27, pp. 103–4. For background information concerning the practice of squatting, or obtaining land by adverse possession, see John A. Caplen, "Camp Big Thicket, Life in the Piney Woods, in Eastern Texas," *Sunny South*, November 5, 1887, p. 1; and Robert W. McCluggage, "The Pioneer Squatter," *Illinois Historical Journal* 82, no. 1 (1989): 47–54.

32. Dave Kenley oral history interview with John Larson, 1954, Lufkin, Texas, Interview 14a, The History Center, Diboll, 1. Dave Kenley's recollections dated back to 1908, but his brother R. O.'s involvement dated to at least 1906. See a two-page letter from the law offices of Greer, Minor, and Miller of Beaumont, Texas, to Southern Pine Lumber Company offices at Texarkana, April 25, 1908, ETRC, box 18, folder 1. For a summary of the legal issues, see Southern Pine Lumber Company vs. Consolidated Louisiana Lumber Company, Circuit Court of Appeals, Fifth District, October 5, 1914, in *United States Circuit Court of Appeals Reports* (St. Paul: West Publishing Company, 1915): 479–86.

33. See correspondence between Vansau and Kenley, which pertains to their business relationship in ETRC, box 3, folder 9.

34. Letters, R. E. Minton to L. D. Gilbert, September 6, 1916, ETRC, box 15, folder 2; G. C. Greer to J. W. Minton, November 7, 1916, ETRC, box 16, folder 5; Greer, Minor, and Miller to Southern Pine Lumber Company, April 25, 1908, ETRC, box 18, folder 1; Trinity County District Clerk Civil Minutes (August 1917), vol. J, 187–89; Southern Pine Lumber Company vs. Consolidated Louisiana Lumber Company, in *United States Circuit Court of Appeals Reports*, 479–86; Southern Pine Lumber Company Land Records, Trinity County Volume, twenty-one pages of Sepulveda survey notes.

35. Dave Kenley oral history interview with John Larson, 1954, Lufkin, Texas, Interview 14a, The His-

tory Center, Diboll, 1. There are many other notable land stories, some of which survive in lumber company surveyor's notebooks. In addition to measuring, marking, and drawing property lines, surveyors often researched genealogies of landowners. In one surveyor's book that survives among R. E. Minton's papers at The History Center in Diboll is a narrative explaining how one family came to Texas from Kentucky in 1835, settling in Nacogdoches, where Dr. J. J. Porter became a merchant. The notebook explains that in September 1836 Dr. Porter "met an early and shocking death" while he was returning home late at night while "all others were asleep." He passed the Old Stone Fort and walked into the arms of a large bear that had been captured and chained to a tree, perhaps as a novelty. The book states that Dr. Porter "was killed before his cries could bring help." See Judge Minton Survey Book, vol. 5, in Southern Pine Lumber Company Land Records (1993:015), p. 151K. The bear story originates in Glenn Dora Fowler Arthur, *Annals of the Fowler Family* (Austin: Glenn Dora Fowler Arthur, 1901), 128–29.

36. The small tract of land is today identified by the GLO as the northeast corner of the Alexander Henry survey (Trinity A-822). Temple Industries registered a deed as recently as 1972, accepting a warranty deed from Rachel Burke and Marjorie Youman for 40 acres out of the northeast corner of a 160 acre tract in the Sepulveda north league, or the Alexander Henry survey. See Southern Pine Lumber Company Land Records, Trinity County Volume, file H-12, deed number 2; Trinity County Deed Records, TCCA, vol. 210, p. 632, and vol. 128, p. 25.

37. Trinity County Deed Records, TCCA, book U, 596. See also book R, 402–3, where W. E. Johnson obtained 1,107 acres in the Sanchez survey in 1898. The Walker survey was only 4,605 acres, whereas the 1902 deed called for 5,759 acres.

38. See Trinity County Deed Records, TCCA, vol. D, 464–65; vol. G, 322–23; and vol. S, 125–26. By 1865, J. M. Walker had sold at least 1,500 acres out of his grant "to various parties," as one deed acknowledged, and another 3,150 acres had been purchased by the Houston, East & West Texas Railway Company in 1883. The math rarely worked out when figuring the acreage amounts, which had to be reconciled later. A court decision in February 1905 upheld Southern Pine's title

in the HE&WT Railway Company lands. See Trinity County District Court Minutes, vol. H, 49–50.

39. Southern Pine Lumber Company, Land Record Volumes (1993:015), Trinity County Volume, J. M. Walker pages, The History Center, Diboll; J. M. Walker Abstract of Title Files, Trinity County Abstract Company, TCAC; Trinity County Deed Records, TCCA, vol. D, 466–67, and 537–38; vol. E, 381–85; vol. G, pp. 319–23.

40. Southern Pine Lumber Company, Land Record Volumes (1993:015), Trinity County Volume, Candido Sanches pages, The History Center, Diboll.

41. See Scrip File 593, W. W. Alston, Trinity County, and School Land File 118590, Joseph A. Martin (Abstract 939), Trinity County, General Land Office (hereafter GLO) files, Austin Texas.

42. H. W. Pennington, "Sketch of W. W. Alston Survey in Trinity County, October 1886," Scrip File 593, Trinity County, GLO; Gerland, "Boggy Slough Island, 1886," *Pine Bough Magazine*, December 2016, pp. 30–31.

43. Kenley's November 10, 1910, "Meanderings of Boggy Slough" is also found in Southern Pine Lumber Company Land Record Volumes, Trinity County, W.W. Alston Grantee, at The History Center, Diboll. In 1929 Kenley revisited the streams, confirmed his earlier findings, and filed his survey and witness testimonies for public record at Groveton and at Austin. His 1929 filing, in which he says his earlier survey was done in the summer of 1911, not in November 1910, is in School Land File 118590, Joseph A. Martin (Abstract 939), Trinity County, at the GLO office in Austin.

44. "To Drill Near Lufkin," *Houston Post*, August 24, 1904, p. 3; "Oil Abounds Near Lufkin, Government Expert Making Topographic Survey of Section," *Houston Post*, July 12, 1907, p. 15.

45. Dumble, *Geology of East Texas*, 313; Margie Kirkland, "Bonner Family a Lufkin Name That's Here to Stay," *Lufkin Daily News*, May 7, 2006, pp. 12B; "B. F. Bonner," in American Lumberman, *American Lumbermen*, 293–96; "Oil Abounds Near Lufkin, Government Expert Making Topographic Survey of Section," *Houston Post*, July 12, 1907, p. 15.

46. Two of the Bonner timber deeds from February 1902 concerning the S. F. Harding survey are in

Trinity County Deed Records, TCCA, vol. 30, p. 180, and vol. 38, p. 624. For the two tracts of BBB&C Railroad surveys, see Trinity County Deed Records, TCCA, vol. 33, p. 157.

47. A list of Bluff Prairie Oil Company's partners is found in a June 28, 1904, Power of Attorney instrument recorded in the Trinity County Deed Records, TCCA, vol. 31, pp. 186–87. For the names of the various oil producers and wildcatters, including L. B. Clark, W. C. Best, J. A. Paulhamus, W. L. Douglass, and R. A. McLeod, see numerous legal documents dated between 1903 and 1905 in Trinity County Deed Records, TCCA, vol. 29, pp. 566, 569; vol. 30, pp. 593, 594–96; and vol. 31, pp. 189, 193–94, 196, 198, 200–206; and vol. 52, p. 501.

48. "A Big Gas Blowout," *Houston Post*, October 8, 1904, p. 7.

49. Southern Pine Lumber Company obtained the lands from W. H. Bonner, Nat Wright, William Ashford, and E. J. Eyres. See Trinity County Deed Records, TCCA, vol. 33, pp. 157, 519; vol. 39, p. 557; and vol. 52, pp. 501–2, 552. See also entries for S. F. Harding (Abstract 280), BBB&C (Abstract 113), and BBB&C (Abstract 118) in Trinity Volume in Southern Pine Lumber Company Land Record Volumes, The History Center, Diboll.

50. Letter, P. M. Albritton to L. D. Gilbert and D. C. Kenley, January 3, 1921 (the letter is erroneously typed with the year as 1921; the intended year is 1922), ETRC, box 20, folder 6; and box 2, folder 6; letters, Kenley to Albritton, January 9, 1922, and Kenley to Gilbert January 28, 1922, ETRC, box 30, folder 5; and box 20, folder 6; and box 2, folder 6; letters, Albritton to Kenley, January 21 and 25, 1922, ETRC, box 20, folder 6; letters, Kenley to Gilbert, February 15, 1922, ETRC, box 2, folder 6; letters, Gilbert to Kenley, February 16, 1922, ETRC, box 2, folder 6.

51. Letter, Gilbert to Kenley, February 16, 1922, ETRC, box 2, folder 6.

52. "Bluff Prairie Saline Prospect," in *Murray-Atkinson Subdivision of Southern Pine Lumber Company Lands*, August 6, 1938, Trinity County, County Clerk's Office, Groveton.

53. Letters, Minton to Kenley, July 27 and August 10, 1923, in ETRC, box 26, folder 4; Trinity County

Deed Records, TCCA, vol. 66, pp. 233, 481–87; Trinity County District Court Rulings, Civil Minutes, vol. J, 516; Trinity County Abstract 953, School Land 131493, GLO Case Files, Austin, Texas; correspondence between Jonathan Gerland and Patrick Walsh of the GLO, Austin, April 26, 2018, author's collection. See also letter, Kenley to Gilbert, August 1, 1923, SFASU, box 26, folder 8. Minton estimated the entire cost of the acquisition, including travel and court costs, to be less than $4.00 an acre. For changes in School Land laws, especially pertaining to lands with timber, see Cooper, *Permanent School Fund*, 64–68.

54. See GLO land records for R. E. Minton, Trinity County Abstract 934, in Austin, and Southern Pine Lumber Company Land Records, Trinity County Volume, Minton Survey, The History Century.

55. The company had earlier purchased some of the tract's timber from the Louisiana and Texas Lumber Company in 1912. Southern Pine Lumber Company Land Records, Trinity County Volume, Hampton Survey, The History Center, Diboll; Trinity County Deed Records, TCCA, vol. 67, p. 419; Houston County Deed Records, HCC, vol. 89, p. 490; Hampton Abstract 259 Files, Trinity County Abstract Company, TCAC; Zlatkovich, *Texas Railroads*, 47. For logging the Hampton Survey in 1948, see Charlie Harber interview with Jonathan Gerland, Interview 157d, pp. 4–5, The History Center, Diboll, and photographs of large gum logs in *Diboll Buzz Saw*, October 30, 1948, p. 7.

56. Most of this data was obtained from Southern Pine Lumber Company Land Record Ledgers (1993:016), Trinity County and Houston County, The History Center, Diboll, and from title abstracts on file at Trinity County Abstract Company, TCAC. See also Letter, D. C. Kenley to Ratcliff State Bank, October 1, 1918, ETRC, box 20, folder 10; Letter, Kenley to C. R. Rushing, Druso, January 27, 1919, ETRC, box 20, folder 10; Lufkin National Bank to Southern Pine Lumber Company, January 30, 1919, ETRC, box 19, folder 4; and Kenley to Moore, March 17, 1919, ETRC, box 19, folder 5.

57. The route of the Eastern Texas Railroad and the various wagon roads are shown on the large map from *McCarthy's Map of Angelina County, Texas*, by P. A. McCarthy & Son, Lufkin, Texas, November 1904, at The History Center, Diboll.

58. "Work on the Eastern Texas," *Houston Daily Post*, March 29, 1901. Grantors generally gave 100-foot-wide rights-of-way for as little as one dollar, except for Lufkin town lots. For right-of-way deeds granted at one dollar, see Angelina County Deed Records, Angelina County Courthouse, Lufkin (hereafter ACC), vol. 7, pp. 21, 32, 93, 166, 287, 343–44, 346, 428, 432, 471. For R-O-W deeds granted for considerably more, up to $666, see Angelina County Deed Records, ACC, vol. 4, p. 168; vol. 6, pp. 232–33; vol. 7, pp. 24, 28, 30, 34, 39, 41, 167; vol. 10, p. 215; vol. 16, p. 381. See also *Finance Docket No. 4, Application for Abandonment, Eastern Texas Railroad Company, September 27, 1920*, in Interstate Commerce Commission Records (RG-134), National Archives II, College Park, MD, copies provided by Murry Hammond, Pasadena, California. Construction of the railroad was completed in December 1901, with the first train between Lufkin and Kennard running on December 21. Most of the machinery for the mill was delivered and installed after completion of the road, and the mill was not completed until May 1902. See *American Lumberman*, November 1, 1902, p. 62.

59. Schivelbusch, *Railway Journey*, 89–92; Ralph Waldo Emerson set nature and steam railroads together in his chapter "Commodity," in *Nature*, 17; Fiege, *Republic of Nature*, 228–65; Wells SW, Texas, Quadrant, USGS 7.5 minute topographical map, edition of 1951. The route of the Eastern Texas Railroad through Angelina County is shown well in P. A. McCarthy and Sons, *McCarthy's Map of Angelina County, Texas* (Lufkin: City of Lufkin, November 1904), The History Center, Diboll. McCarthy served as civil engineer of the Eastern Texas Railroad during its construction.

60. The river bridge measurements are from "Statement of Bridge Repairs Required for Safe Operation on Eastern Texas RR, Year 1920," in Cotton Belt Bridge Supervisor J. E. Enwright's Exhibit 11, *Finance Docket No. 4, Application for Abandonment, Eastern Texas Railroad Company, September 27, 1920*, in Interstate Commerce Commission Records (RG-134), National Archives II, College Park, MD, copies provided by Murry Hammond, Pasadena, California; see Enwright's testimony there also, p. 51.

61. In Texas Southeastern Railroad Records (1993:022), at The History Center, Diboll, see "Map of Yard at Neff, November 1909," box 1, folder 19; and Agreement

between Eastern Texas Railroad Company and Texas Southeastern Railroad Company, June 23, 1909, box 1, folder 18. The TSE crossing of the Eastern Texas was at a point 708 feet west of Eastern Texas milepost 17. The succession of creeks crossed, going westward, was Bristow, Copperas, Indian, Brushy, and Hagers.

62. *The Railway Age*, November 30, 1900, p. 437; February 1, 1901, p. 85; February 15, 1901, p. 128; March 1, 1901, p. 170; March 15, 1901, p. 260; January 6, 1905, p. 25; April 28, p. 707; May 12, 1905, p. 773.

63. While working out of Lufkin, McCarthy also served as an engineer for other railroads in 1905, including the Colorado, Oklahoma & Southeastern in Oklahoma and the Texas Short Line and the Gulf & Northwestern in Texas. See *The Railway Age*, March 24, 1905, pp. 434 and 436. For McCarthy and the GL&N, see *Official Guide of the Railways*, January 1909, p. 883. By 1910, McCarthy was living in Houston, Harris County, according to the 1910 census.

64. The original 1900 charter was amended in April and November of 1906. In November 1908, TSE directors voted to renew that charter, which expired in November 1907, for fifty years, beginning from November 1907. The original charter's expiration was discovered to the "utter astonishment" of T. L. L. Temple's agents in 1908, when they went to Austin seeking authorization to issue bonds. See seven-page letter from Greer, Minor, and Miller, attorneys of Beaumont, to T. L. L. Temple, April 9, 1908, ETRC, box 18, folder 1. TSE's corporation papers are contained in the records of the secretary of state in Austin; see pp. 336–39 for 1900; 243–45 and 303–5 for 1906; 497–502 for 1908; and 618–20 for 1909.

65. "To Be Extended to Waco," *Palestine Daily Herald*, October 26, 1908, p. 2; "New Road for Crockett," *Houston Post*, September 19, 1908, p. 8; "May Build to Palestine," *Houston Post*, November 24, 1910, p. 8; "To Extend Texas Southeastern," *Houston Post*, November 1, 1908, p. 19.

66. Morgan branch is identified in "Map of Yard at Neff, November 1909," in Texas Southeastern Railroad Records (1993:022), box 1, folder 19, at The History Center, Diboll.

67. Gerland, "A Brief Chronicle of Texas South-Eastern Railroad of Diboll, Texas," *Pine Bough* 5, no. 2 (2000):

2–9. Dave Kenley wrote a description of the TSE Railroad's route along the Neches River in a letter to Rand, McNally Map Company in August 1932. He said the Neches River was visible from the mile 35 board to the mile 39 board, the track being on the west side of the river. At the mile 39 board, the road crossed the river again and went up the east side. At the mile 45 board, the river became visible again. At the mile 49 board was the log camp of Fastrill, which contained a hundred houses. The railroad continued up the east side of the river and crossed the Texas State Railroad three-quarters of a mile east of the river. See D. C. Kenley to Rand, McNally and Company, Chicago, August 18, 1932, ETRC, box 55, folder 1.

68. "Neches Valley Pine," *American Lumberman*, January 18, 1908, p. 91, stated the Neches River provided water for Camp 1. Clyde Thompson later said the 640-acre Rayville Pasture, which enclosed the former site of Camp 1 in 1913, "included one or more springs." See an untitled typescript on the "Game Situation" at Boggy Slough in Thompson's 1961 Wilderness Bill Correspondence within the Clyde Thompson Papers (2004:014c), box 33, folders 19 and 20, The History Center, Diboll. There remains today a small spring just north of the 1941–66 clubhouse ruins.

69. "Neches Valley Pine," *American Lumberman*, January 18, 1908, p. 98.

70. Ibid., 91.

71. Bryant, *Logging*, 1st ed., 129–30.

72. Southern Pine Lumber Company's Shay Engine No. 8 was photographed while logging Boggy Slough in November 1907. See the *American Lumberman* Photographic Collection image numbers 334 (at Vair Station) and 338 (in a hardwood forest) at The History Center, Diboll. The standard work on the Shay Locomotive is Koch, *Shay Locomotive*.

73. Jonathan K. Gerland, "A Logging Camp Vignette," *Pine Bough* 4, no. 1 (1999): 30–31.

74. Ibid.; Maxwell and Baker, *Sawdust Empire*, 51–69; Sitton and Conrad, *Nameless Towns*, 148–53; Bryant, *Logging*, 1st ed., 56–70.

75. "Neches Valley Pine," *American Lumberman*, January 18, 1908, p. 86; "News and Notices: Bureau Work in Texas," *Forest Quarterly of the New York State College of Forestry* 1, no. 3 (1903): 114–15; Maxwell and Baker,

Sawdust Empire, 55–56; Walker, *Axes, Oxen, and Men*, 39. Some trees were old enough to have been diseased with red heart rot.

76. "Neches Valley Pine," *American Lumberman*, January 18, 1908, p. 86.

77. Bryant, *Logging*, 1st ed., 183; Williams, *Americans and Their Forests*, 251.

78. Bryant, *Logging*, 1st ed., 188–89; Williams, *Americans and Their Forests*, 251. Advertisements appearing in trade journals during the 1900s and 1910s included Southern Pine Lumber Company endorsements of the Lindsey Wagon. See Sawmill Data Base Project notes from 1993 at the Texas Forestry Museum, Lufkin.

79. Williams, *Americans and Their Forests*, 252; "Southern Pine from Forest to Retailer," *American Lumberman*, April 16, 1904; "Neches Valley Pine," *American Lumberman*, January 18, 1908; American Lumberman Photographs of Southern Pine Lumber Company Operations, 1903 and 1907 (1994:004), The History Center, Diboll.

80. "News and Notices: Bureau Work in Texas," *Forest Quarterly of the New York State College of Forestry* 1, no. 3 (1903): 114–15; "Neches Valley Pine," *American Lumberman*, January 18, 1908, pp. 86, 90–92.

81. "Neches Valley Pine," *American Lumberman*, January 18, 1908, p. 92. For an example of the sizes of ties and the prices paid, see a Cotton Belt "Cross Tie Circular" in ETRC, box 19, folder 6.

82. "TSE Railroad, 100 Years, 1900–2000," *Pine Bough* 5, no. 2 (2000): 36–42; "Neches Valley Pine," *American Lumberman*, January 18, 1908, pp. 70, 86; "Texas Southeastern Railroad Steam Locomotive Roster," *Journal of Texas Shortline Railroads* 2, no. 4 (1998): 58.

83. All four skidders were ten by ten in size. Southern Pine's skidders were Clyde winch numbers 2315 and 2316 (order number 263), and Temple Lumber's winch numbers were 2369 and 2370 (order number 266). Southern Pine's skidders were built in August 1914 and delivered at Neff in September 1914. Temple Lumber's were built in December 1914 and delivered at Pineland in January 1915. See the typescript, "List of Clyde Railroad Mounted Skidders Built between 1908 and 1927," provided the author by the Texas Forestry Museum, Lufkin, Texas, in September 2007.

84. Bryant, *Logging*, 1st ed., 204–7; Brown, *Logging*, 173.

85. Quoted in Robert S. Maxwell, "One Man's Legacy: W. Goodrich Jones and Texas Conservation," *Southwestern Historical Quarterly* 77, no. 3 (1974): 360.

86. See page 2 of a three-page letter, L. D. Gilbert to R. D. Forbes of the US Forest Service, August 25, 1921, ETRC, box 4, folder 13.

87. Gilbert to R. D. Forbes, USFS, August 25, 1921, ETRC, box 4, folder 13; Gerland, "A Brief History of Temple Land Ownership," 14; Correspondence between H. G. Temple and Arthur Temple Sr. in 1940, especially on August 10, 1940, ETRC, boxes 138 and 143; correspondence between Henry Gresham Temple and L. D. Gilbert, March 1 and 6 and April 16, 1926, ETRC, box 45, folder 2.

88. "Neches Valley Pine," *American Lumberman*, January 18, 1908, p. 84; Spaight, *Resources, Soil, and Climate*, 153–55, 311–12; Foster and Rozek, *Forgotten Texas Census*, 110–12 and 217–18.

89. "Overcup Oak," in Burns and Honkala, *Silvics of North America: Hardwoods*.

90. Vintage prints and typed notes from *American Lumberman's* photographer, J. D. Cress, are included in the American Lumberman Collection at The History Center, Diboll. See photographic prints and notes for images 301–4.

91. "Sweet Gum," in Peattie, *Natural History of Trees*, 307–11.

92. An employee of TSE Railroad, R. M. Maberry, was injured while driving piling for a bridge across Boggy Slough on July 24, 1909. See R. M. Maberry Accident File, in papers pertaining to a 1911 lawsuit, in Texas Southeastern Railroad Company Records (1993:022), The History Center, Diboll. When Dave Kenley surveyed the meanderings of Boggy Slough in November 1910, he recorded the location of the bridge, which corresponds to the location of the dam today. Southern Pine Lumber Company Land Record Volumes (1993:015), Trinity County Volume 11, The History Center, Diboll.

93. "Neches Valley Pine," *American Lumberman*, January 18, 1908, pp. 93–101, 104.

94. See especially letters from Watson Walker to T. L. L. Temple dated January 3, June 14, October 11,

November 17, November 22, 1919, and February 16, 1920, ETRC, box 18, folder 1.

95. See correspondence concerning hardwood logging in ETRC, box 18, folder 1; box 19, folder 10; box 20, folder 2; box 22, folder 7; box 26, folder 9; and box 42, folder 2.

96. Watson Walker to T. L. L. Temple, March 30, 1926, ETRC, box 42, folder 7.

97. Watson Walker to T. L. L. Temple, November 7, 1925, ETRC, box 42, folder 7.

98. T. L. L. Temple to Watson Walker, October 8, 1925, ETRC, box 42, folder 7.

99. T. L. L. Temple similarly advised Henry Temple at the Pineland and Hemphill hardwood mills and flooring plants, especially concerning oak and beech logs. Temple wrote Henry often to remind him to have plenty of hardwood logs out of the bottoms in the fall, before rising streams overflowed. Henry always replied that he kept between one and two million board feet of hardwood logs on hand at all times. Concerning ash logs, Henry once conceded that "the small, crooked ones being brought in are not worth fooling with," yet woods sawyers were usually instructed to "cut it" when in doubt. Temple reminded Henry that oaks needed greater attention to quality and lengths. For hickory and beech, Temple said that nothing should be brought to the mill smaller than fifteen inches diameter at the *small* end. Instead of continuing to skid logs 32 feet in length, "with more than half the log in most cases small and knotty," Temple said sawyers must focus on getting "one good short cut" and leave the poorer sections in the woods, with logging foremen grading their hardwood logs "along the track and in the woods, marking cull those which should not be brought to the mill." For red gum and magnolia, Temple felt they could "afford to saw down to a twelve inch top." See multiple letters between T. L. L. Temple and Henry G. Temple in ETRC, box 42, folder 2, especially those dated November 3 and 4 (two letters on November 4), 1925, and October 16 and 19, 1926. See also a two-page letter from H. G. Temple to E. M. Jackson and J. J. Pollard, March 19, 1926, ETRC, box 45, folder 1.

100. Most of the black walnut in Texas had been removed by 1905, according to botanist William L. Bray of Austin, who wrote that the state's best stands were "largely cut out" as a sacrifice to Texas' expanding agricultural pursuits. Bray, *Forest Resources of Texas*, 18–19.

101. G. W. Cleveland to US senator Morris Sheppard, Washington, DC, April 1, 1918, ETRC, box 17, folder 10; R. C. Bryant, "The War and the Lumber Industry," *Journal of Forestry* 17, no. 2 (1919): 127. Southern Pine Lumber Company was then cutting hardwood timber from its own lands as well as from the lands of others, such as Pine Island, east of Boggy Slough.

102. Jackson and Wheat, *Texas by Terán*, 72; see also pp. 139–41.

103. Edward W. Berry, "Notes on the Geological History of the Walnuts and Hickories," *Plant World* 15, no. 10 (1912): 225–40. Helpful in my geographic and ecological understanding of the various walnuts and hickories were professors Charles Lafon of Texas A&M University at College Station; Kathryn Kidd and Jeremy P. Stovall of Stephen F. Austin State University; Francis X. Galan of the University of Texas at San Antonio; and Francis De La Teja of Texas State University at San Marcos, who corresponded with me during April and May 2017, author's collections.

104. Spurr and Barnes, *Forest Ecology*, 61, 309. See also the entry for black walnut in US Forest Service, *Silvics Manual*, vol. 2, *Hardwoods*.

105. Typescript of testimony of E. J. Mantooth before the Interstate Commerce Commission, Washington, DC, in "Stenographers' Minutes before the Interstate Commerce Commission, Finance Docket No. 4, Application for Abandonment, Eastern Texas Railroad Company, September 27, 1920," p. 529, Murry Hammond Collection, Pasadena, California. Mantooth's entire testimony is on pp. 499–530. See also Gilbert to Kenley, July 31, 1922, ETRC, box 2, folder 6.

106. Letter, Dave Kenley to E. J. Mantooth, July 14, 1920, ETRC, box 19, folder 4.

107. See at least twenty-five pages of correspondence among Dave Kenley, L. D. Gilbert, E. J. Irving, R. F. Vinson, Charley Palmer, and others concerning crosstie production and delivery to the Cotton Belt along the Eastern Texas Railroad right-of-way at mileposts 16 and 17, which were inside Boggy Slough Conservation Area, and at other locations in Angelina County, between August 1920 and March 1921, in ETRC, box 19, folder 6. The name of the man who ran the

sawmill was L. P., or P. L., Fore. See also a Cotton Belt "Cross Tie Circular" in the same folder. Earlier, in September 1919, Gilbert had consulted with Lufkin Land and Lumber Company about that company's use of several crosstie mills in East Texas and Louisiana. See Long-Bell Lumber Company to L. D. Gilbert, September 20, 1919, in ETRC, box 19, folder 4.

108. "Neches Valley Pine," *American Lumberman*, January 18, 1908, pp. 71, 74–79, 88, 94–101. J. D. Cress was the photographer. His notes that accompanied vintage prints of his photographs are at The History Center, Diboll. The 38-inch longleaf pine was designated a co-champion tree by the Texas Forest Service in June 2017. Observations of large longleaf pines in East Texas were numerous. One of the earliest mentions of trees larger than 48 inches and 130 feet in height was made by S. B. Buckley, the assistant state geologist in 1868. See Buckley, "Pine Lands of South-Eastern Texas," 91–92.

109. "Neches Valley Pine," *American Lumberman*, January 18, 1908, pp. 71, 74–79, 88, and 94–101. See also J. D. Cress's photographs and notes, The History Center, Diboll.

110. "Lone Star Pine," *American Lumberman*, September 26, 1908, pp. 67–151, esp. pp. 78–80, 85–86, 91.

111. L. D. Gilbert explained the diameter cut reasoning to R. D. Forbes of the US Forest Service in a letter of August 25, 1921, in ETRC, box 4, folder 13.

112. "Neches Valley Pine," *American Lumberman*, January 18, 1908, p. 84.

113. Aldo Leopold, "The Conservation Ethic," *Journal of Forestry* 31, no. 6 (1933): 636; Aldo Leopold, "A Biotic View of Land," *Journal of Forestry* 37, no. 9 (1939): 727–30; Leopold, *Sand County Almanac*.

114. Dionne, "Lumber History of Texas," 342–43.

115. "Gossip of the Corridors," *Houston Post*, January 9 1908, p. 6.

116. Kellogg, *Timber Supply*, 15–23.

117. Dana and Fairfax, *Forest and Range Policy*, 92–93; Davidson's and Jones's speeches are in Blanchard, *Proceedings of a Governors Conference*, 190–91 and 223–26.

118. "Southwest Mill Men on Reforestation," *Houston Post*, August 30, 1908, p. 11.

119. Ibid. The same news story, "Southwest Mill Men on Reforestation," appeared in *Southern Industrial and Lumber Review*, August 1908, pp. 44–45.

Chapter 6. The Land Fenced

1. Letter, E. C. Durham to John F. Fannelly, associate editor of *Commerce & Finance*, New York, April 9, 1926, Temple Industries Records at the East Texas Research Center, Nacogdoches (hereafter ETRC), box 44, folder 4; L. D. Gilbert, "Grazing Cut-Over Lands," *Cut-Over Lands* 1, no. 8 (1918): 20.

2. Tharp, *Structure of Texas Vegetation*, 31; F. V. Emerson, "The Southern Long-Leaf Pine Belt," *Geographical Review* 7, no. 2 (1919): 83–84.

3. Tharp, *Structure of Texas Vegetation*, 31, 38–39; Chapman, "Is the Longleaf Type a Climax?" 329–30; Stewart, "Burning and Natural Vegetation in the United States," 318. Yale University forester Herman Chapman said that the bluestem grasses "dry out so rapidly after rain that within an hour a hot fire can be on its way." See H. H. Chapman, "The Place of Fire in the Ecology of Pines," *Bartonia* no. 26 (1952): 42.

4. Edd Kenley interview with Jonathan Gerland, October 5, 2000, Interview 158a, The History Center, Diboll, 2; "Pioneer Etex Rancher Dead," *Lufkin Daily News* clipping, February 28, 1941, author's possession; Paine, *Captain Bill McDonald*, 265–72, 433–36; Gilbert, "Grazing Cut-Over Lands," 20. Ray was included in the 1910 census, at Malvern, Arkansas, in Hot Springs County, Enumeration District 88, sheet 6A, line 36.

5. Some of these details are contained in a two-page typescript on the "game situation" at Boggy Slough, ca. 1961, in the Clyde Thompson Collection (2004:014c), at The History Center, Diboll, see the folder, "Correspondence, 1961, Wilderness Bill." Some of the pear trees were still growing during the author's first visit to Rayville with Charlie Harber in 2000. Placing corn in silos is also mentioned in a letter from L. D. Gilbert to T. L. L. Temple, July 10, 1917, ETRC, box 18, folder 2. For the stump pullers, see Dave Kenley to Ray, June 27, 1919, ETRC, box 20, folder 10.

6. Two multiple-page letters from E. C. Durham to T. L. L. Temple, July 19 and 25, 1916, ETRC, box 18a, folder 4.

7. Ibid.

8. "Memoranda with reference to fencing different portions of the Ranch of Southern Pine Lumber Company in Trinity and Houston Counties," three-page manuscript in Clyde Thompson's 1943 Correspondence Files (2004:014c), box 4, folder 3, The History Center, Diboll; Gilbert, "Grazing Cut-Over Lands," 20. The lands north of Highway 7 became known as the Malibu Club in the 1930s.

9. Harold E. Grelen, "Forest Grazing in the South," *Journal of Range Management* 31, no. 4 (1978): 248; T. H. Silker, *Forest Grazing*, 11.

10. Odom, *Over on Cochino*, 71.

11. Calf crops were generally better than 60 percent.

12. Letter, D. C. Kenley to George Huffman, Houston, February 27, 1933, ETRC, box 71, folder 6.

13. Jonathan Gerland's recorded interviews with Joe Silvers (174a, November 12, 2008) and Charlie Harber (157a–d, 2000–2002), and notes from conversations with Mytrle Nolen Rushing on June 20 and 21, 2000, all at The History Center, Diboll. J. J. Ray and J. J. Ray Jr. are buried beside each other in the Knight-Glendale Cemetery at Lufkin.

14. Gerland, "The Lonesomest Place in the World," *Pine Bough* 13, no. 1 (2008):15–17. Much of the material concerning Charlie Harber's memories was gathered from notes made during personal and telephone visits between 2000 and 2006 as well as from four recorded interviews: Interviews 157a (May 4, 2000), 157b (May 26, 2000), 157c (October 13, 2000), and 157d (March 27, 2002), which are preserved and transcribed at The History Center, Diboll.

15. Author's conversations with Charlie Harber between 2000 and 2006.

16. Ibid. For other assessments of Robinson, see interviews with Joe Silvers (transcript 174a, November 12, 2008), and John Booker (transcript 224b, September 23, 2014) at The History Center, Diboll. Morgan branch is identified in "Map of Yard at Neff, November 1909," in Texas Southeastern Railroad Records (1993:022), box 1, folder 19.

17. John O. Booker Jr. interview with Jonathan Gerland, September 23, 2014, Interview 224b, pp. 20–25, The History Center, Diboll.

18. Gerland, "Lonesomest Place in the World," 5–7.

19. Charlie Harber quoted in Sitton, *Backwoodsmen*, 227, and in conversations with Jonathan Gerland, 2000–2005.

20. Charlie Harber, Interview 157a, May 4, 2000, by Jonathan Gerland, The History Center, Diboll, 2–3; Sitton, *Backwoodsmen*, 256–70.

21. Gilbert, "Grazing Cut-Over Lands," 20.

22. Jim Rushing interview, Transcript 90a, p. 2, The History Center, Diboll.

23. Notes made by Dan Lay from a conversation with Clyde Thompson and others, from a typed manuscript, "X: Special Places," page 3 of "Boggy Slough," in Dan Lay Collection, box 4, folder 19, East Texas Research Center, Stephen F. Austin State University, Nacogdoches (hereafter SFASU).

24. The tenancy system was common to all Southern Pine Lumber Company lands. Company correspondence is replete with mentions of the practice. Lists of various tenancies and other land leases can be found in the Land Record volumes of Southern Pine Lumber Company, The History Center, Diboll. The quotes come from a lease from 1932, in ETRC, box 55, folder 1.

25. Pyne, *Fire in America*, 129–30.

26. Letter, Kenley to G. I. Huffman, Houston, February 27, 1933, ETRC, box 71, folder 6.

27. Letter, D. C. Kenley to J. J. Ray, April 23, 1919, ETRC box 20, folder 10.

28. Letter, T. L. L. Temple to Watson Walker, October 11, 1926, ETRC, box 42, folder 7.

29. Letter, L. D. Gilbert to T. L. L. Temple, April 18, 1917, ETRC, box 18, folder 1; "Distribution of Boll Weevil," 10, and "Condition of Crop," 10–11, both in *Galveston Daily News*, July 26, 1904.

30. See especially correspondence between Gus Rounsaville of Continental State Bank of Alto and D. C. Kenley, January 19 and 20, 1922, in ETRC, box 19, folder 7.

31. Charlie Harber, interviewed by Jonathan Gerland, May 4, 2000, Interview 157a, pp. 6–7, The History

Center, Diboll. See also Charlie Harber, interviewed by Jonathan Gerland, March 27, 2002, Interview 157d, pp. 13–15, The History Center, Diboll.

32. "Turnip Grows Big," *Lubbock Morning Avalanche*, March 21, 1931.

33. See multi-page letters from E. C. Durham to L. D. Gilbert, September 22, 1916, ETRC, box 18a, folder 6, and to T. L. L. Temple, October 18, 1917, ETRC, box 18a, folder 1. See also letters from Watson Walker to T. L. L. Temple, February 5, 1919, ETRC, box 18, folder 1, and D. C. Kenley to L. D. Gilbert, January 2, 1922, ETRC, box 30, folder 5.

34. Annual Report of Texas Southeastern Railroad to the Railroad Commission of Texas for the Year 1924, The History Center, Diboll; letter, E. C. Durham to L. D. Gilbert, November 2, 1926, ETRC, box 44, folder 3.

35. Letter, E. C. Durham to T. L. L. Temple, October 27, 1919, ETRC, box 18a, folder 4.

36. Letter, Kenley to Gilbert, July 14, 1923, ETRC, box 26, folder 7.

37. Letter, E. C. Durham to John F. Fannelly, associate editor of *Commerce & Finance*, New York, April 9, 1926, ETRC, box 44, folder 4.

38. Campbell, "Grazing in Southern Pine Forests," 13–20; Grelen and Duvall, *Common Plants*, 7, 8, and 12; Guldin, "Ecology of Shortleaf Pine," 25–40; Tharp, *Structure of Texas Vegetation*, 23–40; Tharp, *Vegetation of Texas*; Bray, *Forest Resources of Texas*, 23–25; Don C. Bragg, "Reference Conditions for Old-Growth Pine Forests in the Upper West Gulf Coastal Plain," *Journal of the Torrey Botanical Society* 129, no. 4 (2002): 261–88; Silker, *Forest Grazing*, 4–34; Don C. Bragg, "Structure and Dynamics of a Pine-Hardwood Old-Growth Remnant in Southern Arkansas," *Journal of the Torrey Botanical Society* 131, no. 4 (2004): 320–36; Barbara R. MacRoberts and Michael H. MacRoberts, "Floristics of Upland Shortleaf Pine/Oak-Hickory Forest in Northwestern Louisiana," *Journal of the Botanical Research Institute of Texas* 3, no. 1 (2009): 367–74; MacRoberts and MacRoberts, "Plant Ecology and Phytogeography," 7–28.

39. Hatcher and Foik, "The Expedition of Don Domingo Teran," 30.

40. O. Gordon Langdon, Miriam A. Bomhard, and John T. Cassady, *Field Book of Forage Plants*, 95. Photographs showing goat weed at Boggy Slough from the 1910s through the 1960s is in the Daniel W. Lay Collection at SFASU, box 4, folder 30, and in the Silvers Family and J. Shirley Daniel photographic collections at The History Center, Diboll.

41. Hogan, *Some Especially Valuable Grasses*, 28–30; Vasey, *Grasses of the South*, 8–9; Langdon, Bomhard, and Cassady, *Field Book of Forage Plants*, 38–39; Grelen and Duvall, *Common Plants*, 26; Shaw, *Guide to Texas Grasses*, 246; Hatch, Umphries, and Ardoin, *Field Guide*, 67; Silker, *Forest Grazing*, 22–24; Weaver, *Manual of Forestry*, 118–20.

42. Letter, D. C. Kenley to Austin Cary, USFS, March 27, 1923, ETRC, box 4, folder 12. See also undated notes from Cary to Kenley in the same folder. Responding to Cary's questions on grazing practices, Kenley said it was true that a pasture grazed more would have more carpet grass and less "sage" grass, especially if grazed early in the spring. Kenley added that burning in the spring would have the same effect as grazing in the spring, and if pastures of sage grass were not burned in the spring, they should be grazed. See also Grelen and Duvall, *Common Plants*, 26.

43. Ousley, *Grasses for Pastures and Hay*, 6; *Modern Silage Methods*, 133–42, 152–53.

44. Letter, L. D. Gilbert to J. J. Ray, April 12, 1918, ETRC, box 20, folder 10; L. D. Gilbert, "Grazing Cut-Over Lands," 20; news items in *Cut-Over Lands*, April 1918, pp. 6–7; May 1918, pp. 16–17; June 1918, p. 15; September 1918, p. 16; and November 1918, p. 20; Kittredge, *Forest Influences*, 330; Bill Finch, "The True Story of Kudzu, the Vine That Never Truly Ate the South, *Smithsonian Magazine*, September 2015.

45. Letter, Longview Cotton Oil Company to D. C. Kenley, December 4, 1922, ETRC, box 3, folder 3; *Cut-Over Lands*, April 1918, pp. 6–7; May 1918, pp. 16–17; June 1918, p. 15; and September 1918, p. 16; Emerson, "Southern Long-Leaf Pine Belt," 89.

46. Letter, L. D. Gilbert to E. C. Durham, October 11, 1922, ETRC, box 30, folder 1.

47. Bray, *Forest Resources of Texas*, 21–25; William T. Chambers, "Pine Woods Region of Southeastern Texas," *Economic Geography*, 10, no. 3 (1934): 308;

Frank Heyward, "The Relation of Fire to Stand Composition of Longleaf Pine Forests," *Ecology* 20, no. 2 (1939): 287–304 (esp. 290).

48. Mohr, *Timber Pines*, 97.

49. See Thoreau's journal entries of May 13, 1856, and September 24, 1857, in *The Journal, 1837–1861*, by Henry David Thoreau, ed. Damion Searls, 385–86, 454–55; Thoreau, *Succession of Forest Trees*, 38–39; Spurr, *Forest Ecology*, 400–401.

50. Chambers, "Pine Woods Region," 308; Tharp, *Structure of Texas Vegetation*, 23, 31, 36, 38–40.

51. Gilbert, "Grazing Cut-Over Lands," 20.

52. Letters, E. C. Durham to T. L. L. Temple, November 2 and 26 and December 6, 1916; January 25, March 5 and 7, and December 17 and 30, 1917; February 15, May 7, June 4 and 19, October 14 and 22, and November 30, 1918; and March 10, 1919; in ETRC, box 18a, folders 1, 2, 3, and 7; Silker, *Forest Grazing*, 21.

53. Letter, E. C. Durham to T. L. L. Temple, May 7, 1918, ETRC, box 18a, folder 2; letter, Parker Bros. to Southern Pine Lumber Company, May 18, 1918, ETRC, box 19, folder 1.

54. Letters, P. V. Pardon to D. C. Kenley, April 11, 1918; D. C. Kenley to P. V. Pardon, April 24, 1918, ETRC, box 19, folder 1. Also getting goats from Pineland, see S. P. McElroy to Kenley, May 18, 1918, and Kenley to McElroy, May 18, 1918, ETRC, box 19, folder 1.

55. Joe Silvers, grandson of Rayville cowboy John Silvers, in his interview with Jonathan Gerland on November 12, 2008 (Interview 174a, The History Center, Diboll, 17), said the ranch held three thousand head of goats. Clyde Thompson is another source for three thousand head of goats, in Clyde Thompson Correspondence 1961, Wilderness Bill notes, 2004:014c, The History Center, Diboll. The source for ten thousand head of goats is Charlie Harber in Sitton, *Backwoodsmen*, 217.

56. Edd Kenley, interviewed by Jonathan Gerland, October 5, 2000, Interview 158a, The History Center, Diboll, 12–13. At least one photograph in the Joe Silvers Photograph Collection (2002:091), The History Center, Diboll, shows the goat house near Ray's house.

57. Kenley correspondence in ETRC, boxes 4, 18, 18a, 19, 20, 22, and 26; Letter, E. C. Durham to John F. Fannelly, April 9, 1926, ETRC, box 44, folder 4; Charlie

Harber interview with Jonathan Gerland, October 13, 2000, Interview 157c, The History Center, Diboll, 2.

58. Letter, E. C. Durham to L. D. Gilbert, post script, November 2, 1926, ETRC, box 44, folder 3.

59. The Silvers Family Photographic Collection (2002:091), The History Center, Diboll, includes a photograph showing Guy Burke, a government trapper, with a red wolf he trapped at Boggy Slough during the 1920s.

60. Letter, E. C. Durham to John F. Fannelly, associate editor of *Commerce & Finance*, New York, April 9, 1926, ETRC, box 44, folder 4.

61. Five-page letter, E. C. Durham to T. L. L. Temple, November 2, 1916, ETRC, box 18a, folder 7.

62. Letters, E. C. Durham to T. L. L. Temple, July 19 and August 21, 1916, p. 2; January 25, March 5 and 7, and December 17, 1917; in ETRC, box 18a, folders 3, 4, and 6.

63. Undated letter from L. D. Gilbert to R. D. Forbes, Forest Service, New Orleans, in reply to Forbes's letter of August 5, 1921, in ETRC, box 4, folder 13.

64. Edd Kenley, son of Dave Kenley, tells of his father going to Laredo to make arrangements for payment with the men's families in Mexico. See Edd Kenley, Interview 158a, October 5, 2000, interviewed by Jonathan Gerland, The History Center, Diboll, 13–14. Company records for 1916 through 1918, housed at ETRC in boxes 18 and 18a, suggest the possibility of some Mexican workers having come through a labor agent at Nacogdoches. Other correspondence among Kenley, Durham, and Gilbert indicated that many of the Mexican workers at Boggy Slough became ill from influenza in 1918 and some died. See multiple letters written in October and November 1918 in ETRC, box 18a, folders 2 and 4. Charlie Harber, born in 1920, told the author during 2000 that he remembered the location of a graveyard for the deceased "Mexican brush choppers." He walked by it often as a child and rode horseback by it frequently as a pasture rider during the 1940s and 1950s. He said dozens of sandstone and iron ore rocks once marked the graves. The author, accompanied by Harber, tried unsuccessfully to locate the gravestones several times during 2000. Unfortunately, a thick pine plantation covered the site as best as Harber could tell.

65. Three-page letter, E. C. Durham to T. L. L. Temple, December 30, 1917, ETRC, box 18a, folder 1. See also

E. C. Durham to T. L. L. Temple, November 2, 1916, ETRC, box 18a, folder 7. Durham hired a crew of Mexicans to help with track work.

66. Undated letter from L. D. Gilbert to R. D. Forbes, Forest Service, New Orleans, in reply to Forbes's letter of August 5, 1921, in ETRC, box 4, folder 13. For numbers of Mexicans hired, see "Life Never Dull for City's Lovable Justice of the Peace," *Diboll Free Press*, September 6, 1961, pp. 1, 6, and a one-page typescript concerning the game situation at Boggy Slough, ca. 1961, in Clyde Thompson Correspondence (2004:014c), 1961 Wilderness Bill folder, The History Center, Diboll.

67. Multiple letters, E. C. Durham to T. L. L. Temple, November 2 and 26 and December 6, 1916; January 25, March 5 and 7, and December 17 and 30, 1917; February 15, June 4 and 19, October 14 and 22, and November 30, 1918; ETRC, box 18a, folders 1, 2, 3, and 7. The logging camp in San Augustine County was known as White City. TSE trains operated over the Cotton Belt between White City and Lufkin.

68. See numerous letters between E. C. Durham and T. L. L. Temple in ETRC, box 18a, folders 1, 2, 3, and 5, especially Durham's letters of October 23, 1917, and January 31, February 15, June 19, July 10 and 13, October 4 and 14, and December 1, 1918. See also correspondence between E. C. Durham and Arthur Temple Sr., February 12 and 14, 1923, ETRC, box 29, folder 4.

69. Letter, J. E. Rhodes of Southern Pine Association to T. L. L. Temple, December 1, 1916, ETRC, box 18; "Development of Cut-Over Lands Plans Approved: Utilization of South's Immense Acreage for Farming and Stock Raising Will Meet Demand," *Lufkin Daily News*, October 3, 1917; *Southern Lumberman*, February 1, 1919, p. 24; Carter, Kellison, and Wallinger, *Forestry in the U.S. South*, 31; Fickle, *New South*.

70. Gilbert, "Grazing Cut-Over Lands," 6.

71. Ibid., 20.

72. Gilbert was not alone in promoting the ranch, nor its young second-growth timber. Although Santa Fe's interest in purchasing the TSE railroad "from a stock raising and agricultural standpoint" never materialized, E. C. Durham continued to invite the agricultural departments of the railroad companies to visit Boggy Slough and take promotional photographs. Durham sought as much as possible to keep the ranch

in the eyes of industry as well as of the general public. When Arthur Temple Sr. suggested Durham prepare a feature article on the Temple family's sawmilling operations for the trade magazine *Gulf Coast Lumberman* in 1923, Durham accepted the project, especially if he could include a large number of illustrations. In addition to photographs of the Diboll, Hemphill, and Pineland sawmills, which Temple specifically wanted, Durham, whose many hobbies included photography, wanted to include as many images of the ranch and its "young timber" as possible. Temple, who was now head of the lumber sales department, initially sought to feature the manufacturing side of the businesses, while Durham wanted "the ranch" and "some of Mr. Ray's choice cattle" to be the stars of the show. See letters from E. C. Durham to Arthur Temple, February 12, 1923, and from Arthur Temple to E. C. Durham, February 14, 1923, ETRC, box 29, folder 4; Robert M. Hayes, "Squire Durham's 60-Mile Railroad Wins Him Acclaim of East Texans," *Dallas Morning News*, May 30, 1937, p. 14. One such example of a railroad visiting and photographing the ranch was the Missouri Pacific Lines in June 1931. See the Silvers Photographic Collection (2002:091), The History Center, Diboll.

73. See numerous letters between Southern Pine Lumber Company and the state and federal forestry agencies during the 1920s in ETRC, box 4, folders 12 and 13.

74. Three-page undated letter, L. D. Gilbert to R. D. Forbes, USDA Forest Service at New Orleans, in reply to Forbes's August 25, 1921, letter, in ETRC, box 4, folder 13; Letter, Gilbert to E. O. Siecke, February 6, 1923, ETRC, box 4, folder 12; Marilyn D. Rhinehart, "Forestry and Politics," *East Texas Historical Journal* 20, no. 2 (1982): 12.

75. Three-page undated letter, L. D. Gilbert to R. D. Forbes, USDA Forest Service at New Orleans, in reply to Forbes's August 25, 1921, letter, in ETRC, box 4, folder 13.

76. Cary visited Boggy Slough in February 1923, accompanied by E. O. Siecke of the Texas Forest Service. Dave Kenley was their escort. See letter from Dave Kenley to L. D. Gilbert, February 26, 1923, ETRC, box 26, folder 9. For more information on Cary, see Roy R. White, "Austin Cary, the Father of Southern Forestry," *Forest and Conservation History* 5, no. 1 (1961): 2–5.

77. Grelen and Duvall, *Common Plants*, 26; nine-page typescript by Austin Cary, US Forest Service, to Watson Walker, written at Diboll, March 2, 1923, titled, "Notes for Mr. Walker, Diboll, Texas," ETRC, box 4, folder 12; see also there, undated correspondence between Cary and Kenley and between Cary and Walker. Cary said "fire is the only remedy" to maintain a pasture under growing pines. He also said Kenley had told him that stock raising could be profitable in East Texas, especially for "small owners."

78. Letter, Cary to Walker, March 2, 1923, ETRC, box 4, folder 12.

79. Gilbert to Siecke, February 6, 1923, ETRC, box 4, folder 12.

80. Report, USDA Forest Service, RS Annual Investigative Program, Southern Forest Experiment Station, February 10, 1923, pp. 10–11; and letter, R. D. Forbes to L. D. Gilbert, March 14, 1923, both in ETRC, box 4, folder 12.

81. Two-page letter, Austin Cary to Watson Walker, March 26, 1923, ETRC, box 4, folder 12.

82. Several such letters from 1923 are found in ETRC, box 4, folder 12. See also letter from Kenley to Gilbert, May 12, 1926, ETRC, box 44, folder 6.

83. W. B. Greeley, "Back to the Land," *Saturday Evening Post*, March 31, 1923, pp. 21, 58, 60, 62, quote on p. 21. Greeley referenced Rudyard Kipling's poem, "Recessional" (1897).

84. Letter, Dave Kenley to L. D. Gilbert, May 12, 1926, ETRC, box 44, folder 6. See also Kenley's correspondence concerning forestry matters during the early 1920s in ETRC, box 4, folders 12 and 13. For contemporary descriptions of the effects of various types of fires in cutover pine forests in Texas, see "Effects of Fire," *Texas Forest News*, December 1928, p. 3; Tharp, *Structure of Texas Vegetation*, 30; and Forbes, *Timber Growing and Logging*, 22–23.

85. Aldo Leopold, "Wild Followers of the Forest: The Effect of Forest Fires on Game and Fish, the Relation of Forests to Game Conservation," *American Forestry* 29, no. 357 (1923): 515–19, 568; Aldo Leopold, "Piute Forestry vs. Forest Fire Prevention," *Southwestern Magazine* 2, no. 3 (1920): 12–13; "Editors' Notes on 'Piute Forestry vs. Forest Fire Prevention,'"

in Brown and Carmony, *Aldo Leopold's Wilderness*, 143–45; William B. Greeley, "Piute Forestry or the Fallacy of Light Burning, from *The Timberman*, March 1920," *Forest History Today* (Spring 1999): 33–37; Chapman and Bryant, *Prolonging the Cut*. Pyne (*Fire in America*, 100–122) traces the spread of the light-burning "controversy" from California to the South.

86. Chapman and Bryant, *Prolonging the Cut*, 17; Chapman, "The Place of Fire in the Ecology of Pines," 39–44; Chapman, "Fire and Pines," 62–64, 91–93; Chapman, "Is the Longleaf Type a Climax?," 328–34; H. H. Chapman, "Some Further Relations of Fire to Longleaf Pine," *Journal of Forestry* 30, no. 5 (1932): 602–4. Austin Cary advised Southern Pine Lumber Company against "precautionary fire" for a number of reasons in 1923, but he later changed his views. See nine-page typescript by Austin Cary, US Forest Service, to Watson Walker, written at Diboll, March 2, 1923, titled, "Notes for Mr. Walker, Diboll, Texas," ETRC, box 4, folder 12; White, "Austin Cary," 3–4; and Austin Cary, "Some Relations of Fire to Longleaf Pine," *Journal of Forestry* 30, no. 5 (1932): 594–601.

87. Three-page letter, Gilbert to R. D. Forbes, August 25, 1921, ETRC, box 4, folder 13. In 1923, R. E. Minton advised Kenley to begin removing the word "merchantable" from timber deeds, which would allow future growth of small timber and long-term reserves. Letter, Minton to Kenley, January 19, 1923, ETRC, box 26, folder 8.

88. "Gilbert Heads Forestry Department, East Texas C. C.," *Bryan Eagle*, October 18, 1926, p. 2; "Warden Named as Member of Forestry Committee E. T. C.," *Marshall News Messenger*, December 7, 1926; "Texas Forestry Association Holds Fourteenth Annual Meeting," *Texas Forest News*, December 1929, pp. 1, 3, and 4; "East Texas Chamber of Commerce Outlines Farm Forestry Program," *Texas Forest News*, April 1930, p. 3; "Hochwald to Preside at Park Meeting," *Marshall News Messenger*, August 11, 1931. See also letter from E. C. Durham to John F. Fannelly, April 9, 1926, ETRC, box 44, folder 4. Bernard Fernow delivered an address titled "Timber as a Crop" at the World's Fair Congress in October 1893. See Fernow, "Timber as a Crop," 142–47.

89. Letter, E. C. Durham to John F. Fannelly, April 9, 1926, ETRC, box 44, folder 4; "Private Interest in Forestry," *Texas Forest News*, May 1926, p. 3, col. 2. Watson Walker, as vice president of the Texas Forestry Association, declared at TFA's annual meeting in 1926 that Southern Pine Lumber Company had, as "their final decision," recently turned "to reforestation instead of grazing" on most of their cutover lands.

90. Two-page letter, Arthur Temple Sr. to W. H. McKinney, October 22, 1936, ETRC, box 104, folder 6.

91. Letters and statements, Hintz, Walker-Kenley Cattle Company, 1918–1920, Hintz to Kenley, January 29, 1920, and Kenley to Gilbert, March 24, 1920, ETRC, box 4, folder 6.

92. See three letters from D. C. Kenley: one to L. D. Gilbert on December 30, 1925; one to Gilbert, Walker, and Hintz on December 30; and one to Gilbert, Hintz, Ray, and Walker on December 31; all in ETRC, box 44, folder 6.

93. See multiple lease agreements and tenancy contracts from the 1920s and 1930s in ETRC, box 78, folder 6. See also Kenley cattle and hog business statements and correspondence from the 1910s and 1920s in ETRC, box 4, folder 6; and box 19, folder 5; and, from the 1940s, in ETRC, box 153, folders 2 and 6.

94. Edd Kenley, Interview 158a transcript, 14, The History Center, Diboll.

95. Letter, Kenley to T. L. L. Temple, April 28, 1922, ETRC, box 30, folder 5; letter, Kenley to William Clayton of Rosenberg, January 28, 1922, ETRC, box 19, folder 7.

96. Letter, Kenley to Gilbert, September 8, 1922, ETRC, box 30, folder 4.

97. See multiple letters among R. E. Minton, Dave Kenley, and J. J. Ray, February 23 and 26, 1923, in ETRC, box 22, folders 10 and 11. Whether a lease became effective at this time is unknown. Minton's main concern was the cost of adequately fencing the 3,700 acres, which he estimated at $1,000, which would be lost if Henderson sold the land during the time of the lease.

98. Angelina County Deed Records, Angelina County Courhouse, Lufkin, vol. 63, pp. 390–99; Letter, P. M. Albritton to Dave Kenley, April 15, 1923, ETRC,

box 2, folder 12. Renfro wanted $10 per acre, or more than $90,000, but Kenley and Albritton got the price down to less than $8 per acre, as Renfro was in considerable debt.

99. Letter, Kenley to Gilbert, May 14, 1923, ETRC, box 26, folder 9.

100. Letter, Kenley to Gilbert, August 3, 1923, ETRC, box 26, folder 8.

101. Letter, Gilbert to Kenley and Ray, August 6, 1923, ETRC, box 26, folder 8.

102. Ibid.

103. Kenley mentions his cattle and his "place at Cotulla" often in correspondence. See especially D. C. Kenley letter to Arthur Temple, August 12, 1939, in ETRC, box 126, folder 4. Kenley's ranch was southwest of Fowlerton.

104. Fox and Cox, *Archaeological and Historical Investigations*, 1–6; Dimmitt County Deed Records, Dimmitt County Courthouse, Carrizo Springs, vol. 58, pp. 598–606, and vol. 69, pp. 124–26. Many details about the purchase of the ranch from J. Shugar of Dallas County, the ranch's transfer from Temple Lumber Company to Southern Pine Lumber Company, attempts to lease the ranch (including a lease to A. E. Gates), the sale of the ranch to George W. Lyles, and nagging tax issues and threats of lawsuits that lingered into 1938 are included in dozens of letters written by Arthur Temple Sr., Dave Kenley, and R. E. Minton, among others, between 1932 and 1938, contained in ETRC, box 55, folder 2; box 71, folder 6; box 90, folder 7; box 104, folder 6; box 123, folder 8. See especially letters of May 28–31, June 3, 6, 20, 24, and 25, and July 8, 1932; February 14, June 19, and December 19 and 20, 1933; March 16, April 17, July 18 and 22, July 31, and August 5 and 8, 1935; February 20 and 21, March 3, 21, 25, May 15, June 23 and 25, July 6 and 29, August 6, September 10, and October 15, 19, 21, 22, and 24, 1936; and January 19, February 18 and 21, March 12, 21, 25, and 31, 1938. Southern Pine Lumber Company sold the ranch for $5.50 an acre, while carrying it on the financial books at $13.50 an acre. See letter from Arthur Temple Sr. to W. H. McKinney, October 22, 1936, ETRC, box 104, folder 6.

105. "L. D. Gilbert Passes On," *Texas Forest News*, December 1931, p. 3.

Chapter 7. The Fenced Land

1. Letter, General Terán to the President of Mexico, June 30, 1828, in Jackson and Wheat, *Texas by Terán*, 101.

2. Doughty, *Wildlife and Man in Texas*; Aldo Leopold, *Game Management*, xxxi, 3–21.

3. Charlie Harber quoted in Sitton, *Backwoodsmen*, 257–58. Charlie Harber told Jonathan Gerland similar stories between 2000 and 2005 during numerous visits. See also the recorded and transcribed interviews with Harber, 157a (May 4, 2000), 157b (May 26, 2000), 157c (October 13, 2000), and 157d (May 27, 2002) at The History Center, Diboll.

4. Leopold, *Game Management*; Worster, *Nature's Economy*, 269–73; Doughty, *Wildlife and Man in Texas*, 195–97; Tharp, *Structure of Texas Vegetation*, 23, 31–32; Tharp, *Vegetation of Texas*, 37–38; Daniel W. Lay, "Deer Range Appraisal in East Texas," *Journal of Wildlife Management* 31, no. 3 (1967): 428. Some of the woody vegetation most useful to deer were yaupon, sweetgum, the oaks, white ash, and persimmon.

5. Letters, E. C. Durham to T. L. L. Temple, August 21, 1916, and John F. Lehane of Cotton Belt Lines to E. C. Durham, September 16, 1916, both in Temple Industries Records at the East Texas Research Center, Nacogdoches (hereafter ETRC), box 18a, folder 6.

6. "East Texas Railroad Man Finds Time for Sport" and Robert M. Hayes, "Squire Durham's 60-Mile Railroad Wins Him Acclaim of East Texans," in *Dallas Morning News*, May 30, 1937, p. 14.

7. For example, see Senator George Moffett's guest card and invitation for November 20–23, 1949, in Arthur Temple Jr. Papers (2004:014a), box 9, folder 24, The History Center, Diboll.

8. A sample of hunting invitations and acceptance letters are contained in Arthur Temple Jr. Papers (2004:014a), box 2, folder 12; box 9, folder 24; box 19, folders 24–25; box 23, folder 11; box 24, folder 3; box 26, folder 17; box 27, folder 8; box 32, folder 4; box 32, folder 5; box 43, folder 13; box 48, folder 13; box 49, folder 24; box 54, folder 22; box 59, folder 12; box 60, folder 26; box 67, folder 32; box 73, folder 17; box 75, folder 8; box 82, folder 13; and box 87, folder 9, The History Center, Diboll. See esp. box 37, folder 18 and box 75, folder 8.

9. W. E. Merrem, *Thirty-Seven Years with the Houston Oil Company of Texas, Southwestern Settlement and Development Company, and East Texas Pulp and Paper Company* (Houston: privately published, January 1975), 31–32; Letter, Kenneth Nelson to Arthur Temple, January 23, 1965, Arthur Temple Jr. Papers (2004:014a), box 89, folder 2. Among the wives of company executives who especially enjoyed hunting at Boggy Sough were Mrs. R. E. Minton and Lottie Temple.

10. The original clubhouse was located about 220 yards southwest of where the trail to Deer Stand 71 is today. Along with Robert Sanders and Richard Donovan, the author came across scattered bricks, a concrete footing, and a surplus World War I field oven at the site in the spring of 2018. An H. M. Spain and Company timber type map created for Southern Pine Lumber Company in 1945 shows the former slough clubhouse location, as does a modified aerial photograph from 1948, written on by Carroll Allen. The timber type map is part of Collection 1993:015 at The History Center in Diboll. The original clubhouse is shown on page 52 and the hilltop clubhouse is shown on page 53, both in the Trinity County maps section. A copy of the Carroll Allen photograph is in the author's possession, provided by Stan Cook in 2016.

11. Two-page typescript by Clyde Thompson, "The Boggy Slough Hunting and Fishing Club," ca. 1934, in Clyde Thompson Correspondence, Boggy Slough folder; and one-page typescript and two pages of handwritten papers, "Memoranda with reference to fencing different portions of the Ranch," in 1943 correspondence folder, both in Collection 2004:014c, The History Center, Diboll. The trolley trotline was described to the author by Charlie Harber during site visits in 2000.

12. Constitution, Bylaws, and Rules of the Boggy Slough Hunting and Fishing Club, October 31, 1933, in ETRC, box 72, folder 9.

13. For instance, see letter from Kermit Schafer to Arthur Temple Sr., December 10, 1941, ETRC, box 155, folder 13, and letter from George Crowson to Clyde Thompson, December 18, 1942, in Clyde Thompson Papers (2004:014c), box 4, folder 3.

14. Arthur Temple, Interview 56b, p. 19, The History Center, Diboll.

15. T. L. L. Temple correspondence with Latane Temple, 1925–1926, ETRC, box 43, folder 1; letter, Arthur Temple Sr. to Dave Kenley, November 4, 1933, ETRC, box 71, folder 5.

16. Author's visits with the families of Buddy and Ellen Temple and Chotsy Temple, 2014–19.

17. Descriptions of early hunts are in ETRC, boxes 19, 20, 26, and 30, including Gilbert's letter to Kenley of November 6, 1923.

18. Letter, T. L. L. Temple to Watson Walker, November 27, 1925, ETRC, box 42, folder 7.

19. Letter, Kenley to Gilbert, December 1, 1926, ETRC, box 44, folder 4.

20. Letter, Kenley to Gilbert, December 11, 1926, ETRC, box 44, folder 4.

21. "Deer Hunter Drops Dead," *Taylor Daily Press*, November 17, 1931, p. 1; Edd Kenley interview with Jonathan Gerland, October 5, 2000, Interview 158a, p. 16, The History Center, Diboll. Edd Kenley said that his mother found seven pecans in a pocket of the hunting coat and after she planted them in the family's yard at Lufkin "every one of them made a tree."

22. Judge Minton kept lists of names of more than three hundred persons he had enjoined from entering the Boggy Slough pastures, mostly during the 1920s, after they had been caught inside the ranch's fences. Among the husbands of the Christie sisters who were enjoined were those of Jessie, Maud, Beulah, and Evie. "Defendants Enjoined," R. E. Minton's Correspondence, 1936, ETRC, box 104, folder 6.

23. Sitton, *Backwoodsmen*, 260; Steven Hahn, "Hunting, Fishing, and Foraging: Common Rights and Class Relations in the Postbellum South," *Radical History Review* 26 (1982): 37–64; numerous conversations between the author and Charlie Harber between 2000 and 2008 and with Jerry Lee during the summer of 2018, especially concerning Walter James, who was killed in Boggy Slough in 1932, and how his family thought of the killing, or "assassination."

24. *Review of Texas Wild Life and Conservation: Protective Efforts from 1879 to the Present Time, and Operations of the Fiscal Year Ending August 31, 1929* (Austin: Texas Game, Fish and Oyster Commission, 1929), 86–90.

25. Ibid.

26. Foster, Krausz, and Johnson, *Forest Resources of Eastern Texas*, 9, 24, 52.

27. Letters, Dave Kenley to H. G. Temple, May 26, 1933, and to Arthur Temple Sr., June 2, 1933, ETRC, box 71, folder 6.

28. Hahn, "Hunting, Fishing, and Foraging," 37–64; Steinberg, *Down to Earth*, 104–11; Sitton, *Backwoodsmen*, 233–44, 252–72; J. Crawford King, "The Closing of the Southern Range: An Exploratory Study," *Journal of Southern History*, 48, no. 1 (1982): 53–70; "Results of the Stock Law Held March 21," *Crockett Courier*, April 1, 1892; "The Razor-Back Hog," *Liberty Vindicator*, March 23, 1900, p. 2; "Stock Law Election," *Dallas Morning News*, June 21, 1901, p. 7; "South Austin People Anxious for a Hog Law," *Austin American-Statesman*, February 25, 1903, p. 2; "Would You Want a County Hog Law?" *Liberty Vindicator*, August 27, 1909, p. 3; "Stock Law Elections Carry in Houston County," *Houston Post*, October 25, 1924, p. 3; "Nacogdoches County Defeats Stock Law," *Dallas Morning News*, June 2, 1930; "Wolthers' Hog Law His Chief Achievement," *Fort Worth Star Telegram*, May 11, 1935, p. 2; "State Stock Law Is Being Enforced Now," *Tyler Daily Courier-Times*, June 16, 1935, p. 18; "Stock Law Applies to State Highways Only," *Austin American-Statesman*, August 15, 1935, p. 3; "Livestock on Highways Now Illegal," *Longview News-Journal*, July 1, 1960, p. 1

29. Austin Cary's notes for Mr. Walker, Diboll, Texas, March 2, 1923, pp. 8–9, in ETRC, box 4, folder 12.

30. Ibid.; Tilda Mims, "Evan Frank Allison: Pioneer in Conservation, 1865–1937," *Alabama's Treasured Forests* (Summer 2003): 28–30.

31. L. D. Gilbert, "Grazing Cut-Over Land," 20.

32. Ibid.; author's conversations with Alan Miller, 1999–2006; Gerland, "A Brief History of Temple Land Ownership," 20–22, 29; Alan Miller, Interview 171a, pp. 6–7; Joe Denman, Interview 79b, p. 3; and Horace Stubblefield, Interview 132a, pp. 20–21, all three at The History Center, Diboll.

33. For example, see Arthur Temple Jr.'s interview with Megan Lambert on July 11, 1985, Interview 56b, p. 16, The History Center, Diboll.

34. Ibid.; "Deer Not Always Plentiful Here, Says Mr. Minton," *Diboll News-Bulletin*, November 14, 1957, p. 1; "Wise Management Results in Plentiful Deer Population," *Diboll Free Press*, October 9, 1969; Jim Rushing, Oral History Interview 90a, January 13, 1986, at The History Center, Diboll.

35. Letter, Watson Walker to T. L. L. Temple, September 22, 1925, ETRC, box 42, folder 7.

36. "Pioneer Etex Rancher Dead: J. J. Ray, 72, Succumbs at Fort Worth," *Lufkin News*, February 28, 1941. Clipping on file at The History Center, Diboll.

37. Four-page letter, E. C. Durham to T. L. L. Temple, April 26, 1917, ETRC, box 18a, folder 5.

38. "H. L. Robb Is Dead: Three Men Are Charged," *Houston Post*, May 3, 1907, p. 4. See also chapter 5 in this book.

39. Letter and enclosures titled "Defendants Enjoined," R. E. Minton to Clyde Thompson, August 11, 1936, and letter and enclosure, R. E. Minton to Arthur Temple, December 9, 1936, ETRC, box 104, folder 6. The names of those enjoined are cited in the enclosures, many of which were enjoined in Angelina County. The enclosures suggest that maybe 25 percent of the injunctions were later dismissed. In 2001, Jonathan Gerland and former Temple family and company attorney Ward Burke attempted to locate official records concerning the injunctions that were filed at the Trinity County courthouse, but they were successful in finding only a handful of them, and some of them occurred after Minton's time. See also, "History of Boggy Slough Game Preserve, Written by Judge R. E. Minton, December 28, 1956," p. 2, manuscript in author's possession, provided by Ward Burke in 2000, reprinted in *Diboll Free Press* as, Jonathan Gerland, "Judge a Historian for Boggy Slough," March 28, 2002, p. 3B, and "Wildlife Prospered in Boggy Slough," April 4, 2002, p. 3B.

40. Letter and enclosures, "Defendants Enjoined," R. E. Minton to Clyde Thompson, August 11, 1936, ETRC, box 104, folder 6.

41. Letter, R. E. Minton to J. J. Ray, September 19, 1922, ETRC, box 3, folder 3.

42. Gilbert, "Grazing Cut-Over Lands," 20.

43. Trinity County Deed Records, Trinity County Courthouse Annex, Groveton, (hereafter TCCA),

vol. 58, pp. 121–22; Southern Pine Lumber Company Land Records (1993:015), Trinity County Volume, IGN RR sections 22 and 47, and the William Johnson survey, The History Center, Diboll; "Defendants Enjoined," R. E. Minton to Clyde Thompson, August 11, 1936, ETRC, box 104, folder 6.

44. Frank Ashby account in Sitton, *Backwoodsmen*, 256–57. In an interview with Jonathan Gerland, Charlie Harber discredited this account, saying he personally knew that Southern Pine Lumber Company compensated settlers for their hog claims. See Charlie Harber, Interview 157d (March 27, 2002), The History Center, Diboll, 5–6.

45. Letter, R. E. Minton to J. J. Ray, January 2, 1923, ETRC box 3, folder 3.

46. Letter, R. E. Minton to Clyde Thompson, August 11, 1936, ETRC, box 104, folder 6.

47. The dates of the injunctions were May 2 and 12 and November 28, 1922. Jack Shotwell was enjoined on April 3, 1923.

48. Three-page letter, R. E. Minton to Arthur Temple Sr., December 9, 1936, ETRC, box 104, folder 6; letter and two pages of attachments, being lists of injunctions filed in Angelina, Houston, and Trinity Counties, R. E. Minton to Clyde Thompson, August 11, 1936, ETRC, box 104, folder 6.

49. Three-page letter, R. E. Minton to Arthur Temple Sr., December 9, 1936, ETRC, box 104, folder 6.

50. Correspondence between Arthur Temple Sr. and Dave Kenley in ETRC, box 126, folder 4, especially letters of November 4 and 6, 1939; correspondence between Arthur Temple Sr. and Jr., 1946–50, in Collection 2006:016, especially letters of December 9, 10, and 20, 1946; November 4, 1949; and November 13, 1950; conversations of the author with Jerry Lee of Hudson, June 2018. Jean Shotwell was a great deer hunter and a member of several hunting clubs, including the Dollarhide and Hi-Lo clubs in Angelina County. He named one of his sons after his friend Ned Shands Jr. See Arthur Temple Jr., Interview 56b, p. 16, The History Center, Diboll; "Hunting Clubs Are Center of Outdoor Life," *Lufkin Daily News*, August 16, 1936, Centennial Edition, section 11, p. 1; "Let's Think This Over" and "Diboll to Have Dial Telephones," *Diboll Buzz Saw*, March 31, 1949, pp. 2 and 4. Arthur

Temple Jr. corresponded with and mentioned both men throughout his papers. See Arthur Temple Jr. Papers (2004:014a), The History Center, Diboll.

51. For a history of the early Neches valley hunting clubs and their membership, beginning with the Dollar-Hide Hunting and Fishing Club in 1910, see "Hunting Clubs Are Center of Outdoor Life," *Lufkin Daily News*, 1–2. Minton's old clubhouse went through various modifications and owners or tenants through the years and is now owned by John McClain.

52. Arthur Temple Jr., Interview 56d, p. 9; Gerland, "Judge a Historian for Boggy Slough," 3B; Lay, "Bottomland Hardwoods in East Texas"; Daniel W. Lay, "Outdoors in East Texas Then and Now," *East Texas Historical Journal* 40, no. 2 (2002): 53–62.

53. Letter, R. E. Minton to L. D. Gilbert, December 7, 1922, ETRC, box 19, folder 10.

54. Conversations with Charlie Harber during the early 2000s and with Jerry Lee in 2018.

55. Jerry Lee conversations and interviews with Jonathan Gerland, June 2018; document, "Jerry Lee versus Southern Pine Lumber Company and Elmer Cutler, Trinity County Cause No. 11,109, Release, November 4, 1966, notarized by Louis A. Bronaugh," copy in the possession of Jonathan Gerland, provided by Jerry Lee, July 2018.

56. Odom, *Over on Cochino*, pp. 61–63.

57. "Boggy Slough Campsites Are Cleared," *Diboll Buzz Saw*, July 1951, p. 8.

58. Letter, Kenley to Ray, July 12, 1932, ETRC, box 55, folder 2.

59. Charlie Harber, Interview 157d, March 27, 2002, The History Center, Diboll.

60. Specific and general details about the various poaching activities in this paragraph are in a two-page letter from Minton to H. G. Temple and Arthur Temple, January 14, 1939, ETRC, box 126, folder 5.

61. Charlie Harber interview with Jonathan Gerland at Boggy Slough, March 27, 2002, Interview 157d, pp. 1–4, The History Center, Diboll. The guns of the William Penn Hotel hotels were a 12-gauge shotgun and a .30-30 lever action. Harber said he mainly carried a 9mm pistol.

62. See especially R. E. Minton's multiple-page letters to Arthur Temple, dated December 12 and 17, 1931, in ETRC, box 65, folder 8.

63. E. C. Durham correspondence with Arthur Temple Sr., ETRC, boxes 57, 69, 71, 72, and 82.

64. "Complete Plans for Angelina Preserve," *Dallas Morning News*, February 16, 1926, p. 4; "Contract for Fish and Game Preserve," *Dallas Morning News*, February 21, 1926; "Two New State Game Preserves Announced," *Dallas Morning News*, April 13, 1926. Concerning Southern Pine Lumber Company's lands in the Angelina County preserve, they were mostly tracts recently acquired from John Renfro and his wife, some 9,229 acres known as the John Renfro Ranch. See a copy of the lease to Turner E. Hubby of the Texas Game, Fish, and Oyster Commission dated March 16, 1926, in Clyde Thompson's Papers (2004:014c), box 4, folder 3, The History Center, Diboll. Concerning the Trinity County lands, Minton still owned a former school land tract along Cochino Bayou, and he did not transfer it to the company until 1956.

65. Thompson Brothers Lumber Company established preserves (numbers 32 and 33) on its lands in Walker and San Jacinto Counties just a few weeks after the approval of Southern Pine Lumber Company's No. 27.

66. Texas Game, Fish, and Oyster Commission, *Review of Texas Wild Life*, 91, 94–98; Texas Legislative Council of the 53rd Legislature of Texas, *Wildlife Management in Texas*, 21.

67. "State Game Preserves Will Restore Wild Animal Life for Texas Nature Lovers," *Dallas Morning News*, July 11, 1926; "Deer Taken to Game Preserve," *Fredericksburg Standard*, March 25, 1932; "Herds of Deer to Be Increased," *Hearne Democrat*, June 13, 1930; Texas Legislative Council of the 53rd Legislature of Texas, *Wildlife Management in Texas*, 19–21.

68. "Contract Closed for State Game Preserve," *Lufkin Daily News*, February 16, 1926, pp. 1, 6.

69. "Complete Plans for Angelina Preserve," *Dallas Morning News*, February 16, 1926, p. 4.

70. Texas Game, Fish, and Oyster Commission, *Review of Texas Wild Life*, 96.

71. For instance, see "Herds of Deer To Be Increased," *Hearne Democrat*, June 13, 1930, and "Deer Taken to

Game Preserve," *Fredericksburg Standard*, March 25, 1932. See also, Texas Legislative Council of the 53rd Legislature of Texas, *Wildlife Management in Texas*, 19.

72. Email letters from Don Dietz and Bill Goodrum to Jonathan Gerland, both dated August 14, 2017, author's possession. Spencer, *Pineywoods Deer Herd Status Report* (2), provides statistics dating only to 1938. See also, Charles E. Boyd, "Of Woods and Wildlife," *Texas Parks and Wildlife*, November 1967, pp. 6–9. A few deer were trapped in Refugio County and released in Boggy Slough during the 1970s, according to Carter Smith of the Texas Parks & Wildlife Department. Letter from Carter Smith, executive director of Texas Parks & Wildlife, to Jonathan Gerland, dated April 27, 2016, author's possession.

73. Sitton, *Backwoodsmen*, 257–58, 291; Claude Welch Sr., Interview 27a by Becky Bailey, January 5, 1983, p. 1, The History Center, Diboll.

74. Notes made by the author during conversations with Charlie Harber from 2000 to 2008. See also, Charlie Harber recorded interview with Jonathan Gerland, May 4, 2000, Interview 157a, p. 3, The History Center, Diboll.

75. Charlie Harber, interviewed by Jonathan Gerland, May 4, 2000, Interview 157a, pp. 6–7, The History Center, Diboll; notes by the author from conversations with Charlie Harber, March 28 and May 16, 2008; Buddy Temple interview with Jonathan Gerland, August 11, 2014, Interview 263c, pp. 17–18, The History Center, Diboll.

76. See especially the two-page letter of Arthur Temple to R. E. Minton and E. C. Durham, March 17, 1932, ETRC, box 65, folder 8.

77. "History of Boggy Slough Game Preserve, Written by Judge R. E. Minton, December 28, 1956," p. 2, manuscript in author's possession, provided by Ward Burke in 2000.

78. Letter, Kenley to George Huffman of Houston, February 27, 1933, ETRC, box 71.

79. *Annual Report, Game, Fish and Oyster Commission for the Fiscal Year 1936–1937*, p. 8, in Dan Lay Collection, East Texas Research Center, Nacogdoches; Robert Hayes, "Squire Durham's 60-Mile Railroad Wins Him Acclaim of East Texans," *Dallas Morning News*, May 30, 1937, p. 14.

80. *Annual Report, Game, Fish and Oyster Commission For the Fiscal Year 1936–1937*, p. 8, in Dan Lay Collection, East Texas Research Center, Nacogdoches.

81. "Logging Train Gets Credit for First Deer of Season at Lufkin," *Dallas Morning News*, November 18, 1939.

82. The moral complexities of state involvement in game management is discussed in Texas Legislative Council of the 53rd Legislature of Texas, *Wildlife Management in Texas* (esp. 19–27); Sitton, *Backwoodsmen*; Warren, *The Hunter's Game*; and Karl Jacoby, *Crimes against Nature*.

83. Sitton, *Backwoodsmen*; notes made during conversations between Jerry Lee of Hudson and Jonathan Gerland, July and August 2018.

84. Walter James's mother was Mary Miranda Christie, who was Henry Lafayette Christie's youngest sister.

85. The details of the shooting are contained in chapter 8.

86. Texas Death Certificate for Walter Marion James, August 19, 1932, Trinity County certificate number 36442, Department of Health, Bureau of Vital Statistics, Austin.

87. E. C. Durham headed up one of the publicity campaigns in support of continued protection of wildlife. The text of one of his widely distributed letters was copied into his letter to Arthur Temple Sr., September 12, 1932, ETRC, box 57, folder 1.

88. Texas Legislative Council of the 53rd Legislature of Texas, *Wildlife Management in Texas*, 19–27.

89. Ibid., table II, p. 23.

90. Claude Davenport was earlier convicted of perjury in a hog theft trial. See Trinity County District Court Case 5199, September 1938, Criminal Minutes vol. 3, printed page number 161, handwritten page number 210, Trinity County Courthouse, Groveton. Jay Boren's violent past is referenced in Jim Ligon interview with Jonathan Gerland, November 6, 2009, Interview 185a, pp. 30–35, and Leamon Ligon and Cleveland Mark interview with Jonathan Gerland, September 14, 2017, Interview 285a, pp. 45–47, both at The History Center, Diboll. Also, see "Jay Boren: Man Who Never Backed Down Retires Back to the Farm," *Diboll Free Press*, October 15, 1970; "Special Ranger Guards Diboll Plants, Mill," *Lufkin Daily News*, October 11, 1942. For Davenport, see also "Pasture

Rider Attacked Here," *Lufkin Daily News*, Decmber 16, 1957, p. 1; "Man Fined $100, Sentenced to 30 Days in Attack Here," *Lufkin Daily News*, December 17, 1957, p. 1; "New Trial Is Denied Lufkin Man," *Lufkin Daily News*, December 18, 1957, pp. 1, 7; "Services Held for Claude Davenport," *Silsbee Bee*, March 30, 1989, p. 1.

91. Jerry Lee interview with Jonathan Gerland, June 21, 2018, Intervew 288a (Restricted access), The History Center, Diboll, and later visits and conversations with Lee at his home in Hudson and by telephone; Sitton, *Backwoodsmen*, 267–68.

92. Author's conversations with Arthur Temple in 1999 and 2000.

93. In 1950 Temple still held Kenley responsible for the riders. See letter, Arthur Temple Jr. to D. C. Kenley, October 30, 1950, Arthur Temple Jr. Papers (2004:014a), box 9, folder 27. This had changed by 1955.

94. Letter, Arthur Temple Jr. to Jay Boren, Claude Davenport, and Elmer Cutler, April 1, 1955, Arthur Temple Jr. Papers (2004:014a), box 26, folder 6.

95. Two-page document, "To those employed to prevent trespassing and protect the property of Southern Pine Lumber," Arthur Temple Jr. Papers (2004:014a), box 135, folder 15. For the pasture riders signing the document, see written communications between Temple and Dave Kenley, February 28, 1956, Arthur Temple Jr. Papers (2004:014a), box 32, folder 11.

96. Dwight T. Smith Sr., "Earl Smith," in Hensley, *Trinity County Beginnings*, 699–700.

97. Author's conversations with Charlie Harber of Lufkin between 2000 and 2008 and with Jerry Lee of Hudson in 2018.

98. Jerry Lee interview with Jonathan Gerland, June 21, 2018, Interview 288a (Restricted access), The History Center, Diboll, and later visits and conversations with Lee at his home in Hudson and by telephone.

99. Smith, "Earl Smith," in Hensley, Hensley, and Trinity County Book Committee, *Trinity County Beginnings*, 699.

100. "Two Wounded in Trinity County as Gunfire Breaks Out on Road," *Lufkin Daily News*, August 11, 1962, pp. 1, 8; "Man Charged in Forest Shooting," *Dallas Morning News*, August 12, 1962, p. 20; "Game Warden Held in Shooting," *Brownsville Herald*, August 12, 1962, p. 12.

101. "Deputy Game Warden Charged after Shooting Apple Springs Constable," *Trinity Standard*, August 17, 1962, p. 1.

102. Author's conversations with Ward Burke in 2000. Burke said that Sheriff Lynn Evans allowed him to visit with Davenport at his home on the night of the shooting before Davenport was taken into custody. Records of the District Clerk's Office in Trinity County are incomplete for the time of the shooting. The author made thorough searches and inquiries during 2017 and 2018. Most likely Temple's influence prevented prosecution. Author's correspondence with Groveton attorney Joe Scott Evans, a nephew of Sheriff Lynn Evans, in October 2018 and June and August 2019, author's possession.

103. Letters, Ward Burke to Arthur Temple, August 13 and 16 and October 23, 1962, and Ward Burke to Howard Hargrove, November 13, 1962, box 66, folder 20; letters between Claude Davenport and Arthur Temple, December 1 and 3, 1962, box 67, correspondence D-I, 1962; "List of Hunting Clubs on Southern Pine Lumber Company Lands (1962), box 70, folder 6, all in Arthur Temple Jr. Papers (2004:014a), The History Center, Diboll.

104. Author's conversations with Ward Burke in 2000. For post-shooting-incident instructions to rider Elmer Cutler, who took Davenport's position at Boggy Slough, see four-page letter from Arthur Temple to Elmer Cutler, October 31, 1962, Arthur Temple Jr. Papers (2004:014a), box 66, folder 25, The History Center, Diboll.

105. Leopold, *Game Management*, 129–31.

106. Letter, E. C. Durham to T. L. L. Temple, September 4, 1916, ETRC, box 18a, folder 6.

107. Temple once sent a bird dog to Dave Kenley. See Kenley to T. L. L. Temple, June 14, 1918, ETRC, box 15, folder 5.

108. Letter, T. L. L. Temple to Watson Walker, November 27, 1925, ETRC, box 42, folder 7. Henry Gresham Temple once invited Arthur Temple to hunt quail illegally in January 1926. After telling him the season

had just closed, Henry raved on the many coveys that remained around a particular cutover spot near Pineland where they had hunted before. He said the spot held nine coveys with between twenty-five to forty birds each. Henry wrote that they could go "in a Ford" and "put up the curtains and not be seen." Henry said he would certainly go if Arthur went with him, but he did not think he would break the law without him. See letter, Henry Gresham Temple to Arthur Temple, January 16, 1926, ETRC, box 45, folder 2.

109. Dwight M. Moore, "Grassy Lake: A Biologists' Paradise," *Journal of the Arkansas Academy of Science* 3, article 14 (1950): 41–43; Jeannie Nuss, "Rich Hunters, Poor Town Clash over Power Plant," Associated Press article, March 29, 2011, www.nbcnews.com.

110. Letter, Arthur Temple to E. C. Durham, November 2, 1933, ETRC, box 72, folder 9.

111. Southern Pine Lumber Company granted easements through the Walker and Sanchez surveys to the Shell Pipeline Corporation in May 1937 and to Pan American Pipeline Company in October 1940. See Trinity County Deed Records, TCCA, vol. 88, p. 571; and vol. 94, p. 120. Charlie Harber said he remembered seeing the pipe for one of the pipelines, which he called Pan American, shipped by railroad to Vair, where it was transferred to trucks in 1939. See Interview 157d, The History Center, Diboll.

112. Letter, Arthur Temple Sr. to Dave Kenley, January 28, 1938, ETRC, box 123, folder 8. See Kenley's reply of August 18, 1938. He neglected to return the literature and did not do the planting, saying he simply forgot.

113. Letter, Kenley to Arthur Temple, November 2, 1939, ETRC, box 126, folder 4.

114. Letter, Kenley to Thompson, Farley, O'Hara, Minton, Judd, and Temple, October 25, 1940, ETRC, box 143, folder 1.

115. Letter, Thompson to Kenley, October 26, 1940, ETRC, box 143, folder 1.

116. Letter, Temple to Kenley, October 28, 1940, ETRC, box 143, folder 1.

117. Letter, Temple to Kenley, November 27, 1940, ETRC, box 143, folder 1.

118. Letter, Kenley to Temple, December 2, 1940, ETRC, box 143, folder 1.

119. Letter, Temple to Kenley, December 5, 1940, ETRC, box 143, folder 1. Aldo Leopold discussed the differences between what he called "game farmers," who sought "to produce merely something to shoot," and "wild lifers," who sought to perpetuate a sample of all wildlife, "game and non-game," in the April 1919 publication, *Bulletin of the American Game Protective Association*, reprinted as "Wild Lifers vs. Game Farmers: A Plea for Democracy in Sport," in Meine, *Aldo Leopold*, 198–204.

120. Letters, Dave Kenley to Arthur Temple and Henry G. Tempe, December 10, 1940, and Arthur Temple to Kenley, December 13, 1940, ETRC, box 143, folder 1.

121. Letter, Kenley to Arthur Temple, Deember 10, 1940, ETRC, box 143, folder 1.

122. Quotes are from the letter, Arthur Temple Sr. to D. C. Kenley, March 26, 1941, ETRC, box 156, folder 6.

123. Ibid.

124. Letter, Kenley to Temple, March 28, 1941, ETRC, box 156, folder 6.

125. Correspondence between Kenley and Temple in ETRC, box 156, folder 6. See especially letters of March 28, December 3, 8, and 10.

126. Letter, Arthur Temple to Dave Kenley, Newman Gregory, and R. E. Minton, December 3, 1941, ETRC, box 156, folder 6.

127. Letter, Kenley to Temple, December 8, 1941, ETRC, box 156, folder 6.

128. Letter, Arthur Temple to Dave Kenley, December 10, 1941, ETRC, box 156, folder 6.

129. Mention of ceasing formal conservation efforts at the state duck preserve is found in box 23, folder 11, Arthur Temple Jr. Papers (2004:014a) within the Boggy Slough Club rules of 1954, The History Center, Diboll.

130. Letters between Dave Kenley and Arthur Temple Sr., October 25 and 28, 1944, ETRC, box 197, folder 2.

131. Letter, Arthur Temple Jr. to Arthur Temple Sr., September 4, 1946, Arthur Temple Sr. and Arthur Jr. Correspondence (2006:016), The History Center, Diboll.

132. Letters of Dave Kenley to Arthur Temple Sr., August 26, 1944 (more than one on this date), ETRC, box 197, folder 2.

133. Letter, Dave Kenley to Arthur Temple Sr., February 17, 1949, Arthur Temple Jr. Papers (2004:014a), box 4, folder 33, The History Center, Diboll.

134. For example, see letter from Arthur Temple Jr. to Kenley, December 6, 1950, Arthur Temple Jr. Papers (2004:14a), box 8, folder 18, The History Center, Diboll.

135. For examples of payments to Edd, see various memos and expense accounts from Dave Kenley to G. S. Smith during 1949, in Arthur Temple Jr. Papers (2004:014a), box 4, folder 33, The History Center, Diboll.

136. Arthur Temple Sr. to Dave Kenley, December 8, 1941, ETRC, box 156, folder 6. The restocking was part of renewed cooperation with the federal government, which matched state monies three to one. "Texas Game Restoration," *Dallas Morning News*, February 9, 1940; Bill McClanahan, "With Hunter and Fisher—Texas Game Project," *Dallas Morning News*, March 10, 1940; Bill McClanahan, "Hunter and Fisher," *Dallas Morning News*, February 11, 1940; "More Wildlife for East Texas Goal of Program Under Way in 45 Counties," *Dallas Morning News*, September 23, 1940.

137. Arthur Temple interview with Carolyn Elmore, ca. 1993, Interview 56e, pp. 6–7, The History Center, Diboll. See also Texas Legislative Council of the 53rd Legislature of Texas, *Wildlife Management in Texas*, 30.

138. Email communications with former Temple wildlife biologist Don Dietz during April 2019. See also, Eugene A. Walker, "Distribution and Management of the Wild Turkey in Texas," *Texas Game and Fish* 22, no. 8 (1954): 12–14, 22, 26.

139. Letter, Dave Kenley to Arthur Temple, May 31, 1938, ETRC, box 123, folder 8; page 2 of a four-page letter, letter and drafts of notes, Kenley to Arthur and H. G. Temple, December 17, 1940, ETRC, box 143, folder 1; letter, Kenley to Arthur Temple, July 18, 1941, ETRC, box 156, folder 6.

Chapter 8. The Land for Sale

1. For an example of price valuations, see multiple letters exchanged among Arthur Temple, Dave Kenley, and E. C. Durham in January and February 1935, concerning a possible sale to N. S. Locke of Gladewater, in Temple Industries Records at the East Texas Research Center, Nacogdoches (hereafter ETRC), box 98, folder 8.

2. "L. D. Gilbert Passes On," *Texas Forest News*, December 1931, p. 3. Edd Kenley told the author in 2000 that Gilbert was wearing one of his father's hunting jackets at the time of his death, and when Edd's mother found seven pecans in the pockets of the jacket she planted them at their home in Lufkin and "all of them made a tree." Edd Kenley, Interview 158a, p. 16, The History Center, Diboll.

3. For examples of Kenley's communications concerning land and timber buying, see his correspondence with L. D. Gilbert in ETRC, boxes 26 (especially folders 6–8) and 44. For the quotes, see the handwritten note from Kenley to Gilbert, May 2, 1923, in ETRC, box 26, folder 8.

4. See especially the interviews with Arthur Temple Jr., numbers 56a, 56b, and 56d, at The History Center, Diboll.

5. See the father and son correspondence in Collection 2006:016, especially Arthur Temple Sr.'s letter of February 7, 1948, The History Center, Diboll.

6. For example, see letter, Arthur Temple Sr. to R. E. Minton, June 14, 1939, ETRC, box 126, folder 5.

7. For example, see letters between Kenley and Gilbert, dated April 18, 21, and 27, and May 1, 1926, in ETRC, box 44, folder 6. See also Kenley's and Gilbert's land "partnership firm" and Kenley's wishes to confine the land acquisitions to East Texas, instead of expanding into Arkansas, in letter, Kenley to Gilbert, December 2, 1923, ETRC, box 26, folder 9.

8. Letters, Kenley to J. F. Judd in Texarkana, April 2, 1923; Kenley to Gilbert, April 3, 1923; Kenley to Gilbert, April 6, 1923; and Kenley to Gilbert, May 2, 1923; in ETRC, box 26, folder 8; Kenley to Gilbert, May 21, 1923, ETRC, box 26, folder 7 (and a copy in box 19, folder 11); and Gilbert to Kenley, April 10, 1923, ETRC, box 19, folder 10.

9. Letter, Dave Kenley and E. B. Hinkle to Arthur Temple, April 28, 1934, ETRC, box 81, folder 6.

10. For the transformation of the Oil Field Lumber Company into Temple Builder's Supply, see the cor-

respondence between Arthur Temple Sr. and Jr. in Collection 2006:016 at The History Center, Diboll, especially the letters dated July 10 and December 11, 1950; and January 19 and 25, March 13, April 4 and 9, March 5, 7, 10, 17, 18, 21, 23, 25, and 28, June 28 and 30, July 6, and August 13 and 14, 1951.

11. Carter, Kellison, and Wallinger, *Forestry in the U.S. South*, 52.

12. Southern Pine Lumber Company and Texas Southeastern Railroad each borrowed tens of thousands of dollars from the Reconstruction Finance Corporation specifically to pay off loans from banks. Local individuals approached for loans included Sam Hyman and John Oliver of Lufkin. See various letters, especially Durham to Temple, July 25 and 27, 1935; and Temple to Durham, July 30, 1935; in ETRC, box 98, folder 8; and Durham to Temple, July 25, September 8, and October 15, 1934; and Temple to Durham, July 27, October 8 and 12, 1934; and telegram from Durham to Temple, October 13, 1934; in ETRC, box 82, folder 2.

13. Letter, Durham to Arthur Temple, June 29, 1933, ETRC, box 72, folder 9.

14. Letter, E. C. Durham to Arthur Temple, December 19, 1931, ETRC, box 57, folder 2.

15. Two-page letter, R. E. Minton to Arthur Temple, December 12, 1931, ETRC, box 65, folder 8.

16. Letter, Arthur Temple to R. E. Minton, December 15, 1931, ETRC, box 65, folder 8.

17. Two-page letter, R. E. Minton to Arthur Temple, December 17, 1931, ETRC, box 65, folder 8.

18. Ibid.

19. Letter, Arthur Temple to R. E. Minton, December 21, 1931, ETRC, box 65, folder 8; E. C. Durham to Arthur Temple, December 19, 1931, ETRC, box 57, folder 2.

20. Letter, Arthur Temple to E. C. Durham, March 15, 1932, ETRC, box 57, folder 2.

21. Letter, E. C. Durham to Arthur Temple, "Personal and Confidential," March 16, 1932, ETRC, box 65, folder 8.

22. Two-page letter, Arthur Temple to R. E. Minton, March 17, 1932, ETRC, box 65, folder 8.

23. See the correspondence of Kenley and other officials during 1932 in ETRC, boxes 55–69, esp. box 55.

24. Letter, Kenley to Temple, October 7, 1932, and Temple to Kenley, October 10, 1932, ETRC, box 55, folder 1.

25. This particular phrasing is in Temple's letter to Dave Kenley dated June 2, 1932, ETRC, box 55, folder 2.

26. Letter, E. C. Durham to T. L. L. Temple, November 2, 1926, ETRC, box 44, folder 3; Kenley to McFarland, March 6, 1934, ETRC, box 81, folder 6.

27. Letter, Kenley to Temple, February 17, 1932, and Temple to Kenley, February 22, 1932, ETRC, box 55, folder 3.

28. Letter, John F. Renfro and Arkansas Renfro to Southern Pine Lumber Company, June 1, 1925, Angelina County Deed Records, Angelina County Courthouse, Lufkin, vol. 63, pp. 390–99.

29. Letter, Kenley to J. M. West, March 30, 1932, ETRC, box 55, folder 2.

30. E. C. Durham correspondence with Arthur Temple Sr., ETRC, box 57, folders 1 and 2, and box 55, folders 1–3.

31. According to company records, Southern Pine Lumber Company borrowed $4,000 in 1932 and $12,500 in 1933 and $15,000 in 1934 from a Mr. Oliver "of Lufkin," possibly John Oliver. Arthur Temple Sr. and Dave Kenley both wanted to keep the transactions out of the public records. Oliver wanted land or timber as security in the form of deeds of trust, while Temple wanted to put up company stock as security. Most of the loans were payable in six months at 6 percent interest. Roy Kurth of Lufkin's First National Bank did not approve of the second loan in January 1933, but the company transacted one with Oliver anyway in December 1933, with T. L. L. Temple, Arthur Temple, and Henry Gresham Temple signing the note. See multiple letters, D. C. Kenley to Arthur Temple, January 3, 9, and 17, 1933; D. C. Kenley to T. L. L. Temple, December 30, 1933; Arthur Temple to D. C. Kenley, January 4 and 18, 1933; all in ETRC, box 71, folders 5 and 6; and D. C. Kenley to Arthur Temple, January 2, 1935, ETRC, box 90, folder 7. For later memories of the loans, see Biesele, *Cornbread Whistle*, 67–68.

32. Most of the information concerning Ray's leaving is found in correspondence among Dave Kenley, Arthur Temple, E. C. Durham, J. J. Ray, and J. M. West.

For 1932, see ETRC, box 55, folders 1–3; and box 57, folders 1–2. For 1933, see ETRC, box 71, folder 6.

33. Letter, Durham to Temple, June 22, 1932, ETRC, box 57, folder 1.

34. Ibid.

35. Kenley's letters are in ETRC, box 55, folders 1–3, and box 71, folder 6.

36. "Walter Jones Found Dead This Morning," *Lufkin Daily News*, August 20, 1932.

37. "Investigate Shooting on Hunting Preserve," *Dallas Morning News*, August 21, 1932.

38. "Three Arrested in Connection with Death of Walter James," *Lufkin Daily News*, August 22, 1932. Arthur Temple Jr. told the author once that J. J. Collins was "the best trial lawyer East Texas ever had."

39. Letter, Durham to Arthur Temple, August 22, 1932, ETRC, box 57, folder 1. Midkiff was earlier one of Dave Kenley's personal employees, in the 1910s and 1920s, when Midkiff worked Kenley's cattle and hogs on lands Kenley owned and leased in Houston County. See multiple letters between Dave Kenley and E. C. Midkiff, 1918–19, ETRC, box 19, folder 5. See also E. C. Midkiff and Emory C. Midkiff in the 1920 and 1930 US Census population schedules for Houston County.

40. Letter, Temple to Durham, August 23, 1932, ETRC, box 57, folder 1.

41. Letter, Durham to Temple, August 24, 1932, ETRC, box 57, folder 1.

42. Bureau of Vital Statistics, Certificate of Death, Trinity County, Texas, No. 36442, Walter Marion James, Groveton, Texas, August 19, 1932, copy provided by Suzanne Waller of Trinity County Historical Commission in October 2017.

43. Sitton, *Backwoodsmen*, 260.

44. Trinity County District Court Criminal Minutes, Trinity County Museum, vol. K, 141–42, 144–46. For identification of the families of Walter James and Dema Moore, see the US Census Population Schedules for Trinity County in 1910, 1920, and 1930.

45. For many years Collins was held on retainer by nearly every industrial corporation in central East Texas simply to prevent him from representing plaintiffs against them. Letter, Arthur Temple Jr. to Arthur Temple Sr., June 22, 1950 (yellow sheet) in Collection 2006:016, The History Center, Diboll, and author's conversations with Arthur Temple Jr. in 2000. Invoices for monthly retainers paid by five of the Temple businesses to Collins during 1947 are in ETRC, box 176, folder 14.

46. Charlie Harber conversations with the author, 2000–2005.

47. Text of the letter was copied into a letter from E. C. Durham to Arthur Temple, September 12, 1932, ETRC, box 57, folder 1.

48. "Hunting Clubs Are Center of Outdoor Life," *Lufkin Daily News*, August 16, 1936, Centennial Edition, Section 11, pp. 1–2, online version, TheHistory-CenterOnline.com.

49. Letter, Kenley to Arthur Temple Sr., October 19, 1932, with attachments, ETRC, box 55, folder 1.

50. Ibid.

51. Letter, Arthur Temple Sr. to Kenley, October 28, 1932, ETRC, box 55, folder 1.

52. Ibid.

53. Letter, Kenley to Arthur Temple Sr., November 2, 1938, ETRC, box 123, folder 8. See also letters, Kenley to Temple, November 2, 1939, and November 6, 1939, box 126, folder 4.

54. Letters, Kenley to Arthur Temple Sr., 1938 and 1939, ETRC, boxes 123 and 126.

55. Letters, Arthur Temple Sr. to Kenley, November 4, 1939, and Kenley to Arthur Temple Sr., November 6, 1939, ETRC, box 126, folder 4.

56. Letter, Durham to Minton, January 19, 1933, ETRC, box 72, folder 9.

57. See especially the two-page letter from Kenley to Judge Rolston and Commissioners Odom, Sayers, and Barge of Angelina County, March 12, 1932, ETRC, box 55, folder 3.

58. Minton to Kenley, November 14, 1932, ETRC, box 65, folder 8.

59. At this time Minton also protested his personal property taxes, including the tract he owned in Boggy Slough. See the tax judgements against Minton and his wife Lucy in Trinity County District Court Minutes,

Trinity County courthouse, vol. M, 146, 201–2, and vol. N, 18.

60. Letter, Arthur Temple to Kenley, February 25, 1935, ETRC, box 90, folder 7.

61. Letter, Arthur Temple to Dave Kenley, August 23, 1934, ETRC, box 81, folder 5.

62. Letter, Kenley to Temple, February 28, 1935, ETRC, box 990, folder 7.

63. Letters, Temple to Kenley, March 2 and 8, 1935, ETRC, box 90, folder 7.

64. Undated four-page memorandum by Dave Kenley to Arthur Temple and a letter referencing the memo written by Arthur Temple to Kenley, February 7, 1938, ETRC, box 123, folder 8.

65. Letter, Kenley to Arthur Temple, April 6, 1935, ETRC, box 90, folder 7. By one estimate in 1935, at least forty million acres of forest land in the United States had been forfeited because of nonpayment of taxes. Ronald Craig, "The South's No-Man's Land" *American Forests* 41, no. 12 (1935): 684–85, 712.

66. Letter, Kenley to Temple, May 4, 1935, ETRC, box 90, folder 7.

67. Letters, Kenley to Temple, April 17 and 29 and May 4, 1935, and Temple to Kenley, May 6, 1935, ETRC, box 90, folder 7.

68. Letter, E. C. Durham to Arthur Temple, December 30, 1933, ETRC, box 82, folder 2; email, Tom Middlebrook to Jonathan Gerland, October 18, 2017, author's possession. Tragically, Hall suffered from severe mental illness and in 1935 slit the throat of his three-year-old son before taking his own life. Tom Middlebrook tells of this in his email communication above. Kenneth Nelson, one of Hall's coworkers, also tells of the tragedy in his 1985 oral history interview with Megan Lambert. See Kenneth Nelson, Interview 75a, pp. 3–4, The History Center, Diboll. Hall was actually sent to Kenley in 1926 by L. D. Gilbert, because Hall was then doing "re-forestation" work for several lumber companies in Arkansas at the time and he felt his experience would benefit Kenley. See letters between Kenley and Gilbert, dated January 25 and 30, 1926, in ETRC, box 44, folder 6.

69. Letter, Arthur Temple to Dave Kenley, January 20, 1933, ETRC, box 71, folder 6.

70. Letters, Kenley to J. S. Miller, of Dallas, January 5, 1933; Kenley to Arthur Temple Sr., January 18, February 22 and 27, May 25, 1933; Kenley to I. B. McFarland, of Houston, January 13, 1933; Arthur Temple to Kenley, January 20, 1933; George Huffman, of Houston, to Kenley, February 25, 1933; Kenley to George Huffman, of Houston, February 27, 1933, all in ETRC, box 71, folder 6.

71. See especially the letter from Kenley to George Huffman, Houston, February 27, 1933, ETRC, box 71, folder 6.

72. Letter, Kenley to Temple, February 2, 1933, ETRC, box 71, folder 6.

73. Letter, Arthur Temple to Kenley, February 6, 1933, ETRC, box 71, folder 6.

74. The enabling measure was Senate Concurrent Resolution No. 73, filed in the Department of State on May 26, 1933, with the governor's signature. For Kenley's involvement with the federal agents, see multiple letters in Kenley's correspondence of 1932, 1933, 1934, and 1935, in ETRC, boxes 55, 71, 81, and 90. For an interesting study of the legality and efficacy of the enabling law, see Frost and Hursey, *Texas National Forest Study.*

75. Letter, Kenley to Arthur Temple Sr., November 16, 1933, ETRC, box 71, folder 5.

76. Letter, Kenley to H. G. Temple, December 13, 1933, ETRC, box 71, folder 5.

77. The federal agent was a Mr. Beaumont. See especially two letters and copies attached, from Dave Kenley to H. G. Temple and Arthur Temple, March 13, 1934, ETRC, box 81, folder 6.

78. Letter, Kenley to Arthur Temple, April 19, 1934, ETRC, box 81, folder 6. For the description of the map see two letters from Kenley to Temple, dated March 17 and March 31, 1934, ETRC, box 81, folder 6.

79. Letters, Arthur Temple to Dave Kenley, June 30 and July 10, 1933; and Dave Kenley to Arthur Temple, July 4 and 8, 1933, all in ETRC, box 71, folder 5. See also Arthur Temple to J. H. Kurth Jr., July 11, 1935, ETRC, box 90, folder 4.

80. Letter, Kenley to Temple, July 4, 1933, ETRC, box 71, folder 5.

81. Letter, Temple to Kenley, March 14, 1934, ETRC, box 81, folder 6.

82. Letter, Temple to Kenley, March 19, 1934, ETRC, box 81, folder 6.

83. Edna Mae Dean, "Texas Rural Communities," 126–28; Michael G. Wade, "Back to the Land: The Woodlake Community, 1933–1943," *East Texas Historical Journal* 21, no. 2 (1983): 46–56; Joseph W. Hensley, "Woodlake," in Hensley, *Trinity County Beginnings*, 157–58; "Plan Colony in Trinity County," *Fort Worth Star-Telegram*, January 19, 1934, p. 8.

84. Multiple-page letters, Dave Kenley to Arthur Temple, March 13, 15, 17 (two on this date), 30, and 31, 1934; and Temple to Kenley, March 14, 19, and 28, 1934, ETRC, box 81, folder 6. See also Angelina County/Lufkin Chamber of Commerce Board of Directors Meeting Minutes, March 9 and June 13, 1934, and February 15, 1935, Collection 2018:001, The History Center, Diboll.

85. "For College Land," *Diboll Free Press*, March 16, 1967, p.1; "College Deed Signed," *Lufkin Daily News*, May 25, 1967, p. 1; "Crown Colony Country Club: New Club Seems Assured," *Diboll Free Press*, April 14, 1977, p. 1; "Crown Colony CC Opening Saturday," *Diboll Free Press*, April 12, 1979, pp. 1, 8.

86. Letter, Temple to Kenley, March 28, 1934, and clippings from *Texarkana Daily News*, March 27, 1934, ETRC, box 81, folder 6.

87. Letter, Temple to Kenley, April 21 and May 28, 1934, ETRC, box 81, folder 6.

88. Letter, Temple to Kenley, May 28, 1934, first letter of this date, ETRC, box 81, folder 6.

89. Letter, Temple to Kenley, May 28, 1934, second letter of this date, ETRC, box 81, folder 6.

90. Letters, Dave Kenley to Arthur Temple, June 13, 1934, and Temple to Kenley, June 14, 1934, ETRC, box 81, Folder 6.

91. Letter, E. C. Durham to Arthur Temple, December 30, 1933, ETRC, box 82, folder 2.

92. Letter, Arthur Temple to E. C. Durham, January 2, 1934, ETRC, box 82, folder 2.

93. Letter, Dave Kenley to Arthur Temple, December 30, 1933, ETRC, box 82, folder 2; Wallace Scott McFarlane, "Oil on the Farm: The East Texas Oil Boom and the Origins of an Energy Economy," *Journal of Southern History* 83, no. 4 (2017): 853–88.

94. Letter, Durham to Temple, December 30, 1933.

95. Letter, Kenley to Temple, February 7, 1935, ETRC, box 90, folder 7.

96. Letters, E. C. Durham to Arthur Temple, January 17, 25, and 29, 1935, and Arthur Temple to E. C. Durham, January 18 and 28, and February 1, 1935, ETRC, box 98, folder 8. See also a news clipping, "U.S. Will Buy Land in Texas," January 24, 1935, and a letter from Joseph Kircher of the USDA Forest Service at Atlanta to Temple Lumber Company at Diboll, January 21, 1935, in Dave Kenley's correspondence in ETRC, box 90, folder 7.

97. Letter, U.S. Forest Service at Atlanta to Temple Lumber Company at Diboll, January 21, 1935, ETRC, box 90, folder 7; Maxwell and Martin, *Short History*, 37–38; Gerland, "A Brief History of Temple Land Ownership," 12.

98. Letters, E. C. Durham to Arthur Temple, January 17, 25, and 29, 1935, and Arthur Temple to E. C. Durham, January 18 and 28, and February 1, 1935, ETRC, box 98, folder 8. See also a news clipping, "U.S. Will Buy Land in Texas," January 24, 1935, and a letter from Joseph Kircher of the USDA Forest Service at Atlanta to Temple Lumber Company at Diboll, January 21, 1935, in Dave Kenley's correspondence in ETRC, box 90, folder 7.

99. Letter, Dave Kenley to Arthur Temple, January 17, 1935, ETRC, box 90, folder 7.

100. Letters, Kenley to Arthur Temple, January 18, 1935, and Temple to Kenley, January 22, 1935, ETRC, box 90, folder 7.

101. Two page letter, E. C. Durham to Arthur Temple, February 16, 1935, ETRC box 98, folder 8.

102. Letter, Arthur Temple to E. C. Durham, February 14, 1935, ETRC box 98, folder 8.

103. Letter, Arthur Temple to E. C. Durham, February 18, 1935, ETRC, box 98, folder 8. Kenley had invited Hinkle's involvement, but Kenley did not think the Apple Springs activity was anything serious. See Kenley's letters to Hinkle and Temple, February 4 and 7, 1935, ETRC, box 90, folder 7.

104. Letter, Kenley to Temple, February 7, 1935, ETRC, box 90, folder 7.

105. Letter, Dave Kenley to Arthur Temple, April 6, 1935, ETRC, box 90, folder 7.

106. Letter, Arthur Temple to Dave Kenley, April 26, 1935, ETRC, box 90, folder 7.

107. Letter of Dave Kenley, one of several on the same date, to Arthur Temple, May 15, 1935, ETRC, box 990, folder 7.

108. Kenley to A. G. T. Moore, SPA, at New Orleans, May 15, 1935, ETRC, box 90, folder 7.

109. Undated four-page memorandum by Dave Kenley to Arthur Temple and a letter referencing the memo written by Arthur Temple to Kenley, February 7, 1938, ETRC, box 123, folder 8.

110. Letters, Dave Kenley to Arthur Temple, May 15 (two letters this date), July 22, and November 1, 1935, and Arthur Temple to Dave Kenley, October 29, 1935, ETRC, box 90, folder 7.   `

Chapter 9. Whose Land Is It?

1. Nine-page typescript memo by Austin Cary, US Forest Service, to Watson Walker, written at Diboll, March 2, 1923, titled, "Notes for Mr. Walker, Diboll, Texas," in Temple Industries Records at the East Texas Research Center, Nacogdoches (hereafter ETRC), box 4, folder 12.

2. Hidalgo in Hatcher, "Descriptions of the Tejas," no. 1 (July 1927): 56–57.

3. Postscript note to a letter from E. C. Durham to L. D. Gilbert, November 2, 1926, ETRC, box 44, folder 3.

4. Two-page letter, Arthur Temple to R. E. Minton, March 17, 1932, ETRC, box 65, folder 8; "Deer Not Always Plentiful Here, Says Mr. Minton," *Diboll News-Bulletin*, November 14, 1957, p. 1; "History of Boggy Slough Game Preserve, Written by Judge R. E. Minton, December 28, 1956," manuscript provided to the author by Ward Burke in August 2000.

5. Worster, *Nature's Economy*, 269.

6. Letter, Dave Kenley to Arthur Temple Sr., May 31, 1938, ETRC, box 123, folder 8.

7. Letters, Kenley to Arthur Temple Sr., March 2, 1938, and Kenley to H. G. Temple, June 15, 1938, ETRC, box 123, folder 8; Kenley to Arthur Temple Jr., May 27, 1961, Arthur Temple Jr. Papers (2004:014), box 62, folder 15, The History Center, Diboll.

8. Three-page, single-spaced, typed letter, Dave Kenley to Arthur Temple, Sr., August 18, 1944, ETRC, box 197, folder 2; letter, Dave Kenley to Arthur Temple Sr., June 7, 1948, Arthur Temple Jr. Papers (2004:014), box 4, folder 33, The History Center, Diboll; three-page letter, R. E. Minton to Arthur Temple Sr., December 9, 1936, ETRC, box 104, folder 6.

9. For instance, see Arthur Temple Sr. to R. E. Minton, September 23, 1936, ETRC, box 104, folder 6.

10. Arthur Temple Jr., in spite of his many disagreements with Kenley and Minton, always cited them, along with Captain Ray, as the ones most responsible for protecting the land and game at Boggy Slough, "at great personal cost." See his interviews with Megan Lambert in 1985 and with Jonathan Gerland in 2000, Interview 56b, pp. 11–19, and Interview 56d, pp. 5–9, The History Center, Diboll.

11. Charlie Harber in multiple conversations with Jonathan Gerland in 2000 through 2008.

12. See *Dallas Morning News*, "State Highway No. 7 Designated," December 29, 1917, p. 3; and "Routes for Forty-Five Highways Designated by State Commission, Highway 7, Central Texas Highway," October 5, 1919, p. 29.

13. R. E. Minton Survey, A-934 Trinity County, Scrap File 9790, School Land Files, Texas General Land Office (hereafter GLO), Austin; Trinity County Deed Records, vol. 135, p. 23.

14. Letter, R. E. Minton to H. G. Temple and Arthur Temple, February 22, 1936, ETRC, box 104, folder 7; Trinity County Deed Records, vol. 135, p. 23.

15. William Hampton Survey, File H-11 Trinity, Deed No. 3, Southern Pine Lumber Company Land Records, GLO; R. E. Minton Survey, A-934 Trinity County, Scrap File 9790, School Land Files, GLO.

16. Sullivan's Ferry Road is identified on *McCarthy's Map of Angelina County, Texas*, by P. A. McCarthy & Son, Lufkin, Texas, November 1904, at The History Center, Diboll; and P. A. McCarthy, "Angelina County,

Texas, Good Road System No. 233 (1919) Revised," reprinted on page 44 of Lufkin Genealogical and Historical Society, *History of Angelina County*.

17. The quote is from Arthur Temple Jr. in his interview with Jonathan Gerland, June 2000, Interview 56d, p. 9, The History Center, Diboll. See also Jonathan Gerland, "Judge a Historian for Boggy Slough," *Free Press*, March 28, 2002, p. 3B.

18. "Opposing Sides in Highway 103 Fight Stick to Demands," *Lufkin Daily News*, April 14, 1937, clipping in Minton correspondence, Temple Industries Records, ETRC, box 110, folder 5.

19. At the time of the lease, J. W. Austin resided in San Antonio. He had earlier lived in Jacksonville and eventually moved to Humble's offices in Houston. Letter, E. C. Durham to Arthur Temple, November 26, 1913, ETRC Box 98, folder 8.

20. Two-page letter, R. E. Minton to Arthur Temple, December 17, 1931, ETRC, box 65, folder 8.

21. Worster, *Nature's Economy*, 267–73; Leopold, *Game Management*, 3–21.

22. Worster, *Nature's Economy*, 272–73; Leopold, *Game Management*, 3 and 20–21. Leopold's letters to his mother and father during his time in Tyler County, Texas, are preserved in the Aldo Leopold Archives at the University of Wisconsin. Digital copies of them were obtained by the author.

23. Four letters, R. E. Minton to D. A. Nunn, February 2, 1937; D. A. Nunn to R. E. Minton, February 10, 1937; Arthur Temple to R. E. Minton, May 5, 1937; and R. E. Minton to Arthur Temple, May 8, 1937, all in ETRC, box 110, folder 5.

24. See one letter from Kenley to Judge Rolston, March 12, 1932, ETRC, box 55, folder 3. Minton, too, protested his personal property taxes, including the tract he owned in Boggy Slough. See the tax judgements against Minton and his wife Lucy in Trinity County District Court Minutes, vol. M, 146, 201–2; and vol. N, 18. See also letter, Minton to Kenley, November 14, 1932, ETRC, box 65, folder 8.

25. "Hunting Club Protest on Highway Project 'Height of Absurdity,'" *Lufkin Daily News*, April 16, 1937, clipping in Minton correspondence, Temple Industries Records, ETRC, box 110, folder 5.

26. Ibid.

27. Clipping, "Opposing Sides Argue Road Project before Commission," *Lufkin Daily News*, April 20, 1937, loose clipping in Minton correspondence, ETRC, box 110, folder 5.

28. Ibid.

29. Ibid.

30. Ibid.

31. Minton to Arthur Temple Sr., April 27, 1937, ETRC, box 110, folder 5.

32. Ibid.

33. Letter, Athur Temple Sr. to R. E. Minton, May 5, 1937, ETRC, box 110, folder 5.

34. Ibid.

35. Two-page letter, Minton to Temple, May 8, 1937, ETRC, box 110, folder 5.

36. Letter, Arthur Temple to R. E. Minton, May 18, 1937, ETRC, box 110, folder 5.

37. "Action on Lufkin Road Project Urged by Group," *Vernon Daily Record*, July 24, 1937, p. 4; "Hearing Is Set on Highway 103 Issue," *Lufkin Daily News*, May 25, 1937, p. 1.

38. In numerous conversations between 2000 and 2008, Charlie Harber told Jonathan Gerland often of Minton's, as well as Dave Kenley's, resentment of the highway going through North Boggy and their prolonged opposition to it.

39. Kenley was not initially included, but he was added after the first meeting.

40. Letter and attachment, R. E. Minton to Arthur Temple, Clyde Thompson, and E. C. Durham, February 24, 1941, ETRC, box 155, folder 3. See also letters between Arthur Temple and Minton, January 25 and 27 and February 25, 1941, ETRC, box 155, folder 3.

41. Letter, R. E. Minton to hunting clubs, riders, and Dan Lay, May 13, 1941, ETRC, box 155, folder 3.

42. Letter and attachment, R. E. Minton to Arthur Temple, Clyde Thompson, and E. C. Durham, February 24, 1941, ETRC, box 155, folder 3.

43. Letter, Minton to Arthur Temple, Clyde Thompson, D. C. Kenley, and E. C. Durham, July 30, 1941;

and letter, Minton to J. B. Nabers, State Highway Dept., Lufkin, August 19, 1941; both in ETRC, box 155, folder 3.

44. Dave Kenley, Oral History Interview 14a (1954), p. 1, at The History Center, Diboll.

45. Kenley received his diploma from Sam Houston Normal Institute in 1909, minoring in vocational agriculture, having earlier earned his teaching certificate in 1907. Five-page typescript, "David Crockett Kenley, An Address by Jonathan Gerland on the Occasion of Kenley's Induction into the Texas Forestry Hall of Fame, Sponsored by the Texas Forestry Museum, at the Lufkin Civic Center, on October 4, 2012," in D. C. Kenley Biographical Files, The History Center, Diboll. See also prints of an email and attachments from Barbara Kievit-Mason, University Archivist, SHSU, to Emily Hyatt, Archivist, The History Center, September 27, 2012, The History Center, Diboll. Kenley's hire date of May 1, 1908, is listed in a memo from Vernon Burkhalter to Arthur Temple Jr., November 14, 1967, in Arthur Temple Jr. Business Papers (2004:014), The History Center, Diboll.

46. "Handles Play Major Role in Waste Utilization," *Buzz Saw*, April 30, 1949, pp. 2, 4.

47. Letter and drafts of notes, Kenley to Arthur and Henry Temple, December 17, 1940, ETRC, box 143, folder 1.

48. Letter, D. C. Kenley to B. F. Hines, November 18, 1944; letter, Arthur Temple to D. C. Kenley, November 23, 1944; letter, D. C. Kenley to Arthur Temple, November 27, 1944, box 197, folder 2.

49. Letters and attachments of Silsbee news clipping and a CIO pamphlet, H. G. Temple to Arthur Temple, June 6, 1941, Arthur Temple to R. E. Minton, June 9, 1941, box 155, folder 3.

50. "Southern Pine Employees Form Own Hunting and Fishing Club," *Buzz Saw*, November 30, 1948, p. 4. For expansion of hunting to the general public, see Kenneth Nelson's correspondence for 1951 in Arthur Temple Jr. Business Papers (2004:014), box 12, folder 32, The History Center, Diboll. By the 1970s, many of Temple's lands were open to the general public. See the pamphlet, "Guide to Good Hunting in East Texas 1977," in Arthur Temple Jr.'s Papers (2004:014a), The History Center, Diboll, box 184, folder 10.

51. Letter, Kenley to Arthur Temple Sr., March 2, 1938, ETRC, box 123, folder 8.

52. Kenley's and Arthur Temple's views on forest fire protection are discussed in numerous letters, especially in E. O. Siecke to Kenley, January 13, 1932; and Kenley to Arthur Temple, February 3, 1932; ETRC, box 55, folder 3; Kenley to H. G. Temple, November 19, 1932, ETRC, box 55, folder 1; Kenley to Arthur Temple, January 20, 1933; Arthur Temple to Kenley, February 11, 1933; Kenley to H. G. Temple, February 14, 1933; and Kenley to W. E. White of the Texas Forest Service, February 14, 1933; all in ETRC, box 71, folder 6; Kenley to H. G. Temple, March 17, 1934, ETRC, box 81, folder 6.

53. Two-page letter, Dave Kenley to Arthur Temple, May 31, 1938, ETRC, box 123, folder 8.

54. Letter, Arthur Temple to Kenley, March 5, 1938, ETRC, box 123, folder 8.

55. See multiple letters written between Arthur Temple, Dave Kenley, and Henry Temple in ETRC, box 123, folder 8, especially Temple to Kenley, March 5, 1938.

56. Letter, D. C. Kenley to H. G. Temple, June 15, 1938, ETRC, box 123, folder 8.

57. Letter, D. C. Kenley to H. G. Temple, June 10, 1939, ETRC, box 126, folder 4; Kenley to Henry Temple, March 10, 1938, ETRC, box 123, folder 8; Lay, "Recovery of a Southern Forest," 73.

58. Letter, Kenley to Arthur Temple Sr., August 26, 1944 (second letter of this date), ETRC, box 197, folder 2; three-page letter, J. J. Collins to Arthur Temple Jr., April 19, 1950; and letter, Arthur Temple Sr. to Arthur Temple Jr., April 27, 1950; both in Arthur Temple Jr. Papers (2004:014a) at The History Center, Diboll; Kenneth Nelson, Interview 75a, August 17, 1985, pp. 4 and 9, The History Center, Diboll. Arthur Temple Jr. usually claimed that Kenley "use[d] the land for grazing for nothing" and "wound up with free leases on a hell of a lot of land." See Arthur Temple, Interview 56b, p. 13, The History Center, Diboll.

59. Letter, Kenley to Arthur Temple Sr., August 26, 1944 (second letter of this date), ETRC, box 197, folder 2; three-page letter, J. J. Collins to Arthur Temple Jr., April 19, 1950; and letter, Arthur Temple Sr. to Arthur Temple Jr., April 27, 1950; both in Arthur Temple Jr. Papers (2004:014a) at The History Center, Diboll.

60. Three-page letter, Kenley to Arthur Temple Sr., August 18, 1944; and two-page letter, Kenley to Arthur Temple Sr., second letter of August 26, 1944; both in ETRC, box 197, folder 2.

61. Letter, Kenley to Henry Temple, July 26, 1943, ETRC, box 186, folder 9.

62. Charlie Harber, interviewed by Jonathan Gerland, March 27, 2002, Interview 157d, pp. 13–15, The History Center, Diboll.

63. Charlie Harber told the author about the rye grass planting during site visits in 2000. See also Arthur Temple interview with Jonathan Gerland, Interview 56d, p. 9, The History Center, Diboll. The author visited and photographed the harvesting operations with Buddy Temple in early August 2014. Buddy Temple interview with Jonathan Gerland, August 11, 2014, Interview 263c, pp. 17–18, The History Center, Diboll.

64. Letter, Kenley to Henry Temple, July 26, 1943, ETRC, box 186, folder 9.

65. Letter, Kenley to Arthur Temple Sr., August 26, 1944 (second letter of this date), ETRC, box 197, folder 2.

66. Letter, Kenley to Arthur Temple, January 22, 1943, ETRC, box 186, folder 9. For more on Durham's Shawnee Creek Ranch, see Robert M. Hayes, "Squire Durham's 60-Mile Railroad Wins Him Acclaim of East Texans," *Dallas Morning News*, May 30, 1937, p. 14.

67. Letter, Temple to Kenley, January 23, 1943, ETRC, box 186, folder 9.

68. Letters, Kenley to Arthur Temple, January 25 and February 3, 1943, ETRC, box 186, folder 9.

69. Hayes, "Squire Durham's 60-Mile Railroad Wins Him Acclaim of East Texans," p. 14; Jonathan Gerland's interview with Arthur Temple, June 2000, Interview 56d, p. 25, The History Center, Diboll.

70. Letters, between Arthur Temple Sr. and Dave Kenley, October 11 and 16, 1943, ETRC, box 186, folder 9.

71. Letter, Arthur Temple to Kenley, August 14, 1944, ETRC, box 197, folder 2.

72. Ibid.

73. Kenneth Nelson, Interview 75a, August 17, 1985, p. 4, The History Center, Diboll.

74. Kenley wrote a nearly 1,600-word letter to Arthur Temple Sr. on August 18, 1944, and two shorter letters on August 26, all in ETRC, box 197, folder 2.

75. Three-page, single-spaced, typed letter, Kenley to Temple, August 18, 1944, ETRC, box 197, folder 2.

76. Ibid.

77. Ibid.

78. Ibid.

79. Letter, Kenley to Temple, August 26, 1944 (first letter of this date), ETRC, box 197, folder 2.

80. Ibid.

81. Dave Kenley to Arthur Temple Sr., second letter of August 26, 1944, ETRC, box 197, folder 2.

82. Letters, Kenley to Arthur Temple Sr., August 26, 1944 (first and second letters of this date), ETRC, box 197, folder 2.

83. Letter, Kenley to Arthur Temple Sr., August 26, 1944 (first letter of this date), ETRC, box 197, folder 2.

84. Letters, Arthur Temple Sr. to Dave Kenley, August 21 and 28, 1944, ETRC, box 197, folder 2.

85. In addition to the land-buying activities mentioned in chapter 10, Gilbert allowed Kenley, as well as his brother-in-law R. E. Minton, to hire unscrupulous land agents from time to time. In October 1923, Kenley shared with Gilbert that one of his agents bribed a state penitentiary commissioner, paying the state official $500 to "swing the deal," but Kenley reimbursed the agent only $250, arguing that the agent could have bought the commissioner for less. Kenley was trying to purchase state lands connected with the operations of the Texas State Railroad and the Rusk state prison iron works in a way that would prevent the lands from being offered at a public auction. In the end, the plan was foiled and the desired lands became part of the I. D. Fairchild State Forest in 1925. Interestingly, Fairchild was a former schoolteacher in Diboll and had become a state senator by 1925. See letters, Kenley to R. E. Minton, May 24, 1923, ETRC, box 22, folder 11; Kenley to Gilbert, October 10, 1923, ETRC, box 26, folder 8; Gilbert to Kenley, October 12, 1923, ETRC, box 26, folder 8; Kenley to Gilbert, November 6, 1923, ETRC, box 26, folder 9.

86. Letters, Gilbert to Kenley, May 1, July 6, and December 17, 1923, ETRC, box 26, folders 7 and 8.

87. Letter, Arthur Temple Sr. to Dave Kenley, February 7, 1938, ETRC, box 123, folder 8.

88. Correspondence among Arthur Temple, Henry Temple, and Dave Kenley in ETRC, box 123, folder 8. See especially Arthur Temple to D. C. Kenley, February 11, 1938.

89. Undated four-page typescript memorandum, authored by Kenley, filed with a February 7, 1938, letter from Arthur Temple Sr. to Kenley, Temple Records, ETRC, box 123, folder 8. See also letters, Arthur Temple to Kenley, February 11, 1938, and Kenley to Temple, February 17, 1938, Temple Records, ETRC, box 123, folder 8.

90. Undated four-page typescript memorandum, authored by Kenley, filed with a February 7, 1938, letter from Arthur Temple Sr. to Kenley, ETRC, box 123, folder 8, and letter, Kenley to Temple, February 17, 1938. Kenley identified the stockman as "old man McConnico" and the timber as "the Lacy timber" on behalf of Temple Lumber Company.

91. In the February 1938 memo, Kenley mentioned John Hyden and Hyden's kinsmen as being friends with Temple Lumber Company as a result of Kenley's cattle business relationships. Kenley later claimed during the 1940s that some county commissioners "teased" him about having company lands appraised on the books at valuations of $4 to $7 per acre, when they knew they were worth at least $100 an acre. See Kenley correspondence in ETRC, boxes 123, 142, 143, 153, 156, 164, 165, 171, 172, 186, 195, 197, 200, 206, 248, and 255.

92. Kenley correspondence in ETRC, boxes 123, 142, 143, 153, 156, 164, 165, 171, 172, 186, 195, 197, 200, 206, 248, and 255.

93. Kenley correspondence in ETRC, boxes 123, 142, 143, 153, 156, 164, 165, 171, 172, 186, 195, 197, 200, 206, 248, and 255.

94. Kenley said the lease was on the Newton Survey in Cherokee County, at $500 an acre.

95. Kenley correspondence in ETRC, boxes 123, 142, 143, 153, 156, 164, 165, 171, 172, 186, 195, 197, 200, 206, 248, and 255.

96. See the correspondence of Dave Kenley as well as Southern Pine Association circulars pertaining to selective logging in 1938 in ETRC, box 123, folder 8. See also, letter, Dave Kenley to Arthur Temple Jr., June 25, 1949, ETRC, box 255, folder 9, in which Kenley reports that Southern Pine Lumber Company cut an average of 9,445,000 board feet of timber per year from the beginnings of selective cutting in October 1940 through the end of 1948. See also, Kenneth Nelson, Interview 75b, September 27, 1985, pp. 18–19, The History Center, Diboll.

97. See several multipage letters and reports, especially a two-page letter from E. O. Siecke to D. C. Kenley, April 26, 1939, in ETRC, box 126, folder 4. See also a *Texarkana Gazette* clipping, "New York Day By Day," in the June 1946 correspondence between Arthur Temple Sr. and Jr. (accession 2006:016), at The History Center, Diboll, in which Arthur Temple Sr. explained selective cutting to a journalist.

98. Kenley correspondence, ETRC, box 44, folder 6, and box 126, folder 4; Billings, *Century of Forestry*, 52, 73; Gerland, "A Brief History of Temple Land Ownership," 11–14. Paul Hursey, hired by Angelina County Lumber Company in 1937, is considered the first professional forester hired by a Texas lumber company for more duties than merely buying, selling, and cutting timber.

99. Letter, Temple to Kenley, July 6, 1944, ETRC, box 197, folder 2. For more on B. Koontz, see *Marshall News Messenger*, "Timber Talk from the Lookout Tower," January 23, 1944, p. 14; and "300 On Hand for Forest Field Day Demonstrations," May 27, 1941, p. 1.

100. Letter, Kenley to Temple, July 15, 1944, ETRC, box 197, folder 2.

101. Ibid. See also Temple to Kenley, July 17, 1944, and Kenley to Temple, July 25, 1944.

102. "Cattle in the Pines: Once Viewed as an Unnecessary Evil, Woods Grazing Is Emerging under the Stimulus of Research and Management as an Important Forest Industry," *American Forests* 50, no. 5 (1944): 238–39, 260–64; nine-page typescript memo by Austin Cary, US Forest Service, to Watson Walker, written at Diboll, March 2, 1923, "Notes for Mr. Walker, Diboll, Texas," ETRC, box 4, folder 12.

103. Letter, H. G. Temple to Richie Wells and others, May 2, 1946, in Kenneth Nelson Collection (1985:P008); Kenneth Nelson, Interview 75b, September 27, 1985, p. 18; both in The History Center, Diboll.

104. "Company to Give Scholarship to Stephen F. Austin College," *Buzz Saw* (Diboll), June 30, 1948, p. 2; letter, Arthur Temple Sr. to Arthur Temple Jr., June 18, 1948, Arthur Temple Sr. and Arthur Temple Jr. Correspondence (2006:016), The History Center, Diboll. See also McDonald et al., *Arthur Temple College of Forestry*, 20–21. The earliest full-time college graduate forester was Stephen F. Austin State College graduate Bill Nichols. Bill Fulmer of Syracuse University was hired shortly after Nichols, and Dennis Maynard of Stephen F. Austin University made the seventh college graduate hired by Nelson's forestry department. See Jonathan Gerland's interview with Joe Ruby, September 13, 2012, Interview 136b, The History Center, Diboll; *Diboll Free Press* articles of August 4, 1988 (pertaining to Bill Nichols's retirement party), and June 12, 1986 (pertaining to Bill Fulmer's retirement); and "Dennis Maynard Is New Office Forester," *Buzz Saw* (Diboll), March 1951, p. 3.

105. Some of the activities of the early foresters can be found throughout the J. Shirley Daniel Photographic Collection and related *Buzz Saw* newspaper articles from 1948 to 1951, The History Center, Diboll. For example, see "Tree Planting Program Is Inaugurated by Southern Pine," *Buzz Saw*, November 30, 1950, p. 6.

106. Some of Kenley's extensive cattle business records during the time are in ETRC, boxes 154, 164, 165, 171, 172, and 195. Some of his partners included Grady Singletary of Alto, W. R. Beaumier of Lufkin, and Roy Treadwell of Burke. Employees included his son Edd (who did not receive a salary), Charlie Harber and Tom Gay of Apple Springs, L. C. Dominy of Groveton, and C. G. Davenport of Lufkin.

107. Letter, Arthur Temple Sr. to Dave Kenley, September 24, 1949, ETRC, box 255, folder 9; Arthur Temple Sr. to Arthur Temple Jr., October 1, 1949, Arthur Temple Sr. and Jr. Correspondence (2006:016), The History Center, Diboll.

108. For instance, see letters, E. L. Kurth to D. C. Kenley, July 8, 1941, ETRC, box 156, folder 6; Kenley to Arthur Temple Sr., August 28, 1944, ETRC, box 197; and Arthur Temple Sr. to Dave Kenley, April 2, 1948, Arthur Temple Sr. Letters (1993:016), The History Center, Diboll. Also, see Kenley's correspondence with Arthur Temple Sr. and H. G. Temple in 1948, in ETRC, box 248, folder 6. Kenley was a harsh negotiator and often used racial slurs such as "nigger" and "darkey" in his dealings, bragging that he "used a whip" on various individuals and was particularly harsh to members of the Jewish community in Lufkin. See his correspondence in ETRC, box 4, folder 4; box 19, folder 3; box 22, folder 11; box 44, folder 6; box 55, folder 1; and box 71, folder 6.

109. There were other examples of misunderstandings between Arthur Temple Sr. and Dave Kenley during the 1940s. One of the more interesting ones concerned rights-of-way and easements which Kenley had granted the Rural Electrification Administration and Texas Power & Light Company following World War II without charge. Arthur Sr. felt that the company should have received compensation, but Kenley explained that although he at first felt the same way, upon "full investigation" he learned that the burden had been placed on the farmers to secure the rights-of-way. He said that the utility companies told the farmers to "wire up their houses" and the lines would come. Then after the houses were wired, the farmers were told to secure the rights-of-way from their neighbors; it was no difficult matter for the farmers to grant themselves the needed rights-of-way, until finally the only obstacle to electric service was a big landowner like Southern Pine Lumber Company in the middle. Even bankers, Kenley said, had granted rights-of-way across their unoccupied lands for free, so when the farmers pleaded with Kenley he figured "we couldn't afford to antagonize anybody about it." Kenley said he reasoned that as long as he got the timber off the right-of-way or was paid for the timber, all was well and fair. He did not think a fee for the easement itself was necessary or even possible. Besides, Kenley explained that the highline rights-of-way made excellent fire lanes as well as logging roads, and by opening up the forest they actually helped the timber on either side of the right-of-way to grow faster. Kenley claimed that if the company ever "antagonized just one man enough to set the woods afire at the right time of the year," it would cost the company more than anything they could have ever received in the way of easement payments. Besides, demanding money for easements might have caused someone "to be unfriendly to us on the Board of Equalization." Furthermore, Kenley said that "Mr. Kurth and the paper mill" had not granted easements, and they were taking a bad public relations

hit because of it. After several letters were exchanged, and after Arthur Jr. agreed with Kenley, Arthur Sr. said that he regretted having "made a mountain out of a mole hill" and reluctantly accepted "these utility lines as a necessary evil." Letters, Dave Kenley to Arthur Temple Sr., April 24 and 28 (dictated on the 27th), 1948; and Arthur Temple Sr. to Dave Kenley, April 26 and 29, 1948; all in ETRC, box 248, folder 6; letter, Arthur Temple Jr. to Sr., April 29, 1948, in Collection 2006:016, The History Center, Diboll.

110. Four letters, Arthur Temple Sr. to Dave Kenley, September 24 and October 14 and 25, 1949, and Kenley to Temple, October 5, 1949, ETRC, box 255, folder 9.

111. Letter, Temple to Kenley, October 25, 1949, ETRC, box 255, folder 9.

112. Undated, handwritten note by Kenley, addressed to "Mr. Arthur," and letter from Arthur Temple Sr. to Dave Kenley, October 28, 1949, both in ETRC, box 255, folder 9; letter, Vernon Burkhalter to Arthur Temple Jr., November 14, 1967, Arthur Temple Jr. Business Papers (2004:014), The History Center, Diboll. See also Arthur Temple Sr. to Arthur Temple Jr., March 16 and August 17, 1950 (2006:016), The History Center, Diboll.

113. Two-page letter, Arthur Temple Sr. to R. E. Minton, March 22, 1933, ETRC, box 78, folder 6.

114. Letter, R. E. Minton to Arthur Temple Sr., March 23, 1933, ETRC, box 78, folder 6.

115. Letter, Arthur Temple Sr. to Arthur Temple Jr., August 17, 1950, Arthur Temple Sr. and Arthur Temple Jr. Correspondence; letter, Vernon Burkhalter to Arthur Temple Jr., November 14, 1967, Arthur Temple Jr. Papers, box 101, folder 6; both at The History Center, Diboll.

116. Letter, Arthur Temple Jr. to Arthur Temple Sr., November 4, 1949, Arthur Temple Sr. and Arthur Temple Jr. Correspondence (2006:016), The History Center, Diboll.

117. Letter, Arthur Temple Sr. to Arthur Temple Jr., November 7, 1949 (2006:016), The History Center, Diboll.

118. Multiple letters, Dave Kenley to L. D. Gilbert, May 21 and July 23, 1923, ETRC, box 26, folder 7, and copies in box 19, folder 11; Kenley to Hintz, November 29, 1923, ETRC, box 26, folder 9; multiple letters between Dave Kenley and L. D. Gilbert, April 18, 21, and 27, and May 1, 1926, ETRC, box 44, folder 6; Arthur Temple Sr. to Arthur Temple Jr., February 20, 1950, Arthur Temple Sr. and Jr. Correspondence (2006:016), The History Center, Diboll. For the various laws affecting school fund lands that contained timber, see Cooper, *Permanent School Fund*, 64–68. Email communications to the author from General Land Office employees in 2017 and 2018, author's possession.

119. For instance, see letters between L. D. Gilbert and Dave Kenley, November 5 and 6, 1923, which pertained to one of C. H. Kenley's timber sales, in ETRC, box 26, folder 8; also, see C. H. Kenley to D. C. Kenley, November 4, 1922, ETRC, box 20, folder 2. For early "home place" purchases during the 1910s, see numerous letters between the Kenley brothers and R. E. Minton in ETRC, box 3, folder 8; and box 4, folder 6. For Gilbert's detailed knowledge of the Kenleys' purchasing activities concerning state land, see letters between Gilbert and Kenley in ETRC, box 44, folder 6, esp. those dated April 18, 21, and 27, and May 1926.

120. Numerous conversations with Charlie Harber between 2000 and 2005 and Charlie Harber, Interview 157a, p. 20, The History Center, Diboll.

121. Arthur Temple Sr. to Arthur Temple Jr., July 14, 1948, Arthur Sr. and Jr. Correspondence (2006:016), The History Center, Diboll.

122. Jonathan Gerland's interview with Arthur Temple, June 2, 2000, Interview 56d, p. 9; and Megan Lambert's interview with Arthur Temple, July 11, 1985, Interview 56b, p. 14, both at The History Center, Diboll; letter, Kenneth Nelson to A. G. Johnson, December 9, 1958, Arthur Temple's Papers (2004:014a), box 45, folder 4. For more details about the cattle and their relationship to pine and hardwood regeneration, see Lay, "Recovery of a Southern Forest," 73–95.

123. A thirteen-page typescript, "Plant Composition and Vegetative Alteration under Deer and Cattle Utilization in a Pine-Hardwood Forest Area of East Texas, by Claude A. McLeod, September 1960," in Daniel W. Lay Collection, ETRC, box 3, un-numbered folder.

124. Ibid., especially pp. 4–12. Even after pines were planted at Boggy Slough, cows continued to be a detriment to their success. See correspondence between

Kenneth Nelson and Arthur Temple in 1958 and 1960, especially letters and notes of October 31, 1958, in box 45, folder 4, and February 20, 1960, in box 56, folder 8, in Arthur Temple Jr. Papers (2004:014), The History Center, Diboll. Also see Lay, "Recovery of a Southern Forest," p. 73.

125. Arthur Temple, Interview 56b, pp. 14 and 16, and Arthur Temple Interview 56d, p. 9, The History Center, Diboll. Details concerning the cattle removal in 1961 can be found in letters and multiple handwritten notes between Kenley, Arthur Temple, and Kenneth Nelson, dated May 14 and 27, June 2, and June 11 in Arthur Temple Jr.'s Papers (2004:014a), box 62, folder 15, The History Center, Diboll.

Chapter 10. The Ranch Becomes Boggy Slough

1. Letters, Arthur Temple to R. E. Minton, November 10, 1936, and R. E. Minton to Arthur Temple, November 12, 1936, in Temple Industries Records at the East Texas Research Center, Nacogdoches (hereafter ETRC), box 104, folder 6.

2. Two-page letter, Arthur Temple to R. E. Minton, November 21, 1936, ETRC, box 104, folder 6.

3. One of his mother's uncles was Caspar William Whitney, friend of Theodore Roosevelt, explorer, and outdoors journalist and author.

4. "Arthur Temple," *The Pine Bough*, December 2006, pp. 10–19; "Temple Lumber Company, History of Retail Division, 1920–1944," a 50-page manuscript at The History Center, Diboll; Clurman, *To the End of Time*, 42–43; letter, Arthur Temple Sr. to Arthur Temple Jr., September 6, 1950, Arthur Temple Sr. and Arthur Temple Jr. Correspondence (2006:016), The History Center, Diboll; correspondence between the author and Ellen Temple, September 2018, author's possession.

5. "Arthur Temple," *Pine Bough*, December 2006, p. 11. During the 1950s, Arthur Temple Jr. served on at least eight Angelina Chamber of Commerce committees, often at the same time, including committees on agriculture, aviation, forestry, highways, industry, retail, merchants, and legislative and national affairs. Angelina Chamber of Commerce Records (2018:001), The History Center, Diboll. He was also active in other chambers, including the East Texas Chamber of Commerce.

6. For example, see the Arthur Sr.'s letters of April 11, 1947, and September 10, 1948, Arthur Temple Sr. and Jr. Correspondence (2006:016), The History Center, Diboll.

7. Ibid.

8. Letter, Arthur Temple Sr. to Arthur Temple Jr., December 20, 1946, Arthur Temple Sr. and Arthur Temple Jr. Correspondence (2006:016), hereafter (2006:016), The History Center, Diboll.

9. Letter, Arthur Temple Sr. to Arthur Temple Jr., October 31, 1946 (2006:016).

10. Letter, Arthur Temple Jr. to Arthur Temple Sr., November 9, 1946 (2006:016).

11. Arthur Temple Jr. interview with Jonathan Gerland, June 2, 2000, Interview 56d, The History Center, Diboll.

12. Ibid.

13. John O. Booker interview with Jonathan Gerland, September 23, 2014, Interview 224b, p. 25, The History Center, Diboll.

14. Letter, Arthur Temple Sr. to Kenley, October 28, 1940, ETRC, box 143, folder 1.

15. Ibid. Kenley had earlier written to suggest the construction of a large outdoor open fireplace. See letter, Kenley to Temple, October 25, 1940, ETRC, box 143, folder 1.

16. Trinity County Deed Records, Trinity County Courthouse Annex, Groveton (hereafter TCCA), Book 88, p. 571 and Book 94, p. 120.

17. "Anthony's Second House, Boggy Game Rooms Form Top Feature," *Diboll News-Bulletin*, April 24, 1956, p. 1.

18. For instance, see letter, Kermit Schafer to Arthur Temple Sr., December 10, 1941, ETRC, box 155, folder 13.

19. Letter, Arthur Temple Sr. to Dave Kenley, December 20, 1941, ETRC, box 156, folder 6.

20. Ibid.

21. "Swept Away by Fire: Boggy Slough Is Gone," *Diboll Free Press*, December 15, 1966, p. 1; *Marshall*

News-Messenger, October 17, 1950; *Longview News Journal*, March 25, 1951; "Scout Training Program Set," *Longview News Journal*, March 25, 1951, p. 23; "Explorer Scouts Hold Sport Camp," *Tyler Morning Telegraph*, November 8, 1950, p. 15.

22. Letter, Arthur Temple Sr. to Dave Kenley, Henry Temple, and Arthur Temple Jr., August 14, 1944, ETRC, box 197, folder 2.

23. Ibid.

24. Arthur Temple Jr. interview with Jonathan Gerland, Interview 56d, 2000, The History Center, Diboll.

25. "Boggy Slough Is Gone," *Diboll Free Press*, December 15, 1966. See also correspondence between Walter Trout and Ben Anthony during April 1964 in Arthur Temple Jr. Papers (2004:014), box 82, folder 24, The History Center, Diboll.

26. W. J. Jackson, "The Saga of Professor Jackson, Part Two," *Diboll Buzz Saw*, August 15, 1947, p. 4; Jake Durham, "I Might Be Right," *Diboll Buzz Saw*, November 30, 1947, p. 2; Judith Linsley, "Beaumonter Harry James Personified the Big Band Sound," 2015 manuscript in author's possession; KSPL-Diboll radio interview with Will Jackson, undated, Interview transcription 123a, The History Center, Diboll. Some of the longtime cooks at Boggy Slough were Percy Garrett, A. C. Phillips, Charlie Billy Runnels, and Q. T. Bussey. A photograph of them appeared on page 3 of *Diboll Buzz Saw*, December 31, 1948.

27. For invitations to the "colored choir" to perform before the Texarkana Rotary Club, see letters from Arthur Temple Sr. to Jr., December 4 and 19, 1950; and May 17, 19, and 31, 1951; and from Arthur Temple Jr. to Sr., December 6 and 20, 1950, (2006:016). The idea first came up during Arthur Temple Sr.'s deer-hunting party at Boggy Slough in November 1950. Arthur Jr. encouraged the choir's traveling performances, saying that he thought it was "an excellent thing to have them sing around in this section where they can do us some good."

28. Letter, Senator Howard A. Carney of District 1, Atlanta, to Arthur Temple Jr., November 1, 1949, in Arthur Temple Jr. Papers (2004:014), box 9, folder 24, The History Center, Diboll.

29. Buddy Temple interview with Jonathan Gerland at Boggy Slough, Interview 263c, pp. 6–7, 12, The History Center, Diboll.

30. Letter, Dave Kenley to B. F. Hines, November 18, 1944, ETRC, box 197, folder 2.

31. Boyd, "Of Woods and Wildlife," 6–9.

32. For instance, see "Didn't Get Away," *Lufkin Daily News*, November 21, 1954.

33. Lay, "Recovery of a Southern Forest," 73–98; Kenley letters in ETRC, boxes 50, 55, 71, 81, 90, 123, 126, 142, 143, 153, 154, 156, 164, 165, 171, 172, 186, 195, 200, 206, 248, 255.

34. For examples, see correspondence concerning various hunts in Arthur Temple Jr. Papers (2006:014a), box 19, folders 24–25; and box 60, folder 26.

35. "Boggy Slough Is Gone," *Diboll Free Press*, December 15, 1966. For details concerning sponsored hunting parties from the 1940s through the early 1960s, see Arthur Temple Jr. Papers (2004:014), box 2, folder 12; box 9, folder 24; box 19, folders 24–25; box 19, folder 25; box 23, folder 11; box 23, folder 25; box 24, folder 3; box 26, folder 17; box 27, folder 8; box 32, folder 4; box 32, folder 5; box 37, folder 18; box 43, folder 13; box 48, folder 13; box 49, folder 24; box 54, folder 22; box 59, folder 12; box 60, folder 26; box 67, folder 32; box 73, folder 17; box 75, folder 8; box 80, folder 13; box 82, folder 13; box 87, folder 9; and box 101, folder 8; The History Center, Diboll.

36. For names of invitees, see related correspondence in Arthur Temple Jr. Papers (2004:014a), box 37, folder 18; box 49, folder 24; box 54, folder 22.

37. For example, see the letters from Arthur Temple Sr. to Arthur Temple Jr. dated October 31 and December 9, 1946, and September 21, 1948, Collection 2006:016, The History Center, Diboll.

38. Letter, Arthur Temple Sr. to Arthur Temple Jr., November 17, 1950, The History Center, Diboll.

39. Arthur Sr. had often told Judge Minton that he was "not so much interested in what is done in Texas as what is done in Arkansas." For example, see his letter to Minton of February 26, 1936, ETRC, box 104, folder 7.

40. Letter, Arthur Temple Sr. to Arthur Temple Jr., November 22, 1949, Collection 2006:016, The History Center, Diboll.

41. Letter, Arthur Temple Jr. to Arthur Temple Sr., November 23, 1949, The History Center, Diboll. Details of the senatorial party are in Arthur Temple Jr. Papers (2004:014), box 9, folder 24, The History Center, Diboll.

42. Buddy Temple interview with Jonathan Gerland, August 11, 2014, at Boggy Slough, Interview 263c, pp. 26–27, 30–33, The History Center, Diboll.

43. Letter, Arthur Temple Sr. to Arthur Temple Jr., November 22, 1949, and Arthur Temple Jr. to Arthur Temple Sr., November 23, 1949, Collection 2006:016, The History Center, Diboll.

44. The McDonald case made many newspapers. For example, see "Senator Caught with Deer," *El Paso Times*, December 15, 1954, p. 23; "Solon Charged for Hunting sans License," *Dallas Morning News*, December 15, 1954; "Nab Texas Senator; No Hunting License," *Clovis News-Journal*, December 14, 1954, p. 22; and "State Senator Faces Hunting Law Charges," *Austin American-Statesman*, December 14, 1954, p. 1.

45. "Solon Charged for Hunting sans License," *Dallas Morning News*, December 15, 1954.

46. Buddy Temple interview with Jonathan Gerland, August 11, 2014, Interview 263c, pp. 13–14, The History Center, Diboll.

47. "We Heard," *Liberty Vindicator*, July 21, 1960, p. 1; "Lufkin," *Kilgore News Herald*, June 1, 1960. Photographs of Boggy Slough gatherings and hunting parties during the late 1940s and early 1950s are included throughout the large J. Shirley Daniel Photographic Collection (1994:002) at The History Center, Diboll, especially in binders 1 and 8. Many gatherings were reported as news stories, with photographs in monthly issues of the *Diboll Buzz Saw* newspaper, also at The History Center, Diboll.

48. "Lumbermen Meet at Boggy Slough," *Diboll Buzz Saw*, May 31, 1950, p. 7; "Laredo Congressman Addresses Lumbermen," *Tyler Courier-Times*, May 17, 1953, p. 5; "Daniel Sees Return to Self-Government," *Dallas Morning News*, September 26, 1954.

49. Many meetings were photographed by Southern Pine Lumber Company photographers. See especially the J. Shirley Daniel Photographic Collections at The History Center, Diboll.

50. "Boggy Slough Hunts Slated," *Diboll Free Press*, October 5, 1960.

51. Information about the group can be found in Arthur Temple Jr. Papers (2004:014a), box 23, folder 25.

52. Letters, Dave Kenley to Arthur Temple Jr., December 16, 1954, and Arthur Temple Jr. to Dave Kenley, December 17, 1954, Arthur Temple Jr. Papers (2004:014), box 24, folder 9, The History Center, Diboll. The Pine Island rider was identified as "Williams," who caught "five different trespassers on our side of the river." Kenley requested to provide Williams with $25 for his children's Christmas presents.

53. Letters, Arthur Temple Jr. Papers (2004:014a), box 23, folder 11; box 26, folder 17; and box 27, folder 8.

54. Letters, Arthur Temple Jr. to Dave Kenley, January 29, 1954, box 25, folder 20; and Dave Kenley to J. W. Austin, November 9, 1955, box 27, folder 25, Arthur Temple Jr. Papers (2004:014), The History Center, Diboll. See also box 12, folder 22, where Kenley tells J. W. Austin that his group "are not much hunters," and he just wanted to "show them something."

55. For example, see Senator George Moffett's guest card for November 20–23, 1949, in Arthur Temple Jr.'s Papers (2004:014), box 9, folder 24, The History Center, Diboll. Admonishments to pick up trash were especially prevalent during the 1970s.

56. See the two-page document, "Boggy Slough Club Rules Governing the Membership [1954]," in Arthur Temple Jr. Papers (2004:014), box 23, folder 11, The History Center, Diboll.

57. See "Boggy Slough Game Preserve Rules Governing the Membership and Guests [1963]," "Minutes of a Called Meeting of Boggy Slough Fishing and Hunting Preserve Supervisory Committee Held on March 25, 1963," and a letter from Arthur Temple to Boggy Slough Preserve Committee, October 15, 1963, in Arthur Temple Jr. Papers (2004:014a), box 73, folder 17, The History Center, Diboll.

58. Two letters, Arthur Temple to Bob Burns, Latane Temple, H. C. White, H. G. Stubblefield, Joe C. Denman, Jack Sweeny, Clyde Thompson, Kenneth Nelson, and W. Temple Webber, December 30, 1960, and January 2, 1961, Arthur Temple Jr. Papers (2004:014a), box 59, folder 12, The History Center, Diboll.

59. Letter, Arthur Temple Jr. to Claude Davenport, December 3, 1962, Arthur Temple Jr. Papers (2004:014a), box 67, The History Center, Diboll.

60. Letter, Henry J. LeBlanc, Sr., to Arthur Temple, March 8, 1963, Clyde Thompson Papers (2004:014c), box 35, folder 11, The History Center, Diboll. See also, Fred W. Strong, "Operation Whitetail," *Victoria Advocate*, December 10, 1963, p. 11.

61. Letter, Clyde Thompson to Arthur Temple, March 15, 1963, Clyde Thompson Papers (2004:014c), box 35, folder 11, The History Center, Diboll.

62. Strong, "Operation Whitetail," 11; Fred W. Strong, "Outdoors: Report from SCOT," *Victoria Advocate*, March 28, 1964, p. 8; "Much E-Tex Timber Land Is Open to Public," *San Jacinto News-Times*, October 9, 1969, p. 12; Ray Sasser, "Bow Hunter's Haven," *Port Arthur News*, November 28, 1974, p. 17 "Minutes of Annual Meeting, Sportsmen's Clubs of Texas, Austin, Texas, January 18, 1964," in Clyde Thompson Papers (2004:014c), box 35, folder 11. For further information about Operation Whitetail and Thompson Temple, see correspondence among Arthur Temple, Joe Denman, Gene Samford, and Alan Miller during 1977, in Joe Denman's Papers (2004:014i), box 30, folder 25, The History Center, Diboll.

63. "Memorandum of Lease Agreement between Temple Industries, Inc. and Lufkin Foundry and Machine Company," unexecuted, and letters between Arthur Temple and Walter Trout during April 1964 in Arthur Temple Jr. Papers (2004:014), box 82, folder 24, The History Center, Diboll. See especially Walter Trout to Arthur Temple, April 1 and 20, 1964; Walter Trout to Ben Anthony, April 20, 1964; and Arthur Temple to Walter Trout, April 4, 1964.

64. "Memorandum of Lease Agreement between Temple Industries, Inc. and Lufkin Foundry and Machine Company," unexecuted, and letters between Arthur Temple and Walter Trout during April 1964 in Arthur Temple Jr. Papers (2004:014), box 82, folder 24, The History Center, Diboll. See especially Walter Trout to Arthur Temple, April 1 and 20, 1964; Walter Trout to Ben Anthony, April 20, 1964; and Arthur Temple to Walter Trout, April 4, 1964.

65. "Memorandum of Lease Agreement between Temple Industries, Inc. and Lufkin Foundry and Machine Company," unexecuted, and letters between Arthur Temple and Walter Trout during April 1964 in Arthur Temple Jr. Papers (2004:014), box 82, folder 24, The History Center, Diboll. See especially Walter Trout to Arthur Temple, April 1 and 20, 1964; Walter Trout to Ben Anthony, April 20, 1964; and Arthur Temple to Walter Trout, April 4, 1964.

66. "Historic Boggy Slough Clubhouse Burns; Loss to Exceed $100,000," *Lufkin News*, Evening Edition, December 8, 1966, p. 1. Between 2000 and 2018, the author interviewed a number of people who shared suspicions that the clubhouse was intentionally burned by someone disgruntled, but all of them asked that their own identities as well as the suspected arsonist remain anonymous.

67. "Boggy Slough Is Gone," *Diboll Free Press*, December 15, 1966, p. 1.

68. "Anthony's Second House, Boggy Game Rooms Form Top Feature," *Diboll News-Bulletin*, April 24, 1956, p. 1. As a teenager, Buddy Temple found shed antlers containing thirty-eight points, near Cochino Creek. They were mounted in the clubhouse at the time of the fire. A photograph of them appears in an undated news clipping titled, "Woodland Oddity," in Arthur Temple Jr.'s Scrapbook Collection, The History Center, Diboll; Buddy Temple, Interview 263c, p. 20, also mentions the shed antlers, The History Center, Diboll.

69. Temple briefly addressed this in his interview with Jonathan Gerland, Interview 56d, pp. 5–6; the 1967 clubhouse cost estimate is contained in Arthur Temple Jr. Papers (2004:014), box 101, folder 8; both at The History Center, Diboll.

70. "Minutes of a Special Meeting of Board of Directors of Temple Industries, Inc., Held on July 24, 1967, in the Board Room of Lumbermen's Investment Corporation in Westgate, Austin, Texas," Arthur Temple Jr. Papers, box 102, folder 9, p. 10, The History Center, Diboll.

71. Gerland, "A Brief History of Temple Land Ownership," 15, 18–22, 28–30; Buddy Temple, Interview 263a, pp. 5–6, The History Center, Diboll.

72. Arthur Temple interview with Jonathan Gerland, Interview 56d, p. 6, The History Center, Diboll.

73. Author's conversations with Arthur Temple Jr. in 2000; Buddy Temple, Interview 263c, pp. 27–29, The History Center, Diboll; Bowman, *First of A Kind*, 199–209.

74. See correspondence between Arthur Temple, Kenneth Nelson, and Louis Renfrow, including an inventory of the clubhouse property, in Arthur Temple Jr. Papers (2004:014), box 118, folder 1, The History Center, Diboll.

75. Sportsmen of Boggy Slough, Articles of Incorporation, April 2, 1979, and Bylaws, in Arthur Temple Jr. Papers (2004:014), box 370, folders 5 and 6, The History Center, Diboll.

76. Ibid.; Letter, Ward Burke to Spencer Knutson, February 21, 1980, Collection 2001:034, The History Center, Diboll.

77. Memo, Arthur Temple to Newest Members of SOBS, January 26, 1984, and "SOBS Anthem, written by Charlotte Spencer, 12/31/1979," in Arthur Temple Jr. Papers, box 283, folder 20, The History Center, Diboll; Temple, "Boggy Slough Chili," 41–45.

78. "Bluff Prairie Saline," in Dumble, *Geology of East Texas*, 313; "A Big Gas Blowout," *Houston Post*, October 8, 1904, p. 7; Odom, *Over on Cochino*, 71.

79. John O. Booker interview with Jonathan Gerland, September 23, 2014, Interview 224b, pp. 2–7, The History Center, Diboll; USGS 7.5 Minute Map, *Wells SW Quadrangle*, 1951 ed.; *Davy Crockett National Forest, 1948*, Map by US Department of Agriculture, Forest Service, Lyle F. Watts, Chief, Anthony P. Dean, Chief of Division of Engineering, both maps at The History Center, Diboll.

80. "Timm's Logging Crew Displays Firm Working Form in Their Banking Work at Rayville," *Diboll Buzz Saw*, November 1951, p. 2, at The History Center, Diboll.

81. Water permit, from Texas Water Rights Commission to Temple Industries, July 5, 1966, Trinity County Deed Records, TCCA, vol. 177, p. 254, copy obtained from Groveton Abstract Company.

82. Letter, Arthur Temple to Kenneth Nelson, May 10, 1966, Arthur Temple Jr. Papers (2004:014), box 97, folder 9, The History Center, Diboll; author's correspondence with Ellen Temple, June 2019.

83. Author's correspondence with Don Dietz, June 16, 2019.

84. John O. Booker interviews with Jonathan Gerland, June 20, 2011, Interview 224a, pp. 29–30, and September 23, 2014, Interview 224b, pp. 2–11, both at The History Center, Diboll.

85. John O. Booker, Interview 224b, p. 16, The History Center, Diboll.

86. Ibid., 13–15.

87. Handwritten note by Kenneth Nelson on the typed memo from Arthur Temple to Nelson, dated October 3, 1966, Arthur Temple Jr. Papers (2004:014), box 97, folder 9, The History Center, Diboll.

88. Doughty, *Wildlife and Man in Texas*, 196; Daniel W. Lay, "More Deer in East Texas," *Texas Game and Fish*, December 1954, p. 8.

89. Bill Oaks interviewed by Ellen Temple, October 5, 1978, Interview 17a, pp. 16–17, The History Center, Diboll.

90. W. E. Merrem, *Thirty-Seven Years with the Houston Oil Company of Texas, Southwestern Settlement and Development Company, and East Texas Pulp and Paper Company* (Houston: privately published, January 1975), 31–32, copy at The History Center, Diboll.

91. Arthur Temple Jr.'s correspondence for 1956, Collection 2004:014a, boxes 31–35, The History Center, Diboll.

92. Lay, "Recovery of a Southern Forest," 73, 76.

93. Letters, Arthur Temple to Kenneth Nelson, February 20, 1960, Arthur Temple Jr. Papers (2004:014), box 56, folder 8; see also correspondence between Temple and Nelson in box 45, folder 4; box 62, folder 15; box 97, folder 9; and box 110, folder 12; all at The History Center, Diboll.

94. "History of Boggy Slough Game Preserve, Written by Judge R. E. Minton, December 28, 1956," manuscript provided the author by Ward Burke in August 2000; "Deer Not Always Plentiful Here Says Mr. Minton," *Diboll News Bulletin*, November 14, 1957, pp. 1, 3.

95. Letters, Arthur Temple to Kenneth Nelson, February 20, 1960, box 56, folder 8; and Arthur Temple to members of Boggy Slough, November 10, 1961, box 59, folder 12; Arthur Temple Jr. Papers (2004:014), The History Center, Diboll.

96. 1961 Boggy Slough guest card, in Arthur Temple Jr. Papers (2004:014a), box 135, folder 15, The History Center, Diboll.

97. Letter, Arthur Temple to W. Temple Webber, Clyde Thompson, Latane Temple, Bob Burns, Ed Price, H. C. White Jr., H. G. Stubblefield Jr., Joe Denman, Jack Sweeny, and Ben Anthony, November 10, 1961, Arthur Temple Jr. Papers (2004:014a), box 59, folder 12, The History Center, Diboll.

98. W. C. Roach letter to the editor, *Lufkin Daily News*, April 24, 1962, p. 4; two-page letter, Arthur Temple to W. R. Beaumier, editor, *Lufkin Daily News*, April 25, 1962, Arthur Temple Jr. Papers (2004:014a), box 68, folder 8, The History Center, Diboll.

99. Lay, "Recovery of a Southern Forest," 73–98.

100. "Boggy Slough Is Opened to Trinity Group: Southern Pine Gives Permits for Doe Deer in Public Hunt," *Diboll Free Press*, December 24, 1962, pp. 1, 2.

101. James C. Kroll, "'The Ghost' of Boggy Slough," *North American Whitetail* (November 1988): 44.

102. Email communication, Don Dietz to Jonathan Gerland, April 25, 2019, author's possession.

103. Don Dietz and Darryl Stanley, "South Boggy Slough Browse Utilization Survey, February 1986," Arthur Temple Jr. Papers (2004:014), box 283, folder 21, The History Center, Diboll. In 1984, during a meeting of SOBS members, Temple was so displeased with the state of things that he threatened to use up to $10,000 of "Temple Foundation" funds annually to pay the state to trap the requisite number of remaining does each season and transfer them elsewhere. While the threat of using foundation funds was likely only a threat, the question of what to do with so many deer continued to stump Temple for years to come.

104. Letter, Kenneth Nelson to Arthur Temple, October 17, 1962, Arthur Temple Jr. Papers (2004:014), box 70, folder 6, The History Center, Diboll; "Save the Soil and Save Texas," 1966 Wildlife Awards Nomination for Arthur Temple, a two-page document of the Davy Crockett-Trinity Soil Conservation District No. 404 in Collection 2009:031, The History Center, Diboll.

105. "Haw Prairie," a one-page document attached to a letter from Kenneth Nelson to Arthur Temple, July 1, 1963, Arthur Temple Jr. Papers (2004:014), box 76, folder 13, The History Center, Diboll.

106. Email letter, Clay Kenley to Jonathan Gerland, January 23, 2018, author's possession.

107. See Knutson's correspondence with Dennis Haag and W. J. Gibson in Collection 2011:034, The History Center, Diboll.

108. "Temple, Hunting Clubs Transplanting Hardwoods," *Lufkin Home Banner*, February 5, 1978, p. 1. See also correspondence between Gene Samford and Arthur Temple and Joe Denman during 1977, in Arthur Temple Jr. Papers (2004:014), box 186, folder 15, The History Center, Diboll.

109. The award was the "Save the Soil and Save Texas" program. Two-page document, Davy Crockett-Trinity Soil Conservation District No. 404, Wildlife Award Nomination of Arthur Temple, 1966, in Collection 2009:031, The History Center, Diboll.

110. *Annual Report, Game, Fish and Oyster Commission for the Fiscal Year 1936–1937*, p. 8, in Dan Lay Collection, ETRC; "More Wildlife for East Texas Goal of Program Under Way in 45 Counties," *Dallas Morning News*, September 23, 1940; "Hunter and Fisher," *Dallas Morning News*, February 11, 1940; "With Hunter and Fisher: Texas Game Project," *Dallas Morning News*, March 10, 1940.

111. The three-year study was headed up by Claude A. McLeod. Thirteen-page manuscript, "Plant Composition and Vegetative Alteration under Deer and Cattle Utilization in a Pine-Hardwood Forest Area of East Texas, by Claude A. McLeod, September 1960," in Daniel W. Lay Collection, ETRC, box 3, unnumbered folder. The examination of harvested deer stomachs at Boggy Slough also occurred. See Kenneth Nelson to Ben Anthony, November 8, 1963, Arthur Temple Jr. Papers (2004:014), box 76, folder 13, The History Center, Diboll.

112. Photographs and notes made by Dan Lay during October 1966 at Rayville, in Daniel Lay Collection,

ETRC, box 4, folder 30; Lay, "Recovery of a Southern Forest," 73–98.

113. See correspondence between Arthur Temple and Gene Samford from the late 1970s through 1981 in Arthur Temple Jr. Papers (2004:014), box 191, folder 18; and (2009:030), box 386, folder 21; and box 229, folder 32; all in The History Center, Diboll. Lay, "Recovery of a Southern Forest," p. 78.

114. Two-page memo, Arthur Temple to Boggy Slough Game Committee, August 31, 1976, Joe Denman Papers, box 25, folder 21, The History Center, Diboll. Maps of the Boggy Slough Hunting Club beginning in 1976 also contain the names of the deer stands, including A.T. Area.

115. Author's conversations with John Booker in May 2019; correspondence between Samford and Temple during 1974 in Arthur Temple Jr.'s Papers (2004:014a), box 156, folder 3, The History Center, Diboll. See especially letters of August 1 and 6, where it was stated that "establishing a sound wildlife program" would "benefit us in many ways."

116. *Temple Industries Annual Report for 1970*, p. 8, The History Center, Diboll; Gene Samford's correspondence with Arthur Temple, 1974–1982, Arthur Temple Jr. Papers (2004:014); author's correspondence with wildlife managers Bill Goodrum, Don Dietz, and Robert Sanders, April through June 2019.

117. Letter, Samford to Arthur Temple, February 9, 1978 (2004:014a), box 191, folder 18; author's correspondence with Bill Goodrum in June 2019, author's possession.

118. See correspondence between Arthur Temple and Gene Samford from the late 1970s through 1981 in Arthur Temple Jr. Papers (2004:014), box 191, folder 18; (2009:030), box 386, folder 21; and box 229, folder 32; all at The History Center, Diboll.

119. Author's conversations with Bill Goodrum, June 2019; Donna Parish, "Dr. Deer Lives Here: Father of Modern Deer Management Calls SFA Home," October 12, 2012, print of an online news article from a Stephen F. Austin State University web page, author's possession.

120. "Wildlife Management, Whitetail Deer," *InTouch* 9, no. 4 (1993): 10.

121. "Temple Eastex Transplants Alligators to Boggy Slough," *The EasTexan*, September 1975, p. 11, a newsletter of Temple-Eastex, Inc.

122. News releases from 1977 in Arthur Temple Jr. Papers (2004:014), box 186, folder 15, The History Center, Diboll.

123. Arthur Temple wrote to Claude Davenport on May 11, 1959, instructing him to "make every effort to wipe out the nutria." Letter in Arthur Temple Jr. Papers (2004:014), box 49, folder 1, The History Center, Diboll. See also, "Nutria Hordes" and "Claude Davenport," *Diboll Free Press*, May 20, 1959; "New Assault Seen by Those Nutria," *Austin American Statesman*, June 7, 1959, p. 15; "The Nutria Could Be a Menace," *Austin American Statesman*, March 22, 1959, p. 27.

124. Notes and papers, Spencer Knutson Boggy Slough Collection (2011:034), box 1, folder 3, The History Center, Diboll.

125. Letter, Jonathan Hurst to Arthur Temple, May 1, 1976, Arthur Temple Jr. Papers (2004:014a), box 175, folder 19, The History Center, Diboll; Samford to Temple, June 4, 1982 (2009:030), box 238, folder 3; "South Boggy Newsletter, April and May 1987, by Don Dietz, manager," in Spencer Knutson Boggy Slough Collection (2011:034), The History Center, Diboll. For aerial applications of herbicides, see letters, Arthur Temple Jr. to Kenneth Nelson, July 13, 1958, and Nelson's afternoon reply, in Arthur Temple Jr. Papers (2004:014), box 45, folder 4, and several collections of J. Shirley Daniel photographs, all at The History Center, Diboll. The photographs show the aerial applications of herbicides during the 1950s and 1960s.

126. "South Boggy Newsletter, April and May 1987, by Don Dietz, manager," in Spencer Knutson Papers (2011:034); letters, D. C. Kenley to Arthur Temple Jr., February 17, 1949, Arthur Temple Jr. Papers (2004:014), box 4, folder 33; all in The History Center, Diboll.

127. Letter, Jack R. Stone to Arthur Temple, November 9, 1967, Arthur Temple Jr. Papers (2004:014a), box 103, folder 7, The History Center, Diboll. In the same folder, see related letters to Temple from Leamon Hassell, October 24, 1967, W. G. Dominy, undated; and Arlie R. Bice Jr., October 24, 1967. Stone, *Every Man Dies*.

128. Letters, Arthur Temple Jr. Papers (2004:014a), box 121, folder 13, see especially John Booker to Arthur Temple, July 29, 1970; John Booker to Jewel Brown, August 5, 1970; and drawings of a 32-foot-long holding pen and 55-gallon-drum turkey feeder, The History Center, Diboll.

129. Letters, Arthur Temple Jr. Papers (2004:014), box 135, folder 15, The History Center, Diboll.

130. Author's correspondence with Don Dietz and Bill Goodrum, March through June 2019, author's collection. Quotes are from Bill Goodrum, who is the son of longtime state biologist P. D. Goodrum.

131. Letter, Gene Samford to Joe Denman, February 1, 1979, Arthur Temple Jr. Papers (2009:036), box 386, folder 21; see also Temple-Eastex Press Releases from 1977 in Arthur Temple Jr. Papers (2014:014), box 186, folder 15; both at The History Center, Diboll.

132. Author's correspondence with Don Dietz and Joe Hamrick, June 2019.

133. "South Boggy Newsletter, April and May 1987, by Don Dietz, manager," p. 1, in Spencer Knutson Papers (2011:034), The History Center, Diboll.

134. Author's correspondence with Don Dietz, June 2019, author's collection.

135. Samford and Temple correspondence during 1974 in Collection 2004:014, box 156, folder 3, The History Center, Diboll.

136. Samford and Temple correspondence in Collection 2004:014, box 175, folder 19, The History Center, Diboll.

137. Samford and Temple correspondence in Collection 2004:014, box 191, folder 18, The History Center, Diboll.

138. Ibid., especially Samford to Temple, February 22, 1978. Also see Samford letters to Joe Denman, January 3 and July 6, 1979, The History Center, Diboll.

139. Letter, Gene Samford to Kenneth Nelson, June 9, 1978, Collection 2011:034, box 1, folder 3, The History Center, Diboll. Correspondence with Don Dietz and Bill Goodrum, April through June 2019, author's collection. See also correspondence from 1975 in Joe C. Denman Papers (part of 2004:014i), box 20, folder 9, The History Center, Diboll.

140. Letter, Samford to Denman, May 2, 1980, Arthur Temple Jr. Papers (2009:030), box 393, folder 22, The History Center, Diboll.

141. Author's conversations with John Booker in May 2019; "American Elk in East Texas," *San Jacinto News-Times*, November 16, 1972, p. 16; Arthur Temple and Joe Denman correspondence with Gene Samford, 1974–1982, in Arthur Temple Jr. Papers (2004:014a), especially letters of June 10, 1981 and August 2, 1982, The History Center, Diboll; author's correspondence with Bill Goodrum, May 2019. Oscar Rogers usually worked to "feed, drive, and beg" the animals back into their pens.

142. Five-page document, "Boggy Slough Wildlife Management Plan [1982]," in Spencer Knutson Collection (2011:034), The History Center, Diboll.

143. Author's conversations with Darryl Stanley in 2013 and 2014.

144. Ibid.

145. "South Boggy Newsletter, April and May 1987, by Don Dietz, manager," in Spencer Knutson Papers (2011:034), The History Center, Diboll.

146. Dan Lay, "More Deer in East Texas," *Texas Game and Fish* 22, no. 13 (1954): 26.

147. Ibid., 8, 26.

148. For example, see the letter from Arthur Temple to W. P. Bennett, April 16, 1955, Arthur Temple Jr. Papers (2004:014), box 26, folder 6, The History Center, Diboll.

149. "Boggy Slough Wildlife Management Plan [1982]," p. 4, Collection 2011:034, The History Center, Diboll.

150. Author's correspondence with Bill Goodrum and Robert Sanders, the former and present Boggy Slough managers, April through June 2019, author's collection.

151. "Wildlife Management 'Ideal' at North Boggy," *InTouch* 2, no. 3 (1985): 6; Kroll, "The Ghost of Boggy Slough," 46–47.

152. Leopold, *Game Management*, 130; "Wildlife Management, Quail," *InTouch* 9, no. 4 (1993): 10.

153. "Biologist Studying Quail," *Longview New-Journal*, March 29, 1992, p. 27.

154. Letter, Samford to Arthur Temple, June 4, 1982, Arthur Temple Jr. Papers (2004:014a), box 238, folder 3, The History Center, Diboll.

155. Author's correspondence with Don Dietz, March through June 2019, author's collection.

156. Author's personal observations.

157. Aldo Leopold, in the April 1919 publication, *Bulletin of the American Game Protective Association*, reprinted as "Wild Lifers vs. Game Farmers: A Plea for Democracy in Sport," in Meine, *Aldo Leopold*, 198–204.

158. Author's conversations with Ellen and Buddy Temple in 2013 and 2014.

Chapter 11. Conservation Land

1. Buddy Temple interview with Jonathan Gerland, November 19, 2013, Interview 263b, pp. 1–2, The History Center, Diboll.

2. Ibid.; Buddy Temple interview with Jonathan Gerland, August 11, 2014, Interview 263c, pp. 8–9.

3. Buddy Temple, Interview 263b, October 16 and November 19, 2013, p. 2.

4. Ibid., pp. 1–2; conversations with Buddy Temple in 2014 and with Jack Sweeny and Ellen Temple, 2016–19; author's correspondence with Jack Sweeny, July 2, 2019.

5. Thirty-six page manuscript, "Temple-Inland Forest, The Hardwood Forest, Management Plan, 2001," The History Center, Diboll; author's conversations with Buddy Temple in 2013 and 2014.

6. Buddy Temple, Interview 263b, October 16 and November 19, 2013, p. 4.

7. Gerland, "A Brief History of Temple Land Ownership, 14–21; Franklin Reck and Joseph Shirley Daniel, "Woodsman—Kill This Tree!" *Ford Truck Times* (March-April 1949): 14–17; Jack Sheffield interview with Jonathan Gerland, June 29, 2017, Interview 283a, The History Center, Diboll; photographs of Redgate, *Pine Bough*, December 2017, pp. 38–39.

8. The company had earlier purchased some of the tract's timber from the Louisiana and Texas Lumber Company in 1912 but apparently did not log it at the time. Southern Pine Lumber Company Land Records (1993:015), Trinity County Volume, Hampton Survey, The History Center, Diboll; Trinity County Deed Records, Trinity County Courthouse Annex, Groveton, vol. 67, p. 419; Houston County Deed Records, Houston County Courthouse, Crockett, vol. 89, p. 490; Hampton Abstract 259 Files, Groveton Abstract Company. For logging the Hampton survey in 1948, see Charlie Harber interview with Jonathan Gerland, Interview 157d, pp. 4–5, The History Center, Diboll.

9. Charlie Harber interview with Jonathan Gerland, Interview 157d, pp. 4–5, The History Center, Diboll.

10. The gum logs appear in a photograph published in the *Diboll Buzz Saw*, October 30, 1948, p. 7. Vintage photographs of the logs are in the J. Shirley Daniel Photograph Collection, The History Center, Diboll; see esp. 06:100d.

11. The Cochino loblolly was declared the state champion by the Texas Forest Service in 2017. It measured 133 feet tall, 180 inches in circumference, and 65 feet across, with a 329 index value. "Tall Timber: Texas A&M Forest Service Confirms Loblolly Pine at Boggy Slough as Largest of Its Kind in the State," *Lufkin News*, February 7, 2017, p. 1.

12. Southern Pine Lumber Company and Temple Industries Annual Reports to Shareholders, 1954–1956, The History Center, Diboll.

13. Letter, Kenneth Nelson to Bill Nichols and Bill Fulmer, April 5, 1971, Arthur Temple Jr. Papers (2004:014), box 132, folder 18, The History Center, Diboll.

14. Letter, Arthur Temple to Daniel W. Lay, November 24, 1971, Arthur Temple Jr. Papers (2004:014a), box 133, folder 24, The History Center, Diboll.

15. Norman Davis interview with Jonathan Gerland, February 24, 2017, Interview 282a, pp. 1–6, 13–14, The History Center, Diboll.

16. Letter, Arthur Temple Sr. to Arthur Temple Jr., August 18, 1950 (dictated August 17, 1950), Arthur Temple Sr. and Jr. Correspondence (2006:016); D. C. Kenley to Arthur Temple Jr., August 14, 1950, Arthur Temple Jr. Papers (2004:014), box 9, folder 27; all at The History Center, Diboll.

17. "Notes for Mr. Walker, Diboll, Texas, Cary's Report [March 2, 1923]," pp. 2–3, in Temple Industries Records at the East Texas Research Center, Nacogdoches (hereafter ETRC), box 4, folder 12.

18. Buddy Temple, Interview 263c, p. 23, The History Center, Diboll.

19. "With Reservations ... Timber Owners Pledge Support of Proposed Big Thicket Monument," and "Editorial: The Big Thicket Park," *Diboll Free Press*, June 15, 1967, p. 1; letter, Arthur Temple to Dempsie Henley, June 24, 1967, Arthur Temple Jr. Papers (2004:014), box 101, folder 6; Arthur Temple and Kenneth Nelson correspondence, in Arthur Temple Jr. Papers (2004:014), box 104, folder 12; both at The History Center, Diboll.

20. Letter, Kenneth Nelson to Arthur Temple, May 17, 1967, Arthur Temple Jr. Papers (2004:014), box 104, folder 12, The History Center, Diboll; "With Reservations ... Timber Owners Pledge Support of Proposed Big Thicket Monument," and "Editorial: The Big Thicket Park," *Diboll Free Press*, June 15, 1967, p. 1.

21. Letter, Kenneth Nelson to Arthur Temple, February 6, 1963, along with attachments concerning the Society of American Foresters' definitions of "natural areas" and a letter from W. D. Oliver of International Paper Company to Kenneth Nelson, January 15, 1963, Arthur Temple Jr. Papers (2004:014), box 76, folder 13, The History Center, Diboll.

22. *Temple Industries Annual Report for 1967*, p. 3, The History Center, Diboll; Gunter, *Big Thicket*, 78; Cozine, *Saving the Big Thicket*, 117, 142.

23. Cozine, *Saving the Big Thicket*, 142, 166.

24. For an example of Temple's up and down relationship with some of the Big Thicket supporters, including his threat to Congressman Charles Wilson in 1978 to clear-cut some 5,000 acres of Temple-Eastex lands to prevent the establishment of a "Big Thicket State Park," see letter, Arthur Temple to Charles Wilson, July 6, 1978, "Confidential," and Charlie Wilson to Maxine Johnston, July 20, 1978, in Arthur Temple Jr. Papers (2004:014), "B" file, 1978 Correspondence, The History Center, Diboll; see also the related correspondence and attachments between Temple, Wilson, and Garland Bridges, dated July 5 and 24, 1978. When Temple first supported the smaller 35,500-acre "memorial," rather than an 80,000- or 100,000-acre "preserve," he stated in the pages of the *Diboll Free Press* that he thought there was no need "to set aside 30,000 or 40,000 acres if 5,000 or 10,000 acres will

just as well accomplish the full purpose" of protecting unique ecosystems. See "With Reservations ... ," *Diboll Free Press*, June 15, 1967, p. 1. Author's conversations with Maxine Johnston, 2003–19, and Geraldine Ellis Watson, 2003–4.

25. Letter, Geraldine Watson to Arthur Temple, March 26, 1975, Arthur Temple Jr. Papers (2004:014), box 169, folder 5; letter, Geraldine Watson to the editor of the *Beaumont Enterprise*, March 26, 1975; letter, Geraldine Watson to Arthur Temple, September 5, 1973, Joe Denman Papers (2004:014i), box 9, folder 20; all at The History Center, Diboll.

26. The many and varied details of Temple's "dilemma" concerning the 410-acre tract of timber are best explained in a four-page letter from Ward Burke to Arthur Temple, dated August 11, 1975, in Joe C. Denman Papers (2004:014i), box 20, folder 9, The History Center, Diboll.

27. Ibid.; Gunter, *Big Thicket*, 99; Cozine, *Saving the Big Thicket*, 166.

28. Author's conversations during 1999 to 2007 with Alan O. Miller, former public relations director of Temple Industries, Temple-Eastex, and Temple-Inland.

29. Letters, Arthur Temple to Garland Bridges, July 30, 1973, and Arthur Temple to Geraldine Watson, September 5, 1973, in Joe Denman Papers (2004:014i), box 9, folder 20, The History Center, Diboll.

30. Gerland, "A Brief History of Temple Land Ownership," 28; Cozine, *Saving the Big Thicket*, 236–37.

31. Buddy Temple, Interview 263b, October 16 and November 19, 2013, pp. 2–6, The History Center, Diboll; four-page document, "Conservation / Environmental Grants," made by the T. L. L. Temple Foundation between 1970 and 2015, provided to the author by the foundation.

32. Gerland, "A Brief History of Temple Land Ownership," 18–28; Temple-Inland annual reports, 1968–1972, The History Center, Diboll.

33. Gerland, "A Brief History of Temple Land Ownership," 21–22.

34. Vardaman, *How to Make Money Growing Trees*, 3–4.

35. Gerland, "A Brief History of Temple Land Ownership," 18–28; Temple-Inland annual reports, 1968–1972, The History Center, Diboll.

36. Gerland, "A Brief History of Temple Land Ownership," 28.

37. Eight-page manuscript, "The History of Southwestern Timber Company," prepared ca. 1970, apparently distributed among the directors of Time Inc., who visited southeast Texas at that time, in Temple-Inland Public Affairs Collection (1993:001), box 47, folder 3, The History Center, Diboll. The Arthur Temple Sr. Research Area was a cooperative effort between the Texas Forest Service and Southern Pine Lumber Company. Established in 1952 on leased cutover lands that surrounded the former logging camp of Fastrill, it became the headquarters of the Texas Forest Service's tree improvement research program, the first of its kind in the South, organized by Dr. Bruce Zobel. Many of the seed orchard establishment and management techniques now in common use were first developed at the site. Billings, *Century of Forestry*, 110–11; Gerland, "A Brief History of Temple Land Ownership," 18.

38. Author's conversations with Arthur Temple in 2000.

39. See Temple-Inland's annual reports for 1983 through 1986, The History Center, Diboll. The quotes are from p. 8 of the 1986 report and p. 7 of the 1983 report.

40. Gerland, "A Brief History of Temple Land Ownership," 28–31. By 2007, 65 percent of the Temple-Inland timberlands were pine plantations. See p. 6 of "Temple-Inland Timberlands, April 2007," an eighty-two-page document prepared by Goldman Sachs-Citi, Collection 2008:006, The History Center, Diboll.

41. Author's conversations with Arthur Temple in 2000.

42. Letters, Dave Kenley to P. N. Anger of Beaumont, December 21, 1931, box 55, folders 3 and 5; to Arthur Temple Sr., March 30 and April 19, 1934, box 81, folder 6; and to H. G. Temple, April 7, 1935, box 90, folder 7; and March 21 and December 4 and 6, 1938, box 123, folder 8; all at ETRC.

43. Kenneth Nelson, Interview 75b, pp. 18–19, The History Center, Diboll.

44. Letters in Arthur Temple Jr. Papers (2004:014), between Arthur Temple Jr. and Ernest Kurth, August 17, 18, 27, and 30, and September 7, 1954, box 25, folder 40; E. L. Kurth to Arthur Temple, April 18,

1956, box 34, folder 14; E. L. Kurth to Arthur Temple, May 23, 1958, box 46, folder 17; all at The History Center, Diboll; Bowman, *First of a Kind*, 199–209.

45. Letter, Arthur Temple to Kenneth Nelson, August 25, 1967, Arthur Temple Jr. Papers (2004:014), box 104, folder 12; Kenneth Nelson, Interview 75b, pp. 18–19; Ward Burke, Interview 82a, pp. 14–15; all at The History Center, Diboll; Gerland, "A Brief History of Temple Land Ownership," 15–20. Surveyors' field notes for dams and diversion channels along Cochino Bayou, Franklin Slough, and the river are in Field Book 32 in Temple-Inland Land Department Surveyor Field Notebooks Collection (2007:036) at The History Center, Diboll.

46. Two-page letter, John Courtenay to Kenneth Nelson, January 7, 1971, Arthur Temple Jr. Papers (2004:014), box 132, folder 18, The History Center, Diboll.

47. Letter, Kenneth Nelson to John Courtenay, January 11, 1971, Arthur Temple Jr. Papers (2004:014), box 132, folder 18; Kenneth Nelson, Interview 75b, pp. 18–19; Ward Burke, Interview 82a, pp. 14–15, all at The History Center, Diboll.

48. Carter, Kellison, and Wallinger, *Forestry in the U.S. South*, 294–303.

49. Ibid.; Binkley, *Rise and Fall of Timber Investment*, www.pinchot.org/files/Binkley.DistinguishedLecture.2007.pdf.

50. Temple-Inland Annual Report to Shareholders, 1983, p. 7, The History Center, Diboll.

51. Gerland, "A Brief History of Temple Land Ownership," 8–9; Southern Pine Lumber Company, Temple Industries, Time Inc., and Temple-Inland annual reports to stockholders, The History Center, Diboll; Christine S. Diamond, "Temple-Inland Announces Pending Sale of 1 Million East Texas Timberland Acres," *Lufkin Daily News*, August 6, 2007.

52. Rhonda Oaks, "Temple Foundation Buys Boggy Slough," *Lufkin Daily News*, December 24, 2013; International Paper Press Release, "T. L. L. Temple Foundation, International Paper and The Conservation Fund Announce Landmark Forest Conservation Effort to Protect More Than 19,000 Acres in East Texas," copy in the records of the T. L. L. Temple Foundation

offices, Lufkin; Steve Knight, "International Paper Official: Company Plans to Sell Off Diboll Assets," *Lufkin Daily News*, February 12, 2012; Michael J. de la Merced and Jeffrey Cane, "International Paper Wins Temple-Inland," *New York Times*, September 6, 2011; Steve Knight, "Georgia-Pacific Completes Temple-Inland Building Products Acquisition," *Lufkin Daily News*, July 19, 2013.

53. Shannon Tompkins, "Boggy Slough Gift Is a Win for Conservation," *Houston Chronicle*, January 27, 2016.

54. In 1997 the T. L. L. Temple Foundation gave $4,970,690 to the university to establish an institute for forest ecosystem studies. Other grants from the foundation followed, including $3,641,000 in 1998. Earlier, the foundation had given $1 million to establish a school of forestry chair in 1989 and added another $2 million to the endowment in 2002. T. L. L. Temple Foundation's Conservation and Environmental Grants, provided to the author by the T. L. L. Temple Foundation, Lufkin, in 2016.

55. Author's conversations with Buddy Temple, 2013–14, and with Ellen Temple, 2013–19.

56. Ibid.

57. Author's conversations with Ellen Temple, 2019–20; Ellen Temple, Interview 287a, with Jonathan Gerland, June 8, 2018, The History Center, Diboll.

58. Tartt and Stehling, *The Land*; Ellen Temple conversations with the author in 2019 and 2020.

59. Mike Cox, "Reviving the Ranch: History, Education, and Good Land Management Abound at the Leopold Award-Winning Temple Ranch," *Texas Parks & Wildlife* (November 2011): 40–47; Temple and Hieger, *Temple Ranch Cookbook*.

60. Twenty-one-page document, "Boggy Slough Field Visit Report, May 13–14, 2014, Summary Provided by the Conservation Fund to the T. L. L. Temple Foundation, prepared by Julie Shackelford," copy provided the author by the T. L. L. Temple Foundation.

61. Ibid.; Keith, *Plant Community and Fuel Model Assessment for Temple Boggy Slough*; Keith, *Plant Community and Fuel Model Assessment for T. L. L. Temple*.

62. "Boggy Slough Field Visit Report, May 13–14, 2014." Ironically, Arthur Temple Jr. planted Chinese tallow trees near his Little Boggy clubhouse in 1982. Letter, Arthur Temple Jr. to Gene Samford, April 8, 1982, Arthur Temple Jr. Papers (2004:014), The History Center, Diboll.

63. "Boggy Slough Field Visit Report, May 13–14, 2014"; Larson & McGowin of Mobile, Alabama, "Second Draft, Timber Management Plan of T. L. L. Temple Foundation Boggy Slough Tract, 19,054 Acres, February 22, 2016," p. 14, copy provided the author by the Foundation.

64. "Boggy Slough Field Visit Report."

65. Ibid.

66. Measurements of the hickory, black gum, and red mulberry were made by the author in October 2018. All three were near one another along the winding channels of Cochino Bayou east of the main road. Caddo pottery sherds and other artifacts have been found nearby. The forest composition percentage is based on Larson & McGowin of Mobile, Alabama, "Timber Estimate Report, International Paper, Boggy Slough Tract, March 2013," copy provided by the T. L. L. Temple Foundation.

67. Larson & McGowin of Mobile, Alabama, "Second Draft, Timber Management Plan of T. L. L. Temple Foundation Boggy Slough Tract, 19,054 Acres, February 22, 2016," p. 12, copy provided the author by the Foundation; Keith, *Plant Community and Fuel Model Assessment for T. L. L. Temple*, 2, 38.

68. Damian Mazanet, "Mazanet Seeks Aid for the Tejas Mission, 1693," in Hadley, Naylor, and Schuetz-Miller, *The Presidio and Militia on the Northern Frontier of New Spain*, 346; Jessie Christie, "The Hap's Page, Club Talk," *Houston Post*, April 28, 1912, p. 43.

Appendix

1. Ecological analyses from Texas land survey records include Michael P. Schafale and P. A. Harcombe, "Presettlement Vegetation of Hardin County, Texas," *American Midland Naturalist* 109, no. 2 (1983): 355–66; Indumathi Srinath, "Original Texas Land Survey as a Source for Pre-European Settlement Vegetation Mapping" (master's thesis, Geography, Texas A&M University, December 2009); and Indumathi Srinath and Andrew C. Millington, "Evaluating the

Potential of the Original Texas Land Survey for Mapping Historical Land and Vegetation Cover," *Land* 5, no. 4 (2016): 1–14.

2. Boggy Slough Conservation Area land surveys are in Trinity and Houston Counties. The applicable GLO survey records for Trinity County are filed under abstract numbers 33, 39, 73, 113, 118, 259, 280, 331, 332, 353, 362, 438, 450, 477, 640, 700, 711, 730, 869, 934, 953, Scrip File 593, and School File 118590. Applicable Houston County abstract numbers are 361, 595, 596, 614, 615, 770, 803, 840, 949, 1007, 1041, 1135, 1137, 1271, and 1278. Useful sources in tree ecology and identification are Peattie, *Natural History of Trees* and Stahl and McElvaney, *Trees of Texas*.

3. Cedar Brake Prairie is described in Dumble, *Geology of East Texas*, 313.

4. The original I&GN Railroad surveys utilized stakes, instead of trees, as corners. Southern Pine Lumber Company resurveyed those tracts during the early 1900s and used trees mostly, and those later surveys I included in my overall analysis, omitting the earlier surveys that used stakes instead of trees. The upland hickories were probably pignut and mockernut varieties, which commonly inhabited dry ridges and slopes. The resurveys are in the Houston County Volume (vol. 6) of Southern Pine Lumber Company's Land Record, Ledgers, and Transfer Binders (accession 1993:015), at The History Center, Diboll.

5. Surveyors of the BBB&C land grant (Trinity County Abstract 118, GLO survey files, Austin) set a post "in prairie" for the survey's southwest corner. One of the Sanchez surveys near Cedar Creek also noted a "post in prairie." See the Trinity County Volume in Southern Pine Lumber Company's Land Record (accession 1993:015), The History Center, Diboll.

6. H. W. Pennington's 1886 map of the W. W. Alston Survey in Trinity County is in Texas General Land Office Records, Houston County Scrip File 593 (W. W. Alston).

7. Letters, R. S. Hunnicutt, special state surveyor, to John J. Terrell, Land Office Commissioner, August 29, 1908, in Texas General Land Office Records, Houston County Scrip File 593.

8. Southern Pine Lumber Company Land Record (1993:015), volumes for Houston and Trinity Counties.

9. Stakes and posts were used 36 percent and 46 percent of the time in these later surveys, so they were removed from consideration in the analysis.

10. Stephen H. Spurr and Burton V. Barnes, *Forest Ecology*, 2d ed. (New York: Ronald Press Company, 1973), 475–93.

11. The large black gum and red oak trees were cited in the field notes for the John A. Watson Survey, Angelina County Abstract 648, GLO files, Austin.

Bibliography

Archives, Manuscripts, and Other Records

Angelina County Courthouse (ACC), Lufkin
    Deed Records. Mechanics Lien Records.
        Probate Records, Estate of T. L. L.
        Temple.
Cass County Courthouse, Linden
    Deed Records.
Dimmit County Courthouse, Carrizo Springs
    Deed Records.
East Texas Research Center (ETRC), Stephen F. Austin
   State University (SFASU), Nacogdoches
    Lay, Daniel W. Papers and Collection.
    Sitton, Thad. Oral History Collection.
    Temple Industries (Southern Pine Lumber
        Company) Records.
The History Center, Diboll
    Alevra, Carolyn. Genealogical Collection
        (1999:039 and 2000:027).
    American Lumberman Photographic
        Collection.
    Angelina County Chamber of Commerce
        Records.
    Daniel, J. Shirley. Photographic Collection.
    Denman, Joe. Papers (2004:014i).
    Farrington, Fannie. Scrapbook and Photo-
        graph Album.
    Houston East and West Texas Railway
        Company. Directors' Record,
        1889–1891.
    Knutson, Spencer. Boggy Slough Collection.
    Map Collection.
    Merrem, W. E. Memoirs, 1975.
    Minton, R. E. Papers (2004:014d).
    Munz, Mary. Collection.
    Silvers, Joe. Rayville Ranch Photograph
        Collection.
    Southern Pine Lumber Company Annual
        Reports.

    Southern Pine Lumber Company Land
        Record Ledgers and Timber Type Maps
        (1993:015).
    Temple, Arthur Jr. Business Papers
        (2004:014a).
    Temple, Arthur Jr. Scrapbooks.
    Temple, Arthur Sr., and Arthur Jr.
        Correspondence (2006:016).
    Temple, Arthur Sr. Letters (1993:016).
    Temple Estate Papers (1986:004).
    Temple Family Collection (1986:003).
    Temple Foundation Records.
    Temple Industries Annual Reports.
    Temple-Inland Annual Reports.
    Temple-Inland Land Department Surveyor
        Field Notebooks.
    Temple-Inland Public Affairs Collection.
    Temple Lumber Company Retail Scrapbooks
        (2000:079).
    Temple, William Family Photographs
        (1999:079).
    Texas South-Eastern Railroad Company
        Collection and Records (1993:022 and
        2000:078).
    Thompson, Clyde. Papers (2004:014c).
    Vertical Files.
    Webber, William Temple. Family Photographs.
Houston County Courthouse (HCC), Crockett, Texas
   County School Records.
    Deed Records. District Court Civil and Crimi-
        nal Minutes. Commissioners'
        Court Meeting Minutes.
    Maps and Plats.
Kurth Memorial Library, Lufkin
    Roach, Jack, and Mary Roach. Manuscript,
        "Up on North Cedar, 1856–1998."
National Archives, Washington, DC, and College
   Park, MD
    Civil War Records. Record Group 109:
        Compiled Service Records of Confederate

Soldiers Who Served in Organizations from the State of Texas.

Interstate Commerce Commission Records. Eastern Texas Railroad Company, Finance Docket No. 4, Testimonies and Hearings Pertaining to the Construction, History, and Abandonment of the Railroad; Groveton, Lufkin & Northern Railway Finance Docket No. 8393, Testimonies and Hearings Pertaining to Request for Southern Pacific or Cotton Belt Lines to Operate Its Line; Groveton, Lufkin & Northern Railway Company Finance Docket No. 8629, Testimonies and Hearings Pertaining to the Construction, History, and Abandonment of Its Line; Tap Line Case, Testimonies and Exhibits, Volume 2, Groveton, Lufkin & Northern Railway Company and Texas South-Eastern Railroad Company.

US Census Manuscript Records: Population, Slaves, and Agriculture Schedules for Arkansas, Louisiana, Mississippi, Ohio, Oklahoma, Texas, and Virginia.

World War I Selective Service Draft Registration Records, 1917–1918.

Texas Forestry Museum, Lufkin
Texas Forest News.
East Texas Sawmill Data Base Project Research Notes.

Texas General Land Office (GLO), Austin
Original Land Grants, Surveys, and Maps Records: Angelina, Houston, and Trinity Counties.

Texas Highways Department, Lufkin
Engineer's Records and Drawings, Neches River Bridges and Roads.

Texas Secretary of State, Austin
Business Charters and Articles of Incorporation Records.

Texas State Archives, Austin
Tax Rolls. Angelina, Houston, and Trinity Counties (microfilm).
US Census Schedules for Texas. Population, Industry, Manufactures, and Agriculture (microfilm).

Trinity County Abstract Company, Groveton (TCAC)
Title Abstract Notes and Land Survey Files.

Trinity County Courthouse and Annex (TCCA), Groveton
Deed Records. District Court Civil and Criminal Minutes. Commissioners' Court Meeting Minutes.
Maps and Plats.

Trinity County Museum (TCM), Groveton
County Clerk Records. District Court Records. Kenley Family Vertical Files.

Wilbur Smith Research Library, Texarkana Museums System, Texarkana
Vertical Files. Whitaker Family and T. L. L. Temple.

Newspapers and Other Periodicals

Arkansas
Arkansas Democrat (Little Rock)
Daily Arkansas Gazette (Little Rock)

California
Los Angeles Herald

Illinois
American Lumberman (Chicago)
Railway Age (Chicago)

Missouri
Cut-Over Lands (St. Louis)

New York
Brooklyn Daily Eagle
Brooklyn Life
Brooklyn Times Union
Buffalo Courier
New York Sun
New York Times
Official Guide of the Railways

Texas
Abilene Reporter-News
Abilene Semi Weekly Farm Reporter
Amarillo Daily News
Austin American-Statesman
Beaumont Enterprise
Beaumont Journal
Beaumont News-Beacon

Bryan Eagle

Corpus Christi Caller-Times

Crockett Courier

Dallas Morning News

Diboll Buzz Saw

Diboll Free Press

Diboll News-Bulletin

El Paso Herald

El Paso Times

Fort Worth Star Telegram

Fredericksburg Standard

Galveston Daily News

Gulf Coast Lumberman

Hearne Democrat

Houston Post

Kilgore News-Herald

Longview News-Journal

Lubbock Avalanche Journal

Lufkin Daily News

Lufkin Home Banner

Lufkin News

Lufkin Weekly Tribune

Marshall News Messenger

Neches Valley News (Beaumont)

Pine Bough Magazine

Shiner Gazette

Southern Industrial & Lumber Review (Houston)

Taylor Daily Press

Texas Forest News (College Station)

Trinity County Star

Tyler Courier Times

Tyler Morning Telegraph

Waco News-Tribune

Court Case

"The Southern Pine Lumber Company, a Corporation; T. L. L. Temple, G. W. R. Chinn, and Mrs. G. W. R. Chinn, Plaintiffs in Error and Appellants, Versus W. B. Ward; The Southern Pine Lumber Company, a Partnership Composed of T. L. L. Temple and Benjamin Whitaker; G. M. D. Grigsby and D. J. Grigsby, Partners as Grigsby Brothers; J. W. McNeal, Charles Griswold, J. D. De Bois, Hattie P. De Bois, J. D. Elder, William H. Dugan, Anna Bannister, E. L. Blincole, and the American Exchange Bank, a Corporation, Defendants

in Error, Supreme Court of the United States No. 1483 (1906); October Term 1906, No. 365; and October Term 1907, No. 82." In *The Supreme Court Reporter, Volume 28, Cases Argued and Determined in the United States Supreme Court, October Term 1907*. St. Paul: West Publishing Company, 1908.

Oral Histories

East Texas Research Center (ETRC), Stephen F. Austin State University (SFASU), Nacogdoches

    Allen, Oscar. Recorded interview with Thad Sitton, March 15, 1986.

    Ashby, Frank. Recorded interviews with Thad Sitton, March 16 and 19 and May 6, 1992.

    Boyd, Charles. Recorded interview with Thad Sitton, April 8, 1992.

    Harber, Charlie. Recorded interview with Thad Sitton, February 28, 1992.

    Welch, Claude C. Recorded interview with Thad Sitton, January 17, 1986.

The History Center, Diboll

    Booker, John O. Jr. Recorded interviews with Jonathan Gerland, June 20, 2011 (#224a), and September 23, 2015 (#224b).

    Burke, Ward. Recorded interview with Megan Lambert, October 23, 1985 (#82a).

    Davis, Norman. Recorded interview with Jonathan Gerland, February 24, 2017 (#282a).

    Denman, Joe. Recorded interview with Megan Lambert, October 24, 1985 (#79b).

    Devereaux, Dred D. Recorded interview with John Larson, 1954.

    Dolben, David. Recorded interview with Jonathan Gerland, September 22, 2015.

    Farrington, Fannie. Transcribed interview with John Larson, December 1954 (#11a).

    Hamrick, Joe. Recorded interviews with Jonathan Gerland, March 19 and May 16, 2015.

    Harber, Charlie. Recorded interviews with Jonathan Gerland, May 4 (#157a) and 26, October 13, 2000 (#157c), and March 27, 2002 (#157d).

    Jackson, Will. Interview with KSPL-Diboll Radio (#123a).

    Kenley, Dave. Transcribed interview with John Larson, December 1954 (#14a).

Kenley, Edd. Recorded interview with Jonathan Gerland, October 5, 2000 (#158a).

Knutson, Spencer. Recorded interview with Jonathan Gerland, September 14, 1999.

Lee, Jerry. Recorded interview with Jonathan Gerland, June 21, 2018 (#288a).

Ligon, Jim. Recorded interview with Jonathan Gerland, November 6, 2009 (#185a).

Ligon, Leamon, and Cleveland Mark. Recorded interview with Jonathan Gerland, September 14, 2017 (#285a).

Miller, Alan. Interview with Jonathan Gerland (#171a)

Minton, Mrs. Jewel. Recorded interview with Marie Davis, October 7, 1988.

Monk, John. Recorded interview with Jonathan Gerland, February 26, 2009.

Nelson, Kenneth. Recorded interviews with Megan Lambert, August 17 (#75a) and September 27, 1985, and with Joel Cook, November 30, 1987.

Norman, Jack. Recorded interview with Jonathan Gerland, September 16, 2013.

Oaks, Bill. Recorded interview with Ellen Temple, October 5, 1978 (#17a).

Ruby, Joe. Interview with Jonathan Gerland, September 13, 2012 (#136b).

Rushing, J. B. ("Jim"). Recorded interview with Marie Davis, January 13, 1986 (#90a).

Rushing, Myrtle Nolen. Recorded interview with Marie Davis, March 15, 1986.

Sheffield, Jack. Recorded interview with Jonathan Gerland, June 29, 2017 (#283a).

Silvers, Joe. Recorded interview with Jonathan Gerland, November 12, 2008 (#174a).

Stanley, Darryl. Recorded interview with Jonathan Gerland, October 15, 2014.

Stern, Walter. Recorded interview with Jonathan Gerland, May 3, 2001.

Stubblefield, Horace. Interview with Jonathan Gerland, ca. 1988 (#132a).

Sweeny, Jack C. Recorded interviews with Jonathan Gerland, April 24, May 1, and June 6, 2012.

Temple, Arthur Jr. Recorded interviews with Megan Lambert, May 8 and July 11, 1985 (#56b); with members of the Diboll Historical Society, January 13, 1988; with Carolyn Elmore in 1993 (#56e); and with Jonathan Gerland, June 2, 2000 (#56d).

Temple, Bill. Recorded interview with Jonathan Gerland, July 27, 2001.

Temple, Buddy. Recorded interviews with Jonathan Gerland, October 16 (#263a) and November 19, 2013 (#263b), and August 11, 2014 (#263c).

Temple, Ellen. Recorded interview with Jonathan Gerland, June 8, 2018 (#287a).

Temple, Gresham. Recorded interview with Megan Lambert, August 16, 1985 (#74a).

Temple, Latane. Recorded interviews with Megan Lambert on June 19 and July 14, 1985, and self-interview in December 1985.

Thompson, Clyde. Recorded interviews with John Larson in 1954; with Vivian Holt in 1977; with Becky Bailey on January 14, 1984; and with Megan Lambert on October 25 and 26, 1984.

Webber, W. Temple Jr. Recorded interview with Jonathan Gerland, April 12, 2011.

Welch, Claude Sr. Recorded interview with Becky Bailey, January 5, 1983 (#27a).

Woods, Sadie Estes. Recorded interview with Megan Lambert and Marie Davis, July 18, 1984 (#40a).

Books, Articles, and Other Publications

Abernethy, Francis E., ed. *Tales from the Big Thicket*. Austin: University of Texas Press, 1966.

Abernethy, Francis, Jerry Bryan Lincecum, and Frances B. Vick. *Family Saga: A Collection of Texas Family Legends*. Denton: University of North Texas Press and Texas Folklore Society, 2003.

Abrams, Marc D. "Ecological and Ecophysical Attributes and Responses to Fire in Eastern Oak Forests." In *Fire in Eastern Oak Forests: Delivering Science to Land Managers*, edited by Matthew B. Dickinson, 74–89. Proceedings of a Conference, November 15–17, 2005, Ohio State University. USDA Forest Service, Northern Research Station General Technical Report NRS-P-1.

———. "Fire and the Development of Oak Forests." *BioScience* 42, no. 5 (1992): 346–53.

Abrams, Marc D., and Gregory J. Nowacki. "Native Americans as Active and Passive Promoters of Mast and Fruit Trees in the Eastern USA." *The Holocene* 18, no. 7 (2008): 1123–37.

Abt, Jeffrey, and Leabeth Abt. "Documents: The Gardening Sentiments of an Early Texas Pioneer." *East Texas Historical Journal* 29, no. 1 (1991): 63–70.

Ahlstrom, Sydney E. *A Religious History of the American People.* New Haven: Yale University Press, 1972.

Ainsworth, Jim Tom, and DeLoyd English Rudloff. *Crossing over Cochino: Kennard 1864–1996.* Lufkin: Best of East Texas Publishers, 1997.

Albert, Bruce M. "Climate, Fire, and Land-Use History in the Oak-Pine-Hickory Forests of Northeast Texas during the Past 3500 Years." *Castanea* 72, no. 2 (2007): 82–91.

Aldrich, Armistead Albert. *The History of Houston County, Texas.* San Antonio: Naylor Company, 1943.

Alexander, Bob. *Bad Company and Burnt Powder: Justice and Injustice in the Old Southwest.* Denton: University of North Texas Press, 2014.

Allen, Ruth A. *East Texas Lumber Workers: An Economic and Social Picture, 1870–1950.* Austin: University of Texas Press, 1961.

American Forestry Association. *The American Elm: Its Glorious Past, Its Present Dilemma, Its Hope for Protection.* Washington, DC: American Forestry Association, 1937.

American Lumberman. *American Lumbermen: The Personal History and Public and Business Achievements of One Hundred Eminent Lumbermen of the United States.* 3 vols. Chicago: American Lumberman, 1905–1906.

———. "Lone Star Pine." *American Lumberman,* September 26, 1908, pp. 67–151.

———. "Neches Valley Pine." *American Lumberman,* January 18, 1908, pp. 67–106.

———. "Opportunities of the Present in Making Plans for the Future." *American Lumberman,* January 18, 1908, p. 33.

———. "Southern Pine from Forest to Retailer." *American Lumberman,* April 16, 1904, pp. 35–42.

———. "A Successful Campaign of Conquest in Yellow Pine." *American Lumberman,* January 18, 1908, p. 34.

———. "Western Coal and Lumber Resources, as Exemplified by the Coal Mining and Lumber Manufacturing Departments of the Central Coal and Coke Company of Kansas City, Mo." *American Lumberman,* November 1, 1902.

Anderson, Edgar. "Basswood Bark and Its Use by the Indians." *Arnold Arboretum, Harvard University, Bulletin of Popular Information* 1, no. 7 (series 4, 1933): 33–37.

Anderson, M. K. and T. Oakes. *Plant Guide for Giant Cane Arundinaria gigantea.* USDA Natural Resources Conservation Service at Greensboro, NC, 2011. https://www.nrcs.usda.gov/Internet/FSE_DOCUMENTS/nrcs144p2_002413.pdf.

Armistead, Paul T. "Abandoned Short-Line Railroads of Texas, 1892–1956." Master's thesis, University of Texas, June 1957.

Arnn, John Wesley, III. *Land of the Tejas: Native American Identity and Interaction in Texas, A.D. 1300 to 1700.* Austin: University of Texas Press, 2012.

Arthur, Glenn Dora Fowler. *Annals of the Fowler Family.* Austin: Glenn Dora Fowler Arthur, 1901.

Austin, Stephen F. "Journal of Stephen F. Austin on His First Trip to Texas, 1821." *Quarterly of the Texas State Historical Association* 7, no. 4 (1904): 286–307.

Ayers, Edward L. *The Promise of the New South: Life after Reconstruction.* New York: Oxford University Press, 1992.

Bagur, Jacques D., ed. *Captain W. W. Withenbury's 1838–1842 Red River Reminiscences.* Denton: University of North Texas Press, 2014.

Barr, Juliana. "Geographies of Power: Mapping Indian Borders in the 'Borderlands' of the Early Southwest." *William and Mary Quarterly* 68, no. 1 (2011): 5–46.

Barr, Juliana, and Edward Countryman. *Contested Spaces of Early America.* Philadelphia: University of Pennsylvania Press, 2014.

Bartram, William. *Travels of William Bartram.* Edited by Mark Van Doren. New York: Dover Publications, 1955.

Baxter, David, and Laurence Parent. *Nature of the Forest: Temple-Inland's Timberlands in the Twenty-First Century.* Austin: Temple-Inland, 2002.

Bedichek, Roy. *Adventures with a Texas Naturalist.* Garden City: Doubleday & Company, 1947.

Bell, Kate Atkinson, ed. *Journey to Jubilee: Groveton, Texas, USA.* Groveton: Groveton Ex-Students Association, 1980.

Berry, Edward W. "Notes on the Geological History of the Walnuts and Hickories." *Plant World* 15, no. 10 (1912): 225–40.

Biesele, Megan. *The Cornbread Whistle: Oral History of a Texas Timber Company Town*. Diboll: Diboll Historical Society, 1986.

Billings, Ronald F. *A Century of Forestry, 1914–2014: Texas Forestry Association and Texas A&M Forest Service*. Virginia Beach: Donning Company, 2014.

Binkley, C. S. *The Rise and Fall of Timber Investment Management Organizations: Ownership Changes in US Forestlands*. Pinchot Distinguished Lecture, March 2, 2007, Pinchot Institute for Conservation. www.pinchot.org/files/Binkley .DistinguishedLecture.2007.pdf

Bishop, L. L. "Texas National Forests." *Texas Geographic Magazine* 1, no. 2 (1937): 1–15.

Blackburn, W. "Common Grazing in the Shortleaf Pine-Loblolly Pine-Hardwoods Portion of South Arkansas." *Journal of Farm Economics* 29, no. 2 (1947): 546–53.

Blanchard, Newton, ed. *Proceedings of a Governors Conference in the White House, Washington, D.C., May 13–15, 1908*. Washington: Government Printing Office, 1909.

Block, W. T. *East Texas Mill Towns & Ghost Towns*. 3 vols. Lufkin: Best of East Texas Publishing, 1994, 1995, 1997.

Bolton, Herbert E. *The Hasinais: Southern Caddoans as Seen by the Earliest Europeans*. Norman: University of Oklahoma Press, 2002.

———. "The Native Tribes about the East Texas Missions." *Quarterly of the Texas State Historical Association* 11, no. 4 (1908): 249–76.

———. "Spanish Activities on the Lower Trinity River, 1746–1771." *Southwestern Historical Quarterly* 16, no. 4 (1913): 339–77.

———, ed. *Spanish Exploration in the Southwest, 1542–1706*. New York: Charles Scribner's Sons, 1916.

Bonnell, George W. *Topographical Description of Texas, To Which Is Added an Account of the Indian Tribes*. Austin: Clark, Wing, and Brown, 1840.

Boon, Effie. "The History of Angelina County." Master's thesis, University of Texas, 1937.

Botkin, Daniel B. "The Depth of Walden Pond: Thoreau as a Guide to Solving Twenty-First Century Environmental Problems." *The Concord Saunterer, New Series* 9 (2001): 4–14.

Bowles, Flora G. *A History of Trinity County, Texas, from 1827 to 1928*. Groveton: Groveton Independent School District, 1928, 1966.

Bowman, Bob. *First of a Kind: The Building of the South's First Newsprint Mill*. Lufkin: Best of East Texas Publishers, 2001.

Boyd, Charles E. "Of Woods and Wildlife." *Texas Parks and Wildlife*, November 1967, pp. 6–9.

Boyd, William. *The Slain Wood: Papermaking and Its Environmental Consequences in the American South*. Baltimore: Johns Hopkins University Press, 2015.

Bradley, J. C., R. E. Will, J. F. Stewart, C. D. Nelson, and J. M. Gulding. "Post-Fire Resprouting of Shortleaf Pine Is Facilitated by a Morphological Trait but Fire Eliminates Shortleaf-Loblolly Pine Hybrid Seedlings." *Forest Ecology and Management* 379 (2016): 146–52.

Bragg, Don C. "Composition of a 1930's-Era Pine-Hardwood Stand in Arkansas." *Southeastern Naturalist* 3, no. 2 (2004): 327–44.

———. "Presettlement Features of the Ashley County, Arkansas Area." *American Midland Naturalist* 149, no. 1 (2003): 1–20.

———. "The Prominence of Pine in the Upper West Gulf Coastal Plain during Historical Times." In *Bulletin of the Museum of Life Sciences, Number 14, Freeman and Custis Red River Expedition of 1806: Two Hundred Years Later, A Symposium, June 14–17, 2006*, edited by Laurence M. Hardy, 29–54. Shreveport: Museum of Life Sciences, Louisiana State University in Shreveport, 2008.

———. "Reference Conditions for Old-Growth Pine Forests in the Upper West Gulf Coastal Plain." *Journal of the Torrey Botanical Society* 129, no. 4 (2002): 261–88.

———. "Structure and Dynamics of a Pine-Hardwood Old-Growth Remnant in Southern Arkansas." *Journal of the Torrey Botanical Society* 131, no. 4 (2004): 320–36.

Bragg, Louis H. "Morphogeography of Four Grass Taxa in North-Central and Eastern Texas." *Southwestern Naturalist* 9, no. 4 (1964): 219–31.

Brakie, Melinda. *American Beautyberry Plant Fact Sheet*. USDA Natural Resources Conservation Service at Nacogdoches, TX, 2010. https://www.nrcs.usda.gov/Internet /FSE_PLANTMATERIALS/publications /etpmcfs10015.pdf.

Braun, E. Lucy. *The Deciduous Forests of the Eastern United States*. Philadelphia: Blakiston Company, 1950.

Bray, William L. *Distribution and Adaptation of the Vegetation of Texas*. Bulletin of the University of Texas No. 82, Scientific Series 1, no. 10. Austin: University of Texas, 1906.

———. *Forest Resources of Texas*. US Department of Agriculture, Bureau of Forestry Bulletin No. 47. Washington: Government Printing Office, 1904.

Bridges, Katherine, and Winston DeVille. "Natchitoches and the Trail to the Rio Grande: Two Early Eighteenth-Century Accounts by the Sieur Derbanne." *Louisiana History* 8, no. 3 (1967): 239–59.

Briegleb, Philip A. *Forests of East Texas, 1953–1955*. Forest Survey Release 77. New Orleans: Southern Forest Experiment Station, Forest Service, US Department of Agriculture, June 1956.

Brosius, J. B. "Cut-Over Problems That Must Be Solved." *Cut-Over Lands*, October 1918.

Brown, David E., and Neil B. Carmony, eds. *Aldo Leopold's Wilderness: Selected Early Writings by the Author of A Sand County Almanac*. Harrisburg: Stackpole Books, 1990.

Brown, Nelson Courtlandt. *Logging—Principles and Practices in the United States and Canada*. New York: John Wiley & Sons, 1934.

———. *Timber Products and Industries*. New York: John Wiley & Sons, 1937.

Bryant, Ralph Clement. *Logging: The Principles and General Methods of Operation in the United States*. 1st ed. New York: John Wiley & Sons, 1914.

———. *Logging: The Principles and General Methods of Operation in the United States*. 2d ed. New York: John Wiley & Sons, 1923.

———. "The War and the Lumber Industry." *Journal of Forestry* 17, no. 2 (1919): 125–34.

Buckley, Eleanor Claire. "The Aguayo Expedition into Texas and Louisiana, 1719–1722." *Quarterly of the Texas State Historical Association* 15, no. 1 (1911): 1–65.

Buckley, S. B. "Pine Lands of South-Eastern Texas." In *The Texas Almanac for 1868*, 91–92. Galveston: W. Richardson and Company, 1868.

Bunkśe, Edmunds V. "Commoner Attitudes toward Landscape and Nature." *Annals of the Association of American Geographers* 68, no. 4 (1978): 551–66.

———. "Feeling Is Believing, or Landscape as a Way of Being in the World." *Geografiska Annaler. Series B, Human Geography* 89, no. 3 (2007): 219–31.

Burka, Paul. "The King of the Forest." *Texas Monthly* 10, no. 8 (1982): 114–23, 196–208, and 214.

Burns, Russell M. and Barbara H. Honkala. *Silvics of North America: Conifers*. Washington: U. S. Department of Agriculture, Forest Service, 1990.

———. *Silvics of North America: Hardwoods*. Washington: U. S. Department of Agriculture, Forest Service, 1990.

Buttrick, P. L. "Forest Growth on Abandoned Agriculture Land." *Scientific Monthly* 5, no. 1 (1917): 80–91.

Campbell, Randolph B. *An Empire for Slavery: The Peculiar Institution in Texas, 1821–1865*. Baton Rouge: Louisiana State University Press, 1989.

Campbell, R. S., and H. H. Biswell. "Cattle in the Pines." *American Forests* 50, no. 5 (1944): 238–39, 260–62, 264.

Campbell, Robert S. "Grazing in Southern Pine Forests." In *Special Problems in Southern Forest Management, Proceedings of the Sixth Annual Forestry Symposium, Baton Rouge, Louisiana*, 13–20. Baton Rouge: Louisiana State University School of Forestry, April 4–5, 1957.

Caplen, John A. "Camp Big Thicket: Life in the Piney Woods, in Eastern Texas, A Graphically Written and Interesting Letter." *Sunny South* 13, no. 625 (1887): 1.

Carlson, Paul H. *Texas Woollybacks: The Range Sheep and Goat Industry*. College Station: Texas A&M University Press, 1982.

Carter, Cecile Elkins. *Caddo Indians: Where We Came From*. Norman: University of Oklahoma Press, 1995.

Carter, Mason C., Robert C. Kellison, and R. Scott Wallinger. *Forestry in the U.S. South: A History*. Baton Rouge: Louisiana State University Press, 2015.

Carter, William T., and A. E. Kocher. "Soil Survey of Houston County, Texas, 1905." In *Field Operations of the Bureau of Soils, 1905 (Seventh Report)*, 537–65. Washington: US Department of Agriculture Bureau of Soils and Government Printing Office, 1907.

Cary, Austin. "Some Relations of Fire to Longleaf Pine." *Journal of Forestry* 30, no. 5 (1932): 594–601.

Catlin, George. *Letters and Notes on the Manners, Customs, and Condition of the North American Indians*. 2 vols. New York: Wiley and Putnam, 1841.

Céliz, Francisco. *Diary of the Alarcon Expedition into Texas, 1718–1719*. Edited by Fritz Leo Hoffman. Los Angeles: The Quivira Society, 1935.

Chambers, William T. "Divisions of the Pine Belt of East Texas." *Economic Geography* 6, no. 1 (1930): 94–103.

———. "Pine Woods Region of Southeastern Texas." *Economic Geography* 10, no. 3 (1934): 302–18.

Chapman, Brian R., and Eric G. Bolen. *The Natural History of Texas*. College Station: Texas A&M University Press, 2018.

Chapman, Herman H. "An Experiment in Logging Longleaf Pine." *Forest Quarterly* 7, no. 4 (1909): 385–95.

———. "Fire and Pines." *American Forests* 50 (February 1944): 62–64, 91–93.

———. "Forest Taxation." *Bulletin of the National Tax Association* 5, no. 4 (1920): 109–16.

———. "Is the Longleaf Type a Climax?" *Ecology* 13, no. 4 (1932): 328–34.

———. "Natural Areas." *Ecology* 28, no. 2 (1947): 193–94.

———. "The Place of Fire in the Ecology of Pines." *Bartonia* no. 26 (1952): 39–44.

———. "Public Ownership of Forest Land." *American Forests* (January 1932): 7–9.

———. "Some Further Relations of Fire to Longleaf Pine." *Journal of Forestry* 30, no. 5 (1932): 602–4.

Chapman, Herman H., and Ralph C. Bryant. *Prolonging the Cut of Southern Pine*. Yale University Forest School Bulletin 2. New Haven: Yale University Press, April 1913.

Chapman, Herman H., J. H. Foster, Philip W. Ayres, and Louis S. Murphy. "The Taxation of Forest Property." *Proceedings of the Annual Conference on Taxation under the Auspices of the National Tax Association* 14 (September 12–16, 1921): 36–58.

Christensen, Norman L. "Landscape History and Ecological Change." *Journal of Forest History* 33, no. 3 (1989): 116–25.

Clark, Thomas D. *The Greening of the South: The Recovery of Land and Forests*. Lexington: University Press of Kentucky, 1984.

Clurman, Richard M. *To the End of Time: The Seduction and Conquest of a Media Empire*. New York: Simon & Schuster, 1993.

Collier, G. Loyd. "The Evolving East Texas Woodland." PhD diss., University of Nebraska, Lincoln, Department of Geography, April 1964.

Cooper, Lewis B. *The Permanent School Fund of Texas*. Fort Worth: Texas State Teachers Association, 1934.

Cowdrey, Albert E. *This Land, This South: An Environmental History*. Rev. ed. Lexington: University Press of Kentucky, 1996.

Cox, Isaac Joslin, ed. *The Journeys of Rene Robert Cavelier, Sieur de La Salle*. 2 vols. New York: Allerton Book Company, 1922.

Cox, Mike. "Reviving the Ranch: History, Education, and Good Land Management Abound at the Leopold Award-Winning Temple Ranch." *Texas Parks & Wildlife*, November 2011, pp. 40–47.

Cox, Thomas R. *The Lumberman's Frontier: Three Centuries of Land Use, Society, and Change in America's Forests*. Corvallis: Oregon State University Press, 2010.

Cozine, James J., Jr. *Saving the Big Thicket: From Exploration to Preservation, 1685–2003*. Denton: University of North Texas Press, 2004.

Craig, Ronald. "The South's No-Man's Land." *American Forests* 41, no. 12 (1935): 684–85, 712.

Craig, Ronald B. "The Forest Tax Delinquency Problem in the South." *Southern Economic Journal* 6, no. 2 (1939): 145–64.

Cram, George Franklin. *Cram's Rail Road and Township Map of Texas*. New York: Cram Atlas Company, 1875.

Cravens, John N. *Between Two Rivers: A History of Wells, Texas*. Wichita Falls: Humphrey Printing Company, 1974.

———. *A History of Three Ghost Towns of East Texas near the Cherokee and Angelina County Line*. Abilene: Abilene Printing and Stationery Company, 1970.

Cronon, William. "Caretaking Tales." In *The Story Handbook: Language and Storytelling for Land Conservationists*, edited by Helen Whybrow, 87–93. San Francisco: The Trust for Public Land, 2002.

———. *Changes in the Land: Indians, Colonists, and the Ecology of New England*. 1983. New York: Hill and Wang, 2003.

———. "Modes of Prophecy and Production: Placing Nature in History." *Journal of American History* 76, no. 4 (1990): 1122–31.

———. *Nature's Metropolis: Chicago and the Great West*. New York: W. W. Norton and Company, 1991.

———. "A Place for Stories: Nature, History, and Narrative." *Journal of American History* 78, no. 4 (1992): 1347–76.

———, ed. *Uncommon Ground: Rethinking the Human Place in Nature.* New York: W. W. Norton & Company, 1995.

———. "The Uses of Environmental History." *Environmental History Review* 17, no. 3 (1993): 1–22.

Crook, Betty Ross, and Billie Dean Watson Brem. *Houston County, Texas, Newspaper Abstracts, 1890–1901, from the Crockett Courier.* 2 vols. Waco: Central Texas Genealogical Society, 2002, 2006.

Cruikshank, J. W., and I. F. Eldredge. *Forest Resources of Southeastern Texas, United States Department of Agriculture Miscellaneous Publication No. 326, February 1939.* Washington: Government Printing Office, 1939.

Dana, Samuel Trask, and Sally K. Fairfax. *Forest and Range Policy: Its Development in the United States.* 2d ed. New York: McGraw-Hill Book Company, 1980.

Davis, Richard C., ed. *Encyclopedia of American Forest and Conservation History.* 2 vols. New York: Macmillan Publishers, 1983.

Day, Gordon M. "The Indian as an Ecological Factor in the Northeastern Forest." *Ecology* 43, no. 2 (1953): 329–46.

Dean, Edna Mae. "Texas Rural Communities in Trinity County." In *A History of Trinity County, Texas, From 1827 to 1928,* edited by Flora G. Bowles, 126–28. Groveton: Groveton Independent School District, 1928, 1966.

De Cordova, Jacob. *Texas: Her Resources and Her Public Men.* Philadelphia: J. B. Lippincott & Company, 1858.

Defebaugh, James Elliott. *History of the Lumber Industry of America.* 2d ed. Chicago: American Lumberman, 1906.

Deffenbaugh, Daniel G. "The Ecological Indian Revisited." *Soundings: An Interdisciplinary Journal* 83, no. 2 (2000): 477–85.

Delanglez, Jean. *The Journal of Jean Cavelier: The Account of a Survivor of LaSalle's Texas Expedition, 1684–1688.* Chicago: Institute of Jesuit History, 1938.

Demmon, E. L. *East Texas Forests and the Future.* Occasional Paper No. 103, US Department of Agriculture, Forest Service. New Orleans: Southern Forest Experiment Station, 1943.

———. "The Piney Woods' Challenge to Research." *American Forests* 50 (May 1944): 234–36, 256, 258.

Diamond, Jared. *Guns, Germs, and Steel: The Fates of Human Societies.* New York: W. W. Norton & Company, 1999.

Diggs, George M., Jr., Barney L. Lipscomb, Monique D. Reed, and Robert J. O'Kennon. *Illustrated Flora of East Texas.* Fort Worth: Botanical Research Institute of Texas and Austin College, Center for Environmental Studies, 2006.

Dionne, J. C. "The Lumber History of Texas for 1909." *Bulletin of the Texas Department of Agriculture Year Book 1909* 13 (May-June 1910): 337–47.

Donovan, Richard. *Paddling the Wild Neches.* College Station: Texas A&M University Press, 2006.

Douay, Anastasius. "Narrative of La Salle's Attempt to Ascend the Mississippi in 1687." In *The Journeys of Rene Robert Cavelier Sieur de LaSalle,* vol. 1, edited by Isaac Joslin Cox, 222–47. New York: Allerton Book Company, 1922.

Doughty, Robin W. *At Home in Texas: Early Views of the Land.* College Station: Texas A&M University Press, 1987.

———. "Settlement and Environmental Change in Texas, 1820–1900." *Southwestern Historical Quarterly* 89, no. 4 (1986): 423–42.

———. *Wildlife and Man in Texas: Environmental Change and Conservation.* College Station: Texas A&M University Press, 1983.

Dugas, Vera Lea. "Texas Industry, 1860–1880." *Southwestern Historical Quarterly* 59, no. 2 (1955): 151–83.

Dumble, Edwin T. *The Geology of East Texas.* University of Texas Bulletin No. 1869, Bureau of Economic Geology and Technology, December 10, 1918.

Eakin, William L. "The Kingdom of the Tejas: The Hasinai Indians at the Crossroads of Change." PhD diss., University of Kansas, 1997.

Earley, Lawrence S. *Looking for Longleaf: The Fall and Rise of an American Forest.* Chapel Hill: University of North Carolina Press, 2004.

Easton, Hamilton Pratt. "The History of the Texas Lumbering Industry." PhD diss., University of Texas, 1947.

Emerson, F. V. "The Southern Long-Leaf Pine Belt." *Geographical Review* 7, no. 2 (1919): 81–90.

Emerson, Ralph Waldo. *Nature.* Boston: James Munroe and Company, 1836.

Espinosa, Isidro Felix De. "Ramon Expedition: Espinosa's Diary of 1716." *Preliminary Studies of the Texas Catholic Historical Society* 1, no. 4. Translated by Gabriel Tous. Texas Knights of Columbus Historical Commission, April 1930.

Evans, C. F. "Can the South Conquer the Fire Scourge?" *American Forests* 50 (May 1944): 227–29, 265, 267.

Ewers, John C., ed., and Patricia Reading Leclerq. *The Indians of Texas in 1830 by Jean Louis Berlandier.* Washington, DC: Smithsonian Institution Press, 1969.

Fehrenbach, T. R. *Lone Star: A History of Texas and the Texans.* New York: Tess Press, 2000.

Fernow, Bernard E. "Outlook of the Timber Supply in the United States." *Forest Quarterly of the New York State College of Forestry* 1, no. 2 (1903): 41–49.

———. "Timber as a Crop." *Proceedings of the American Forestry Association, Volume X,* 142–47. Washington: Government Printing Office, 1894.

Fickle, James E. *The New South and the "New Competition": Trade Association Development in the Southern Pine Industry.* Chicago: Forest History Society and University of Illinois Press, 1980.

———. "Reflections upon the Past and Present in Southern Forest History." *East Texas Historical Journal* 40, no. 2 (2002): 4–11.

Fiege, Mark. *The Republic of Nature: An Environmental History of the United States.* Seattle: University of Washington Press, 2012.

Finch, Bill. "The True Story of Kudzu, the Vine That Never Truly Ate the South." *Smithsonian Magazine,* September 2015.

Finney, John H. "Forest Resources and Conservation." *Annals of the American Academy of Political and Social Science, Vol. 35, No. 1, The New South* (1910): 67–76.

Flores, Dan. "An Argument for Bioregional History." *Environmental History Review* 18, no. 4 (1994): 1–18.

———, ed. *Southern Counterpart to Lewis & Clark: The Freeman & Custis Expedition of 1806.* Red River Books edition. Norman: University of Oklahoma Press, 2001.

Forbes, R. D. "The Passing of the Piney Woods." *American Forestry* 29, no. 351 (1923): 131–36, 185–86.

———. *Timber Growing and Logging and Turpentining Practices in the Southern Pine Region: Measures Necessary to Keep Forest Land Productive and to Produce Full Timber Crops.* Technical Bulletin No. 204, October 1930. Washington: United States Department of Agriculture, 1930.

Forrestal, Peter P., trans. "Peña's Diary of the Aguayo Expedition." *Preliminary Studies of the Texas Catholic Historical Society* 2, no. 7 (1935).

Foster, J. H., H. B. Krausz, and George W. Johnson. *Forest Resources of Eastern Texas.* Bulletin of the Agricultural and Mechanical College of Texas 3, no. 10, Forestry Bulletin no. 5 (3d series, 1917).

Foster, J. H., H. B. Krausz, and A. H. Leidigh. *A General Survey of Texas Woodlands, Including a Study of the Commercial Possibilities of Mesquite.* Bulletin of the Agricultural and Mechanical College of Texas 3, Forestry Bulletin no. 3 (3d series, 1917).

Foster, L. L., and Barbara J. Rozek. *Forgotten Texas Census: First Annual Report of the Agricultural Bureau of the Department of Agriculture, Insurance, Statistics, and History.* Austin: Texas State Historical Association, 2001.

Foster, William C. *Spanish Expeditions into Texas, 1689–1768.* Austin: University of Texas Press, 1995.

Foster, William C., Jack Jackson, and Ned F. Brierley. "The 1693 Expedition of Gregario de Salinas Varona to Sustain the Missionaries among the Tejas Indians." *Southwestern Historical Quarterly* 97, no. 2 (1993): 264–311.

Foster, William C., ed., and Johanna S. Warren, trans. *The LaSalle Expedition to Texas: The Journal of Henri Joutel, 1684–1687.* Austin: Texas State Historical Association, 1998.

Fox, Anne A., and I. Wayne Cox, with an appendix by Thomas R. Hester. *Archaeological and Historical Investigations at the Valenzuela Ranch, Dimmit County, Texas.* Archaeological Survey Report No. 126. San Antonio: Center for Archaeological Research, University of Texas at San Antonio, 1983.

Fritz, Edward C. *Clearcutting: A Crime against Nature.* Austin: Eakin Press, 1989.

Frost, Sherman L., and Paul F. Hursey. *Texas National Forest Study.* Longview: East Texas Chamber of Commerce, 1954.

Garren, Kenneth H. "Effects of Fire on Vegetation of the Southeastern United States." *Botanical Review* 9, no. 9 (1943): 617–54.

Gerland, Jonathan K. "A Brief Chronicle of Texas Southeastern Railroad of Diboll, Texas." *Pine Bough* 5, no. 2 (2000): 2–9.

———. "A Brief History of Temple Land Ownership and Management in East Texas, 1893–2007." *Pine Bough* 12, no. 1 (2007): 8–33.

———. "Judge a Historian for Boggy Slough." *Diboll Free Press*, March 28, 2002.

———. "Living in the Land of the Tejas: An East Texas Twenty-First Century Re-Discovery of the Beginnings of a Place Called Texas." *Pine Bough* 17 (2012): 2–11.

———. "A Logging Camp Vignette." *Pine Bough* 4, no. 1 (1999): 30–31.

———. "'The Lonesomest Place in the World': A Photographic History of the Rayville Ranch." *Pine Bough* 13, no. 1 (2008): 2–21.

———. "Sawdust City: Beaumont, Texas, On the Eve of the Petroleum Age." *Texas Gulf Historical & Biographical Record* 32 (November 1996): 20–47.

———. *Steam in the Pines: A History of the Texas State Railroad*. Nacogdoches: East Texas Historical Association, 2004.

Gilbert, L. D. "Grazing Cut-Over Lands." *Cut-Over Lands* 1, no. 8 (1918): 20.

Glitzenstein, Jeff S., Paul A. Harcombe, and Donna R. Streng. "Disturbance, Succession, and Maintenance of Species Diversity in an East Texas Forest." *Ecological Monographs* 56, no. 3 (1986): 243–58.

Goldsmith, Oliver. "The Deserted Village." In *English Romantic Poetry and Prose*, edited by Russell Noyes, 88–93. New York: Oxford University Press, 1956.

Gordon, Greg. *When Money Grew On Trees: A. B. Hammond and the Age of the Timber Baron*. Norman: University of Oklahoma Press, 2014.

Gow, James E. "An Ecological Study of the Sabine and Neches Valleys, Texas." In *Proceedings of the Iowa Academy of Sciences for 1904, Vol. 12*, 39–50. Des Moines: State of Iowa, 1905.

Graves, Henry S. "Private Forestry." *Journal of Forestry* 17, no. 2 (1919): 113–21.

Gray, Glenn A. *Gazetteer of Streams of Texas*. United States Geological Survey Water-Supply Paper 448. Washington: Government Printing Office, 1919.

Gray, Thomas. "Elegy Written in a Country Church-Yard." *In English Romantic Poetry and Prose,* edited by Russell Noyes, 47–49. New York: Oxford University Press, 1956.

Greeley, William B. "Piute Forestry or the Fallacy of Light Burning, From *The Timberman*, March 1920." *Forest History Today* (Spring 1999): 33–37.

Greeley, W. B. "Back to the Land." *Saturday Evening Post*, March 31, 1923, pp. 21, 58, 60, 62.

Grelen, Harold E. "Forest Grazing in the South." *Journal of Range Management* 31, no. 4 (1978): 244–50.

Grelen, Harold E., and Vinson L. Duvall. *Common Plants of Longleaf Pine-Bluestem Range*. US Forest Service Research Paper SO-23. Southern Forest Experiment Station, US Department of Agriculture, 1966.

Griffith, William Joyce. *The Hasinai Indians of East Texas as Seen by Europeans, 1687–1772*. Philological and Documentary Studies, vol. 2, no. 3. Middle American Research Institute. New Orleans: Tulane University, 1954.

Guldin, James M. "Ecology of Shortleaf Pine." In *Proceedings of Symposium on the Shortleaf Pine Ecosystem, Little Rock, Arkansas, March 31–April 2, 1986*, edited by Paul A. Murphy, 25–40. Monticello: Arkansas Cooperative Extension Service, 1986.

———. "Restoration and Management of Shortleaf Pine in Pure and Mixed Stands: Science, Empirical Observation, and the Wishful Application of Generalities." In *Shortleaf Pine Restoration and Ecology in the Ozarks: Proceedings of a Symposium, November 7–9, 2006*. Edited by John M. Kabrick, Daniel C. Dey, and David Gwaze, 47–58. Newton Square, PA: USDA Forest Service, 2007.

Guldin, James M., John Strom, Warren Montague, and Larry D. Hedrick. "Shortleaf Pine-Bluestem Habitat Restoration in the Interior Highlands: Implications for Stand Growth and Regeneration." In *Silviculture in Special Places: Proceedings of the 2003 National Silviculture Workshop*. Edited by Wayne D. Shepperd and Lane G. Eskew, 182–90. Fort Collins, CO: USDA Forest Service, 2004.

Gulf Coast Lumberman. "A Sturdy Tree Has Fallen: Death Takes T. L. L. Temple Sr. of Texarkana." *Gulf Coast Lumberman*, October 15, 1935, pp. 14–15.

Gunter, Pete A. Y. *The Big Thicket: An Ecological Re-evaluation*. Denton: University of North Texas Press, 1993.

Hackett, Charles W. "The Marquis of San Miguel de Aguayo and His Recovery of Texas from the

French, 1719–1723." *Southwestern Historical Quarterly* 49, no. 2 (1945): 193–214.

Hadley, Diana, Thomas H. Naylor, and Mardith K. Schuetz-Miller, comps. and eds. *The Presidio and Militia on the Northern Frontier of New Spain: A Documentary History, Volume Two, Part Two, The Central Corridor and the Texas Corridor, 1700–1765.* Tucson: University of Arizona Press, 1997.

Hahn, Steven. "Hunting, Fishing, and Foraging: Common Rights and Class Relations in the Postbellum South." *Radical History Review* 26 (1982): 37–64.

———. *The Roots of Southern Populism: Yeoman Farmers and the Transformation of the Georgia Upcountry, 1850–1890.* New York: Oxford University Press, 1983.

Hale, Leon. "A Sad Story in an Old Graveyard." *Houston Post*, June 24, 1977, p. 3E.

Halls, Lowell K. "Browse Use by Deer in an East Texas Forest." In *Proceedings of the Twentieth-Eighth Annual Conference, Southeastern Association of Game and Fish Commissioners*, 557–62. FAP W-91-R. Nacogdoches: Stephen F. Austin State University, 1975.

———. *Flowering and Fruiting of Southern Browse Species.* USDA Forest Service Research Paper SO-90. Southern Forest Experiment Station, 1973.

Haltom. R. W. *History and Description of Angelina County, Texas.* Lufkin: Lufkin Leader, 1888.

Haney, Lewis H., ed. *Studies in the Land Problem in Texas.* Bulletin of the University of Texas, July 1915, no. 39. Austin: University of Texas, 1915.

Harper, Roland M. "A Week in Eastern Texas." *Bulletin of the Torrey Botanical Club* 47, no. 7 (1920): 289–317.

Hatch, Stephan L., Kelly C. Umphries, and A. Jenet Ardoin. *Field Guide to Common Texas Grasses.* College Station: Texas A&M University Press, 2015.

Hatcher, Mattie Austin. "Descriptions of the Tejas or Asinai Indians, 1691–1722, in Four Parts." *Southwestern Historical Quarterly* 30, no. 3 (January 1927): 206–18; 30, no. 4 (April 1927): 283–304; 31, no. 1 (July 1927): 50–62; 31, no. 2 (October 1927): 150–80.

Hatcher, Mattie Austin, trans., and Paul J. Foik, ed. "The Expedition of Don Domingo Teran de Los Rios into Texas (1691–1692)." *Preliminary Studies of the Texas Catholic Historical Society* 2, no. 1 (1932).

Hayes, Robert M. "Squire Durham's 60-Mile Railroad Wins Him Acclaim of East Texans." *Dallas Morning News*, May 30, 1937.

Hearn, W. Edward, and James L. Burgess. "Soil Survey of the Nacogdoches Area, Texas, 1903." In *Field Operations of the Bureau of Soils, 1903 (Fifth Report)*, 487–99. Washington: US Department of Agriculture Bureau of Soils and Government Printing Office, 1904.

Hearn, W. Edward, and Party. "Soil Survey of the Lufkin Area, Texas, 1903." In *Field Operations of the Bureau of Soils, 1903 (Fifth Report)*, 501–10. Washington: US Department of Agriculture Bureau of Soils and Government Printing Office, 1904.

Hensley, Patricia, Joseph Hensley, and the Trinity County Book Committee. *Trinity County Beginnings.* Dallas: Curtis Media Corporation, 1987.

Heyward, Frank. "The Relation of Fire to Stand Composition of Longleaf Pine Forests." *Ecology* 20, no. 2 (1939): 287–304.

Hickerson, Daniel A. "Historical Processes, Epidemic Disease, and the Formation of the Hasinai Confederacy." *Ethnohistory* 44, no. 1 (1997): 31–52.

Hickman, Nollie. *Mississippi Harvest: Lumbering in the Longleaf Pine Belt, 1840–1915.* Oxford: University of Mississippi Press, 1962.

Higgins, Richard. *Thoreau and the Language of Trees.* Oakland: University of California Press, 2017.

Hitchcock, A. S. *Manual of the Grasses of the United States.* United States Department of Agriculture Misc. Publication No. 200. Washington: Government Printing Office, 1935.

Hogan, George H. *Some Especially Valuable Grasses in Texas.* Texas Department of Agriculture Bulletin No. 20 (July-August 1911). Austin: Austin Printing Company, 1911.

Holley, Mary Austin. *Texas.* Lexington: J. Clarke & Company, 1836.

Houston County Historical Commission. *History of Houston County, 1687–1979.* Tulsa: Heritage Publishing Company, 1979.

Howard, William B., and J. M. K., Jr. "News and Notices: Bureau Work in Texas." *Forest Quarterly of the New York State College of Forestry* 1, no. 3 (1903): 113–15.

Hudson, Charles. *Knights of Spain, Warriors of the Sun: Hernando de Soto and the South's Ancient Chiefdoms*. Athens: University of Georgia Press, 1997.

Hunter, R. T., trans. "The Interrogation of the Talon Brothers, 1698: Expedition to the Mississippi River by Way of the Gulf of Mexico." *Iowa Review* 15, no. 2 (1985): 99–139.

Hyde, Samuel C., Jr. "Backcountry Justice in the Piney-Woods South." In *Plain Folk of the South Revisited*, edited by Samuel C. Hyde Jr., 228–49. Baton Rouge: Louisiana State University Press, 1997.

Isern, Thomas D., and Raymond Wilson, "Lone Star: The Thompson Timber Interests of Texas." *Red River Valley Historical Review* 6, no. 4 (1981).

Jackson, Jack. *Indian Agent: Peter Ellis Bean in Mexican Texas*. College Station: Texas A&M University Press, 2005.

———. *Los Mesteños: Spanish Ranching in Texas, 1721–1821*. College Station: Texas A&M University Press, 1986.

———. *Shooting the Sun: Cartographic Results of Military Activities in Texas, 1689–1829*. 2 vols. Lubbock: Book Club of Texas, 1999.

Jackson, Jack, and John Wheat. *Almonte's Texas: Juan N. Almonte's 1834 Inspection, Secret Report and Role in the 1836 Campaign*. Austin: Texas State Historical Association, 2003.

———. *Texas by Teran: The Diary Kept by General Manuel de Mier y Teran on His 1828 Inspection of Texas*. Austin: University of Texas Press, 2000.

Jackson, Jack, ed., and William C. Foster. *Imaginary Kingdom: Texas as Seen by the Rivera and Rubi Military Expeditions, 1727 and 1767*. Austin: Texas State Historical Association, 1995.

Jackson, John Brickerhoff. *A Sense of Place, a Sense of Time*. New Haven: Yale University Press, 1994.

Jacoby, Karl. *Crimes against Nature: Squatters, Poachers, Thieves, and the Hidden History of American Civilization*. Berkeley: University of California Press, 2001.

Jelks, Edward B. "The Archaeology of Sam Rayburn Reservoir." *CRHR Research Reports: Vol. 3, Article 1*. Nacogdoches: Center for Regional Heritage Research, 2017.

Jennings, Nancy Moores Watts. *Texarkana Pioneer Family Histories*. Texarkana: Texarkana Pioneer Association, 1961.

John, Elizabeth A. H. *Storms Brewed in Other Men's Worlds: The Confrontations of Indians, Spanish, and French in the Southwest, 1540–1795*. Lincoln: University of Nebraska Press, 1975.

Johnson, Melvin C., and Jonathan K. Gerland. "Tapping Green Gold: The Steam Rail and Logging Tram Roads of East Texas." *Environmental History* 1, no. 4 (1996): 46–65.

Johnson, R. L., and R. M. Krinard. *Hardwood Regeneration after Seed Tree Cutting*. US Department of Agriculture Forest Service Research Paper SO-123. New Orleans: Southern Forest Experiment Station, 1976.

Jordan, Terry G. "The Origin of Anglo-American Cattle Ranching in Texas: A Documentation of Diffusion from the Lower South." *Economic Geography* 45, no. 1 (1969): 63–87.

———. "Pioneer Evaluation of Vegetation in Frontier Texas." *Southwestern Historical Quarterly* 76, no. 3 (1973): 233–54.

———. *Texas Log Buildings: A Folk Architecture*. Austin: University of Texas Press, 1978.

———. *Trails to Texas: Southern Roots of Western Cattle Ranching*. Lincoln: University of Nebraska Press, 1981.

Jordan, Terry G., John L. Bean Jr., and William M. Holmes. *Texas: A Geography*. Boulder: Westview Press, 1984.

Jurney, David, Rob Evans, John Ippolito, Velicia Bergstrom. "The Role of Wildland Fire in Southeastern North America." In *Fire in Temperate, Boreal, and Montane Ecosystems: An International Symposium*, 95–116. Proceedings from the Tall Timbers Fire Ecology Conference, 22. Tallahassee: Tall Timbers Research Station and Land Conservancy, 2004.

Jurney, David H., John Ippolito, and Velicia Bergstrom. "The Frequency of Fire in East Texas Forests." *Journal of Northeast Texas Archaeology* 13 (2000): 40–49.

Kehr, Kurt. "Walden Three: Ecological Changes in the Landscape of Henry David Thoreau." *Journal of Forest History* 27, no. 1 (1983): 28–33.

Keith, Eric. *Plant Community and Fuel Model Assessment for Temple Boggy Slough, Trinity County, Texas*. Huntsville: Raven Environmental Services, 2015.

———. *Plant Community and Fuel Model Assessment for T. L. L. Temple Foundation's Boggy Slough in Houston and Trinity Counties, Texas*. Huntsville: Raven Environmental Services, 2015.

Keller, John Esten. "The Subsistence Paleoecology of the Middle Neches Region of Eastern Texas." PhD diss., University of Texas, Austin, 1974.

Kellogg, R. S. *The Timber Supply of the United States*. US Department of Agriculture, Forest Service Circular 166. Washington: Government Printing Office, 1909.

Kerr, Homer L. "Migration into Texas, 1860–1880." *Southwestern Historical Quarterly* 70, no. 2 (1966): 184–216.

Kimball, J. P., trans. *Laws and Decrees of the State of Coahuila and Texas, in Spanish and English*. Houston: Telegraph Power Press, 1839.

King, J. Crawford, Jr. "The Closing of the Southern Range: An Exploratory Study." *Journal of Southern History* 48, no. 1 (1982): 53–70.

Kircher, Joseph C. "Uncle Sam in the Piney Woods: What He Is Doing and How He Views Southern Forest Possibilities." *American Forests* 50 (May 1944): 217–19, 254–55.

Kittredge, Joseph. *Forest Influences*. New York: McGraw-Hill, 1948.

Koch, Michael. *The Shay Locomotive: Titan of the Timber*. Denver: World Press, 1971.

Korstain, Clarence F. "Grazing Practice on the National Forests and Its Effect on Natural Conditions." *Scientific Monthly* 13, no. 3 (1921): 275–81.

Krech, Shepard III. "Reflections on Conservation, Sustainability, and Environmentalism in Indigenous North America." *American Anthropologist* 107, no. 1 (2005): 78–86.

Kroll, James C. "'The Ghost' of Boggy Slough." *North American Whitetail* (November 1988): 44.

———. "The Saga of Boggy Slough's Monster Buck." *Texas Sportsman* (August 1988): 34–39.

Kroll, James C., William D. Goodrum, and Pamela J. Behrman. "Implications to White-Tailed Deer Management on Wilderness Areas." In *Wilderness Natural Areas in the Eastern United States: A Management Challenge*, edited by David L. Kulhavy and Richard N. Conner, 294–303. Nacogdoches: Center for Applied Studies, Stephen F. Austin State University, 1986.

Kurth, Ernest. "Pine Growers." *American Forests* 50 (May 1944): 224.

Kush, John S., Ralph S. Meldahl, Charles K. McMahon, and William D. Boyer. "Longleaf Pine: A Sustainable Approach for Increasing Terrestrial Carbon in the Southern United States." *Environmental Management* 33, supplement 1 (December 2004): S139–S147.

Lack, Paul D. "The Cordova Revolt." In *Tejano Journey, 1770–1850*, edited by Gerald E. Poyo, 89–109. Austin: University of Texas Press, 1996.

Langdon, O. Gordon, Miriam A. Bomhard, and John T. Cassady. *Field Book of Forage Plants on Longleaf Pine-Bluestem Ranges*. Forest Service, USDA, Occasional Paper 127. New Orleans: Southern Forest Experiment Station, 1952.

Lathrop, Barnes F. "Migration into East Texas, 1835–1860, in Three Parts." *Southwestern Historical Quarterly* 52, no. 1 (July 1948): 1–31; 52, no. 2 (October 1948): 184–208; 52, no. 3 (January 1949): 325–48.

La Vere, David. *Caddo Chiefdoms: Caddo Economics and Politics, 700–1835*. Lincoln: University of Nebraska Press, 1998.

Lay, Daniel W. "Bottomland Hardwoods in East Texas: An Historical Overview." In *Bottomland Hardwoods in Texas: Proceedings of an Interagency Workshop on Status and Ecology, May 6–7, 1986, Nacogdoches, Texas*. Austin: Texas Parks and Wildlife, 1987.

———. "Browse Quality and the Effects of Prescribed Burning in Southern Pine Forests." *Journal of Forestry* 55, no. 5 (1967): 342–47.

———. "Deer Range Appraisal in East Texas." *Journal of Wildlife Management* 31, no. 3 (1967): 426–32.

———. "Effects of Prescribed Burning on Forage and Mast Production in Southern Pine Forests." *Journal of Forestry* 54, no. 9 (1956): 582–84.

———. "Fruit Utilization by Deer in Southern Forests." *Journal of Wildlife Management* 29, no. 2 (1965): 370–75.

———. "How Valuable Are Woodland Clearings to Birdlife?" *Wilson Bulletin* 50, no. 4 (1938): 254–56.

———. "More Deer in East Texas." *Texas Game and Fish* 22, no. 13 (1954): 8, 26.

———. "Outdoors in East Texas Then and Now." *East Texas Historical Journal* 40, no. 2 (2002): 53–62.

———. "Recovery of a Southern Forest from Excessive Utilization: An Example of Good Deer Management." *The White-Tailed Deer: Its Problems and Potentials. Proceedings of the Wildlife Conference, June 29–30, 1966*, 73–95. College Station: Texas A&M University Press, 1966.

Lay, Daniel W., and Dennis N. Russell. "Notes on the Red-Cockaded Woodpecker in Texas." *The Auk* 87, no. 4 (1970): 781–86.

Leithead, Horace L., Lewis L. Yartlett, and Thomas N. Shiflet. *100 Native Forage Grasses in 11 Southern States.* Agriculture Handbook No. 389. Washington, DC: Soil Conservation Service, US Department of Agriculture, 1971.

Leopold, Aldo. "A Biotic View of Land." *Journal of Forestry* 37, no. 9 (1939): 727–30.

———. "The Conservation Ethic." *Journal of Forestry* 31, no. 6 (1933): 634–43.

———. *Game Management.* 1933. Reprint. Madison: University of Wisconsin Press, 1986.

———. "Grass, Brush, Timber, and Fire in Southern Arizona." *Journal of Forestry* 22, no. 6 (1924): 1–10.

———. "The National Forests: The Last Free Hunting Grounds of the Nation." *Journal of Forestry* 17, no. 2 (1919): 150–53.

———. "Piute Forestry vs. Forest Fire Prevention." *Southwestern Magazine* 2, no. 3 (1920): 12–13.

———. *A Sand County Almanac and Sketches Here and There.* London: Oxford University Press, 1949.

———. "A Survey of Over-Populated Deer Ranges in the United States." *Journal of Wildlife Management* 11, no. 2 (1947): 162–77.

———. "The Wilderness and Its Place in Forest Recreational Policy." *Journal of Forestry* 19 no. 7 (1921): 718–21.

———. "Wild Followers of the Forest: The Effect of Forest Fires on Game and Fish, the Relation of Forests to Game Conservation." *American Forestry* 29, no. 357 (1923): 515–19, 568.

———. "Wildlife in American Culture." *Journal of Wildlife Management* 7, no. 1 (1943): 1–6.

Lincecum, Gideon, A. L. Bradford, and T. N. Campbell. "Journal of Lincecum's Travels in Texas, 1835." *Southwestern Historical Quarterly* 53, no. 2 (1949): 180–201.

Ludwig, Wayne. *The Old Chisholm Trail: From Cow Path to Tourist Stop.* College Station: Texas A&M University Press, 2018.

Lufkin Genealogical and Historical Society. *The History of Angelina County, Texas, 1846–1991.* Dallas: Curtis Media Company, 1992.

MacRoberts, Barbara R., and Michael H. MacRoberts. "Floristics of Upland Shortleaf Pine/Oak-Hickory Forest in Northwestern Louisiana." *Journal of the Botanical Research Institute of Texas* 3, no. 1 (2009): 367–74.

———. "Plant Ecology and Phytogeography of the West Gulf Coastal Plain: An Overview." In *Bulletin of the Museum of Life Sciences, Number 14, Freeman and Custis Red River Expedition of 1806: Two Hundred Years Later, A Symposium, June 14–17, 2006,* edited by Laurence M. Hardy, 7–28. Shreveport: Museum of Life Sciences, Louisiana State University in Shreveport, 2008.

Mann, Charles C. *1491: New Revelations of the Americas before Columbus.* New York: Vintage Books, 2011.

Manzanet, Don Damian, and Lilia M. Casis, trans. "Carta de Don Damian Manzanet á Don Carlos Sobre el Descubrimiento de la Bahía del Espíruto / Letter of Don Damian Manzanet to Don Carlos de Siguenza Relative to the Discovery of the Bay of Espiritu Santo." *Quarterly of the Texas State Historical Association* 2, no. 4 (1899): 253–312.

Marsh, George P. *Man and Nature, or Physical Geography as Modified by Human Action.* New York: Charles Scribner, 1864.

Marx, Leo. *The Machine in the Garden: Technology and the Pastoral Ideal in America.* 1964. New York: Oxford University Press, 2000.

Mathews, Archie Birdsong. "The Economic Development of Angelina County." Master's thesis, University of Texas, Austin, 1952.

Maxwell, Hu. "The Use and Abuse of Forests by the Virginia Indians." *William and Mary Quarterly* 19, no. 2 (1910): 73–103.

Maxwell, Robert S. "The Impact of Forestry on the Gulf South." *Forest History Newsletter* 17, no. 1 (1973): 30–35.

———. "Lumbermen of the East Texas Frontier." *Forest History Newsletter* 9, no. 1 (1965): 12–16.

———. "One Man's Legacy: W. Goodrich Jones and Texas Conservation." *Southwestern Historical Quarterly* 77, no. 3 (1974): 355–80.

———. *Whistle in the Piney Woods: Paul Bremond and the Houston, East and West Texas Railway.* Houston: Texas Gulf Coast Historical Association, 1963.

Maxwell, Robert S., and Robert D. Baker. *Sawdust Empire: The Texas Lumber Industry, 1830–1940.* College Station: Texas A&M University Press, 1983.

Maxwell, Robert S., and James W. Martin. *A Short History of Forest Conservation in Texas, 1880–1940.* School of Forestry Bulletin 20, Stephen F. Austin State University, 1970.

Maynard, W. Barksdale. *Walden Pond: A History.* New York: Oxford University Press, 2004.

McClintock, William A. "Journal of a Trip through Texas and Northern Mexico in 1846–1847: I." *Southwestern Historical Quarterly* 34, no. 1 (1930): 20–37.

McCluggage, Robert W. "The Pioneer Squatter." *Illinois Historical Journal* 82, no. 1 (1989): 47–54.

McDaniel, Robert Cecil. *Sabine County, Texas: The First One Hundred and Fifty Years.* Waco: Texian Press, 1990.

McDanield, H. F., and N. A. Taylor. *The Coming Empire, Or Two Thousand Miles in Texas on Horseback.* New York: A. S. Barnes & Company, 1877.

McDermid, Robert W., ed. *The Upland Hardwood Problem in Southern Woodlands: Technical Papers Presented at the Second Annual Symposium, School of Forestry, Louisiana State University.* Baton Rouge: Louisiana State University, April 14–15, 1953.

McDonald, Archie P., with James E. Fickle, R. Scott Beasley, R. Montague Whiting Jr., Kent T. Adair, Robert D. Baker, Billy J. Earley, et al. *Arthur Temple College of Forestry: The Story of Forestry at SFA.* Nacogdoches: Stephen F. Austin State University, 2004.

McDonald, Forrest, and Grady McWhiney. "The Antebellum Southern Herdsman: A Reinterpretation." *Journal of Southern History* 41, no. 2 (1975): 147–66.

McFarlane, Wallace Scott. "Oil on the Farm: The East Texas Oil Boom and the Origins of an Energy Economy." *Journal of Southern History* 83, no. 4 (2017): 853–88.

McKitrick, Reuben. *The Public Land System of Texas, 1823–1910.* Bulletin of the University of Wisconsin, No. 905. Economics and Political Science Series 9, no. 1. Madison: University of Wisconsin, 1918.

McMahan, Craig A., and Roy G. Frye, eds. *Bottomland Hardwoods in Texas: Proceedings of an Interagency Workshop on Status and Ecology, May 6–7, 1986, Nacogdoches, Texas.* PWD-RP-7100-133-3/87. Austin: Texas Parks and Wildlife Department, Wildlife Division, 1987.

McWhiney, Grady. *Cracker Culture: Celtic Ways in the Old South.* Tuscaloosa: University of Alabama Press, 1988.

Meine, Curt, ed. *Aldo Leopold: A Sand County Almanac & Other Writings on Ecology and Conservation.* New York: Library of America, 2013.

Meinig, D. W. "The Beholding Eye: Ten Versions of the Same Thing." *Landscape Architecture Magazine* 66, no. 1 (1976): 47–54.

Miller, James H. *Nonnative Invasive Plants of Southern Forests: A Field Guide for Identification and Control.* Rev. ed. General Technical Report SRS-62. Ashville: US Department of Agriculture, Forest Service, Southern Forest Research Station, 2003.

Mims, Tilda. "Evan Frank Allison: Pioneer in Conservation, 1865–1937." *Alabama's Treasured Forests* (Summer 2003): 28–30.

Mitchell, Margaret. *Gone with the Wind.* New York: Macmillan, 1936.

Modern Silage Methods: Feeders' and Dairymens' Guide, 8th ed. Salem, OH: Silver Manufacturing Company, 1911.

Mohr, Charles. "The Interest of the Individual in Forestry in View of the Present Condition of the Lumber Interest." In *Proceedings of the American Forestry Congress at Its Meeting Held in Atlanta, Georgia, December 1888,* pp. 36–38. Washington, D.C.: Gibson Bros., 1889.

———. *The Timber Pines of the Southern United States.* USDA, Forestry Division, Bulletin No. 13. Washington: Government Printing Office, 1897.

Moore, A. G. T. "Cut-Over Pine Land Plans." *Cut-Over Lands* 1, no. 3 (1918): 21.

Moore, Dwight M. "Grassy Lake: A Biologist's Paradise." *Journal of the Arkansas Academy of Sciences* 3, article 14 (1950): 41–43.

Munns, Edward N. "Women in Southern Lumbering Operations." *Journal of Forestry* 17, no. 2 (1919): 144–49.

Murphy, Louis S. "Forest Taxation Experiences of the States and Conclusions Based on Them." *Journal of Forestry* 22, no. 5 (1924): 453–63.

Nance, Joseph Milton. *After San Jacinto: The Texas-Mexican Frontier, 1836–1841.* Austin: University of Texas Press, 1963.

Nash, Roderick Frazier. *Wilderness and the American Mind.* 5th ed. New Haven: Yale University Press, 2014.

Neal, Jim, and Jeff Haskins. "Bottomland Hardwoods: Ecology, Management, and Preservation." In *Wilderness Natural Areas in the Eastern United States: A Management Challenge*, edited by David L. Kulhavy and Richard N. Conner, 311–22. Nacogdoches: Center for Applied Studies, Stephen F. Austin State University, 1986.

Newcomb, W. W., Jr. *The Indians of Texas: From Prehistoric to Modern Times*. Austin: University of Texas Press, 1961.

Newell, H. Perry, and Alex D. Krieger. *The George C. Davis Site, Cherokee County, Texas*. Memoirs of the Society for American Archaeology, Number 5. Published Jointly by the Society for American Archaeology and the University of Texas, 1949.

Newkumet, Vynola Beaver, and Howard L. Meredith. *Hasinai: A Traditional History of the Caddo Confederacy*. College Station: Texas A&M University Press, 2009.

Norris, Lola Orellano, ed. and trans. *General Alonso de Leon's Expeditions into Texas, 1686–1690*. College Station: Texas A&M University Press, 2017.

Nowacki, Gregory J., and Marc D. Abrams. "The Demise of Fire and 'Mesophication' of Forests in the Eastern United States." *BioScience* 58, no. 2 (2008): 123–38.

Odom, Harrell. *Cecil Creek Echoes: Memos from a Schoolteacher's Notebook*. New York: Vantage Press, 1991.

———. *Over on Cochino*. Waco: Texian Press, 1980.

Odum, Eugene P. *Ecology: A Bridge between Science and Society*. Sunderland, MA: Sinauer Associates, 1997.

Olmsted, Frederick Law. *A Journey through Texas; Or, A Saddle-Trip on the Southwestern Frontier*. New York: Dix, Edwards & Co., 1857.

Otto, John Solomon. "The Migration of the Southern Plain Folk: An Interdisciplinary Synthesis." *Journal of Southern History* 51, no. 2 (1985): 183–200.

Ousley, Clarence. *Grasses for Pasture and Hay in Texas*. Bulletin of the Agricultural and Mechanical College of Texas, B-32. College Station: Extension Service, November 1916.

Owen, C. O. and Company. *Portrait and Biographical Record of Guernsey County, Ohio, Containing Biographical Sketches of Prominent and Representative Citizens of the County*. Chicago: C. O. Owen & Co., 1895.

Owsley, Frank L. *Plain Folk of the Old South*. Baton Rouge: Louisiana State University Press, 1949.

Page, Frederic Benjamin. *Prairiedom: Rambles and Scrambles in Texas or New Estremadura*. 2d ed. New York: Paine & Burgess, 1846.

Paine, Albert Bigelow. *Captain Bill McDonald, Texas Ranger: A Story of Frontier Reform*. New York: J. J. Little & Ives Co., 1909.

Parker, A. A. *A Trip to the West and Texas*. 2d ed. Concord, NH: William White, 1836.

Patterson, William A. "The Paleoecology of Fire and Oaks in Eastern Forests." In *Fire in Eastern Oak Forests: Delivering Science to Land Managers*, edited by Matthew B. Dickinson, 2–19. Proceedings of a Conference, November 15–17, 2005, Ohio State University. USDA Forest Service, Northern Research Station General Technical Report NRS-P-1.

Pearce, J. E. "The Archaeology of East Texas." *American Anthropologist* 34, no. 4 (1932): 670–87.

———. "Indian Mounds and Other Relics of Indian Life in Texas." *American Anthropologist* 21, no. 3 (1919): 223–34.

Peattie, Donald Culross. *A Natural History of Trees of Eastern and Central North America*. 2d ed. New York: Bonanza Books, 1966.

Peña, Juan Antonio de La, and Peter P. Forrestal, trans. "Peña's Diary of the Aguayo Expedition." *Preliminary Studies of the Texas Catholic Historical Society* 2, no. 7 (1935).

Perttula, Timothy K. *Caddo Landscapes in the East Texas Forests*. Havertown, PA: Oxbow Books: 2017.

———. "41AG22: An Historic Caddo Allen Phase Caddo Site in the Neches River Basin, Angelina County, Texas." *TARL Newsletter* (March 2018).

———. "How Texas Historians Write about the Pre-A.D. 1685 Caddo Peoples of Texas." *Southwestern Historical Quarterly* 115, no. 4 (2012): 364–76.

Post, Richard H. *Notes on Quogue, 1659–1959*. Quogue: Quogue Tercentenary Committee, 1959.

Power, Ronald Allen. "Protecting Texas Forests: The Texas Forestry Association, 1914–1997." Master's thesis, Texas Tech University, 1998.

Pyne, Stephen J. *Fire in America: A Cultural History of Wildland and Rural Fire*. Princeton: Princeton University Press, 1982.

———. "No Fuel Like an Old Fuel." *Fire Management Today* 60, no. 4 (2000): 4–5.

Quogue Historical Society. *Quogue, 1659–1984, The 325th Anniversary of the Purchase of Its Lands from the Shinnecock Indians: A Mini History*. Quogue: Quogue Historical Society, 1984.

Raines, C. W. *Year Book for Texas, 1901*. 2 vols. Austin: Gammel Book Company, 1902.

Ramón, Domingo. "The Domingo Ramon Diary of the 1716 Expedition into the Province of the Tejas Indians: An Annotated Translation." Edited by Debbie S. Cunningham. *Southwestern Historical Quarterly* 110, no. 1 (2006): 39–67.

Rankin, Melinda. *Texas in 1850*. Boston: Damrell & Moore, 1852.

"Rattlesnake and Its Congeners." *Harper's New Monthly Magazine* 10, no. 58 (1855): 470–83.

Reck, Franklin, and Joseph Shirley Daniel. "Woodsman—Kill This Tree!" *Ford Truck Times*, March-April 1949, pp. 14–17.

Reed, S. G. *A History of Texas Railroads and of Transportation Conditions under Spain and Mexico and the Republic and the State*. Houston: St. Clair Publishing Co., 1941.

Reid, Vincent H., and Phil D. Goodrum. "Factors Influencing the Yield and Wildlife Use of Acorns." In *Special Problems in Southern Forest Management, Proceedings of the Sixth Annual Forestry Symposium, Baton Rouge, Louisiana*, edited by William C. Hopkins, 46–79. Baton Rouge: Louisiana State University School of Forestry, April 4–5, 1957.

Rhinehart, Marilyn D. "Forestry and Politics in Texas, 1915–1921." *East Texas Historical Journal* 20, no. 2 (1982): 6–17.

Rideout, Sandra, and Brian P. Oswald. "Effects of Prescribed Burning on Vegetation and Fuel Loading in Three East Texas State Parks." *Texas Journal of Science* 54, no. 3 (2002): 211–26.

Rienstra, Ellen Walker, and Jo Ann Stiles. *The Long Shadow: The Lutcher-Stark Lumber Dynasty*. Austin: University of Texas Press, 2016.

Roberts, O. M. *A Description of Texas, Its Advantages and Resources, with Some Account of Their Development, Past, Present, and Future*. St. Louis: Gilbert Book Company, 1881.

Row, J. M. and W. A. Geyer. *Plant Fact Sheet for Chickasaw plum (Prunus angustifolia)*. USDA Natural Resources Conservation Service at Manhattan, KS, 2010. https://www.nrcs.usda.gov/Internet /FSE_PLANTMATERIALS/publications /kspmcfs10101.pdf.

Runte, Alfred. *Allies of the Earth: Railroads and the Soul of Preservation*. Kirksville: Truman State University Press, 2006.

Russell, Edmund, James Allison, Thomas Finger, John K. Brown, Brian Balogh, and W. Branard Carson. "The Nature of Power: Synthesizing the History of Technology and Environmental History." *Technology and Culture* 52, no. 2 (2011): 246–59.

Russell, Emily W. B. "Fires in the Forests of the Northeastern United States." *Ecology* 64, no. 1 (1983): 78–88.

Rutkow, Eric. *American Canopy: Trees, Forests, and the Making of a Nation*. New York: Scribner, 2012.

Sain, Melody P. "Distinguishing the Neches River Rose Mallow, *Hibiscus dasycalyx*, from Its Congeners Using DNA Sequence Data and Niche Modeling Methods." PhD diss., University of Texas at Tyler, 2015.

Sánchez, José María, and Carlos E. Castaneda. "A Trip to Texas in 1828." *Southwestern Historical Quarterly* 29, no. 4 (1926): 249–88.

Santos, Richard G. *Aguayo Expedition into Texas, 1721: An Annotated Translation of the Five Versions of the Diary Kept by Juan Antonio de La Peña*. Austin: Jenkins Publishing Company, 1981.

Sargent, Charles S. "The American Elm." *Garden and Forest*, June 11, 1890, pp. 281–82.

Sargent, Charles S. *Report on the Forests of North America (Exclusive of Mexico), Tenth Census of the United States, Vol. 9, Forests*. Washington: Government Printing Office, 1884.

Sawyer, R. K. *A Hundred Years of Texas Waterfowl Hunting: The Decoys, Guides, Clubs, and Places, 1870s to 1970s*. College Station: Texas A&M University Press, 2012.

Schafale, Michael P., and P. A. Harcombe. "Presettlement Vegetation of Hardin County, Texas." *American Midland Naturalist* 109, no. 2 (1983): 355–66.

Schama, Simon. *Landscape and Memory*. New York: Alfred A. Knopf, 1996.

Schivelbusch, Wolfgang. *The Railway Journey: The Industrialization of Time and Space in the 19th Century*. Berkeley: University of California Press, 1986.

Schmidly, David J. *Texas Natural History: A Century of Change*. Lubbock: Texas Tech University Press, 2002.

Schimdt, Walter G. *An Encyclopedia of Texas Post Offices: Texas Post Offices under Five Flags*. Chicago: Collectors' Club of Chicago, 1993.

Schultz, Robert. *Loblolly Pine: The Ecology and Culture of Loblolly Pine*. Agricultural Handbook 713. New Orleans: Southern Forest Experiment Station, US Department of Agriculture, 1997.

Shackford, Martha Hale. "A Definition of the Pastoral Idyll." *PMLA* 19, no. 4 (1904): 583–92.

Silker, T. H. *Forest Grazing in the Pine-Hardwood and Bottomland Hardwood Types of Southeast Texas*. Texas Forest Service Bulletin No. 47. College Station: Texas A&M College, July 1955.

———. "Prescribed Burning for Control of Understory Hardwoods Invading Southern Pine Stands." *The Upland Hardwood Problem in Southern Woodlands: Technical Papers Presented at the Second Annual Symposium, School of Forestry, Louisiana State University*. Baton Rouge: Louisiana State University Press, 1953.

Simonds, Frederic William. *The Geography of Texas, Physical and Political*. New York: Ginn & Company, 1905.

Sitton, Thad. *Backwoodsmen: Stockmen and Hunters along a Big Thicket River Valley*. Norman: University of Oklahoma Press, 1995.

Sitton, Thad, and James H. Conrad. *Nameless Towns: Texas Sawmill Communities, 1880–1942*. Austin: University of Texas Press, 1998.

Sjoberg, Andrée F. "The Bidai Indians of Southeastern Texas." *Southwestern Journal of Anthropology* 7, no. 4 (1951): 391–400.

Smith, Bruce D. "A Comparison of Niche Construction Theory and Diet Breadth Models as Explanatory Frameworks for the Initial Domestication of Plants and Animals." *Journal of Archaeological Research* 23, no. 3 (2015): 215–62.

Smith, F. Todd. *The Caddo Indians: Tribes at the Convergence of Empires, 1542–1854*. College Station: Texas A&M University Press, 1995.

———. *From Dominance to Disappearance: The Indians of Texas and the Near Southwest, 1786–1859*. Lincoln: University of Nebraska Press, 2005.

Smith, Jared G. *Grazing Problems in the Southwest and How to Meet Them*. US Department of Agriculture, Division of Agrostology, Bulletin No. 16. Washington: Government Printing Office, 1899.

Smither, Harriet. "The Alabama Indians of Texas." *Southwestern Historical Quarterly* 36, no. 2 (1932): 83–108.

Solís, Gaspar José de. "Diary of a Visit of Inspection of the Texas Missions Made by Fray Gaspar Jose de Solis in the Year 1767–1767. Translated by Margaret Kenney Kress with Introductory Note by Mattie Austin Hatcher." *Southwestern Historical Quarterly* 35, no. 1 (1931): 28–76.

———. "The Solís Diary of 1767." *Preliminary Studies of the Texas Catholic Historical Society* 1, no. 6 (1931): 355–96. Translated by Peter P. Forrestal and edited by Paul J. Foik.

Spaight, Ashley W. *The Resources, Soil, and Climate of Texas: A Report of the Commissioner of Insurance, Statistics and History*. Galveston: A. H. Belo, 1882.

Spencer, Gary E. *Pineywoods Deer Herd Status Report*. Austin: Texas Parks and Wildlife Department, 1992.

Spratt, John Strickland. *The Road to Spindletop: Economic Change in Texas, 1875–1901*. Austin: University of Texas Press, 1955.

Spurr, Stephen H. *Forest Ecology*. New York: Ronald Press Company, 1964.

Spurr, Stephen H., and Burton V. Barnes. *Forest Ecology*, 3d ed. New York: John Wiley & Sons, 1980.

Srinath, Indumathi. "Original Texas Land Survey as a Source for Pre-European Settlement Vegetation Mapping." Master's thesis, Texas A&M University, Department of Geography, December 2009.

Srinath, Indumathi, and Andrew C. Millington. "Evaluating the Potential of the Original Texas Land Survey for Mapping Historical Land and Vegetation Cover." *Land* 5, no. 4 (2016): 1–14.

Stahl, Carmine, and Ria McElvaney. *Trees of Texas: An Easy Guide to Leaf Identification*. College Station: Texas A&M University Press, 2003.

Stanturf, John A., Dale D. Wade, Thomas A. Waldrop, Deborah K. Kennard, and Gary L. Actemeier. "Fire in Southern Forest Landscapes." In *Southern Forest Resource Assessment. General Technical Report SRS-53*, edited by David N. Wear and John G. Greis, 607–30. Asheville: US Department of Agriculture, Forest Service, Southern Research Station, 2002.

Steinberg, Ted. *Down to Earth: Nature's Role in American History*. 2d ed. New York: Oxford University Press, 2009.

Sterne, Adolphus, and Archie P. McDonald, ed. 1969. *Hurrah for Texas: The Diary of Adolphus Sterne, 1838–1851*. Austin: Nortex Press, 1986.

Sternitzke, Herbert E. *East Texas Pineywoods*. USDA Forest Service Resource Bulletin SO-10. New Orleans: Southern Forest Experiment Station, 1967.

Stewart, George R. 1945. *Names on the Land: A Historical Account of Placenaming in the United States.* New York: New York Review of Books, 2008.

Stewart, Omer C. "Burning and Natural Vegetation in the United States." *Geographical Review* 41, no. 2 (1951): 317–20.

Stoddard, H. L., Sr. "Use of Fire in Pine Forests and Game Lands of the Deep Southeast." In *Proceedings of the First Tall Timbers Fire Ecology Conference,* 31–42. Tallahassee: Tall Timbers Research Station, 1962.

Stone, Jack R. *Every Man Dies, Not Every Man Lives.* Bloomington: iUniverse, 2011.

Stover, John F. *American Railroads.* 2d ed. Chicago: University of Chicago Press, 1997.

Strapac, Joseph A. *Cotton Belt Locomotives.* Huntington Beach: Shade Tree Books, 1977.

Strickland, Arvarh E. "The Strange Affair of the Boll Weevil: The Pest as Liberator." *Agricultural History* 68, no. 2 (1994): 157–68.

Strickland, Rex W. "Moscoso's Journey through Texas." *Southwestern Historical Quarterly* 46, no. 2 (1942): 109–37.

Strong, Fred W. "Outdoors: Operation Whitetail." *Victoria Advocate,* December 10, 1963, p. 11.

Swanton, John R. *Source Material on the History and Ethnology of the Caddo Indians.* Norman: University of Oklahoma Press, 1996.

Tartt, Alison, and Evelyn Stehling, eds. *The Land: The Philosophical Society of Texas Proceedings of the Annual Meeting at Austin, November 30—December 2, 2001.* Austin: Philosophical Society of Texas, 2002.

Taylor, Rick. 1991. *The Feral Hog in Texas.* Austin: Texas Parks & Wildlife, 2003.

Temple, Ellen. "Boggy Slough Chili—50 Years of Chili Makin' in East Texas." In *Tales of Texas Cooking: Stories and Recipes from the Trans Pecos to the Piney Woods and High Plains to the Gulf Prairies,* edited by Frances B. Vick, 41–45. Denton: University of North Texas Press, 2015.

Temple, Ellen, and Patrick Hieger. *Temple Ranch Cookbook: A Tradition of Texas Conservation and Cuisine.* Austin: Emerald Book Company, 2013.

Temple Industries. *A Look into the Past.* Diboll: The Free Press, 1969.

Texas Almanac for 1873, and Emigrant's Guide to Texas. Galveston: Richardson, Belo & Company, 1873.

Texas Game, Fish and Oyster Commission. *Principal Game Birds and Mammals of Texas: Their Distribution and Management.* Austin: Texas Game, Fish and Oyster Commission, 1945.

Texas Game, Fish and Oyster Commission. *Review of Texas Wild Life and Conservation: Protective Efforts from 1879 to the Present Time, and Operations of the Fiscal Year Ending August 31, 1929.* Austin: Texas Game, Fish and Oyster Commission, 1929.

Texas Legislative Council of the 53rd Legislature of Texas. *Wildlife Management in Texas.* Austin: Texas Legislative Council, 1954.

Tharp, Benjamin Carroll. *Structure of Texas Vegetation East of the 98th Meridian.* Bulletin No. 2606. Austin: University of Texas Press, 1926.

———. *Texas Range Grasses.* Austin: University of Texas Press, 1952.

———. *The Vegetation of Texas.* Houston: Anson Jones Press and Texas Academy of Science, 1939.

Thoreau, Henry D. "Autumnal Tints." *Atlantic Monthly,* October 1862, pp. 385–402.

———. *The Succession of Forest Trees and Wild Apples.* Boston: Houghton, Mifflin and Company, 1887.

———. *Walden; or, Life in the Woods.* 1854. Reprint. Franklin Center: The Franklin Library, 1976.

———. *A Week on the Concord and Merrimack Rivers.* 1849. Reprint. Franklin Center: The Franklin Library, 1983.

Thoreau, Henry D., and Damion Searls, ed. *The Journal, 1837–1861.* New York: New York Review of Books, 2009.

Tippah County Historical and Genealogical Society. *The History of Tippah County, Mississippi.* Dallas: Tippah County Historical and Genealogical Society and National ShareGraphics, 1981.

Trinity Historical Society. *A History of Trinity, Texas: The First One Hundred Years and More.* Crockett: Publications Development Company of Texas, 1984.

Truett, Joe C. *Circling Back: Chronicle of a Texas River Valley.* Iowa City: University of Iowa Press, 1996.

Truett, Joe C., and Daniel W. Lay. *Land of Bears and Honey: A Natural History of East Texas.* Austin: University of Texas Press, 1984.

Turner, Ellen Sue, Thomas R. Hester, and Richard L. McReynolds. *Stone Artifacts of Texas Indians.* Lanham: Taylor Trade Publishing, 2011.

U. S. Bureau of Corporations, Department of Commerce and Labor. *The Lumber Industry, Part 1, Standing Timber.* Washington: Government Printing Office, 1913.

U. S. Bureau of Corporations, Department of Commerce and Labor. *The Lumber Industry, Part 2, Concentration of Timber Ownership in Important Selected Regions, and Part 3, Land Holdings of Large Timber Owners.* Washington: Government Printing Office, 1914.

Utley, Dan K. "A Gathering in the Woods." In *History Ahead: Stories beyond the Texas Roadside Markers,* edited by Dan K. Utley and Cynthia J. Beeman, 132–47. College Station: Texas A&M University Press, 2010.

———. "With the Yalies in the Deep Woods, May 10–13, 1909." In *Eavesdropping on Texas History,* edited by Mary L. Scheer, 133–153. Denton: University of North Texas Press, 2017.

Vardaman, James M. *How to Make Money Growing Trees.* New York: Wiley, 1989.

Varner, J. Morgan, III, and John S. Kush. "Remnant Old-Growth Longleaf Pine Savannas and Forests of the Southeastern USA: Status and Threats." *Natural Areas Journal* 24, no. 2 (2004): 141–49.

Vasey, George. *Grasses of the South: A Report on Certain Grasses and Forage Plants for Cultivation in the South and Southwest.* Department of Agriculture, Botanical Division Bulletin No. 3. Washington: Government Printing Office, 1887.

Vines, Robert A. *Trees, Shrubs and Woody Vines of the Southwest.* Austin: University of Texas Press, 1960.

Wade, Michael G. "Back to the Land: The Woodlake Community, 1933–1943." *East Texas Historical Journal* 21, no. 2 (1983): 46–56.

Walker, Eugene. "Distribution and Management of the Wild Turkey in Texas." *Texas Game and Fish* 22, no. 8 (1954): 12–14, 22, 26.

Walker, Laurence C. *Axes, Oxen, and Men: A Pictorial History of Southern Pine Lumber Company.* Diboll: Angelina Free Press, 1975.

———. *The Southern Forest: A Chronicle.* Austin: University of Texas Press, 1991.

Warren, Louis S. *The Hunter's Game: Poachers and Conservationists in Twentieth-Century America.* New Haven: Yale University Press, 1997.

Waterman, Todd. "Rail Fences: Their History and Construction." *Bittersweet* 9, no. 1 (1981): 4–15.

Way, Albert G. "Burned to Be Wild: Herbert Stoddard and the Roots of Ecological Conservation in the Southern Longleaf Pine Forest." *Environmental History* 11, no. 3 (2006): 500–26.

Weaver, Howard E., ed. *A Manual of Forestry, with Special Reference to Forestry Problems in East Texas.* Bulletin 45. College Station: Texas Forest Service, 1952.

Weber, David J. *The Spanish Frontier in North America.* New Haven: Yale University Press, 1992.

Weddle, Robert S., ed. *La Salle, the Mississippi, and the Gulf: Three Primary Documents.* College Station: Texas A&M University Press, 1987.

Welch, William C., and Greg Grant. *Heirloom Gardening in the South.* College Station: Texas A&M University Press, 2011.

Weniger, Del. *The Explorers' Texas: The Animals They Found.* Austin: Eakin Press, 1997.

———. *The Explorers' Texas: The Lands and Waters.* Austin: Eakin Press, 1984.

West, Robert C. "The Term 'Bayou' in the United States: A Study in the Geography of Place Names." *Annals of the Association of American Geographers* 44, no. 1 (1954): 63–74.

White, David L., and F. Thomas Lloyd. *An Old-Growth Definition for Dry and Dry-Mesic Oak-Pine Forests.* United States Department of Agriculture, Forest Service, General Technical Report SRS-23. Asheville: Southern Forest Research Station, 1998.

White, Roy R. "Austin Cary, the Father of Southern Forestry." *Forest and Conservation History* 5, no. 1 (1961): 2–5.

White-Tailed Deer in the Southern Forest Habitat, Proceedings of a Symposium at Nacogdoches, Texas, March 25–26, 1969. Southern Forest Experiment Station, Forest Service, US Department of Agriculture, 1969.

Whitford, Kathryn. "Thoreau and the Woodlots of Concord." *New England Quarterly* 23, no. 3 (1950): 291–306.

Whitney, Gordon G., and William C. Davis. "From Primitive Woods to Cultivated Woodlots: Thoreau and the Forest History of Concord, Massachusetts." *Journal of Forest History* (1986): 70–81.

Wilkins, J. W. "Pisgah Cemetery." *Records of East Texas* 6, no. 1 (1971): 16–17.

Williams, Jeffrey M. "GIS Aided Archaeological Research of El Camino Real de Los Tejas with Focus on the Landscape and River Crossings along El

Camino Carretera." Master's thesis, Stephen F. Austin State University, 2007.

Williams, Michael. *Americans and Their Forests: A Historical Geography*. Cambridge, UK: Cambridge University Press, 1989.

———. *Deforesting the Earth: From Prehistory to Global Crisis, An Abridgment*. Chicago: University of Chicago Press, 2006.

Williams, Raymond. *The Country and the City*. New York: Oxford University Press, 1973.

———. "Ideas of Nature." In *Problems in Materialism and Culture: Selected Essays*, by Raymond Williams, 67–85. London: Verso Books, 1980.

Winfrey, Dorman. "Chief Bowles of the Texas Cherokee." *Chronicles of Oklahoma* 32, no. 1 (1954): 29–41.

Winkler, Ernest William. "The Cherokee Indians in Texas." *Quarterly of the Texas State Historical Association* 7, no. 2 (1903): 95–165.

Woldert, Albert. "The Expedition of Luis de Moscoso in Texas in 1542." *Southwestern Historical Quarterly* 46, no. 2 (1942): 158–66.

Wolters, Gale L., Alton Martin Jr., and Warren P. Clary. "Timber, Browse, and Herbage on Selected Loblolly-Shortleaf Pine-Hardwood Forest Stands." *Southern Forest Experiment Station Research Note*, USDA Publication SO-223, 1977.

Woodall, Joe Ned. "Cultural Ecology of the Caddo." PhD diss., Southern Methodist University, Dallas, 1969.

Woodhead, D. "The Hardwood Wealth of Texas." *Texas Almanac and State Industrial Guide for 1904*, 146–147. Galveston: A. H. Belo & Co., 1904.

Woodruff, George W. *Federal and State Forest Laws*. US Department of Agriculture Bureau of Forestry Bulletin No. 57. Washington: Government Printing Office, 1904.

Woods, John B. "Texas Timberlands and State Forestry." *American Forests* (June 1946): 270–73, 278, 295–96.

Worster, Donald. *Nature's Economy: A History of Ecological Ideas*. 2d ed. New York: Cambridge University Press, 1994.

Wright, Charles. "Deer and Deer-Hunting in Texas." *American Naturalist* 2, no. 9 (1869): 466–76.

Wright, Nathan Dawson. In *East Texas: Its History and Its Makers*, vol. 4, edited by Dabney White, 392–93. New York: Lewis Historical Publishing Company, 1940.

Wright, Solomon Alexander. *My Rambles as East Texas Cowboy, Hunter, Fisherman, Tie-Cutter*. Austin: Texas Folklore Society, 1942.

Zlatkovich, Charles P. *Texas Railroads: A Record of Construction and Abandonment*. Austin: Bureau of Business Research, University of Texas, and Texas State Historical Association, 1981.

Zon, Raphael. *Loblolly Pine in Eastern Texas*. USDA, Forest Service Bulletin No. 64. Washington: Government Printing Office, 1905.

Index

Page numbers in italics refer to illustrations.

Southern Pine Association (SPA), 119, 173, 211

Southern Pine Lumber Company, 240; conservation efforts by, 140; debt owed by, 159, 299n12, 299n31; employee treatment at, 46–47, 66–68, *67*, 184–85; Forestry School Scholarship established by, 195; founding of, 57–60; Highway 103 project opposed by, 177–82; hunts hosted by, 3, 128–31, 143; impact of railroads on, 58–60; land acquisition by, 3–4, 33, 35, 51, 73–83, 125, 159; land title litigation by, 79–83; property taxes of, 62, 162–65; prospective sale of cutover lands of, 165–74; speculative ventures of, 153–54; sustained-yield policy of, 122–26, 236; Temple mill at Diboll, 60–62; tenancy system of, 112, 285n24. *See also* cattle grazing operations; logging operations; Rayville Ranch

Southland Paper Mills, 80, 235, 240

South Texas Native Seeds Project, 244

Southwestern Settlement and Development Company, 128, 222

Southwestern Timber Company, 226, 239, 320n37

Spencer, Spence, 226, 243

split rail fences, 24, 30, 34, 36–37, 44, 74, 79

Sportsmen of Boggy Slough (SOBS), 218–19, 315n103

Sportsmen's Clubs of Texas, Inc. (SCOT), 215

Spurr, Stephen, 12

St. Louis Southwestern Railway of Texas (SSW). *See* Cotton BeltStanley, Darryl, 229

Starr, Amory R., 59

state highway through Boggy Slough, opposition to, 177–82

steam shovels, 85, *85*

Stephen F. Austin State University, vii, 195, *205*, 211, 224, 226–227, 231, 242, 244, 321n54

Stern, Libby, 243

Stillwell, Charles, 208

stock dogs, 44, *108*, 111, 127, 129, 132–33

Stone, Jack R., 227–28

Stone, O. M., 123

stone hunting points, 8–9, *9*, 253nn6–7

Strauss, P. H., 129

Stubblefield, Gandy, 226

Stubblefield, Horace "Stubby," 226

sugarcane, 30–31, 36, 46

Sullivan, Charles Benjamin, 41, 264n89

Sullivan, Edmund J., 251n7

Sullivan, Edward, 42

Sullivan, Ella Doxie, 48

Sullivan, John Calvin, 39, 41

Sullivan, Laura Alice, 39, 48

Sullivan, Leonidas, 41

Sullivan, Lucinda, 37–38

Sullivan, Mary Eliza, 262n64

Sullivan, Samuel Doxie, 37–38, 39, 41, 263n82, 264n89

Sullivan, Samuel T., 262n64

Sullivan, Susan L., 42, 251n7

Sullivan, William Luther, 41

Sullivan, William Rufus, 41, 251n7

Sullivan's Bluff, 26–27, *37*, 41–42, 251n7, 265n114; crime and family feud in, 47–51; Highway 103 project and, 177–82

Sullivan's Ferry, 39, 41–42

Sunny South, 36

surveys, Texas General Land Office: ecological analysis from, 13, 22, 249–50; filing numbers of, 322n2; land features recorded in, 254n12; land grants based on, 31–36; place names used in, 2; title issues with, 79–81

sustained-yield policy, development of: in logging operations, 99–102, 171, 173, 194–95, 236; at Rayville Ranch, 122–26

Swanton, John R., 23

Sweeny, Jack, 226, 234, 243

sweetgum (*Liquidambar styraciflua*): impact of fire on, 13; impact on habitat, 11; industrial logging of, 94–95, 236, 237, 291n4; in original Texas Land surveys, 13, 249; in settlement homesteads, 53

switch cane, 32, 34, 39, 94, *95*, 114–16. *See also* giant cane

switchgrass (*P. virgatum*), 34

taxes: after World War II, 202; of Boggy Slough Hunting and Fishing Club, 215; of Copes Estate, 62, 270n46; of leased lands, 125, 217; Minton's personal property, 300n59; of owners of inholdings, 104; on Phelps land, 271n56; as reason against reforestation, 123; of settlers, 36, 42, 50–51, 263n75; of Southern Pine Lumber Company, 163–64, 179, 301n65; of Temple businesses, 154, 159, 171–73, 184, 192–94; T. L. L. Temple's income, 70–71; of TSE Railroad, 119

Taylor, Melinda E., 243

Tejas people. *See* Hasinai Confederacy of Caddo peoples

Temple, Ann, 274n113

Temple, Arthur III ("Buddy"), 4, *130*, 201, 210–11, *210*, 226, 244, 251n10; birth and childhood of, 233, *234*; Boggy Slough Hunting and Fishing Club and, 130–31; Buddy's Pond named for, 150; death of, 244; health of, 243; Kurth and, 240; philanthropy and conservation work of, 233–34, 242–44, 247, 319n24